# Beg the Question

*Also by Bob Fingerman:*
Minimum Wage Book One
White Like She
Finger Filth
You Deserved It

Zombie World: Winter's Dregs and Other Stories
(Title story scripted by Fingerman; art by Tommy Lee Edwards)

# Beg the Question

# Bob Fingerman

FANTAGRAPHICS BOOKS

BEG THE QUESTION was originally released as a graphic novel
(*Minimum Wage Book One*) and a subsequent series of ten *Minimum Wage* comics,
the first five of which were collected as *Minimum Wage Book Two*.
The present volume collects nine of the ten comics and includes a new opening
chapter (which condenses and revises *Minimum Wage Book One* in the continuity),
a new closing chapter, and a few additional sequences; all of the pages
have been reworked, most of them substantially, for this edition.

Visit our web site at **www.fantagraphics.com**
**To order a free copy of our full-color catalogue call 1-800-657-1100.**

Designed by Bob Fingerman and Greg Sadowski
Production by Paul Baresh
Promotion by Eric Reynolds
Thanks to Peppy White
Published by Gary Groth and Kim Thompson
Distributed by W.W. Norton

ISBN: 1-56097-685-3
First Hardcover printing: October 2002
First Softcover Printing: July 2005
Printed in Korea through PRINT VISION

For Michele,
without whom
there'd frankly be no point.

# Hey, Bob, Who Ya Calling "Loser"?

## by Penn Jillette

YOU'RE ABOUT TO READ A GREAT BOOK. I've been led to believe it's autobiographical. So, it's a funny book about my new friend, Bob. Even if you don't have the pleasure of meeting Bob personally and exchanging emails in which he begs you to write a foreword for him, the book is a great way to learn about a new friend.

There is one thing that I learned from this book about Bob and his NYC friends that I don't understand at all. All the characters we like and identify with in this book consider themselves to be losers. All the sympathetic characters are obsessed with how inadequate they are in every way.*

Is Bob a loser? Is Rob, the lead character in this book, a loser? Well, they're both Atheists. They don't pray to imaginary friends to solve their problems. They work on the problems themselves. Losers don't work on solving their problems themselves. Atheists are not losers. Bob and Rob both have healthy attitudes towards sex. They're not hung up about pornography. Rob works at *Pork Magazine*; it's not the job he wants, but it helps him pay the bills. Bob worked at *Screw* magazine. Bob and I both know Al Goldstein. Al is the founder of *Screw*. He's a very good friend of mine, and a pig. I'm Al's friend; Bob was paid to be around him. Getting paid for what I do for free – that's not a loser. At least not to me.

Rob has trouble with big questions like marriage and kids. Those are big questions; everyone should have big problems with those big questions. I think those choices are hard for anyone who isn't a loser.

Losers think "beg the question" means "to bring up another question." Losers are wrong. Bob knows what it really means and he puts it right in the front of his book.

Bob can write. His ear for dialogue is perfect. In just one panel of dialogue you hear another thousand conversations that these characters had or will have and a gachillion things you said, had said to you, thought, had thought about you, should have said, or should have had said to you.

Bob can draw. The pictures are beautiful. They tell the whole story without being redundant to the words. It's art, dude, it really is.

So, Bob and Rob are right about everything. That's good. They're living life in a fine straightforward manner, honest with themselves and others. An examined life is worth living. That's enough to be a winner.

Bob and Rob are really talented writers and artists. That counts for nothing. If you talk to people in line at the DMV, they all think they have talent.

But, Bob and Rob can prove they have talent. They get books done. They delivered their talent into your hands. Losers can't do that.

Maybe the loser stuff is meant to be ironic (a word that Bob can probably use correctly, but I'm not sure I can) or sarcastic or something. I don't know. But, this all begs the question: if he thinks he's a loser, what does he think of the rest of us? Huh?

His standards are too high. Maybe we don't want to be his friend. But, we sure want to read his loser book.

– Penn Jillette

Las Vegas, May 12, 2005

*There's an exception for the lead character's sex scenes. Rob isn't a loser in bed. He does fine. Make a note right now: if you're working on a piece that is transparently autobiographical, remember to make the lead character at least pretty good at sex. If you don't, it might come back to not bite you in the ass.

**Beg the question:**
to assume the truth of the very point raised in a question.

*– Webster's New Universal Unabridged Dictionary*

# CHAPTER ONE

# PATCHOULI VAPOR TRAIL

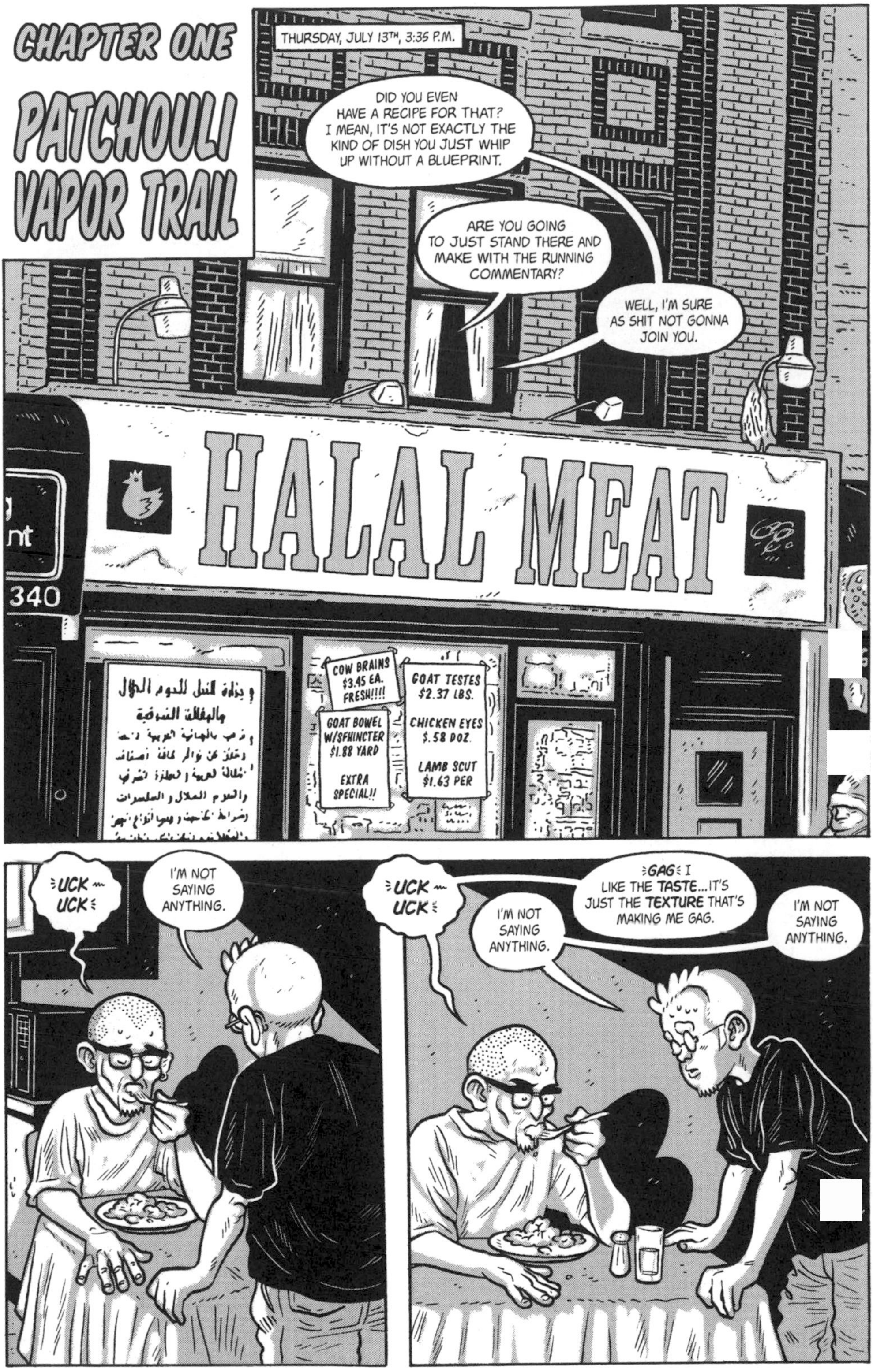
THURSDAY, JULY 13TH, 3:35 P.M.
DID YOU EVEN HAVE A RECIPE FOR THAT? I MEAN, IT'S NOT EXACTLY THE KIND OF DISH YOU JUST WHIP UP WITHOUT A BLUEPRINT.
ARE YOU GOING TO JUST STAND THERE AND MAKE WITH THE RUNNING COMMENTARY?
WELL, I'M SURE AS SHIT NOT GONNA JOIN YOU.
HALAL MEAT
340
COW BRAINS $3.45 EA. FRESH!!!!
GOAT TESTES $2.37 LBS.
GOAT BOWEL W/SFHINCTER $1.88 YARD
EXTRA SPECIAL!!
CHICKEN EYES $.58 DOZ.
LAMB SCUT $1.63 PER
UCK UCK
I'M NOT SAYING ANYTHING.
UCK UCK
I'M NOT SAYING ANYTHING.
GAG I LIKE THE TASTE...IT'S JUST THE TEXTURE THAT'S MAKING ME GAG.
I'M NOT SAYING ANYTHING.

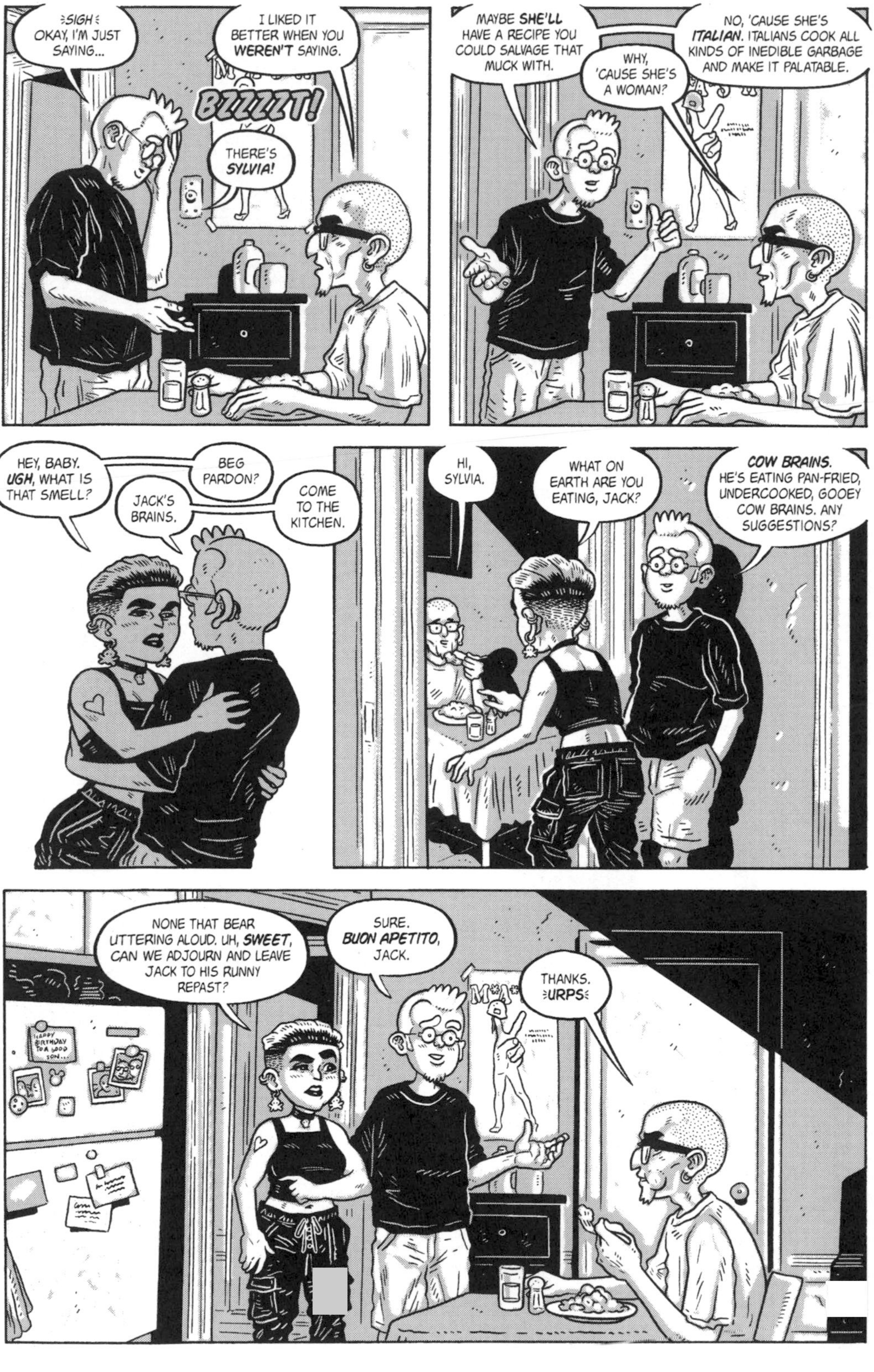

≶SIGH≷ OKAY, I'M JUST SAYING...
I LIKED IT BETTER WHEN YOU **WEREN'T** SAYING.
BZZZZZT!
THERE'S ***SYLVIA!***
MAYBE **SHE'LL** HAVE A RECIPE YOU COULD SALVAGE THAT MUCK WITH.
WHY, 'CAUSE SHE'S A WOMAN?
NO, 'CAUSE SHE'S ***ITALIAN.*** ITALIANS COOK ALL KINDS OF INEDIBLE GARBAGE AND MAKE IT PALATABLE.
HEY, BABY. ***UGH***, WHAT IS THAT SMELL?
BEG PARDON?
JACK'S BRAINS.
COME TO THE KITCHEN.
HI, SYLVIA.
WHAT ON EARTH ARE YOU EATING, JACK?
***COW BRAINS.*** HE'S EATING PAN-FRIED, UNDERCOOKED, GOOEY COW BRAINS. ANY SUGGESTIONS?
NONE THAT BEAR UTTERING ALOUD. UH, ***SWEET***, CAN WE ADJOURN AND LEAVE JACK TO HIS RUNNY REPAST?
SURE. ***BUON APETITO***, JACK.
THANKS. **URPS**
HAPPY BIRTHDAY TO A GOOD SON...

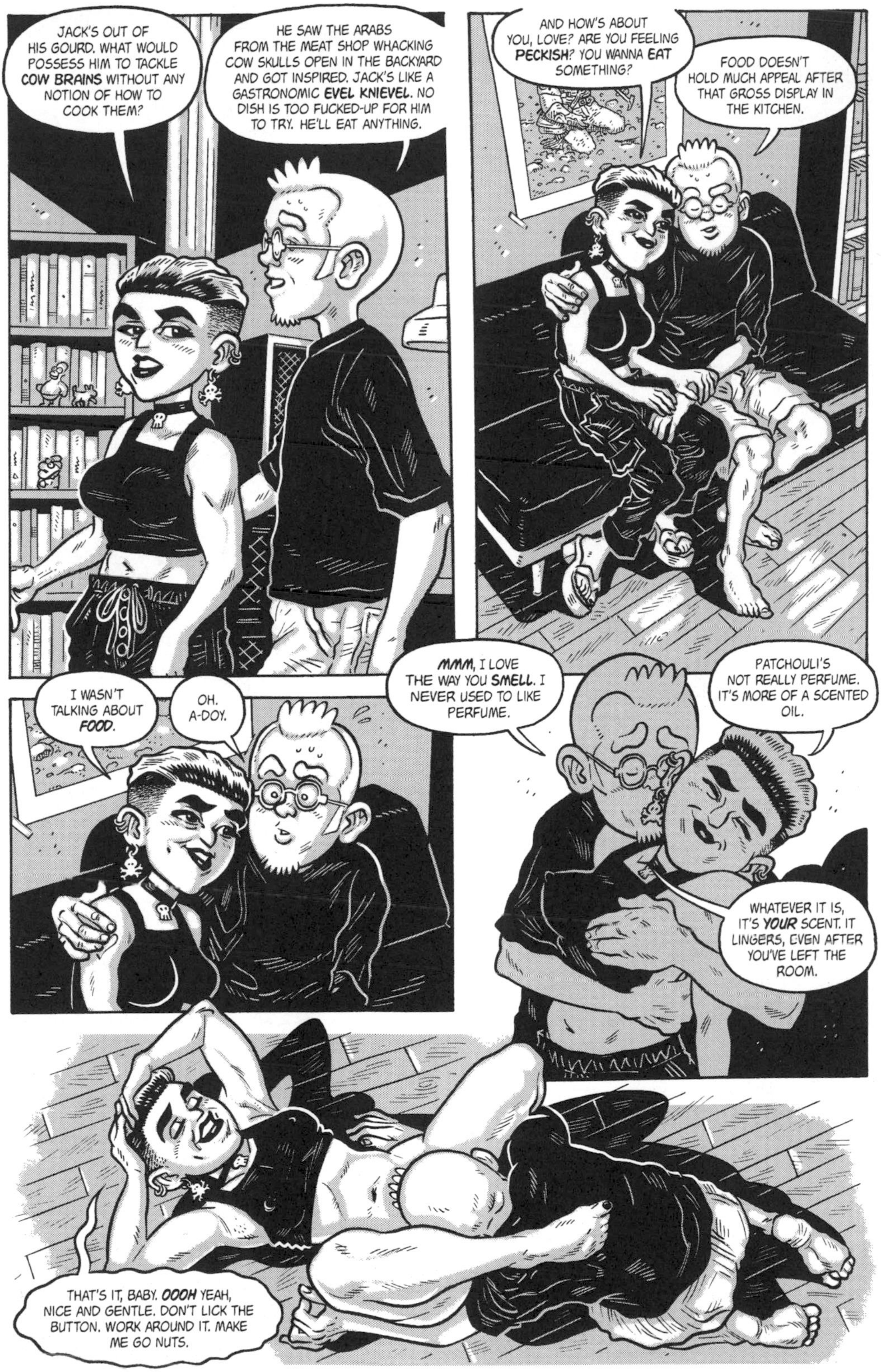
JACK'S OUT OF HIS GOURD. WHAT WOULD POSSESS HIM TO TACKLE **COW BRAINS** WITHOUT ANY NOTION OF HOW TO COOK THEM?
HE SAW THE ARABS FROM THE MEAT SHOP WHACKING COW SKULLS OPEN IN THE BACKYARD AND GOT INSPIRED. JACK'S LIKE A GASTRONOMIC **EVEL KNIEVEL**. NO DISH IS TOO FUCKED-UP FOR HIM TO TRY. HE'LL EAT ANYTHING.
AND HOW'S ABOUT YOU, LOVE? ARE YOU FEELING **PECKISH**? YOU WANNA **EAT** SOMETHING?
FOOD DOESN'T HOLD MUCH APPEAL AFTER THAT GROSS DISPLAY IN THE KITCHEN.
I WASN'T TALKING ABOUT ***FOOD***.
OH. A-DOY.
***MMM***, I LOVE THE WAY YOU **SMELL**. I NEVER USED TO LIKE PERFUME.
PATCHOULI'S NOT REALLY PERFUME. IT'S MORE OF A SCENTED OIL.
WHATEVER IT IS, IT'S ***YOUR*** SCENT. IT LINGERS, EVEN AFTER YOU'VE LEFT THE ROOM.
THAT'S IT, BABY. ***OOOH*** YEAH, NICE AND GENTLE. DON'T LICK THE BUTTON. WORK AROUND IT. MAKE ME GO NUTS.

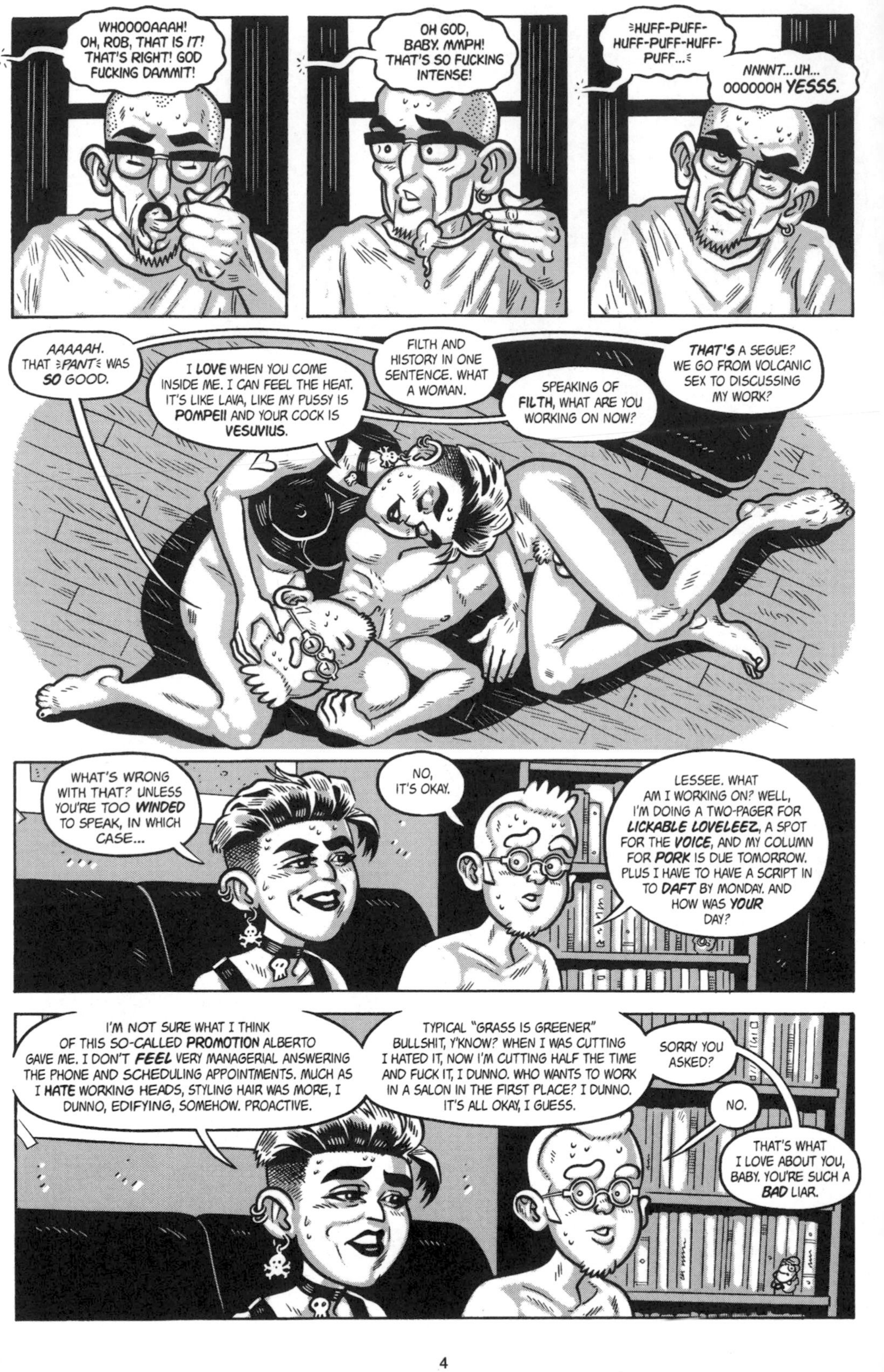
WHOOOOAAAH! OH, ROB, THAT IS IT! THAT'S RIGHT! GOD FUCKING DAMMIT!
OH GOD, BABY. MMPH! THAT'S SO FUCKING INTENSE!
HUFF-PUFF-HUFF-PUFF-HUFF-PUFF...
NNNNT...UH... OOOOOOH YESSS.
AAAAAH. THAT PANT WAS SO GOOD.
I LOVE WHEN YOU COME INSIDE ME. I CAN FEEL THE HEAT. IT'S LIKE LAVA, LIKE MY PUSSY IS POMPEII AND YOUR COCK IS VESUVIUS.
FILTH AND HISTORY IN ONE SENTENCE. WHAT A WOMAN.
SPEAKING OF FILTH, WHAT ARE YOU WORKING ON NOW?
THAT'S A SEGUE? WE GO FROM VOLCANIC SEX TO DISCUSSING MY WORK?
WHAT'S WRONG WITH THAT? UNLESS YOU'RE TOO WINDED TO SPEAK, IN WHICH CASE...
NO, IT'S OKAY.
LESSEE. WHAT AM I WORKING ON? WELL, I'M DOING A TWO-PAGER FOR LICKABLE LOVELEEZ, A SPOT FOR THE VOICE, AND MY COLUMN FOR PORK IS DUE TOMORROW. PLUS I HAVE TO HAVE A SCRIPT IN TO DAFT BY MONDAY. AND HOW WAS YOUR DAY?
I'M NOT SURE WHAT I THINK OF THIS SO-CALLED PROMOTION ALBERTO GAVE ME. I DON'T FEEL VERY MANAGERIAL ANSWERING THE PHONE AND SCHEDULING APPOINTMENTS. MUCH AS I HATE WORKING HEADS, STYLING HAIR WAS MORE, I DUNNO, EDIFYING, SOMEHOW. PROACTIVE.
TYPICAL "GRASS IS GREENER" BULLSHIT, Y'KNOW? WHEN I WAS CUTTING I HATED IT, NOW I'M CUTTING HALF THE TIME AND FUCK IT, I DUNNO. WHO WANTS TO WORK IN A SALON IN THE FIRST PLACE? I DUNNO. IT'S ALL OKAY, I GUESS.
SORRY YOU ASKED?
NO.
THAT'S WHAT I LOVE ABOUT YOU, BABY. YOU'RE SUCH A BAD LIAR.

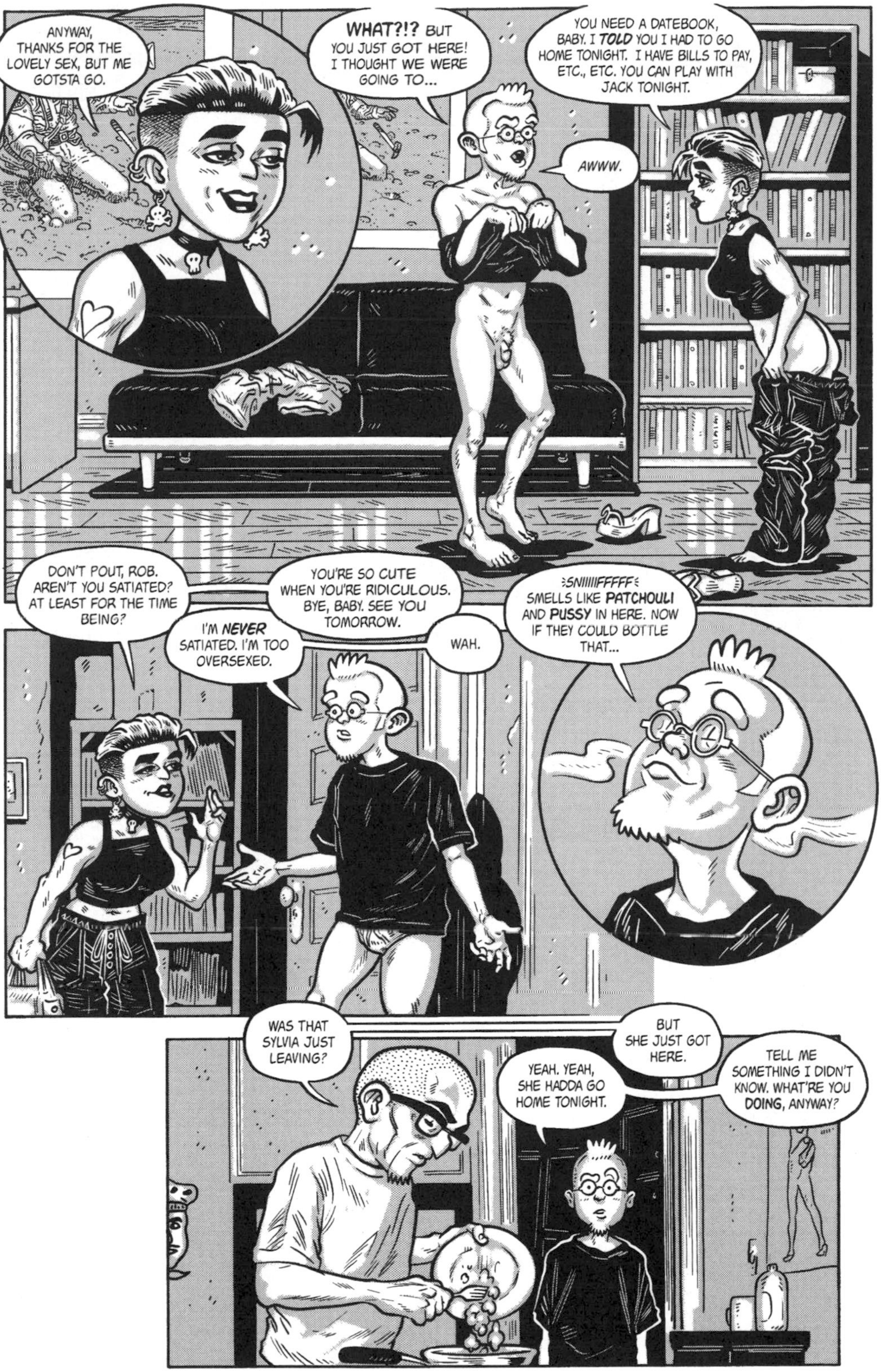
ANYWAY, THANKS FOR THE LOVELY SEX, BUT ME GOTSTA GO.
WHAT?!? BUT YOU JUST GOT HERE! I THOUGHT WE WERE GOING TO...
YOU NEED A DATEBOOK, BABY. I TOLD YOU I HAD TO GO HOME TONIGHT. I HAVE BILLS TO PAY, ETC., ETC. YOU CAN PLAY WITH JACK TONIGHT.
AWWW.
DON'T POUT, ROB. AREN'T YOU SATIATED? AT LEAST FOR THE TIME BEING?
I'M NEVER SATIATED. I'M TOO OVERSEXED.
YOU'RE SO CUTE WHEN YOU'RE RIDICULOUS. BYE, BABY. SEE YOU TOMORROW.
WAH.
SNIIIIIFFFFF
SMELLS LIKE PATCHOULI AND PUSSY IN HERE. NOW IF THEY COULD BOTTLE THAT...
WAS THAT SYLVIA JUST LEAVING?
YEAH. YEAH, SHE HADDA GO HOME TONIGHT.
BUT SHE JUST GOT HERE.
TELL ME SOMETHING I DIDN'T KNOW. WHAT'RE YOU DOING, ANYWAY?

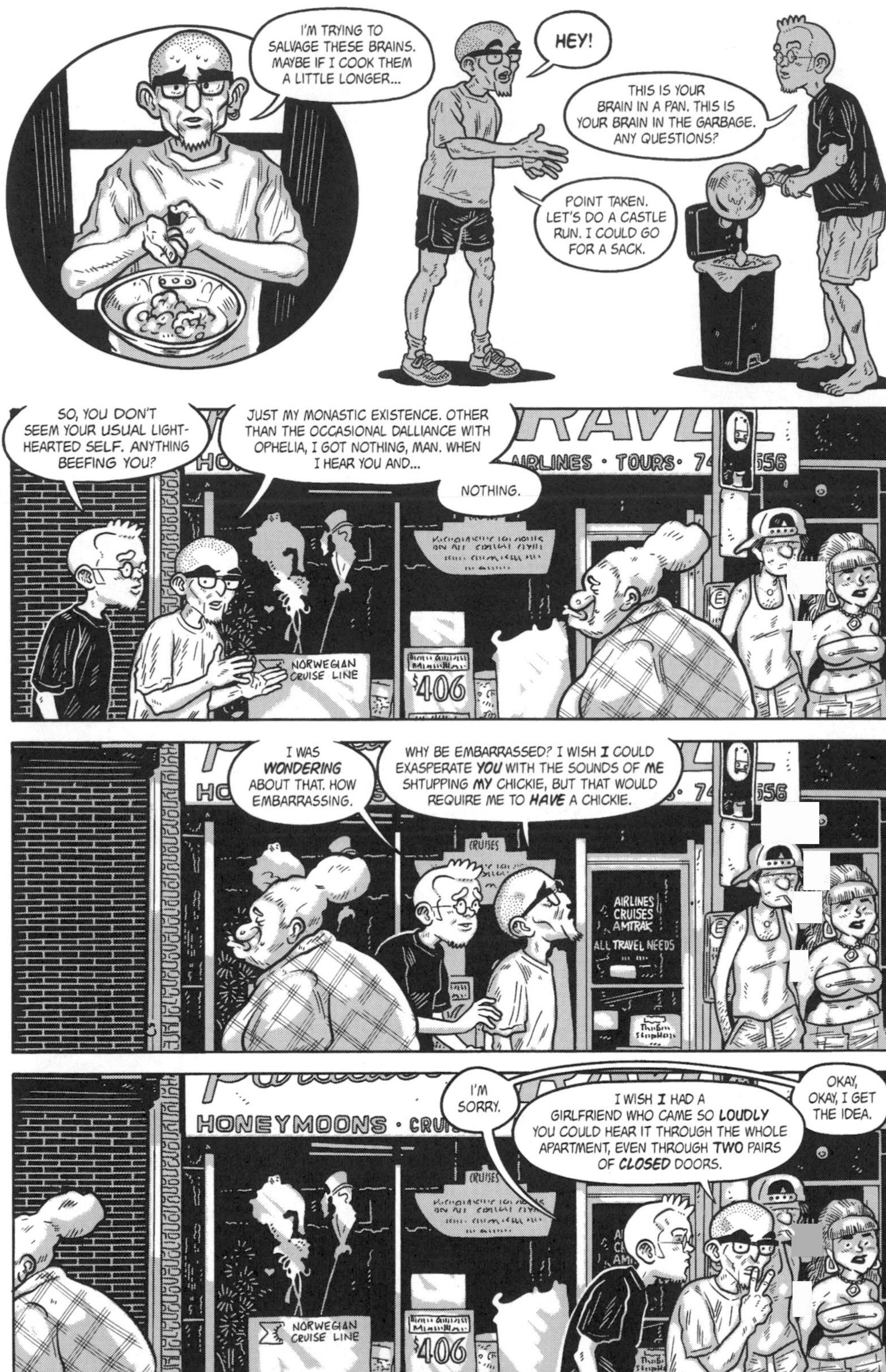
I'M TRYING TO SALVAGE THESE BRAINS. MAYBE IF I COOK THEM A LITTLE LONGER...
HEY!
THIS IS YOUR BRAIN IN A PAN. THIS IS YOUR BRAIN IN THE GARBAGE. ANY QUESTIONS?
POINT TAKEN. LET'S DO A CASTLE RUN. I COULD GO FOR A SACK.
SO, YOU DON'T SEEM YOUR USUAL LIGHT-HEARTED SELF. ANYTHING BEEFING YOU?
JUST MY MONASTIC EXISTENCE. OTHER THAN THE OCCASIONAL DALLIANCE WITH OPHELIA, I GOT NOTHING, MAN. WHEN I HEAR YOU AND...
NOTHING.
AIRLINES · TOURS · 74 556
NORWEGIAN CRUISE LINE
$406
I WAS WONDERING ABOUT THAT. HOW EMBARRASSING.
WHY BE EMBARRASSED? I WISH I COULD EXASPERATE YOU WITH THE SOUNDS OF ME SHTUPPING MY CHICKIE, BUT THAT WOULD REQUIRE ME TO HAVE A CHICKIE.
CRUISES
AIRLINES
CRUISES
AMTRAK
ALL TRAVEL NEEDS
HONEYMOONS · CRUI
I'M SORRY.
I WISH I HAD A GIRLFRIEND WHO CAME SO LOUDLY YOU COULD HEAR IT THROUGH THE WHOLE APARTMENT, EVEN THROUGH TWO PAIRS OF CLOSED DOORS.
OKAY, OKAY, I GET THE IDEA.
CRUISES
NORWEGIAN CRUISE LINE
$406

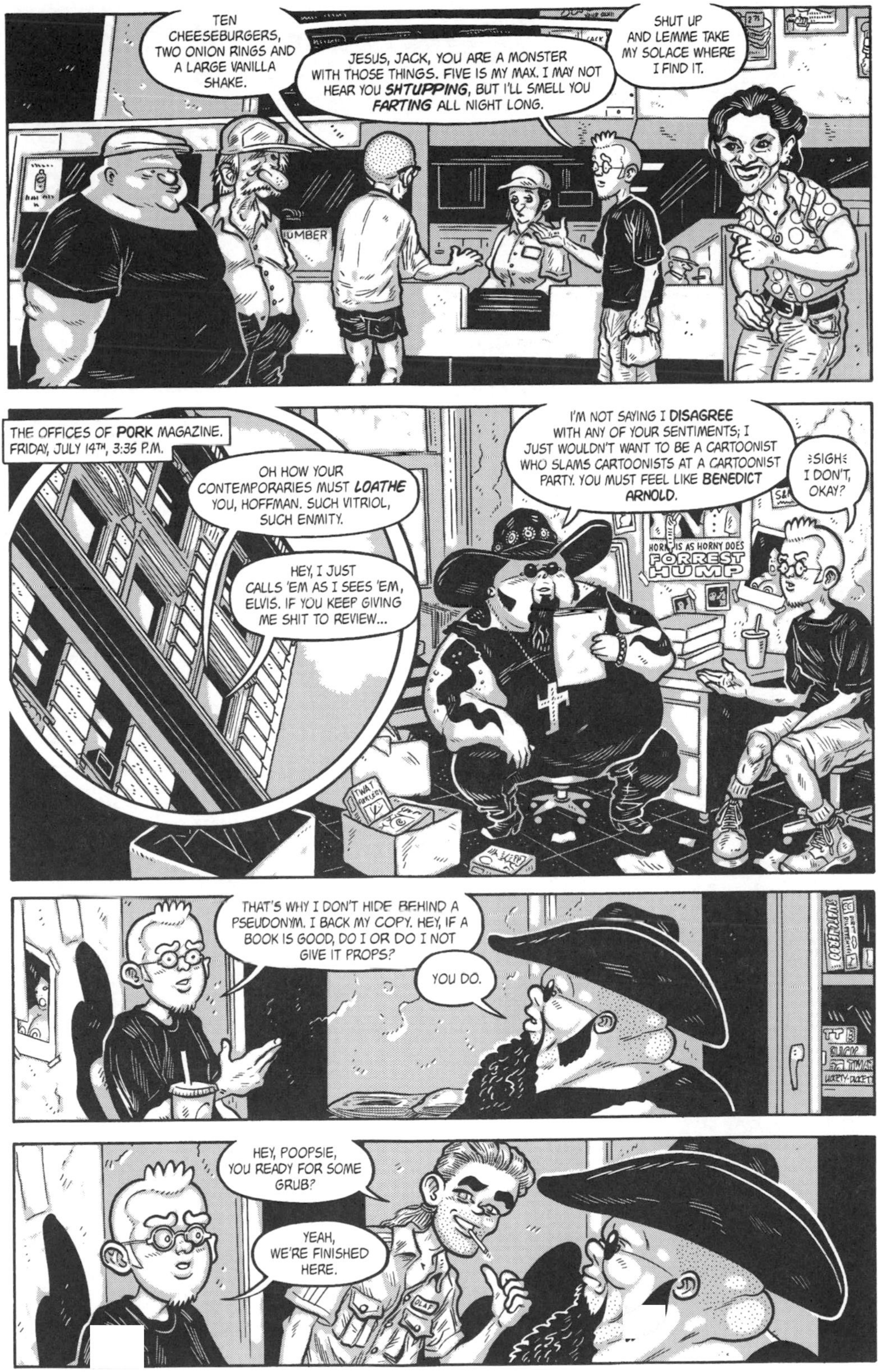

TEN CHEESEBURGERS, TWO ONION RINGS AND A LARGE VANILLA SHAKE.
JESUS, JACK, YOU ARE A MONSTER WITH THOSE THINGS. FIVE IS MY MAX. I MAY NOT HEAR YOU **SHTUPPING**, BUT I'LL SMELL YOU **FARTING** ALL NIGHT LONG.
SHUT UP AND LEMME TAKE MY SOLACE WHERE I FIND IT.
THE OFFICES OF **PORK** MAGAZINE. FRIDAY, JULY 14TH, 3:35 P.M.
OH HOW YOUR CONTEMPORARIES MUST **LOATHE** YOU, HOFFMAN. SUCH VITRIOL, SUCH ENMITY.
HEY, I JUST CALLS 'EM AS I SEES 'EM, ELVIS. IF YOU KEEP GIVING ME SHIT TO REVIEW...
I'M NOT SAYING I **DISAGREE** WITH ANY OF YOUR SENTIMENTS; I JUST WOULDN'T WANT TO BE A CARTOONIST WHO SLAMS CARTOONISTS AT A CARTOONIST PARTY. YOU MUST FEEL LIKE **BENEDICT ARNOLD**.
SIGH I DON'T, OKAY?
FORREST HUMP
THAT'S WHY I DON'T HIDE BEHIND A PSEUDONYM. I BACK MY COPY. HEY, IF A BOOK IS GOOD, DO I OR DO I NOT GIVE IT PROPS?
YOU DO.
HEY, POOPSIE, YOU READY FOR SOME GRUB?
YEAH, WE'RE FINISHED HERE.
OLAF

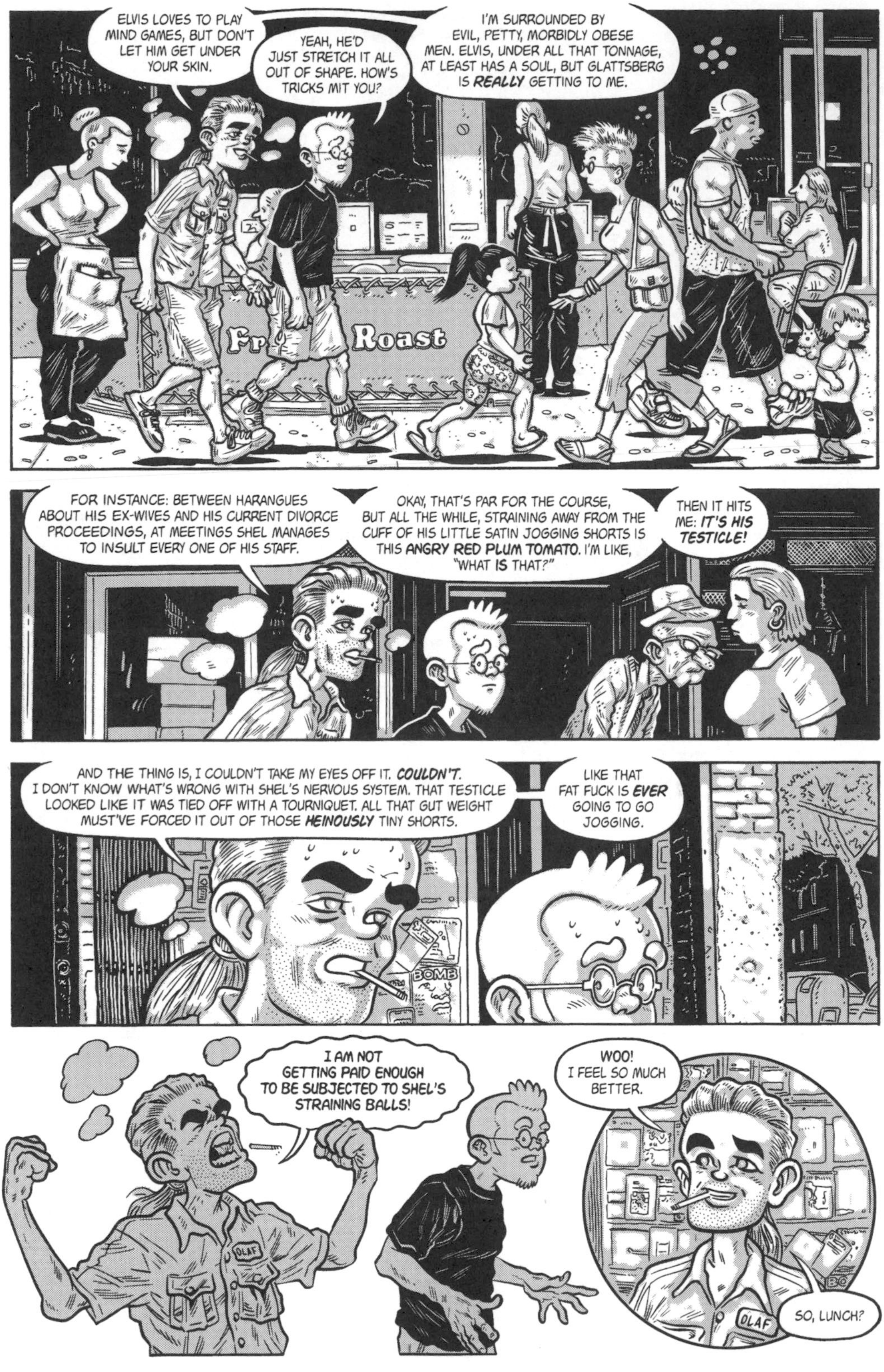
ELVIS LOVES TO PLAY MIND GAMES, BUT DON'T LET HIM GET UNDER YOUR SKIN.
YEAH, HE'D JUST STRETCH IT ALL OUT OF SHAPE. HOW'S TRICKS MIT YOU?
I'M SURROUNDED BY EVIL, PETTY, MORBIDLY OBESE MEN. ELVIS, UNDER ALL THAT TONNAGE, AT LEAST HAS A SOUL, BUT GLATTSBERG IS REALLY GETTING TO ME.
Fr Roast
FOR INSTANCE: BETWEEN HARANGUES ABOUT HIS EX-WIVES AND HIS CURRENT DIVORCE PROCEEDINGS, AT MEETINGS SHEL MANAGES TO INSULT EVERY ONE OF HIS STAFF.
OKAY, THAT'S PAR FOR THE COURSE, BUT ALL THE WHILE, STRAINING AWAY FROM THE CUFF OF HIS LITTLE SATIN JOGGING SHORTS IS THIS ANGRY RED PLUM TOMATO. I'M LIKE, "WHAT IS THAT?"
THEN IT HITS ME: IT'S HIS TESTICLE!
AND THE THING IS, I COULDN'T TAKE MY EYES OFF IT. COULDN'T. I DON'T KNOW WHAT'S WRONG WITH SHEL'S NERVOUS SYSTEM. THAT TESTICLE LOOKED LIKE IT WAS TIED OFF WITH A TOURNIQUET. ALL THAT GUT WEIGHT MUST'VE FORCED IT OUT OF THOSE HEINOUSLY TINY SHORTS.
LIKE THAT FAT FUCK IS EVER GOING TO GO JOGGING.
BOMB
I AM NOT GETTING PAID ENOUGH TO BE SUBJECTED TO SHEL'S STRAINING BALLS!
OLAF
WOO! I FEEL SO MUCH BETTER.
OLAF
SO, LUNCH?

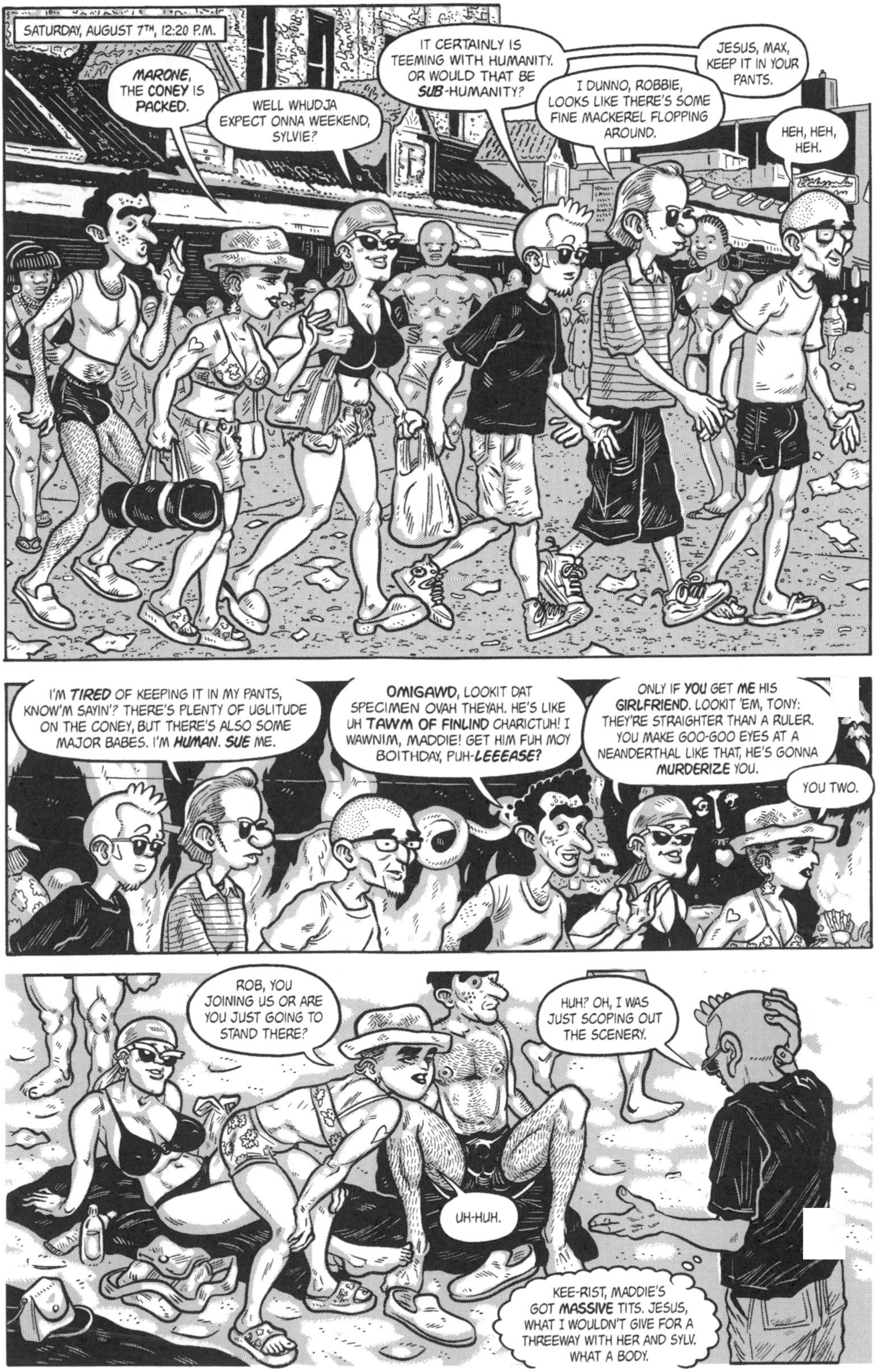
SATURDAY, AUGUST 7TH, 12:20 P.M.
MARONE, THE CONEY IS PACKED.
WELL WHUDJA EXPECT ONNA WEEKEND, SYLVIE?
IT CERTAINLY IS TEEMING WITH HUMANITY. OR WOULD THAT BE SUB-HUMANITY?
I DUNNO, ROBBIE, LOOKS LIKE THERE'S SOME FINE MACKEREL FLOPPING AROUND.
JESUS, MAX, KEEP IT IN YOUR PANTS.
HEH, HEH, HEH.
I'M TIRED OF KEEPING IT IN MY PANTS, KNOW'M SAYIN'? THERE'S PLENTY OF UGLITUDE ON THE CONEY, BUT THERE'S ALSO SOME MAJOR BABES. I'M HUMAN. SUE ME.
OMIGAWD, LOOKIT DAT SPECIMEN OVAH THEYAH. HE'S LIKE UH TAWM OF FINLIND CHARICTUH! I WAWNIM, MADDIE! GET HIM FUH MOY BOITHDAY, PUH-LEEEASE?
ONLY IF YOU GET ME HIS GIRLFRIEND. LOOKIT 'EM, TONY: THEY'RE STRAIGHTER THAN A RULER. YOU MAKE GOO-GOO EYES AT A NEANDERTHAL LIKE THAT, HE'S GONNA MURDERIZE YOU.
YOU TWO.
ROB, YOU JOINING US OR ARE YOU JUST GOING TO STAND THERE?
HUH? OH, I WAS JUST SCOPING OUT THE SCENERY.
UH-HUH.
KEE-RIST, MADDIE'S GOT MASSIVE TITS. JESUS, WHAT I WOULDN'T GIVE FOR A THREEWAY WITH HER AND SYLV. WHAT A BODY.

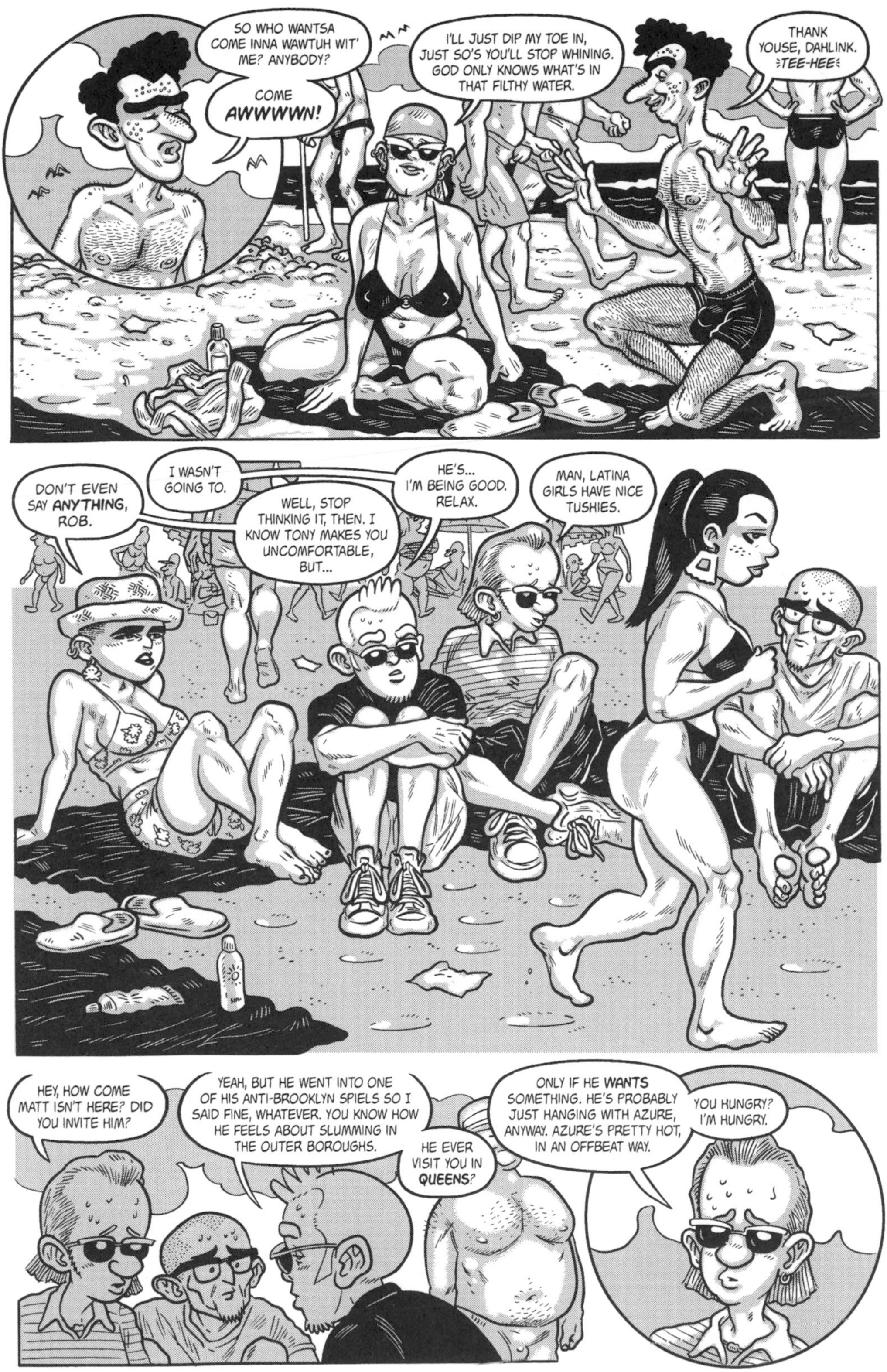

SO WHO WANTSA COME INNA WAWTUH WIT' ME? ANYBODY?
COME AWWWWN!
I'LL JUST DIP MY TOE IN, JUST SO'S YOU'LL STOP WHINING. GOD ONLY KNOWS WHAT'S IN THAT FILTHY WATER.
THANK YOUSE, DAHLINK. TEE-HEE
DON'T EVEN SAY ANYTHING, ROB.
I WASN'T GOING TO.
WELL, STOP THINKING IT, THEN. I KNOW TONY MAKES YOU UNCOMFORTABLE, BUT...
HE'S... I'M BEING GOOD. RELAX.
MAN, LATINA GIRLS HAVE NICE TUSHIES.
HEY, HOW COME MATT ISN'T HERE? DID YOU INVITE HIM?
YEAH, BUT HE WENT INTO ONE OF HIS ANTI-BROOKLYN SPIELS SO I SAID FINE, WHATEVER. YOU KNOW HOW HE FEELS ABOUT SLUMMING IN THE OUTER BOROUGHS.
HE EVER VISIT YOU IN QUEENS?
ONLY IF HE WANTS SOMETHING. HE'S PROBABLY JUST HANGING WITH AZURE, ANYWAY. AZURE'S PRETTY HOT, IN AN OFFBEAT WAY.
YOU HUNGRY? I'M HUNGRY.

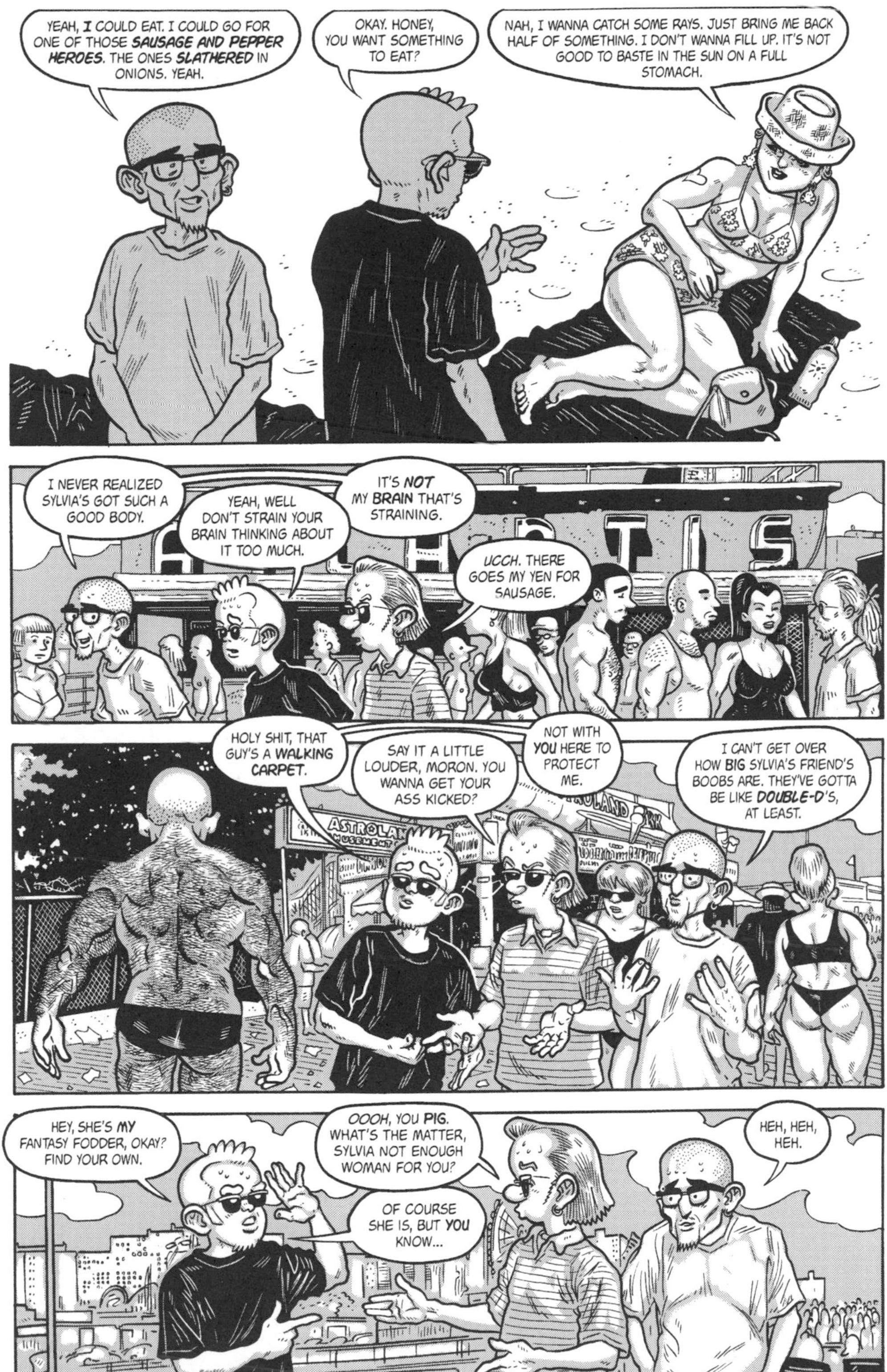
YEAH, I COULD EAT. I COULD GO FOR ONE OF THOSE SAUSAGE AND PEPPER HEROES. THE ONES SLATHERED IN ONIONS. YEAH.
OKAY. HONEY, YOU WANT SOMETHING TO EAT?
NAH, I WANNA CATCH SOME RAYS. JUST BRING ME BACK HALF OF SOMETHING. I DON'T WANNA FILL UP. IT'S NOT GOOD TO BASTE IN THE SUN ON A FULL STOMACH.
I NEVER REALIZED SYLVIA'S GOT SUCH A GOOD BODY.
YEAH, WELL DON'T STRAIN YOUR BRAIN THINKING ABOUT IT TOO MUCH.
IT'S NOT MY BRAIN THAT'S STRAINING.
UCCH. THERE GOES MY YEN FOR SAUSAGE.
HOLY SHIT, THAT GUY'S A WALKING CARPET.
SAY IT A LITTLE LOUDER, MORON. YOU WANNA GET YOUR ASS KICKED?
NOT WITH YOU HERE TO PROTECT ME.
I CAN'T GET OVER HOW BIG SYLVIA'S FRIEND'S BOOBS ARE. THEY'VE GOTTA BE LIKE DOUBLE-D'S, AT LEAST.
HEY, SHE'S MY FANTASY FODDER, OKAY? FIND YOUR OWN.
OOOH, YOU PIG. WHAT'S THE MATTER, SYLVIA NOT ENOUGH WOMAN FOR YOU?
OF COURSE SHE IS, BUT YOU KNOW...
HEH, HEH, HEH.

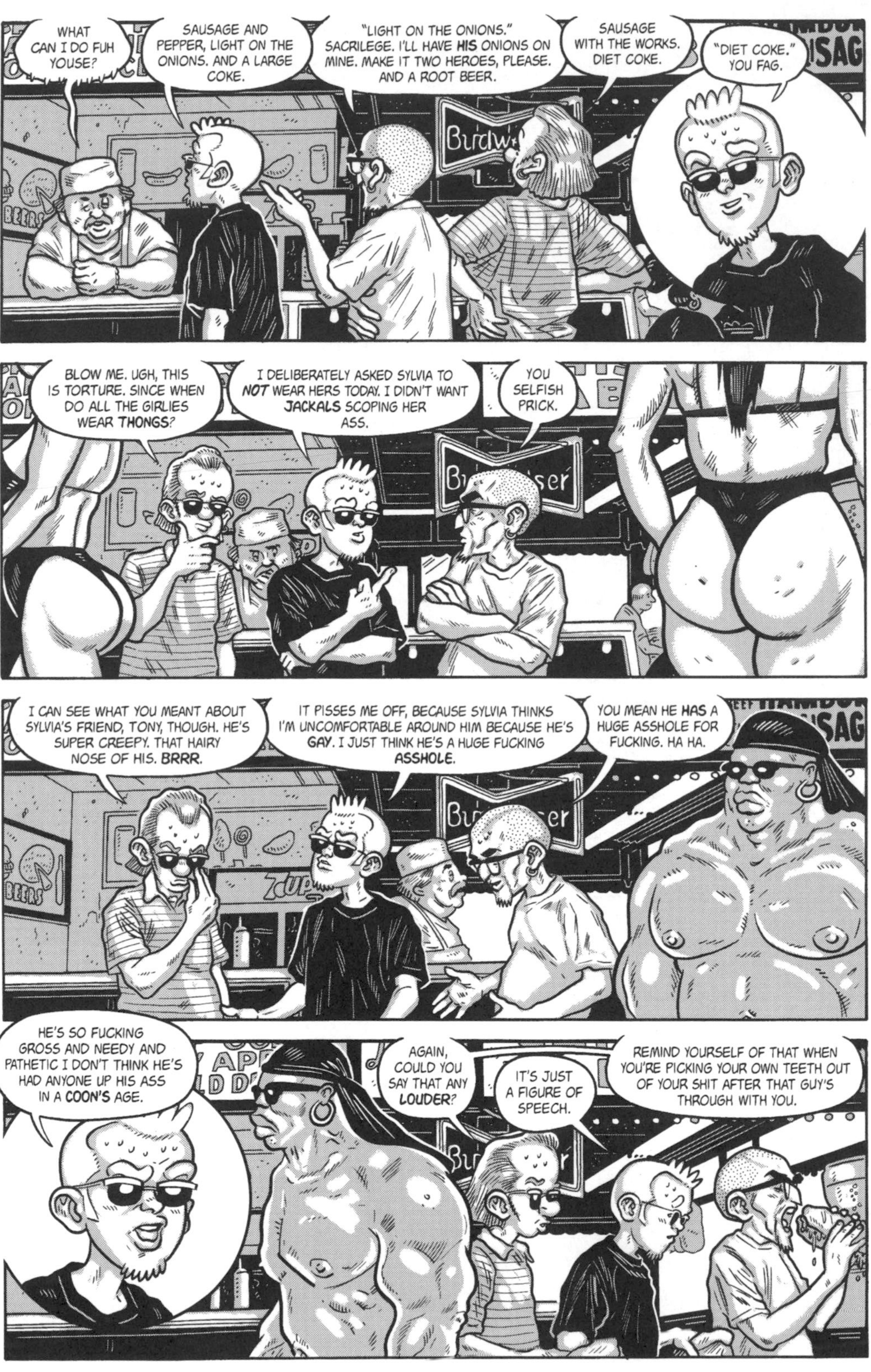
WHAT CAN I DO FUH YOUSE?
SAUSAGE AND PEPPER, LIGHT ON THE ONIONS. AND A LARGE COKE.
"LIGHT ON THE ONIONS." SACRILEGE. I'LL HAVE HIS ONIONS ON MINE. MAKE IT TWO HEROES, PLEASE. AND A ROOT BEER.
SAUSAGE WITH THE WORKS. DIET COKE.
"DIET COKE." YOU FAG.
BLOW ME. UGH, THIS IS TORTURE. SINCE WHEN DO ALL THE GIRLIES WEAR THONGS?
I DELIBERATELY ASKED SYLVIA TO NOT WEAR HERS TODAY. I DIDN'T WANT JACKALS SCOPING HER ASS.
YOU SELFISH PRICK.
I CAN SEE WHAT YOU MEANT ABOUT SYLVIA'S FRIEND, TONY, THOUGH. HE'S SUPER CREEPY. THAT HAIRY NOSE OF HIS. BRRR.
IT PISSES ME OFF, BECAUSE SYLVIA THINKS I'M UNCOMFORTABLE AROUND HIM BECAUSE HE'S GAY. I JUST THINK HE'S A HUGE FUCKING ASSHOLE.
YOU MEAN HE HAS A HUGE ASSHOLE FOR FUCKING. HA HA.
HE'S SO FUCKING GROSS AND NEEDY AND PATHETIC I DON'T THINK HE'S HAD ANYONE UP HIS ASS IN A COON'S AGE.
AGAIN, COULD YOU SAY THAT ANY LOUDER?
IT'S JUST A FIGURE OF SPEECH.
REMIND YOURSELF OF THAT WHEN YOU'RE PICKING YOUR OWN TEETH OUT OF YOUR SHIT AFTER THAT GUY'S THROUGH WITH YOU.

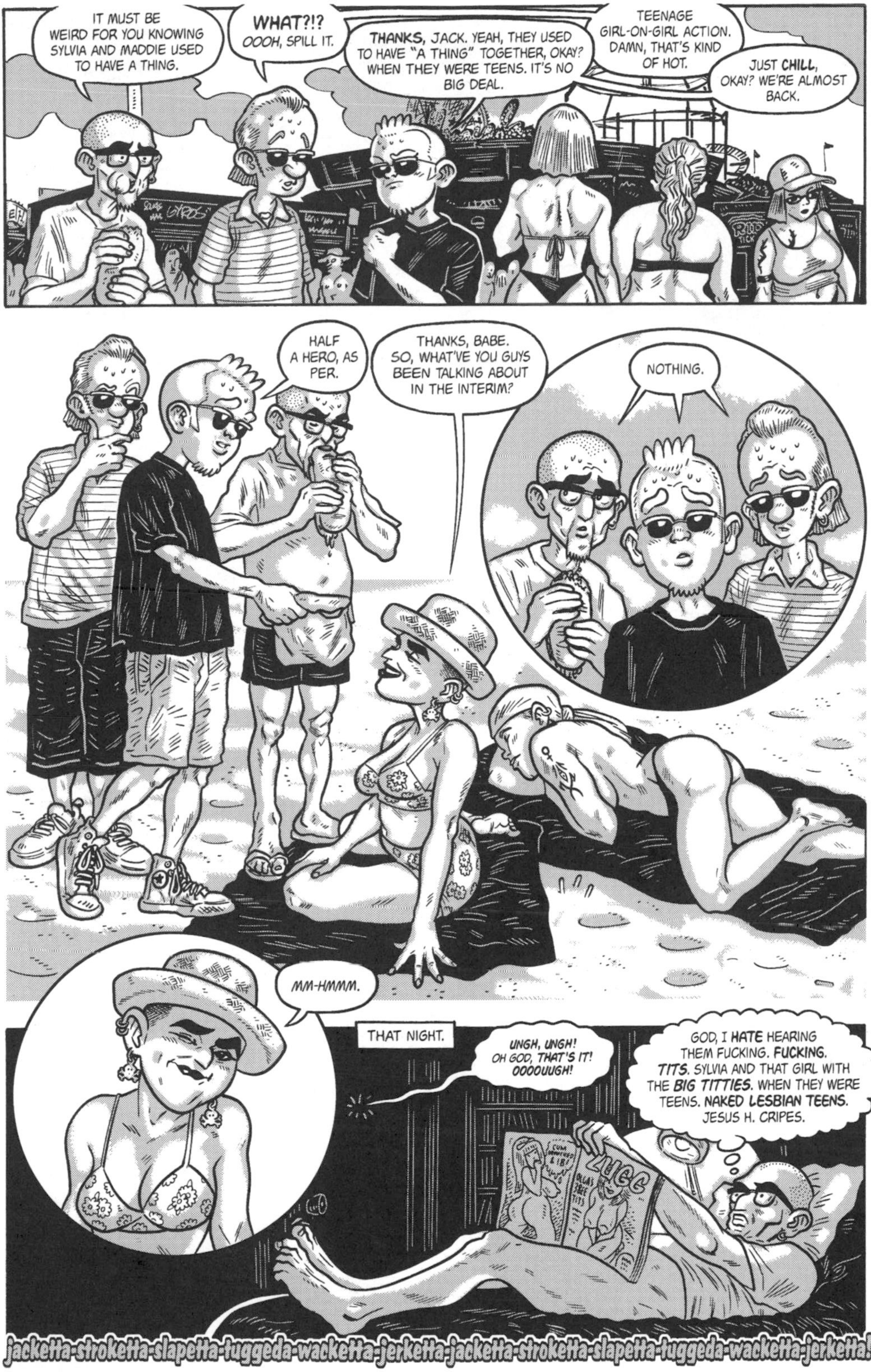
IT MUST BE WEIRD FOR YOU KNOWING SYLVIA AND MADDIE USED TO HAVE A THING.
WHAT?!? OOOH, SPILL IT.
THANKS, JACK. YEAH, THEY USED TO HAVE "A THING" TOGETHER, OKAY? WHEN THEY WERE TEENS. IT'S NO BIG DEAL.
TEENAGE GIRL-ON-GIRL ACTION. DAMN, THAT'S KIND OF HOT.
JUST CHILL, OKAY? WE'RE ALMOST BACK.
GYROS
HALF A HERO, AS PER.
THANKS, BABE. SO, WHAT'VE YOU GUYS BEEN TALKING ABOUT IN THE INTERIM?
NOTHING.
MM-HMMM.
THAT NIGHT.
UNGH, UNGH! OH GOD, THAT'S IT! OOOOUUGH!
GOD, I HATE HEARING THEM FUCKING. FUCKING. TITS. SYLVIA AND THAT GIRL WITH THE BIG TITTIES. WHEN THEY WERE TEENS. NAKED LESBIAN TEENS. JESUS H. CRIPES.
ZUGG
jacketta-stroketta-slapetta-tuggeda-wacketta-jerketta-jacketta-stroketta-slapetta-tuggeda-wacketta-jerketta!

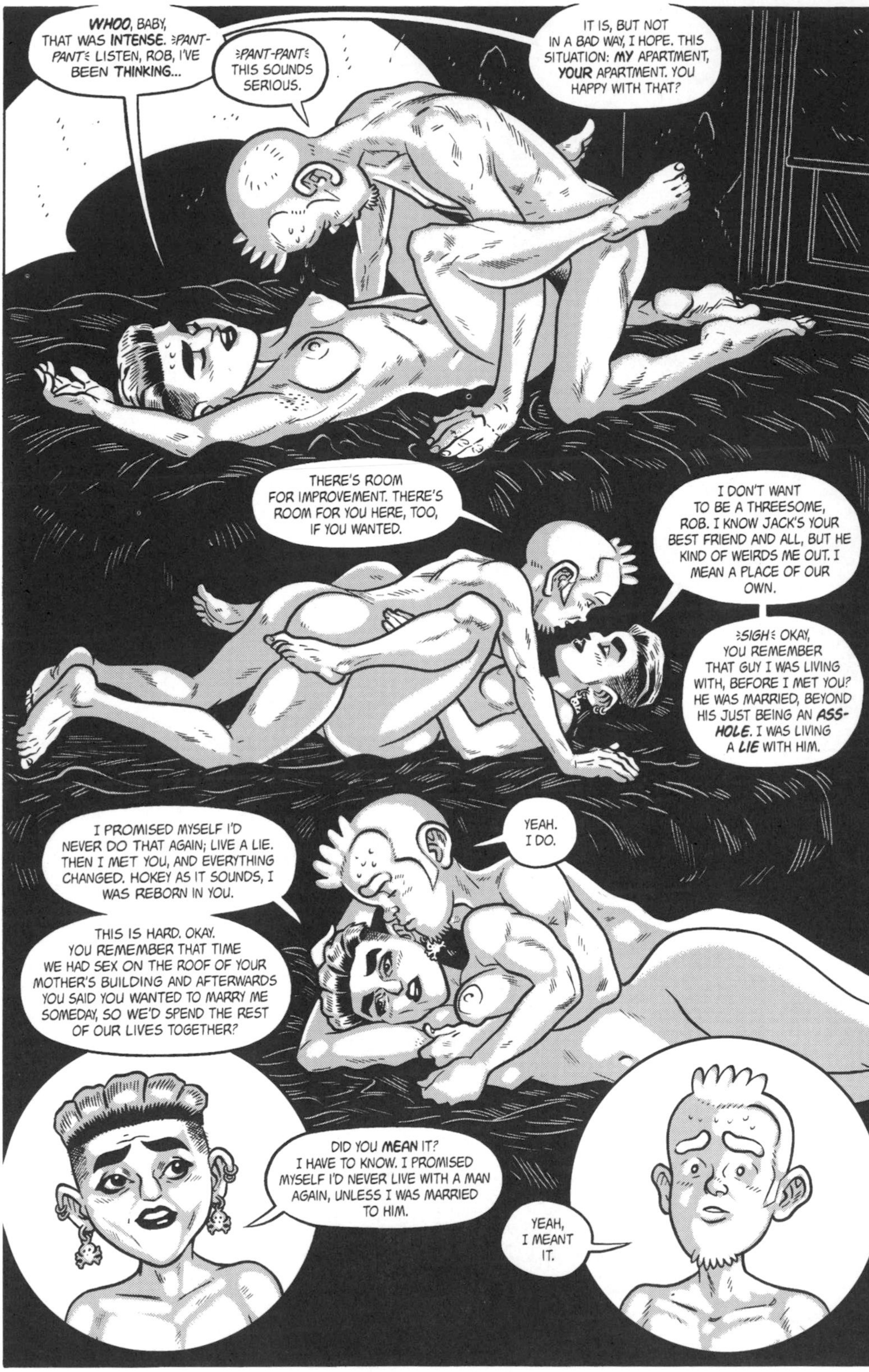
WHOO, BABY, THAT WAS INTENSE. PANT-PANT LISTEN, ROB, I'VE BEEN THINKING...
PANT-PANT THIS SOUNDS SERIOUS.
IT IS, BUT NOT IN A BAD WAY, I HOPE. THIS SITUATION: MY APARTMENT, YOUR APARTMENT. YOU HAPPY WITH THAT?
THERE'S ROOM FOR IMPROVEMENT. THERE'S ROOM FOR YOU HERE, TOO, IF YOU WANTED.
I DON'T WANT TO BE A THREESOME, ROB. I KNOW JACK'S YOUR BEST FRIEND AND ALL, BUT HE KIND OF WEIRDS ME OUT. I MEAN A PLACE OF OUR OWN.
SIGH OKAY, YOU REMEMBER THAT GUY I WAS LIVING WITH, BEFORE I MET YOU? HE WAS MARRIED, BEYOND HIS JUST BEING AN ASS-HOLE. I WAS LIVING A LIE WITH HIM.
I PROMISED MYSELF I'D NEVER DO THAT AGAIN; LIVE A LIE. THEN I MET YOU, AND EVERYTHING CHANGED. HOKEY AS IT SOUNDS, I WAS REBORN IN YOU.
THIS IS HARD. OKAY. YOU REMEMBER THAT TIME WE HAD SEX ON THE ROOF OF YOUR MOTHER'S BUILDING AND AFTERWARDS YOU SAID YOU WANTED TO MARRY ME SOMEDAY, SO WE'D SPEND THE REST OF OUR LIVES TOGETHER?
YEAH. I DO.
DID YOU MEAN IT? I HAVE TO KNOW. I PROMISED MYSELF I'D NEVER LIVE WITH A MAN AGAIN, UNLESS I WAS MARRIED TO HIM.
YEAH, I MEANT IT.

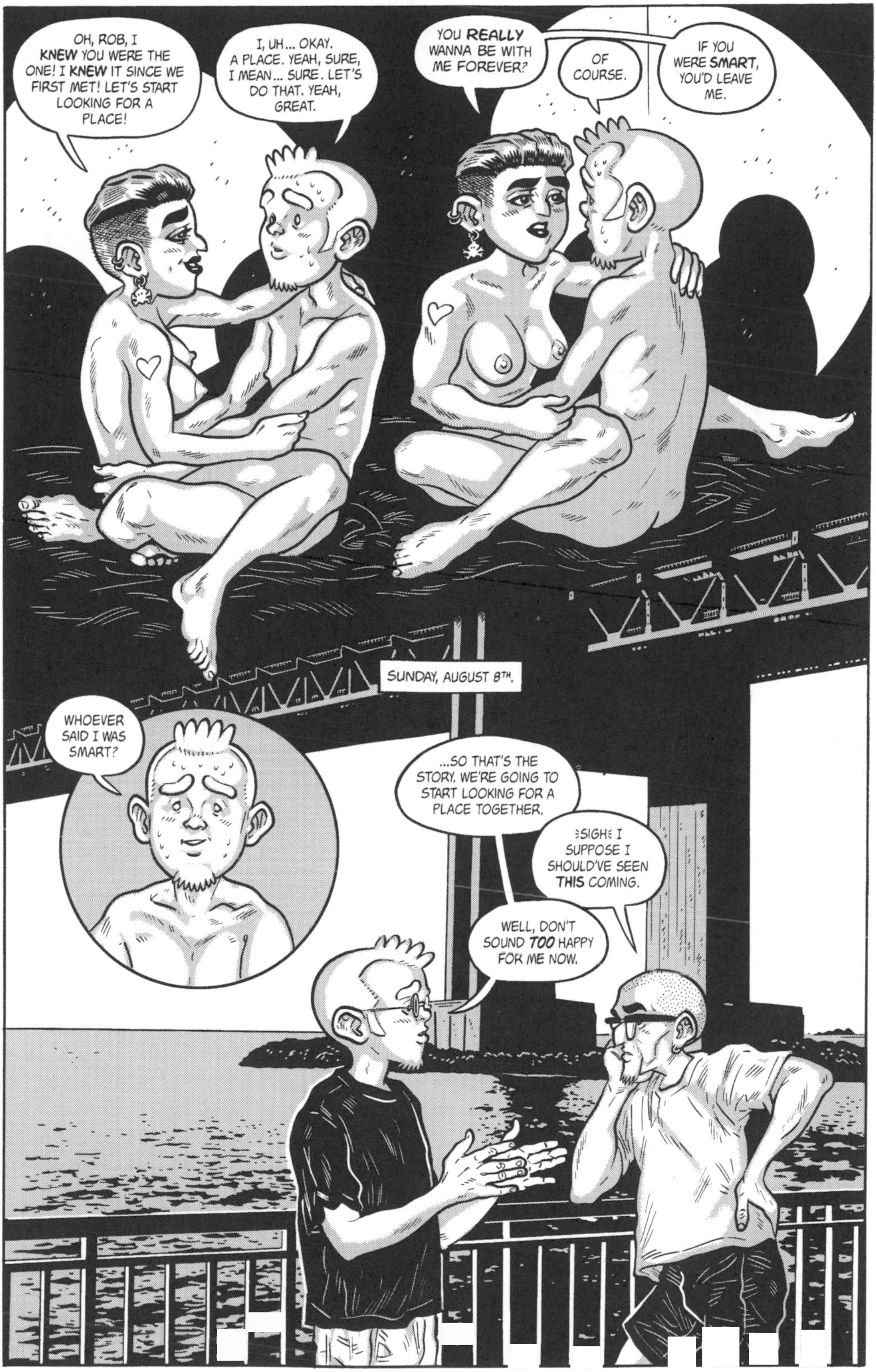
OH, ROB, I KNEW YOU WERE THE ONE! I KNEW IT SINCE WE FIRST MET! LET'S START LOOKING FOR A PLACE!
I, UH... OKAY. A PLACE. YEAH, SURE, I MEAN... SURE. LET'S DO THAT. YEAH, GREAT.
YOU REALLY WANNA BE WITH ME FOREVER?
OF COURSE.
IF YOU WERE SMART, YOU'D LEAVE ME.
SUNDAY, AUGUST 8TH.
WHOEVER SAID I WAS SMART?
...SO THAT'S THE STORY. WE'RE GOING TO START LOOKING FOR A PLACE TOGETHER.
SIGH I SUPPOSE I SHOULD'VE SEEN THIS COMING.
WELL, DON'T SOUND TOO HAPPY FOR ME NOW.

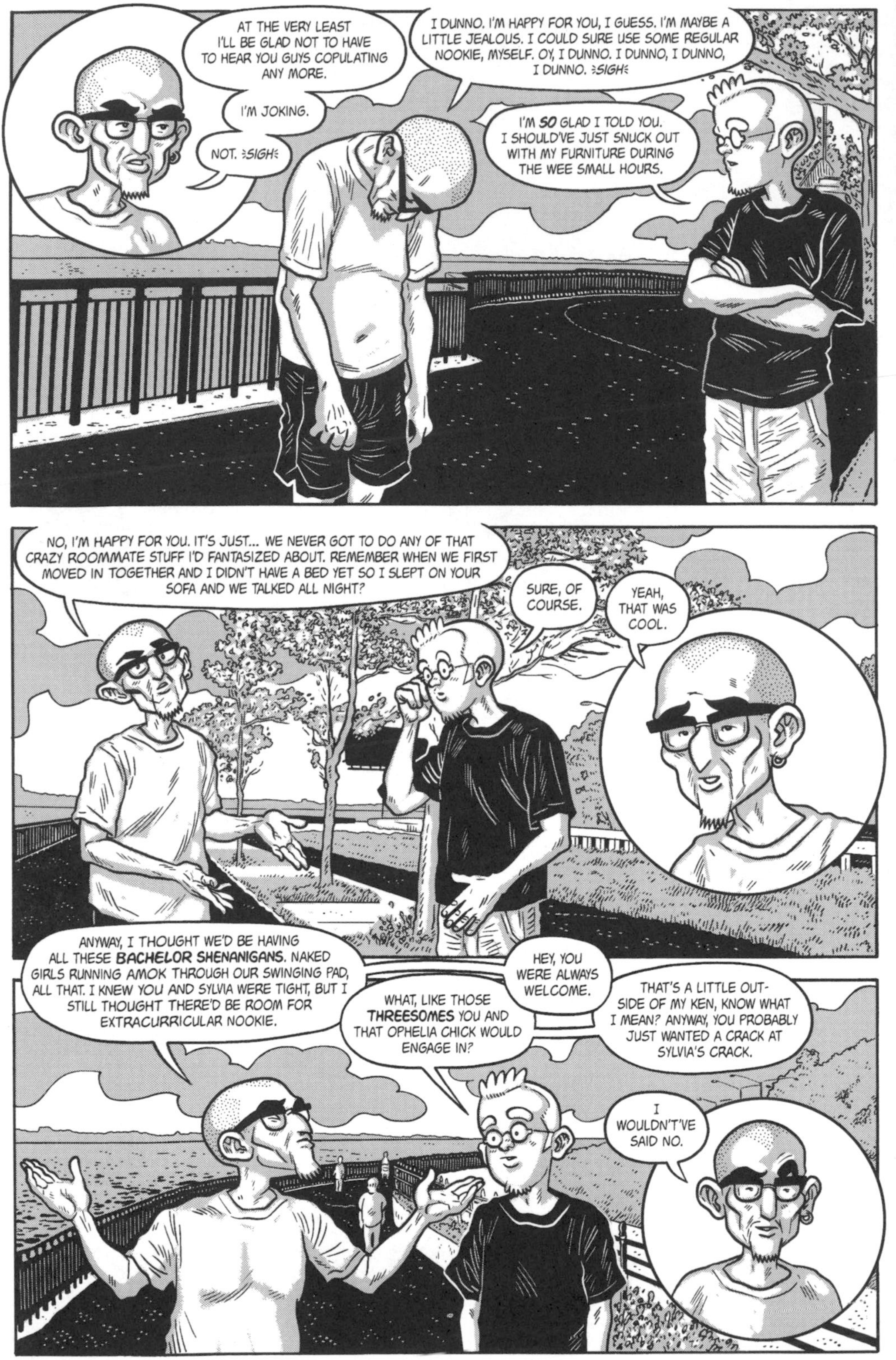
AT THE VERY LEAST I'LL BE GLAD NOT TO HAVE TO HEAR YOU GUYS COPULATING ANY MORE.
I'M JOKING.
NOT. ≷SIGH≶
I DUNNO. I'M HAPPY FOR YOU, I GUESS. I'M MAYBE A LITTLE JEALOUS. I COULD SURE USE SOME REGULAR NOOKIE, MYSELF. OY, I DUNNO. I DUNNO, I DUNNO, I DUNNO. ≷SIGH≶
I'M SO GLAD I TOLD YOU. I SHOULD'VE JUST SNUCK OUT WITH MY FURNITURE DURING THE WEE SMALL HOURS.
NO, I'M HAPPY FOR YOU. IT'S JUST... WE NEVER GOT TO DO ANY OF THAT CRAZY ROOMMATE STUFF I'D FANTASIZED ABOUT. REMEMBER WHEN WE FIRST MOVED IN TOGETHER AND I DIDN'T HAVE A BED YET SO I SLEPT ON YOUR SOFA AND WE TALKED ALL NIGHT?
SURE, OF COURSE.
YEAH, THAT WAS COOL.
ANYWAY, I THOUGHT WE'D BE HAVING ALL THESE BACHELOR SHENANIGANS. NAKED GIRLS RUNNING AMOK THROUGH OUR SWINGING PAD, ALL THAT. I KNEW YOU AND SYLVIA WERE TIGHT, BUT I STILL THOUGHT THERE'D BE ROOM FOR EXTRACURRICULAR NOOKIE.
WHAT, LIKE THOSE THREESOMES YOU AND THAT OPHELIA CHICK WOULD ENGAGE IN?
HEY, YOU WERE ALWAYS WELCOME.
THAT'S A LITTLE OUT-SIDE OF MY KEN, KNOW WHAT I MEAN? ANYWAY, YOU PROBABLY JUST WANTED A CRACK AT SYLVIA'S CRACK.
I WOULDN'T'VE SAID NO.

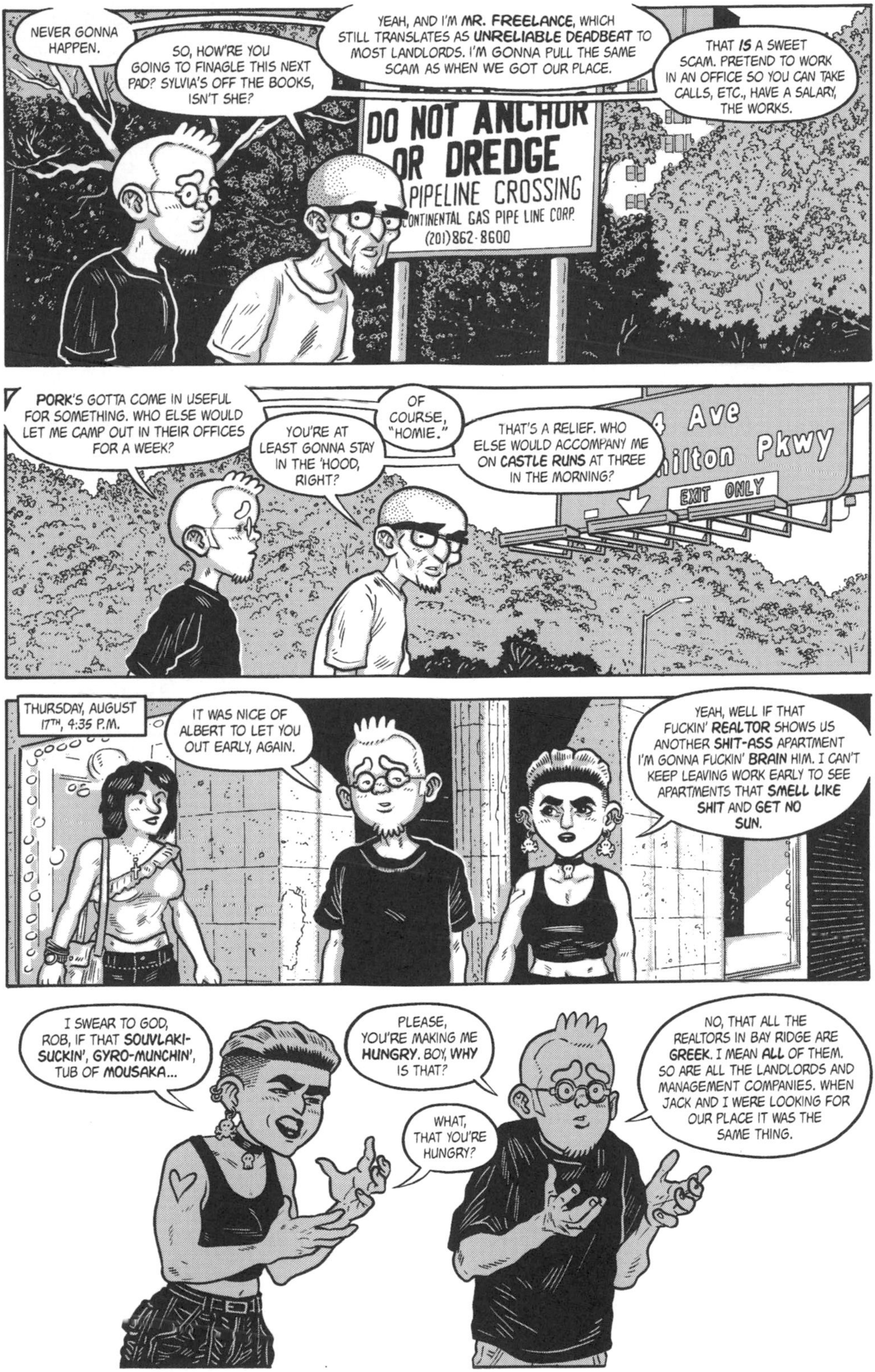
NEVER GONNA HAPPEN.
SO, HOW'RE YOU GOING TO FINAGLE THIS NEXT PAD? SYLVIA'S OFF THE BOOKS, ISN'T SHE?
YEAH, AND I'M MR. FREELANCE, WHICH STILL TRANSLATES AS UNRELIABLE DEADBEAT TO MOST LANDLORDS. I'M GONNA PULL THE SAME SCAM AS WHEN WE GOT OUR PLACE.
THAT IS A SWEET SCAM. PRETEND TO WORK IN AN OFFICE SO YOU CAN TAKE CALLS, ETC., HAVE A SALARY, THE WORKS.
DO NOT ANCHOR OR DREDGE
PIPELINE CROSSING
CONTINENTAL GAS PIPE LINE CORP.
(201) 862-8600
PORK'S GOTTA COME IN USEFUL FOR SOMETHING. WHO ELSE WOULD LET ME CAMP OUT IN THEIR OFFICES FOR A WEEK?
YOU'RE AT LEAST GONNA STAY IN THE 'HOOD, RIGHT?
OF COURSE, "HOMIE."
THAT'S A RELIEF. WHO ELSE WOULD ACCOMPANY ME ON CASTLE RUNS AT THREE IN THE MORNING?
4 Ave
ilton Pkwy
EXIT ONLY
THURSDAY, AUGUST 17TH, 4:35 P.M.
IT WAS NICE OF ALBERT TO LET YOU OUT EARLY, AGAIN.
YEAH, WELL IF THAT FUCKIN' REALTOR SHOWS US ANOTHER SHIT-ASS APARTMENT I'M GONNA FUCKIN' BRAIN HIM. I CAN'T KEEP LEAVING WORK EARLY TO SEE APARTMENTS THAT SMELL LIKE SHIT AND GET NO SUN.
I SWEAR TO GOD, ROB, IF THAT SOUVLAKI-SUCKIN', GYRO-MUNCHIN', TUB OF MOUSAKA...
PLEASE, YOU'RE MAKING ME HUNGRY. BOY, WHY IS THAT?
WHAT, THAT YOU'RE HUNGRY?
NO, THAT ALL THE REALTORS IN BAY RIDGE ARE GREEK. I MEAN ALL OF THEM. SO ARE ALL THE LANDLORDS AND MANAGEMENT COMPANIES. WHEN JACK AND I WERE LOOKING FOR OUR PLACE IT WAS THE SAME THING.

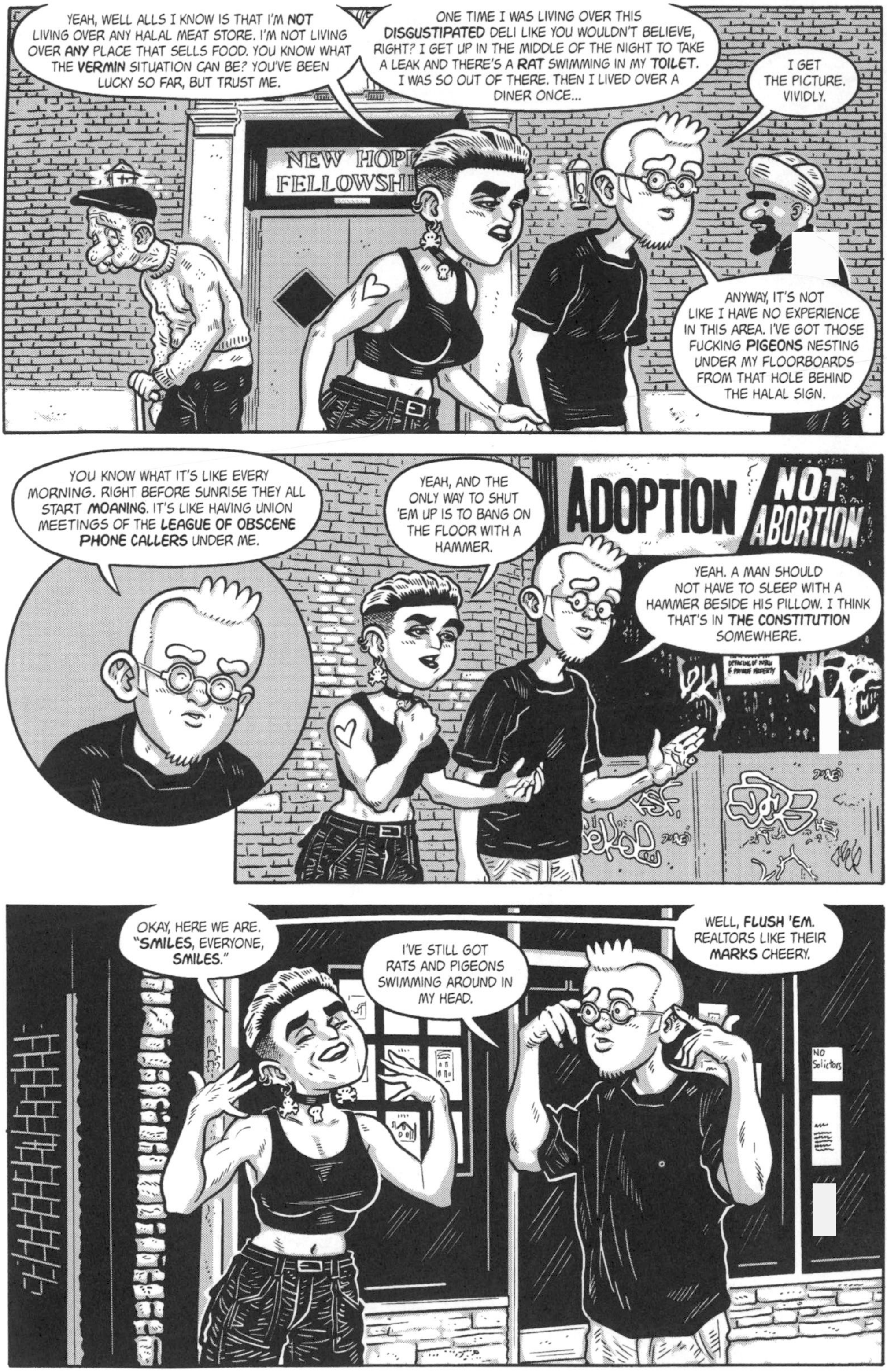
YEAH, WELL ALLS I KNOW IS THAT I'M NOT LIVING OVER ANY HALAL MEAT STORE. I'M NOT LIVING OVER ANY PLACE THAT SELLS FOOD. YOU KNOW WHAT THE VERMIN SITUATION CAN BE? YOU'VE BEEN LUCKY SO FAR, BUT TRUST ME.
ONE TIME I WAS LIVING OVER THIS DISGUSTIPATED DELI LIKE YOU WOULDN'T BELIEVE, RIGHT? I GET UP IN THE MIDDLE OF THE NIGHT TO TAKE A LEAK AND THERE'S A RAT SWIMMING IN MY TOILET. I WAS SO OUT OF THERE. THEN I LIVED OVER A DINER ONCE...
I GET THE PICTURE. VIVIDLY.
NEW HOPE FELLOWSHI
ANYWAY, IT'S NOT LIKE I HAVE NO EXPERIENCE IN THIS AREA. I'VE GOT THOSE FUCKING PIGEONS NESTING UNDER MY FLOORBOARDS FROM THAT HOLE BEHIND THE HALAL SIGN.
YOU KNOW WHAT IT'S LIKE EVERY MORNING. RIGHT BEFORE SUNRISE THEY ALL START MOANING. IT'S LIKE HAVING UNION MEETINGS OF THE LEAGUE OF OBSCENE PHONE CALLERS UNDER ME.
YEAH, AND THE ONLY WAY TO SHUT 'EM UP IS TO BANG ON THE FLOOR WITH A HAMMER.
ADOPTION NOT ABORTION
YEAH. A MAN SHOULD NOT HAVE TO SLEEP WITH A HAMMER BESIDE HIS PILLOW. I THINK THAT'S IN THE CONSTITUTION SOMEWHERE.
OKAY, HERE WE ARE. "SMILES, EVERYONE, SMILES."
I'VE STILL GOT RATS AND PIGEONS SWIMMING AROUND IN MY HEAD.
WELL, FLUSH 'EM. REALTORS LIKE THEIR MARKS CHEERY.
NO Solicitors

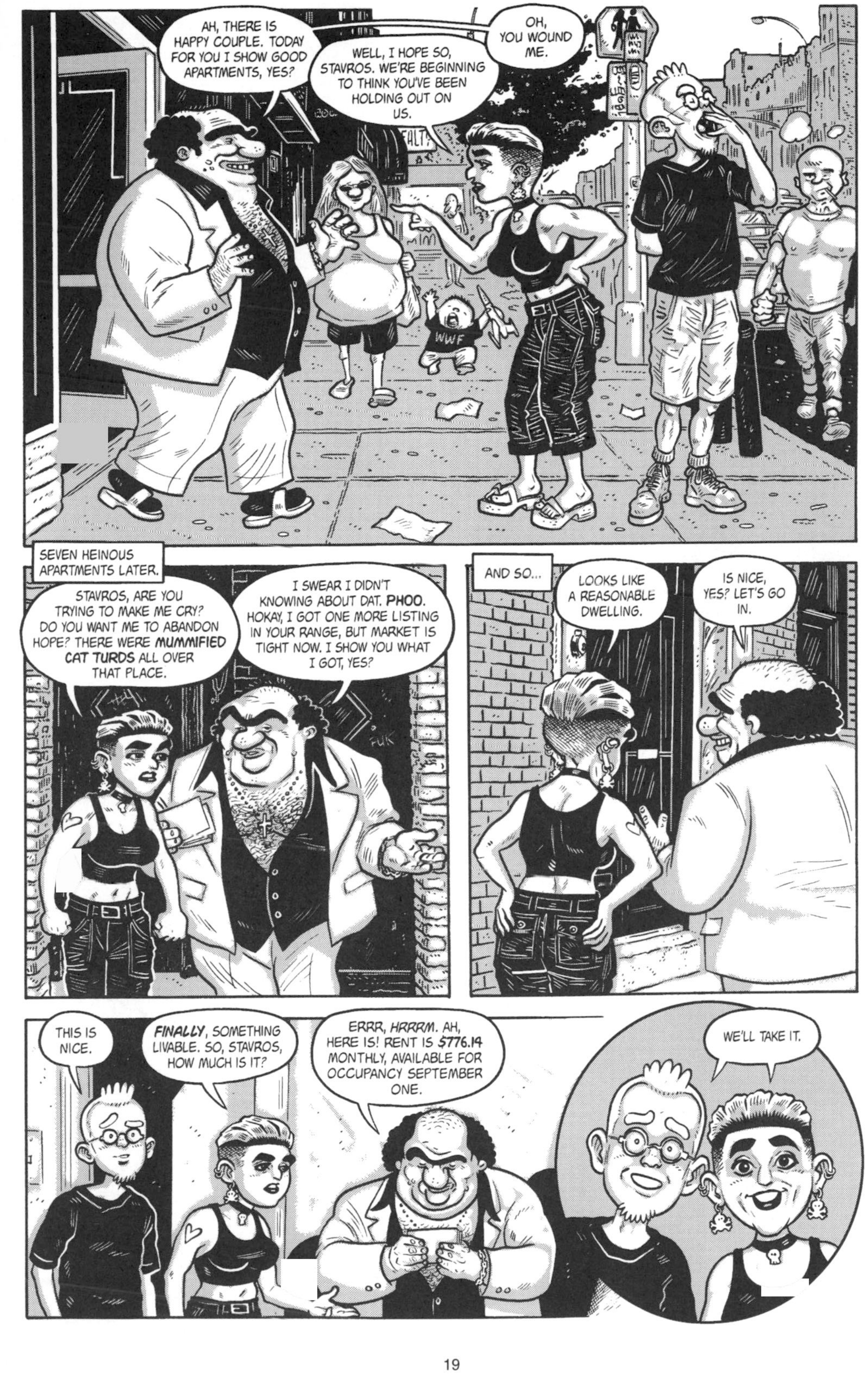
AH, THERE IS HAPPY COUPLE. TODAY FOR YOU I SHOW GOOD APARTMENTS, YES?
WELL, I HOPE SO, STAVROS. WE'RE BEGINNING TO THINK YOU'VE BEEN HOLDING OUT ON US.
OH, YOU WOUND ME.
WWF
SEVEN HEINOUS APARTMENTS LATER.
STAVROS, ARE YOU TRYING TO MAKE ME CRY? DO YOU WANT ME TO ABANDON HOPE? THERE WERE **MUMMIFIED CAT TURDS** ALL OVER THAT PLACE.
I SWEAR I DIDN'T KNOWING ABOUT DAT. **PHOO.** HOKAY, I GOT ONE MORE LISTING IN YOUR RANGE, BUT MARKET IS TIGHT NOW. I SHOW YOU WHAT I GOT, YES?
FUK
AND SO...
LOOKS LIKE A REASONABLE DWELLING.
IS NICE, YES? LET'S GO IN.
THIS IS NICE.
***FINALLY***, SOMETHING LIVABLE. SO, STAVROS, HOW MUCH IS IT?
ERRR, ***HRRRM***. AH, HERE IS! RENT IS **$776.14** MONTHLY, AVAILABLE FOR OCCUPANCY SEPTEMBER ONE.
WE'LL TAKE IT.

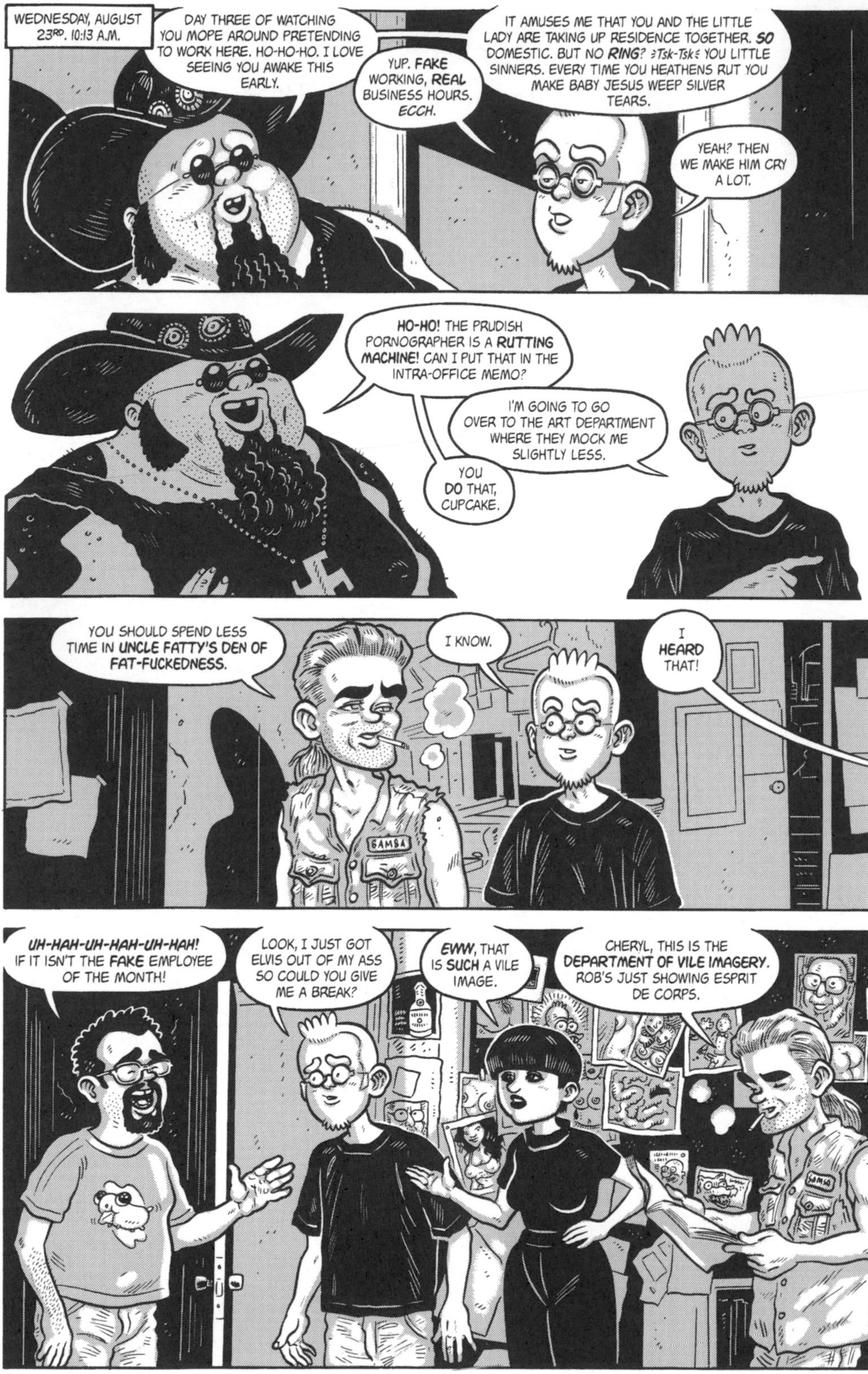
WEDNESDAY, AUGUST 23RD. 10:13 A.M.
DAY THREE OF WATCHING YOU MOPE AROUND PRETENDING TO WORK HERE. HO-HO-HO. I LOVE SEEING YOU AWAKE THIS EARLY.
YUP. FAKE WORKING, REAL BUSINESS HOURS. ECCH.
IT AMUSES ME THAT YOU AND THE LITTLE LADY ARE TAKING UP RESIDENCE TOGETHER. SO DOMESTIC. BUT NO RING? Tsk-Tsk YOU LITTLE SINNERS. EVERY TIME YOU HEATHENS RUT YOU MAKE BABY JESUS WEEP SILVER TEARS.
YEAH? THEN WE MAKE HIM CRY A LOT.
HO-HO! THE PRUDISH PORNOGRAPHER IS A RUTTING MACHINE! CAN I PUT THAT IN THE INTRA-OFFICE MEMO?
I'M GOING TO GO OVER TO THE ART DEPARTMENT WHERE THEY MOCK ME SLIGHTLY LESS.
YOU DO THAT, CUPCAKE.
YOU SHOULD SPEND LESS TIME IN UNCLE FATTY'S DEN OF FAT-FUCKEDNESS.
I KNOW.
I HEARD THAT!
UH-HAH-UH-HAH-UH-HAH! IF IT ISN'T THE FAKE EMPLOYEE OF THE MONTH!
LOOK, I JUST GOT ELVIS OUT OF MY ASS SO COULD YOU GIVE ME A BREAK?
EWW, THAT IS SUCH A VILE IMAGE.
CHERYL, THIS IS THE DEPARTMENT OF VILE IMAGERY. ROB'S JUST SHOWING ESPRIT DE CORPS.

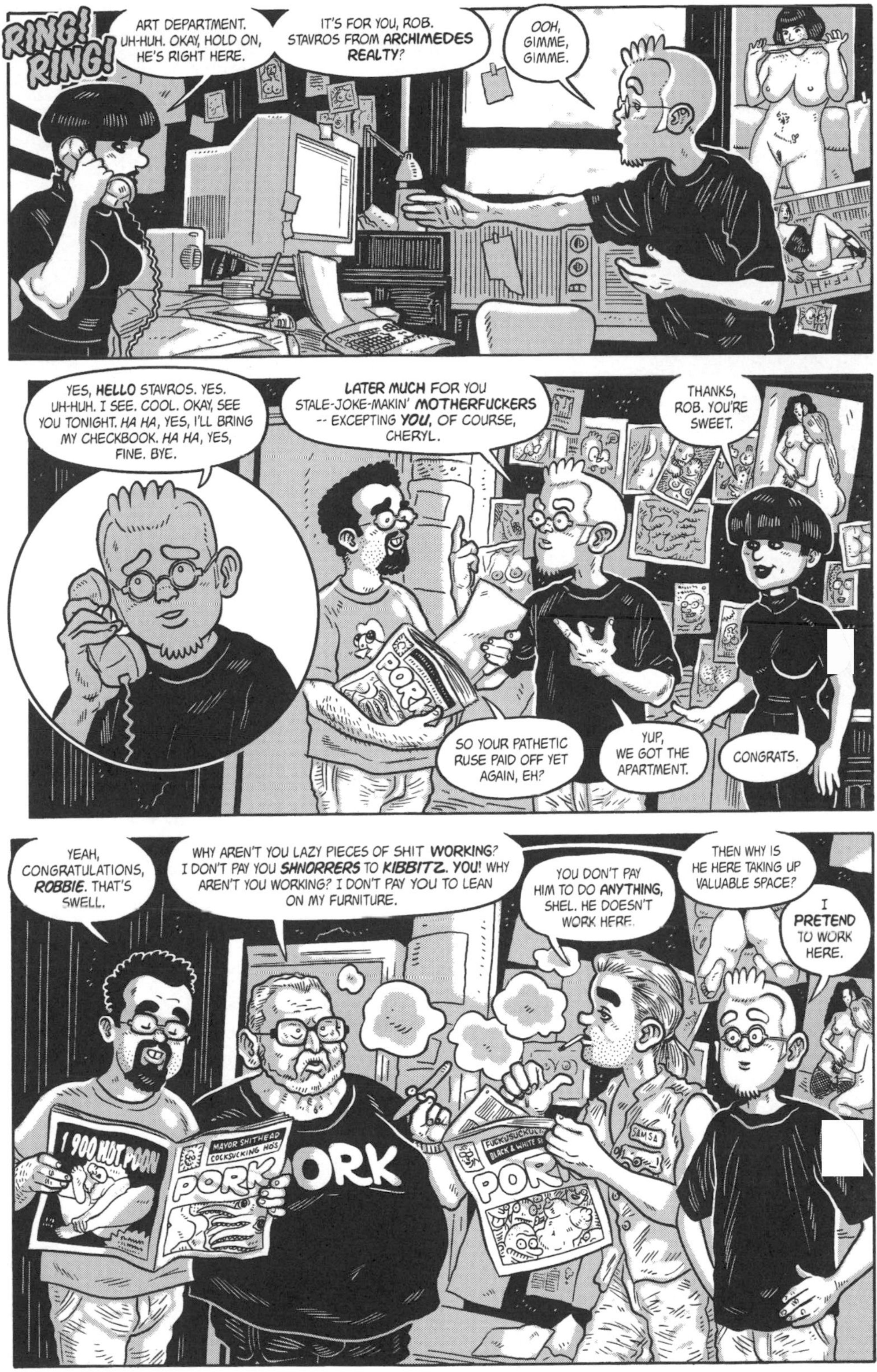
RING! RING!
ART DEPARTMENT. UH-HUH. OKAY, HOLD ON, HE'S RIGHT HERE.
IT'S FOR YOU, ROB. STAVROS FROM ARCHIMEDES REALTY?
OOH, GIMME, GIMME.
YES, HELLO STAVROS. YES. UH-HUH. I SEE. COOL. OKAY, SEE YOU TONIGHT. HA HA, YES, I'LL BRING MY CHECKBOOK. HA HA, YES, FINE. BYE.
LATER MUCH FOR YOU STALE-JOKE-MAKIN' MOTHERFUCKERS -- EXCEPTING YOU, OF COURSE, CHERYL.
THANKS, ROB. YOU'RE SWEET.
SO YOUR PATHETIC RUSE PAID OFF YET AGAIN, EH?
YUP, WE GOT THE APARTMENT.
CONGRATS.
YEAH, CONGRATULATIONS, ROBBIE. THAT'S SWELL.
WHY AREN'T YOU LAZY PIECES OF SHIT WORKING? I DON'T PAY YOU SHNORRERS TO KIBBITZ. YOU! WHY AREN'T YOU WORKING? I DON'T PAY YOU TO LEAN ON MY FURNITURE.
YOU DON'T PAY HIM TO DO ANYTHING, SHEL. HE DOESN'T WORK HERE.
THEN WHY IS HE HERE TAKING UP VALUABLE SPACE?
I PRETEND TO WORK HERE.
1 900 HOT POON
MAYOR SHITHEAD
COCKSUCKING HOS
PORK
ORK
BLACK & WHITE
SAMSA

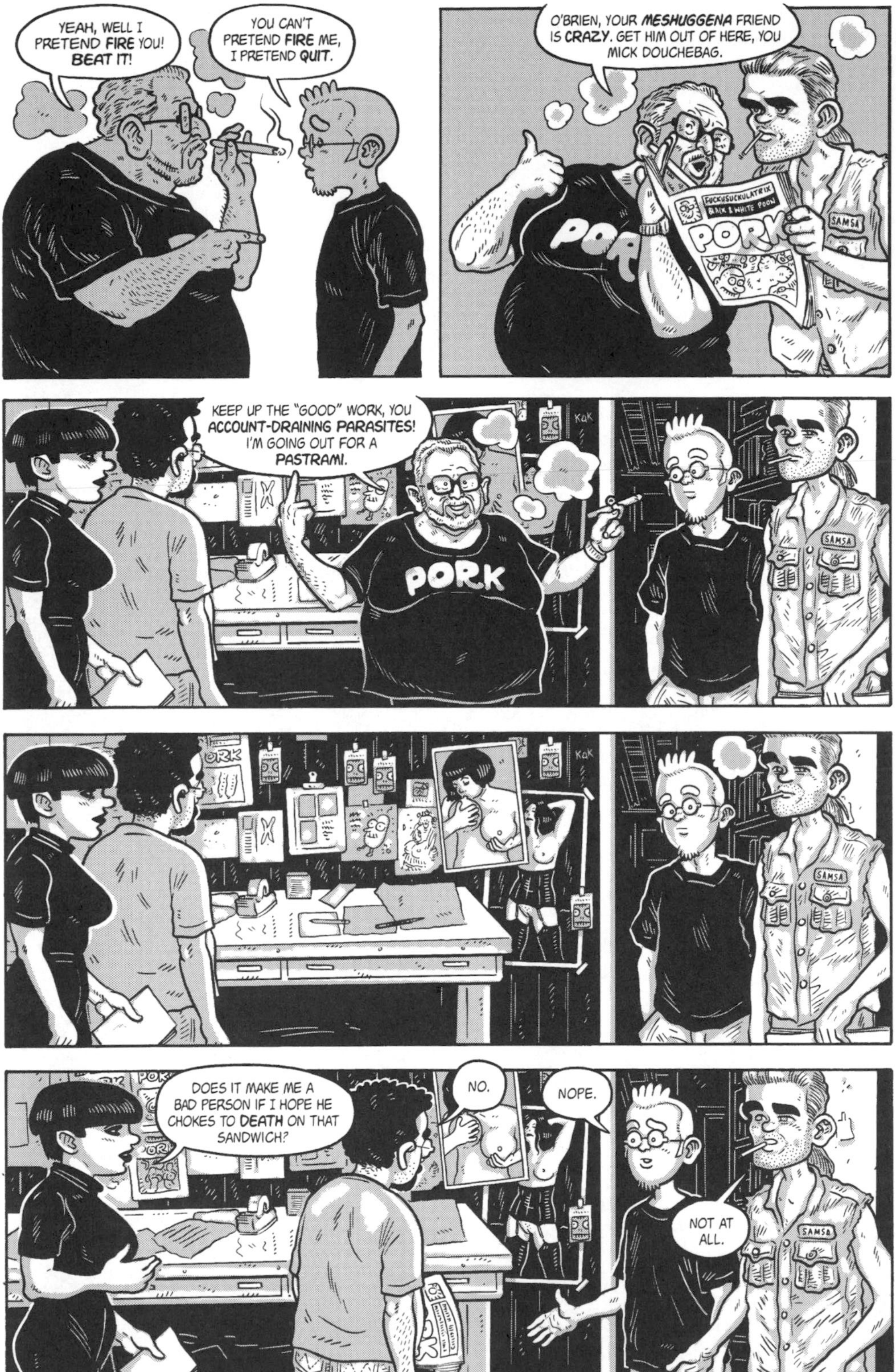
YEAH, WELL I PRETEND **FIRE** YOU! **BEAT IT**!
YOU CAN'T PRETEND **FIRE** ME, I PRETEND **QUIT**.
O'BRIEN, YOUR ***MESHUGGENA*** FRIEND IS **CRAZY**. GET HIM OUT OF HERE, YOU MICK DOUCHEBAG.
FUCKUSUCKULATRIX
BLACK & WHITE POON
PORK
SAMSA
PORK
KEEP UP THE "GOOD" WORK, YOU **ACCOUNT-DRAINING PARASITES!** I'M GOING OUT FOR A **PASTRAMI**.
KAK
SAMSA
KAK
SAMSA
DOES IT MAKE ME A BAD PERSON IF I HOPE HE CHOKES TO **DEATH** ON THAT SANDWICH?
NO.
NOPE.
NOT AT ALL.
SAMSA

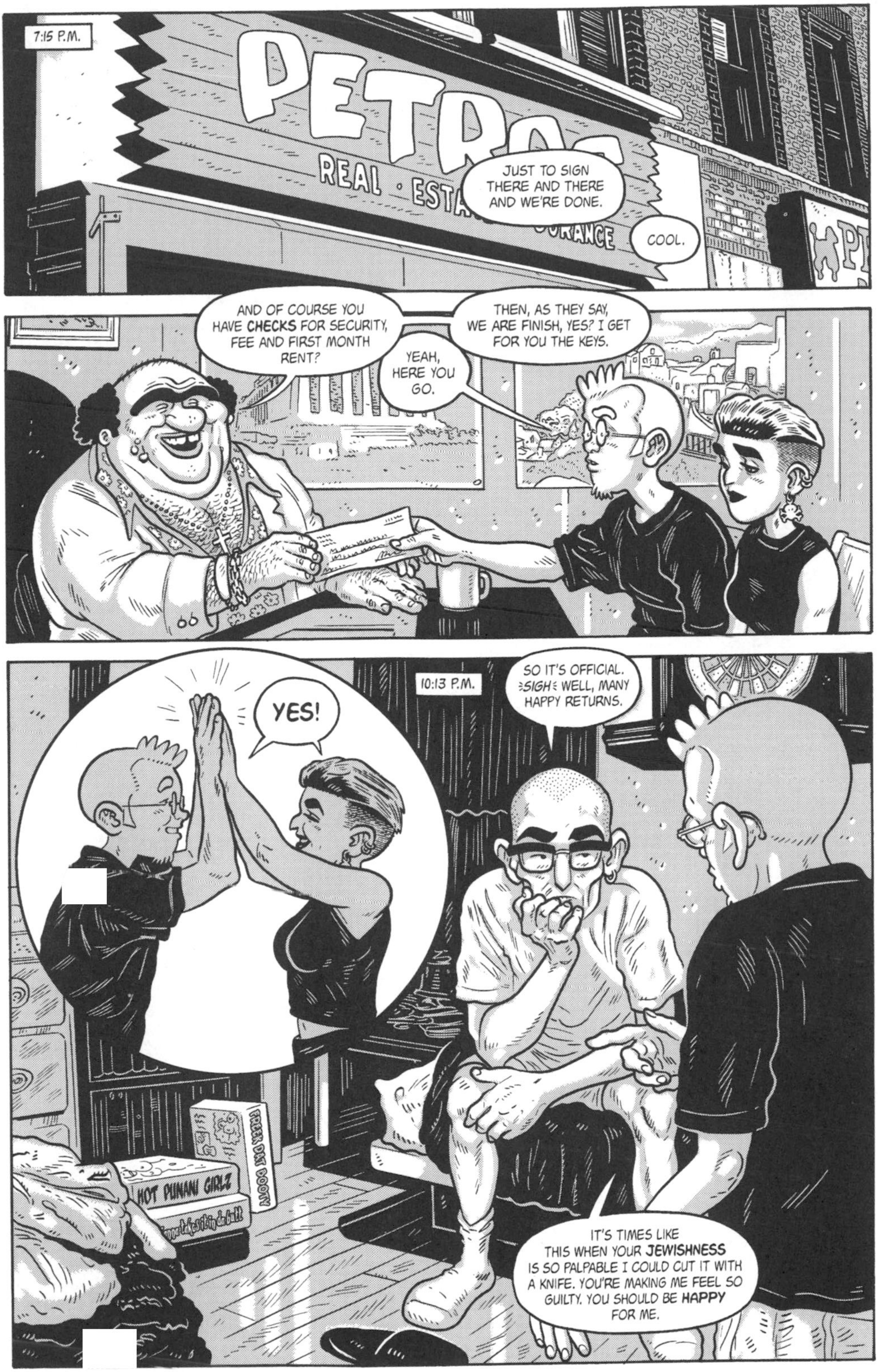
7:15 P.M.
JUST TO SIGN THERE AND THERE AND WE'RE DONE.
COOL.
AND OF COURSE YOU HAVE CHECKS FOR SECURITY, FEE AND FIRST MONTH RENT?
YEAH, HERE YOU GO.
THEN, AS THEY SAY, WE ARE FINISH, YES? I GET FOR YOU THE KEYS.
10:13 P.M.
YES!
SO IT'S OFFICIAL. SIGH WELL, MANY HAPPY RETURNS.
HOT PUNANI GIRLZ
FREAK DAT BOOTY
IT'S TIMES LIKE THIS WHEN YOUR JEWISHNESS IS SO PALPABLE I COULD CUT IT WITH A KNIFE. YOU'RE MAKING ME FEEL SO GUILTY. YOU SHOULD BE HAPPY FOR ME.

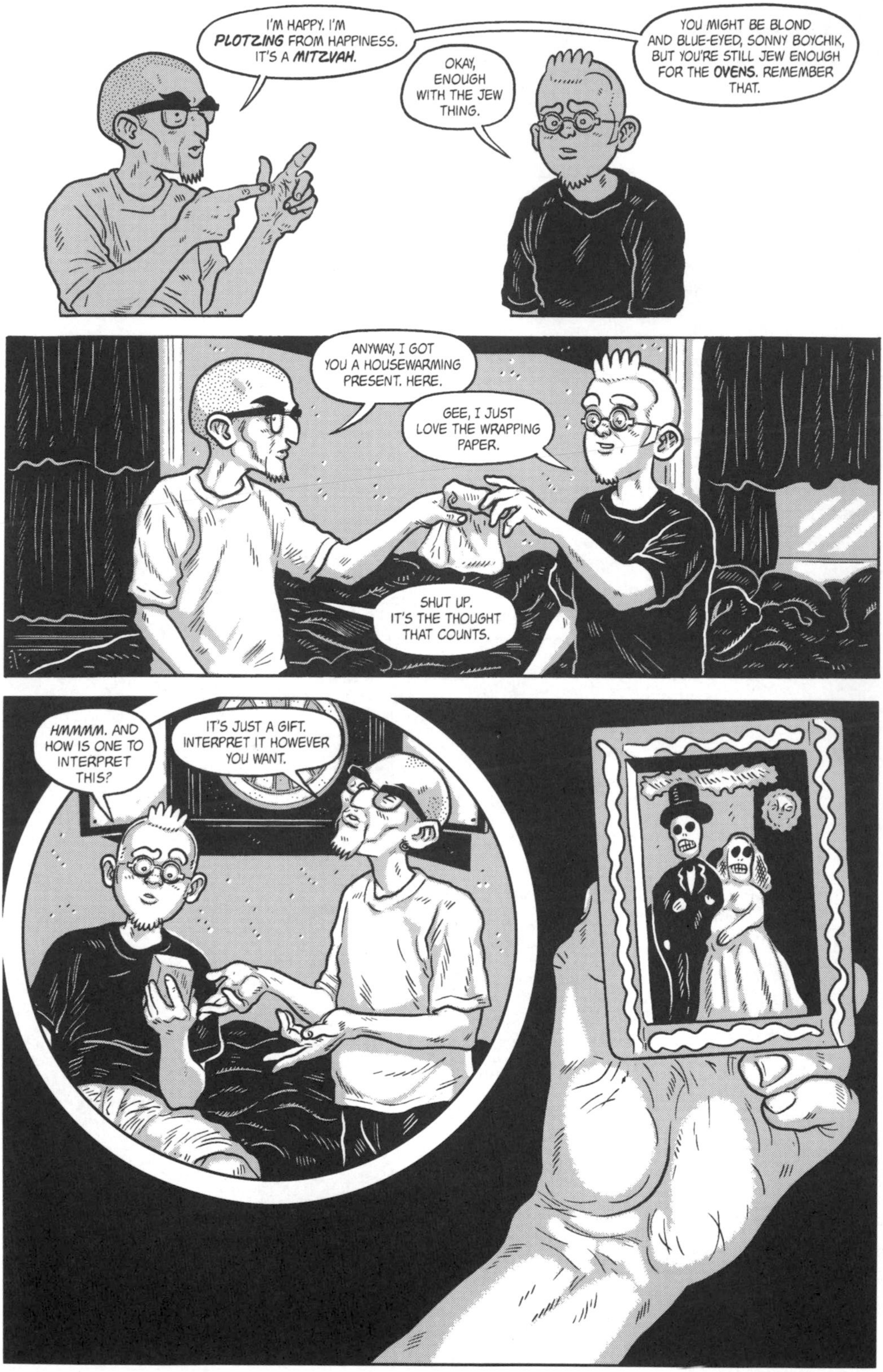
I'M HAPPY. I'M PLOTZING FROM HAPPINESS. IT'S A MITZVAH.
OKAY, ENOUGH WITH THE JEW THING.
YOU MIGHT BE BLOND AND BLUE-EYED, SONNY BOYCHIK, BUT YOU'RE STILL JEW ENOUGH FOR THE OVENS. REMEMBER THAT.
ANYWAY, I GOT YOU A HOUSEWARMING PRESENT. HERE.
GEE, I JUST LOVE THE WRAPPING PAPER.
SHUT UP. IT'S THE THOUGHT THAT COUNTS.
HMMMM. AND HOW IS ONE TO INTERPRET THIS?
IT'S JUST A GIFT. INTERPRET IT HOWEVER YOU WANT.

# CHAPTER TWO
# BELABORED DAY WEEKEND

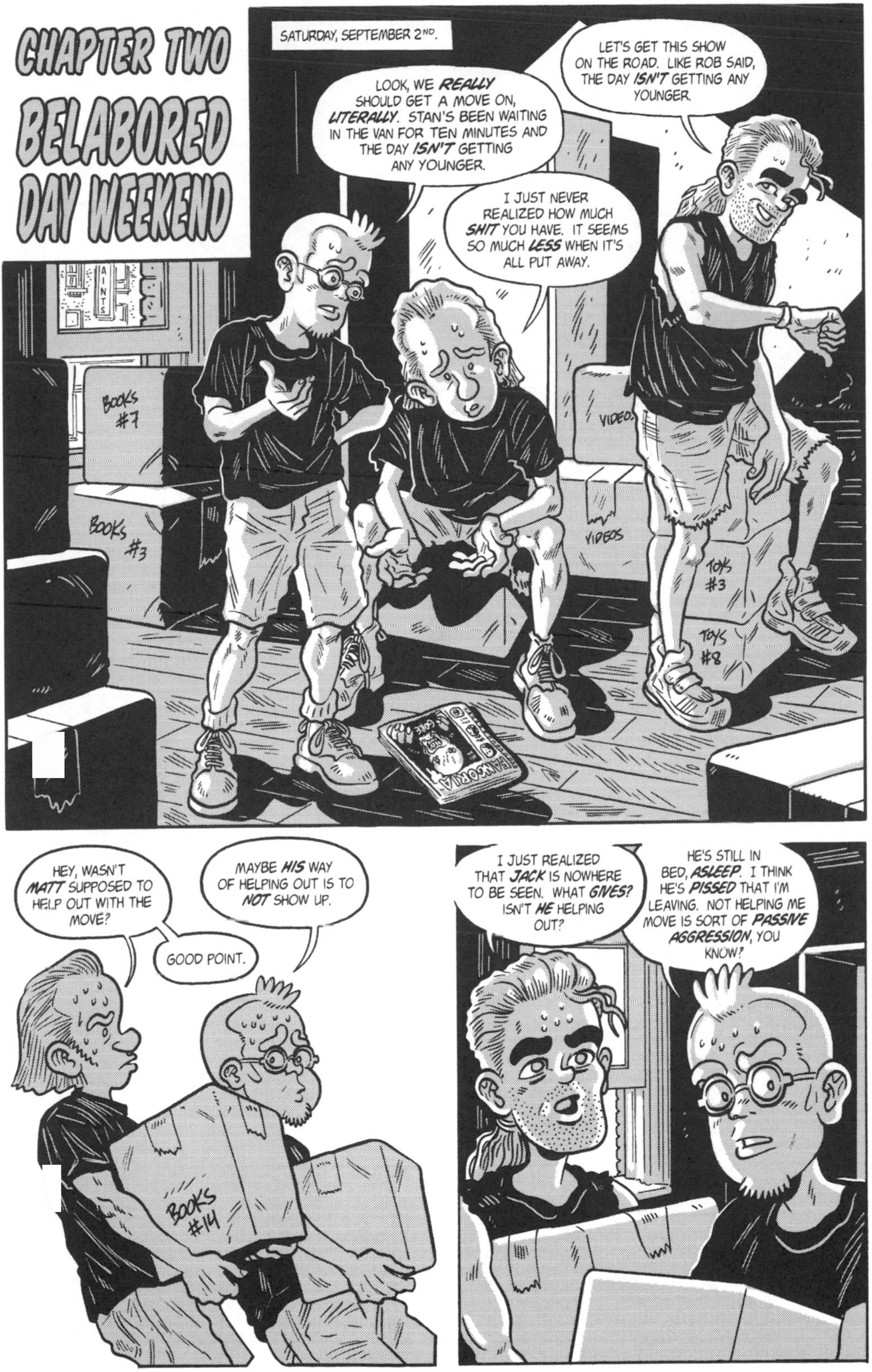

SATURDAY, SEPTEMBER 2ND.
LOOK, WE REALLY SHOULD GET A MOVE ON, LITERALLY. STAN'S BEEN WAITING IN THE VAN FOR TEN MINUTES AND THE DAY ISN'T GETTING ANY YOUNGER.
LET'S GET THIS SHOW ON THE ROAD. LIKE ROB SAID, THE DAY ISN'T GETTING ANY YOUNGER.
I JUST NEVER REALIZED HOW MUCH SHIT YOU HAVE. IT SEEMS SO MUCH LESS WHEN IT'S ALL PUT AWAY.
BOOKS #7
BOOKS #3
VIDEOS
VIDEOS
TOYS #3
TOYS #8
FANGORIA
HEY, WASN'T MATT SUPPOSED TO HELP OUT WITH THE MOVE?
MAYBE HIS WAY OF HELPING OUT IS TO NOT SHOW UP.
GOOD POINT.
BOOKS #14
I JUST REALIZED THAT JACK IS NOWHERE TO BE SEEN. WHAT GIVES? ISN'T HE HELPING OUT?
HE'S STILL IN BED, ASLEEP. I THINK HE'S PISSED THAT I'M LEAVING. NOT HELPING ME MOVE IS SORT OF PASSIVE AGGRESSION, YOU KNOW?

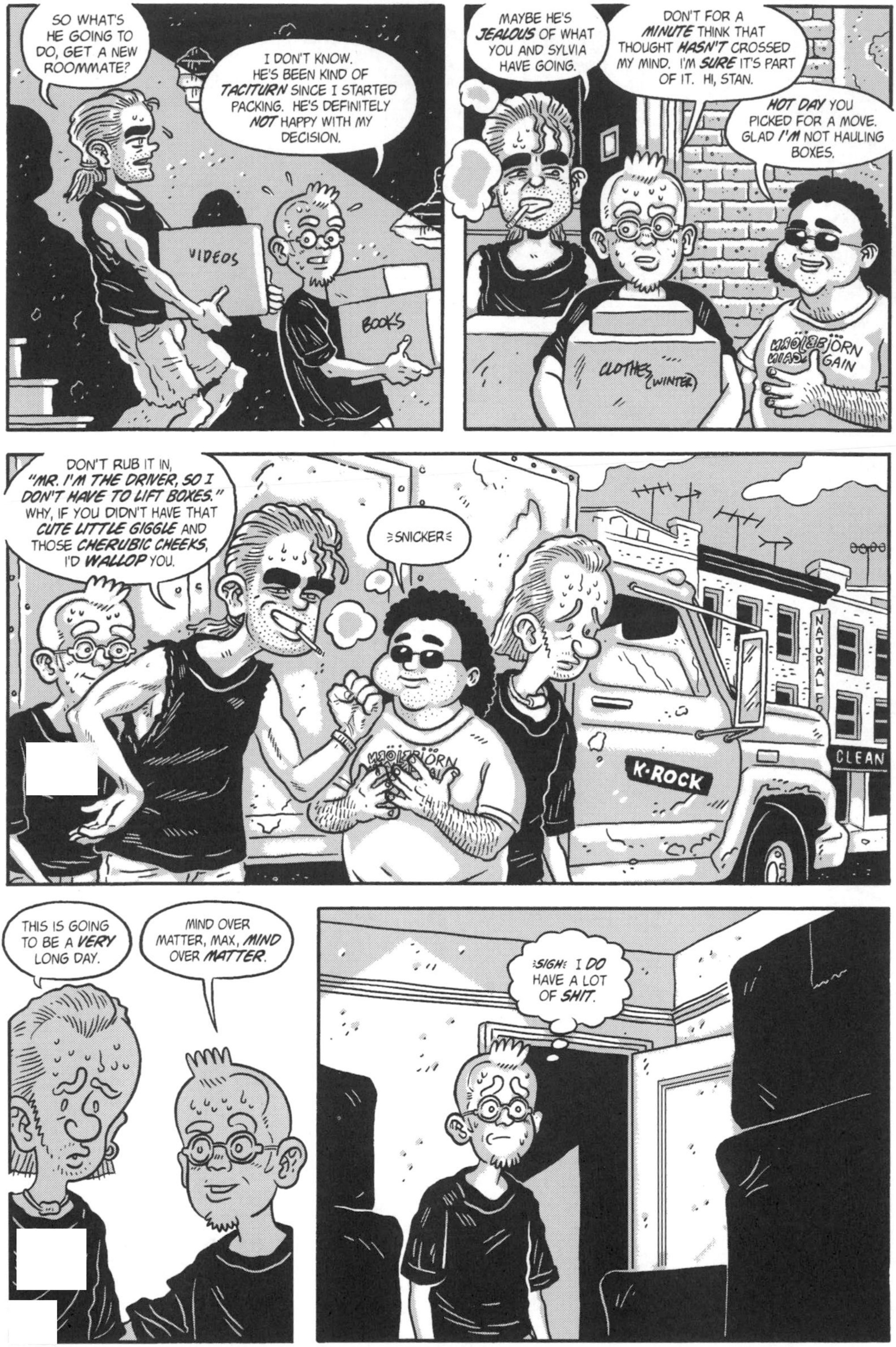
SO WHAT'S HE GOING TO DO, GET A NEW ROOMMATE?
I DON'T KNOW. HE'S BEEN KIND OF *TACITURN* SINCE I STARTED PACKING. HE'S DEFINITELY *NOT* HAPPY WITH MY DECISION.
VIDEOS
BOOKS
MAYBE HE'S *JEALOUS* OF WHAT YOU AND SYLVIA HAVE GOING.
DON'T FOR A *MINUTE* THINK THAT THOUGHT *HASN'T* CROSSED MY MIND. I'M *SURE* IT'S PART OF IT. HI, STAN.
*HOT DAY* YOU PICKED FOR A MOVE. GLAD *I'M* NOT HAULING BOXES.
CLOTHES (WINTER)
DON'T RUB IT IN, ***"MR. I'M THE DRIVER, SO I DON'T HAVE TO LIFT BOXES."*** WHY, IF YOU DIDN'T HAVE THAT ***CUTE LITTLE GIGGLE*** AND THOSE ***CHERUBIC CHEEKS***, I'D ***WALLOP*** YOU.
SNICKER
K-ROCK
CLEAN
THIS IS GOING TO BE A *VERY* LONG DAY.
MIND OVER MATTER, MAX, *MIND* OVER *MATTER*.
*SIGH* I *DO* HAVE A LOT OF *SHIT*.

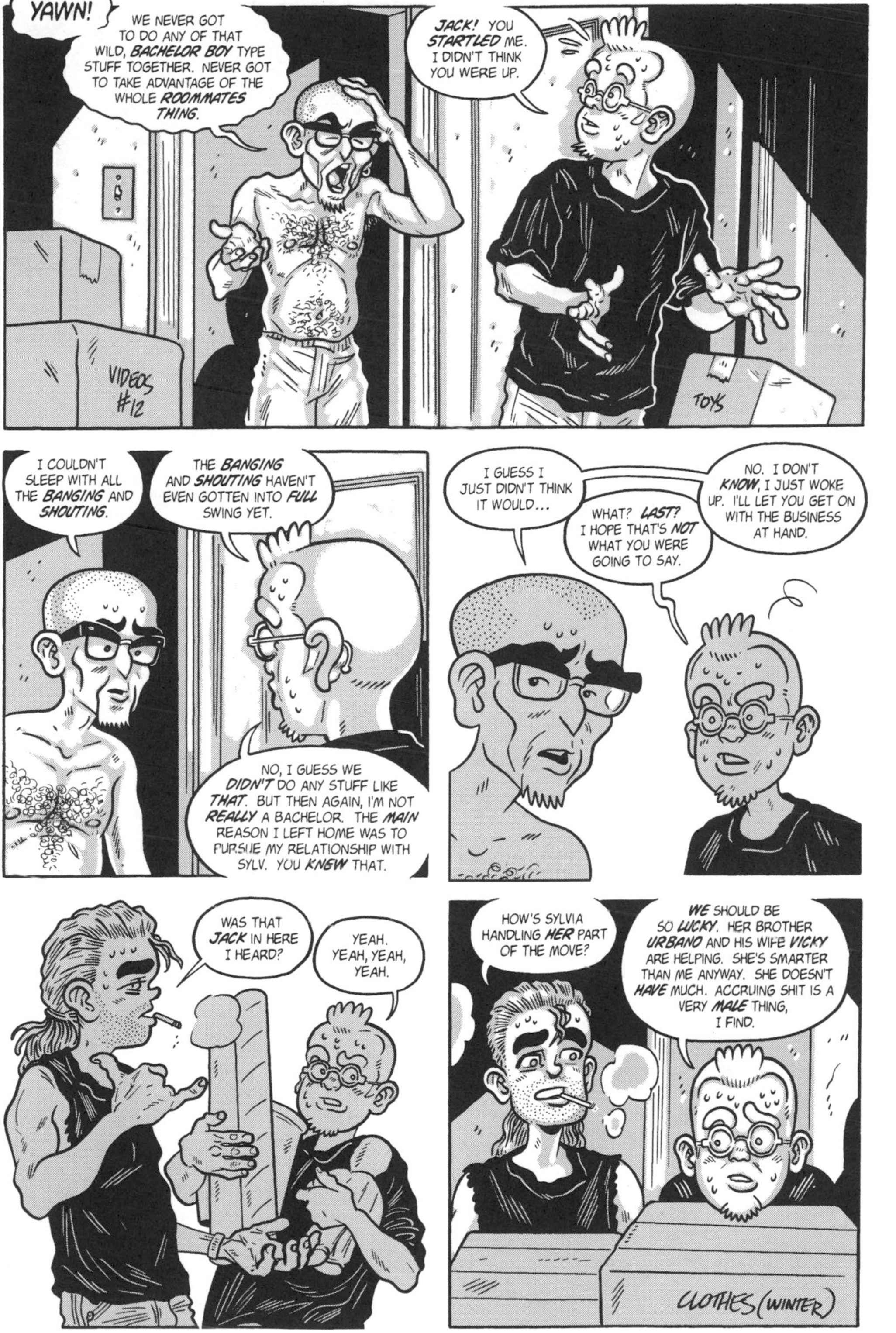
YAWN!
WE NEVER GOT TO DO ANY OF THAT WILD, BACHELOR BOY TYPE STUFF TOGETHER. NEVER GOT TO TAKE ADVANTAGE OF THE WHOLE ROOMMATES THING.
JACK! YOU STARTLED ME. I DIDN'T THINK YOU WERE UP.
VIDEOS #12
TOYS
I COULDN'T SLEEP WITH ALL THE BANGING AND SHOUTING.
THE BANGING AND SHOUTING HAVEN'T EVEN GOTTEN INTO FULL SWING YET.
NO, I GUESS WE DIDN'T DO ANY STUFF LIKE THAT. BUT THEN AGAIN, I'M NOT REALLY A BACHELOR. THE MAIN REASON I LEFT HOME WAS TO PURSUE MY RELATIONSHIP WITH SYLV. YOU KNEW THAT.
I GUESS I JUST DIDN'T THINK IT WOULD...
WHAT? LAST? I HOPE THAT'S NOT WHAT YOU WERE GOING TO SAY.
NO. I DON'T KNOW, I JUST WOKE UP. I'LL LET YOU GET ON WITH THE BUSINESS AT HAND.
WAS THAT JACK IN HERE I HEARD?
YEAH. YEAH, YEAH, YEAH.
HOW'S SYLVIA HANDLING HER PART OF THE MOVE?
WE SHOULD BE SO LUCKY. HER BROTHER URBANO AND HIS WIFE VICKY ARE HELPING. SHE'S SMARTER THAN ME ANYWAY. SHE DOESN'T HAVE MUCH. ACCRUING SHIT IS A VERY MALE THING, I FIND.
CLOTHES (WINTER)

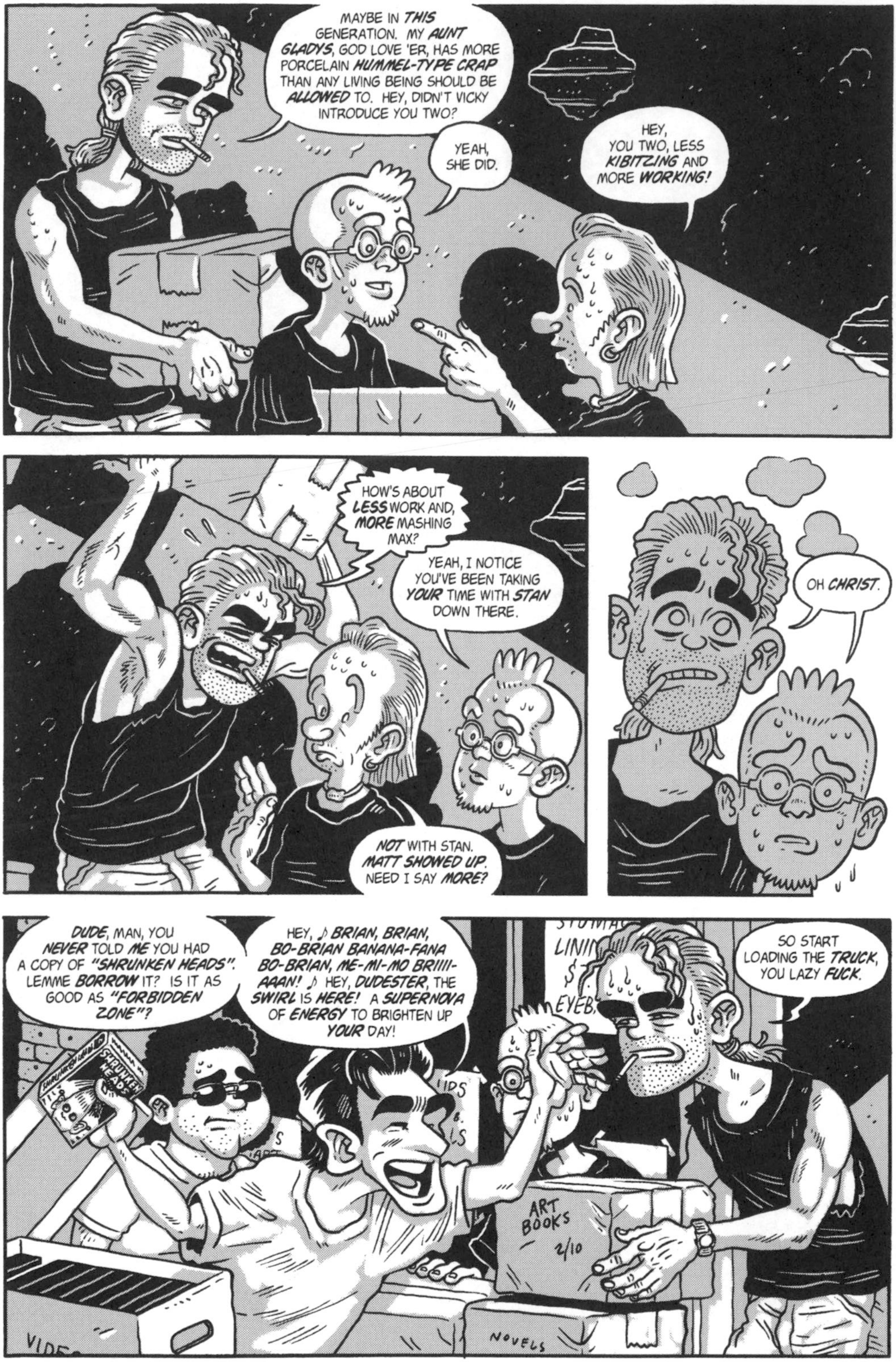
MAYBE IN THIS GENERATION. MY AUNT GLADYS, GOD LOVE 'ER, HAS MORE PORCELAIN HUMMEL-TYPE CRAP THAN ANY LIVING BEING SHOULD BE ALLOWED TO. HEY, DIDN'T VICKY INTRODUCE YOU TWO?
YEAH, SHE DID.
HEY, YOU TWO, LESS KIBITZING AND MORE WORKING!
HOW'S ABOUT LESS WORK AND, MORE MASHING MAX?
YEAH, I NOTICE YOU'VE BEEN TAKING YOUR TIME WITH STAN DOWN THERE.
NOT WITH STAN. MATT SHOWED UP. NEED I SAY MORE?
OH CHRIST.
DUDE, MAN, YOU NEVER TOLD ME YOU HAD A COPY OF "SHRUNKEN HEADS". LEMME BORROW IT? IS IT AS GOOD AS "FORBIDDEN ZONE"?
HEY, ♪ BRIAN, BRIAN, BO-BRIAN BANANA-FANA BO-BRIAN, ME-MI-MO BRIIII-AAAN! ♪ HEY, DUDESTER, THE SWIRL IS HERE! A SUPERNOVA OF ENERGY TO BRIGHTEN UP YOUR DAY!
SO START LOADING THE TRUCK, YOU LAZY FUCK.
SHRUNKEN HEADS
ART BOOKS 2/10
NOVELS

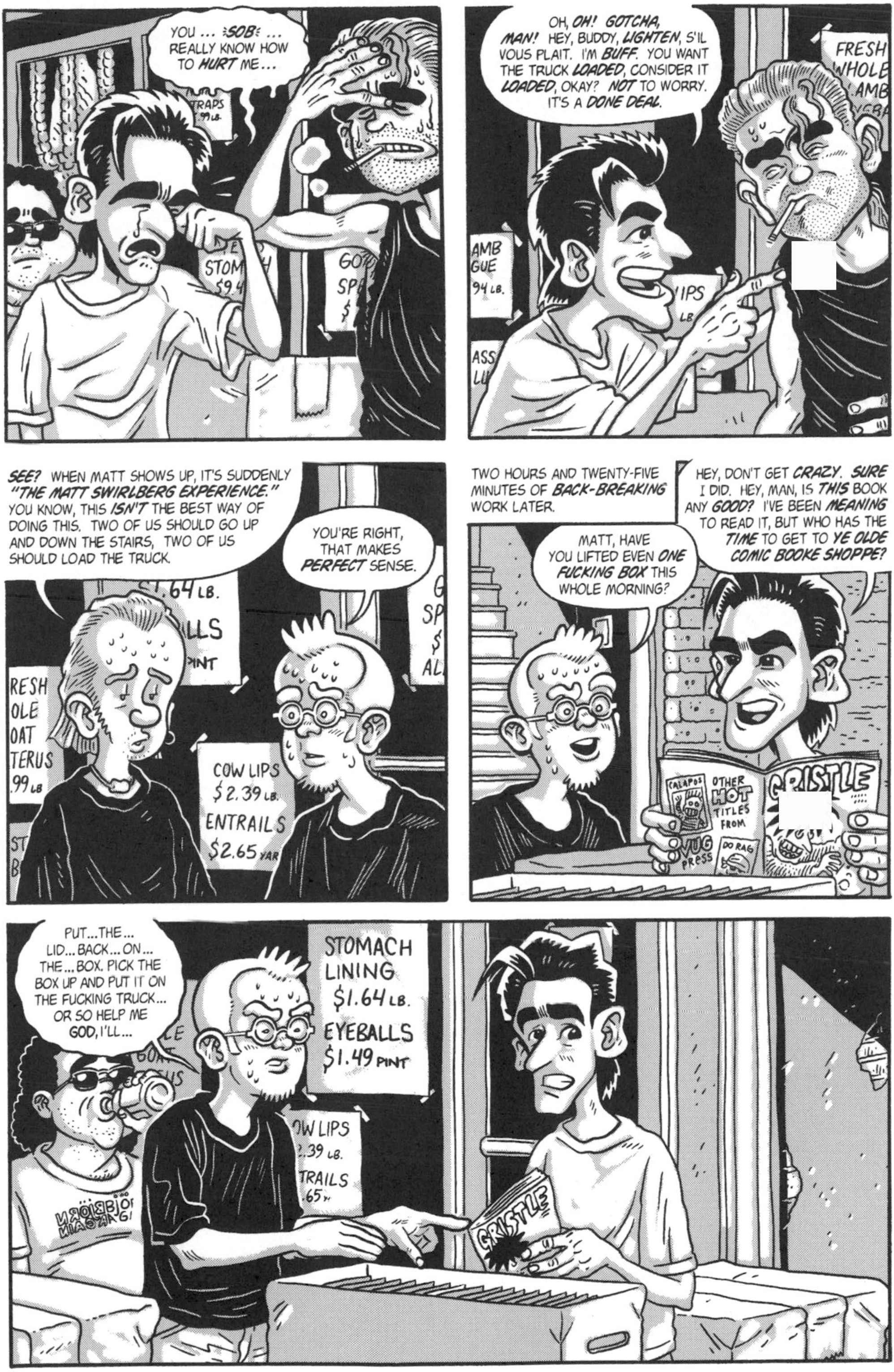

YOU ... SOB ... REALLY KNOW HOW TO HURT ME...
TRAPS 99 LB.
OH, OH! GOTCHA, MAN! HEY, BUDDY, LIGHTEN, S'IL VOUS PLAIT. I'M BUFF. YOU WANT THE TRUCK LOADED, CONSIDER IT LOADED, OKAY? NOT TO WORRY. IT'S A DONE DEAL.
FRESH WHOLE LAMB
SEE? WHEN MATT SHOWS UP, IT'S SUDDENLY "THE MATT SWIRLBERG EXPERIENCE." YOU KNOW, THIS ISN'T THE BEST WAY OF DOING THIS. TWO OF US SHOULD GO UP AND DOWN THE STAIRS, TWO OF US SHOULD LOAD THE TRUCK.
YOU'RE RIGHT, THAT MAKES PERFECT SENSE.
COW LIPS $2.39 LB.
ENTRAILS $2.65
TWO HOURS AND TWENTY-FIVE MINUTES OF BACK-BREAKING WORK LATER.
MATT, HAVE YOU LIFTED EVEN ONE FUCKING BOX THIS WHOLE MORNING?
HEY, DON'T GET CRAZY. SURE I DID. HEY, MAN, IS THIS BOOK ANY GOOD? I'VE BEEN MEANING TO READ IT, BUT WHO HAS THE TIME TO GET TO YE OLDE COMIC BOOKE SHOPPE?
GRISTLE
OTHER HOT TITLES FROM VUG PRESS
PUT...THE... LID...BACK...ON... THE...BOX. PICK THE BOX UP AND PUT IT ON THE FUCKING TRUCK... OR SO HELP ME GOD, I'LL...
STOMACH LINING $1.64 LB.
EYEBALLS $1.49 PINT
GRISTLE

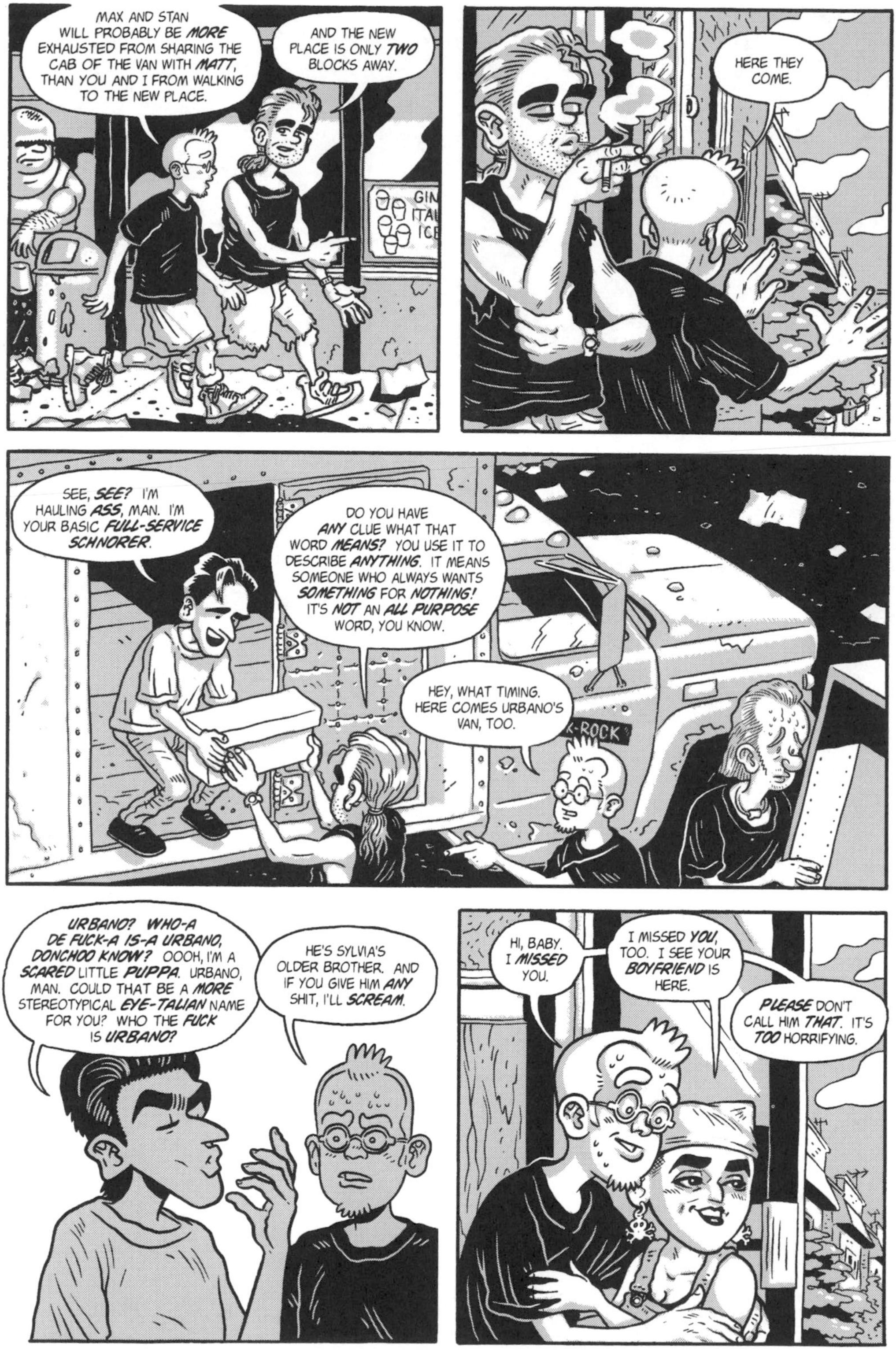
MAX AND STAN WILL PROBABLY BE MORE EXHAUSTED FROM SHARING THE CAB OF THE VAN WITH MATT, THAN YOU AND I FROM WALKING TO THE NEW PLACE.
AND THE NEW PLACE IS ONLY TWO BLOCKS AWAY.
GIN ITAL ICE
HERE THEY COME.
SEE, SEE? I'M HAULING ASS, MAN. I'M YOUR BASIC FULL-SERVICE SCHNORER.
DO YOU HAVE ANY CLUE WHAT THAT WORD MEANS? YOU USE IT TO DESCRIBE ANYTHING. IT MEANS SOMEONE WHO ALWAYS WANTS SOMETHING FOR NOTHING! IT'S NOT AN ALL PURPOSE WORD, YOU KNOW.
HEY, WHAT TIMING. HERE COMES URBANO'S VAN, TOO.
K-ROCK
URBANO? WHO-A DE FUCK-A IS-A URBANO, DONCHOO KNOW? OOOH, I'M A SCARED LITTLE PUPPA. URBANO, MAN. COULD THAT BE A MORE STEREOTYPICAL EYE-TALIAN NAME FOR YOU? WHO THE FUCK IS URBANO?
HE'S SYLVIA'S OLDER BROTHER. AND IF YOU GIVE HIM ANY SHIT, I'LL SCREAM.
HI, BABY. I MISSED YOU.
I MISSED YOU, TOO. I SEE YOUR BOYFRIEND IS HERE.
PLEASE DON'T CALL HIM THAT. IT'S TOO HORRIFYING.

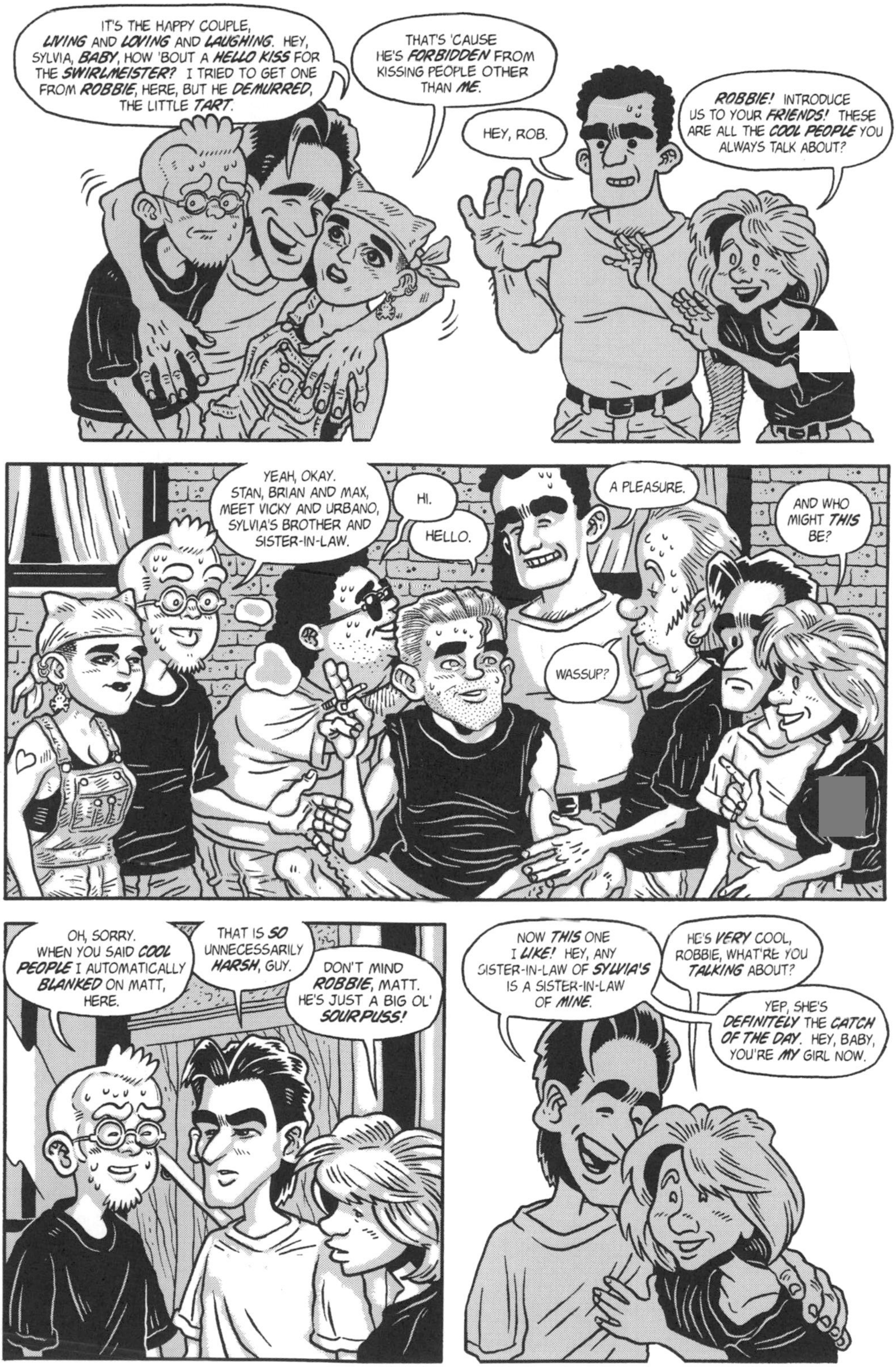

IT'S THE HAPPY COUPLE, LIVING AND LOVING AND LAUGHING. HEY, SYLVIA, BABY, HOW 'BOUT A HELLO KISS FOR THE SWIRLMEISTER? I TRIED TO GET ONE FROM ROBBIE, HERE, BUT HE DEMURRED, THE LITTLE TART.
THAT'S 'CAUSE HE'S FORBIDDEN FROM KISSING PEOPLE OTHER THAN ME.
HEY, ROB.
ROBBIE! INTRODUCE US TO YOUR FRIENDS! THESE ARE ALL THE COOL PEOPLE YOU ALWAYS TALK ABOUT?
YEAH, OKAY. STAN, BRIAN AND MAX, MEET VICKY AND URBANO, SYLVIA'S BROTHER AND SISTER-IN-LAW.
HI.
HELLO.
A PLEASURE.
AND WHO MIGHT THIS BE?
WASSUP?
OH, SORRY. WHEN YOU SAID COOL PEOPLE I AUTOMATICALLY BLANKED ON MATT, HERE.
THAT IS SO UNNECESSARILY HARSH, GUY.
DON'T MIND ROBBIE, MATT. HE'S JUST A BIG OL' SOURPUSS!
NOW THIS ONE I LIKE! HEY, ANY SISTER-IN-LAW OF SYLVIA'S IS A SISTER-IN-LAW OF MINE.
HE'S VERY COOL, ROBBIE, WHAT'RE YOU TALKING ABOUT?
YEP, SHE'S DEFINITELY THE CATCH OF THE DAY. HEY, BABY, YOU'RE MY GIRL NOW.

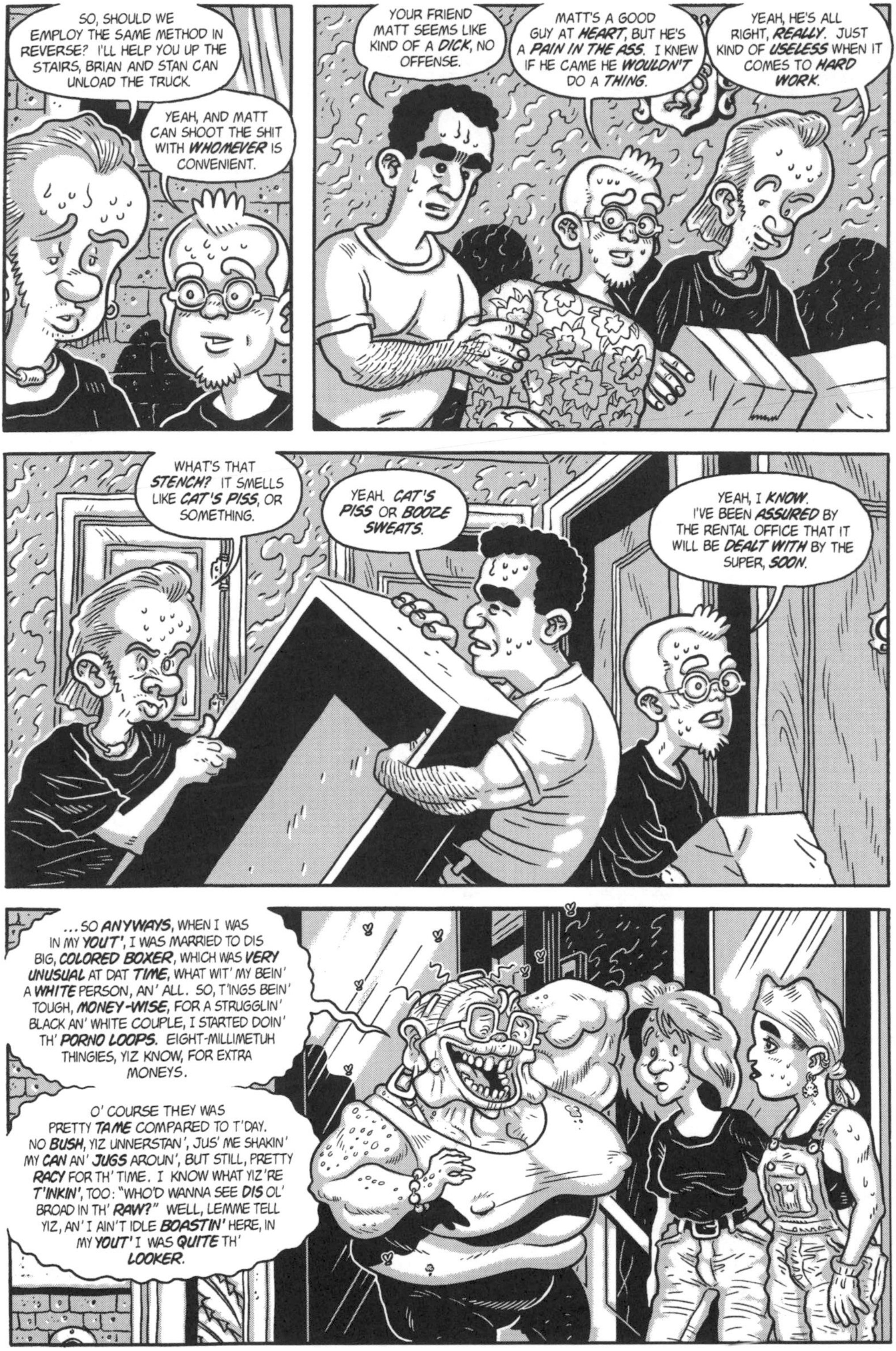
SO, SHOULD WE EMPLOY THE SAME METHOD IN REVERSE? I'LL HELP YOU UP THE STAIRS, BRIAN AND STAN CAN UNLOAD THE TRUCK.
YEAH, AND MATT CAN SHOOT THE SHIT WITH WHOMEVER IS CONVENIENT.
YOUR FRIEND MATT SEEMS LIKE KIND OF A DICK, NO OFFENSE.
MATT'S A GOOD GUY AT HEART, BUT HE'S A PAIN IN THE ASS. I KNEW IF HE CAME HE WOULDN'T DO A THING.
YEAH, HE'S ALL RIGHT, REALLY. JUST KIND OF USELESS WHEN IT COMES TO HARD WORK.
WHAT'S THAT STENCH? IT SMELLS LIKE CAT'S PISS, OR SOMETHING.
YEAH. CAT'S PISS OR BOOZE SWEATS.
YEAH, I KNOW. I'VE BEEN ASSURED BY THE RENTAL OFFICE THAT IT WILL BE DEALT WITH BY THE SUPER, SOON.
...SO ANYWAYS, WHEN I WAS IN MY YOUT', I WAS MARRIED TO DIS BIG, COLORED BOXER, WHICH WAS VERY UNUSUAL AT DAT TIME, WHAT WIT' MY BEIN' A WHITE PERSON, AN' ALL. SO, T'INGS BEIN' TOUGH, MONEY-WISE, FOR A STRUGGLIN' BLACK AN' WHITE COUPLE, I STARTED DOIN' TH' PORNO LOOPS. EIGHT-MILLIMETUH THINGIES, YIZ KNOW, FOR EXTRA MONEYS.
O' COURSE THEY WAS PRETTY TAME COMPARED TO T'DAY. NO BUSH, YIZ UNNERSTAN', JUS' ME SHAKIN' MY CAN AN' JUGS AROUN', BUT STILL, PRETTY RACY FOR TH' TIME. I KNOW WHAT YIZ'RE T'INKIN', TOO: "WHO'D WANNA SEE DIS OL' BROAD IN TH' RAW?" WELL, LEMME TELL YIZ, AN' I AIN'T IDLE BOASTIN' HERE, IN MY YOUT' I WAS QUITE TH' LOOKER.

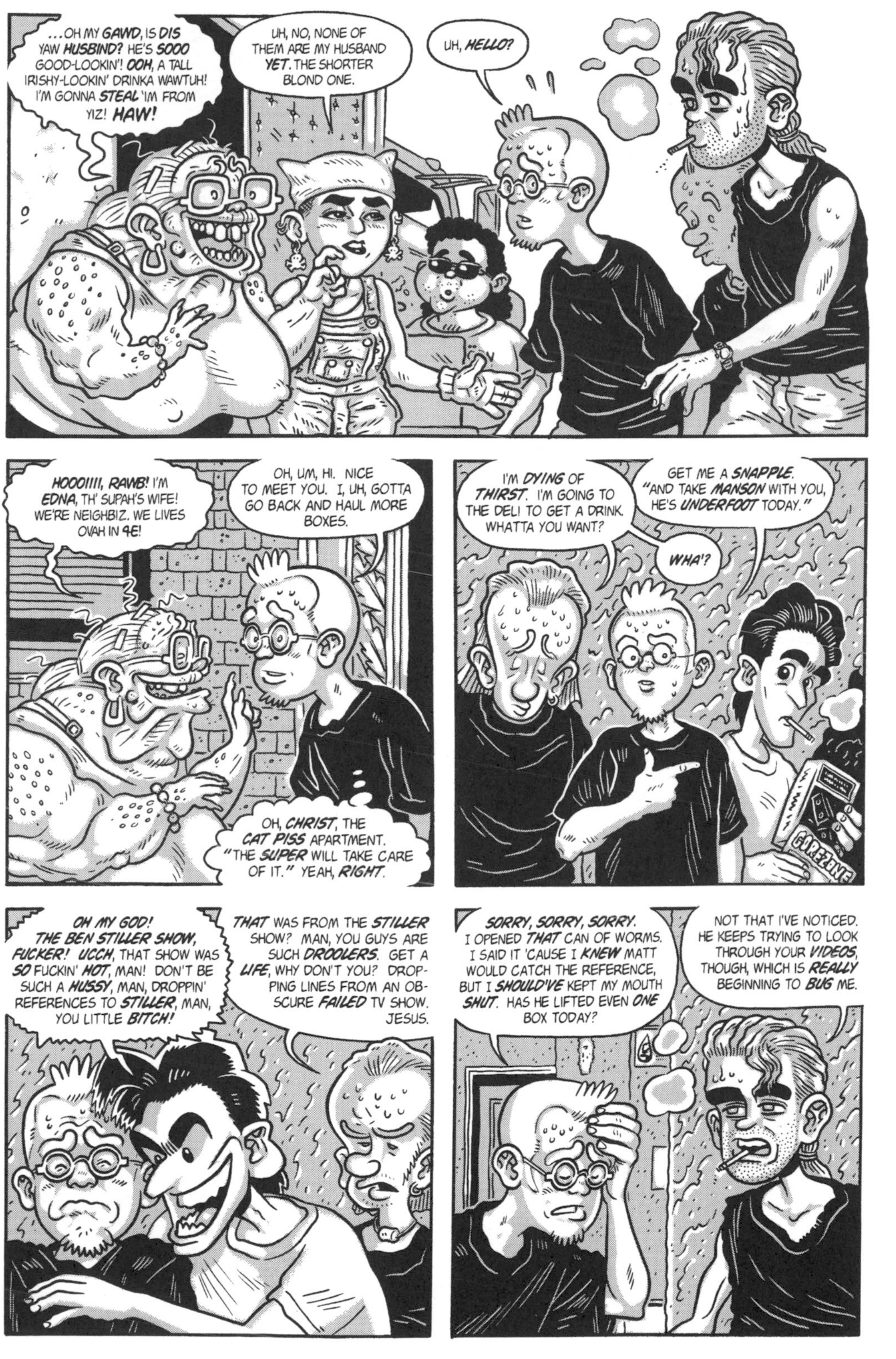
...OH MY GAWD, IS DIS YAW HUSBIND? HE'S SOOO GOOD-LOOKIN'! OOH, A TALL IRISHY-LOOKIN' DRINKA WAWTUH! I'M GONNA STEAL 'IM FROM YIZ! HAW!
UH, NO, NONE OF THEM ARE MY HUSBAND YET. THE SHORTER BLOND ONE.
UH, HELLO?
HOOOIIII, RAWB! I'M EDNA, TH' SUPAH'S WIFE! WE'RE NEIGHBIZ. WE LIVES OVAH IN 4E!
OH, UM, HI. NICE TO MEET YOU. I, UH, GOTTA GO BACK AND HAUL MORE BOXES.
OH, CHRIST, THE CAT PISS APARTMENT. "THE SUPER WILL TAKE CARE OF IT." YEAH, RIGHT.
I'M DYING OF THIRST. I'M GOING TO THE DELI TO GET A DRINK. WHATTA YOU WANT?
GET ME A SNAPPLE. "AND TAKE MANSON WITH YOU, HE'S UNDERFOOT TODAY."
WHA'?
GOREZONE
OH MY GOD! THE BEN STILLER SHOW, FUCKER! UCCH, THAT SHOW WAS SO FUCKIN' HOT, MAN! DON'T BE SUCH A HUSSY, MAN, DROPPIN' REFERENCES TO STILLER, MAN, YOU LITTLE BITCH!
THAT WAS FROM THE STILLER SHOW? MAN, YOU GUYS ARE SUCH DROOLERS. GET A LIFE, WHY DON'T YOU? DROPPING LINES FROM AN OBSCURE FAILED TV SHOW. JESUS.
SORRY, SORRY, SORRY. I OPENED THAT CAN OF WORMS. I SAID IT 'CAUSE I KNEW MATT WOULD CATCH THE REFERENCE, BUT I SHOULD'VE KEPT MY MOUTH SHUT. HAS HE LIFTED EVEN ONE BOX TODAY?
NOT THAT I'VE NOTICED. HE KEEPS TRYING TO LOOK THROUGH YOUR VIDEOS, THOUGH, WHICH IS REALLY BEGINNING TO BUG ME.

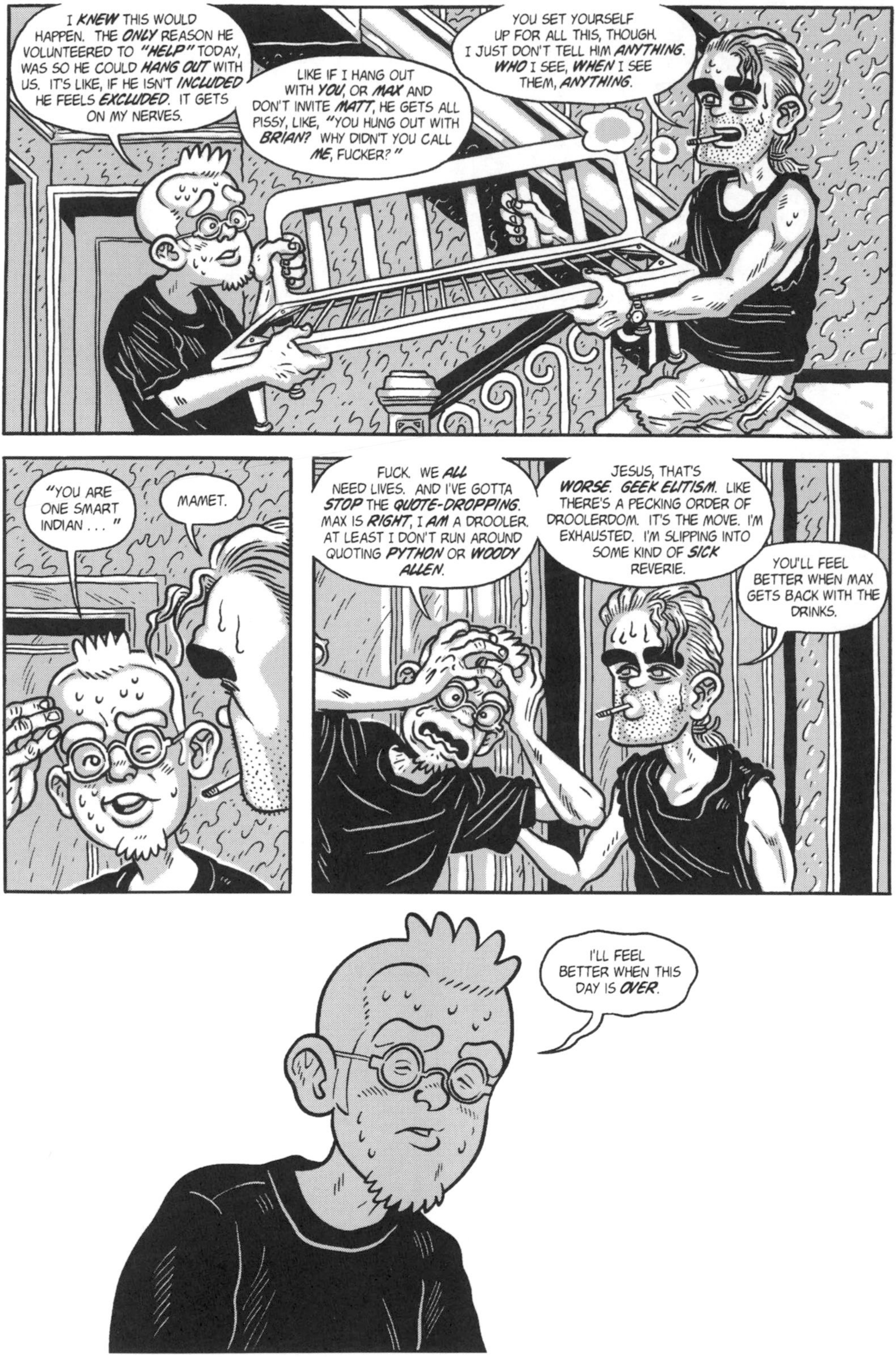
I KNEW THIS WOULD HAPPEN. THE ONLY REASON HE VOLUNTEERED TO "HELP" TODAY, WAS SO HE COULD HANG OUT WITH US. IT'S LIKE, IF HE ISN'T INCLUDED HE FEELS EXCLUDED. IT GETS ON MY NERVES.
LIKE IF I HANG OUT WITH YOU, OR MAX AND DON'T INVITE MATT, HE GETS ALL PISSY, LIKE, "YOU HUNG OUT WITH BRIAN? WHY DIDN'T YOU CALL ME, FUCKER?"
YOU SET YOURSELF UP FOR ALL THIS, THOUGH. I JUST DON'T TELL HIM ANYTHING. WHO I SEE, WHEN I SEE THEM, ANYTHING.
"YOU ARE ONE SMART INDIAN . . ."
MAMET.
FUCK. WE ALL NEED LIVES. AND I'VE GOTTA STOP THE QUOTE-DROPPING. MAX IS RIGHT, I AM A DROOLER. AT LEAST I DON'T RUN AROUND QUOTING PYTHON OR WOODY ALLEN.
JESUS, THAT'S WORSE. GEEK ELITISM. LIKE THERE'S A PECKING ORDER OF DROOLERDOM. IT'S THE MOVE. I'M EXHAUSTED. I'M SLIPPING INTO SOME KIND OF SICK REVERIE.
YOU'LL FEEL BETTER WHEN MAX GETS BACK WITH THE DRINKS.
I'LL FEEL BETTER WHEN THIS DAY IS OVER.

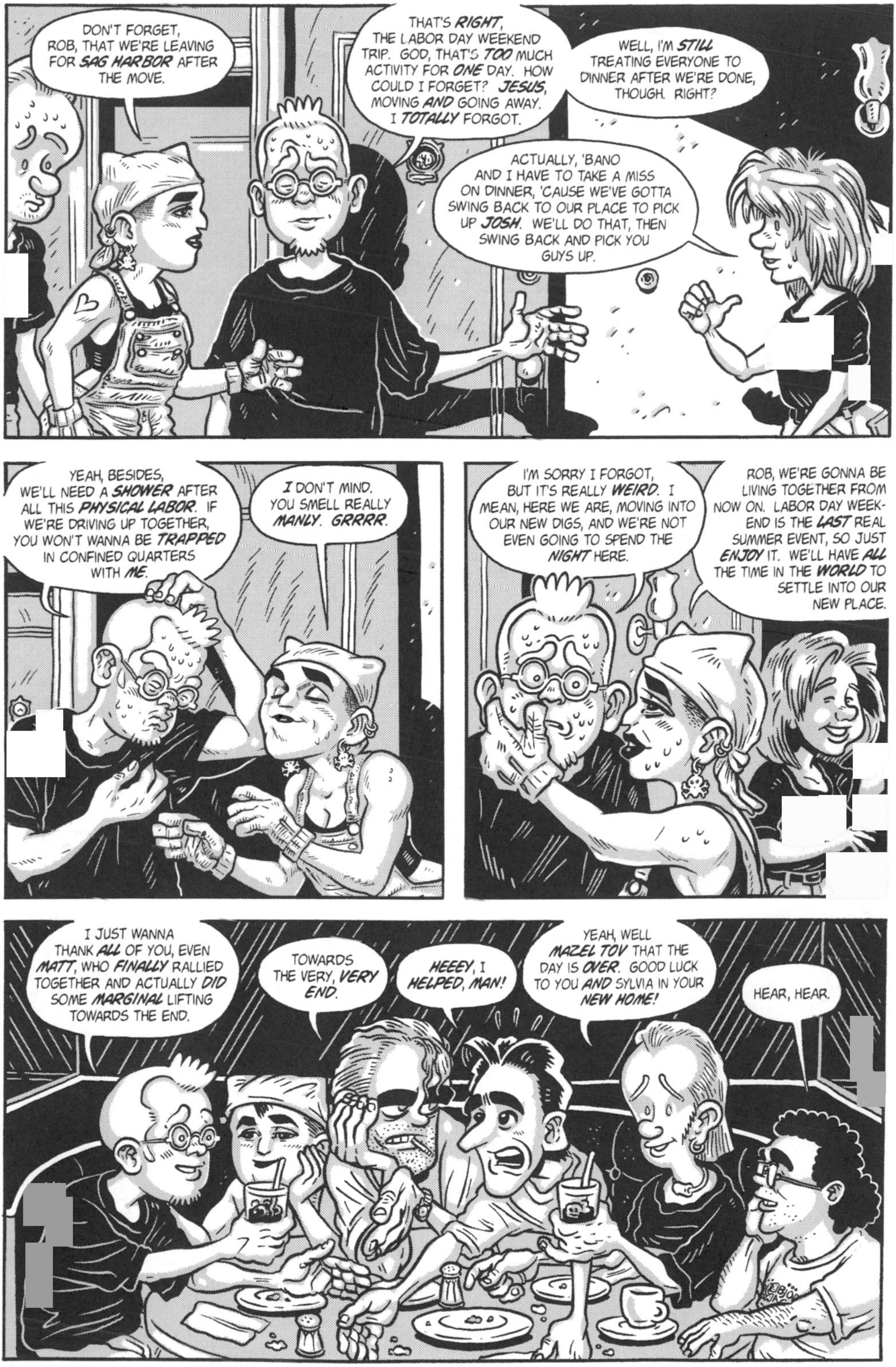
DON'T FORGET, ROB, THAT WE'RE LEAVING FOR SAG HARBOR AFTER THE MOVE.
THAT'S RIGHT, THE LABOR DAY WEEKEND TRIP. GOD, THAT'S TOO MUCH ACTIVITY FOR ONE DAY. HOW COULD I FORGET? JESUS, MOVING AND GOING AWAY. I TOTALLY FORGOT.
WELL, I'M STILL TREATING EVERYONE TO DINNER AFTER WE'RE DONE, THOUGH. RIGHT?
ACTUALLY, 'BANO AND I HAVE TO TAKE A MISS ON DINNER, 'CAUSE WE'VE GOTTA SWING BACK TO OUR PLACE TO PICK UP JOSH. WE'LL DO THAT, THEN SWING BACK AND PICK YOU GUYS UP.
YEAH, BESIDES, WE'LL NEED A SHOWER AFTER ALL THIS PHYSICAL LABOR. IF WE'RE DRIVING UP TOGETHER, YOU WON'T WANNA BE TRAPPED IN CONFINED QUARTERS WITH ME.
I DON'T MIND. YOU SMELL REALLY MANLY. GRRRR.
I'M SORRY I FORGOT, BUT IT'S REALLY WEIRD. I MEAN, HERE WE ARE, MOVING INTO OUR NEW DIGS, AND WE'RE NOT EVEN GOING TO SPEND THE NIGHT HERE.
ROB, WE'RE GONNA BE LIVING TOGETHER FROM NOW ON. LABOR DAY WEEK-END IS THE LAST REAL SUMMER EVENT, SO JUST ENJOY IT. WE'LL HAVE ALL THE TIME IN THE WORLD TO SETTLE INTO OUR NEW PLACE.
I JUST WANNA THANK ALL OF YOU, EVEN MATT, WHO FINALLY RALLIED TOGETHER AND ACTUALLY DID SOME MARGINAL LIFTING TOWARDS THE END.
TOWARDS THE VERY, VERY END.
HEEEY, I HELPED, MAN!
YEAH, WELL MAZEL TOV THAT THE DAY IS OVER. GOOD LUCK TO YOU AND SYLVIA IN YOUR NEW HOME!
HEAR, HEAR.

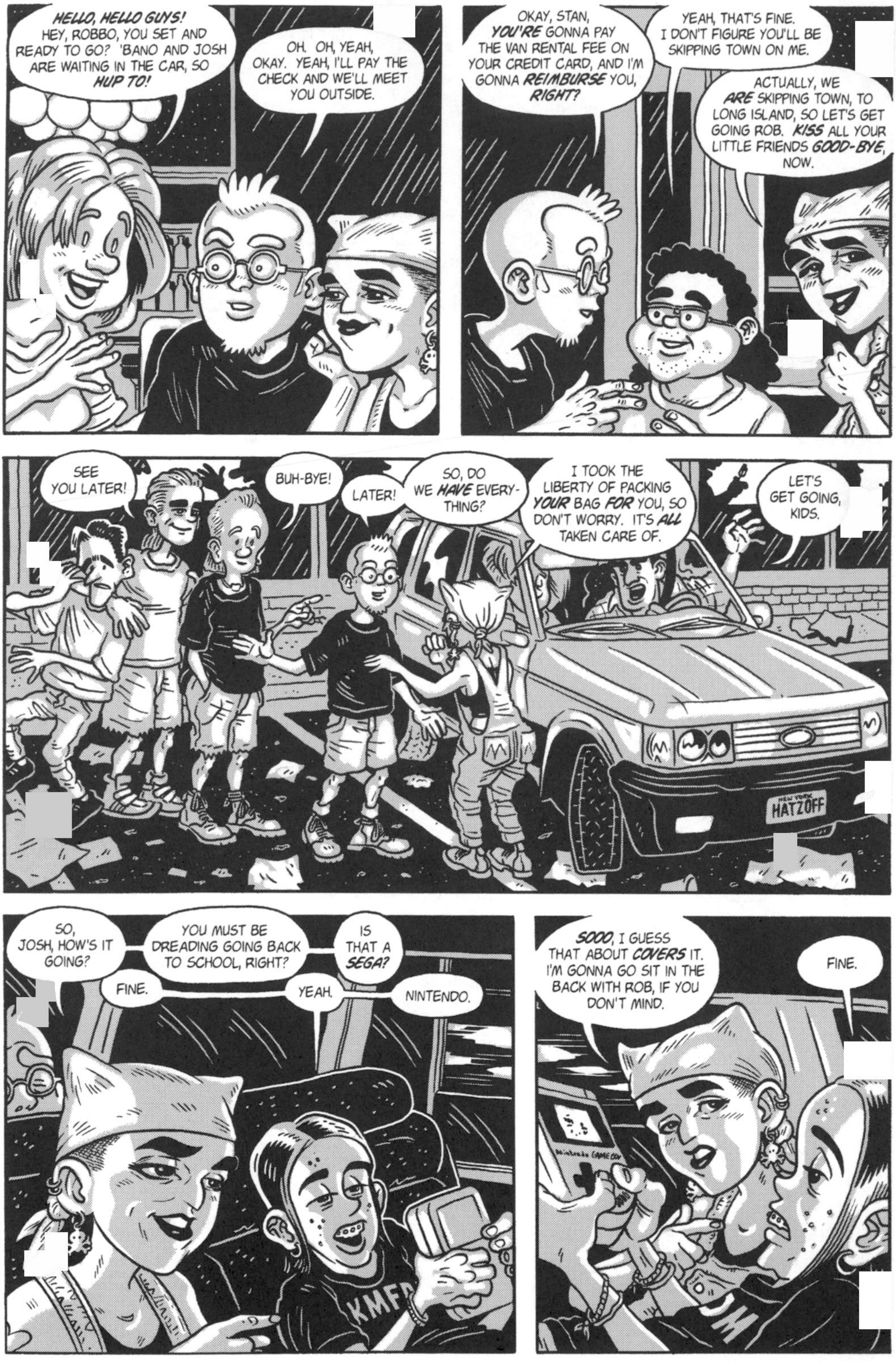
HELLO, HELLO GUYS! HEY, ROBBO, YOU SET AND READY TO GO? 'BANO AND JOSH ARE WAITING IN THE CAR, SO HUP TO!
OH. OH, YEAH, OKAY. YEAH, I'LL PAY THE CHECK AND WE'LL MEET YOU OUTSIDE.
OKAY, STAN, YOU'RE GONNA PAY THE VAN RENTAL FEE ON YOUR CREDIT CARD, AND I'M GONNA REIMBURSE YOU, RIGHT?
YEAH, THAT'S FINE. I DON'T FIGURE YOU'LL BE SKIPPING TOWN ON ME.
ACTUALLY, WE ARE SKIPPING TOWN, TO LONG ISLAND, SO LET'S GET GOING ROB. KISS ALL YOUR LITTLE FRIENDS GOOD-BYE, NOW.
SEE YOU LATER!
BUH-BYE!
LATER!
SO, DO WE HAVE EVERYTHING?
I TOOK THE LIBERTY OF PACKING YOUR BAG FOR YOU, SO DON'T WORRY. IT'S ALL TAKEN CARE OF.
LET'S GET GOING, KIDS.
HATZOFF
SO, JOSH, HOW'S IT GOING?
FINE.
YOU MUST BE DREADING GOING BACK TO SCHOOL, RIGHT?
YEAH.
IS THAT A SEGA?
NINTENDO.
KMF
SOOO, I GUESS THAT ABOUT COVERS IT. I'M GONNA GO SIT IN THE BACK WITH ROB, IF YOU DON'T MIND.
FINE.

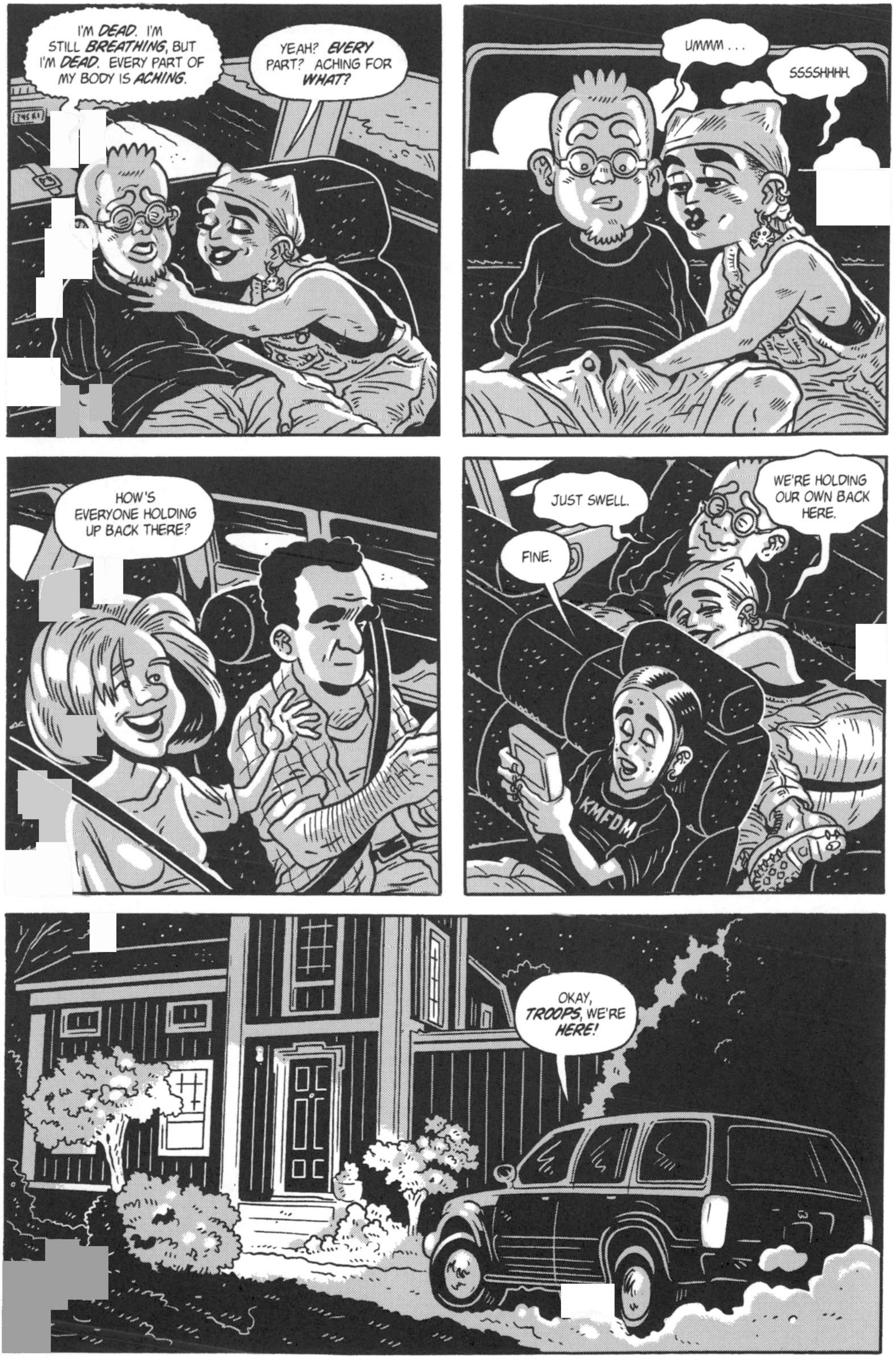
I'M *DEAD*. I'M STILL *BREATHING*, BUT I'M *DEAD*. EVERY PART OF MY BODY IS *ACHING*.
YEAH? *EVERY* PART? ACHING FOR *WHAT?*
UMMM . . .
SSSSHHHH.
HOW'S EVERYONE HOLDING UP BACK THERE?
JUST SWELL.
WE'RE HOLDING OUR OWN BACK HERE.
FINE.
KMFDM
OKAY, *TROOPS*, WE'RE *HERE!*

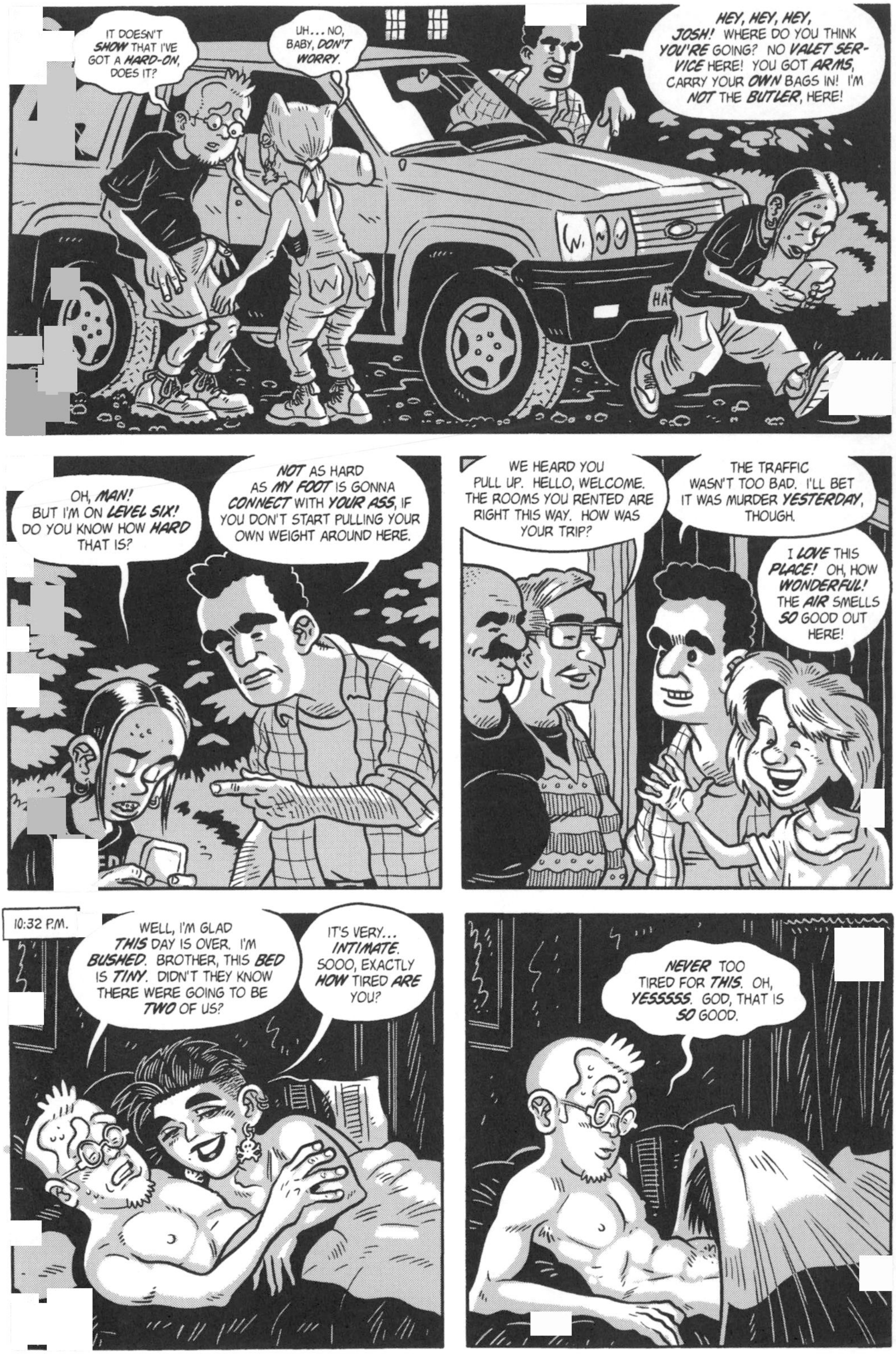
IT DOESN'T SHOW THAT I'VE GOT A HARD-ON, DOES IT?
UH... NO, BABY, DON'T WORRY.
HEY, HEY, HEY, JOSH! WHERE DO YOU THINK YOU'RE GOING? NO VALET SERVICE HERE! YOU GOT ARMS, CARRY YOUR OWN BAGS IN! I'M NOT THE BUTLER, HERE!
OH, MAN! BUT I'M ON LEVEL SIX! DO YOU KNOW HOW HARD THAT IS?
NOT AS HARD AS MY FOOT IS GONNA CONNECT WITH YOUR ASS, IF YOU DON'T START PULLING YOUR OWN WEIGHT AROUND HERE.
WE HEARD YOU PULL UP. HELLO, WELCOME. THE ROOMS YOU RENTED ARE RIGHT THIS WAY. HOW WAS YOUR TRIP?
THE TRAFFIC WASN'T TOO BAD. I'LL BET IT WAS MURDER YESTERDAY, THOUGH.
I LOVE THIS PLACE! OH, HOW WONDERFUL! THE AIR SMELLS SO GOOD OUT HERE!
10:32 P.M.
WELL, I'M GLAD THIS DAY IS OVER. I'M BUSHED. BROTHER, THIS BED IS TINY. DIDN'T THEY KNOW THERE WERE GOING TO BE TWO OF US?
IT'S VERY... INTIMATE. SOOO, EXACTLY HOW TIRED ARE YOU?
NEVER TOO TIRED FOR THIS. OH, YESSSSS. GOD, THAT IS SO GOOD.

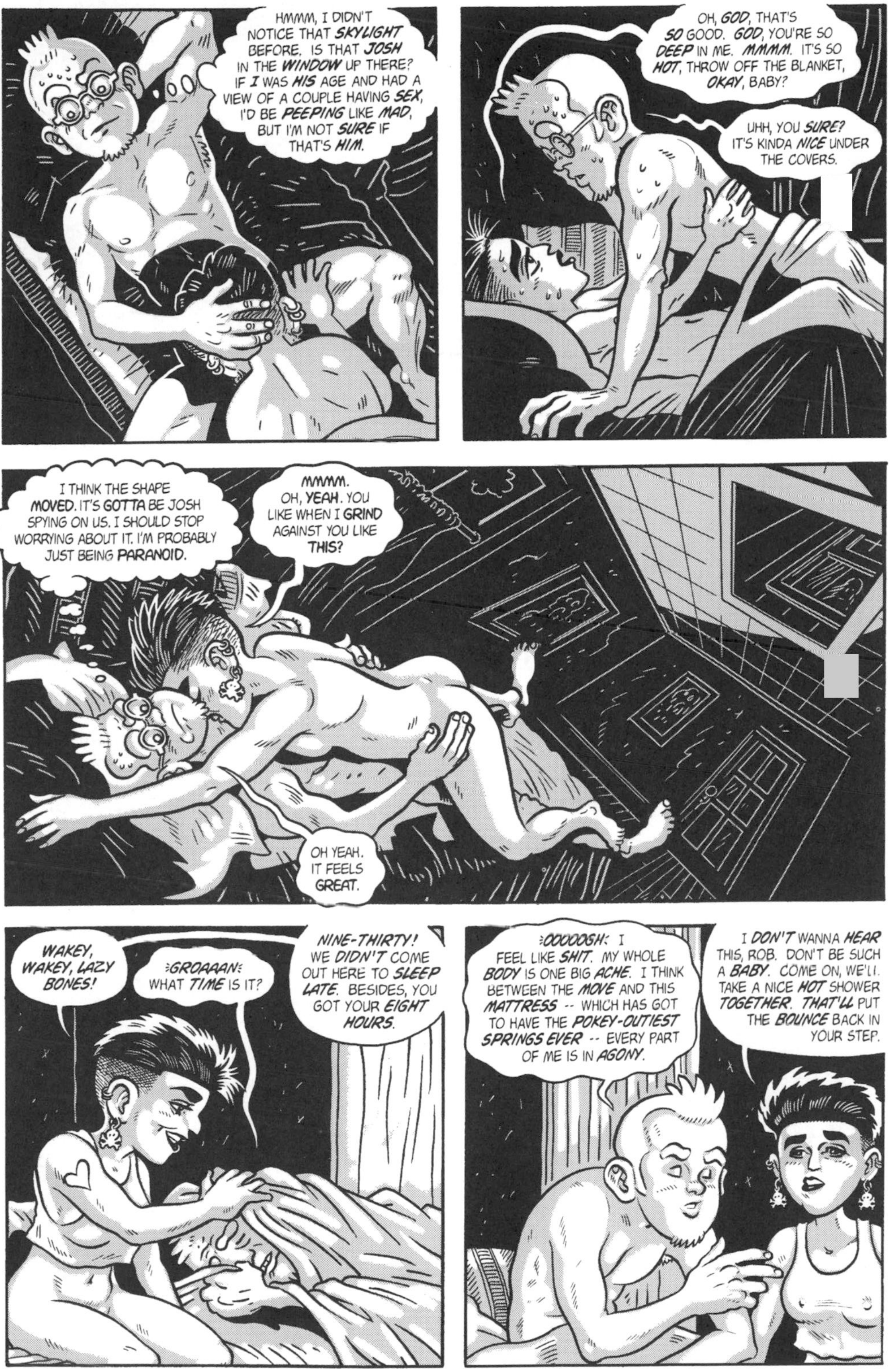

HMMM, I DIDN'T NOTICE THAT SKYLIGHT BEFORE. IS THAT JOSH IN THE WINDOW UP THERE? IF I WAS HIS AGE AND HAD A VIEW OF A COUPLE HAVING SEX, I'D BE PEEPING LIKE MAD, BUT I'M NOT SURE IF THAT'S HIM.
OH, GOD, THAT'S SO GOOD. GOD, YOU'RE SO DEEP IN ME. MMMM. IT'S SO HOT, THROW OFF THE BLANKET, OKAY, BABY?
UHH, YOU SURE? IT'S KINDA NICE UNDER THE COVERS.
I THINK THE SHAPE MOVED. IT'S GOTTA BE JOSH SPYING ON US. I SHOULD STOP WORRYING ABOUT IT. I'M PROBABLY JUST BEING PARANOID.
MMMM. OH, YEAH. YOU LIKE WHEN I GRIND AGAINST YOU LIKE THIS?
OH YEAH. IT FEELS GREAT.
WAKEY, WAKEY, LAZY BONES!
GROAAAN
WHAT TIME IS IT?
NINE-THIRTY! WE DIDN'T COME OUT HERE TO SLEEP LATE. BESIDES, YOU GOT YOUR EIGHT HOURS.
OOOOOSH! I FEEL LIKE SHIT. MY WHOLE BODY IS ONE BIG ACHE. I THINK BETWEEN THE MOVE AND THIS MATTRESS -- WHICH HAS GOT TO HAVE THE POKEY-OUTIEST SPRINGS EVER -- EVERY PART OF ME IS IN AGONY.
I DON'T WANNA HEAR THIS, ROB. DON'T BE SUCH A BABY. COME ON, WE'LL TAKE A NICE HOT SHOWER TOGETHER. THAT'LL PUT THE BOUNCE BACK IN YOUR STEP.

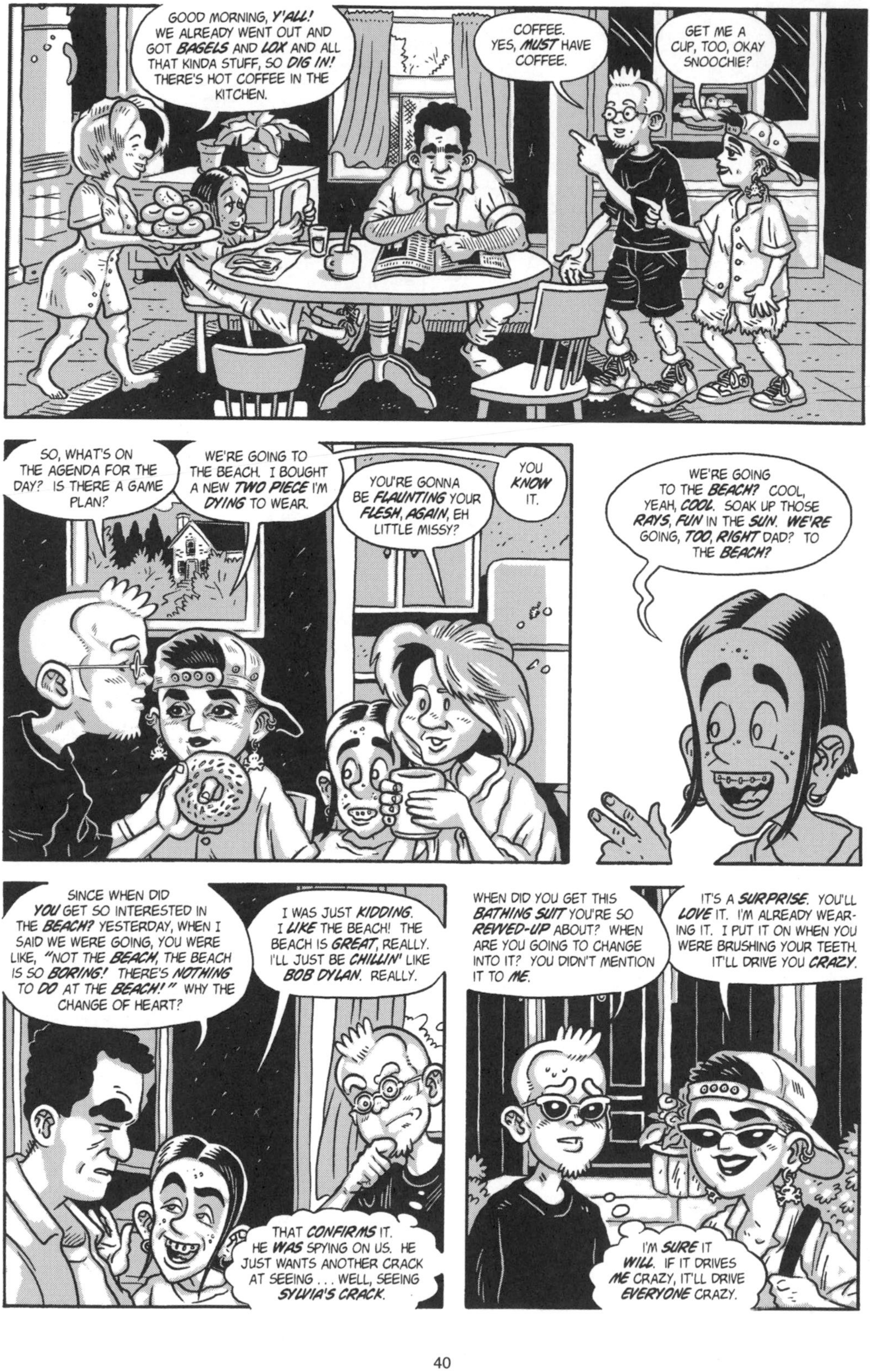
GOOD MORNING, Y'ALL! WE ALREADY WENT OUT AND GOT BAGELS AND LOX AND ALL THAT KINDA STUFF, SO DIG IN! THERE'S HOT COFFEE IN THE KITCHEN.
COFFEE. YES, MUST HAVE COFFEE.
GET ME A CUP, TOO, OKAY SNOOCHIE?
SO, WHAT'S ON THE AGENDA FOR THE DAY? IS THERE A GAME PLAN?
WE'RE GOING TO THE BEACH. I BOUGHT A NEW TWO PIECE I'M DYING TO WEAR.
YOU'RE GONNA BE FLAUNTING YOUR FLESH, AGAIN, EH LITTLE MISSY?
YOU KNOW IT.
WE'RE GOING TO THE BEACH? COOL, YEAH, COOL. SOAK UP THOSE RAYS, FUN IN THE SUN. WE'RE GOING, TOO, RIGHT DAD? TO THE BEACH?
SINCE WHEN DID YOU GET SO INTERESTED IN THE BEACH? YESTERDAY, WHEN I SAID WE WERE GOING, YOU WERE LIKE, "NOT THE BEACH, THE BEACH IS SO BORING! THERE'S NOTHING TO DO AT THE BEACH!" WHY THE CHANGE OF HEART?
I WAS JUST KIDDING. I LIKE THE BEACH! THE BEACH IS GREAT, REALLY. I'LL JUST BE CHILLIN' LIKE BOB DYLAN. REALLY.
THAT CONFIRMS IT. HE WAS SPYING ON US. HE JUST WANTS ANOTHER CRACK AT SEEING . . . WELL, SEEING SYLVIA'S CRACK.
WHEN DID YOU GET THIS BATHING SUIT YOU'RE SO REVVED-UP ABOUT? WHEN ARE YOU GOING TO CHANGE INTO IT? YOU DIDN'T MENTION IT TO ME.
IT'S A SURPRISE. YOU'LL LOVE IT. I'M ALREADY WEARING IT. I PUT IT ON WHEN YOU WERE BRUSHING YOUR TEETH. IT'LL DRIVE YOU CRAZY.
I'M SURE IT WILL. IF IT DRIVES ME CRAZY, IT'LL DRIVE EVERYONE CRAZY.

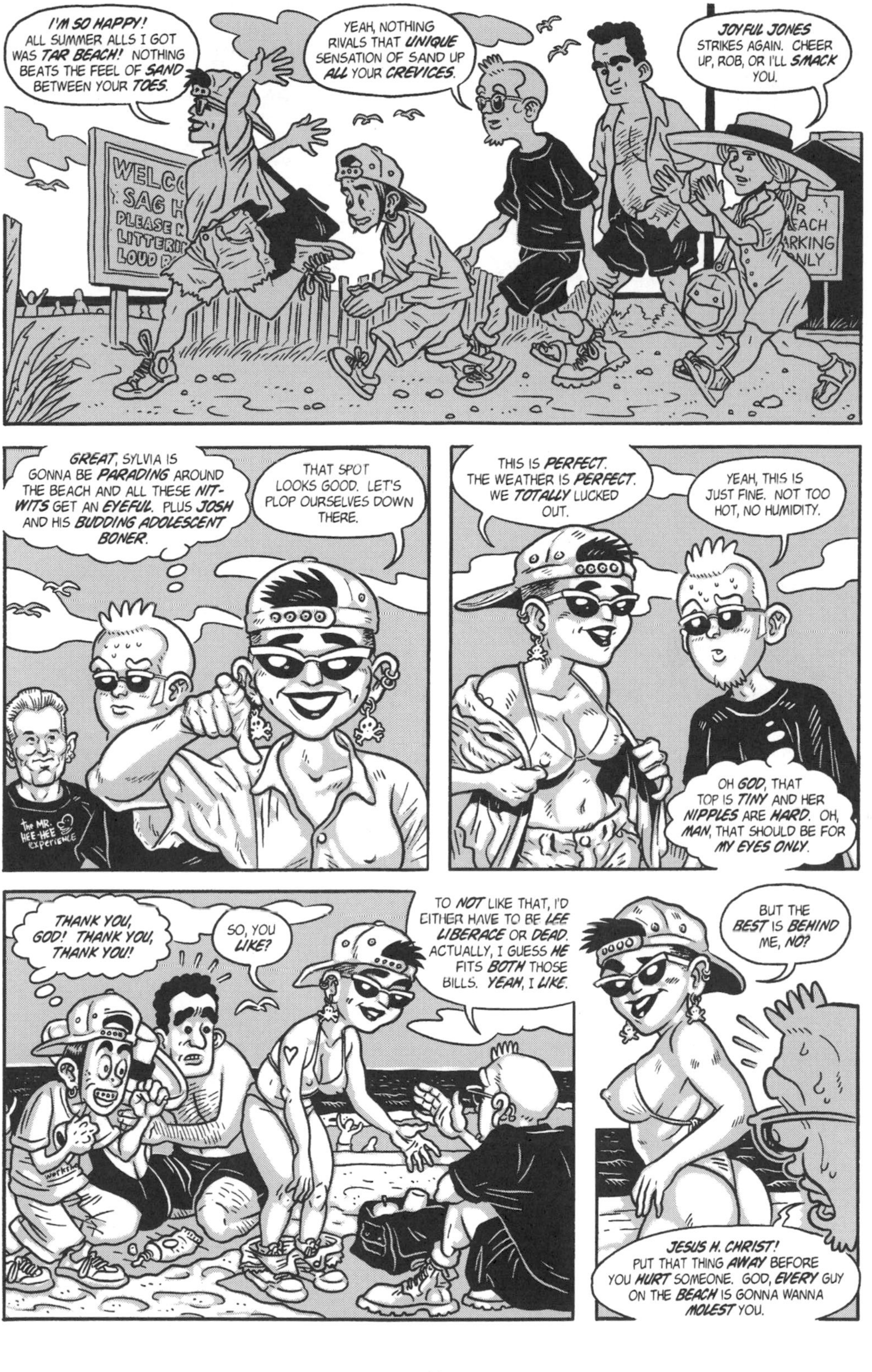

I'M SO HAPPY! ALL SUMMER ALLS I GOT WAS TAR BEACH! NOTHING BEATS THE FEEL OF SAND BETWEEN YOUR TOES.
YEAH, NOTHING RIVALS THAT UNIQUE SENSATION OF SAND UP ALL YOUR CREVICES.
JOYFUL JONES STRIKES AGAIN. CHEER UP, ROB, OR I'LL SMACK YOU.
GREAT, SYLVIA IS GONNA BE PARADING AROUND THE BEACH AND ALL THESE NIT-WITS GET AN EYEFUL. PLUS JOSH AND HIS BUDDING ADOLESCENT BONER.
THAT SPOT LOOKS GOOD. LET'S PLOP OURSELVES DOWN THERE.
The MR. HEE-HEE experience
THIS IS PERFECT. THE WEATHER IS PERFECT. WE TOTALLY LUCKED OUT.
YEAH, THIS IS JUST FINE. NOT TOO HOT, NO HUMIDITY.
OH GOD, THAT TOP IS TINY AND HER NIPPLES ARE HARD. OH, MAN, THAT SHOULD BE FOR MY EYES ONLY.
THANK YOU, GOD! THANK YOU, THANK YOU!
SO, YOU LIKE?
TO NOT LIKE THAT, I'D EITHER HAVE TO BE LEE LIBERACE OR DEAD. ACTUALLY, I GUESS HE FITS BOTH THOSE BILLS. YEAH, I LIKE.
BUT THE BEST IS BEHIND ME, NO?
JESUS H. CHRIST! PUT THAT THING AWAY BEFORE YOU HURT SOMEONE. GOD, EVERY GUY ON THE BEACH IS GONNA WANNA MOLEST YOU.

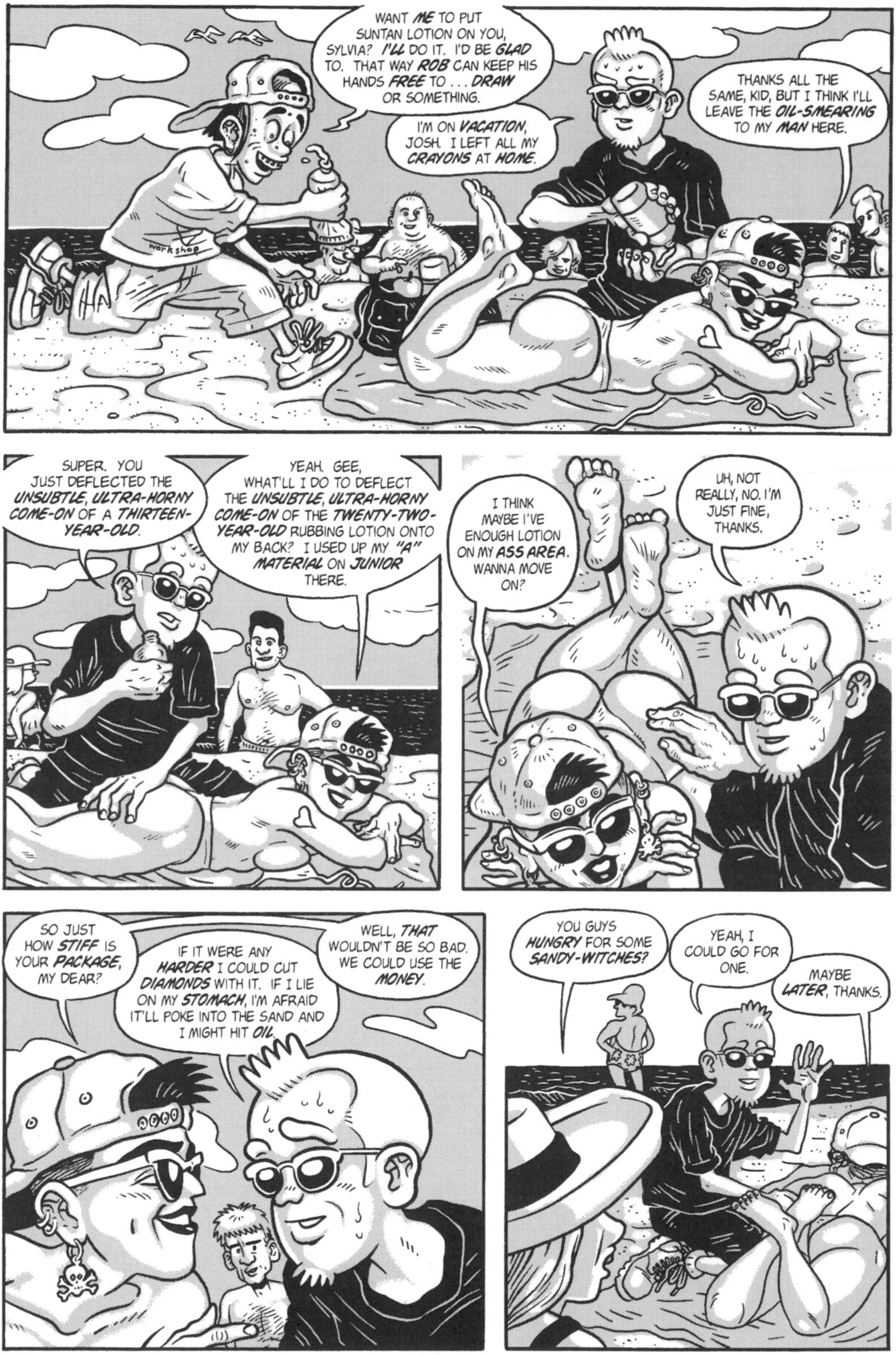
WANT ME TO PUT SUNTAN LOTION ON YOU, SYLVIA? I'LL DO IT. I'D BE GLAD TO. THAT WAY ROB CAN KEEP HIS HANDS FREE TO . . . DRAW OR SOMETHING.
I'M ON VACATION, JOSH. I LEFT ALL MY CRAYONS AT HOME.
THANKS ALL THE SAME, KID, BUT I THINK I'LL LEAVE THE OIL-SMEARING TO MY MAN HERE.
SUPER. YOU JUST DEFLECTED THE UNSUBTLE, ULTRA-HORNY COME-ON OF A THIRTEEN-YEAR-OLD.
YEAH. GEE, WHAT'LL I DO TO DEFLECT THE UNSUBTLE, ULTRA-HORNY COME-ON OF THE TWENTY-TWO-YEAR-OLD RUBBING LOTION ONTO MY BACK? I USED UP MY "A" MATERIAL ON JUNIOR THERE.
I THINK MAYBE I'VE ENOUGH LOTION ON MY ASS AREA. WANNA MOVE ON?
UH, NOT REALLY, NO. I'M JUST FINE, THANKS.
SO JUST HOW STIFF IS YOUR PACKAGE, MY DEAR?
IF IT WERE ANY HARDER I COULD CUT DIAMONDS WITH IT. IF I LIE ON MY STOMACH, I'M AFRAID IT'LL POKE INTO THE SAND AND I MIGHT HIT OIL.
WELL, THAT WOULDN'T BE SO BAD. WE COULD USE THE MONEY.
YOU GUYS HUNGRY FOR SOME SANDY-WITCHES?
YEAH, I COULD GO FOR ONE.
MAYBE LATER, THANKS.

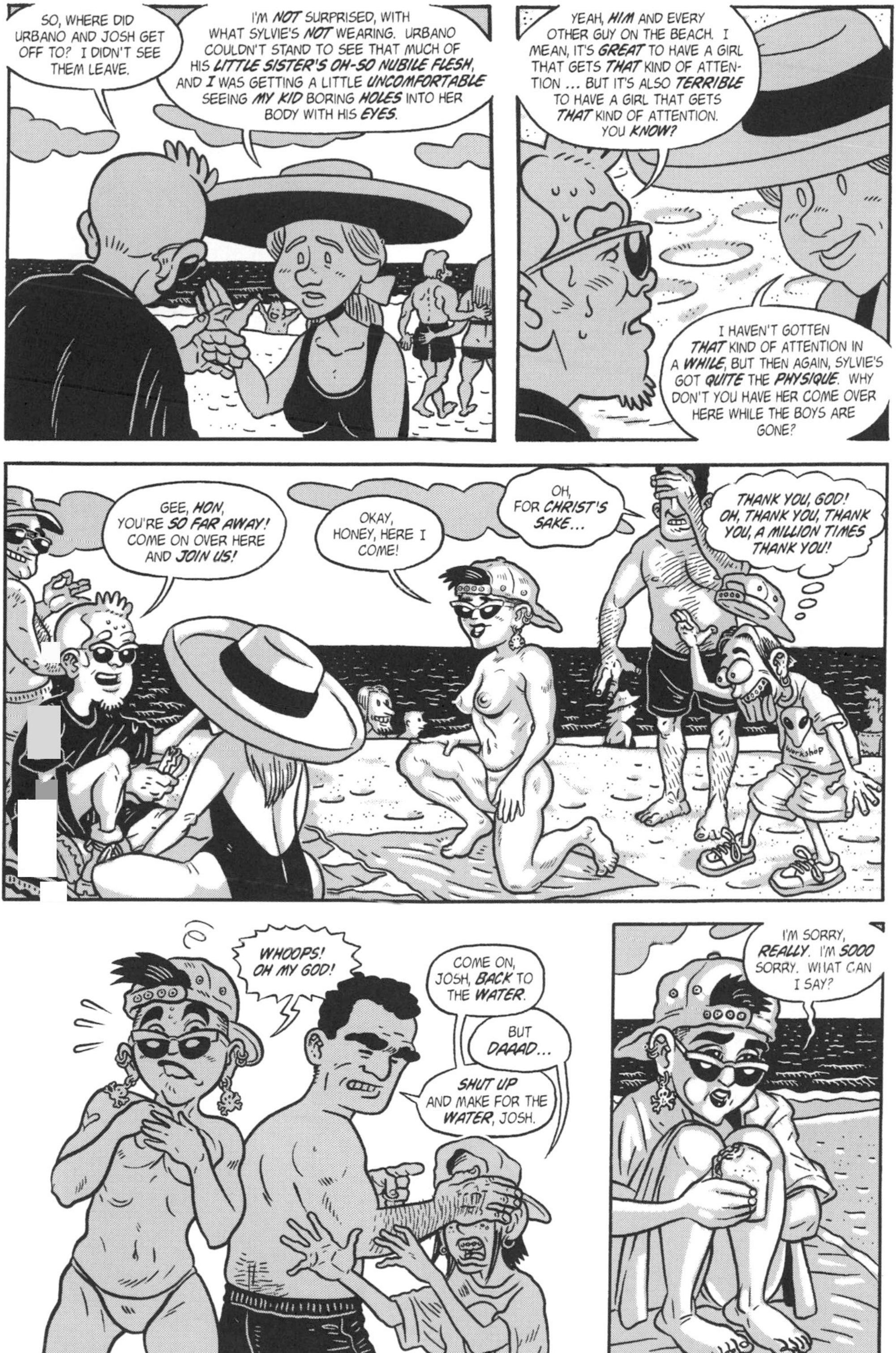
SO, WHERE DID URBANO AND JOSH GET OFF TO? I DIDN'T SEE THEM LEAVE.
I'M NOT SURPRISED, WITH WHAT SYLVIE'S NOT WEARING. URBANO COULDN'T STAND TO SEE THAT MUCH OF HIS LITTLE SISTER'S OH-SO NUBILE FLESH, AND I WAS GETTING A LITTLE UNCOMFORTABLE SEEING MY KID BORING HOLES INTO HER BODY WITH HIS EYES.
YEAH, HIM AND EVERY OTHER GUY ON THE BEACH. I MEAN, IT'S GREAT TO HAVE A GIRL THAT GETS THAT KIND OF ATTENTION ... BUT IT'S ALSO TERRIBLE TO HAVE A GIRL THAT GETS THAT KIND OF ATTENTION. YOU KNOW?
I HAVEN'T GOTTEN THAT KIND OF ATTENTION IN A WHILE, BUT THEN AGAIN, SYLVIE'S GOT QUITE THE PHYSIQUE. WHY DON'T YOU HAVE HER COME OVER HERE WHILE THE BOYS ARE GONE?
GEE, HON, YOU'RE SO FAR AWAY! COME ON OVER HERE AND JOIN US!
OKAY, HONEY, HERE I COME!
OH, FOR CHRIST'S SAKE...
THANK YOU, GOD! OH, THANK YOU, THANK YOU, A MILLION TIMES THANK YOU!
WHOOPS! OH MY GOD!
COME ON, JOSH, BACK TO THE WATER.
BUT DAAAD...
SHUT UP AND MAKE FOR THE WATER, JOSH.
I'M SORRY, REALLY. I'M SOOO SORRY. WHAT CAN I SAY?

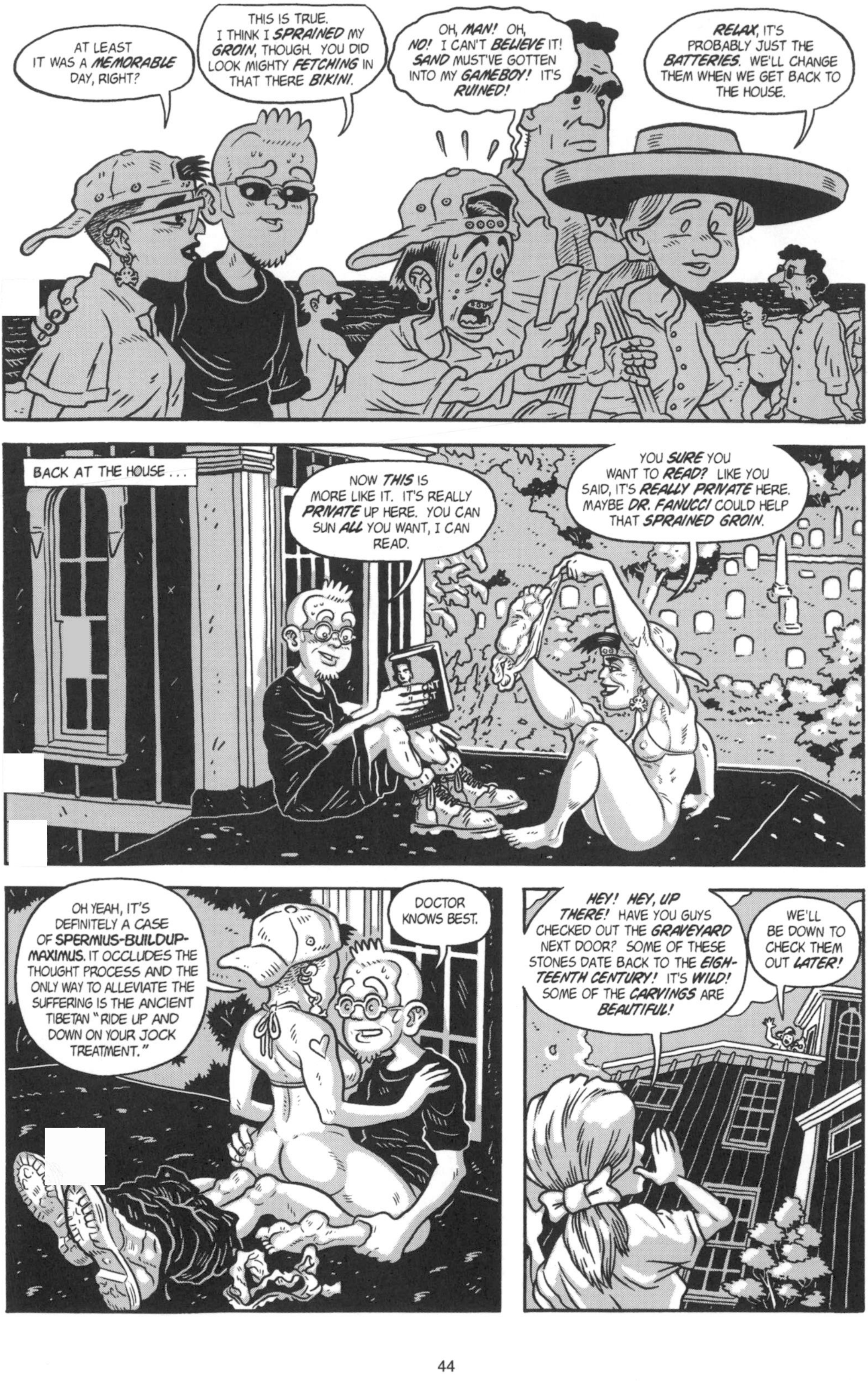
AT LEAST IT WAS A MEMORABLE DAY, RIGHT?
THIS IS TRUE. I THINK I SPRAINED MY GROIN, THOUGH. YOU DID LOOK MIGHTY FETCHING IN THAT THERE BIKINI.
OH, MAN! OH, NO! I CAN'T BELIEVE IT! SAND MUST'VE GOTTEN INTO MY GAMEBOY! IT'S RUINED!
RELAX, IT'S PROBABLY JUST THE BATTERIES. WE'LL CHANGE THEM WHEN WE GET BACK TO THE HOUSE.
BACK AT THE HOUSE . . .
NOW THIS IS MORE LIKE IT. IT'S REALLY PRIVATE UP HERE. YOU CAN SUN ALL YOU WANT, I CAN READ.
YOU SURE YOU WANT TO READ? LIKE YOU SAID, IT'S REALLY PRIVATE HERE. MAYBE DR. FANUCCI COULD HELP THAT SPRAINED GROIN.
OH YEAH, IT'S DEFINITELY A CASE OF SPERMUS-BUILDUP-MAXIMUS. IT OCCLUDES THE THOUGHT PROCESS AND THE ONLY WAY TO ALLEVIATE THE SUFFERING IS THE ANCIENT TIBETAN "RIDE UP AND DOWN ON YOUR JOCK TREATMENT."
DOCTOR KNOWS BEST.
HEY! HEY, UP THERE! HAVE YOU GUYS CHECKED OUT THE GRAVEYARD NEXT DOOR? SOME OF THESE STONES DATE BACK TO THE EIGHTEENTH CENTURY! IT'S WILD! SOME OF THE CARVINGS ARE BEAUTIFUL!
WE'LL BE DOWN TO CHECK THEM OUT LATER!

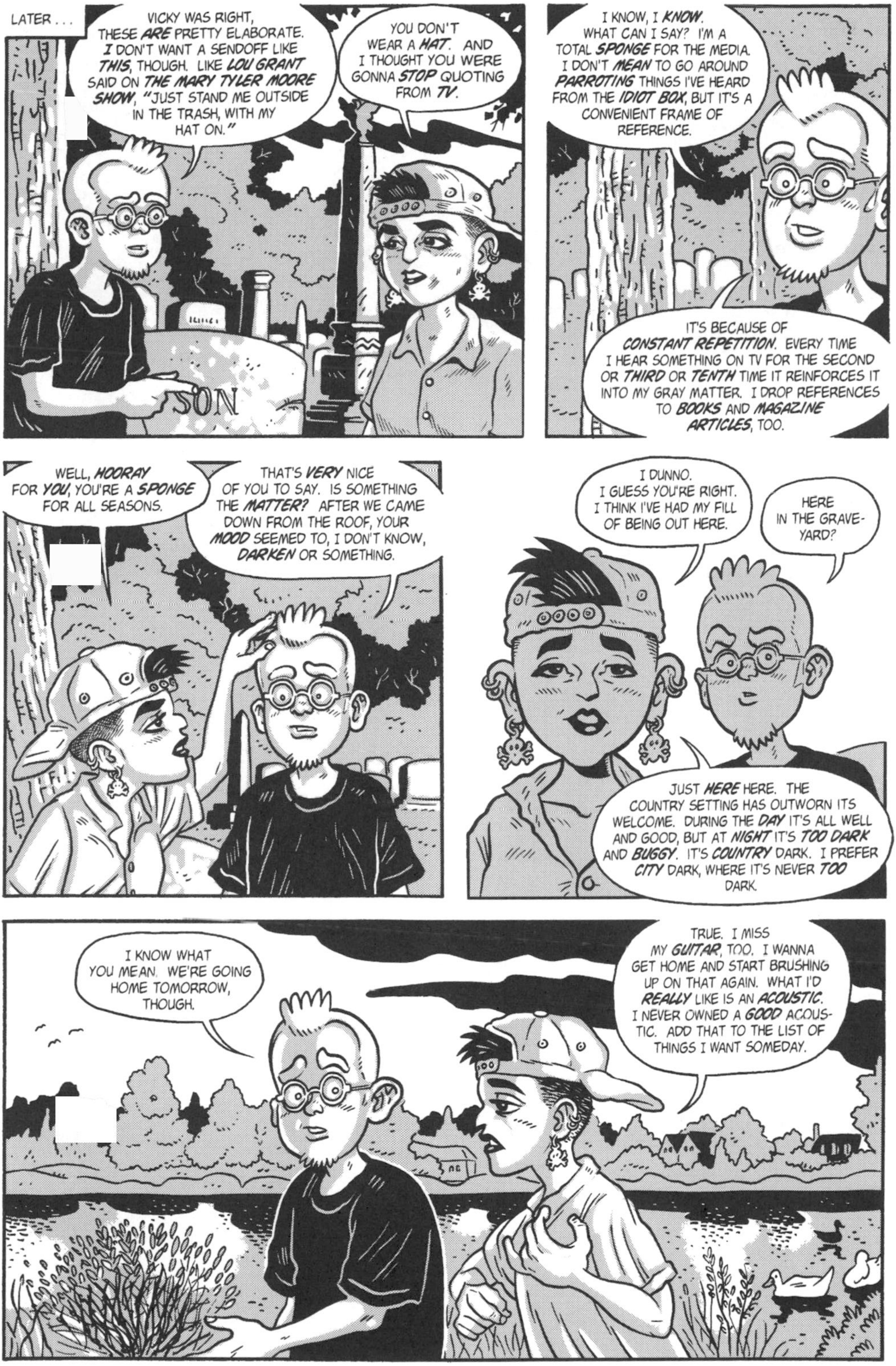
LATER . . .
VICKY WAS RIGHT, THESE ARE PRETTY ELABORATE. I DON'T WANT A SENDOFF LIKE THIS, THOUGH. LIKE LOU GRANT SAID ON THE MARY TYLER MOORE SHOW, "JUST STAND ME OUTSIDE IN THE TRASH, WITH MY HAT ON."
SON
YOU DON'T WEAR A HAT. AND I THOUGHT YOU WERE GONNA STOP QUOTING FROM TV.
I KNOW, I KNOW. WHAT CAN I SAY? I'M A TOTAL SPONGE FOR THE MEDIA. I DON'T MEAN TO GO AROUND PARROTING THINGS I'VE HEARD FROM THE IDIOT BOX, BUT IT'S A CONVENIENT FRAME OF REFERENCE.
IT'S BECAUSE OF CONSTANT REPETITION. EVERY TIME I HEAR SOMETHING ON TV FOR THE SECOND OR THIRD OR TENTH TIME IT REINFORCES IT INTO MY GRAY MATTER. I DROP REFERENCES TO BOOKS AND MAGAZINE ARTICLES, TOO.
WELL, HOORAY FOR YOU, YOU'RE A SPONGE FOR ALL SEASONS.
THAT'S VERY NICE OF YOU TO SAY. IS SOMETHING THE MATTER? AFTER WE CAME DOWN FROM THE ROOF, YOUR MOOD SEEMED TO, I DON'T KNOW, DARKEN OR SOMETHING.
I DUNNO. I GUESS YOU'RE RIGHT. I THINK I'VE HAD MY FILL OF BEING OUT HERE.
HERE IN THE GRAVE-YARD?
JUST HERE HERE. THE COUNTRY SETTING HAS OUTWORN ITS WELCOME. DURING THE DAY IT'S ALL WELL AND GOOD, BUT AT NIGHT IT'S TOO DARK AND BUGGY. IT'S COUNTRY DARK. I PREFER CITY DARK, WHERE IT'S NEVER TOO DARK.
I KNOW WHAT YOU MEAN. WE'RE GOING HOME TOMORROW, THOUGH.
TRUE. I MISS MY GUITAR, TOO. I WANNA GET HOME AND START BRUSHING UP ON THAT AGAIN. WHAT I'D REALLY LIKE IS AN ACOUSTIC. I NEVER OWNED A GOOD ACOUS-TIC. ADD THAT TO THE LIST OF THINGS I WANT SOMEDAY.

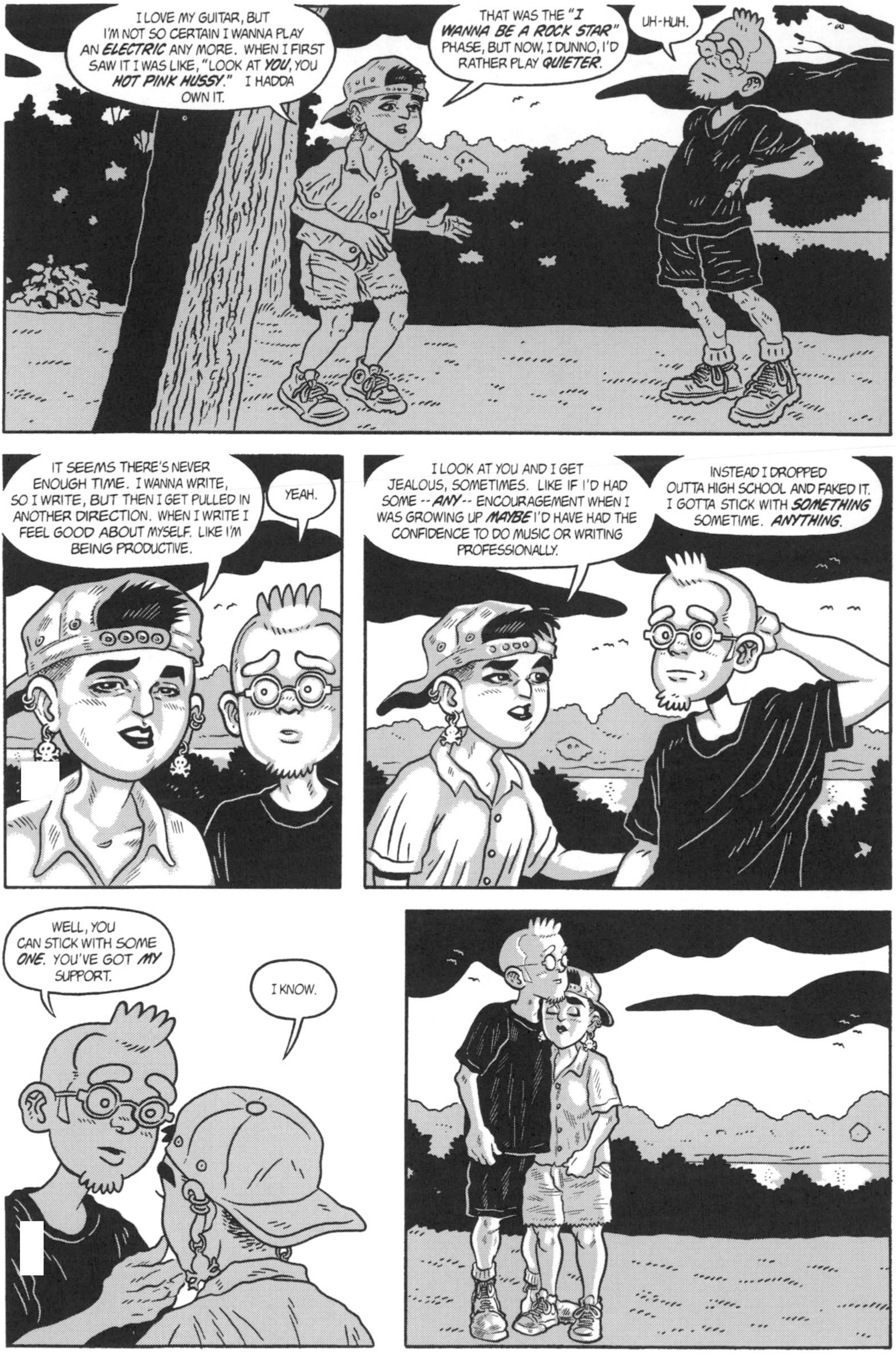
I LOVE MY GUITAR, BUT I'M NOT SO CERTAIN I WANNA PLAY AN ELECTRIC ANY MORE. WHEN I FIRST SAW IT I WAS LIKE, "LOOK AT YOU, YOU HOT PINK HUSSY." I HADDA OWN IT.
THAT WAS THE "I WANNA BE A ROCK STAR" PHASE, BUT NOW, I DUNNO, I'D RATHER PLAY QUIETER.
UH-HUH.
IT SEEMS THERE'S NEVER ENOUGH TIME. I WANNA WRITE, SO I WRITE, BUT THEN I GET PULLED IN ANOTHER DIRECTION. WHEN I WRITE I FEEL GOOD ABOUT MYSELF. LIKE I'M BEING PRODUCTIVE.
YEAH.
I LOOK AT YOU AND I GET JEALOUS, SOMETIMES. LIKE IF I'D HAD SOME -- ANY -- ENCOURAGEMENT WHEN I WAS GROWING UP MAYBE I'D HAVE HAD THE CONFIDENCE TO DO MUSIC OR WRITING PROFESSIONALLY.
INSTEAD I DROPPED OUTTA HIGH SCHOOL AND FAKED IT. I GOTTA STICK WITH SOMETHING SOMETIME. ANYTHING.
WELL, YOU CAN STICK WITH SOME ONE. YOU'VE GOT MY SUPPORT.
I KNOW.

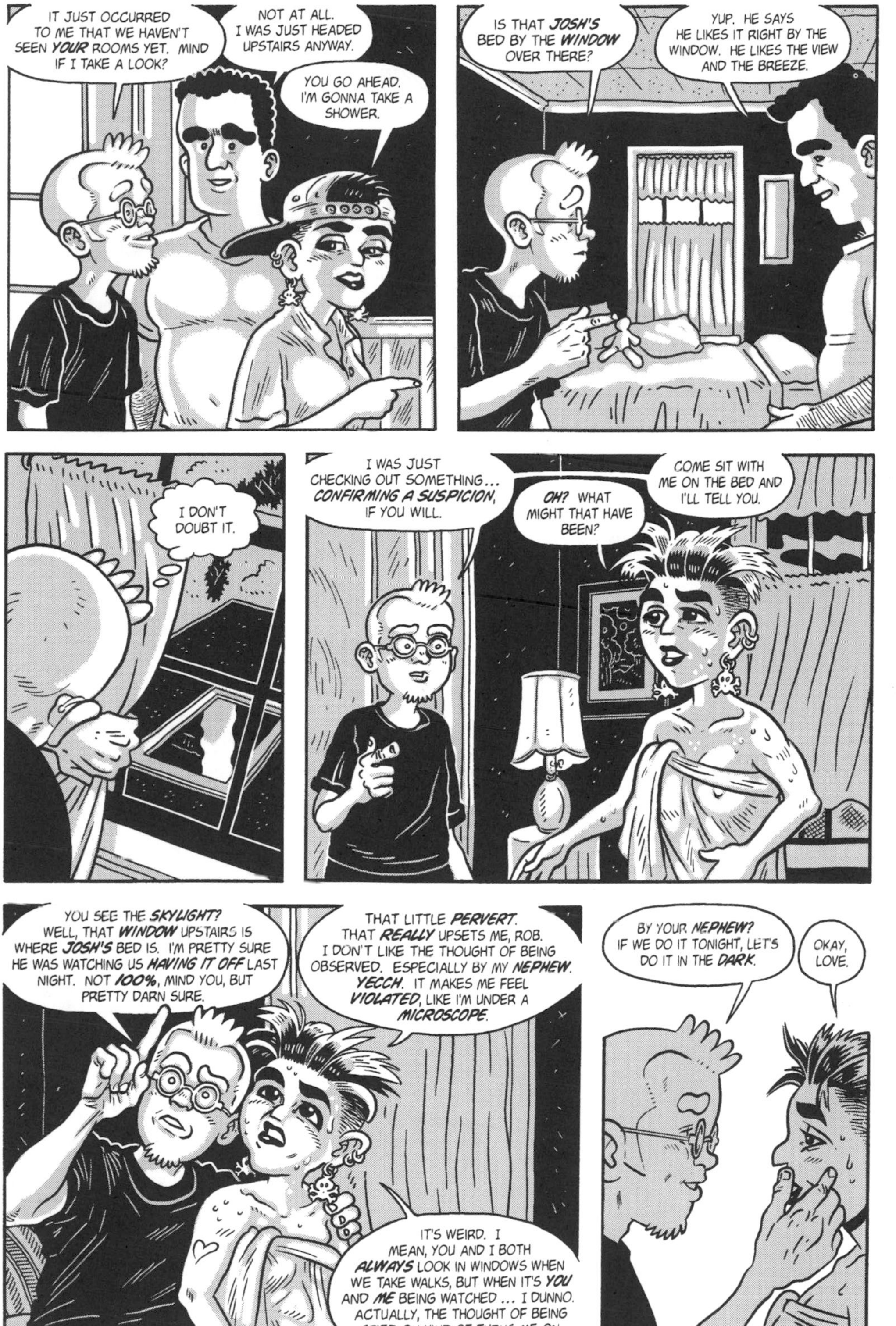
IT JUST OCCURRED TO ME THAT WE HAVEN'T SEEN YOUR ROOMS YET. MIND IF I TAKE A LOOK?
NOT AT ALL. I WAS JUST HEADED UPSTAIRS ANYWAY.
YOU GO AHEAD. I'M GONNA TAKE A SHOWER.
IS THAT JOSH'S BED BY THE WINDOW OVER THERE?
YUP. HE SAYS HE LIKES IT RIGHT BY THE WINDOW. HE LIKES THE VIEW AND THE BREEZE.
I DON'T DOUBT IT.
I WAS JUST CHECKING OUT SOMETHING... CONFIRMING A SUSPICION, IF YOU WILL.
OH? WHAT MIGHT THAT HAVE BEEN?
COME SIT WITH ME ON THE BED AND I'LL TELL YOU.
YOU SEE THE SKYLIGHT? WELL, THAT WINDOW UPSTAIRS IS WHERE JOSH'S BED IS. I'M PRETTY SURE HE WAS WATCHING US HAVING IT OFF LAST NIGHT. NOT 100%, MIND YOU, BUT PRETTY DARN SURE.
THAT LITTLE PERVERT. THAT REALLY UPSETS ME, ROB. I DON'T LIKE THE THOUGHT OF BEING OBSERVED. ESPECIALLY BY MY NEPHEW. YECCH. IT MAKES ME FEEL VIOLATED, LIKE I'M UNDER A MICROSCOPE.
IT'S WEIRD. I MEAN, YOU AND I BOTH ALWAYS LOOK IN WINDOWS WHEN WE TAKE WALKS, BUT WHEN IT'S YOU AND ME BEING WATCHED ... I DUNNO. ACTUALLY, THE THOUGHT OF BEING SPIED ON KIND OF TURNS ME ON.
BY YOUR NEPHEW? IF WE DO IT TONIGHT, LET'S DO IT IN THE DARK.
OKAY, LOVE.

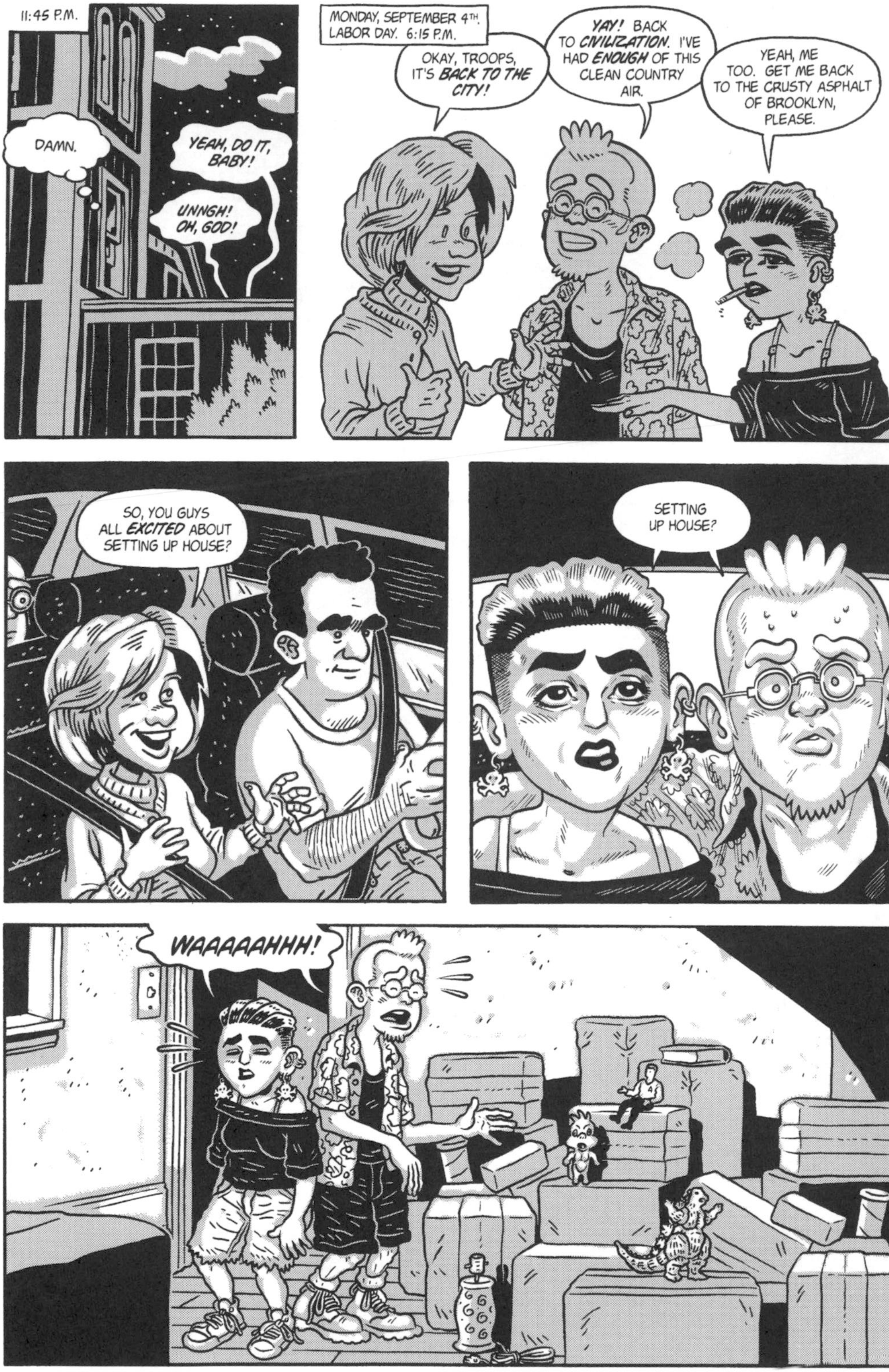
11:45 P.M.
DAMN.
YEAH, DO IT, BABY!
UNNGH! OH, GOD!
MONDAY, SEPTEMBER 4TH. LABOR DAY. 6:15 P.M.
OKAY, TROOPS, IT'S BACK TO THE CITY!
YAY! BACK TO CIVILIZATION. I'VE HAD ENOUGH OF THIS CLEAN COUNTRY AIR.
YEAH, ME TOO. GET ME BACK TO THE CRUSTY ASPHALT OF BROOKLYN, PLEASE.
SO, YOU GUYS ALL EXCITED ABOUT SETTING UP HOUSE?
SETTING UP HOUSE?
WAAAAAHHH!

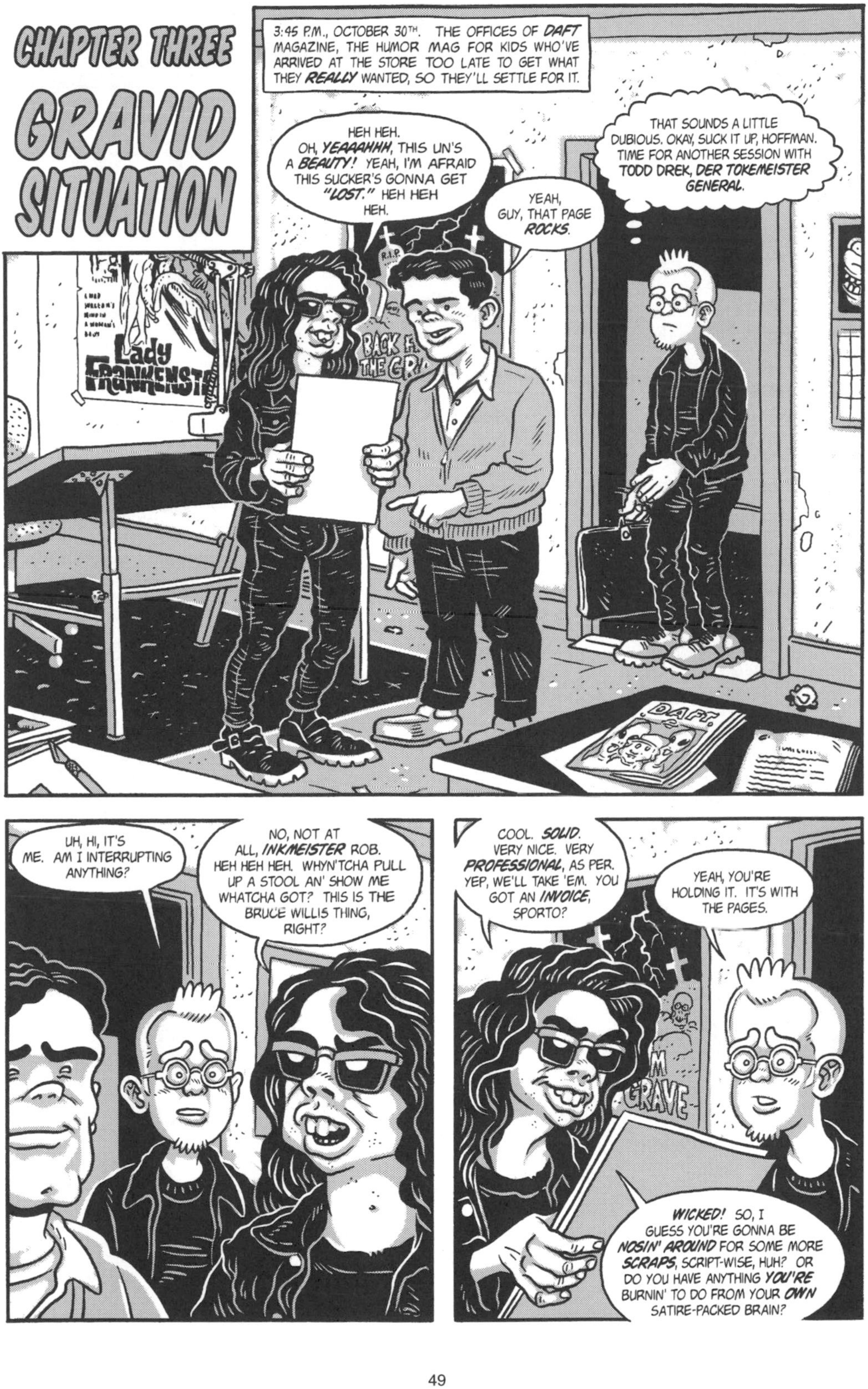
CHAPTER THREE
GRAVID SITUATION
3:45 P.M., OCTOBER 30TH. THE OFFICES OF DAFT MAGAZINE, THE HUMOR MAG FOR KIDS WHO'VE ARRIVED AT THE STORE TOO LATE TO GET WHAT THEY REALLY WANTED, SO THEY'LL SETTLE FOR IT.
HEH HEH. OH, YEAAAHHH, THIS UN'S A BEAUTY! YEAH, I'M AFRAID THIS SUCKER'S GONNA GET "LOST." HEH HEH HEH.
YEAH, GUY, THAT PAGE ROCKS.
THAT SOUNDS A LITTLE DUBIOUS. OKAY, SUCK IT UP, HOFFMAN. TIME FOR ANOTHER SESSION WITH TODD DREK, DER TOKEMEISTER GENERAL.
Lady FRANKENSTEIN
DAFT
UH, HI, IT'S ME. AM I INTERRUPTING ANYTHING?
NO, NOT AT ALL, INKMEISTER ROB. HEH HEH HEH. WHYN'TCHA PULL UP A STOOL AN' SHOW ME WHATCHA GOT? THIS IS THE BRUCE WILLIS THING, RIGHT?
COOL. SOLID. VERY NICE. VERY PROFESSIONAL, AS PER. YEP, WE'LL TAKE 'EM. YOU GOT AN INVOICE, SPORTO?
YEAH, YOU'RE HOLDING IT. IT'S WITH THE PAGES.
WICKED! SO, I GUESS YOU'RE GONNA BE NOSIN' AROUND FOR SOME MORE SCRAPS, SCRIPT-WISE, HUH? OR DO YOU HAVE ANYTHING YOU'RE BURNIN' TO DO FROM YOUR OWN SATIRE-PACKED BRAIN?

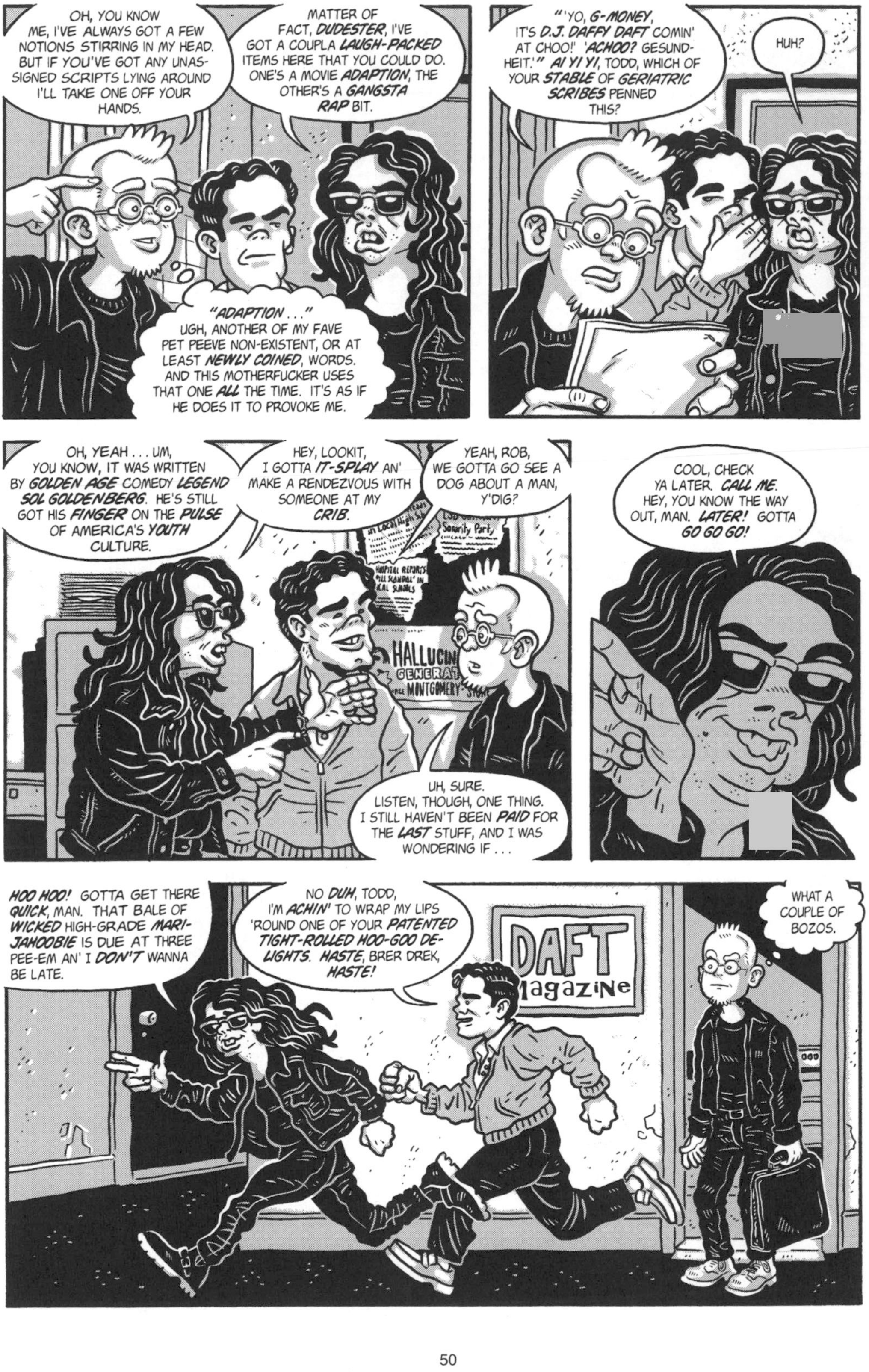
OH, YOU KNOW ME, I'VE ALWAYS GOT A FEW NOTIONS STIRRING IN MY HEAD. BUT IF YOU'VE GOT ANY UNASSIGNED SCRIPTS LYING AROUND I'LL TAKE ONE OFF YOUR HANDS.
MATTER OF FACT, DUDESTER, I'VE GOT A COUPLA LAUGH-PACKED ITEMS HERE THAT YOU COULD DO. ONE'S A MOVIE ADAPTION, THE OTHER'S A GANGSTA RAP BIT.
"ADAPTION . . ." UGH, ANOTHER OF MY FAVE PET PEEVE NON-EXISTENT, OR AT LEAST NEWLY COINED, WORDS. AND THIS MOTHERFUCKER USES THAT ONE ALL THE TIME. IT'S AS IF HE DOES IT TO PROVOKE ME.
"'YO, G-MONEY, IT'S D.J. DAFFY DAFT COMIN' AT CHOO!' 'ACHOO? GESUNDHEIT.'" AI YI YI, TODD, WHICH OF YOUR STABLE OF GERIATRIC SCRIBES PENNED THIS?
HUH?
OH, YEAH . . . UM, YOU KNOW, IT WAS WRITTEN BY GOLDEN AGE COMEDY LEGEND SOL GOLDENBERG. HE'S STILL GOT HIS FINGER ON THE PULSE OF AMERICA'S YOUTH CULTURE.
HEY, LOOKIT, I GOTTA IT-SPLAY AN' MAKE A RENDEZVOUS WITH SOMEONE AT MY CRIB.
YEAH, ROB, WE GOTTA GO SEE A DOG ABOUT A MAN, Y'DIG?
UH, SURE. LISTEN, THOUGH, ONE THING. I STILL HAVEN'T BEEN PAID FOR THE LAST STUFF, AND I WAS WONDERING IF . . .
COOL, CHECK YA LATER. CALL ME. HEY, YOU KNOW THE WAY OUT, MAN. LATER! GOTTA GO GO GO!
HOO HOO! GOTTA GET THERE QUICK, MAN. THAT BALE OF WICKED HIGH-GRADE MARIJAHOOBIE IS DUE AT THREE PEE-EM AN' I DON'T WANNA BE LATE.
NO DUH, TODD, I'M ACHIN' TO WRAP MY LIPS 'ROUND ONE OF YOUR PATENTED TIGHT-ROLLED HOO-GOO DELIGHTS. HASTE, BRER DREK, HASTE!
DAFT Magazine
WHAT A COUPLE OF BOZOS.

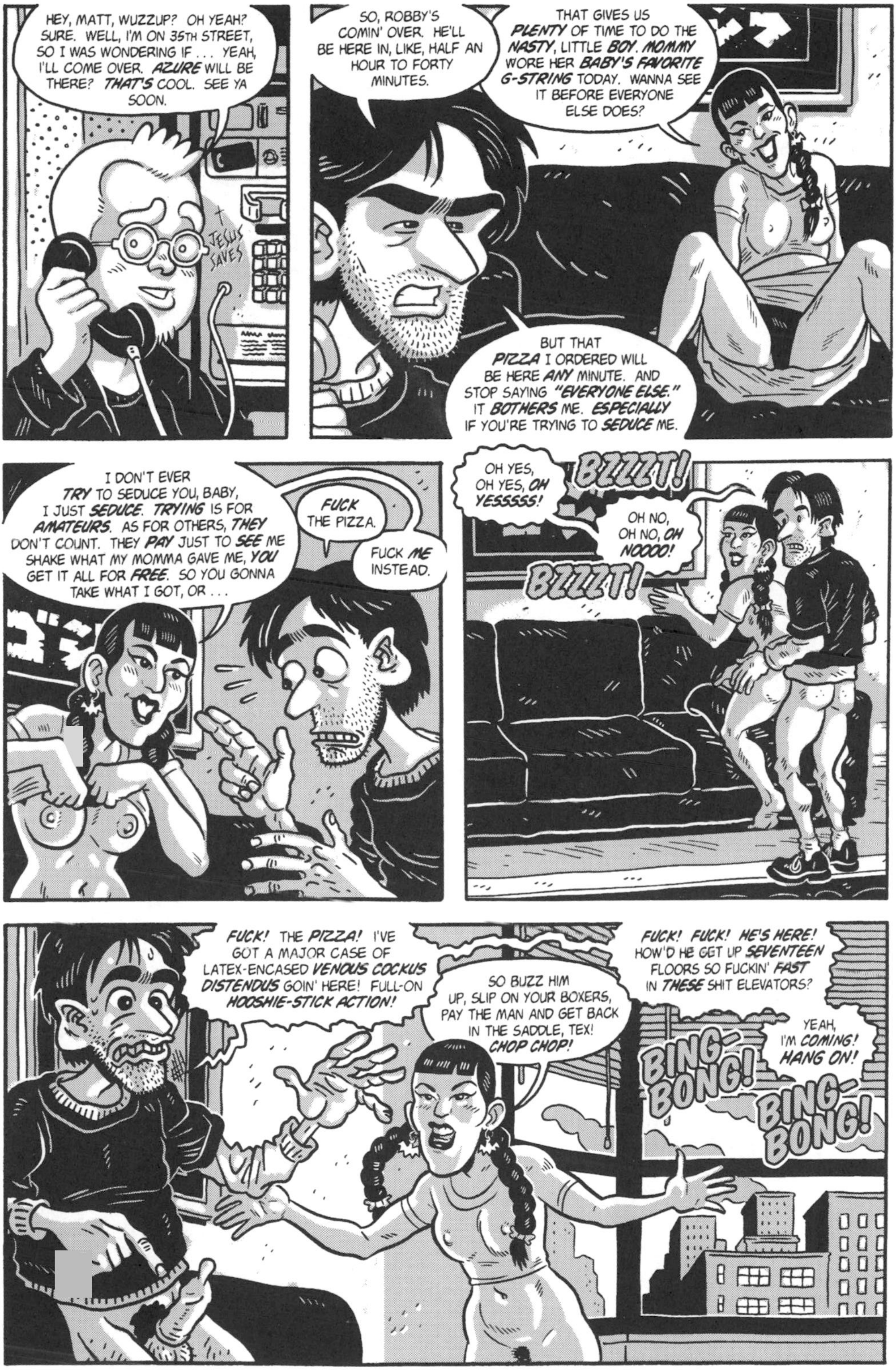
HEY, MATT, WUZZUP? OH YEAH? SURE. WELL, I'M ON 35TH STREET, SO I WAS WONDERING IF . . . YEAH, I'LL COME OVER. AZURE WILL BE THERE? THAT'S COOL. SEE YA SOON.
JESUS SAVES
SO, ROBBY'S COMIN' OVER. HE'LL BE HERE IN, LIKE, HALF AN HOUR TO FORTY MINUTES.
THAT GIVES US PLENTY OF TIME TO DO THE NASTY, LITTLE BOY. MOMMY WORE HER BABY'S FAVORITE G-STRING TODAY. WANNA SEE IT BEFORE EVERYONE ELSE DOES?
BUT THAT PIZZA I ORDERED WILL BE HERE ANY MINUTE. AND STOP SAYING "EVERYONE ELSE." IT BOTHERS ME. ESPECIALLY IF YOU'RE TRYING TO SEDUCE ME.
I DON'T EVER TRY TO SEDUCE YOU, BABY, I JUST SEDUCE. TRYING IS FOR AMATEURS. AS FOR OTHERS, THEY DON'T COUNT. THEY PAY JUST TO SEE ME SHAKE WHAT MY MOMMA GAVE ME, YOU GET IT ALL FOR FREE. SO YOU GONNA TAKE WHAT I GOT, OR . . .
FUCK THE PIZZA.
FUCK ME INSTEAD.
OH YES, OH YES, OH YESSSSS!
BZZZZT!
OH NO, OH NO, OH NOOOO!
BZZZZT!
FUCK! THE PIZZA! I'VE GOT A MAJOR CASE OF LATEX-ENCASED VENOUS COCKUS DISTENDUS GOIN' HERE! FULL-ON HOOSHIE-STICK ACTION!
SO BUZZ HIM UP, SLIP ON YOUR BOXERS, PAY THE MAN AND GET BACK IN THE SADDLE, TEX! CHOP CHOP!
FUCK! FUCK! HE'S HERE! HOW'D HE GET UP SEVENTEEN FLOORS SO FUCKIN' FAST IN THESE SHIT ELEVATORS?
BING-BONG!
YEAH, I'M COMING! HANG ON!
BING-BONG!

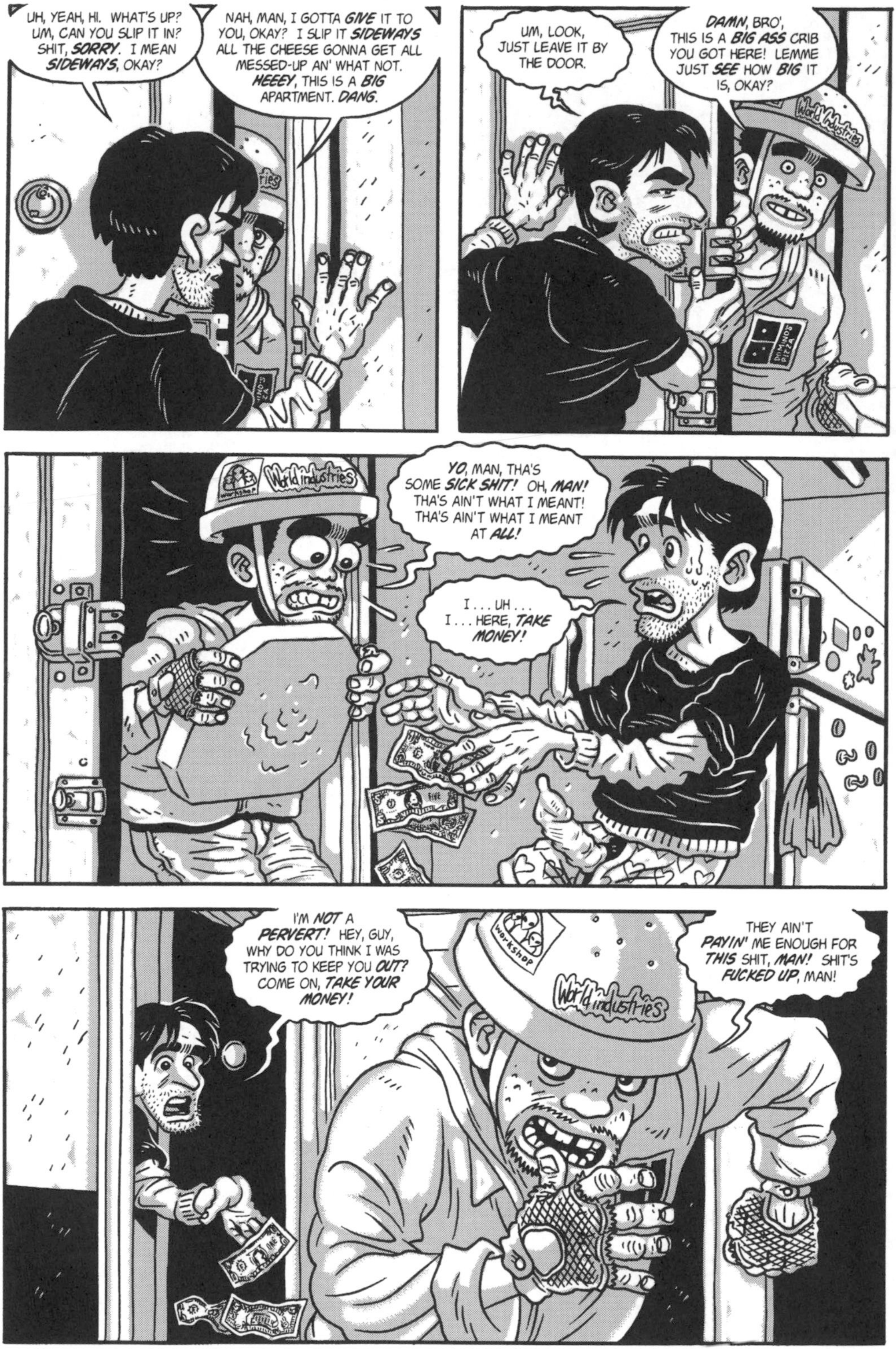
UH, YEAH, HI. WHAT'S UP? UM, CAN YOU SLIP IT IN? SHIT, SORRY. I MEAN SIDEWAYS, OKAY?
NAH, MAN, I GOTTA GIVE IT TO YOU, OKAY? I SLIP IT SIDEWAYS ALL THE CHEESE GONNA GET ALL MESSED-UP AN' WHAT NOT. HEEEY, THIS IS A BIG APARTMENT. DANG.
UM, LOOK, JUST LEAVE IT BY THE DOOR.
DAMN, BRO', THIS IS A BIG ASS CRIB YOU GOT HERE! LEMME JUST SEE HOW BIG IT IS, OKAY?
World Industries
YO, MAN, THA'S SOME SICK SHIT! OH, MAN! THA'S AIN'T WHAT I MEANT! THA'S AIN'T WHAT I MEANT AT ALL!
I . . . UH . . . I . . . HERE, TAKE MONEY!
I'M NOT A PERVERT! HEY, GUY, WHY DO YOU THINK I WAS TRYING TO KEEP YOU OUT? COME ON, TAKE YOUR MONEY!
THEY AIN'T PAYIN' ME ENOUGH FOR THIS SHIT, MAN! SHIT'S FUCKED UP, MAN!

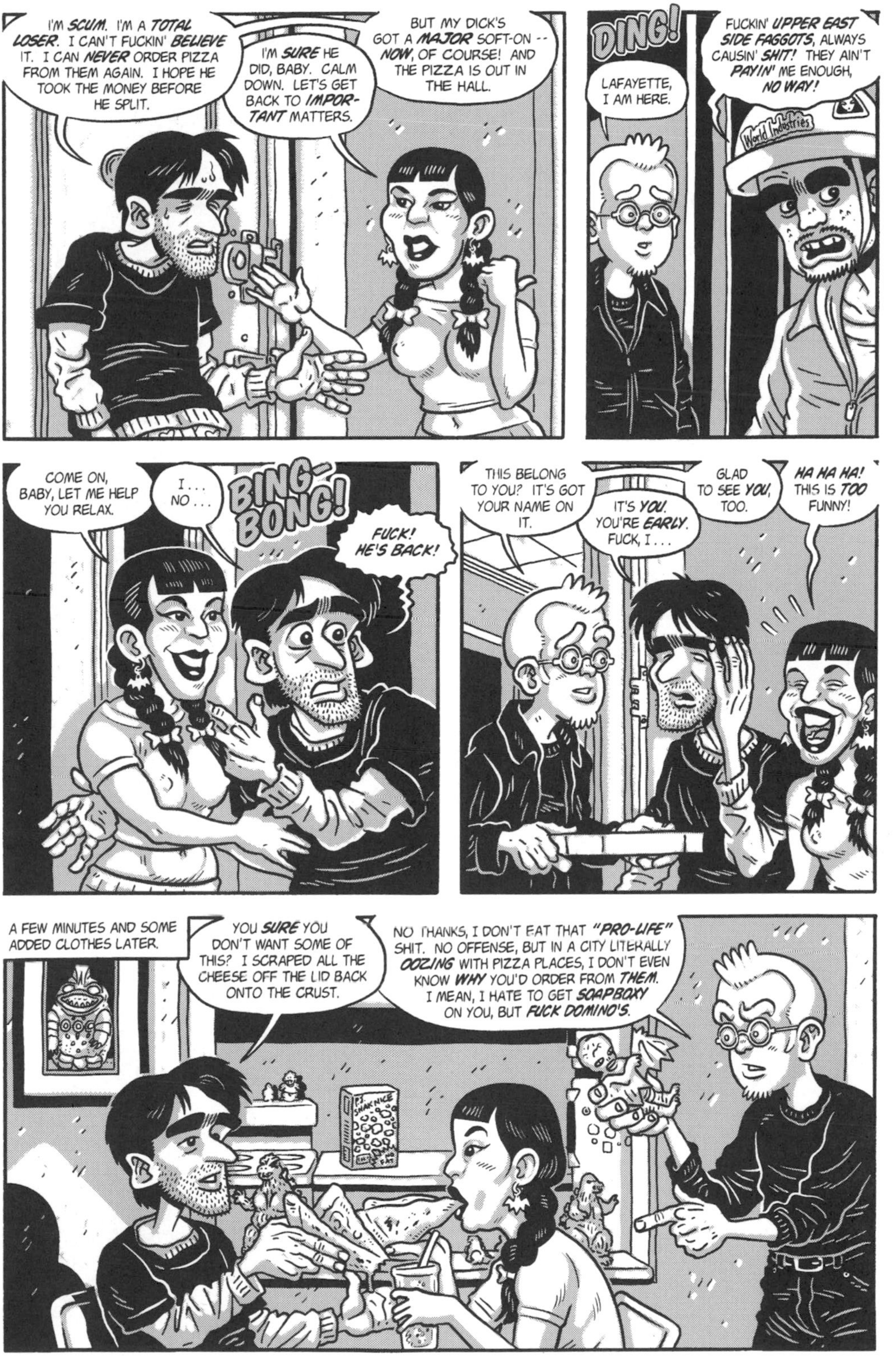
I'M SCUM. I'M A TOTAL LOSER. I CAN'T FUCKIN' BELIEVE IT. I CAN NEVER ORDER PIZZA FROM THEM AGAIN. I HOPE HE TOOK THE MONEY BEFORE HE SPLIT.
I'M SURE HE DID, BABY. CALM DOWN. LET'S GET BACK TO IMPORTANT MATTERS.
BUT MY DICK'S GOT A MAJOR SOFT-ON -- NOW, OF COURSE! AND THE PIZZA IS OUT IN THE HALL.
DING!
LAFAYETTE, I AM HERE.
FUCKIN' UPPER EAST SIDE FAGGOTS, ALWAYS CAUSIN' SHIT! THEY AIN'T PAYIN' ME ENOUGH, NO WAY!
World Industries
COME ON, BABY, LET ME HELP YOU RELAX.
I... NO...
BING-BONG!
FUCK! HE'S BACK!
THIS BELONG TO YOU? IT'S GOT YOUR NAME ON IT.
IT'S YOU. YOU'RE EARLY. FUCK, I...
GLAD TO SEE YOU, TOO.
HA HA HA! THIS IS TOO FUNNY!
A FEW MINUTES AND SOME ADDED CLOTHES LATER.
YOU SURE YOU DON'T WANT SOME OF THIS? I SCRAPED ALL THE CHEESE OFF THE LID BACK ONTO THE CRUST.
NO THANKS, I DON'T EAT THAT "PRO-LIFE" SHIT. NO OFFENSE, BUT IN A CITY LITERALLY OOZING WITH PIZZA PLACES, I DON'T EVEN KNOW WHY YOU'D ORDER FROM THEM. I MEAN, I HATE TO GET SOAPBOXY ON YOU, BUT FUCK DOMINO'S.
SNAK NICE

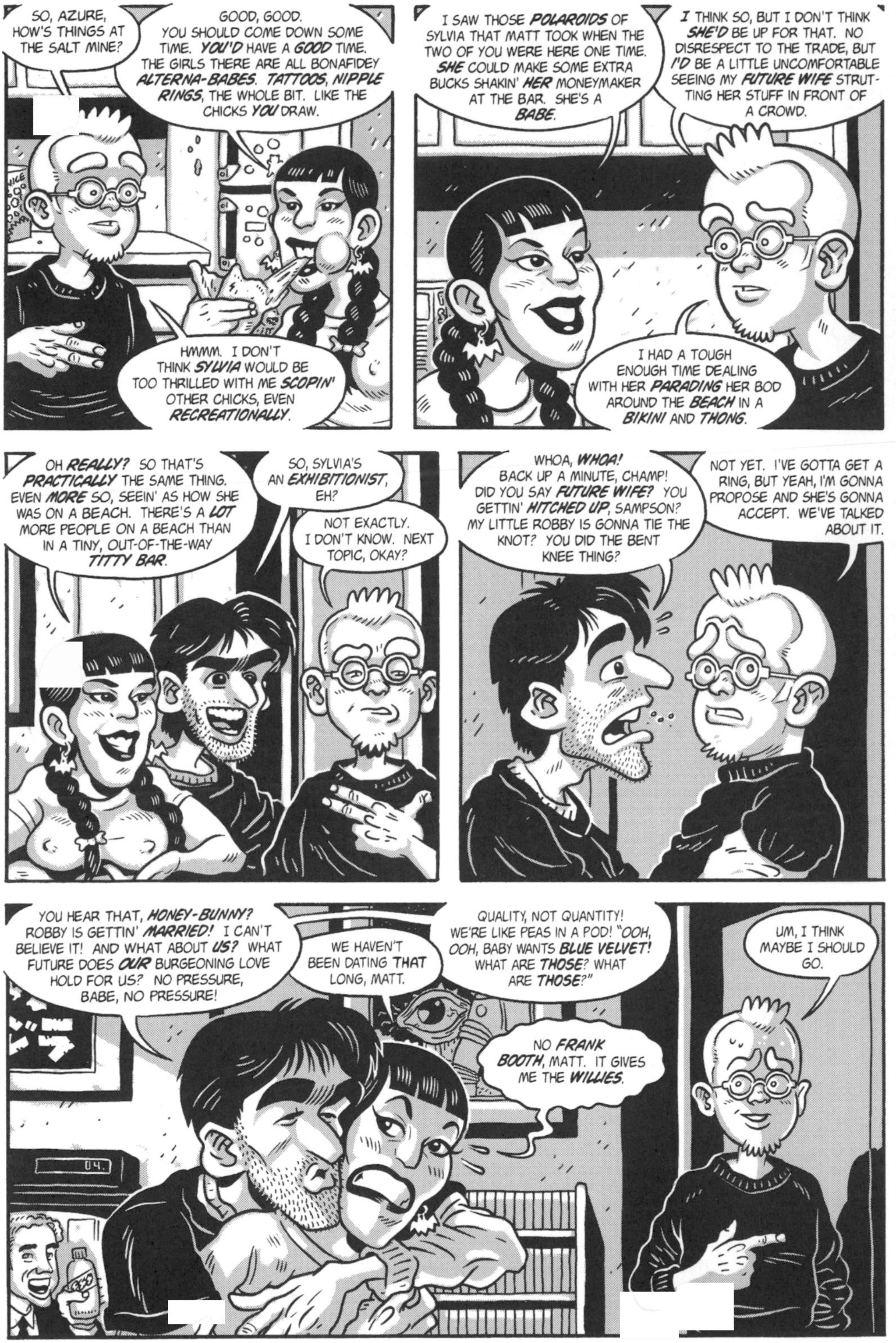
SO, AZURE, HOW'S THINGS AT THE SALT MINE?
GOOD, GOOD. YOU SHOULD COME DOWN SOME TIME. YOU'D HAVE A GOOD TIME. THE GIRLS THERE ARE ALL BONAFIDEY ALTERNA-BABES. TATTOOS, NIPPLE RINGS, THE WHOLE BIT. LIKE THE CHICKS YOU DRAW.
HMMM. I DON'T THINK SYLVIA WOULD BE TOO THRILLED WITH ME SCOPIN' OTHER CHICKS, EVEN RECREATIONALLY.
I SAW THOSE POLAROIDS OF SYLVIA THAT MATT TOOK WHEN THE TWO OF YOU WERE HERE ONE TIME. SHE COULD MAKE SOME EXTRA BUCKS SHAKIN' HER MONEYMAKER AT THE BAR. SHE'S A BABE.
I THINK SO, BUT I DON'T THINK SHE'D BE UP FOR THAT. NO DISRESPECT TO THE TRADE, BUT I'D BE A LITTLE UNCOMFORTABLE SEEING MY FUTURE WIFE STRUTTING HER STUFF IN FRONT OF A CROWD.
I HAD A TOUGH ENOUGH TIME DEALING WITH HER PARADING HER BOD AROUND THE BEACH IN A BIKINI AND THONG.
OH REALLY? SO THAT'S PRACTICALLY THE SAME THING. EVEN MORE SO, SEEIN' AS HOW SHE WAS ON A BEACH. THERE'S A LOT MORE PEOPLE ON A BEACH THAN IN A TINY, OUT-OF-THE-WAY TITTY BAR.
SO, SYLVIA'S AN EXHIBITIONIST, EH?
NOT EXACTLY. I DON'T KNOW. NEXT TOPIC, OKAY?
WHOA, WHOA! BACK UP A MINUTE, CHAMP! DID YOU SAY FUTURE WIFE? YOU GETTIN' HITCHED UP, SAMPSON? MY LITTLE ROBBY IS GONNA TIE THE KNOT? YOU DID THE BENT KNEE THING?
NOT YET. I'VE GOTTA GET A RING, BUT YEAH, I'M GONNA PROPOSE AND SHE'S GONNA ACCEPT. WE'VE TALKED ABOUT IT.
YOU HEAR THAT, HONEY-BUNNY? ROBBY IS GETTIN' MARRIED! I CAN'T BELIEVE IT! AND WHAT ABOUT US? WHAT FUTURE DOES OUR BURGEONING LOVE HOLD FOR US? NO PRESSURE, BABE, NO PRESSURE!
WE HAVEN'T BEEN DATING THAT LONG, MATT.
QUALITY, NOT QUANTITY! WE'RE LIKE PEAS IN A POD! "OOH, OOH, BABY WANTS BLUE VELVET! WHAT ARE THOSE? WHAT ARE THOSE?"
NO FRANK BOOTH, MATT. IT GIVES ME THE WILLIES.
UM, I THINK MAYBE I SHOULD GO.

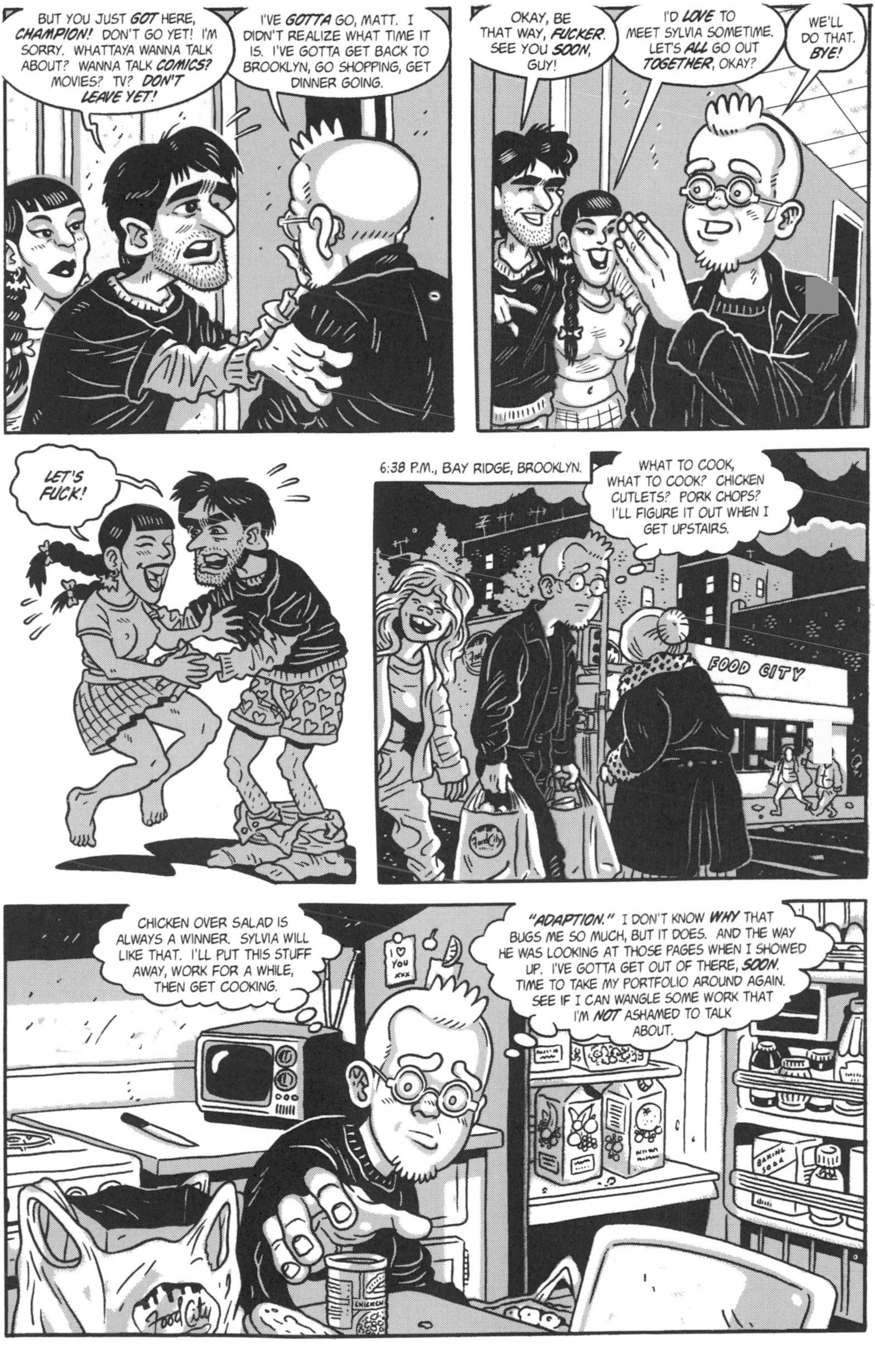
BUT YOU JUST GOT HERE, CHAMPION! DON'T GO YET! I'M SORRY. WHATTAYA WANNA TALK ABOUT? WANNA TALK COMICS? MOVIES? TV? DON'T LEAVE YET!
I'VE GOTTA GO, MATT. I DIDN'T REALIZE WHAT TIME IT IS. I'VE GOTTA GET BACK TO BROOKLYN, GO SHOPPING, GET DINNER GOING.
OKAY, BE THAT WAY, FUCKER. SEE YOU SOON, GUY!
I'D LOVE TO MEET SYLVIA SOMETIME. LET'S ALL GO OUT TOGETHER, OKAY?
WE'LL DO THAT. BYE!
LET'S FUCK!
6:38 P.M., BAY RIDGE, BROOKLYN.
WHAT TO COOK, WHAT TO COOK? CHICKEN CUTLETS? PORK CHOPS? I'LL FIGURE IT OUT WHEN I GET UPSTAIRS.
FOOD CITY
CHICKEN OVER SALAD IS ALWAYS A WINNER. SYLVIA WILL LIKE THAT. I'LL PUT THIS STUFF AWAY, WORK FOR A WHILE, THEN GET COOKING.
"ADAPTION." I DON'T KNOW WHY THAT BUGS ME SO MUCH, BUT IT DOES. AND THE WAY HE WAS LOOKING AT THOSE PAGES WHEN I SHOWED UP. I'VE GOTTA GET OUT OF THERE, SOON. TIME TO TAKE MY PORTFOLIO AROUND AGAIN. SEE IF I CAN WANGLE SOME WORK THAT I'M NOT ASHAMED TO TALK ABOUT.
I ♡ YOU XXX
Food City
BAKING SODA

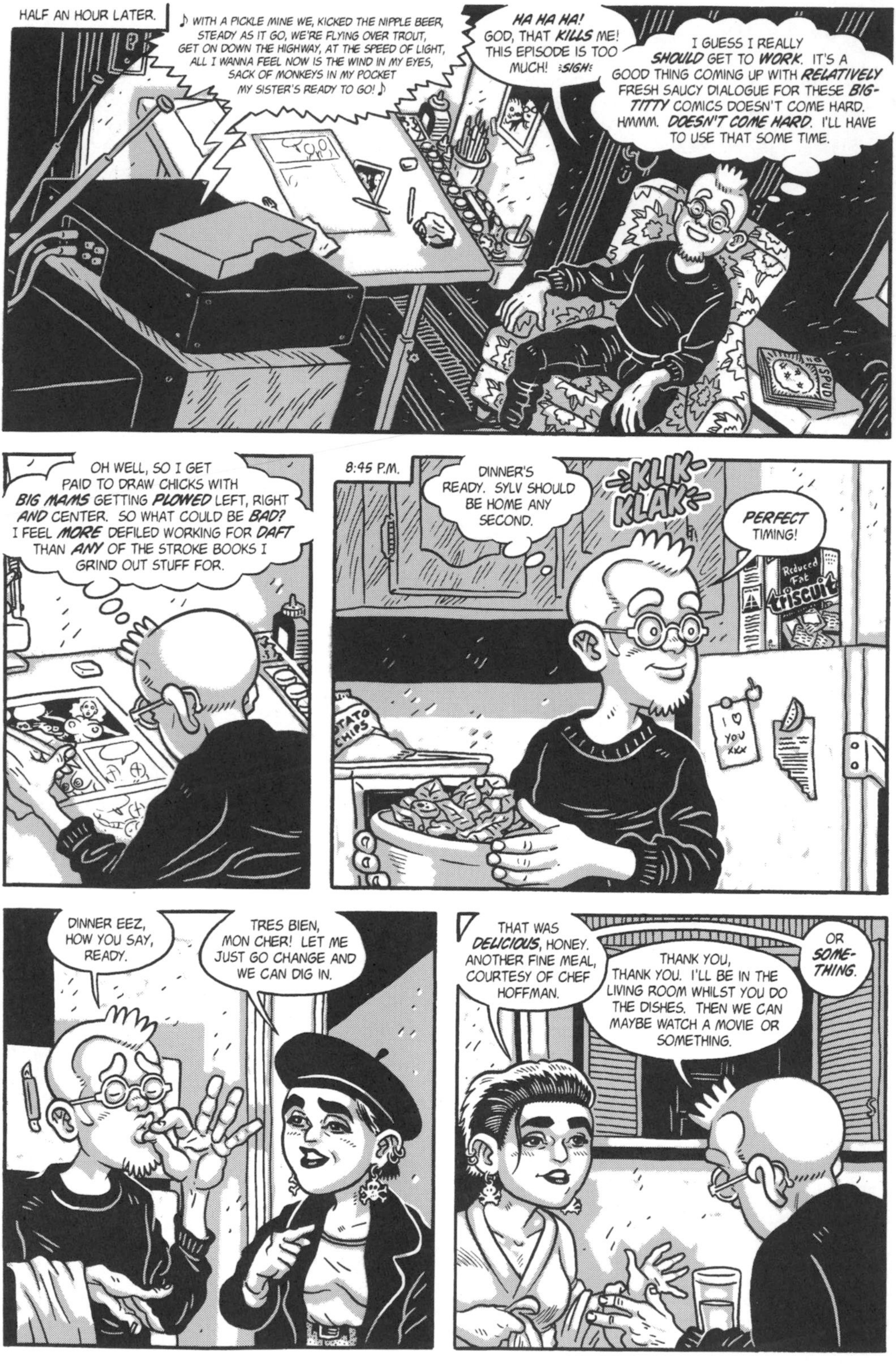
HALF AN HOUR LATER.
♪ WITH A PICKLE MINE WE, KICKED THE NIPPLE BEER, STEADY AS IT GO, WE'RE FLYING OVER TROUT, GET ON DOWN THE HIGHWAY, AT THE SPEED OF LIGHT, ALL I WANNA FEEL NOW IS THE WIND IN MY EYES, SACK OF MONKEYS IN MY POCKET MY SISTER'S READY TO GO! ♪
HA HA HA! GOD, THAT KILLS ME! THIS EPISODE IS TOO MUCH! SIGH
I GUESS I REALLY SHOULD GET TO WORK. IT'S A GOOD THING COMING UP WITH RELATIVELY FRESH SAUCY DIALOGUE FOR THESE BIG-TITTY COMICS DOESN'T COME HARD. HMMM. DOESN'T COME HARD. I'LL HAVE TO USE THAT SOME TIME.
SPUD
OH WELL, SO I GET PAID TO DRAW CHICKS WITH BIG MAMS GETTING PLOWED LEFT, RIGHT AND CENTER. SO WHAT COULD BE BAD? I FEEL MORE DEFILED WORKING FOR DAFT THAN ANY OF THE STROKE BOOKS I GRIND OUT STUFF FOR.
8:45 P.M.
DINNER'S READY. SYLV SHOULD BE HOME ANY SECOND.
KLIK KLAK
PERFECT TIMING!
Reduced Fat triscuit
I ♡ YOU XXX
DINNER EEZ, HOW YOU SAY, READY.
TRES BIEN, MON CHER! LET ME JUST GO CHANGE AND WE CAN DIG IN.
THAT WAS DELICIOUS, HONEY. ANOTHER FINE MEAL, COURTESY OF CHEF HOFFMAN.
THANK YOU, THANK YOU. I'LL BE IN THE LIVING ROOM WHILST YOU DO THE DISHES. THEN WE CAN MAYBE WATCH A MOVIE OR SOMETHING.
OR SOME-THING.

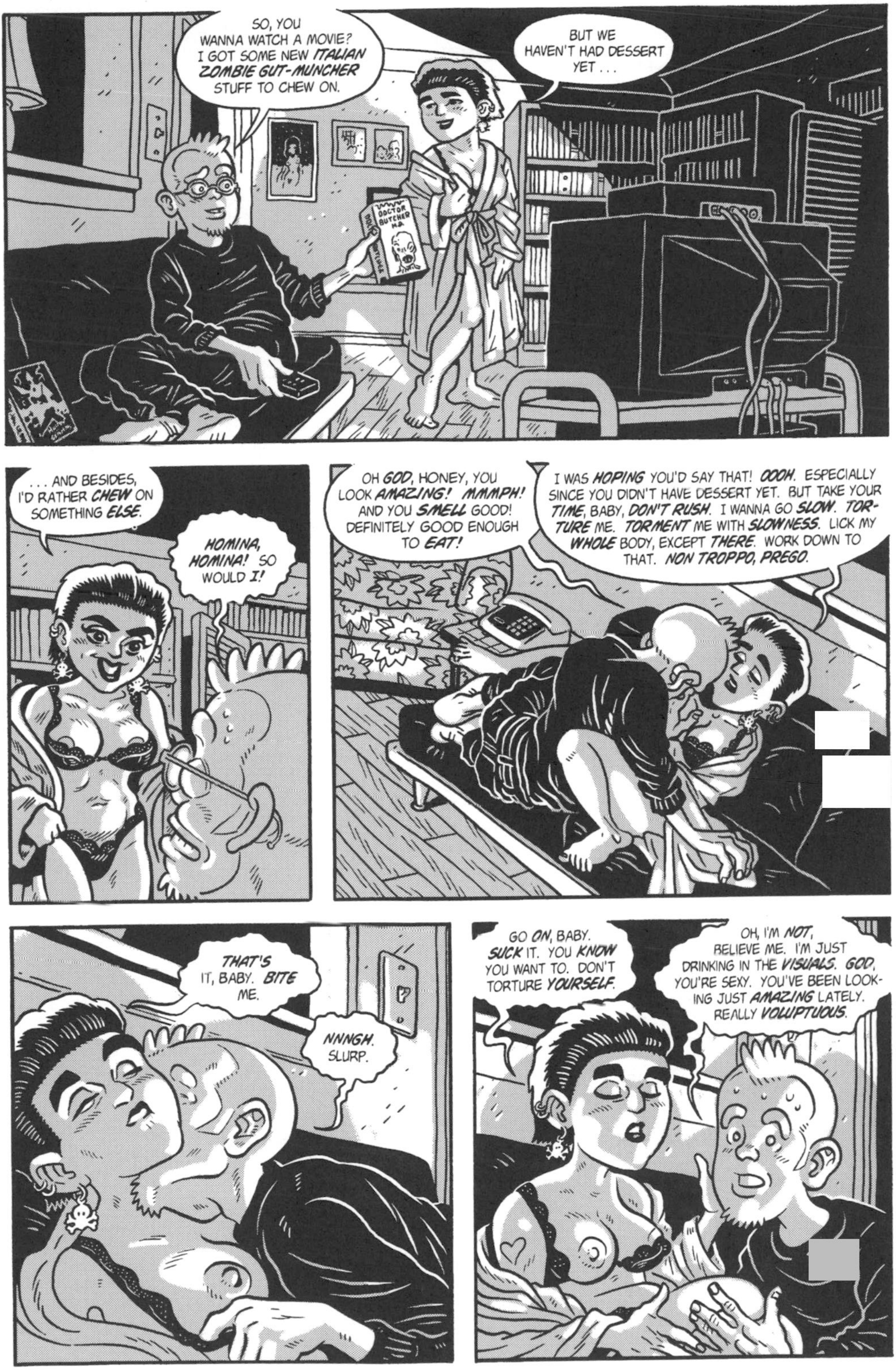
SO, YOU WANNA WATCH A MOVIE? I GOT SOME NEW *ITALIAN ZOMBIE GUT-MUNCHER* STUFF TO CHEW ON.
BUT WE HAVEN'T HAD DESSERT YET . . .
. . . AND BESIDES, I'D RATHER *CHEW* ON SOMETHING *ELSE*.
*HOMINA, HOMINA!* SO WOULD *I!*
OH *GOD*, HONEY, YOU LOOK *AMAZING! MMMPH!* AND YOU *SMELL* GOOD! DEFINITELY GOOD ENOUGH TO *EAT!*
I WAS *HOPING* YOU'D SAY THAT! *OOOH*. ESPECIALLY SINCE YOU DIDN'T HAVE DESSERT YET. BUT TAKE YOUR *TIME*, BABY, *DON'T RUSH*. I WANNA GO *SLOW*. *TORTURE* ME. *TORMENT* ME WITH *SLOWNESS*. LICK MY *WHOLE* BODY, EXCEPT *THERE*. WORK DOWN TO THAT. *NON TROPPO, PREGO.*
*THAT'S* IT, BABY. *BITE* ME.
*NNNGH.* SLURP.
GO *ON*, BABY. *SUCK* IT. YOU *KNOW* YOU WANT TO. DON'T TORTURE *YOURSELF*.
OH, I'M *NOT*, BELIEVE ME. I'M JUST DRINKING IN THE *VISUALS*. *GOD*, YOU'RE SEXY. YOU'VE BEEN LOOKING JUST *AMAZING* LATELY. REALLY *VOLUPTUOUS*.

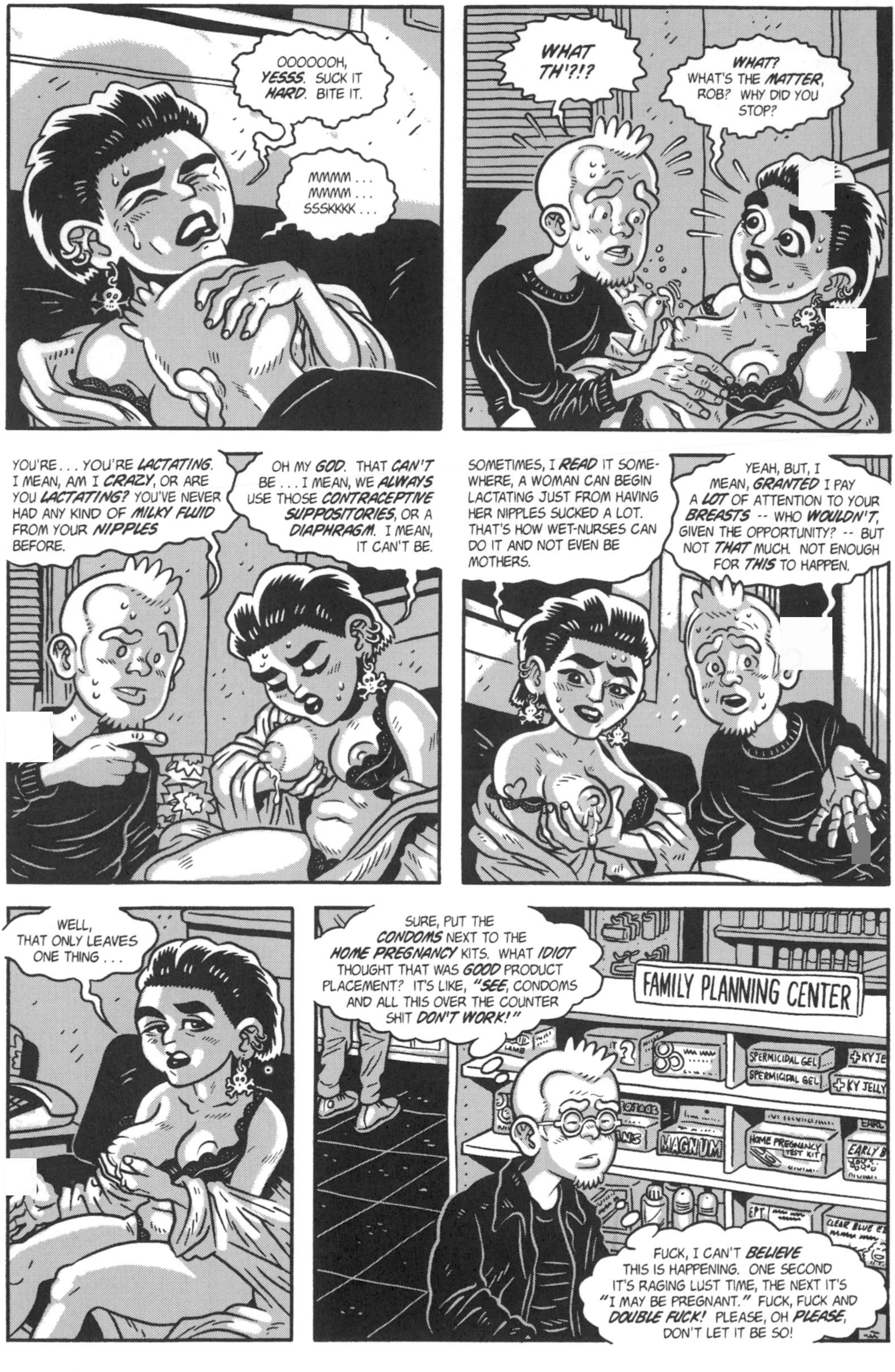
OOOOOOH, YESSS. SUCK IT HARD. BITE IT.
MMMM . . . MMMM . . . SSSKKKK . . .
WHAT TH'?!?
WHAT? WHAT'S THE MATTER, ROB? WHY DID YOU STOP?
YOU'RE . . . YOU'RE LACTATING. I MEAN, AM I CRAZY, OR ARE YOU LACTATING? YOU'VE NEVER HAD ANY KIND OF MILKY FLUID FROM YOUR NIPPLES BEFORE.
OH MY GOD. THAT CAN'T BE . . . I MEAN, WE ALWAYS USE THOSE CONTRACEPTIVE SUPPOSITORIES, OR A DIAPHRAGM. I MEAN, IT CAN'T BE.
SOMETIMES, I READ IT SOMEWHERE, A WOMAN CAN BEGIN LACTATING JUST FROM HAVING HER NIPPLES SUCKED A LOT. THAT'S HOW WET-NURSES CAN DO IT AND NOT EVEN BE MOTHERS.
YEAH, BUT, I MEAN, GRANTED I PAY A LOT OF ATTENTION TO YOUR BREASTS -- WHO WOULDN'T, GIVEN THE OPPORTUNITY? -- BUT NOT THAT MUCH. NOT ENOUGH FOR THIS TO HAPPEN.
WELL, THAT ONLY LEAVES ONE THING . . .
SURE, PUT THE CONDOMS NEXT TO THE HOME PREGNANCY KITS. WHAT IDIOT THOUGHT THAT WAS GOOD PRODUCT PLACEMENT? IT'S LIKE, "SEE, CONDOMS AND ALL THIS OVER THE COUNTER SHIT DON'T WORK!"
FAMILY PLANNING CENTER
SPERMICIDAL GEL
SPERMICIDAL GEL
KY JELLY
MAGNUM
HOME PREGNANCY TEST KIT
FUCK, I CAN'T BELIEVE THIS IS HAPPENING. ONE SECOND IT'S RAGING LUST TIME, THE NEXT IT'S "I MAY BE PREGNANT." FUCK, FUCK AND DOUBLE FUCK! PLEASE, OH PLEASE, DON'T LET IT BE SO!

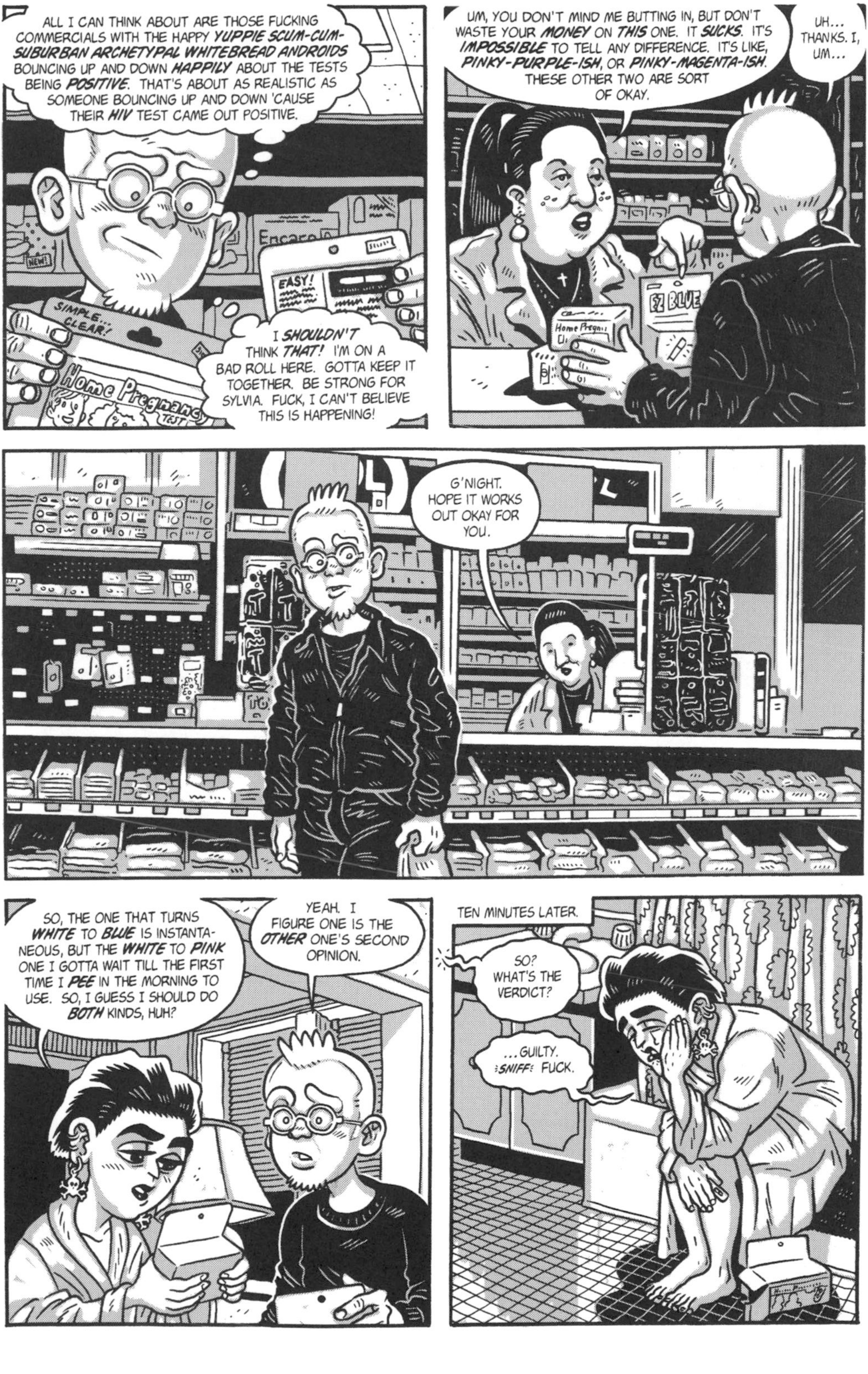
ALL I CAN THINK ABOUT ARE THOSE FUCKING COMMERCIALS WITH THE HAPPY YUPPIE SCUM-CUM-SUBURBAN ARCHETYPAL WHITEBREAD ANDROIDS BOUNCING UP AND DOWN HAPPILY ABOUT THE TESTS BEING POSITIVE. THAT'S ABOUT AS REALISTIC AS SOMEONE BOUNCING UP AND DOWN 'CAUSE THEIR HIV TEST CAME OUT POSITIVE.
EASY!
SIMPLE... CLEAR!
Home Pregnancy TEST
I SHOULDN'T THINK THAT! I'M ON A BAD ROLL HERE. GOTTA KEEP IT TOGETHER. BE STRONG FOR SYLVIA. FUCK, I CAN'T BELIEVE THIS IS HAPPENING!
UM, YOU DON'T MIND ME BUTTING IN, BUT DON'T WASTE YOUR MONEY ON THIS ONE. IT SUCKS. IT'S IMPOSSIBLE TO TELL ANY DIFFERENCE. IT'S LIKE, PINKY-PURPLE-ISH, OR PINKY-MAGENTA-ISH. THESE OTHER TWO ARE SORT OF OKAY.
UH... THANKS. I, UM...
EZ BLUE
G'NIGHT. HOPE IT WORKS OUT OKAY FOR YOU.
SO, THE ONE THAT TURNS WHITE TO BLUE IS INSTANTANEOUS, BUT THE WHITE TO PINK ONE I GOTTA WAIT TILL THE FIRST TIME I PEE IN THE MORNING TO USE. SO, I GUESS I SHOULD DO BOTH KINDS, HUH?
YEAH. I FIGURE ONE IS THE OTHER ONE'S SECOND OPINION.
TEN MINUTES LATER.
SO? WHAT'S THE VERDICT?
...GUILTY. SNIFF FUCK.

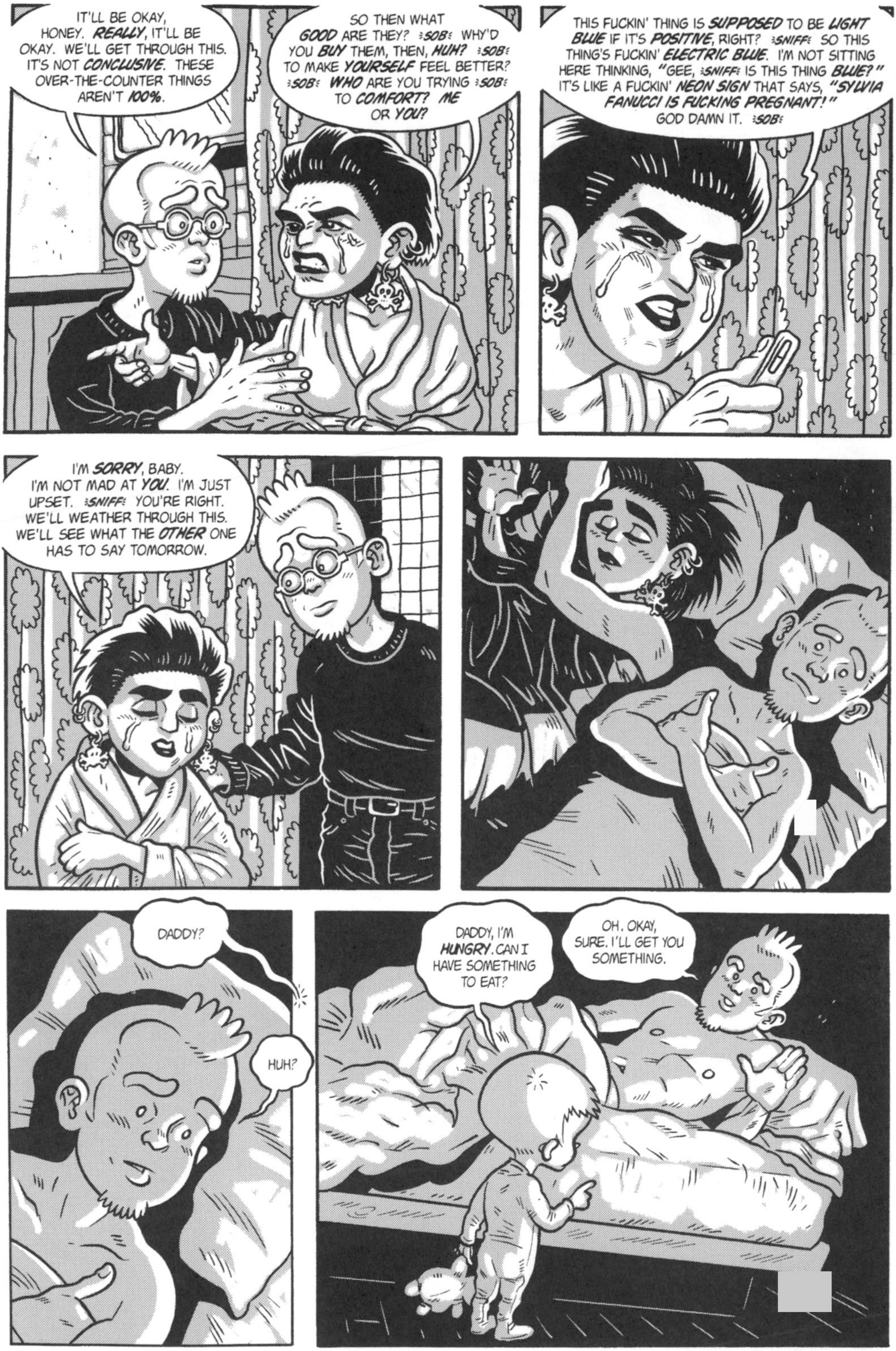

IT'LL BE OKAY, HONEY. REALLY, IT'LL BE OKAY. WE'LL GET THROUGH THIS. IT'S NOT CONCLUSIVE. THESE OVER-THE-COUNTER THINGS AREN'T 100%.
SO THEN WHAT GOOD ARE THEY? SOB WHY'D YOU BUY THEM, THEN, HUH? SOB TO MAKE YOURSELF FEEL BETTER? SOB WHO ARE YOU TRYING SOB TO COMFORT? ME OR YOU?
THIS FUCKIN' THING IS SUPPOSED TO BE LIGHT BLUE IF IT'S POSITIVE, RIGHT? SNIFF SO THIS THING'S FUCKIN' ELECTRIC BLUE. I'M NOT SITTING HERE THINKING, "GEE, SNIFF IS THIS THING BLUE?" IT'S LIKE A FUCKIN' NEON SIGN THAT SAYS, "SYLVIA FANUCCI IS FUCKING PREGNANT!" GOD DAMN IT. SOB
I'M SORRY, BABY. I'M NOT MAD AT YOU. I'M JUST UPSET. SNIFF YOU'RE RIGHT. WE'LL WEATHER THROUGH THIS. WE'LL SEE WHAT THE OTHER ONE HAS TO SAY TOMORROW.
DADDY?
HUH?
DADDY, I'M HUNGRY. CAN I HAVE SOMETHING TO EAT?
OH. OKAY, SURE. I'LL GET YOU SOMETHING.

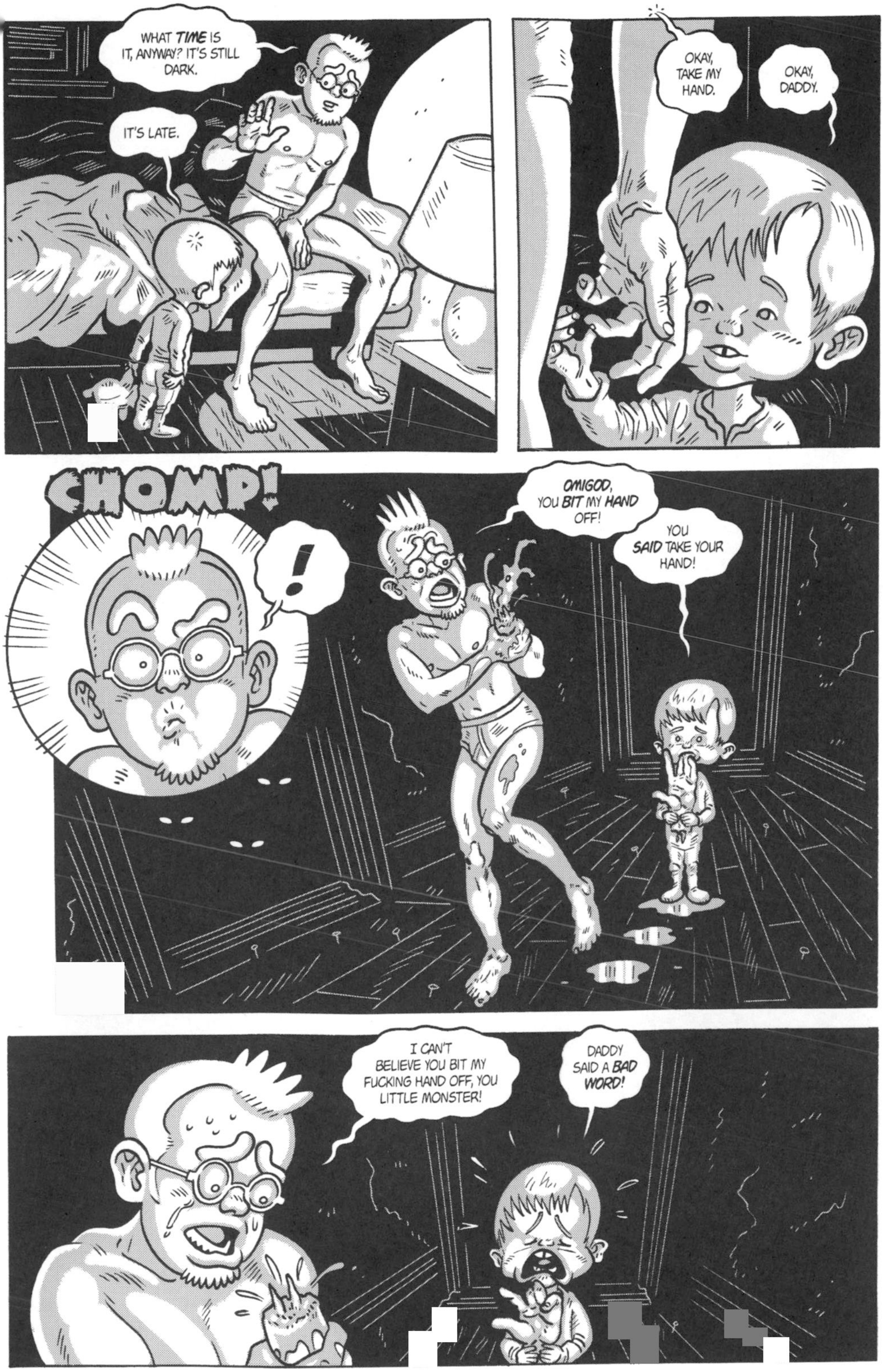
WHAT TIME IS IT, ANYWAY? IT'S STILL DARK.
IT'S LATE.
OKAY, TAKE MY HAND.
OKAY, DADDY.
CHOMP!
!
OMIGOD, YOU BIT MY HAND OFF!
YOU SAID TAKE YOUR HAND!
I CAN'T BELIEVE YOU BIT MY FUCKING HAND OFF, YOU LITTLE MONSTER!
DADDY SAID A BAD WORD!

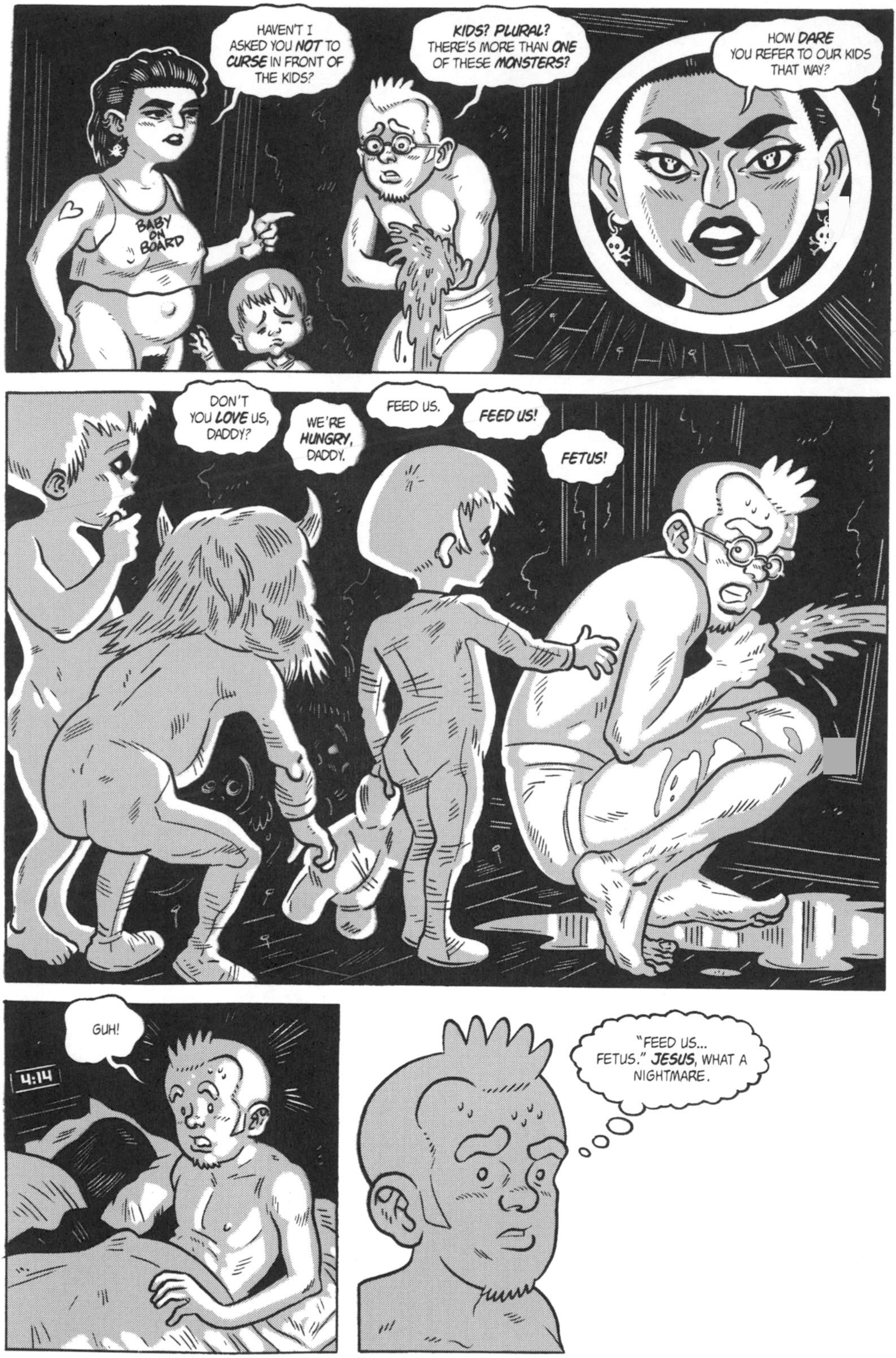
HAVEN'T I ASKED YOU NOT TO CURSE IN FRONT OF THE KIDS?
KIDS? PLURAL? THERE'S MORE THAN ONE OF THESE MONSTERS?
HOW DARE YOU REFER TO OUR KIDS THAT WAY?
BABY ON BOARD
DON'T YOU LOVE US, DADDY?
WE'RE HUNGRY, DADDY.
FEED US.
FEED US!
FETUS!
GUH!
4:14
"FEED US... FETUS." JESUS, WHAT A NIGHTMARE.

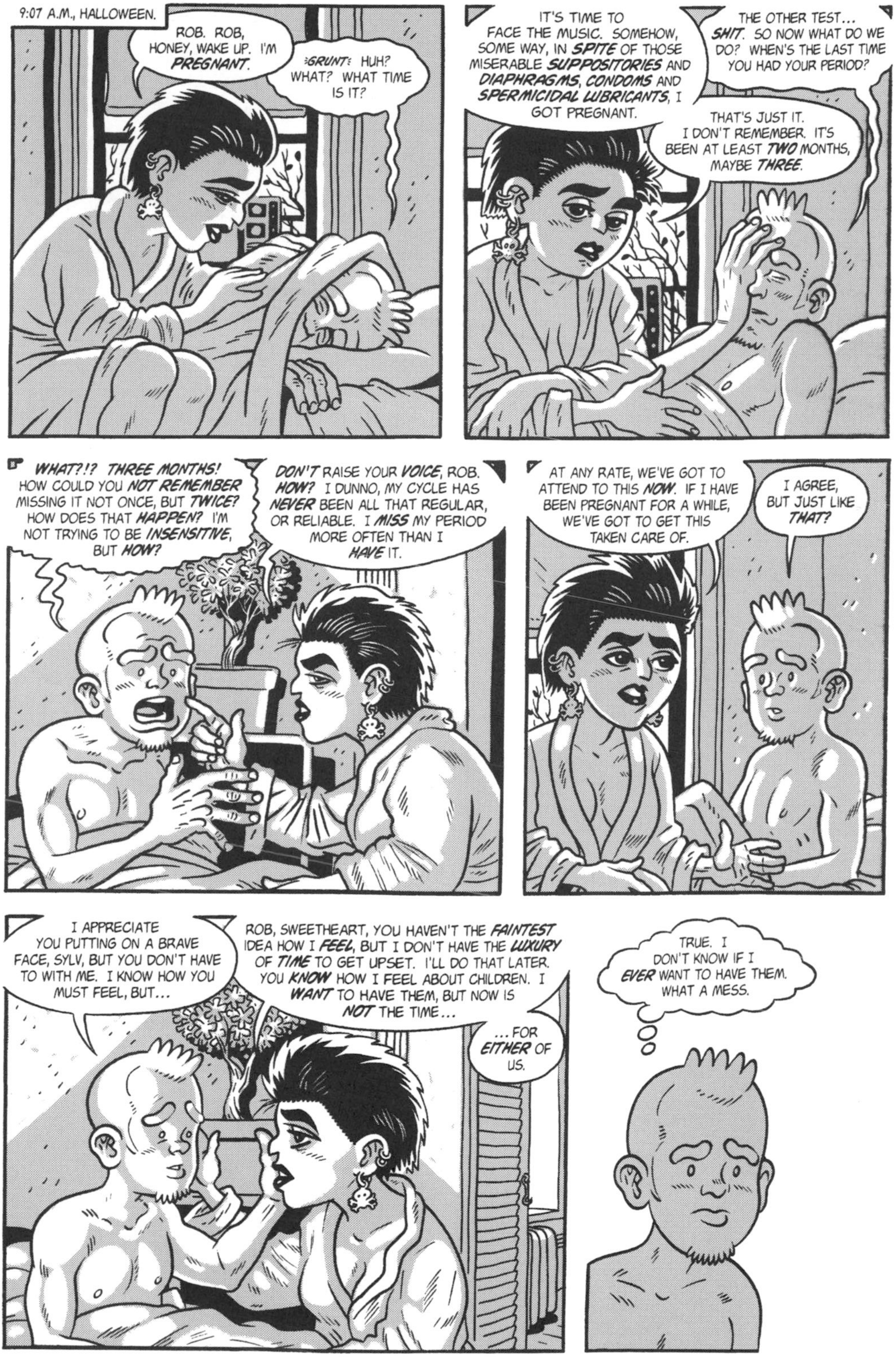
9:07 A.M., HALLOWEEN.
ROB. ROB, HONEY, WAKE UP. I'M PREGNANT.
*GRUNT* HUH? WHAT? WHAT TIME IS IT?
IT'S TIME TO FACE THE MUSIC. SOMEHOW, SOME WAY, IN SPITE OF THOSE MISERABLE SUPPOSITORIES AND DIAPHRAGMS, CONDOMS AND SPERMICIDAL LUBRICANTS, I GOT PREGNANT.
THE OTHER TEST... SHIT. SO NOW WHAT DO WE DO? WHEN'S THE LAST TIME YOU HAD YOUR PERIOD?
THAT'S JUST IT. I DON'T REMEMBER. IT'S BEEN AT LEAST TWO MONTHS, MAYBE THREE.
WHAT?!? THREE MONTHS! HOW COULD YOU NOT REMEMBER MISSING IT NOT ONCE, BUT TWICE? HOW DOES THAT HAPPEN? I'M NOT TRYING TO BE INSENSITIVE, BUT HOW?
DON'T RAISE YOUR VOICE, ROB. HOW? I DUNNO, MY CYCLE HAS NEVER BEEN ALL THAT REGULAR, OR RELIABLE. I MISS MY PERIOD MORE OFTEN THAN I HAVE IT.
AT ANY RATE, WE'VE GOT TO ATTEND TO THIS NOW. IF I HAVE BEEN PREGNANT FOR A WHILE, WE'VE GOT TO GET THIS TAKEN CARE OF.
I AGREE, BUT JUST LIKE THAT?
I APPRECIATE YOU PUTTING ON A BRAVE FACE, SYLV, BUT YOU DON'T HAVE TO WITH ME. I KNOW HOW YOU MUST FEEL, BUT...
ROB, SWEETHEART, YOU HAVEN'T THE FAINTEST IDEA HOW I FEEL, BUT I DON'T HAVE THE LUXURY OF TIME TO GET UPSET. I'LL DO THAT LATER. YOU KNOW HOW I FEEL ABOUT CHILDREN. I WANT TO HAVE THEM, BUT NOW IS NOT THE TIME...
...FOR EITHER OF US.
TRUE. I DON'T KNOW IF I EVER WANT TO HAVE THEM. WHAT A MESS.

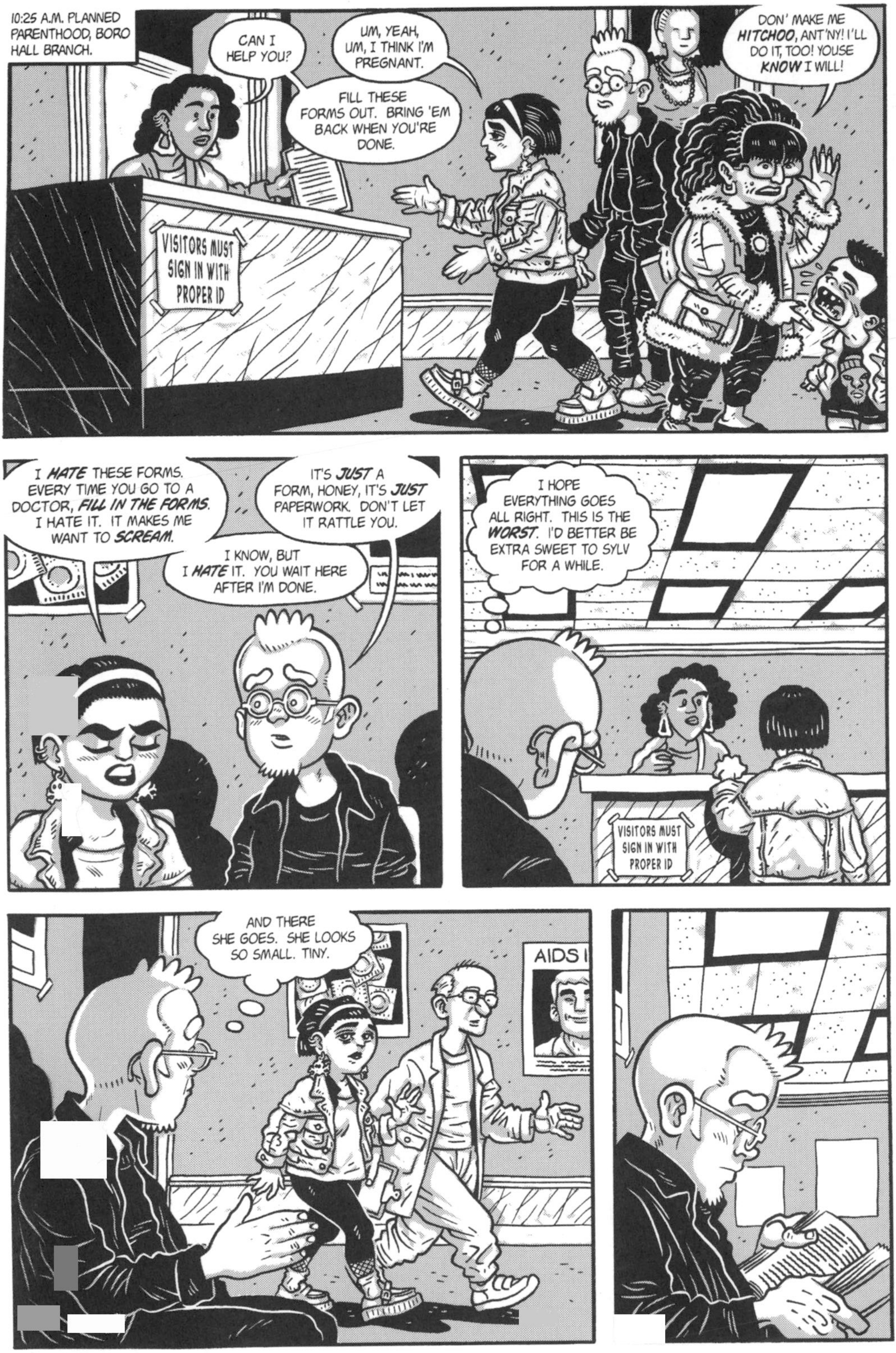
10:25 A.M. PLANNED PARENTHOOD, BORO HALL BRANCH.
CAN I HELP YOU?
UM, YEAH, UM, I THINK I'M PREGNANT.
FILL THESE FORMS OUT. BRING 'EM BACK WHEN YOU'RE DONE.
DON' MAKE ME HITCHOO, ANT'NY! I'LL DO IT, TOO! YOUSE KNOW I WILL!
VISITORS MUST SIGN IN WITH PROPER ID
I HATE THESE FORMS. EVERY TIME YOU GO TO A DOCTOR, FILL IN THE FORMS. I HATE IT. IT MAKES ME WANT TO SCREAM.
IT'S JUST A FORM, HONEY, IT'S JUST PAPERWORK. DON'T LET IT RATTLE YOU.
I KNOW, BUT I HATE IT. YOU WAIT HERE AFTER I'M DONE.
I HOPE EVERYTHING GOES ALL RIGHT. THIS IS THE WORST. I'D BETTER BE EXTRA SWEET TO SYLV FOR A WHILE.
VISITORS MUST SIGN IN WITH PROPER ID
AND THERE SHE GOES. SHE LOOKS SO SMALL. TINY.
AIDS

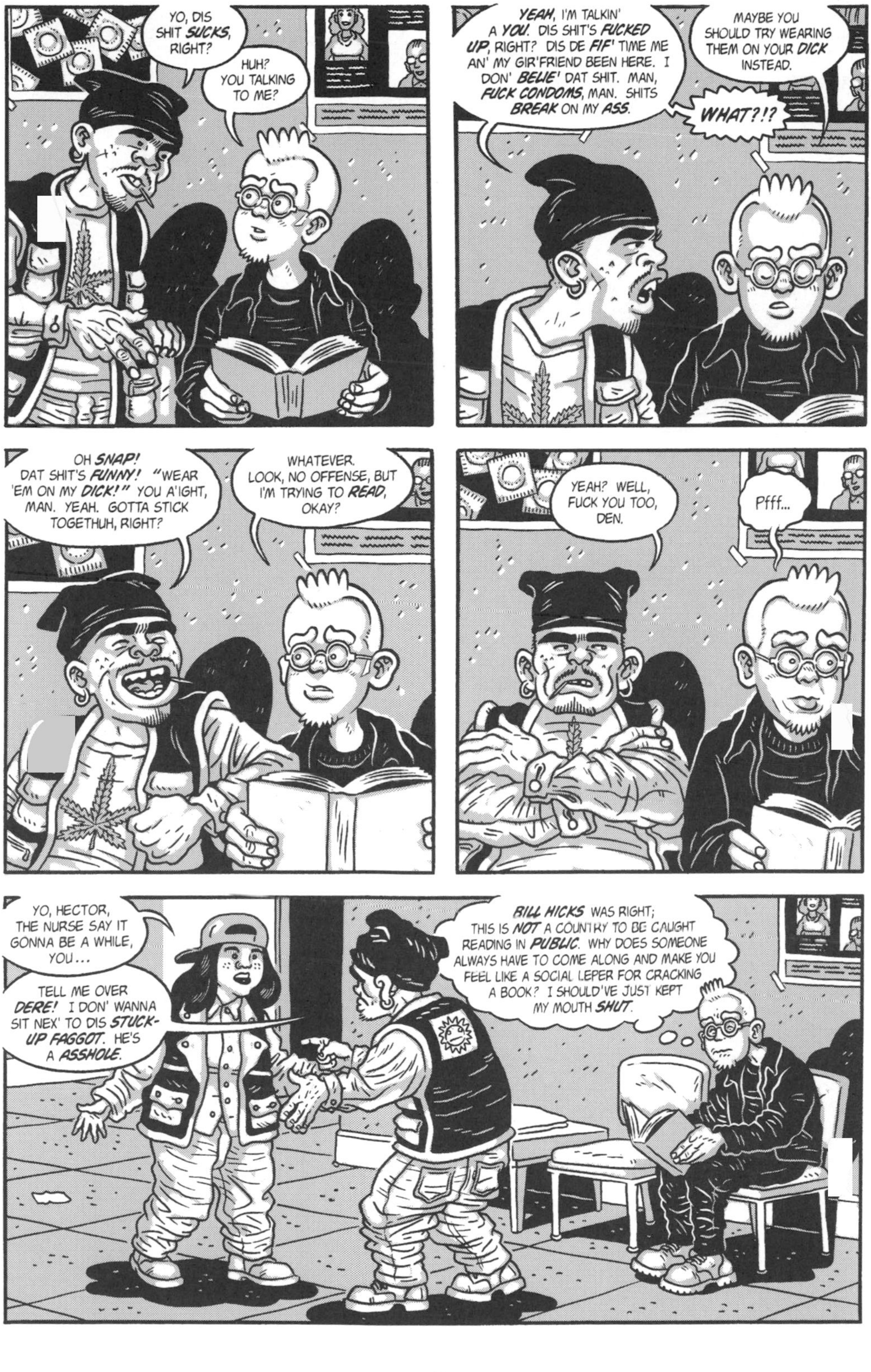
YO, DIS SHIT SUCKS, RIGHT?
HUH? YOU TALKING TO ME?
YEAH, I'M TALKIN' A YOU. DIS SHIT'S FUCKED UP, RIGHT? DIS DE FIF' TIME ME AN' MY GIR'FRIEND BEEN HERE. I DON' BELIE' DAT SHIT. MAN, FUCK CONDOMS, MAN. SHITS BREAK ON MY ASS.
MAYBE YOU SHOULD TRY WEARING THEM ON YOUR DICK INSTEAD.
WHAT?!?
OH SNAP! DAT SHIT'S FUNNY! "WEAR 'EM ON MY DICK!" YOU A'IGHT, MAN. YEAH. GOTTA STICK TOGETHUH, RIGHT?
WHATEVER. LOOK, NO OFFENSE, BUT I'M TRYING TO READ, OKAY?
YEAH? WELL, FUCK YOU TOO, DEN.
Pfff...
YO, HECTOR, THE NURSE SAY IT GONNA BE A WHILE, YOU...
TELL ME OVER DERE! I DON' WANNA SIT NEX' TO DIS STUCK-UP FAGGOT. HE'S A ASSHOLE.
BILL HICKS WAS RIGHT; THIS IS NOT A COUNTRY TO BE CAUGHT READING IN PUBLIC. WHY DOES SOMEONE ALWAYS HAVE TO COME ALONG AND MAKE YOU FEEL LIKE A SOCIAL LEPER FOR CRACKING A BOOK? I SHOULD'VE JUST KEPT MY MOUTH SHUT.

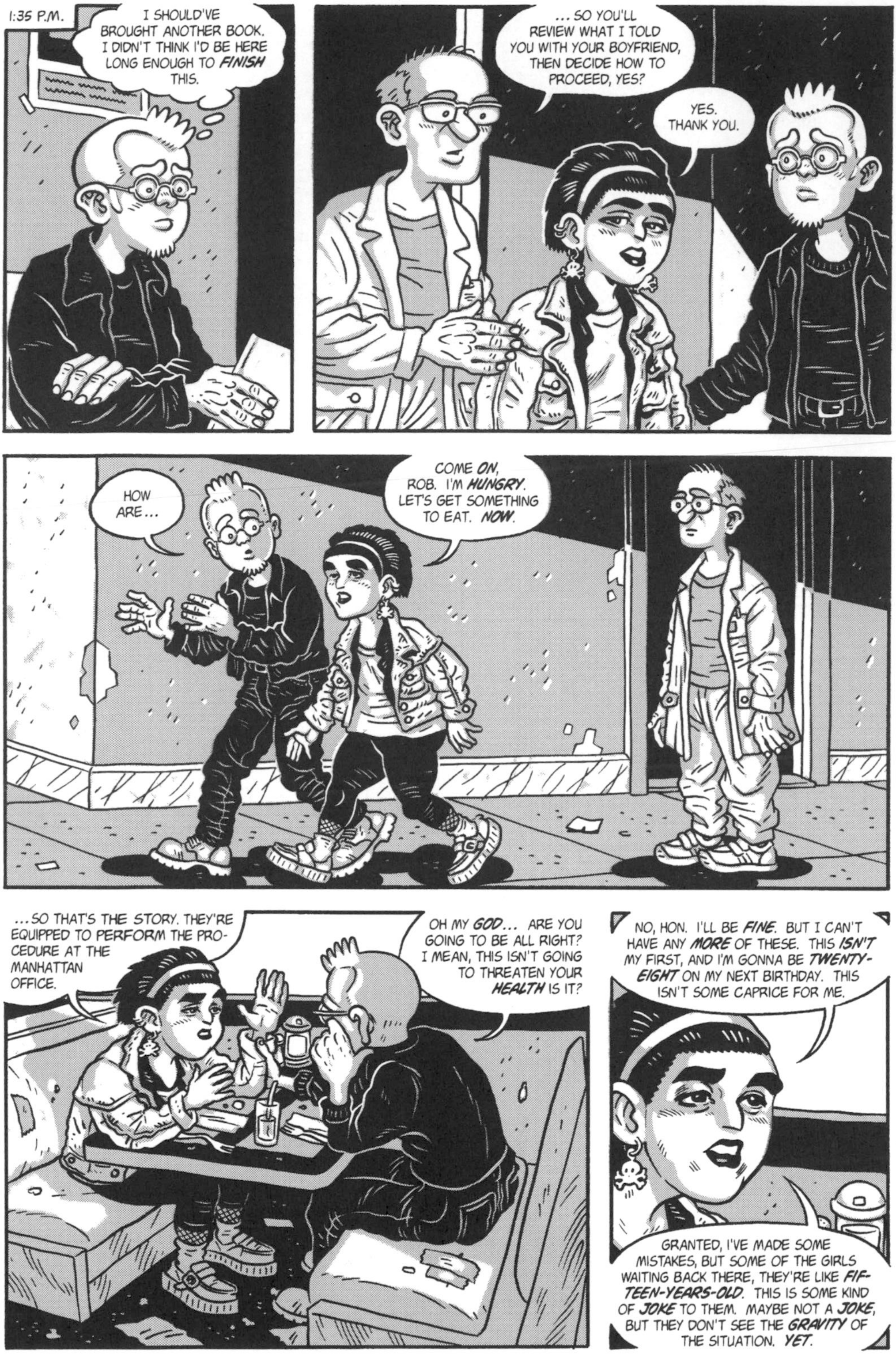
1:35 P.M.
I SHOULD'VE BROUGHT ANOTHER BOOK. I DIDN'T THINK I'D BE HERE LONG ENOUGH TO FINISH THIS.
...SO YOU'LL REVIEW WHAT I TOLD YOU WITH YOUR BOYFRIEND, THEN DECIDE HOW TO PROCEED, YES?
YES. THANK YOU.
HOW ARE...
COME ON, ROB. I'M HUNGRY. LET'S GET SOMETHING TO EAT. NOW.
...SO THAT'S THE STORY. THEY'RE EQUIPPED TO PERFORM THE PROCEDURE AT THE MANHATTAN OFFICE.
OH MY GOD... ARE YOU GOING TO BE ALL RIGHT? I MEAN, THIS ISN'T GOING TO THREATEN YOUR HEALTH IS IT?
NO, HON. I'LL BE FINE. BUT I CAN'T HAVE ANY MORE OF THESE. THIS ISN'T MY FIRST, AND I'M GONNA BE TWENTY-EIGHT ON MY NEXT BIRTHDAY. THIS ISN'T SOME CAPRICE FOR ME.
GRANTED, I'VE MADE SOME MISTAKES, BUT SOME OF THE GIRLS WAITING BACK THERE, THEY'RE LIKE FIFTEEN-YEARS-OLD. THIS IS SOME KIND OF JOKE TO THEM. MAYBE NOT A JOKE, BUT THEY DON'T SEE THE GRAVITY OF THE SITUATION. YET.

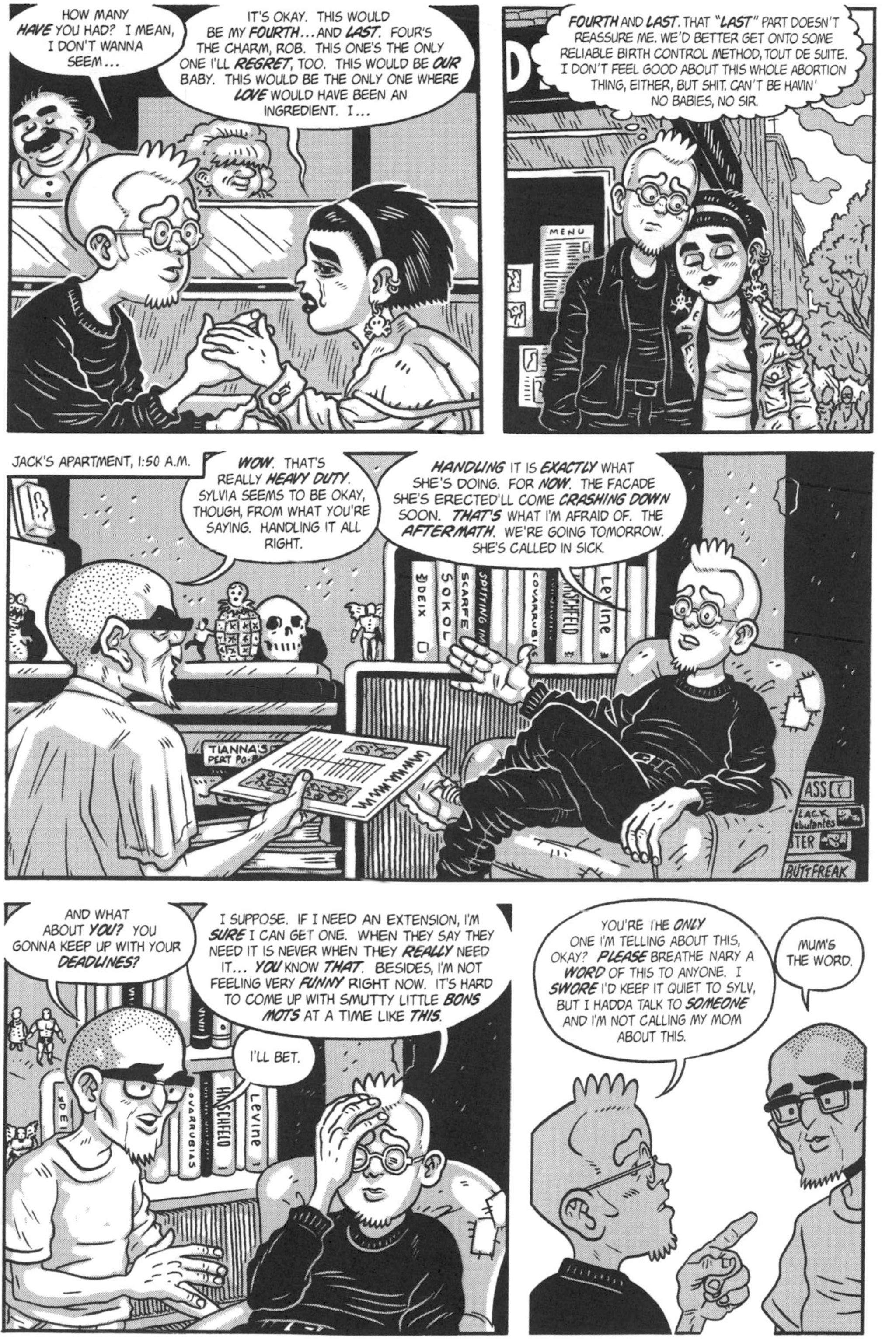

HOW MANY HAVE YOU HAD? I MEAN, I DON'T WANNA SEEM...
IT'S OKAY. THIS WOULD BE MY FOURTH... AND LAST. FOUR'S THE CHARM, ROB. THIS ONE'S THE ONLY ONE I'LL REGRET, TOO. THIS WOULD BE OUR BABY. THIS WOULD BE THE ONLY ONE WHERE LOVE WOULD HAVE BEEN AN INGREDIENT. I...
FOURTH AND LAST. THAT "LAST" PART DOESN'T REASSURE ME. WE'D BETTER GET ONTO SOME RELIABLE BIRTH CONTROL METHOD, TOUT DE SUITE. I DON'T FEEL GOOD ABOUT THIS WHOLE ABORTION THING, EITHER, BUT SHIT. CAN'T BE HAVIN' NO BABIES, NO SIR.
MENU
JACK'S APARTMENT, 1:50 A.M.
WOW. THAT'S REALLY HEAVY DUTY. SYLVIA SEEMS TO BE OKAY, THOUGH, FROM WHAT YOU'RE SAYING. HANDLING IT ALL RIGHT.
HANDLING IT IS EXACTLY WHAT SHE'S DOING. FOR NOW. THE FACADE SHE'S ERECTED'LL COME CRASHING DOWN SOON. THAT'S WHAT I'M AFRAID OF. THE AFTERMATH. WE'RE GOING TOMORROW. SHE'S CALLED IN SICK.
DEIX
SOKOL
SCARFE
Levine
AND WHAT ABOUT YOU? YOU GONNA KEEP UP WITH YOUR DEADLINES?
I SUPPOSE. IF I NEED AN EXTENSION, I'M SURE I CAN GET ONE. WHEN THEY SAY THEY NEED IT IS NEVER WHEN THEY REALLY NEED IT... YOU KNOW THAT. BESIDES, I'M NOT FEELING VERY FUNNY RIGHT NOW. IT'S HARD TO COME UP WITH SMUTTY LITTLE BONS MOTS AT A TIME LIKE THIS.
I'LL BET.
YOU'RE THE ONLY ONE I'M TELLING ABOUT THIS, OKAY? PLEASE BREATHE NARY A WORD OF THIS TO ANYONE. I SWORE I'D KEEP IT QUIET TO SYLV, BUT I HADDA TALK TO SOMEONE AND I'M NOT CALLING MY MOM ABOUT THIS.
MUM'S THE WORD.

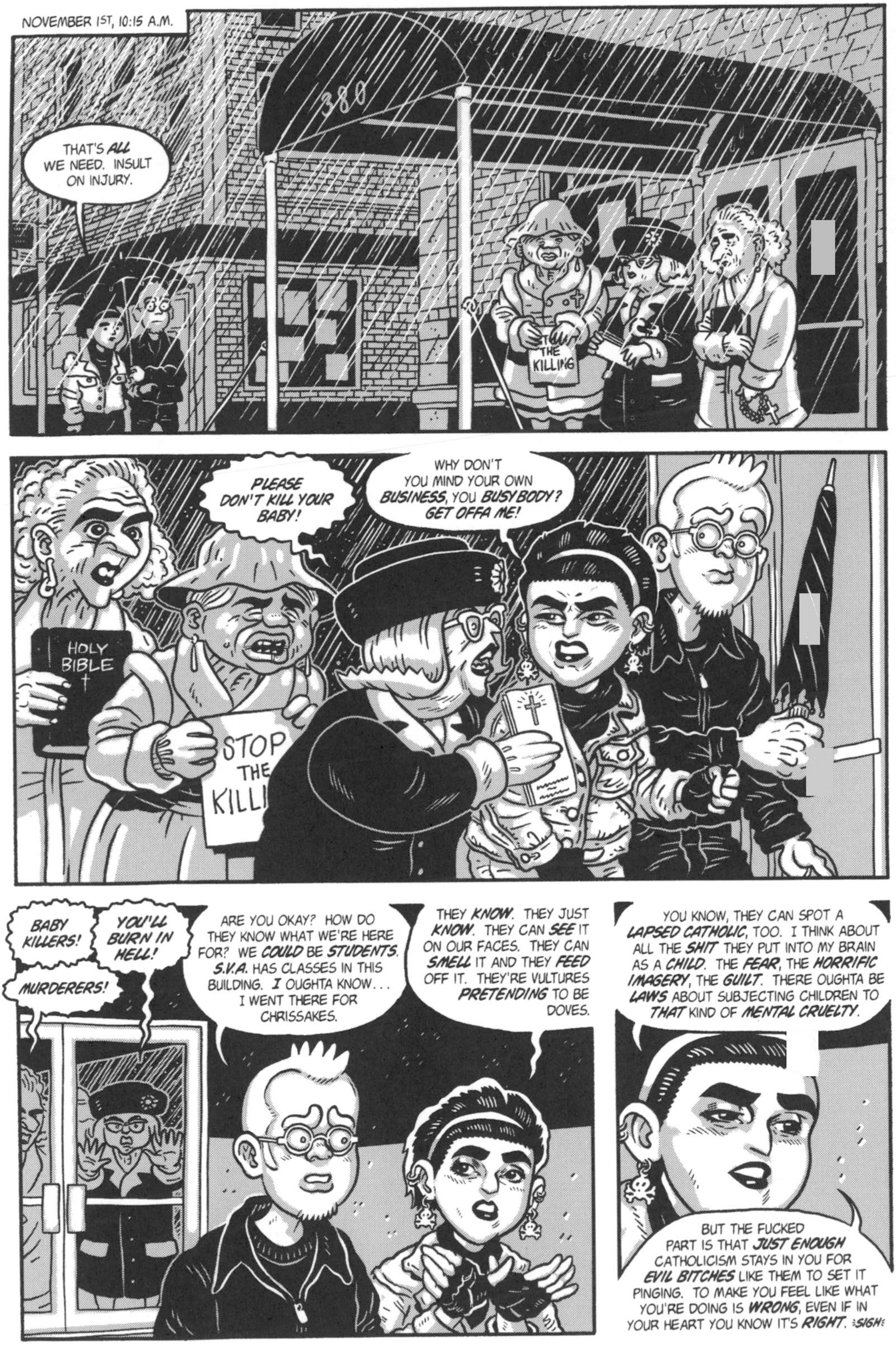
NOVEMBER 1ST, 10:15 A.M.
380
THAT'S ALL WE NEED. INSULT ON INJURY.
THE KILLING
PLEASE DON'T KILL YOUR BABY!
WHY DON'T YOU MIND YOUR OWN BUSINESS, YOU BUSYBODY? GET OFFA ME!
HOLY BIBLE
STOP THE KILLI
BABY KILLERS!
YOU'LL BURN IN HELL!
MURDERERS!
ARE YOU OKAY? HOW DO THEY KNOW WHAT WE'RE HERE FOR? WE COULD BE STUDENTS. S.V.A. HAS CLASSES IN THIS BUILDING. I OUGHTA KNOW... I WENT THERE FOR CHRISSAKES.
THEY KNOW. THEY JUST KNOW. THEY CAN SEE IT ON OUR FACES. THEY CAN SMELL IT AND THEY FEED OFF IT. THEY'RE VULTURES PRETENDING TO BE DOVES.
YOU KNOW, THEY CAN SPOT A LAPSED CATHOLIC, TOO. I THINK ABOUT ALL THE SHIT THEY PUT INTO MY BRAIN AS A CHILD. THE FEAR, THE HORRIFIC IMAGERY, THE GUILT. THERE OUGHTA BE LAWS ABOUT SUBJECTING CHILDREN TO THAT KIND OF MENTAL CRUELTY.
BUT THE FUCKED PART IS THAT JUST ENOUGH CATHOLICISM STAYS IN YOU FOR EVIL BITCHES LIKE THEM TO SET IT PINGING. TO MAKE YOU FEEL LIKE WHAT YOU'RE DOING IS WRONG, EVEN IF IN YOUR HEART YOU KNOW IT'S RIGHT.
SIGH

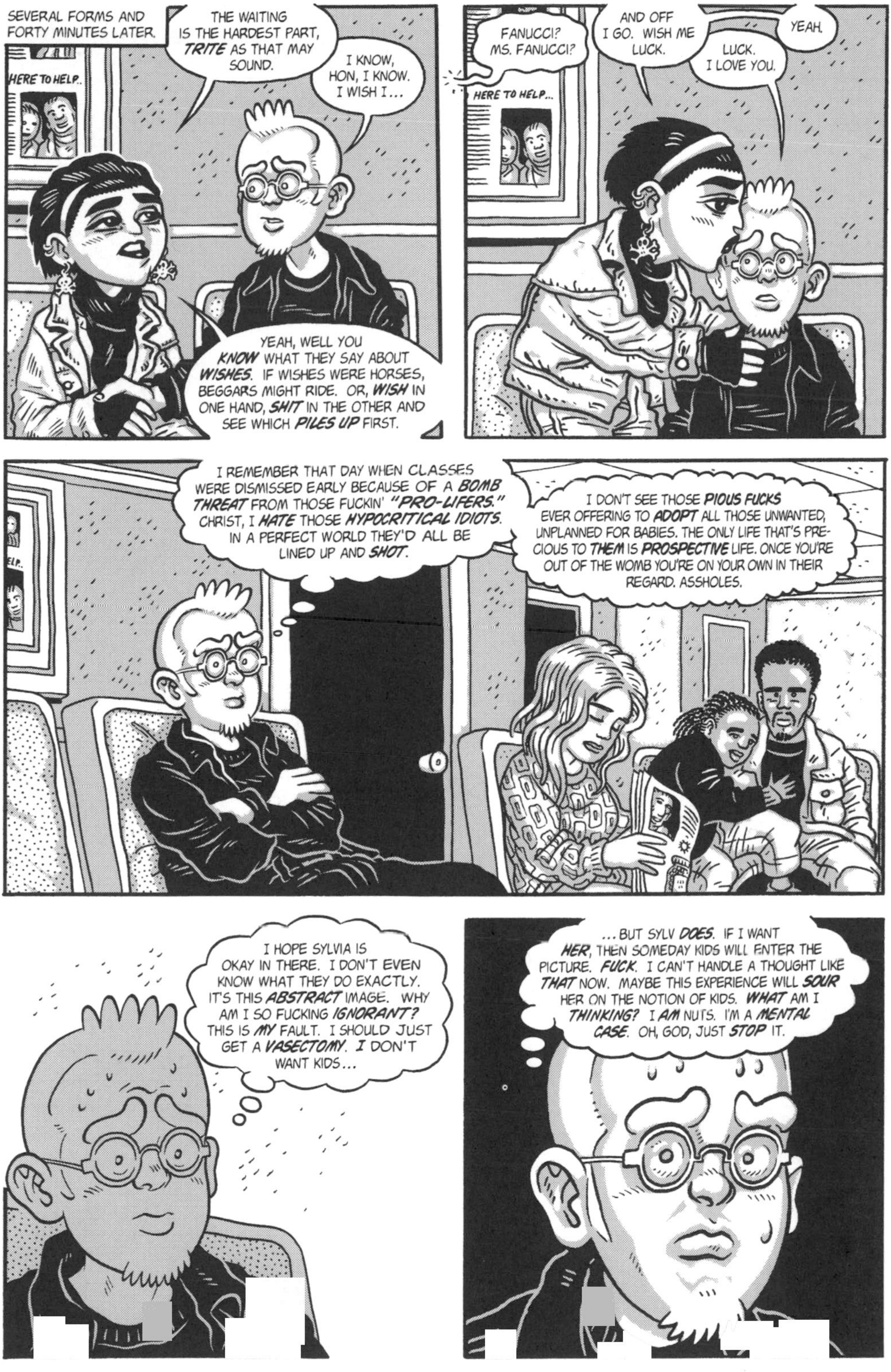
SEVERAL FORMS AND FORTY MINUTES LATER.
HERE TO HELP..
THE WAITING IS THE HARDEST PART, TRITE AS THAT MAY SOUND.
I KNOW, HON, I KNOW. I WISH I...
YEAH, WELL YOU KNOW WHAT THEY SAY ABOUT WISHES. IF WISHES WERE HORSES, BEGGARS MIGHT RIDE. OR, WISH IN ONE HAND, SHIT IN THE OTHER AND SEE WHICH PILES UP FIRST.
FANUCCI? MS. FANUCCI?
HERE TO HELP...
AND OFF I GO. WISH ME LUCK.
LUCK. I LOVE YOU.
YEAH.
I REMEMBER THAT DAY WHEN CLASSES WERE DISMISSED EARLY BECAUSE OF A BOMB THREAT FROM THOSE FUCKIN' "PRO-LIFERS." CHRIST, I HATE THOSE HYPOCRITICAL IDIOTS. IN A PERFECT WORLD THEY'D ALL BE LINED UP AND SHOT.
I DON'T SEE THOSE PIOUS FUCKS EVER OFFERING TO ADOPT ALL THOSE UNWANTED, UNPLANNED FOR BABIES. THE ONLY LIFE THAT'S PRECIOUS TO THEM IS PROSPECTIVE LIFE. ONCE YOU'RE OUT OF THE WOMB YOU'RE ON YOUR OWN IN THEIR REGARD. ASSHOLES.
I HOPE SYLVIA IS OKAY IN THERE. I DON'T EVEN KNOW WHAT THEY DO EXACTLY. IT'S THIS ABSTRACT IMAGE. WHY AM I SO FUCKING IGNORANT? THIS IS MY FAULT. I SHOULD JUST GET A VASECTOMY. I DON'T WANT KIDS...
...BUT SYLV DOES. IF I WANT HER, THEN SOMEDAY KIDS WILL ENTER THE PICTURE. FUCK. I CAN'T HANDLE A THOUGHT LIKE THAT NOW. MAYBE THIS EXPERIENCE WILL SOUR HER ON THE NOTION OF KIDS. WHAT AM I THINKING? I AM NUTS. I'M A MENTAL CASE. OH, GOD, JUST STOP IT.

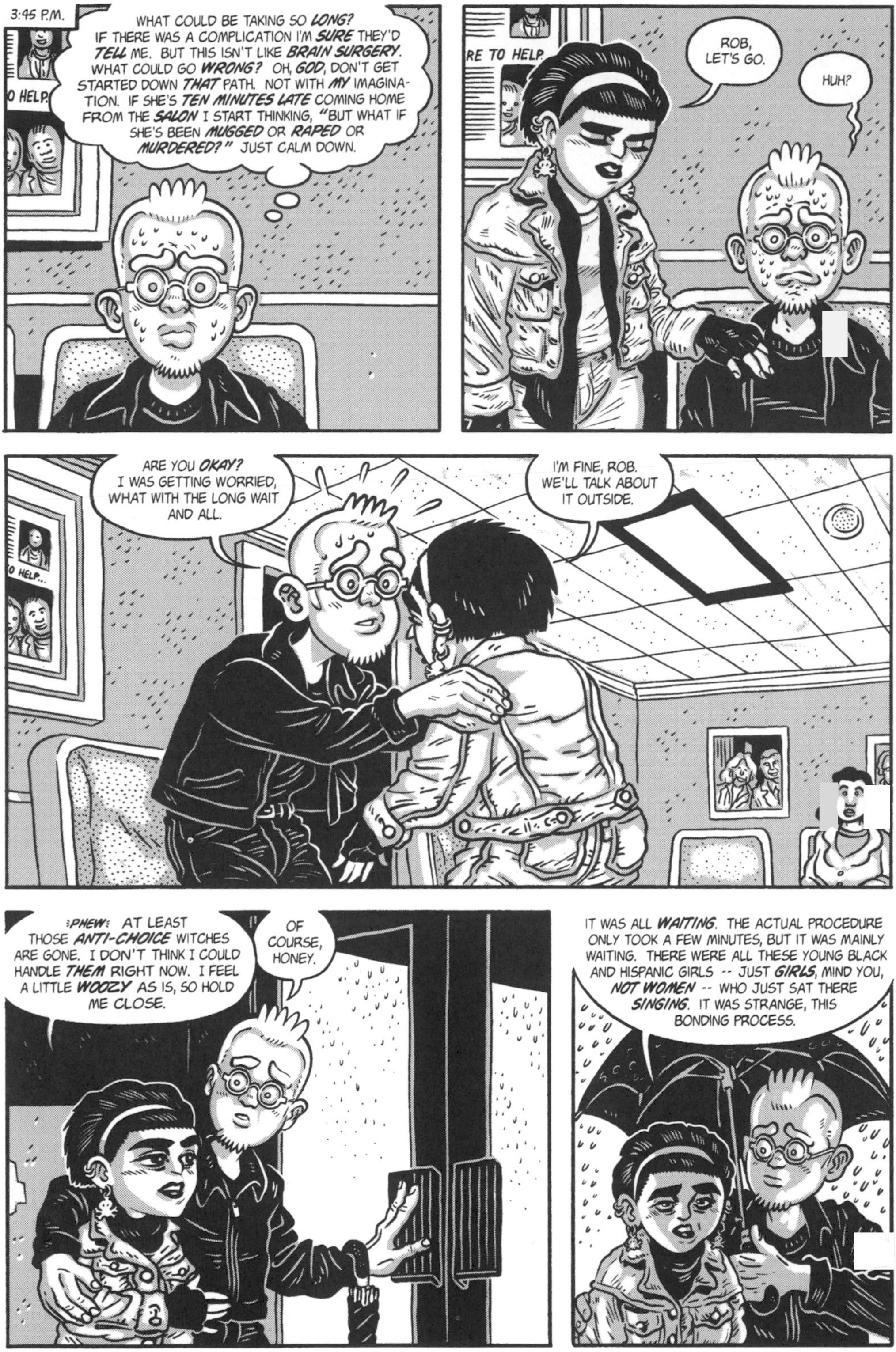

3:45 P.M.
WHAT COULD BE TAKING SO LONG? IF THERE WAS A COMPLICATION I'M SURE THEY'D TELL ME. BUT THIS ISN'T LIKE BRAIN SURGERY. WHAT COULD GO WRONG? OH, GOD, DON'T GET STARTED DOWN THAT PATH. NOT WITH MY IMAGINATION. IF SHE'S TEN MINUTES LATE COMING HOME FROM THE SALON I START THINKING, "BUT WHAT IF SHE'S BEEN MUGGED OR RAPED OR MURDERED?" JUST CALM DOWN.
ROB, LET'S GO.
HUH?
ARE YOU OKAY? I WAS GETTING WORRIED, WHAT WITH THE LONG WAIT AND ALL.
I'M FINE, ROB. WE'LL TALK ABOUT IT OUTSIDE.
PHEW AT LEAST THOSE ANTI-CHOICE WITCHES ARE GONE. I DON'T THINK I COULD HANDLE THEM RIGHT NOW. I FEEL A LITTLE WOOZY AS IS, SO HOLD ME CLOSE.
OF COURSE, HONEY.
IT WAS ALL WAITING. THE ACTUAL PROCEDURE ONLY TOOK A FEW MINUTES, BUT IT WAS MAINLY WAITING. THERE WERE ALL THESE YOUNG BLACK AND HISPANIC GIRLS -- JUST GIRLS, MIND YOU, NOT WOMEN -- WHO JUST SAT THERE SINGING. IT WAS STRANGE, THIS BONDING PROCESS.

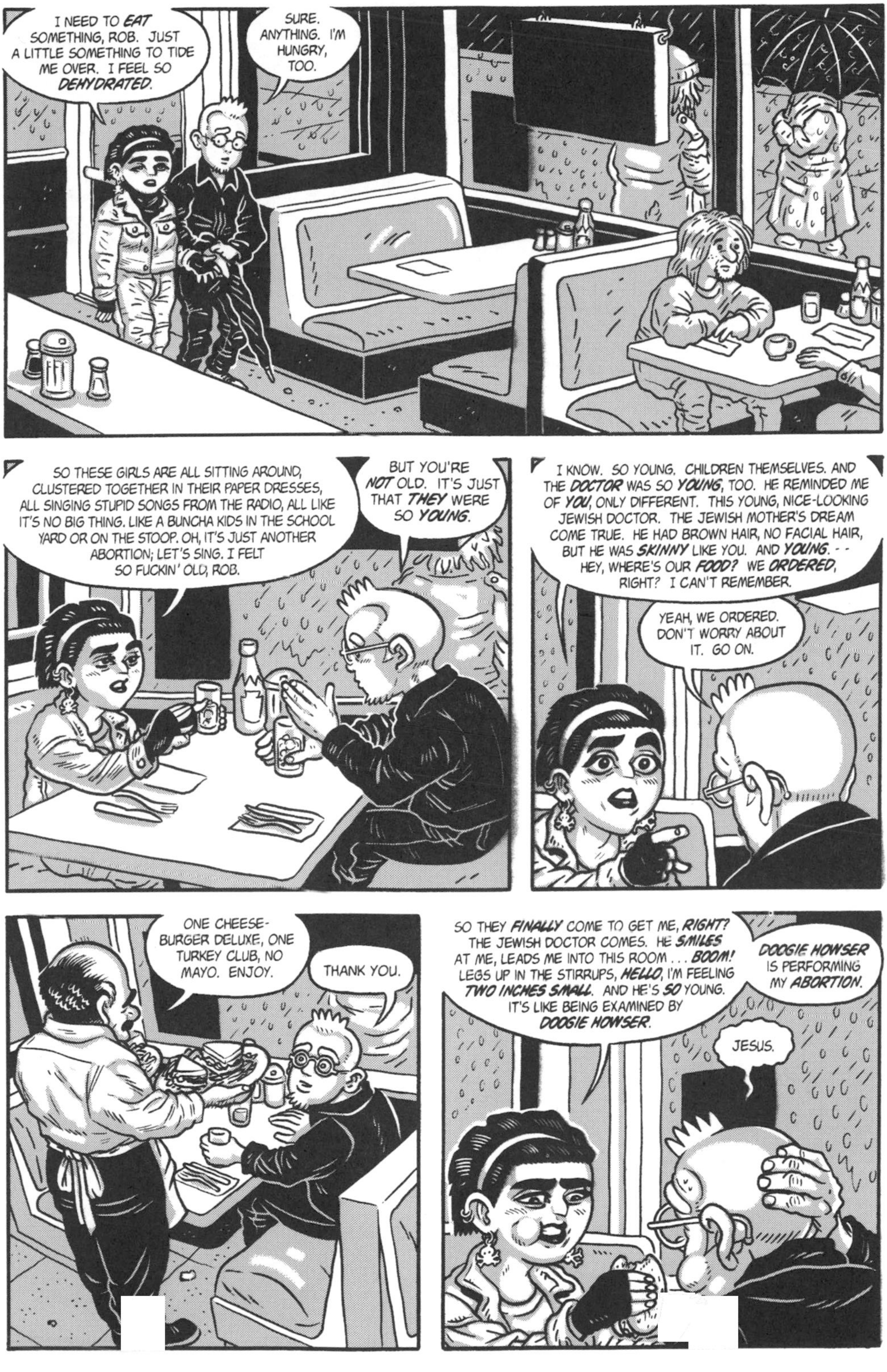
I NEED TO EAT SOMETHING, ROB. JUST A LITTLE SOMETHING TO TIDE ME OVER. I FEEL SO DEHYDRATED.
SURE. ANYTHING. I'M HUNGRY, TOO.
SO THESE GIRLS ARE ALL SITTING AROUND, CLUSTERED TOGETHER IN THEIR PAPER DRESSES, ALL SINGING STUPID SONGS FROM THE RADIO, ALL LIKE IT'S NO BIG THING. LIKE A BUNCHA KIDS IN THE SCHOOL YARD OR ON THE STOOP. OH, IT'S JUST ANOTHER ABORTION; LET'S SING. I FELT SO FUCKIN' OLD, ROB.
BUT YOU'RE NOT OLD. IT'S JUST THAT THEY WERE SO YOUNG.
I KNOW. SO YOUNG. CHILDREN THEMSELVES. AND THE DOCTOR WAS SO YOUNG, TOO. HE REMINDED ME OF YOU, ONLY DIFFERENT. THIS YOUNG, NICE-LOOKING JEWISH DOCTOR. THE JEWISH MOTHER'S DREAM COME TRUE. HE HAD BROWN HAIR, NO FACIAL HAIR, BUT HE WAS SKINNY LIKE YOU. AND YOUNG. - - HEY, WHERE'S OUR FOOD? WE ORDERED, RIGHT? I CAN'T REMEMBER.
YEAH, WE ORDERED. DON'T WORRY ABOUT IT. GO ON.
ONE CHEESE-BURGER DELUXE, ONE TURKEY CLUB, NO MAYO. ENJOY.
THANK YOU.
SO THEY FINALLY COME TO GET ME, RIGHT? THE JEWISH DOCTOR COMES. HE SMILES AT ME, LEADS ME INTO THIS ROOM . . . BOOM! LEGS UP IN THE STIRRUPS, HELLO, I'M FEELING TWO INCHES SMALL. AND HE'S SO YOUNG. IT'S LIKE BEING EXAMINED BY DOOGIE HOWSER.
DOOGIE HOWSER IS PERFORMING MY ABORTION.
JESUS.

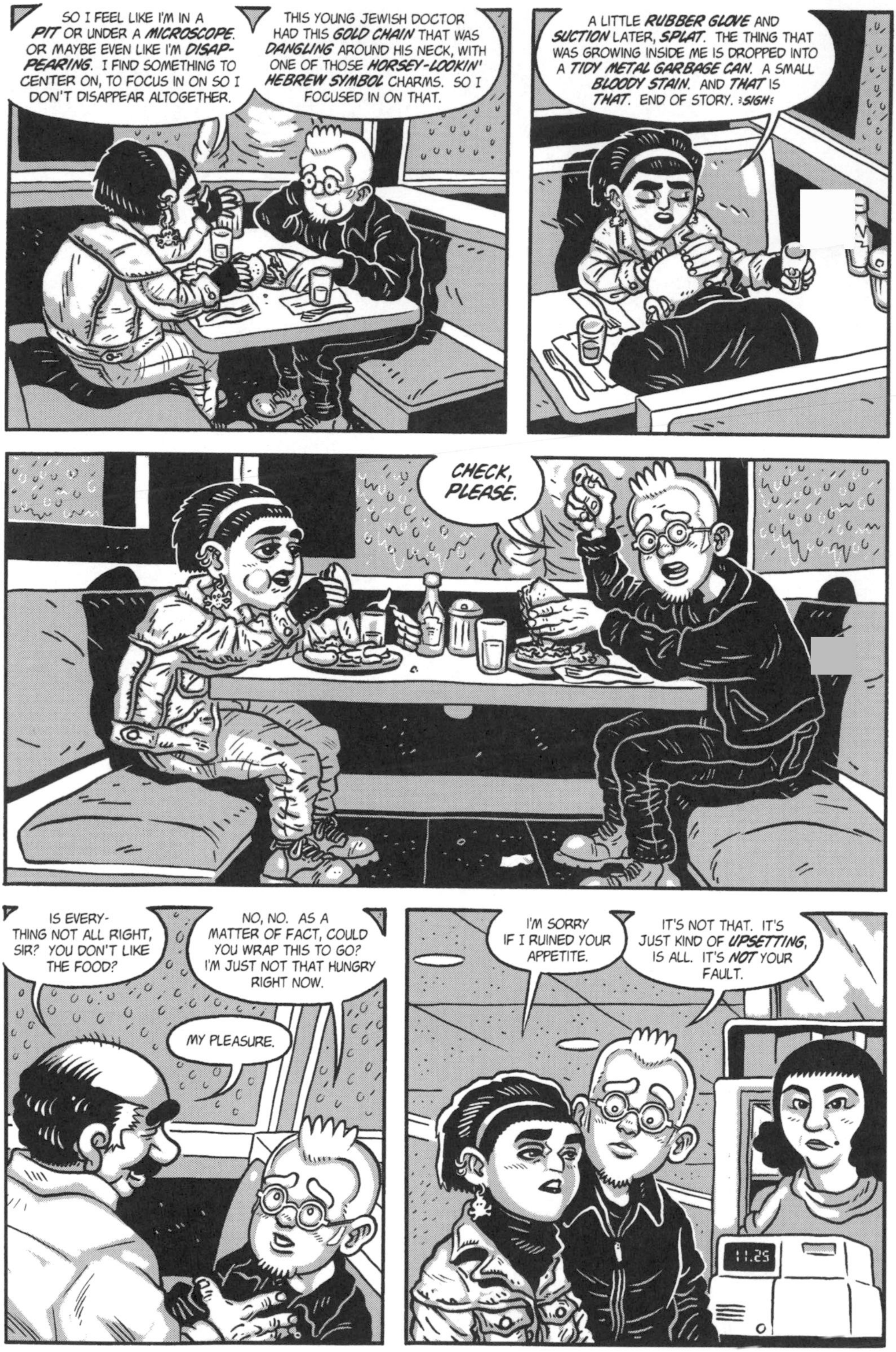
SO I FEEL LIKE I'M IN A PIT OR UNDER A MICROSCOPE. OR MAYBE EVEN LIKE I'M DISAP-PEARING. I FIND SOMETHING TO CENTER ON, TO FOCUS IN ON SO I DON'T DISAPPEAR ALTOGETHER.
THIS YOUNG JEWISH DOCTOR HAD THIS GOLD CHAIN THAT WAS DANGLING AROUND HIS NECK, WITH ONE OF THOSE HORSEY-LOOKIN' HEBREW SYMBOL CHARMS. SO I FOCUSED IN ON THAT.
A LITTLE RUBBER GLOVE AND SUCTION LATER, SPLAT. THE THING THAT WAS GROWING INSIDE ME IS DROPPED INTO A TIDY METAL GARBAGE CAN. A SMALL BLOODY STAIN. AND THAT IS THAT. END OF STORY. SIGH
CHECK, PLEASE.
IS EVERY-THING NOT ALL RIGHT, SIR? YOU DON'T LIKE THE FOOD?
NO, NO. AS A MATTER OF FACT, COULD YOU WRAP THIS TO GO? I'M JUST NOT THAT HUNGRY RIGHT NOW.
MY PLEASURE.
I'M SORRY IF I RUINED YOUR APPETITE.
IT'S NOT THAT. IT'S JUST KIND OF UPSETTING, IS ALL. IT'S NOT YOUR FAULT.
11:25

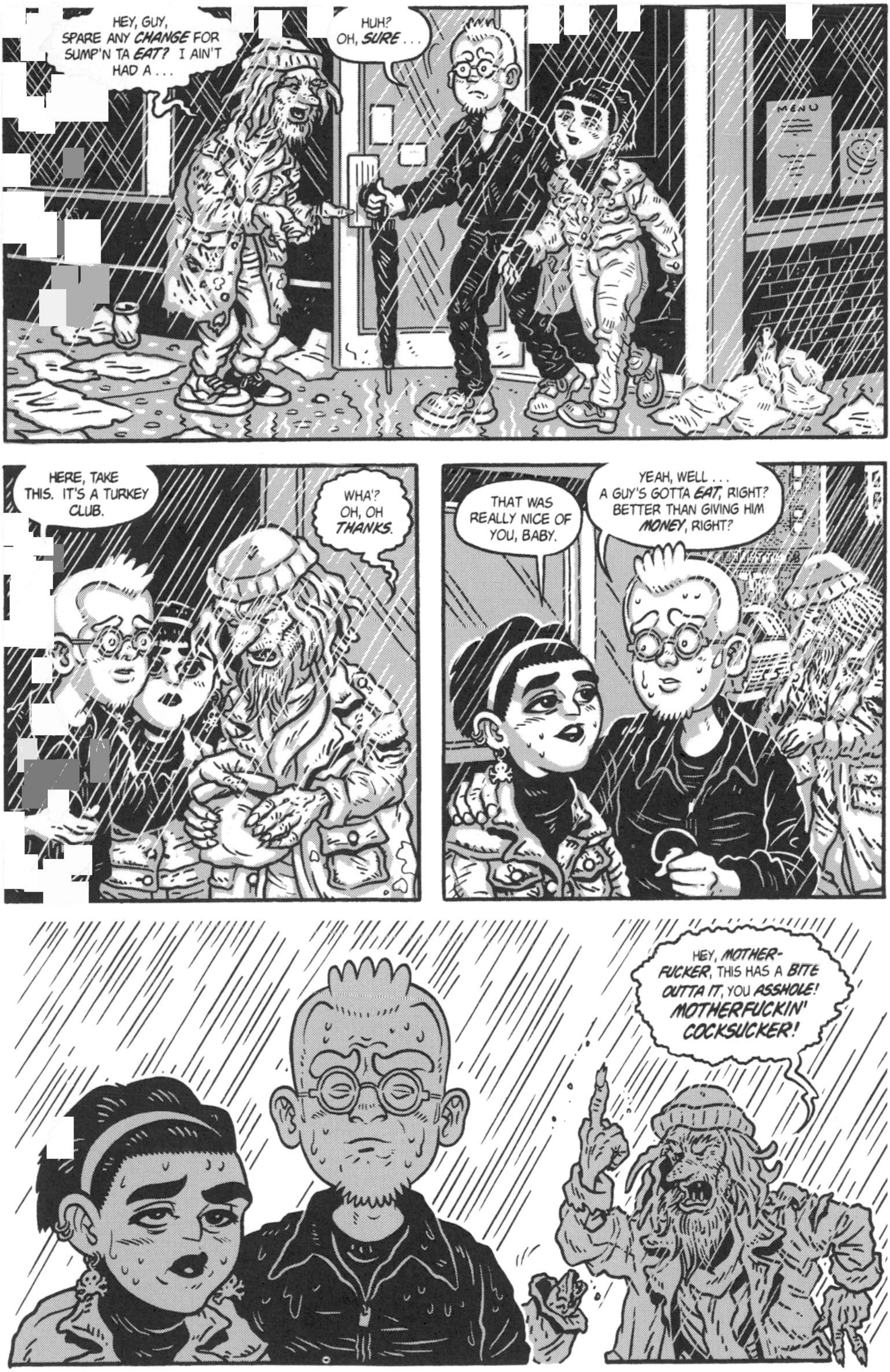
HEY, GUY, SPARE ANY CHANGE FOR SUMP'N TA EAT? I AIN'T HAD A . . .
HUH? OH, SURE . . .
HERE, TAKE THIS. IT'S A TURKEY CLUB.
WHA'? OH, OH THANKS.
THAT WAS REALLY NICE OF YOU, BABY.
YEAH, WELL . . . A GUY'S GOTTA EAT, RIGHT? BETTER THAN GIVING HIM MONEY, RIGHT?
HEY, MOTHER-FUCKER, THIS HAS A BITE OUTTA IT, YOU ASSHOLE! MOTHERFUCKIN' COCKSUCKER!

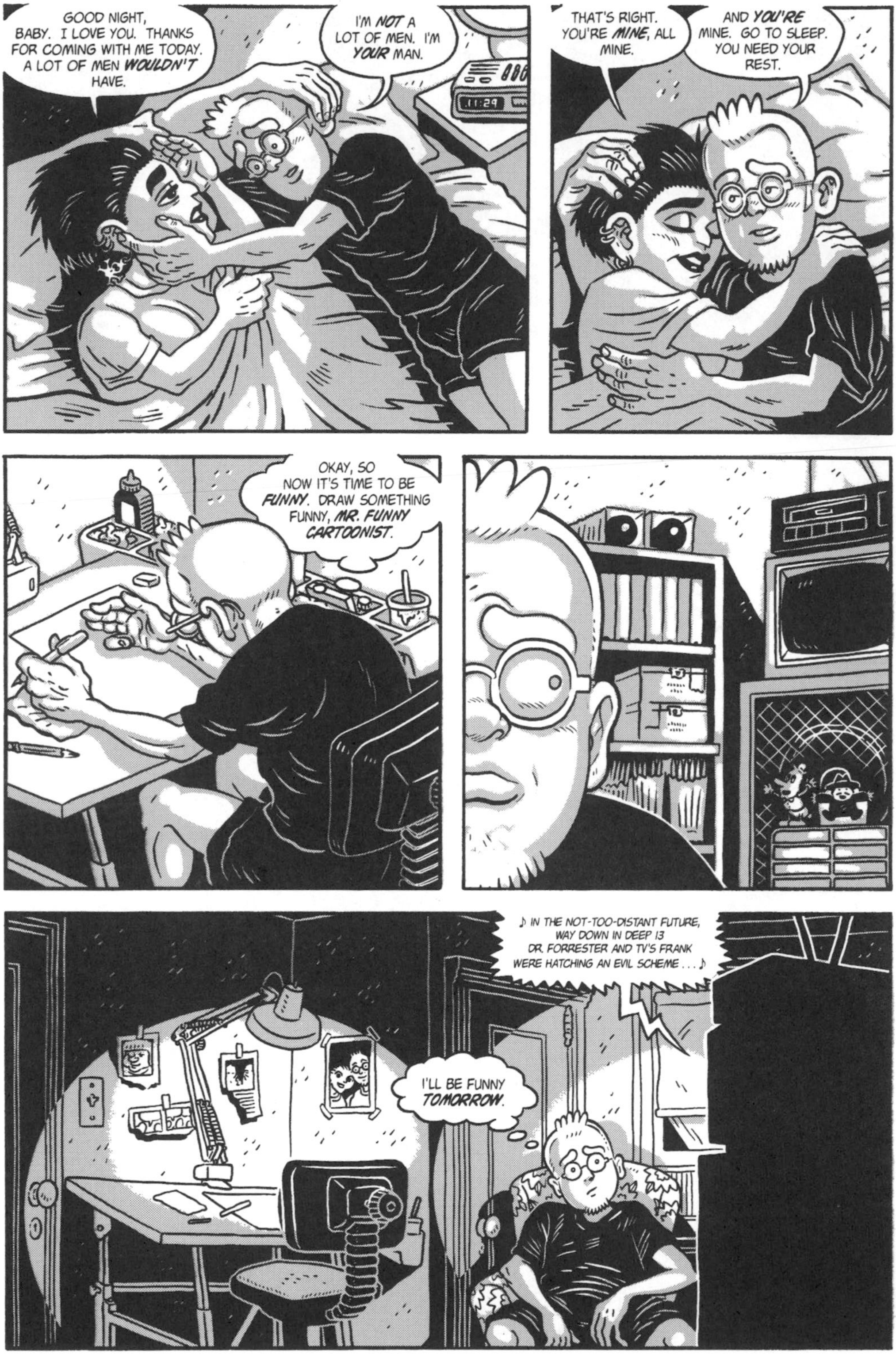
GOOD NIGHT, BABY. I LOVE YOU. THANKS FOR COMING WITH ME TODAY. A LOT OF MEN WOULDN'T HAVE.
I'M NOT A LOT OF MEN. I'M YOUR MAN.
11:29
THAT'S RIGHT. YOU'RE MINE, ALL MINE.
AND YOU'RE MINE. GO TO SLEEP. YOU NEED YOUR REST.
OKAY, SO NOW IT'S TIME TO BE FUNNY. DRAW SOMETHING FUNNY, MR. FUNNY CARTOONIST.
♪ IN THE NOT-TOO-DISTANT FUTURE, WAY DOWN IN DEEP 13 DR. FORRESTER AND TV'S FRANK WERE HATCHING AN EVIL SCHEME . . . ♪
I'LL BE FUNNY TOMORROW.

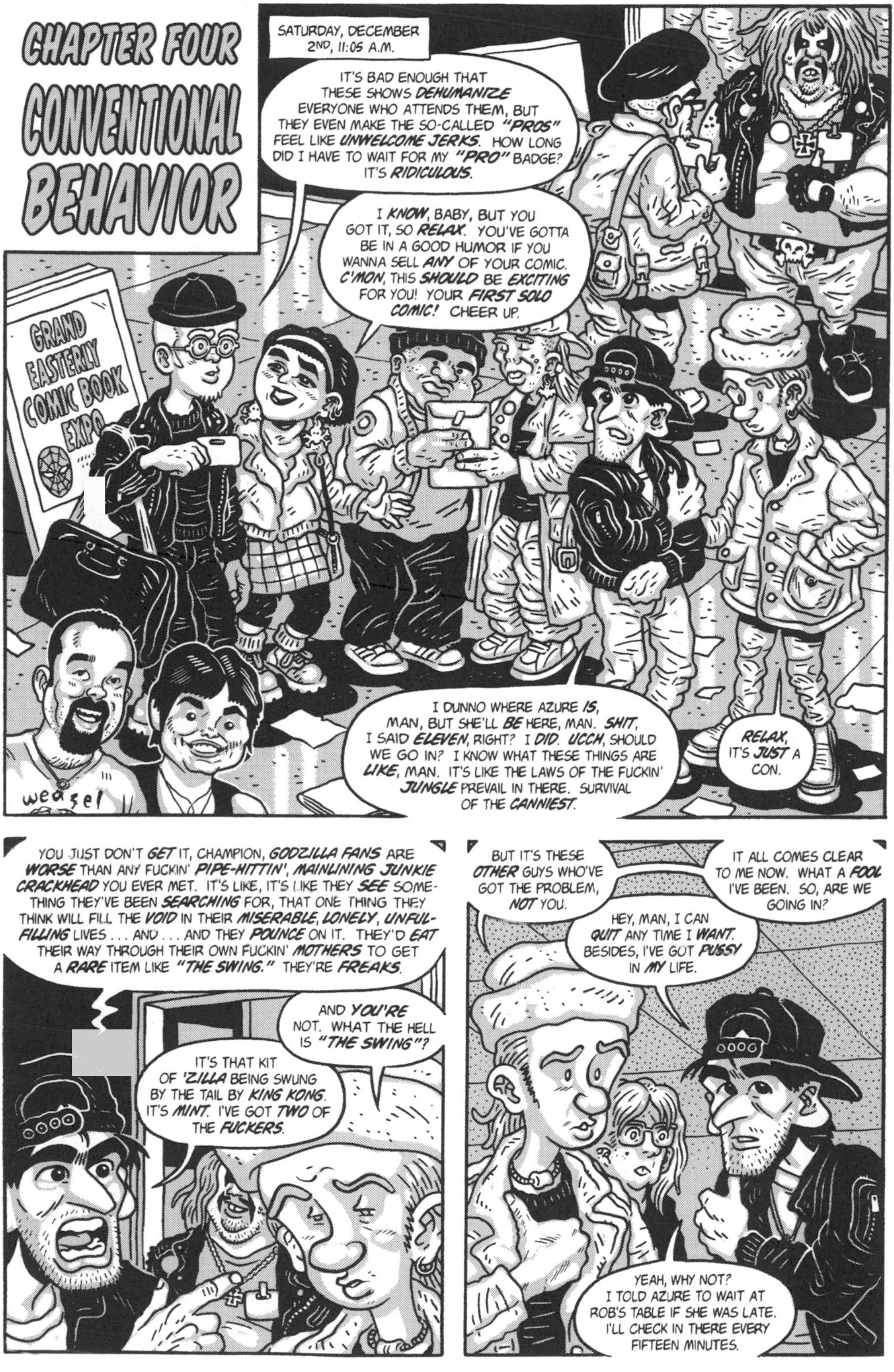
CHAPTER FOUR
CONVENTIONAL BEHAVIOR
SATURDAY, DECEMBER 2ND, 11:05 A.M.
IT'S BAD ENOUGH THAT THESE SHOWS DEHUMANIZE EVERYONE WHO ATTENDS THEM, BUT THEY EVEN MAKE THE SO-CALLED "PROS" FEEL LIKE UNWELCOME JERKS. HOW LONG DID I HAVE TO WAIT FOR MY "PRO" BADGE? IT'S RIDICULOUS.
I KNOW, BABY, BUT YOU GOT IT, SO RELAX. YOU'VE GOTTA BE IN A GOOD HUMOR IF YOU WANNA SELL ANY OF YOUR COMIC. C'MON, THIS SHOULD BE EXCITING FOR YOU! YOUR FIRST SOLO COMIC! CHEER UP.
GRAND EASTERLY COMIC BOOK EXPO
I DUNNO WHERE AZURE IS, MAN, BUT SHE'LL BE HERE, MAN. SHIT, I SAID ELEVEN, RIGHT? I DID. UCCH, SHOULD WE GO IN? I KNOW WHAT THESE THINGS ARE LIKE, MAN. IT'S LIKE THE LAWS OF THE FUCKIN' JUNGLE PREVAIL IN THERE. SURVIVAL OF THE CANNIEST.
RELAX, IT'S JUST A CON.
weasel
YOU JUST DON'T GET IT, CHAMPION, GODZILLA FANS ARE WORSE THAN ANY FUCKIN' PIPE-HITTIN', MAINLINING JUNKIE CRACKHEAD YOU EVER MET. IT'S LIKE, IT'S LIKE THEY SEE SOMETHING THEY'VE BEEN SEARCHING FOR, THAT ONE THING THEY THINK WILL FILL THE VOID IN THEIR MISERABLE, LONELY, UNFULFILLING LIVES . . . AND . . . AND THEY POUNCE ON IT. THEY'D EAT THEIR WAY THROUGH THEIR OWN FUCKIN' MOTHERS TO GET A RARE ITEM LIKE "THE SWING." THEY'RE FREAKS.
AND YOU'RE NOT. WHAT THE HELL IS "THE SWING"?
IT'S THAT KIT OF 'ZILLA BEING SWUNG BY THE TAIL BY KING KONG. IT'S MINT. I'VE GOT TWO OF THE FUCKERS.
BUT IT'S THESE OTHER GUYS WHO'VE GOT THE PROBLEM, NOT YOU.
IT ALL COMES CLEAR TO ME NOW. WHAT A FOOL I'VE BEEN. SO, ARE WE GOING IN?
HEY, MAN, I CAN QUIT ANY TIME I WANT. BESIDES, I'VE GOT PUSSY IN MY LIFE.
YEAH, WHY NOT? I TOLD AZURE TO WAIT AT ROB'S TABLE IF SHE WAS LATE. I'LL CHECK IN THERE EVERY FIFTEEN MINUTES.

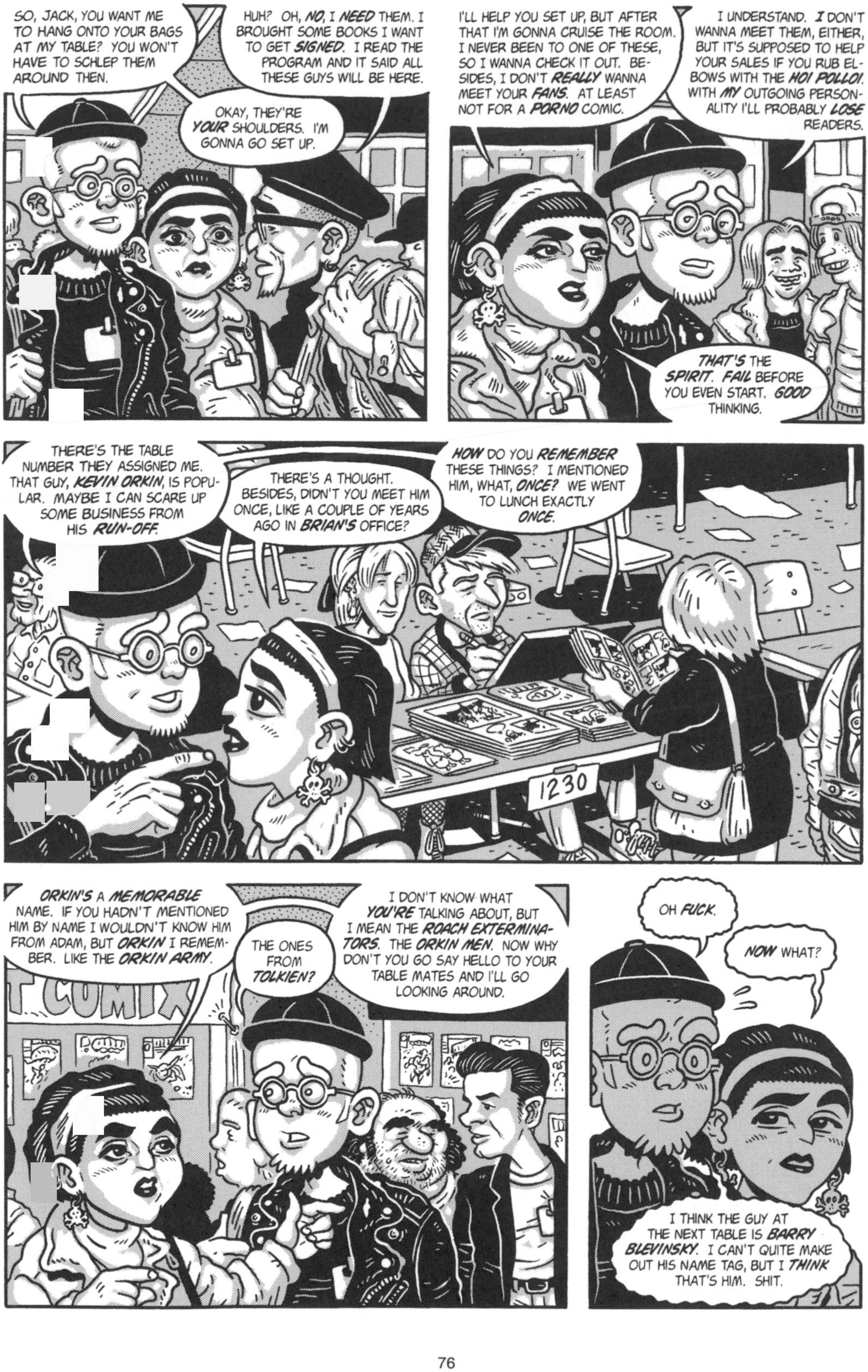
SO, JACK, YOU WANT ME TO HANG ONTO YOUR BAGS AT MY TABLE? YOU WON'T HAVE TO SCHLEP THEM AROUND THEN.
HUH? OH, NO, I NEED THEM. I BROUGHT SOME BOOKS I WANT TO GET SIGNED. I READ THE PROGRAM AND IT SAID ALL THESE GUYS WILL BE HERE.
OKAY, THEY'RE YOUR SHOULDERS. I'M GONNA GO SET UP.
I'LL HELP YOU SET UP, BUT AFTER THAT I'M GONNA CRUISE THE ROOM. I NEVER BEEN TO ONE OF THESE, SO I WANNA CHECK IT OUT. BESIDES, I DON'T REALLY WANNA MEET YOUR FANS. AT LEAST NOT FOR A PORNO COMIC.
I UNDERSTAND. I DON'T WANNA MEET THEM, EITHER, BUT IT'S SUPPOSED TO HELP YOUR SALES IF YOU RUB ELBOWS WITH THE HOI POLLOI. WITH MY OUTGOING PERSONALITY I'LL PROBABLY LOSE READERS.
THAT'S THE SPIRIT. FAIL BEFORE YOU EVEN START. GOOD THINKING.
THERE'S THE TABLE NUMBER THEY ASSIGNED ME. THAT GUY, KEVIN ORKIN, IS POPULAR. MAYBE I CAN SCARE UP SOME BUSINESS FROM HIS RUN-OFF.
THERE'S A THOUGHT. BESIDES, DIDN'T YOU MEET HIM ONCE, LIKE A COUPLE OF YEARS AGO IN BRIAN'S OFFICE?
HOW DO YOU REMEMBER THESE THINGS? I MENTIONED HIM, WHAT, ONCE? WE WENT TO LUNCH EXACTLY ONCE.
1230
ORKIN'S A MEMORABLE NAME. IF YOU HADN'T MENTIONED HIM BY NAME I WOULDN'T KNOW HIM FROM ADAM, BUT ORKIN I REMEMBER. LIKE THE ORKIN ARMY.
THE ONES FROM TOLKIEN?
I DON'T KNOW WHAT YOU'RE TALKING ABOUT, BUT I MEAN THE ROACH EXTERMINATORS. THE ORKIN MEN. NOW WHY DON'T YOU GO SAY HELLO TO YOUR TABLE MATES AND I'LL GO LOOKING AROUND.
COMIX
OH FUCK.
NOW WHAT?
I THINK THE GUY AT THE NEXT TABLE IS BARRY BLEVINSKY. I CAN'T QUITE MAKE OUT HIS NAME TAG, BUT I THINK THAT'S HIM. SHIT.

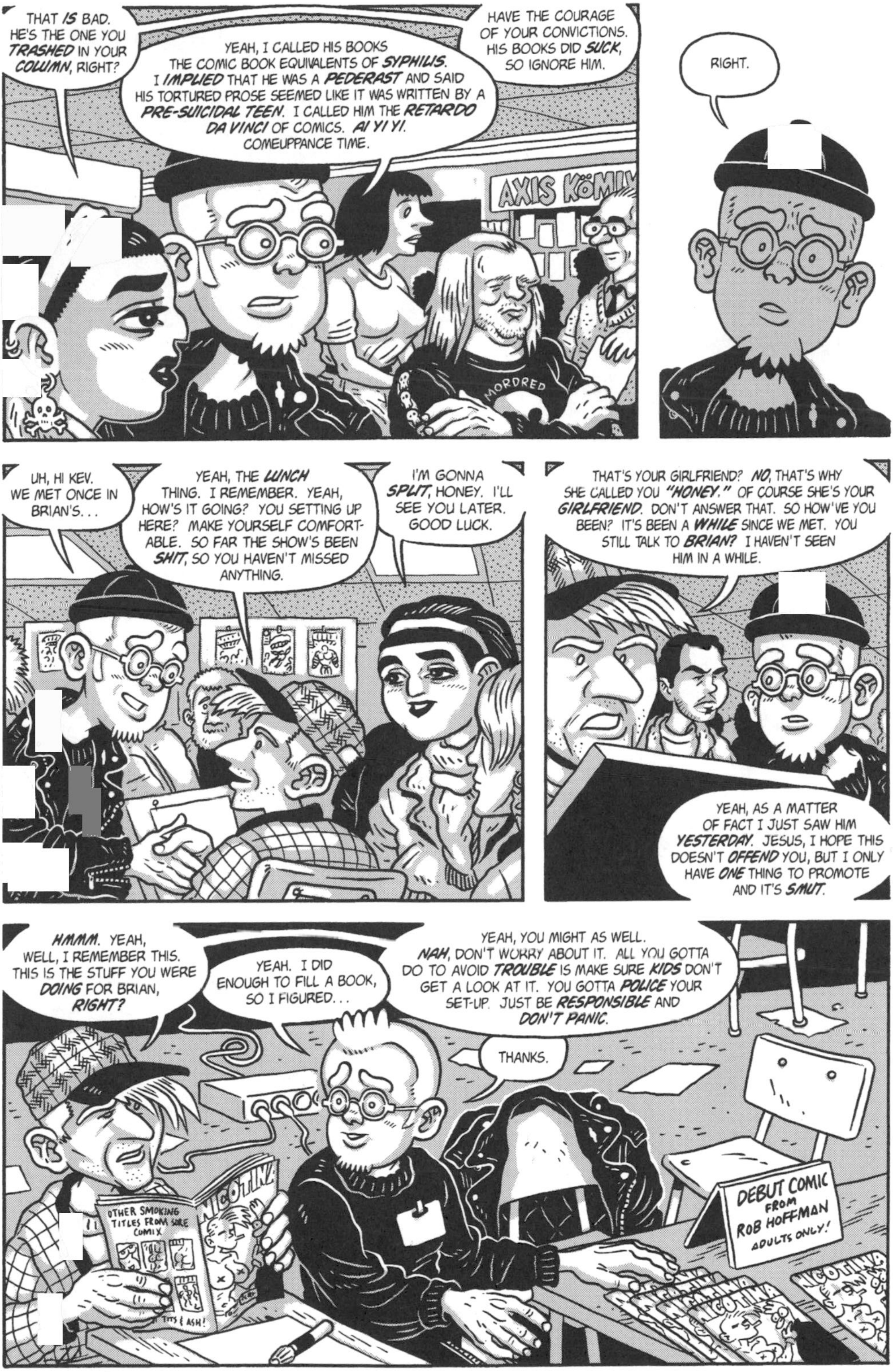
THAT IS BAD. HE'S THE ONE YOU TRASHED IN YOUR COLUMN, RIGHT?
YEAH, I CALLED HIS BOOKS THE COMIC BOOK EQUIVALENTS OF SYPHILIS. I IMPLIED THAT HE WAS A PEDERAST AND SAID HIS TORTURED PROSE SEEMED LIKE IT WAS WRITTEN BY A PRE-SUICIDAL TEEN. I CALLED HIM THE RETARDO DA VINCI OF COMICS. AI YI YI. COMEUPPANCE TIME.
HAVE THE COURAGE OF YOUR CONVICTIONS. HIS BOOKS DID SUCK, SO IGNORE HIM.
AXIS KÖMIX
MORDRED
RIGHT.
UH, HI KEV. WE MET ONCE IN BRIAN'S...
YEAH, THE LUNCH THING. I REMEMBER. YEAH, HOW'S IT GOING? YOU SETTING UP HERE? MAKE YOURSELF COMFORT-ABLE. SO FAR THE SHOW'S BEEN SHIT, SO YOU HAVEN'T MISSED ANYTHING.
I'M GONNA SPLIT, HONEY. I'LL SEE YOU LATER. GOOD LUCK.
THAT'S YOUR GIRLFRIEND? NO, THAT'S WHY SHE CALLED YOU "HONEY." OF COURSE SHE'S YOUR GIRLFRIEND. DON'T ANSWER THAT. SO HOW'VE YOU BEEN? IT'S BEEN A WHILE SINCE WE MET. YOU STILL TALK TO BRIAN? I HAVEN'T SEEN HIM IN A WHILE.
YEAH, AS A MATTER OF FACT I JUST SAW HIM YESTERDAY. JESUS, I HOPE THIS DOESN'T OFFEND YOU, BUT I ONLY HAVE ONE THING TO PROMOTE AND IT'S SMUT.
HMMM. YEAH, WELL, I REMEMBER THIS. THIS IS THE STUFF YOU WERE DOING FOR BRIAN, RIGHT?
YEAH. I DID ENOUGH TO FILL A BOOK, SO I FIGURED...
YEAH, YOU MIGHT AS WELL. NAH, DON'T WORRY ABOUT IT. ALL YOU GOTTA DO TO AVOID TROUBLE IS MAKE SURE KIDS DON'T GET A LOOK AT IT. YOU GOTTA POLICE YOUR SET-UP. JUST BE RESPONSIBLE AND DON'T PANIC.
THANKS.
OTHER SMOKING TITLES FROM SURE COMIX
TITS & ASH!
DEBUT COMIC FROM ROB HOFFMAN ADULTS ONLY!

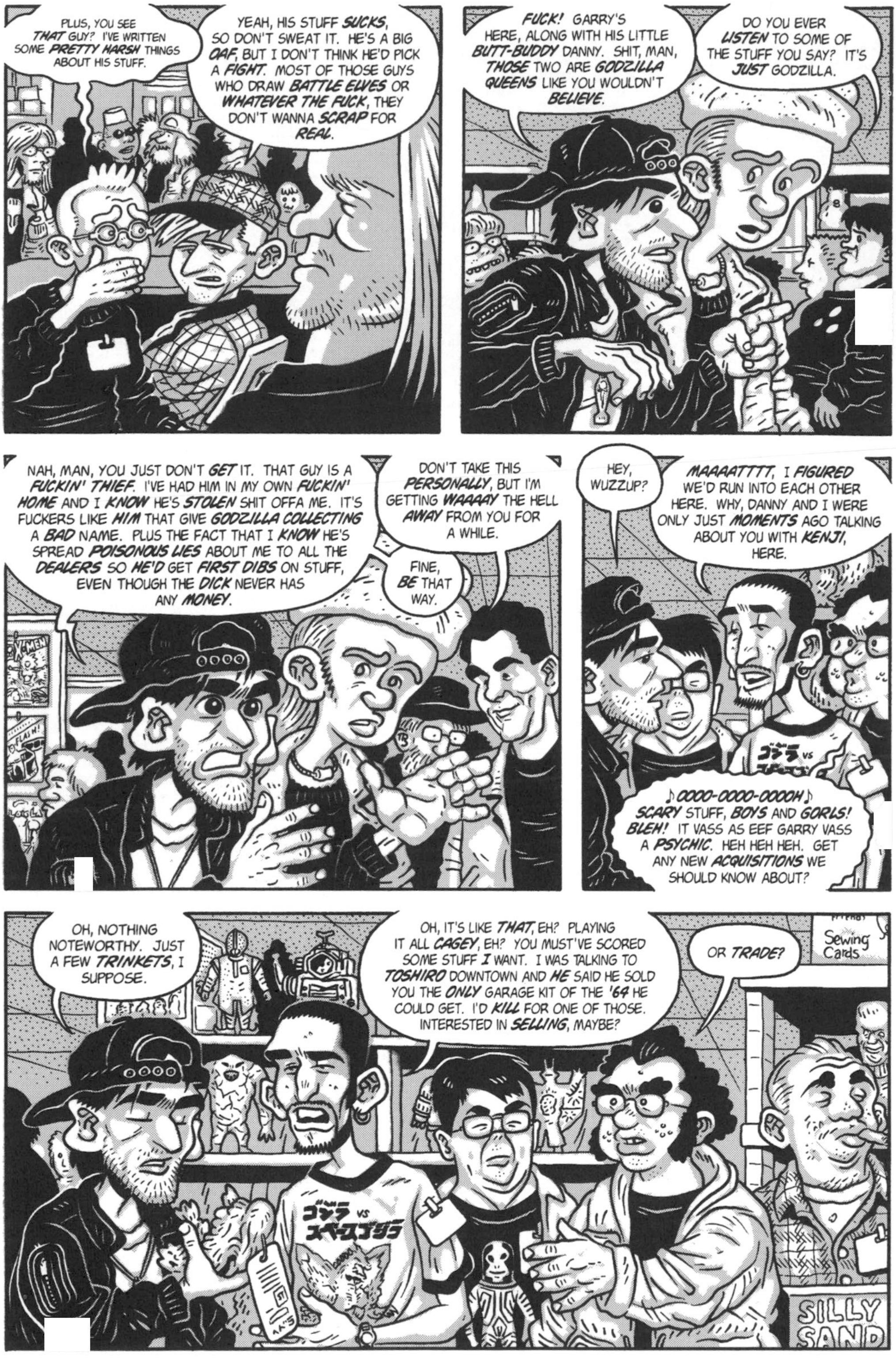
PLUS, YOU SEE ***THAT*** GUY? I'VE WRITTEN SOME ***PRETTY HARSH*** THINGS ABOUT HIS STUFF.
YEAH, HIS STUFF ***SUCKS***, SO DON'T SWEAT IT. HE'S A BIG ***OAF***, BUT I DON'T THINK HE'D PICK A ***FIGHT***. MOST OF THOSE GUYS WHO DRAW ***BATTLE ELVES*** OR ***WHATEVER THE FUCK***, THEY DON'T WANNA ***SCRAP*** FOR ***REAL***.
***FUCK!*** GARRY'S HERE, ALONG WITH HIS LITTLE ***BUTT-BUDDY*** DANNY. SHIT, MAN, ***THOSE*** TWO ARE ***GODZILLA QUEENS*** LIKE YOU WOULDN'T ***BELIEVE***.
DO YOU EVER ***LISTEN*** TO SOME OF THE STUFF YOU SAY? IT'S ***JUST*** GODZILLA.
NAH, MAN, YOU JUST DON'T ***GET*** IT. THAT GUY IS A ***FUCKIN' THIEF***. I'VE HAD HIM IN MY OWN ***FUCKIN' HOME*** AND I ***KNOW*** HE'S ***STOLEN*** SHIT OFFA ME. IT'S FUCKERS LIKE ***HIM*** THAT GIVE ***GODZILLA COLLECTING*** A ***BAD*** NAME. PLUS THE FACT THAT I ***KNOW*** HE'S SPREAD ***POISONOUS LIES*** ABOUT ME TO ALL THE ***DEALERS*** SO ***HE'D*** GET ***FIRST DIBS*** ON STUFF, EVEN THOUGH THE ***DICK*** NEVER HAS ANY ***MONEY***.
DON'T TAKE THIS ***PERSONALLY***, BUT I'M GETTING ***WAAAAY*** THE HELL ***AWAY*** FROM YOU FOR A WHILE.
FINE, ***BE*** THAT WAY.
X-MEN
FLASH!
HEY, WUZZUP?
***MAAAATTTT***, I ***FIGURED*** WE'D RUN INTO EACH OTHER HERE. WHY, DANNY AND I WERE ONLY JUST ***MOMENTS*** AGO TALKING ABOUT YOU WITH ***KENJI***, HERE.
♪***OOOO-OOOO-OOOOH***♪ ***SCARY*** STUFF, ***BOYS*** AND ***GORLS! BLEH!*** IT VASS AS EEF GARRY VASS A ***PSYCHIC***. HEH HEH HEH. GET ANY NEW ***ACQUISITIONS*** WE SHOULD KNOW ABOUT?
OH, NOTHING NOTEWORTHY. JUST A FEW ***TRINKETS***, I SUPPOSE.
OH, IT'S LIKE ***THAT***, EH? PLAYING IT ALL ***CAGEY***, EH? YOU MUST'VE SCORED SOME STUFF ***I*** WANT. I WAS TALKING TO ***TOSHIRO*** DOWNTOWN AND ***HE*** SAID HE SOLD YOU THE ***ONLY*** GARAGE KIT OF THE ***'64*** HE COULD GET. I'D ***KILL*** FOR ONE OF THOSE. INTERESTED IN ***SELLING***, MAYBE?
OR ***TRADE?***
Sewing Cards
ゴジラ VS スペースゴジラ
SILLY SAND

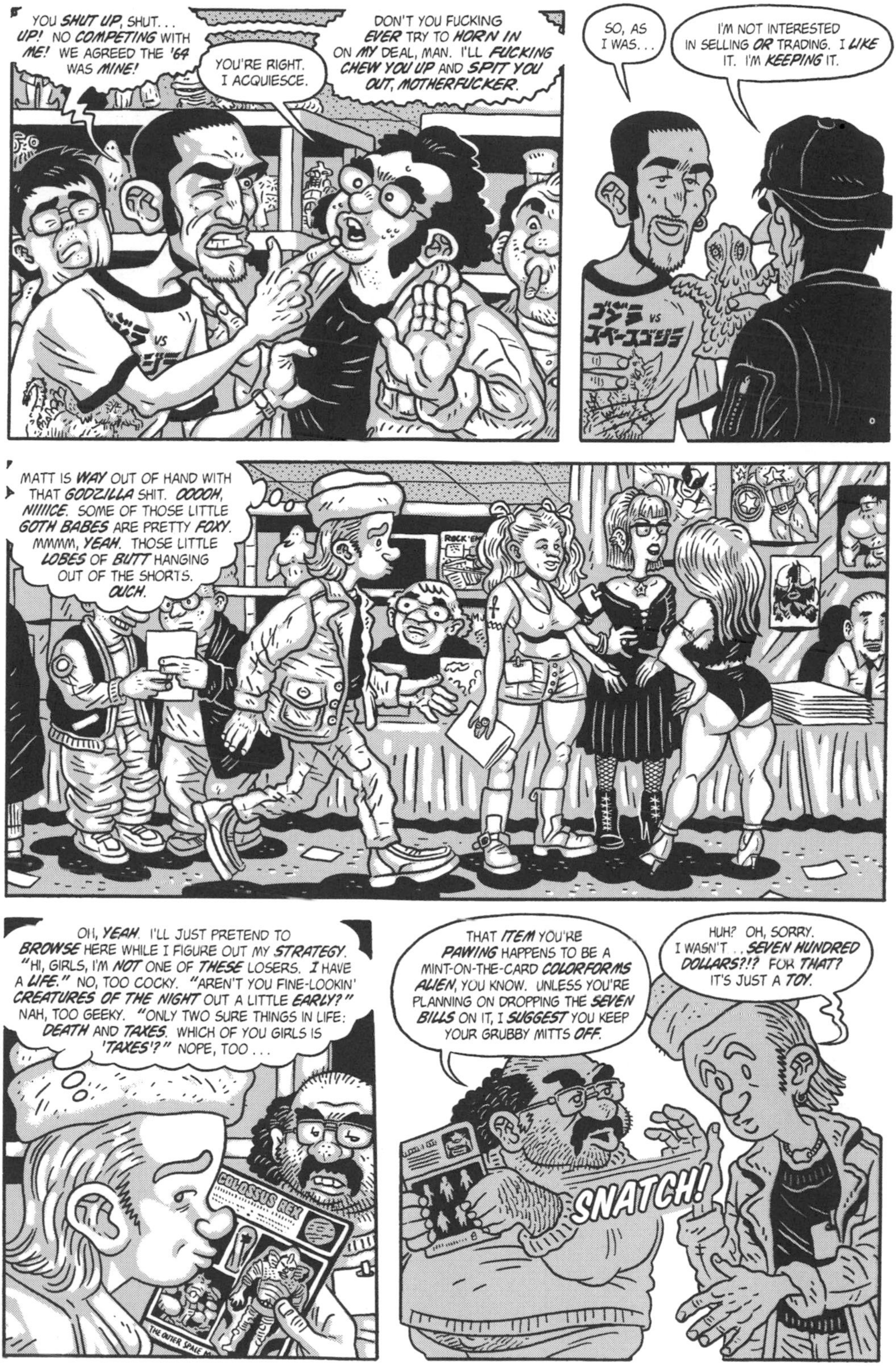

YOU SHUT UP, SHUT... UP! NO COMPETING WITH ME! WE AGREED THE '64 WAS MINE!
YOU'RE RIGHT. I ACQUIESCE.
DON'T YOU FUCKING EVER TRY TO HORN IN ON MY DEAL, MAN. I'LL FUCKING CHEW YOU UP AND SPIT YOU OUT, MOTHERFUCKER.
SO, AS I WAS...
I'M NOT INTERESTED IN SELLING OR TRADING. I LIKE IT. I'M KEEPING IT.
ゴジラ vs スペースゴジラ
MATT IS WAY OUT OF HAND WITH THAT GODZILLA SHIT. OOOOH, NIIIICE. SOME OF THOSE LITTLE GOTH BABES ARE PRETTY FOXY. MMMM, YEAH. THOSE LITTLE LOBES OF BUTT HANGING OUT OF THE SHORTS. OUCH.
OH, YEAH. I'LL JUST PRETEND TO BROWSE HERE WHILE I FIGURE OUT MY STRATEGY. "HI, GIRLS, I'M NOT ONE OF THESE LOSERS. I HAVE A LIFE." NO, TOO COCKY. "AREN'T YOU FINE-LOOKIN' CREATURES OF THE NIGHT OUT A LITTLE EARLY?" NAH, TOO GEEKY. "ONLY TWO SURE THINGS IN LIFE: DEATH AND TAXES. WHICH OF YOU GIRLS IS 'TAXES'?" NOPE, TOO...
COLOSSUS REX
THAT ITEM YOU'RE PAWING HAPPENS TO BE A MINT-ON-THE-CARD COLORFORMS ALIEN, YOU KNOW. UNLESS YOU'RE PLANNING ON DROPPING THE SEVEN BILLS ON IT, I SUGGEST YOU KEEP YOUR GRUBBY MITTS OFF.
HUH? OH, SORRY. I WASN'T... SEVEN HUNDRED DOLLARS?!? FOR THAT? IT'S JUST A TOY.
SNATCH!

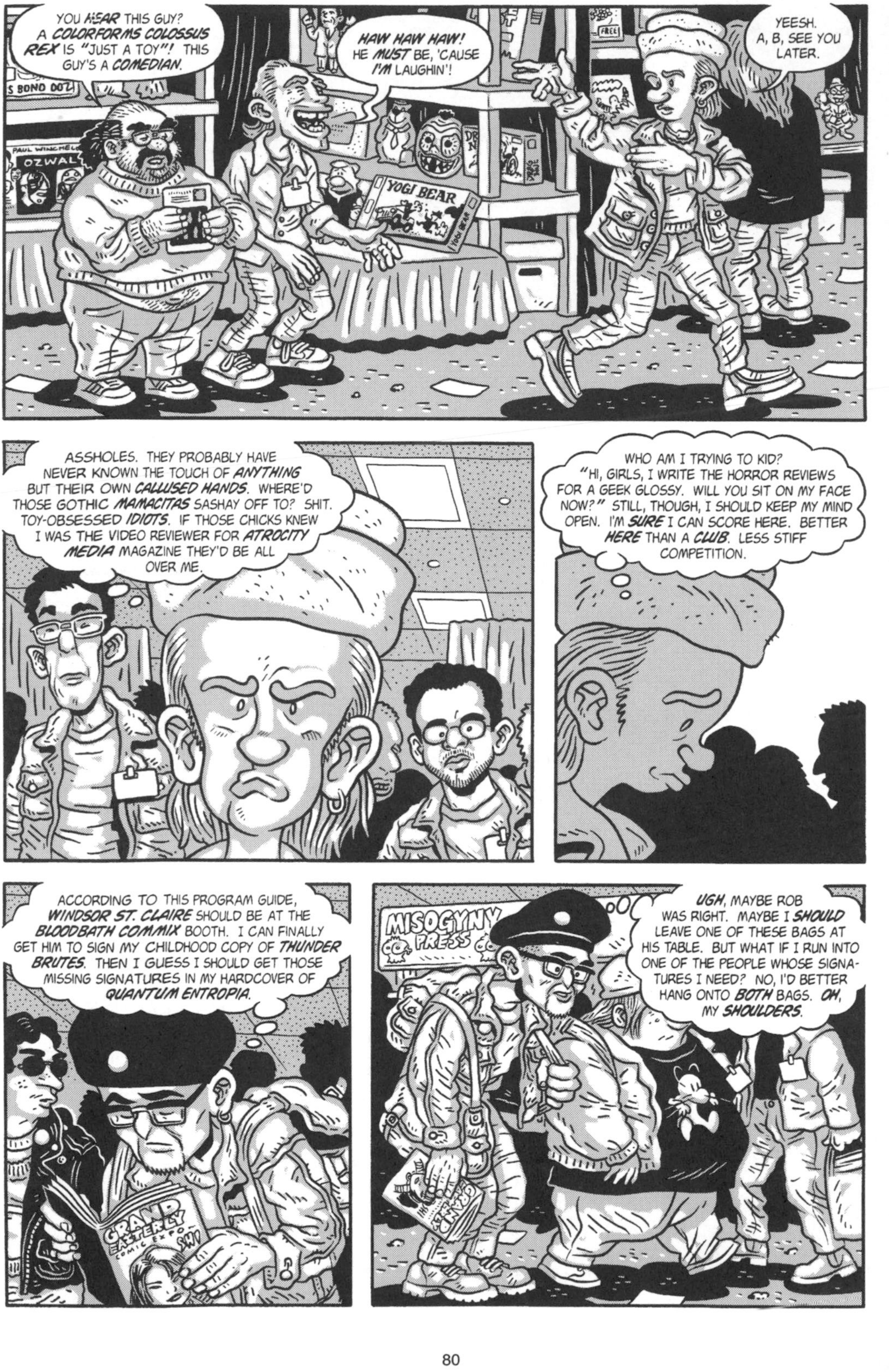
YOU HEAR THIS GUY? A COLORFORMS COLOSSUS REX IS "JUST A TOY"! THIS GUY'S A COMEDIAN.
HAW HAW HAW! HE MUST BE, 'CAUSE I'M LAUGHIN'!
YEESH. A, B, SEE YOU LATER.
YOGI BEAR
FREE
ASSHOLES. THEY PROBABLY HAVE NEVER KNOWN THE TOUCH OF ANYTHING BUT THEIR OWN CALLUSED HANDS. WHERE'D THOSE GOTHIC MAMACITAS SASHAY OFF TO? SHIT. TOY-OBSESSED IDIOTS. IF THOSE CHICKS KNEW I WAS THE VIDEO REVIEWER FOR ATROCITY MEDIA MAGAZINE THEY'D BE ALL OVER ME.
WHO AM I TRYING TO KID? "HI, GIRLS, I WRITE THE HORROR REVIEWS FOR A GEEK GLOSSY. WILL YOU SIT ON MY FACE NOW?" STILL, THOUGH, I SHOULD KEEP MY MIND OPEN. I'M SURE I CAN SCORE HERE. BETTER HERE THAN A CLUB. LESS STIFF COMPETITION.
ACCORDING TO THIS PROGRAM GUIDE, WINDSOR ST. CLAIRE SHOULD BE AT THE BLOODBATH COMMIX BOOTH. I CAN FINALLY GET HIM TO SIGN MY CHILDHOOD COPY OF THUNDER BRUTES. THEN I GUESS I SHOULD GET THOSE MISSING SIGNATURES IN MY HARDCOVER OF QUANTUM ENTROPIA.
GRAND EASTERLY COMIC EXPO
MISOGYNY PRESS
UGH, MAYBE ROB WAS RIGHT. MAYBE I SHOULD LEAVE ONE OF THESE BAGS AT HIS TABLE. BUT WHAT IF I RUN INTO ONE OF THE PEOPLE WHOSE SIGNATURES I NEED? NO, I'D BETTER HANG ONTO BOTH BAGS. OH, MY SHOULDERS.

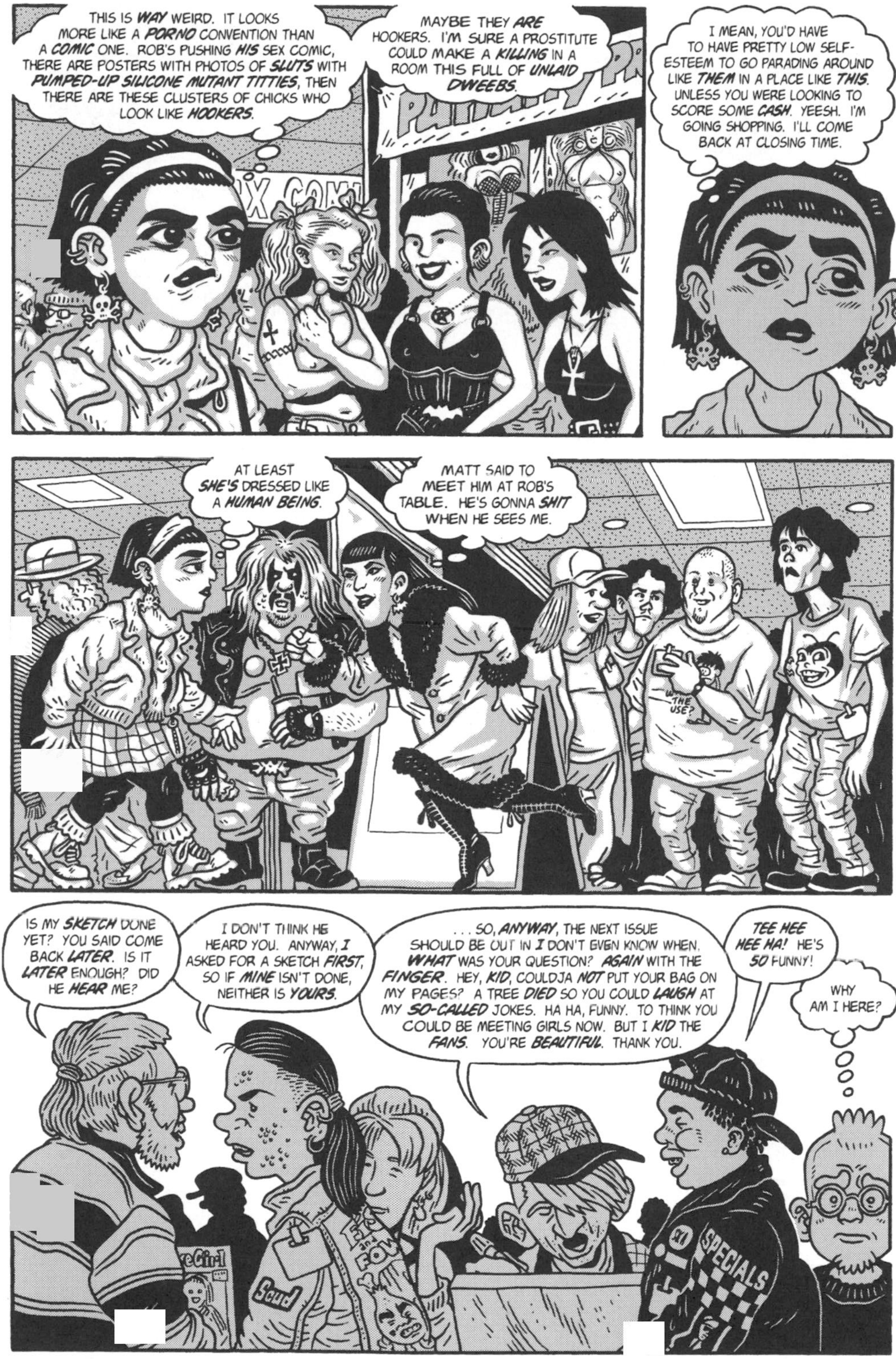
THIS IS WAY WEIRD. IT LOOKS MORE LIKE A PORNO CONVENTION THAN A COMIC ONE. ROB'S PUSHING HIS SEX COMIC, THERE ARE POSTERS WITH PHOTOS OF SLUTS WITH PUMPED-UP SILICONE MUTANT TITTIES, THEN THERE ARE THESE CLUSTERS OF CHICKS WHO LOOK LIKE HOOKERS.
MAYBE THEY ARE HOOKERS. I'M SURE A PROSTITUTE COULD MAKE A KILLING IN A ROOM THIS FULL OF UNLAID DWEEBS.
I MEAN, YOU'D HAVE TO HAVE PRETTY LOW SELF-ESTEEM TO GO PARADING AROUND LIKE THEM IN A PLACE LIKE THIS. UNLESS YOU WERE LOOKING TO SCORE SOME CASH. YEESH. I'M GOING SHOPPING. I'LL COME BACK AT CLOSING TIME.
AT LEAST SHE'S DRESSED LIKE A HUMAN BEING.
MATT SAID TO MEET HIM AT ROB'S TABLE. HE'S GONNA SHIT WHEN HE SEES ME.
IS MY SKETCH DONE YET? YOU SAID COME BACK LATER. IS IT LATER ENOUGH? DID HE HEAR ME?
I DON'T THINK HE HEARD YOU. ANYWAY, I ASKED FOR A SKETCH FIRST, SO IF MINE ISN'T DONE, NEITHER IS YOURS.
. . . SO, ANYWAY, THE NEXT ISSUE SHOULD BE OUT IN I DON'T EVEN KNOW WHEN. WHAT WAS YOUR QUESTION? AGAIN WITH THE FINGER. HEY, KID, COULDJA NOT PUT YOUR BAG ON MY PAGES? A TREE DIED SO YOU COULD LAUGH AT MY SO-CALLED JOKES. HA HA, FUNNY. TO THINK YOU COULD BE MEETING GIRLS NOW. BUT I KID THE FANS. YOU'RE BEAUTIFUL. THANK YOU.
TEE HEE HEE HA! HE'S SO FUNNY!
WHY AM I HERE?
SPECIALS

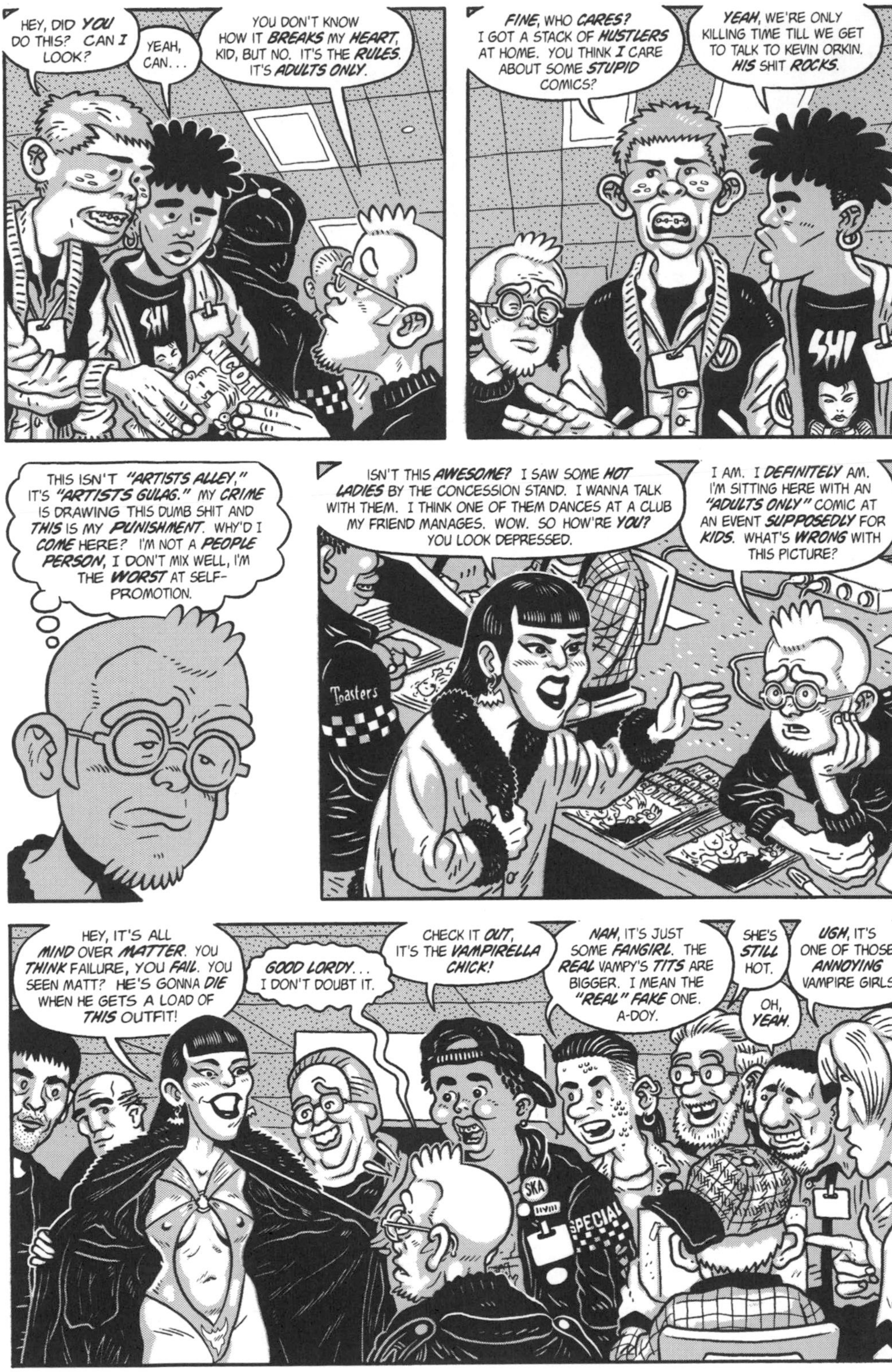
HEY, DID YOU DO THIS? CAN I LOOK?
YEAH, CAN...
YOU DON'T KNOW HOW IT BREAKS MY HEART, KID, BUT NO. IT'S THE RULES. IT'S ADULTS ONLY.
FINE, WHO CARES? I GOT A STACK OF HUSTLERS AT HOME. YOU THINK I CARE ABOUT SOME STUPID COMICS?
YEAH, WE'RE ONLY KILLING TIME TILL WE GET TO TALK TO KEVIN ORKIN. HIS SHIT ROCKS.
THIS ISN'T "ARTISTS ALLEY," IT'S "ARTISTS GULAG." MY CRIME IS DRAWING THIS DUMB SHIT AND THIS IS MY PUNISHMENT. WHY'D I COME HERE? I'M NOT A PEOPLE PERSON, I DON'T MIX WELL, I'M THE WORST AT SELF-PROMOTION.
ISN'T THIS AWESOME? I SAW SOME HOT LADIES BY THE CONCESSION STAND. I WANNA TALK WITH THEM. I THINK ONE OF THEM DANCES AT A CLUB MY FRIEND MANAGES. WOW. SO HOW'RE YOU? YOU LOOK DEPRESSED.
I AM. I DEFINITELY AM. I'M SITTING HERE WITH AN "ADULTS ONLY" COMIC AT AN EVENT SUPPOSEDLY FOR KIDS. WHAT'S WRONG WITH THIS PICTURE?
HEY, IT'S ALL MIND OVER MATTER. YOU THINK FAILURE, YOU FAIL. YOU SEEN MATT? HE'S GONNA DIE WHEN HE GETS A LOAD OF THIS OUTFIT!
GOOD LORDY... I DON'T DOUBT IT.
CHECK IT OUT, IT'S THE VAMPIRELLA CHICK!
NAH, IT'S JUST SOME FANGIRL. THE REAL VAMPY'S TITS ARE BIGGER. I MEAN THE "REAL" FAKE ONE. A-DOY.
SHE'S STILL HOT.
OH, YEAH.
UGH, IT'S ONE OF THOSE ANNOYING VAMPIRE GIRLS.

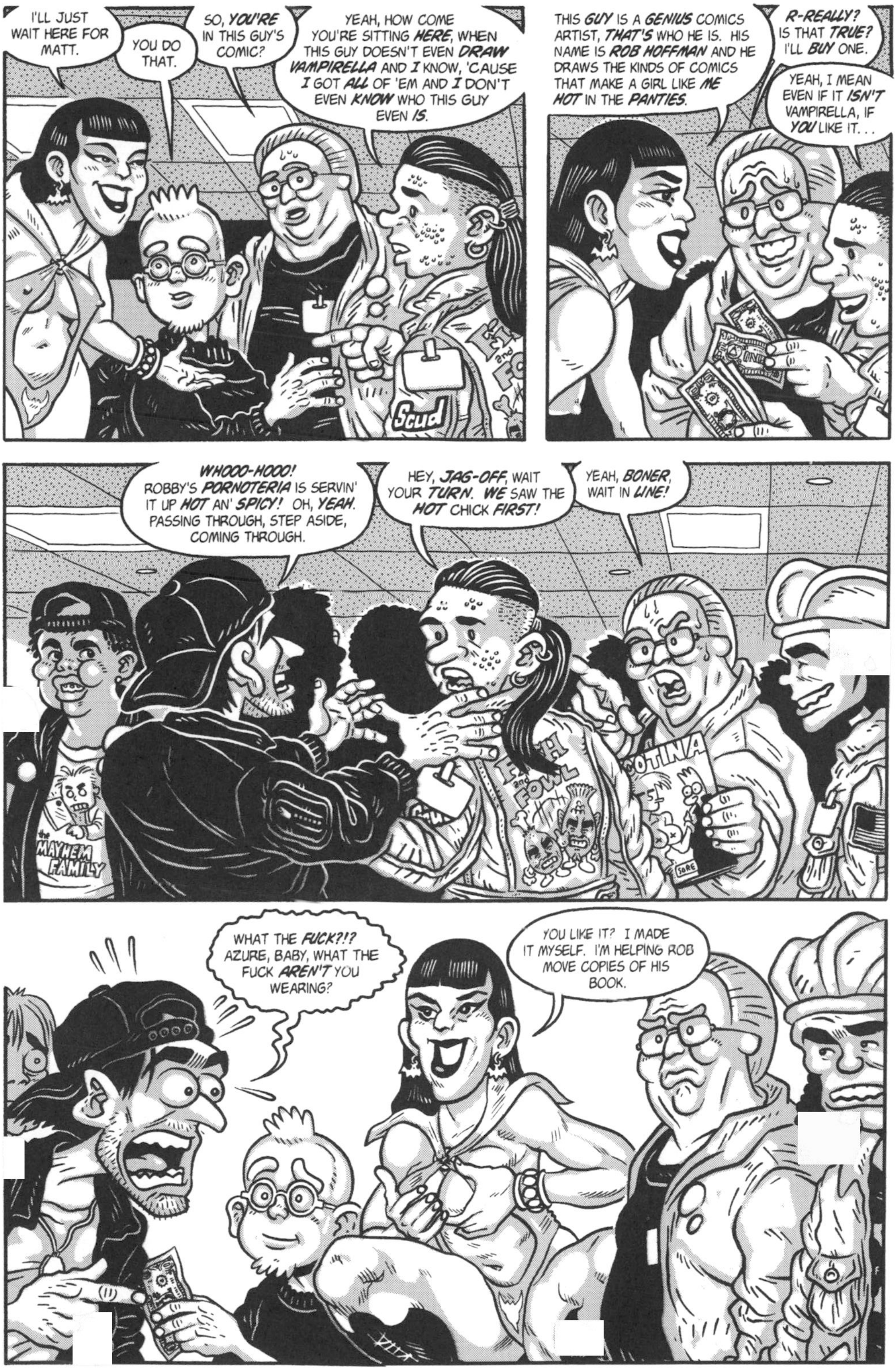

I'LL JUST WAIT HERE FOR MATT.
YOU DO THAT.
SO, *YOU'RE* IN THIS GUY'S COMIC?
YEAH, HOW COME YOU'RE SITTING *HERE*, WHEN THIS GUY DOESN'T EVEN *DRAW VAMPIRELLA* AND *I* KNOW, 'CAUSE *I* GOT *ALL* OF 'EM AND *I* DON'T EVEN *KNOW* WHO THIS GUY EVEN *IS*.
Scud
THIS *GUY* IS A *GENIUS* COMICS ARTIST, *THAT'S* WHO HE IS. HIS NAME IS *ROB HOFFMAN* AND HE DRAWS THE KINDS OF COMICS THAT MAKE A GIRL LIKE *ME HOT* IN THE *PANTIES*.
*R-REALLY?* IS THAT *TRUE?* I'LL *BUY* ONE.
YEAH, I MEAN EVEN IF IT *ISN'T* VAMPIRELLA, IF *YOU* LIKE IT. . .
*WHOOO-HOOO!* ROBBY'S *PORNOTERIA* IS SERVIN' IT UP *HOT* AN' *SPICY!* OH, *YEAH*. PASSING THROUGH, STEP ASIDE, COMING THROUGH.
HEY, *JAG-OFF*, WAIT YOUR *TURN*. *WE* SAW THE *HOT* CHICK *FIRST!*
YEAH, *BONER*, WAIT IN *LINE!*
the MAYHEM FAMILY
WHAT THE *FUCK?!?* AZURE, BABY, WHAT THE FUCK *AREN'T* YOU WEARING?
YOU LIKE IT? I MADE IT MYSELF. I'M HELPING ROB MOVE COPIES OF HIS BOOK.

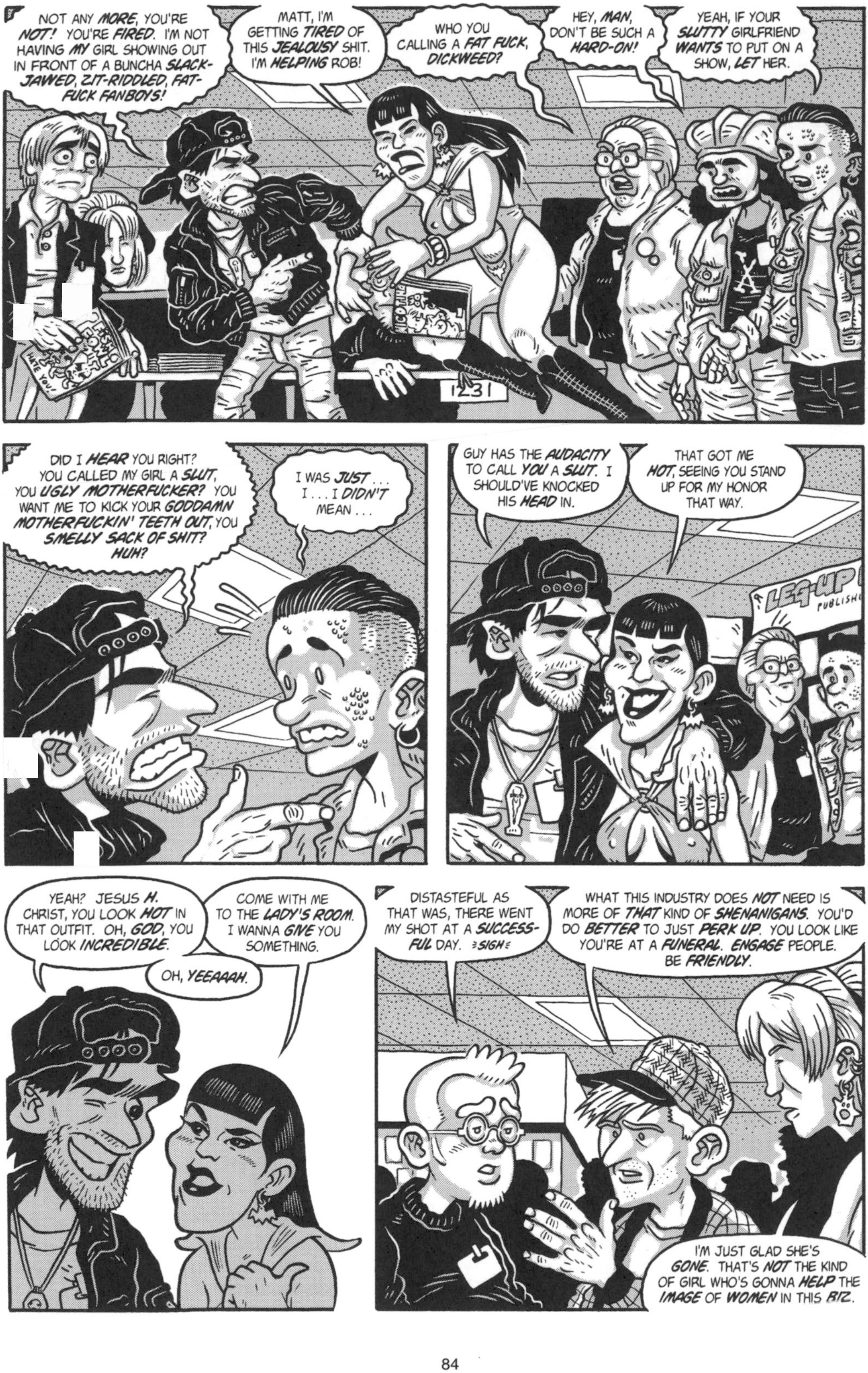
NOT ANY MORE, YOU'RE NOT! YOU'RE FIRED. I'M NOT HAVING MY GIRL SHOWING OUT IN FRONT OF A BUNCHA SLACK-JAWED, ZIT-RIDDLED, FAT-FUCK FANBOYS!
MATT, I'M GETTING TIRED OF THIS JEALOUSY SHIT. I'M HELPING ROB!
WHO YOU CALLING A FAT FUCK, DICKWEED?
HEY, MAN, DON'T BE SUCH A HARD-ON!
YEAH, IF YOUR SLUTTY GIRLFRIEND WANTS TO PUT ON A SHOW, LET HER.
1231
DID I HEAR YOU RIGHT? YOU CALLED MY GIRL A SLUT, YOU UGLY MOTHERFUCKER? YOU WANT ME TO KICK YOUR GODDAMN MOTHERFUCKIN' TEETH OUT, YOU SMELLY SACK OF SHIT? HUH?
I WAS JUST . . . I . . . I DIDN'T MEAN . . .
GUY HAS THE AUDACITY TO CALL YOU A SLUT. I SHOULD'VE KNOCKED HIS HEAD IN.
THAT GOT ME HOT, SEEING YOU STAND UP FOR MY HONOR THAT WAY.
LEG-UP
PUBLISH
YEAH? JESUS H. CHRIST, YOU LOOK HOT IN THAT OUTFIT. OH, GOD, YOU LOOK INCREDIBLE.
COME WITH ME TO THE LADY'S ROOM. I WANNA GIVE YOU SOMETHING.
OH, YEEAAAH.
DISTASTEFUL AS THAT WAS, THERE WENT MY SHOT AT A SUCCESSFUL DAY. SIGH
WHAT THIS INDUSTRY DOES NOT NEED IS MORE OF THAT KIND OF SHENANIGANS. YOU'D DO BETTER TO JUST PERK UP. YOU LOOK LIKE YOU'RE AT A FUNERAL. ENGAGE PEOPLE. BE FRIENDLY.
I'M JUST GLAD SHE'S GONE. THAT'S NOT THE KIND OF GIRL WHO'S GONNA HELP THE IMAGE OF WOMEN IN THIS BIZ.

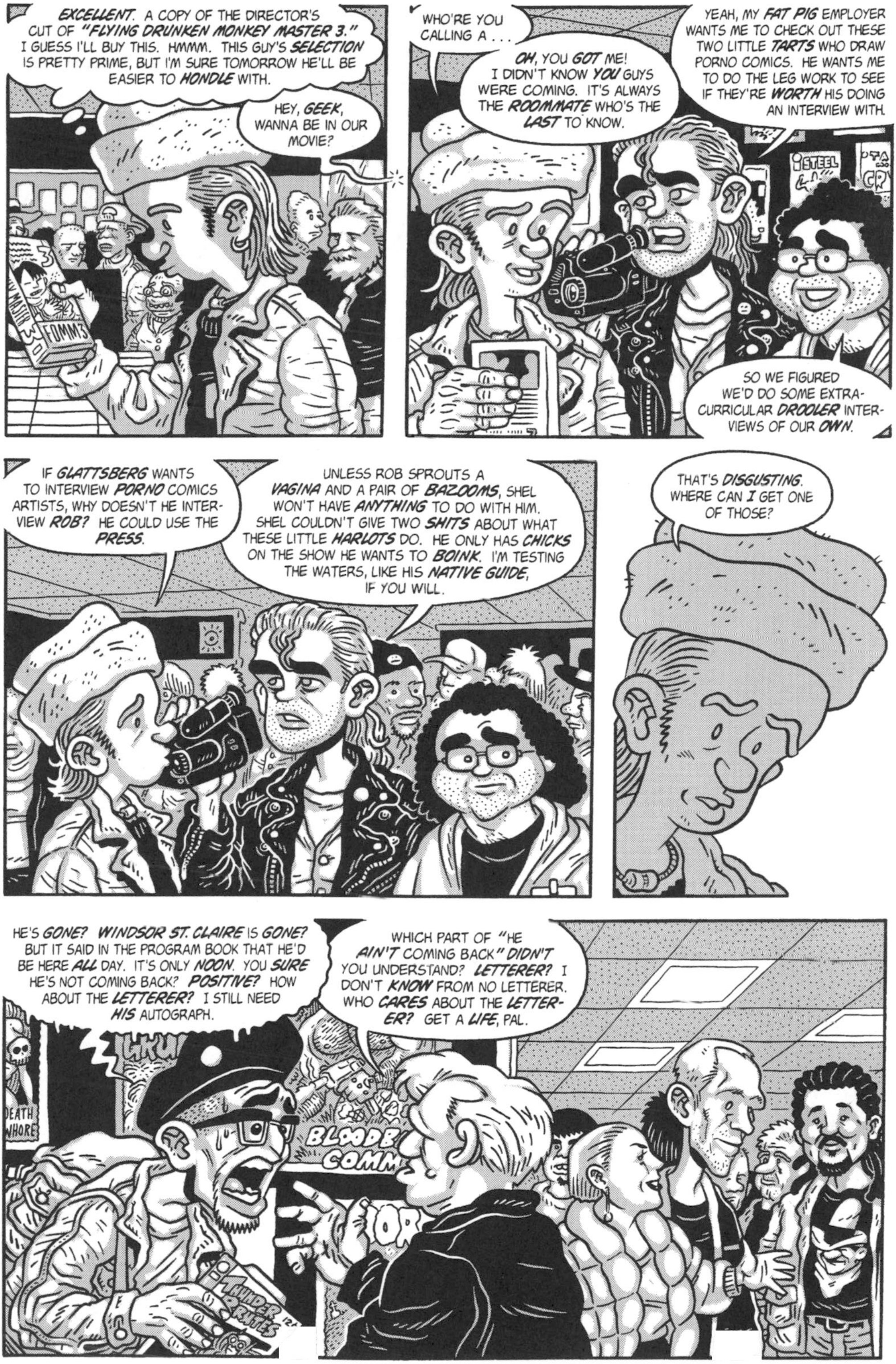
EXCELLENT. A COPY OF THE DIRECTOR'S CUT OF "FLYING DRUNKEN MONKEY MASTER 3." I GUESS I'LL BUY THIS. HMMM. THIS GUY'S SELECTION IS PRETTY PRIME, BUT I'M SURE TOMORROW HE'LL BE EASIER TO HONDLE WITH.
HEY, GEEK, WANNA BE IN OUR MOVIE?
WHO'RE YOU CALLING A . . .
OH, YOU GOT ME! I DIDN'T KNOW YOU GUYS WERE COMING. IT'S ALWAYS THE ROOMMATE WHO'S THE LAST TO KNOW.
YEAH, MY FAT PIG EMPLOYER WANTS ME TO CHECK OUT THESE TWO LITTLE TARTS WHO DRAW PORNO COMICS. HE WANTS ME TO DO THE LEG WORK TO SEE IF THEY'RE WORTH HIS DOING AN INTERVIEW WITH.
SO WE FIGURED WE'D DO SOME EXTRA-CURRICULAR DROOLER INTER-VIEWS OF OUR OWN.
IF GLATTSBERG WANTS TO INTERVIEW PORNO COMICS ARTISTS, WHY DOESN'T HE INTER-VIEW ROB? HE COULD USE THE PRESS.
UNLESS ROB SPROUTS A VAGINA AND A PAIR OF BAZOOMS, SHEL WON'T HAVE ANYTHING TO DO WITH HIM. SHEL COULDN'T GIVE TWO SHITS ABOUT WHAT THESE LITTLE HARLOTS DO. HE ONLY HAS CHICKS ON THE SHOW HE WANTS TO BOINK. I'M TESTING THE WATERS, LIKE HIS NATIVE GUIDE, IF YOU WILL.
THAT'S DISGUSTING. WHERE CAN I GET ONE OF THOSE?
HE'S GONE? WINDSOR ST. CLAIRE IS GONE? BUT IT SAID IN THE PROGRAM BOOK THAT HE'D BE HERE ALL DAY. IT'S ONLY NOON. YOU SURE HE'S NOT COMING BACK? POSITIVE? HOW ABOUT THE LETTERER? I STILL NEED HIS AUTOGRAPH.
WHICH PART OF "HE AIN'T COMING BACK" DIDN'T YOU UNDERSTAND? LETTERER? I DON'T KNOW FROM NO LETTERER. WHO CARES ABOUT THE LETTER-ER? GET A LIFE, PAL.
DEATH WHORE
BLOODB
COMM

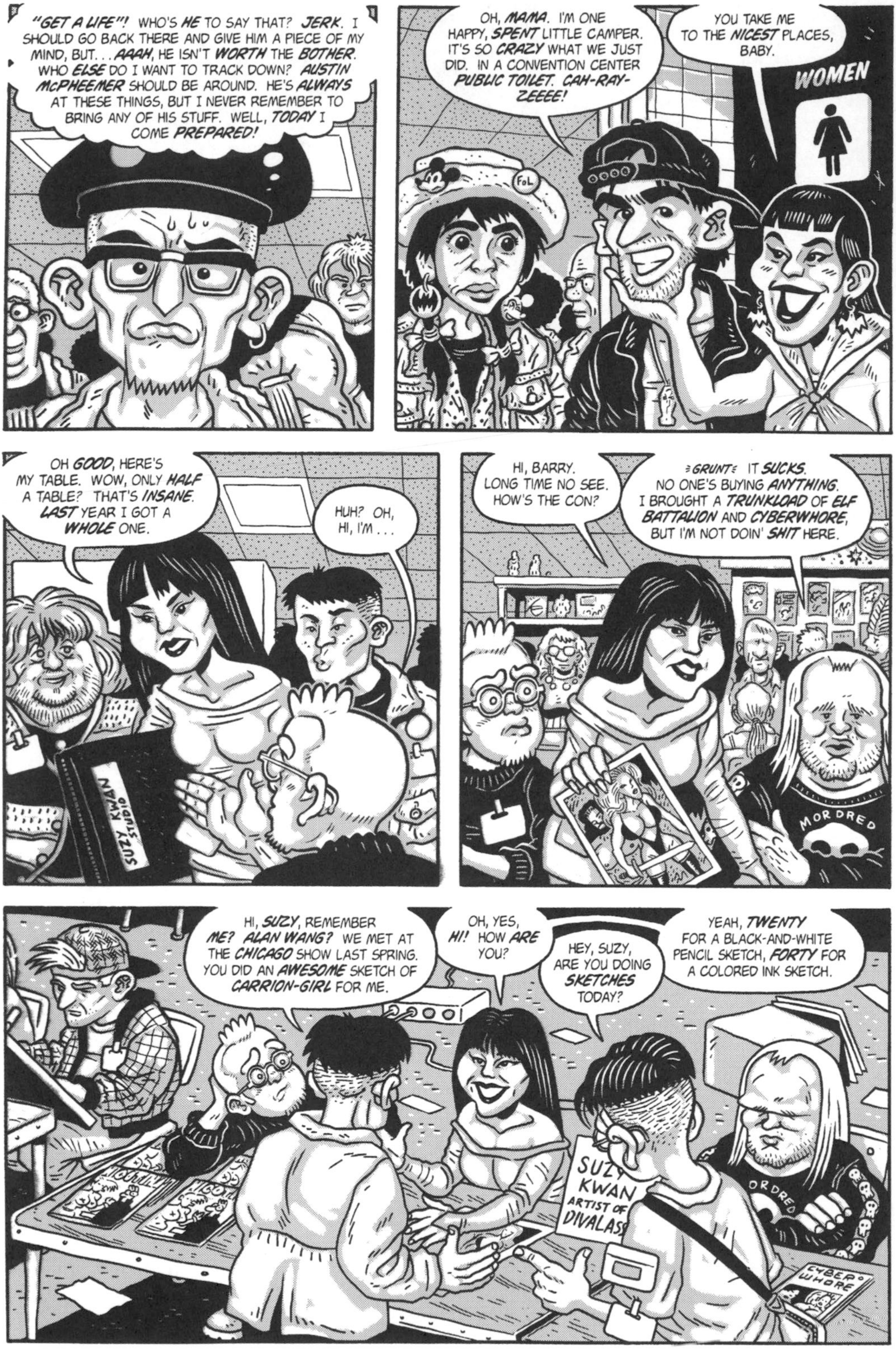
"GET A LIFE"! WHO'S HE TO SAY THAT? JERK. I SHOULD GO BACK THERE AND GIVE HIM A PIECE OF MY MIND, BUT... AAAH, HE ISN'T WORTH THE BOTHER. WHO ELSE DO I WANT TO TRACK DOWN? AUSTIN McPHEEMER SHOULD BE AROUND. HE'S ALWAYS AT THESE THINGS, BUT I NEVER REMEMBER TO BRING ANY OF HIS STUFF. WELL, TODAY I COME PREPARED!
OH, MAMA. I'M ONE HAPPY, SPENT LITTLE CAMPER. IT'S SO CRAZY WHAT WE JUST DID. IN A CONVENTION CENTER PUBLIC TOILET. CAH-RAY-ZEEEE!
YOU TAKE ME TO THE NICEST PLACES, BABY.
WOMEN
OH GOOD, HERE'S MY TABLE. WOW, ONLY HALF A TABLE? THAT'S INSANE. LAST YEAR I GOT A WHOLE ONE.
HUH? OH, HI, I'M . . .
SUZY KWAN STUDIO
HI, BARRY. LONG TIME NO SEE. HOW'S THE CON?
≶GRUNT≶ IT SUCKS. NO ONE'S BUYING ANYTHING. I BROUGHT A TRUNKLOAD OF ELF BATTALION AND CYBERWHORE, BUT I'M NOT DOIN' SHIT HERE.
MORDRED
HI, SUZY, REMEMBER ME? ALAN WANG? WE MET AT THE CHICAGO SHOW LAST SPRING. YOU DID AN AWESOME SKETCH OF CARRION-GIRL FOR ME.
OH, YES, HI! HOW ARE YOU?
HEY, SUZY, ARE YOU DOING SKETCHES TODAY?
YEAH, TWENTY FOR A BLACK-AND-WHITE PENCIL SKETCH, FORTY FOR A COLORED INK SKETCH.
SUZY KWAN ARTIST OF DIVALASS
CYBER WHORE

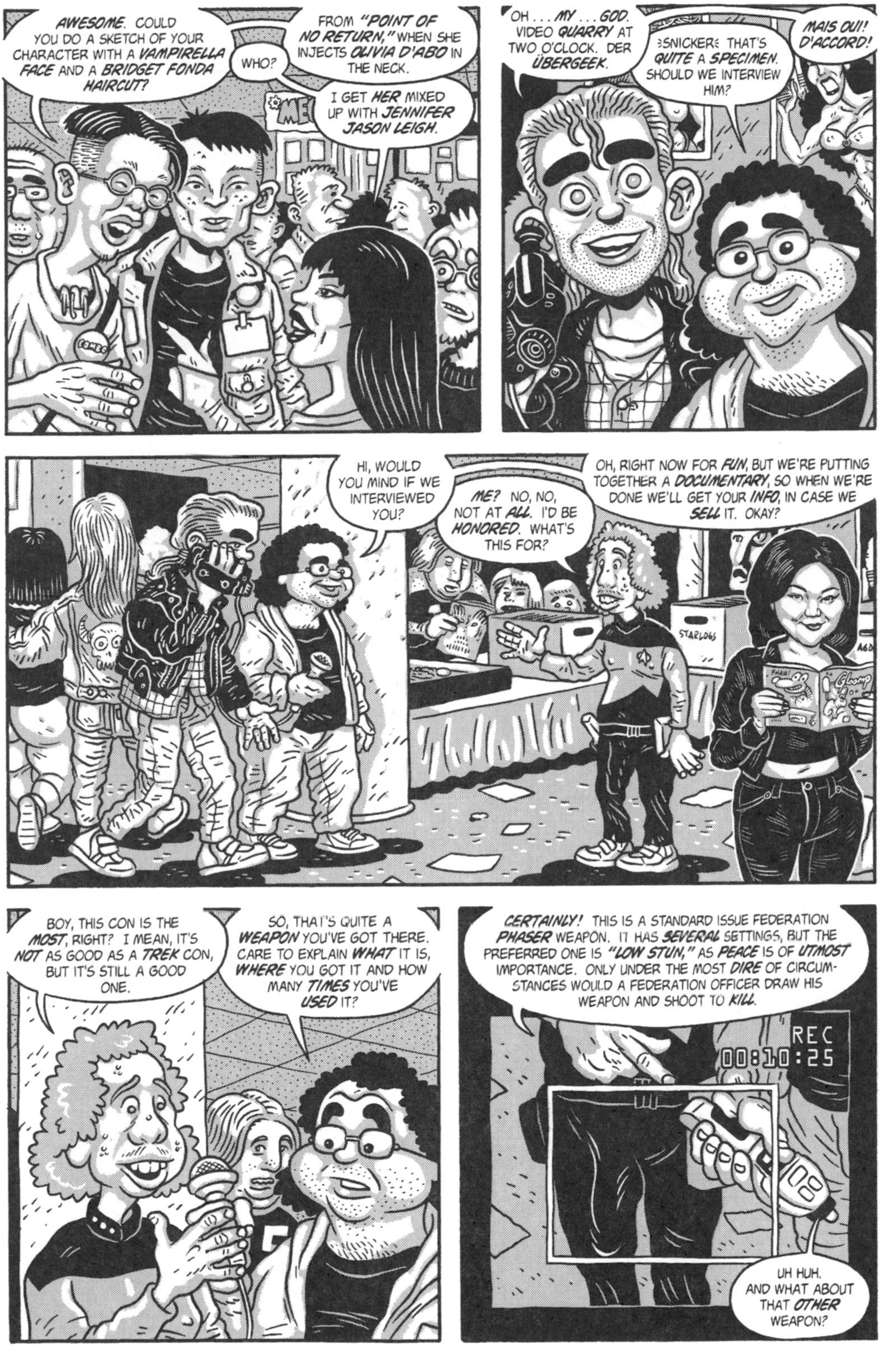
AWESOME. COULD YOU DO A SKETCH OF YOUR CHARACTER WITH A VAMPIRELLA FACE AND A BRIDGET FONDA HAIRCUT?
WHO?
FROM "POINT OF NO RETURN," WHEN SHE INJECTS OLIVIA D'ABO IN THE NECK.
I GET HER MIXED UP WITH JENNIFER JASON LEIGH.
OH . . . MY . . . GOD. VIDEO QUARRY AT TWO O'CLOCK. DER ÜBERGEEK.
SNICKER THAT'S QUITE A SPECIMEN. SHOULD WE INTERVIEW HIM?
MAIS OUI! D'ACCORD!
HI, WOULD YOU MIND IF WE INTERVIEWED YOU?
ME? NO, NO, NOT AT ALL. I'D BE HONORED. WHAT'S THIS FOR?
OH, RIGHT NOW FOR FUN, BUT WE'RE PUTTING TOGETHER A DOCUMENTARY, SO WHEN WE'RE DONE WE'LL GET YOUR INFO, IN CASE WE SELL IT. OKAY?
STARLOGS
BOY, THIS CON IS THE MOST, RIGHT? I MEAN, IT'S NOT AS GOOD AS A TREK CON, BUT IT'S STILL A GOOD ONE.
SO, THAT'S QUITE A WEAPON YOU'VE GOT THERE. CARE TO EXPLAIN WHAT IT IS, WHERE YOU GOT IT AND HOW MANY TIMES YOU'VE USED IT?
CERTAINLY! THIS IS A STANDARD ISSUE FEDERATION PHASER WEAPON. IT HAS SEVERAL SETTINGS, BUT THE PREFERRED ONE IS "LOW STUN," AS PEACE IS OF UTMOST IMPORTANCE. ONLY UNDER THE MOST DIRE OF CIRCUMSTANCES WOULD A FEDERATION OFFICER DRAW HIS WEAPON AND SHOOT TO KILL.
REC
00:10:25
UH HUH. AND WHAT ABOUT THAT OTHER WEAPON?

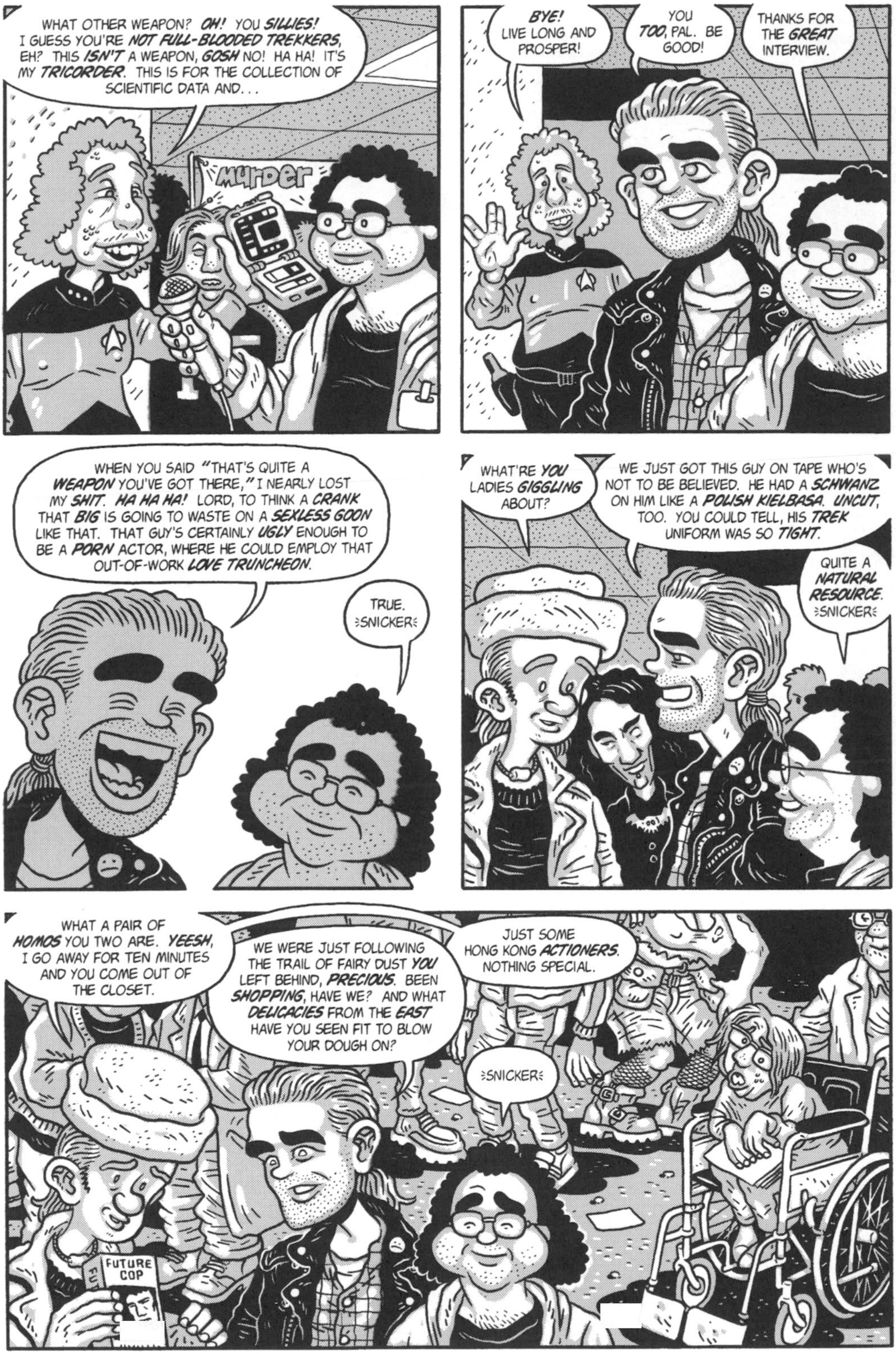
WHAT OTHER WEAPON? *OH!* YOU *SILLIES!* I GUESS YOU'RE *NOT FULL-BLOODED TREKKERS*, EH? THIS *ISN'T* A WEAPON, *GOSH* NO! HA HA! IT'S MY *TRICORDER*. THIS IS FOR THE COLLECTION OF SCIENTIFIC DATA AND...
murder
*BYE!* LIVE LONG AND PROSPER!
YOU *TOO*, PAL. BE GOOD!
THANKS FOR THE *GREAT* INTERVIEW.
WHEN YOU SAID *"THAT'S QUITE A WEAPON* YOU'VE GOT THERE," I NEARLY LOST MY *SHIT*. *HA HA HA!* LORD, TO THINK A *CRANK* THAT *BIG* IS GOING TO WASTE ON A *SEXLESS GOON* LIKE THAT. THAT GUY'S CERTAINLY *UGLY* ENOUGH TO BE A *PORN* ACTOR, WHERE HE COULD EMPLOY THAT OUT-OF-WORK *LOVE TRUNCHEON*.
TRUE. ≷SNICKER≷
WHAT'RE *YOU* LADIES *GIGGLING* ABOUT?
WE JUST GOT THIS GUY ON TAPE WHO'S NOT TO BE BELIEVED. HE HAD A *SCHWANZ* ON HIM LIKE A *POLISH KIELBASA*. *UNCUT*, TOO. YOU COULD TELL, HIS *TREK* UNIFORM WAS SO *TIGHT*.
QUITE A *NATURAL RESOURCE*. ≷SNICKER≷
WHAT A PAIR OF *HOMOS* YOU TWO ARE. *YEESH*, I GO AWAY FOR TEN MINUTES AND YOU COME OUT OF THE CLOSET.
WE WERE JUST FOLLOWING THE TRAIL OF FAIRY DUST *YOU* LEFT BEHIND, *PRECIOUS*. BEEN *SHOPPING*, HAVE WE? AND WHAT *DELICACIES* FROM THE *EAST* HAVE YOU SEEN FIT TO BLOW YOUR DOUGH ON?
JUST SOME HONG KONG *ACTIONERS*. NOTHING SPECIAL.
≷SNICKER≷
FUTURE COP

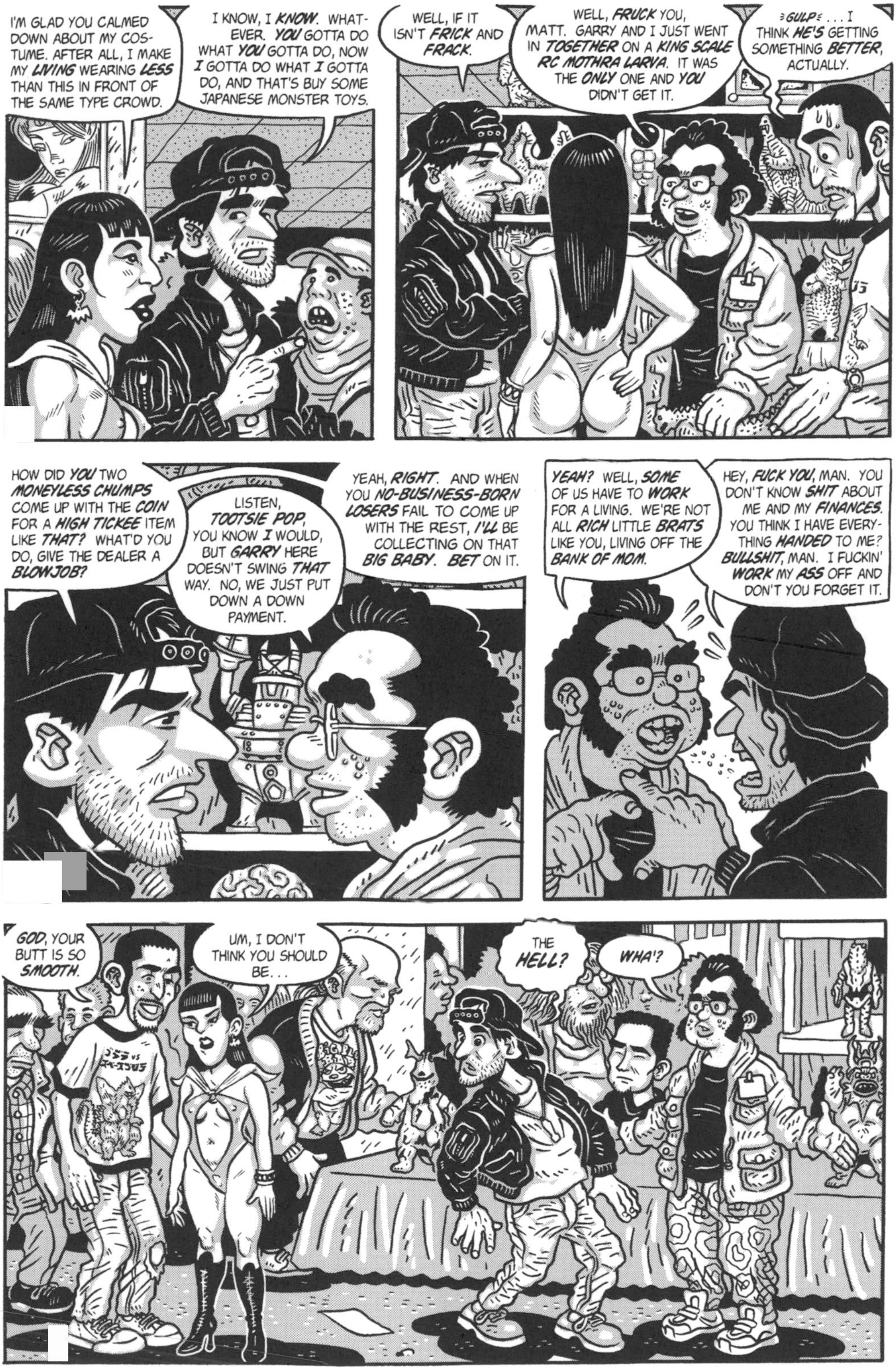
I'M GLAD YOU CALMED DOWN ABOUT MY COS-TUME. AFTER ALL, I MAKE MY LIVING WEARING LESS THAN THIS IN FRONT OF THE SAME TYPE CROWD.
I KNOW, I KNOW. WHAT-EVER. YOU GOTTA DO WHAT YOU GOTTA DO, NOW I GOTTA DO WHAT I GOTTA DO, AND THAT'S BUY SOME JAPANESE MONSTER TOYS.
WELL, IF IT ISN'T FRICK AND FRACK.
WELL, FRUCK YOU, MATT. GARRY AND I JUST WENT IN TOGETHER ON A KING SCALE RC MOTHRA LARVA. IT WAS THE ONLY ONE AND YOU DIDN'T GET IT.
GULP ... I THINK HE'S GETTING SOMETHING BETTER, ACTUALLY.
HOW DID YOU TWO MONEYLESS CHUMPS COME UP WITH THE COIN FOR A HIGH TICKEE ITEM LIKE THAT? WHAT'D YOU DO, GIVE THE DEALER A BLOWJOB?
LISTEN, TOOTSIE POP, YOU KNOW I WOULD, BUT GARRY HERE DOESN'T SWING THAT WAY. NO, WE JUST PUT DOWN A DOWN PAYMENT.
YEAH, RIGHT. AND WHEN YOU NO-BUSINESS-BORN LOSERS FAIL TO COME UP WITH THE REST, I'LL BE COLLECTING ON THAT BIG BABY. BET ON IT.
YEAH? WELL, SOME OF US HAVE TO WORK FOR A LIVING. WE'RE NOT ALL RICH LITTLE BRATS LIKE YOU, LIVING OFF THE BANK OF MOM.
HEY, FUCK YOU, MAN. YOU DON'T KNOW SHIT ABOUT ME AND MY FINANCES. YOU THINK I HAVE EVERY-THING HANDED TO ME? BULLSHIT, MAN. I FUCKIN' WORK MY ASS OFF AND DON'T YOU FORGET IT.
GOD, YOUR BUTT IS SO SMOOTH.
UM, I DON'T THINK YOU SHOULD BE...
THE HELL?
WHA'?

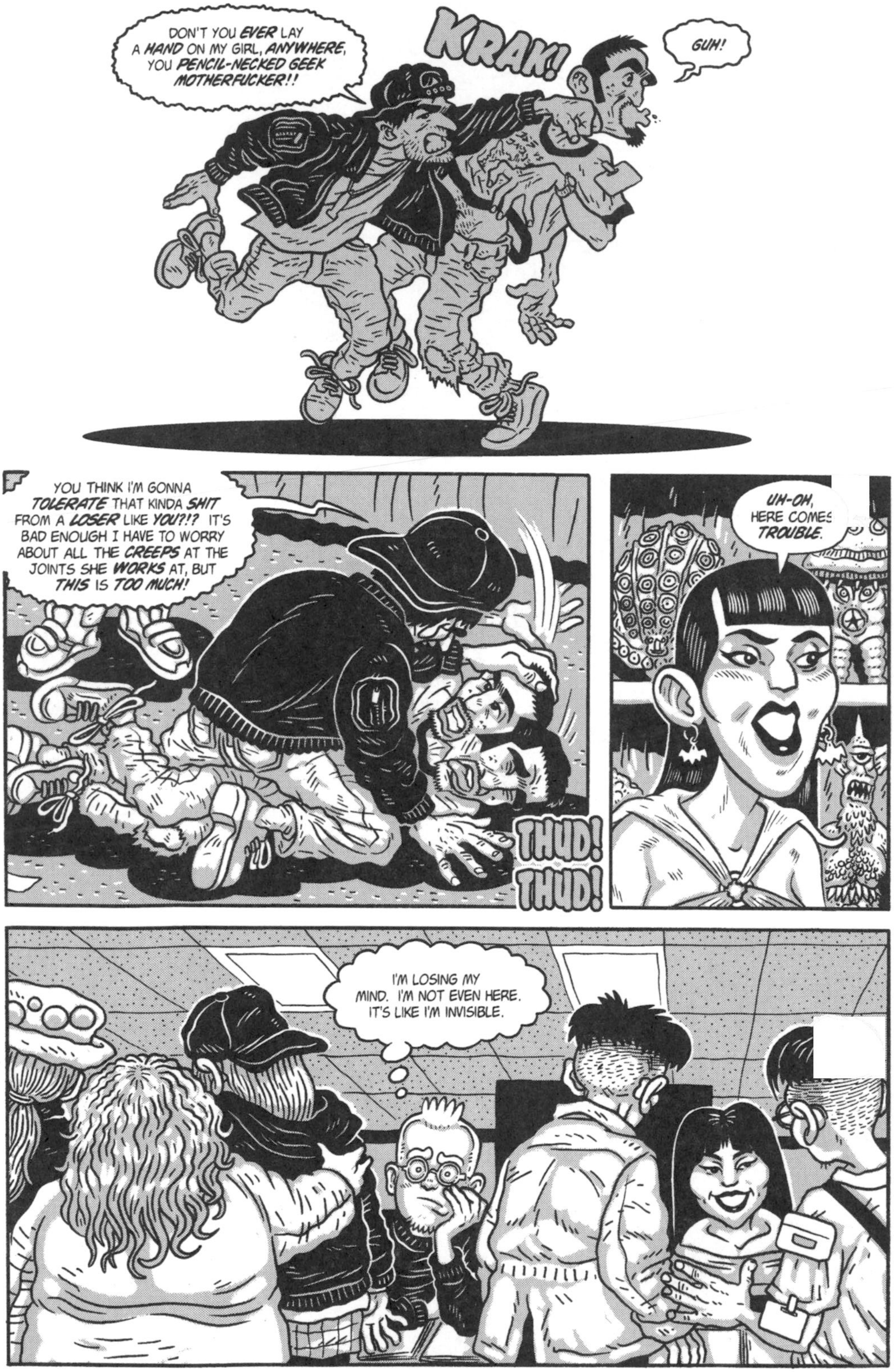
DON'T YOU EVER LAY A HAND ON MY GIRL, ANYWHERE, YOU PENCIL-NECKED GEEK MOTHERFUCKER!!
KRAK!
GUH!
YOU THINK I'M GONNA TOLERATE THAT KINDA SHIT FROM A LOSER LIKE YOU?!? IT'S BAD ENOUGH I HAVE TO WORRY ABOUT ALL THE CREEPS AT THE JOINTS SHE WORKS AT, BUT THIS IS TOO MUCH!
THUD! THUD!
UH-OH, HERE COMES TROUBLE.
I'M LOSING MY MIND. I'M NOT EVEN HERE. IT'S LIKE I'M INVISIBLE.

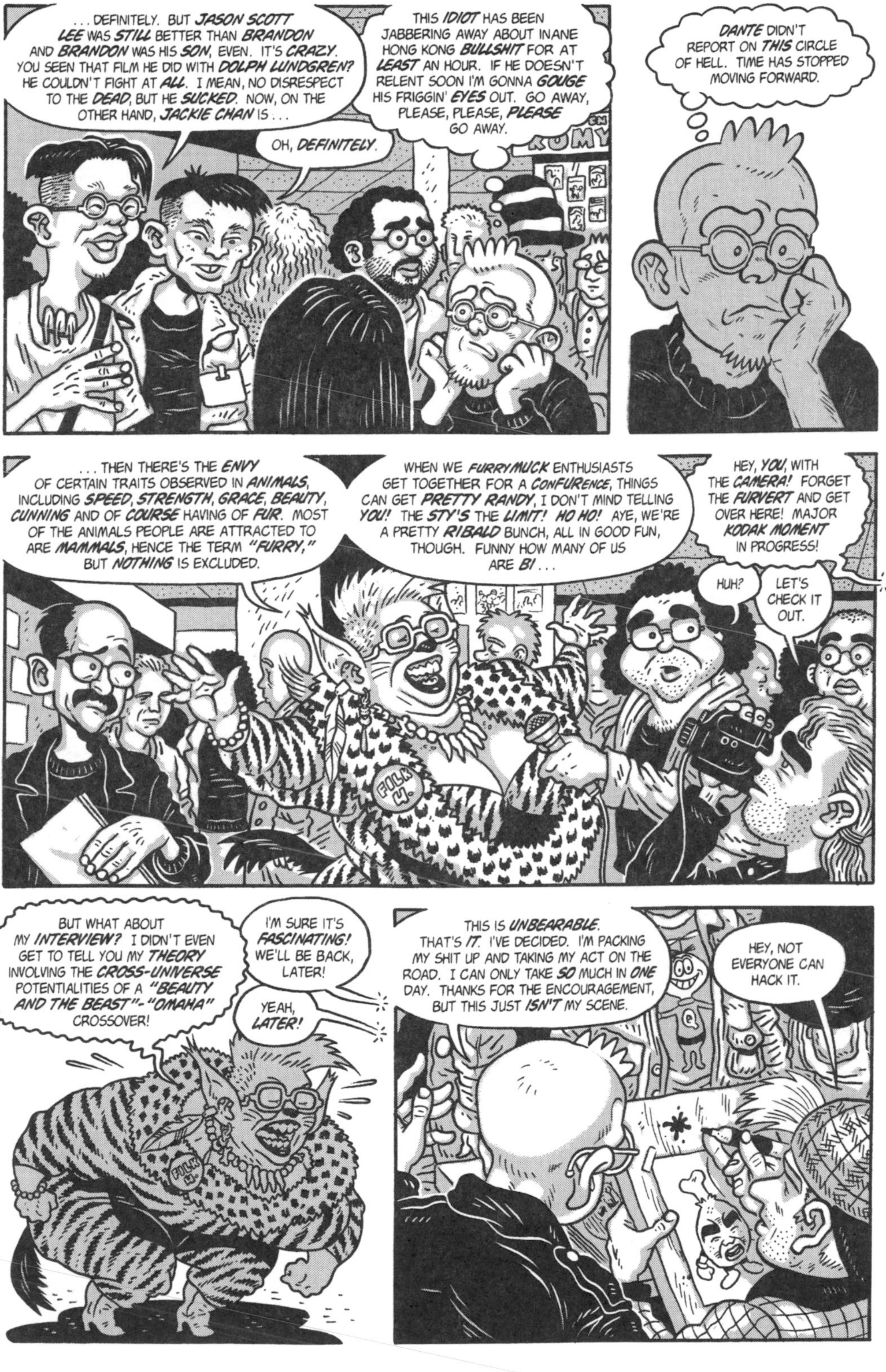
. . . DEFINITELY. BUT JASON SCOTT LEE WAS STILL BETTER THAN BRANDON AND BRANDON WAS HIS SON, EVEN. IT'S CRAZY. YOU SEEN THAT FILM HE DID WITH DOLPH LUNDGREN? HE COULDN'T FIGHT AT ALL. I MEAN, NO DISRESPECT TO THE DEAD, BUT HE SUCKED. NOW, ON THE OTHER HAND, JACKIE CHAN IS . . .
OH, DEFINITELY.
THIS IDIOT HAS BEEN JABBERING AWAY ABOUT INANE HONG KONG BULLSHIT FOR AT LEAST AN HOUR. IF HE DOESN'T RELENT SOON I'M GONNA GOUGE HIS FRIGGIN' EYES OUT. GO AWAY, PLEASE, PLEASE, PLEASE GO AWAY.
DANTE DIDN'T REPORT ON THIS CIRCLE OF HELL. TIME HAS STOPPED MOVING FORWARD.
. . . THEN THERE'S THE ENVY OF CERTAIN TRAITS OBSERVED IN ANIMALS, INCLUDING SPEED, STRENGTH, GRACE, BEAUTY, CUNNING AND OF COURSE HAVING OF FUR. MOST OF THE ANIMALS PEOPLE ARE ATTRACTED TO ARE MAMMALS, HENCE THE TERM "FURRY," BUT NOTHING IS EXCLUDED.
WHEN WE FURRYMUCK ENTHUSIASTS GET TOGETHER FOR A CONFURENCE, THINGS CAN GET PRETTY RANDY, I DON'T MIND TELLING YOU! THE STY'S THE LIMIT! HO HO! AYE, WE'RE A PRETTY RIBALD BUNCH, ALL IN GOOD FUN, THOUGH. FUNNY HOW MANY OF US ARE BI . . .
HEY, YOU, WITH THE CAMERA! FORGET THE FURVERT AND GET OVER HERE! MAJOR KODAK MOMENT IN PROGRESS!
HUH?
LET'S CHECK IT OUT.
FILK 4.
BUT WHAT ABOUT MY INTERVIEW? I DIDN'T EVEN GET TO TELL YOU MY THEORY INVOLVING THE CROSS-UNIVERSE POTENTIALITIES OF A "BEAUTY AND THE BEAST"-"OMAHA" CROSSOVER!
I'M SURE IT'S FASCINATING! WE'LL BE BACK, LATER!
YEAH, LATER!
THIS IS UNBEARABLE. THAT'S IT. I'VE DECIDED. I'M PACKING MY SHIT UP AND TAKING MY ACT ON THE ROAD. I CAN ONLY TAKE SO MUCH IN ONE DAY. THANKS FOR THE ENCOURAGEMENT, BUT THIS JUST ISN'T MY SCENE.
HEY, NOT EVERYONE CAN HACK IT.

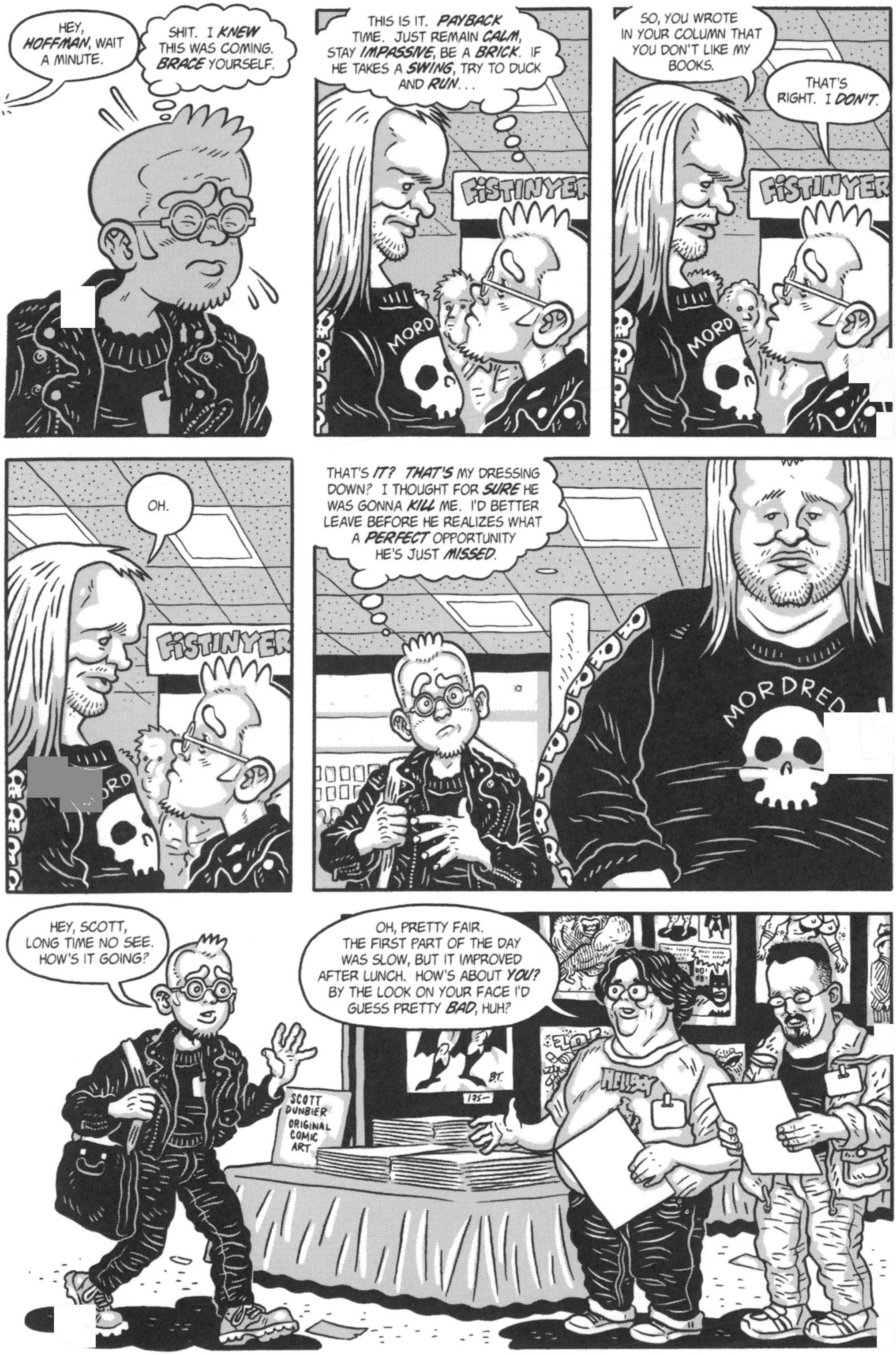
HEY, HOFFMAN, WAIT A MINUTE.
SHIT. I KNEW THIS WAS COMING. BRACE YOURSELF.
THIS IS IT. PAYBACK TIME. JUST REMAIN CALM, STAY IMPASSIVE, BE A BRICK. IF HE TAKES A SWING, TRY TO DUCK AND RUN...
FISTINYER
MORD
SO, YOU WROTE IN YOUR COLUMN THAT YOU DON'T LIKE MY BOOKS.
THAT'S RIGHT. I DON'T.
FISTINYER
MORD
OH.
FISTINYER
THAT'S IT? THAT'S MY DRESSING DOWN? I THOUGHT FOR SURE HE WAS GONNA KILL ME. I'D BETTER LEAVE BEFORE HE REALIZES WHAT A PERFECT OPPORTUNITY HE'S JUST MISSED.
MORDRED
HEY, SCOTT, LONG TIME NO SEE. HOW'S IT GOING?
OH, PRETTY FAIR. THE FIRST PART OF THE DAY WAS SLOW, BUT IT IMPROVED AFTER LUNCH. HOW'S ABOUT YOU? BY THE LOOK ON YOUR FACE I'D GUESS PRETTY BAD, HUH?
SCOTT DUNBIER ORIGINAL COMIC ART
B.T.
175—

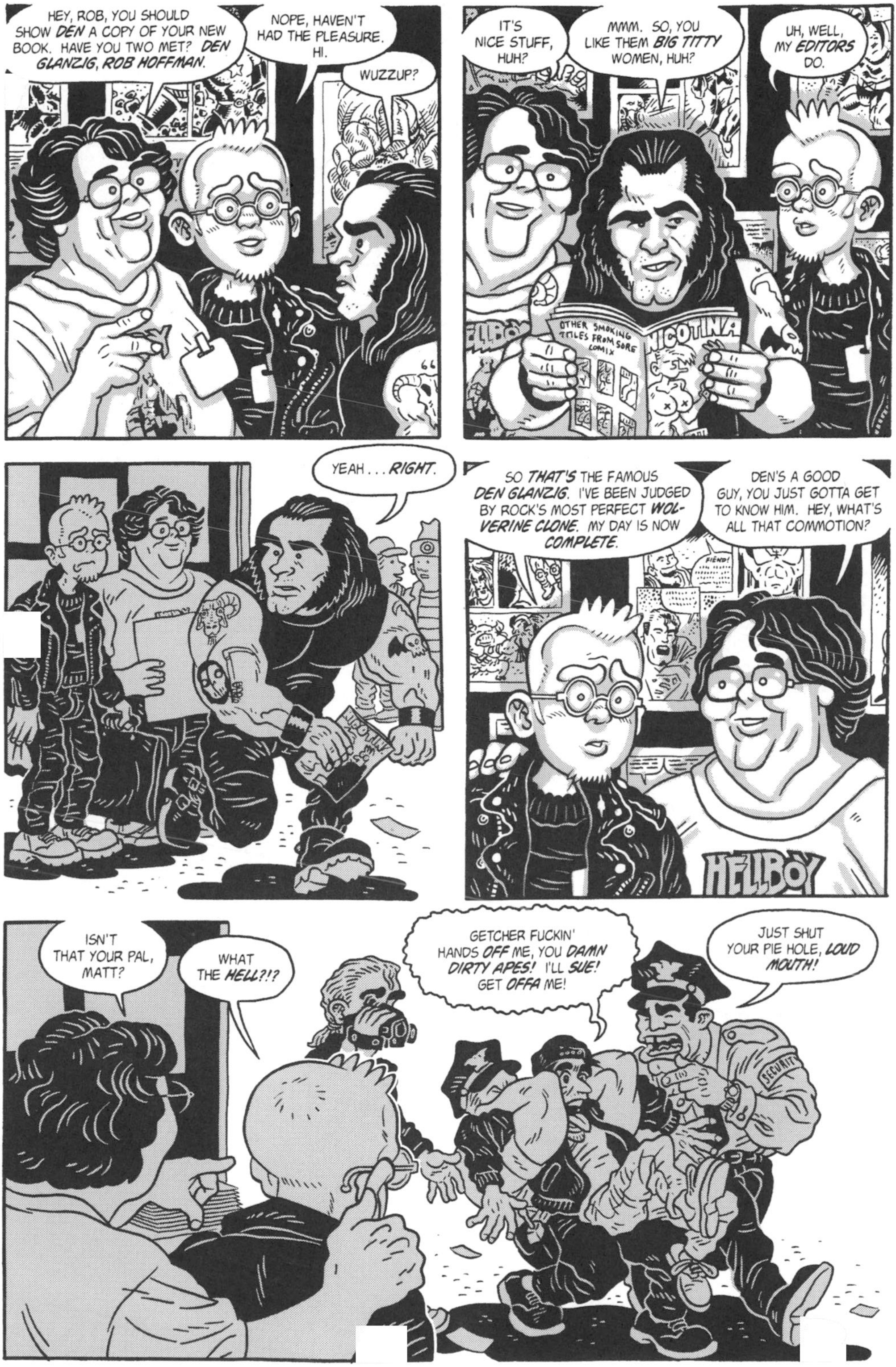
HEY, ROB, YOU SHOULD SHOW DEN A COPY OF YOUR NEW BOOK. HAVE YOU TWO MET? DEN GLANZIG, ROB HOFFMAN.
NOPE, HAVEN'T HAD THE PLEASURE. HI.
WUZZUP?
IT'S NICE STUFF, HUH?
MMM. SO, YOU LIKE THEM BIG TITTY WOMEN, HUH?
UH, WELL, MY EDITORS DO.
OTHER SMOKING TITLES FROM SORE COMIX
NICOTINA
HELLBOY
YEAH . . . RIGHT.
SO THAT'S THE FAMOUS DEN GLANZIG. I'VE BEEN JUDGED BY ROCK'S MOST PERFECT WOLVERINE CLONE. MY DAY IS NOW COMPLETE.
DEN'S A GOOD GUY, YOU JUST GOTTA GET TO KNOW HIM. HEY, WHAT'S ALL THAT COMMOTION?
HELLBOY
ISN'T THAT YOUR PAL, MATT?
WHAT THE HELL?!?
GETCHER FUCKIN' HANDS OFF ME, YOU DAMN DIRTY APES! I'LL SUE! GET OFFA ME!
JUST SHUT YOUR PIE HOLE, LOUD MOUTH!
SECURITY

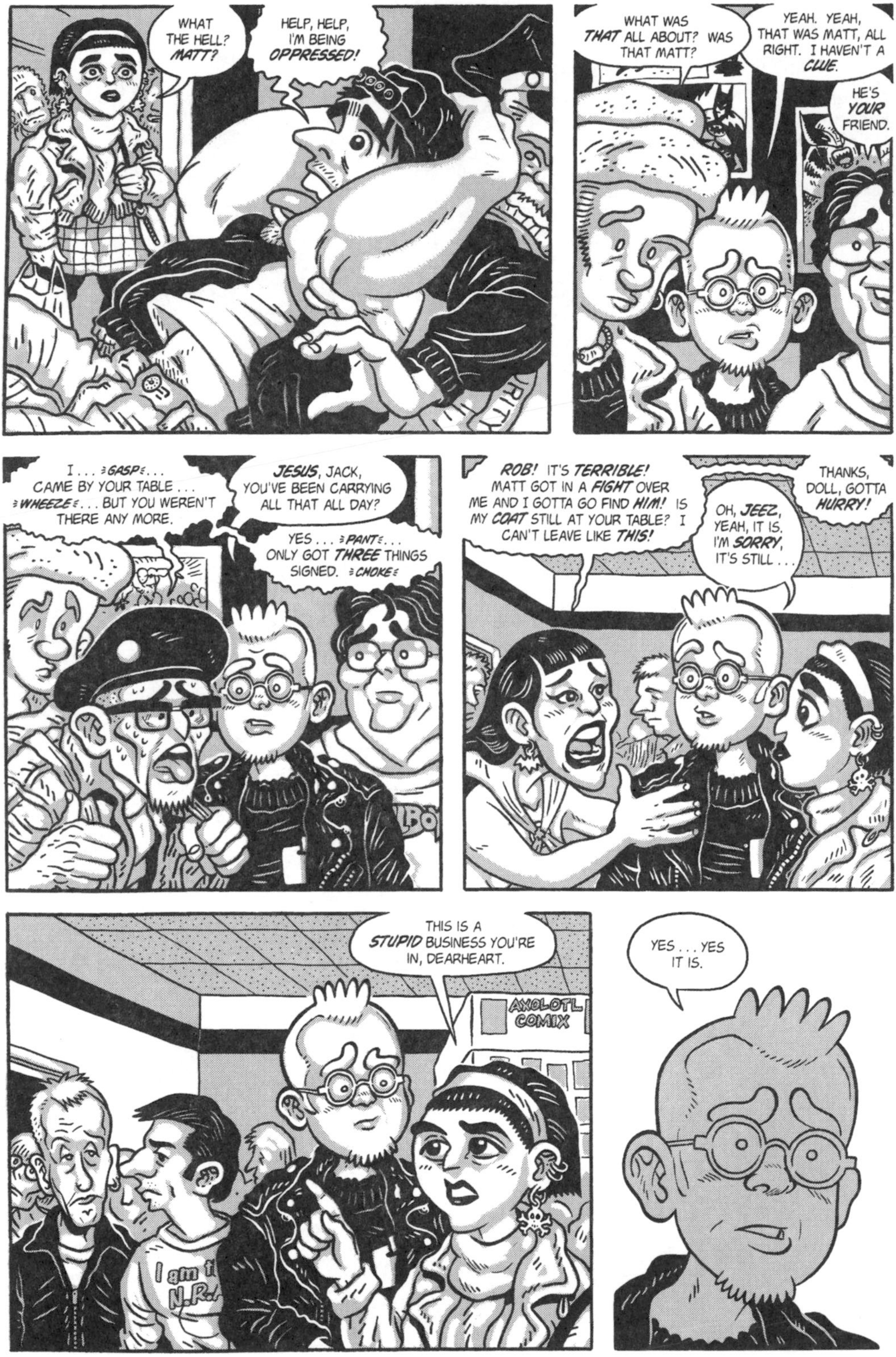
WHAT THE HELL? MATT?
HELP, HELP, I'M BEING OPPRESSED!
WHAT WAS THAT ALL ABOUT? WAS THAT MATT?
YEAH. YEAH, THAT WAS MATT, ALL RIGHT. I HAVEN'T A CLUE.
HE'S YOUR FRIEND.
I . . . GASP . . . CAME BY YOUR TABLE . . . WHEEZE . . . BUT YOU WEREN'T THERE ANY MORE.
JESUS, JACK, YOU'VE BEEN CARRYING ALL THAT ALL DAY?
YES . . . PANT . . . ONLY GOT THREE THINGS SIGNED. CHOKE
ROB! IT'S TERRIBLE! MATT GOT IN A FIGHT OVER ME AND I GOTTA GO FIND HIM! IS MY COAT STILL AT YOUR TABLE? I CAN'T LEAVE LIKE THIS!
OH, JEEZ, YEAH, IT IS. I'M SORRY, IT'S STILL . . .
THANKS, DOLL, GOTTA HURRY!
THIS IS A STUPID BUSINESS YOU'RE IN, DEARHEART.
AXOLOTL COMIX
YES . . . YES IT IS.

# CHAPTER FIVE
# BRUNCH ENGAGEMENT

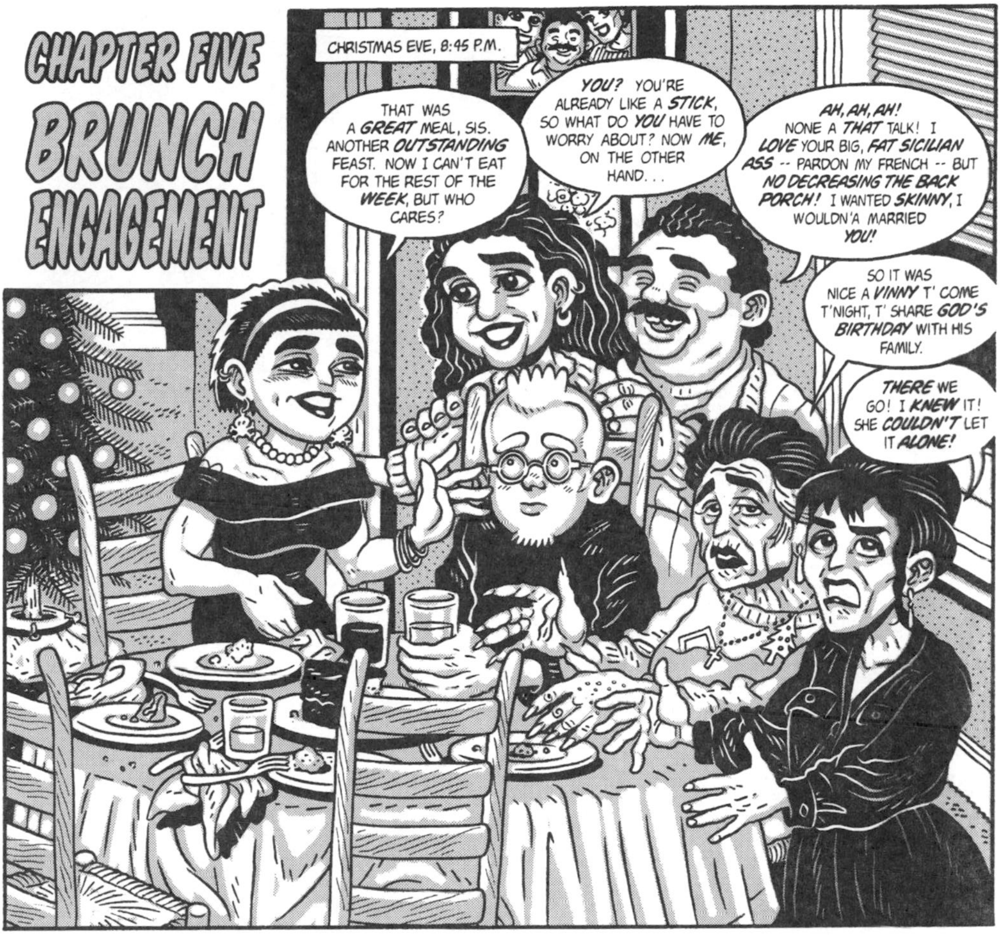
CHRISTMAS EVE, 8:45 P.M.
THAT WAS A GREAT MEAL, SIS. ANOTHER OUTSTANDING FEAST. NOW I CAN'T EAT FOR THE REST OF THE WEEK, BUT WHO CARES?
YOU? YOU'RE ALREADY LIKE A STICK, SO WHAT DO YOU HAVE TO WORRY ABOUT? NOW ME, ON THE OTHER HAND. . .
AH, AH, AH! NONE A THAT TALK! I LOVE YOUR BIG, FAT SICILIAN ASS -- PARDON MY FRENCH -- BUT NO DECREASING THE BACK PORCH! I WANTED SKINNY, I WOULDN'A MARRIED YOU!
SO IT WAS NICE A VINNY T' COME T'NIGHT, T' SHARE GOD'S BIRTHDAY WITH HIS FAMILY.
THERE WE GO! I KNEW IT! SHE COULDN'T LET IT ALONE!

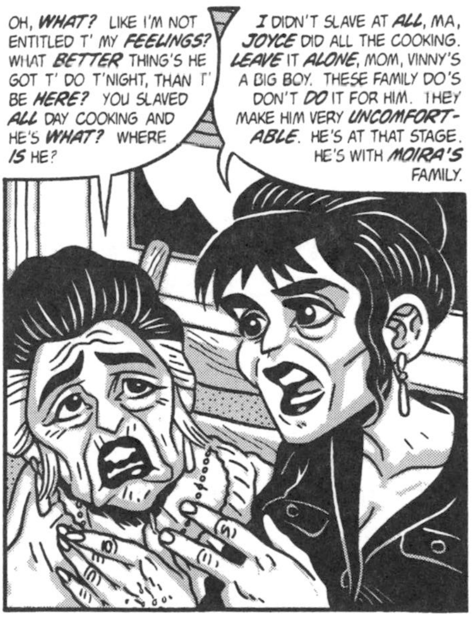
OH, WHAT? LIKE I'M NOT ENTITLED T' MY FEELINGS? WHAT BETTER THING'S HE GOT T' DO T'NIGHT, THAN T' BE HERE? YOU SLAVED ALL DAY COOKING AND HE'S WHAT? WHERE IS HE?
I DIDN'T SLAVE AT ALL, MA, JOYCE DID ALL THE COOKING. LEAVE IT ALONE, MOM, VINNY'S A BIG BOY. THESE FAMILY DO'S DON'T DO IT FOR HIM. THEY MAKE HIM VERY UNCOMFORTABLE. HE'S AT THAT STAGE. HE'S WITH MOIRA'S FAMILY.

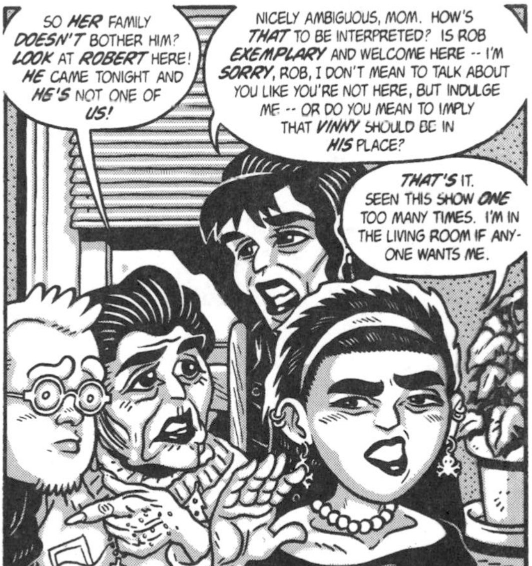
SO HER FAMILY DOESN'T BOTHER HIM? LOOK AT ROBERT HERE! HE CAME TONIGHT AND HE'S NOT ONE OF US!
NICELY AMBIGUOUS, MOM. HOW'S THAT TO BE INTERPRETED? IS ROB EXEMPLARY AND WELCOME HERE -- I'M SORRY, ROB, I DON'T MEAN TO TALK ABOUT YOU LIKE YOU'RE NOT HERE, BUT INDULGE ME -- OR DO YOU MEAN TO IMPLY THAT VINNY SHOULD BE IN HIS PLACE?
THAT'S IT. SEEN THIS SHOW ONE TOO MANY TIMES. I'M IN THE LIVING ROOM IF ANYONE WANTS ME.

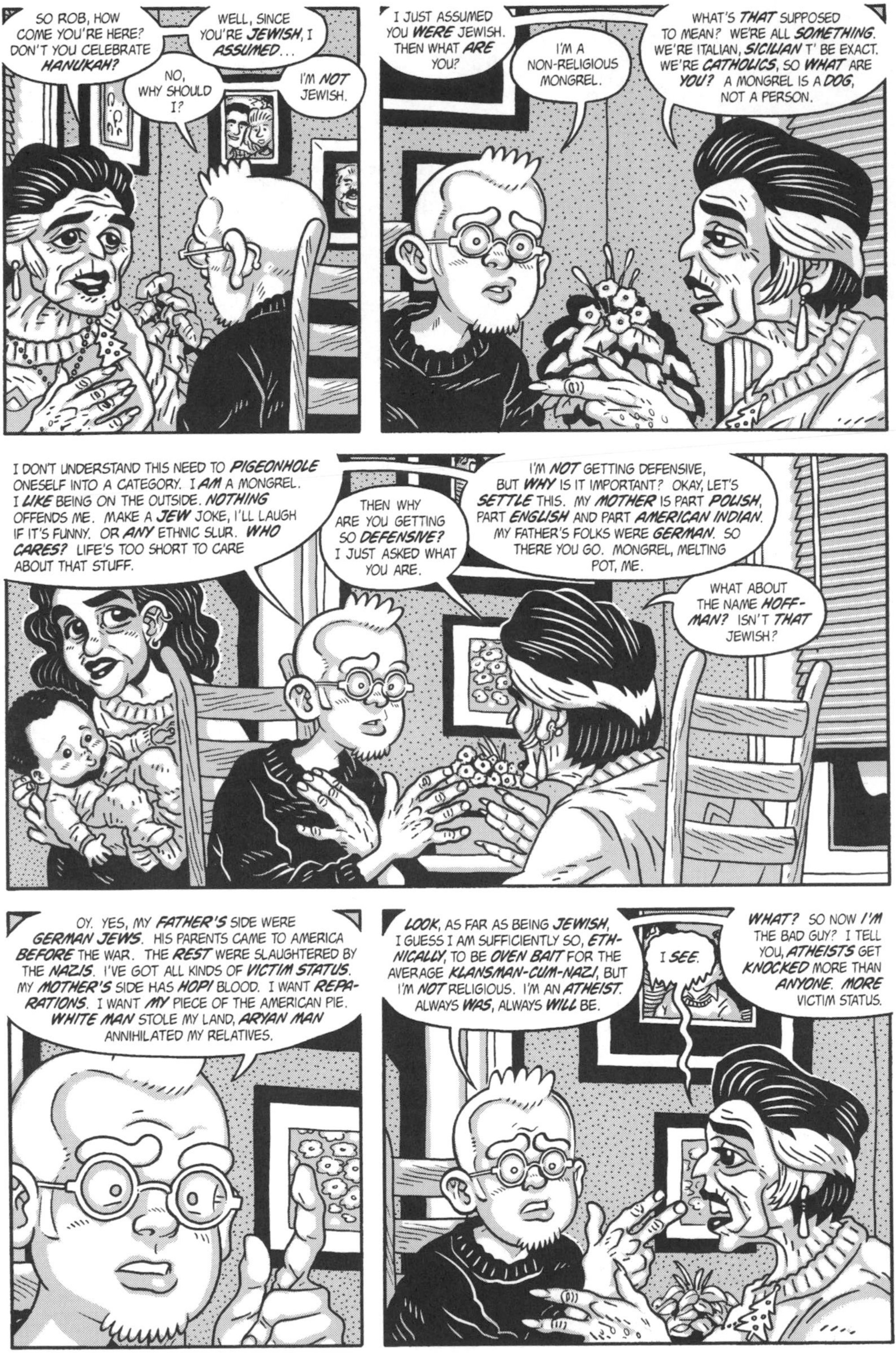
SO ROB, HOW COME YOU'RE HERE? DON'T YOU CELEBRATE HANUKAH?
NO, WHY SHOULD I?
WELL, SINCE YOU'RE JEWISH, I ASSUMED...
I'M NOT JEWISH.
I JUST ASSUMED YOU WERE JEWISH. THEN WHAT ARE YOU?
I'M A NON-RELIGIOUS MONGREL.
WHAT'S THAT SUPPOSED TO MEAN? WE'RE ALL SOMETHING. WE'RE ITALIAN, SICILIAN T' BE EXACT. WE'RE CATHOLICS, SO WHAT ARE YOU? A MONGREL IS A DOG, NOT A PERSON.
I DON'T UNDERSTAND THIS NEED TO PIGEONHOLE ONESELF INTO A CATEGORY. I AM A MONGREL. I LIKE BEING ON THE OUTSIDE. NOTHING OFFENDS ME. MAKE A JEW JOKE, I'LL LAUGH IF IT'S FUNNY. OR ANY ETHNIC SLUR. WHO CARES? LIFE'S TOO SHORT TO CARE ABOUT THAT STUFF.
THEN WHY ARE YOU GETTING SO DEFENSIVE? I JUST ASKED WHAT YOU ARE.
I'M NOT GETTING DEFENSIVE, BUT WHY IS IT IMPORTANT? OKAY, LET'S SETTLE THIS. MY MOTHER IS PART POLISH, PART ENGLISH AND PART AMERICAN INDIAN. MY FATHER'S FOLKS WERE GERMAN. SO THERE YOU GO. MONGREL, MELTING POT, ME.
WHAT ABOUT THE NAME HOFF-MAN? ISN'T THAT JEWISH?
OY. YES, MY FATHER'S SIDE WERE GERMAN JEWS. HIS PARENTS CAME TO AMERICA BEFORE THE WAR. THE REST WERE SLAUGHTERED BY THE NAZIS. I'VE GOT ALL KINDS OF VICTIM STATUS. MY MOTHER'S SIDE HAS HOPI BLOOD. I WANT REPA-RATIONS. I WANT MY PIECE OF THE AMERICAN PIE. WHITE MAN STOLE MY LAND, ARYAN MAN ANNIHILATED MY RELATIVES.
LOOK, AS FAR AS BEING JEWISH, I GUESS I AM SUFFICIENTLY SO, ETH-NICALLY, TO BE OVEN BAIT FOR THE AVERAGE KLANSMAN-CUM-NAZI, BUT I'M NOT RELIGIOUS. I'M AN ATHEIST. ALWAYS WAS, ALWAYS WILL BE.
I SEE.
WHAT? SO NOW I'M THE BAD GUY? I TELL YOU, ATHEISTS GET KNOCKED MORE THAN ANYONE. MORE VICTIM STATUS.

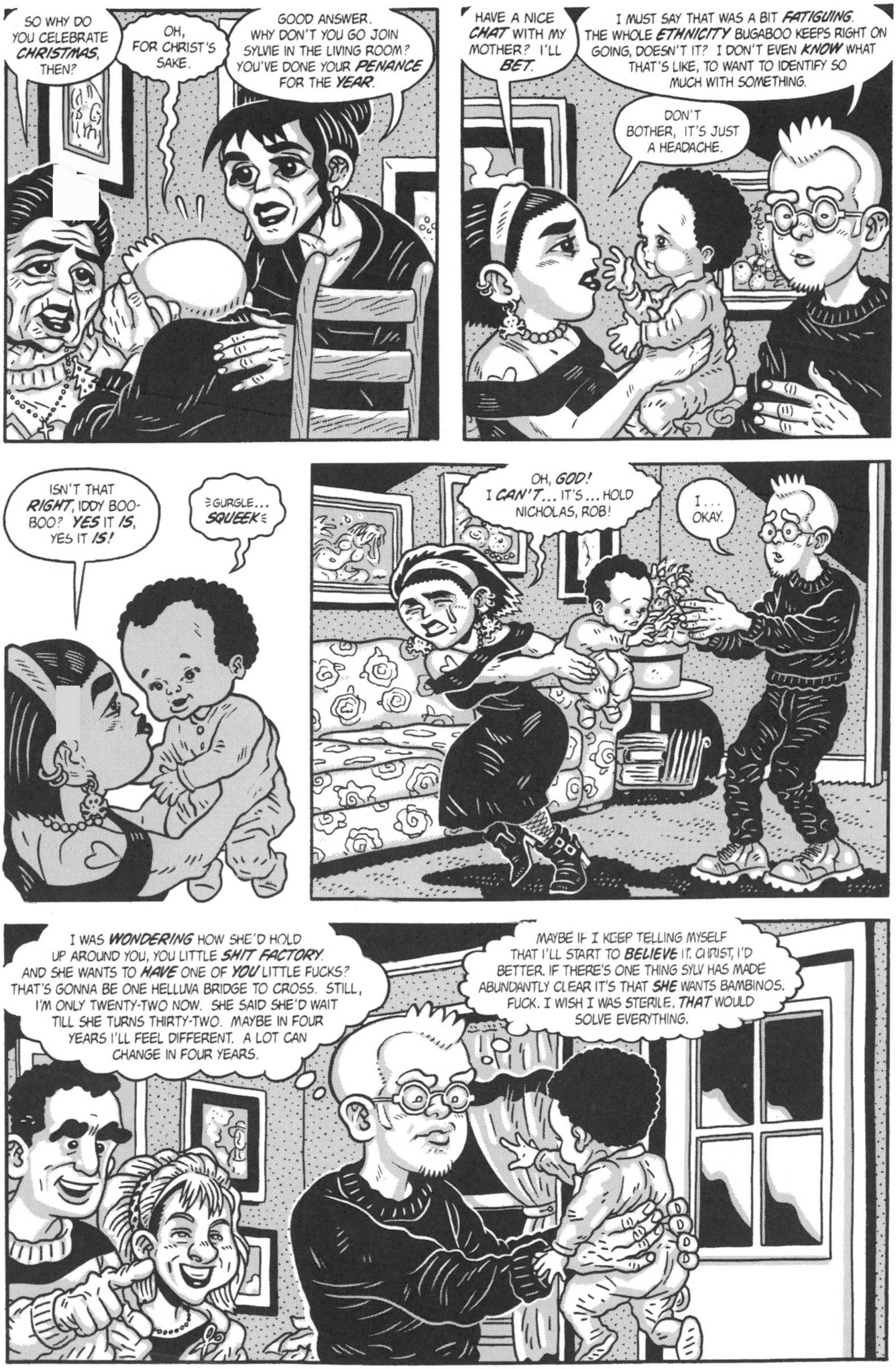
SO WHY DO YOU CELEBRATE CHRISTMAS, THEN?
OH, FOR CHRIST'S SAKE.
GOOD ANSWER. WHY DON'T YOU GO JOIN SYLVIE IN THE LIVING ROOM? YOU'VE DONE YOUR PENANCE FOR THE YEAR.
HAVE A NICE CHAT WITH MY MOTHER? I'LL BET.
I MUST SAY THAT WAS A BIT FATIGUING. THE WHOLE ETHNICITY BUGABOO KEEPS RIGHT ON GOING, DOESN'T IT? I DON'T EVEN KNOW WHAT THAT'S LIKE, TO WANT TO IDENTIFY SO MUCH WITH SOMETHING.
DON'T BOTHER, IT'S JUST A HEADACHE.
ISN'T THAT RIGHT, IDDY BOO-BOO? YES IT IS, YES IT IS!
GURGLE... SQUEEK
OH, GOD! I CAN'T... IT'S... HOLD NICHOLAS, ROB!
I... OKAY.
I WAS WONDERING HOW SHE'D HOLD UP AROUND YOU, YOU LITTLE SHIT FACTORY. AND SHE WANTS TO HAVE ONE OF YOU LITTLE FUCKS? THAT'S GONNA BE ONE HELLUVA BRIDGE TO CROSS. STILL, I'M ONLY TWENTY-TWO NOW. SHE SAID SHE'D WAIT TILL SHE TURNS THIRTY-TWO. MAYBE IN FOUR YEARS I'LL FEEL DIFFERENT. A LOT CAN CHANGE IN FOUR YEARS.
MAYBE IF I KEEP TELLING MYSELF THAT I'LL START TO BELIEVE IT. CHRIST, I'D BETTER. IF THERE'S ONE THING SYLV HAS MADE ABUNDANTLY CLEAR IT'S THAT SHE WANTS BAMBINOS. FUCK. I WISH I WAS STERILE. THAT WOULD SOLVE EVERYTHING.

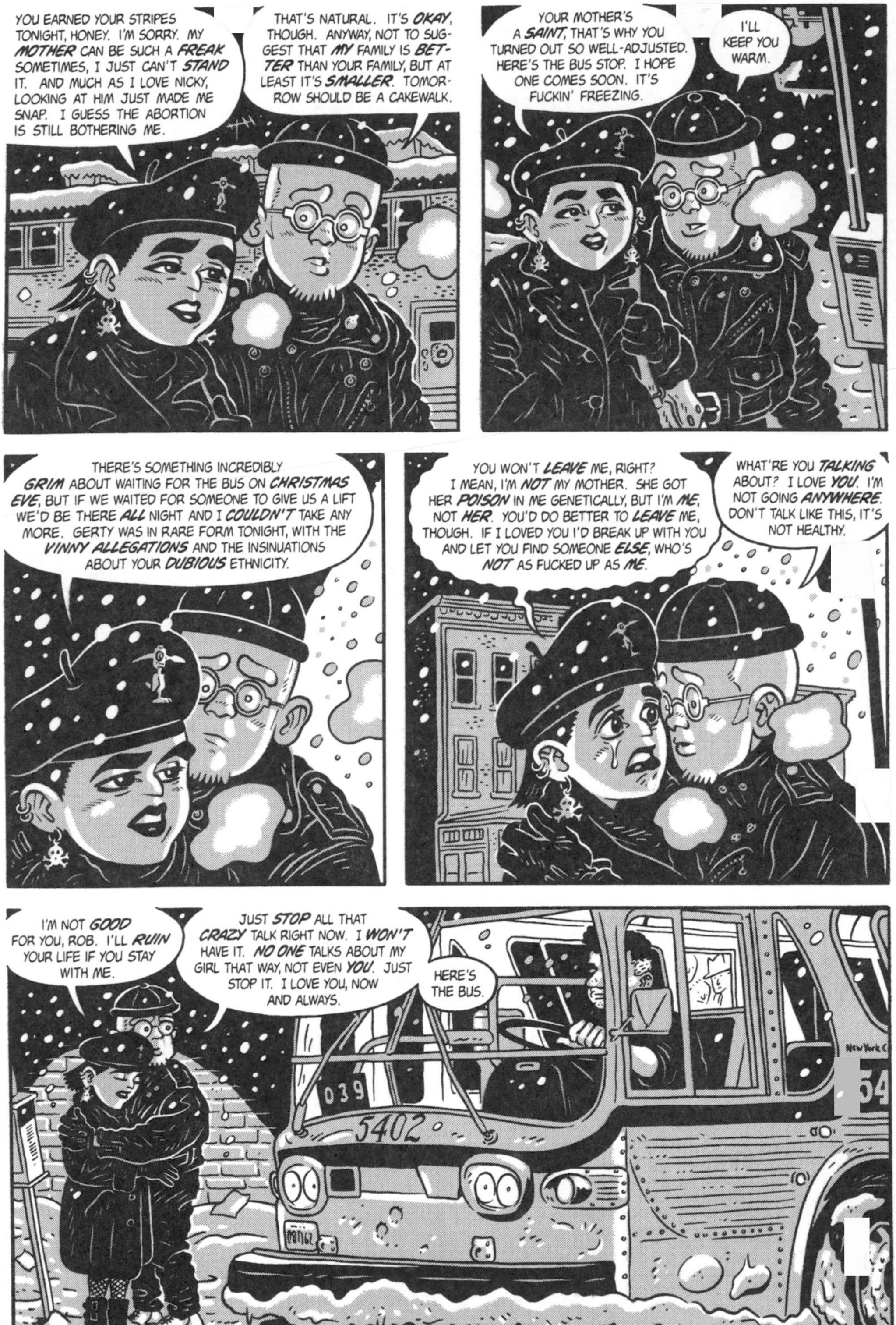
YOU EARNED YOUR STRIPES TONIGHT, HONEY. I'M SORRY. MY MOTHER CAN BE SUCH A FREAK SOMETIMES, I JUST CAN'T STAND IT. AND MUCH AS I LOVE NICKY, LOOKING AT HIM JUST MADE ME SNAP. I GUESS THE ABORTION IS STILL BOTHERING ME.
THAT'S NATURAL. IT'S OKAY, THOUGH. ANYWAY, NOT TO SUGGEST THAT MY FAMILY IS BETTER THAN YOUR FAMILY, BUT AT LEAST IT'S SMALLER. TOMORROW SHOULD BE A CAKEWALK.
YOUR MOTHER'S A SAINT, THAT'S WHY YOU TURNED OUT SO WELL-ADJUSTED. HERE'S THE BUS STOP. I HOPE ONE COMES SOON. IT'S FUCKIN' FREEZING.
I'LL KEEP YOU WARM.
THERE'S SOMETHING INCREDIBLY GRIM ABOUT WAITING FOR THE BUS ON CHRISTMAS EVE, BUT IF WE WAITED FOR SOMEONE TO GIVE US A LIFT WE'D BE THERE ALL NIGHT AND I COULDN'T TAKE ANY MORE. GERTY WAS IN RARE FORM TONIGHT, WITH THE VINNY ALLEGATIONS AND THE INSINUATIONS ABOUT YOUR DUBIOUS ETHNICITY.
YOU WON'T LEAVE ME, RIGHT? I MEAN, I'M NOT MY MOTHER. SHE GOT HER POISON IN ME GENETICALLY, BUT I'M ME, NOT HER. YOU'D DO BETTER TO LEAVE ME, THOUGH. IF I LOVED YOU I'D BREAK UP WITH YOU AND LET YOU FIND SOMEONE ELSE, WHO'S NOT AS FUCKED UP AS ME.
WHAT'RE YOU TALKING ABOUT? I LOVE YOU. I'M NOT GOING ANYWHERE. DON'T TALK LIKE THIS, IT'S NOT HEALTHY.
I'M NOT GOOD FOR YOU, ROB. I'LL RUIN YOUR LIFE IF YOU STAY WITH ME.
JUST STOP ALL THAT CRAZY TALK RIGHT NOW. I WON'T HAVE IT. NO ONE TALKS ABOUT MY GIRL THAT WAY, NOT EVEN YOU. JUST STOP IT. I LOVE YOU, NOW AND ALWAYS.
HERE'S THE BUS.
039
5402

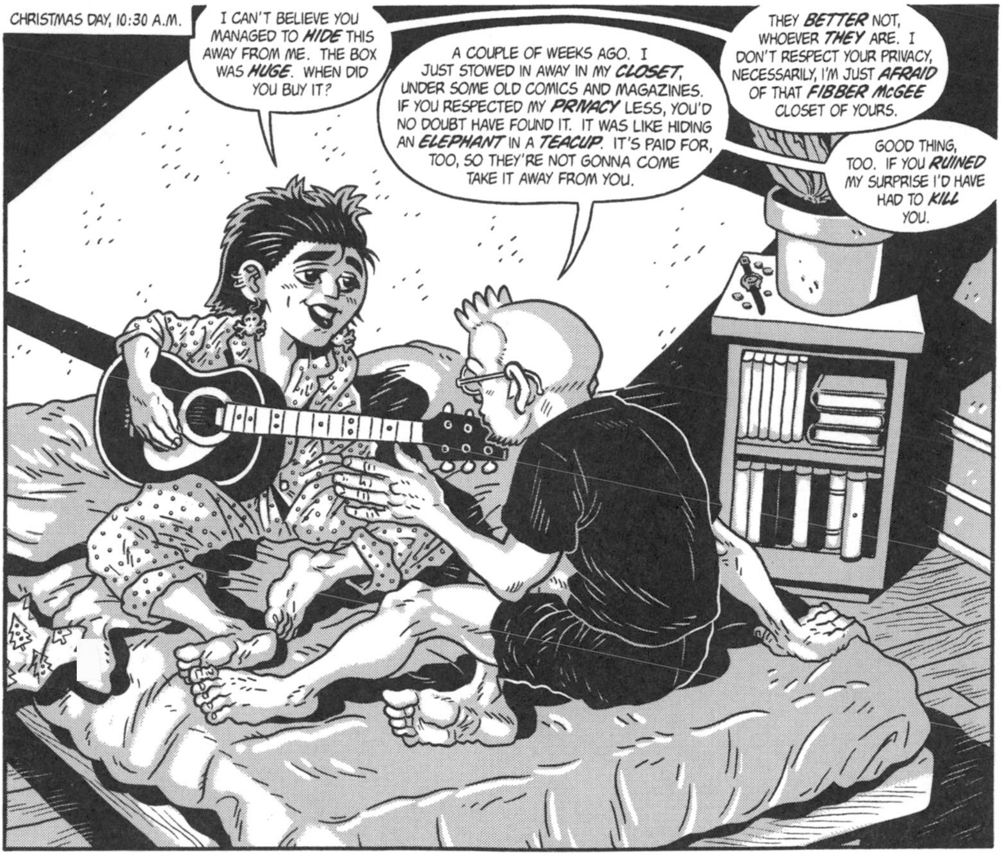
CHRISTMAS DAY, 10:30 A.M.
I CAN'T BELIEVE YOU MANAGED TO HIDE THIS AWAY FROM ME. THE BOX WAS HUGE. WHEN DID YOU BUY IT?
A COUPLE OF WEEKS AGO. I JUST STOWED IN AWAY IN MY CLOSET, UNDER SOME OLD COMICS AND MAGAZINES. IF YOU RESPECTED MY PRIVACY LESS, YOU'D NO DOUBT HAVE FOUND IT. IT WAS LIKE HIDING AN ELEPHANT IN A TEACUP. IT'S PAID FOR, TOO, SO THEY'RE NOT GONNA COME TAKE IT AWAY FROM YOU.
THEY BETTER NOT, WHOEVER THEY ARE. I DON'T RESPECT YOUR PRIVACY, NECESSARILY, I'M JUST AFRAID OF THAT FIBBER McGEE CLOSET OF YOURS.
GOOD THING, TOO. IF YOU RUINED MY SURPRISE I'D HAVE HAD TO KILL YOU.

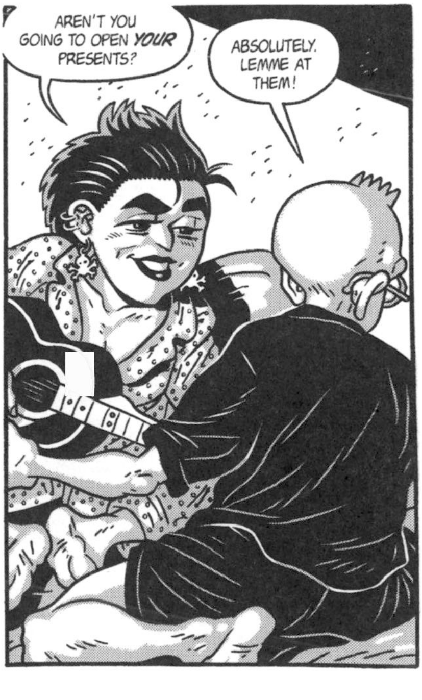
AREN'T YOU GOING TO OPEN YOUR PRESENTS?
ABSOLUTELY. LEMME AT THEM!

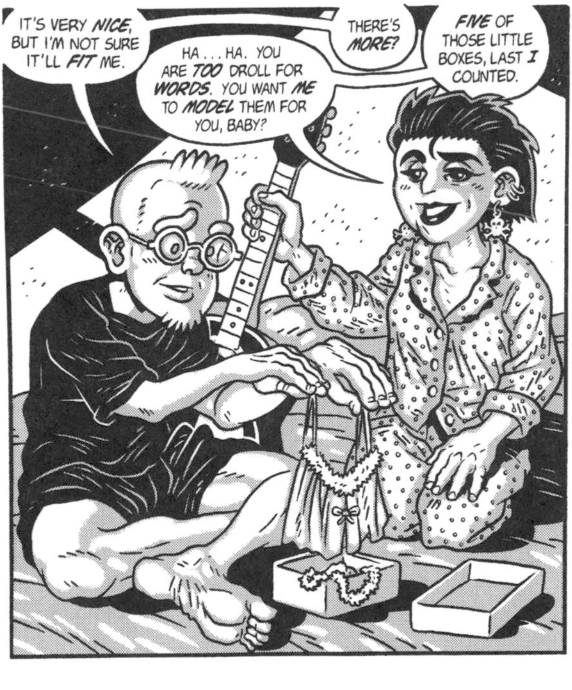
IT'S VERY NICE, BUT I'M NOT SURE IT'LL FIT ME.
HA... HA. YOU ARE TOO DROLL FOR WORDS. YOU WANT ME TO MODEL THEM FOR YOU, BABY?
THERE'S MORE?
FIVE OF THOSE LITTLE BOXES, LAST I COUNTED.

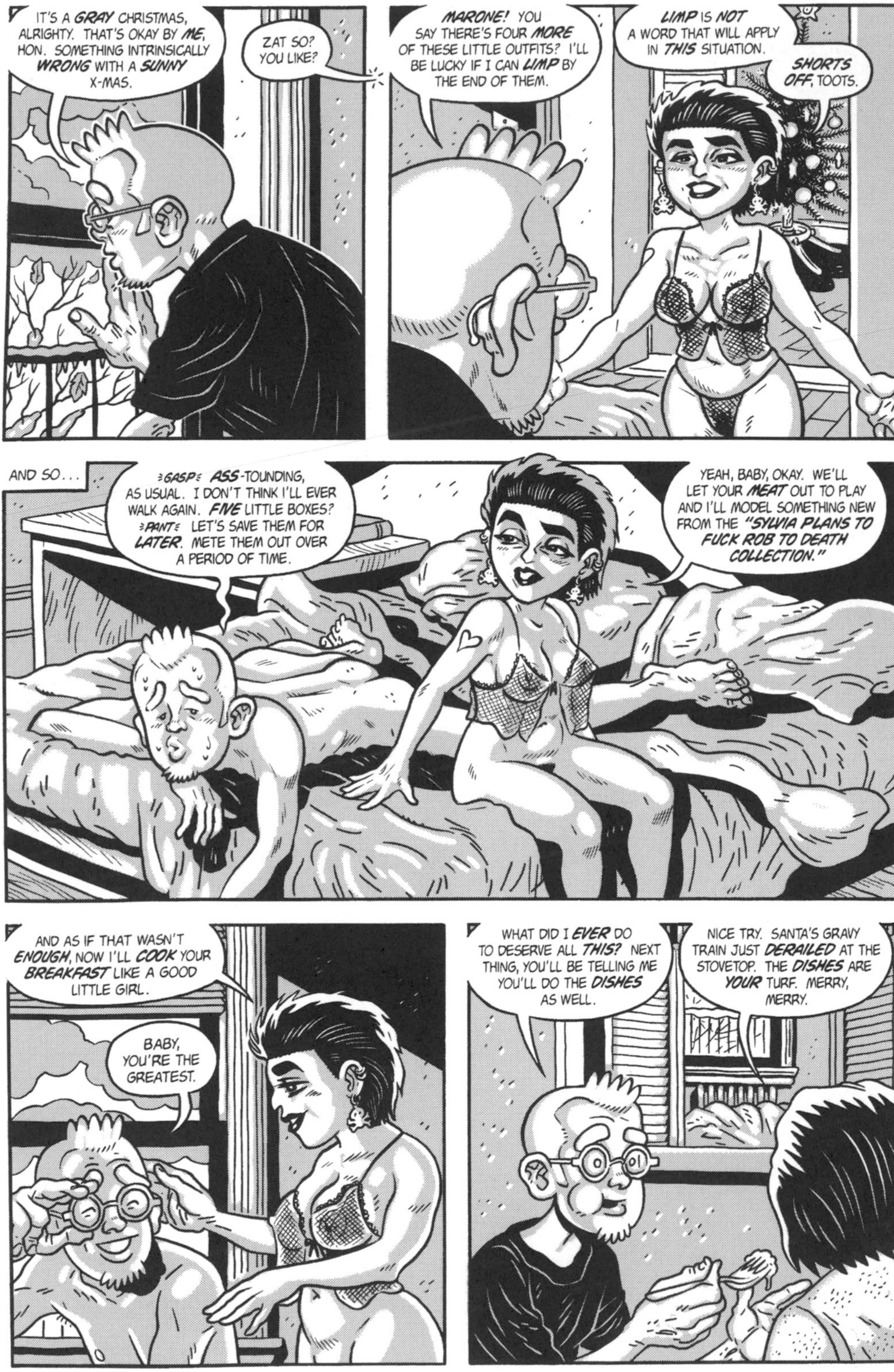
IT'S A GRAY CHRISTMAS, ALRIGHTY. THAT'S OKAY BY ME, HON. SOMETHING INTRINSICALLY WRONG WITH A SUNNY X-MAS.
ZAT SO? YOU LIKE?
MARONE! YOU SAY THERE'S FOUR MORE OF THESE LITTLE OUTFITS? I'LL BE LUCKY IF I CAN LIMP BY THE END OF THEM.
LIMP IS NOT A WORD THAT WILL APPLY IN THIS SITUATION.
SHORTS OFF, TOOTS.
AND SO...
GASP ASS-TOUNDING, AS USUAL. I DON'T THINK I'LL EVER WALK AGAIN. FIVE LITTLE BOXES? PANT LET'S SAVE THEM FOR LATER. METE THEM OUT OVER A PERIOD OF TIME.
YEAH, BABY, OKAY. WE'LL LET YOUR MEAT OUT TO PLAY AND I'LL MODEL SOMETHING NEW FROM THE "SYLVIA PLANS TO FUCK ROB TO DEATH COLLECTION."
AND AS IF THAT WASN'T ENOUGH, NOW I'LL COOK YOUR BREAKFAST LIKE A GOOD LITTLE GIRL.
BABY, YOU'RE THE GREATEST.
WHAT DID I EVER DO TO DESERVE ALL THIS? NEXT THING, YOU'LL BE TELLING ME YOU'LL DO THE DISHES AS WELL.
NICE TRY. SANTA'S GRAVY TRAIN JUST DERAILED AT THE STOVETOP. THE DISHES ARE YOUR TURF. MERRY, MERRY.

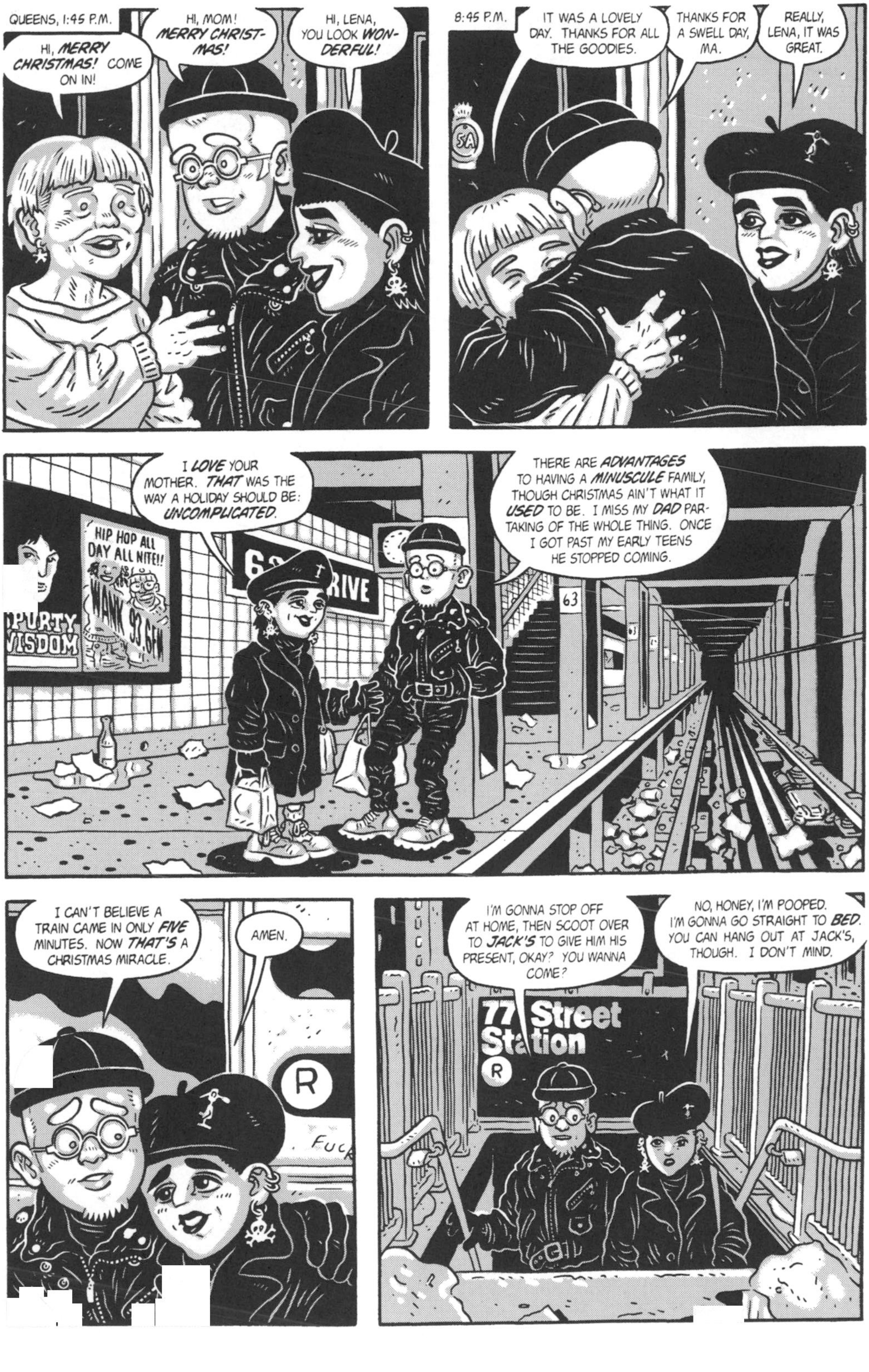
QUEENS, 1:45 P.M.
HI, *MERRY CHRISTMAS!* COME ON IN!
HI, MOM! *MERRY CHRISTMAS!*
HI, LENA, YOU LOOK *WONDERFUL!*
8:45 P.M.
IT WAS A LOVELY DAY. THANKS FOR ALL THE GOODIES.
THANKS FOR A SWELL DAY, MA.
REALLY, LENA, IT WAS GREAT.
I *LOVE* YOUR MOTHER. *THAT* WAS THE WAY A HOLIDAY SHOULD BE: *UNCOMPLICATED*.
HIP HOP ALL DAY ALL NITE!!
WANK 93.6FM
63
THERE ARE *ADVANTAGES* TO HAVING A *MINUSCULE* FAMILY, THOUGH CHRISTMAS AIN'T WHAT IT *USED* TO BE. I MISS MY *DAD* PARTAKING OF THE WHOLE THING. ONCE I GOT PAST MY EARLY TEENS HE STOPPED COMING.
I CAN'T BELIEVE A TRAIN CAME IN ONLY *FIVE* MINUTES. NOW *THAT'S* A CHRISTMAS MIRACLE.
AMEN.
R
I'M GONNA STOP OFF AT HOME, THEN SCOOT OVER TO *JACK'S* TO GIVE HIM HIS PRESENT, OKAY? YOU WANNA COME?
NO, HONEY, I'M POOPED. I'M GONNA GO STRAIGHT TO *BED*. YOU CAN HANG OUT AT JACK'S, THOUGH. I DON'T MIND.
77 Street Station
R

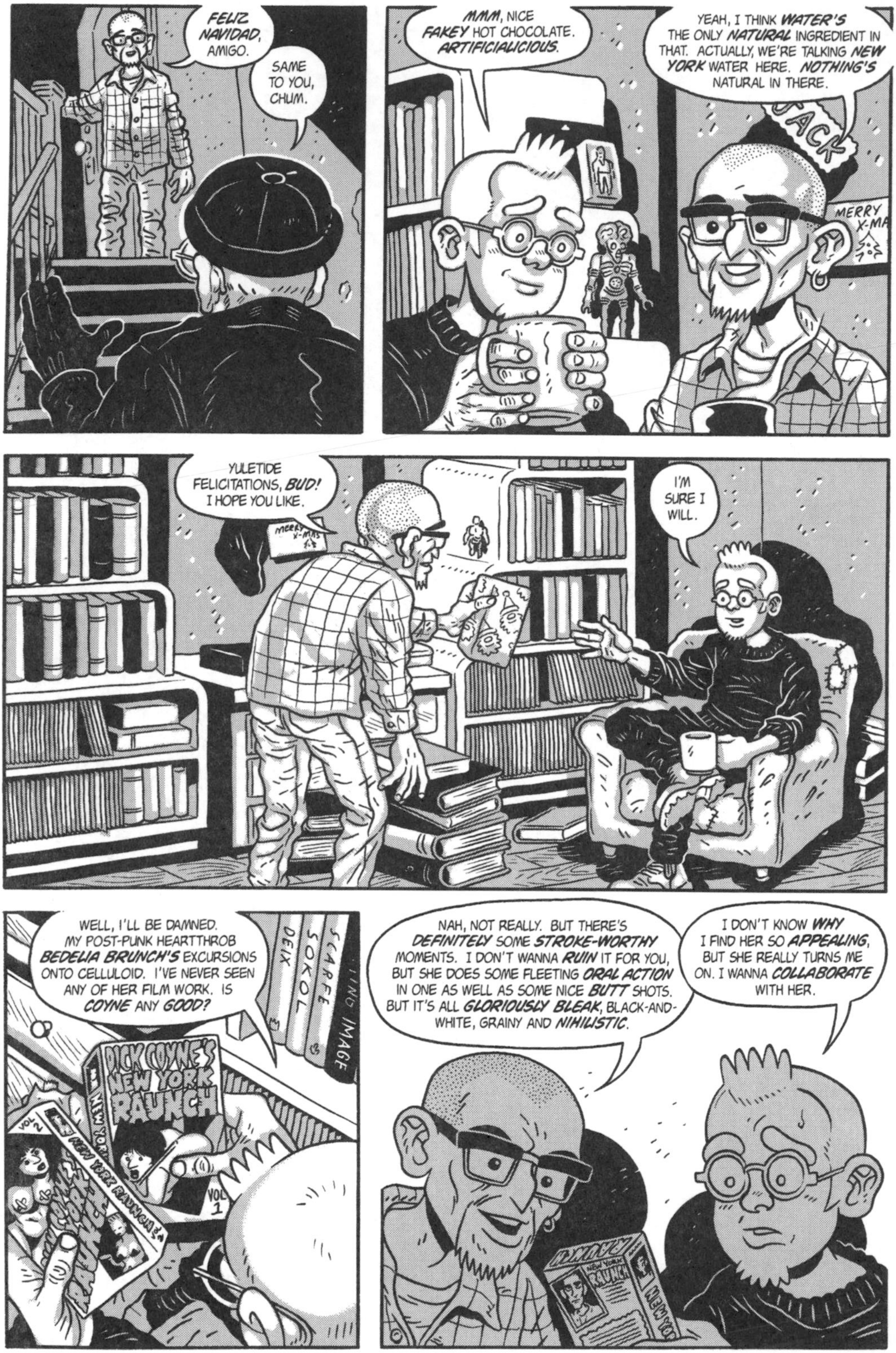
FELIZ NAVIDAD, AMIGO.
SAME TO YOU, CHUM.
MMM, NICE FAKEY HOT CHOCOLATE. ARTIFICIALICIOUS.
YEAH, I THINK WATER'S THE ONLY NATURAL INGREDIENT IN THAT. ACTUALLY, WE'RE TALKING NEW YORK WATER HERE. NOTHING'S NATURAL IN THERE.
YULETIDE FELICITATIONS, BUD! I HOPE YOU LIKE.
I'M SURE I WILL.
WELL, I'LL BE DAMNED. MY POST-PUNK HEARTTHROB BEDELIA BRUNCH'S EXCURSIONS ONTO CELLULOID. I'VE NEVER SEEN ANY OF HER FILM WORK. IS COYNE ANY GOOD?
DICK COYNE'S NEW YORK RAUNCH
NAH, NOT REALLY. BUT THERE'S DEFINITELY SOME STROKE-WORTHY MOMENTS. I DON'T WANNA RUIN IT FOR YOU, BUT SHE DOES SOME FLEETING ORAL ACTION IN ONE AS WELL AS SOME NICE BUTT SHOTS. BUT IT'S ALL GLORIOUSLY BLEAK, BLACK-AND-WHITE, GRAINY AND NIHILISTIC.
I DON'T KNOW WHY I FIND HER SO APPEALING, BUT SHE REALLY TURNS ME ON. I WANNA COLLABORATE WITH HER.

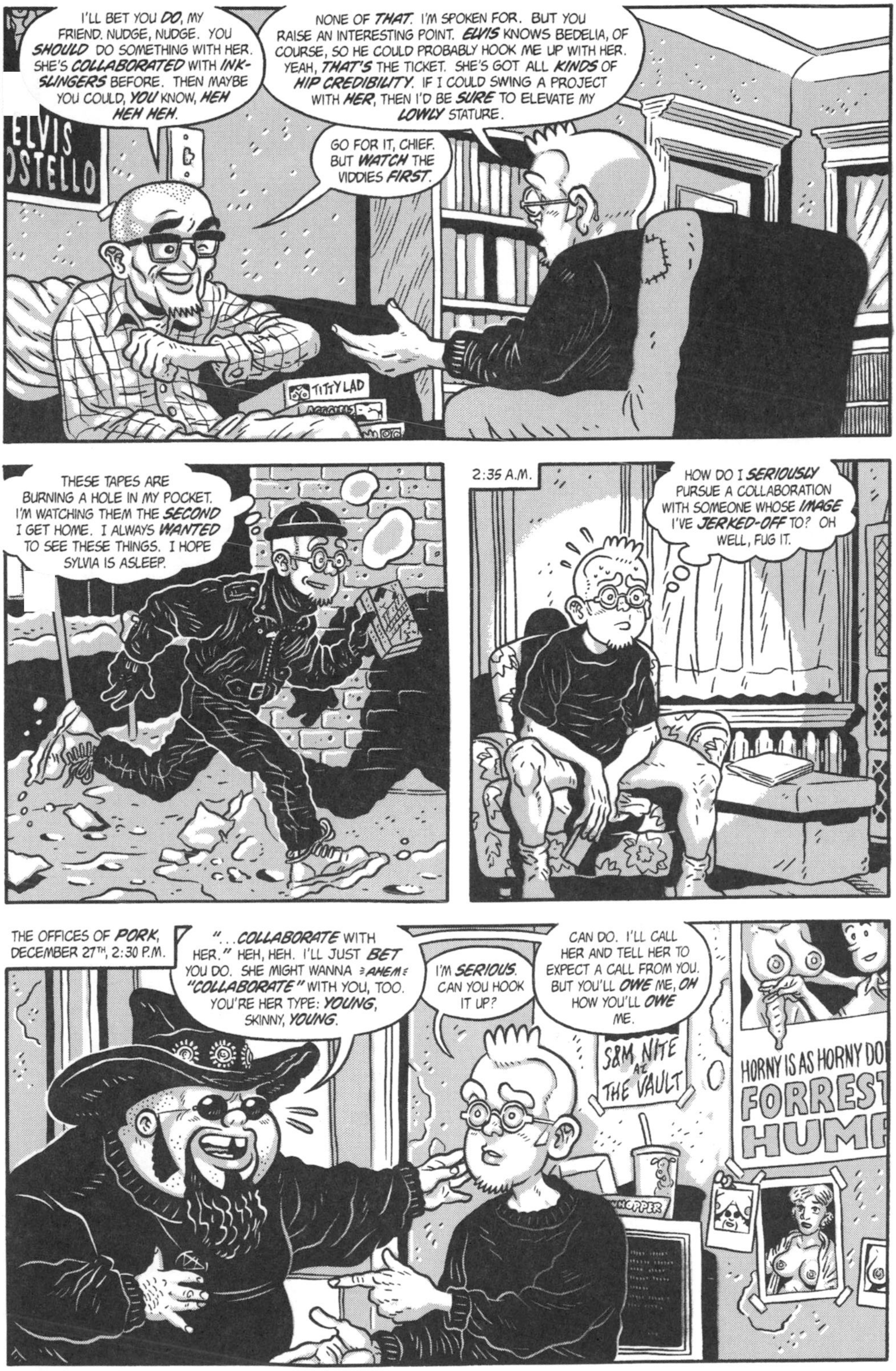
I'LL BET YOU DO, MY FRIEND. NUDGE, NUDGE. YOU SHOULD DO SOMETHING WITH HER. SHE'S COLLABORATED WITH INK-SLINGERS BEFORE. THEN MAYBE YOU COULD, YOU KNOW, HEH HEH HEH.
NONE OF THAT. I'M SPOKEN FOR. BUT YOU RAISE AN INTERESTING POINT. ELVIS KNOWS BEDELIA, OF COURSE, SO HE COULD PROBABLY HOOK ME UP WITH HER. YEAH, THAT'S THE TICKET. SHE'S GOT ALL KINDS OF HIP CREDIBILITY. IF I COULD SWING A PROJECT WITH HER, THEN I'D BE SURE TO ELEVATE MY LOWLY STATURE.
GO FOR IT, CHIEF. BUT WATCH THE VIDDIES FIRST.
ELVIS
OSTELLO
TITTY LAD
THESE TAPES ARE BURNING A HOLE IN MY POCKET. I'M WATCHING THEM THE SECOND I GET HOME. I ALWAYS WANTED TO SEE THESE THINGS. I HOPE SYLVIA IS ASLEEP.
2:35 A.M.
HOW DO I SERIOUSLY PURSUE A COLLABORATION WITH SOMEONE WHOSE IMAGE I'VE JERKED-OFF TO? OH WELL, FUG IT.
THE OFFICES OF PORK, DECEMBER 27TH, 2:30 P.M.
"...COLLABORATE WITH HER." HEH, HEH. I'LL JUST BET YOU DO. SHE MIGHT WANNA ≥AHEM≤ "COLLABORATE" WITH YOU, TOO. YOU'RE HER TYPE: YOUNG, SKINNY, YOUNG.
I'M SERIOUS. CAN YOU HOOK IT UP?
CAN DO. I'LL CALL HER AND TELL HER TO EXPECT A CALL FROM YOU. BUT YOU'LL OWE ME, OH HOW YOU'LL OWE ME.
S&M NITE AT THE VAULT
HORNY IS AS HORNY DO
FORREST HUMP
WHOPPER

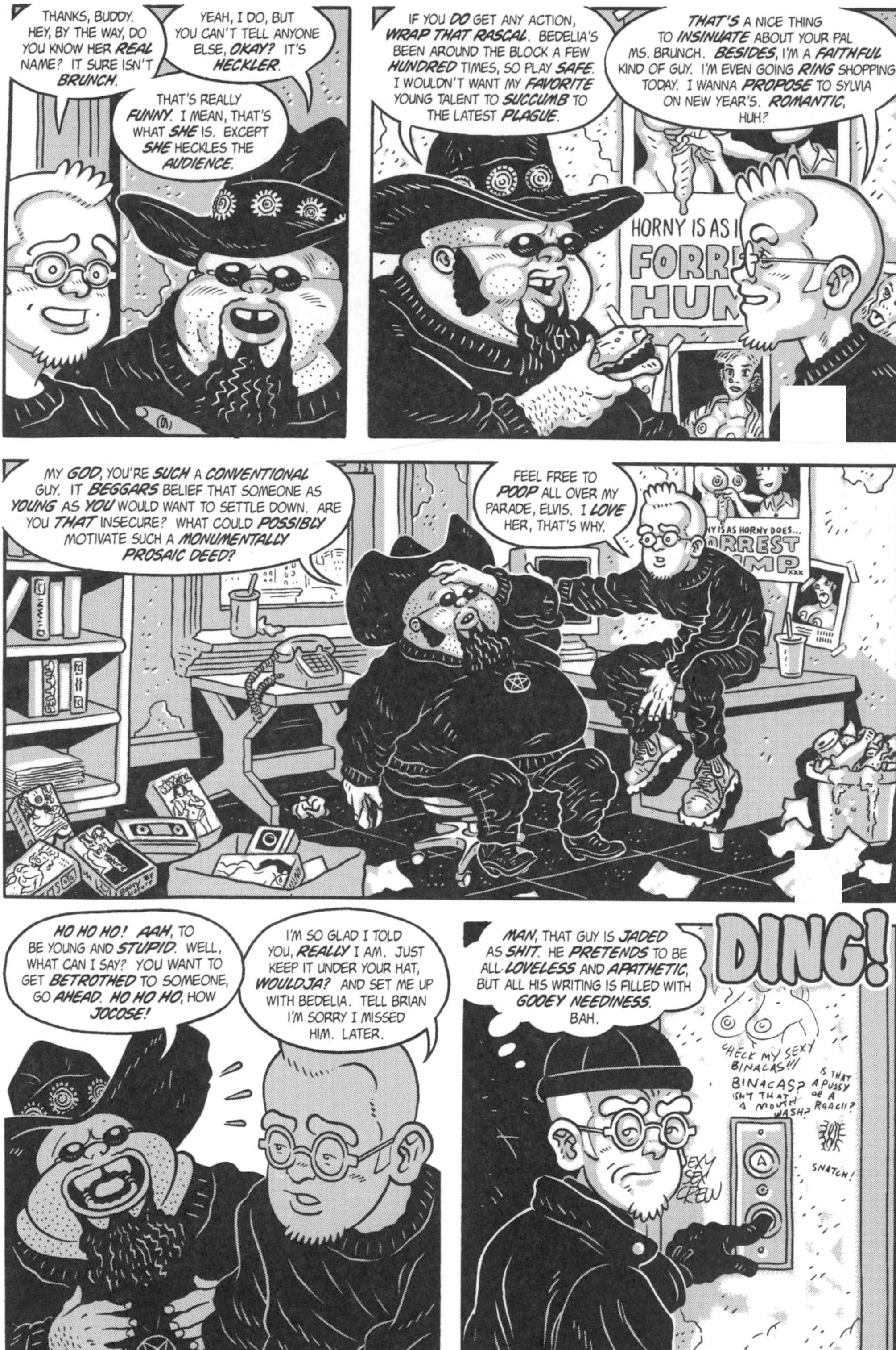
THANKS, BUDDY. HEY, BY THE WAY, DO YOU KNOW HER REAL NAME? IT SURE ISN'T BRUNCH.
YEAH, I DO, BUT YOU CAN'T TELL ANYONE ELSE, OKAY? IT'S HECKLER.
THAT'S REALLY FUNNY. I MEAN, THAT'S WHAT SHE IS. EXCEPT SHE HECKLES THE AUDIENCE.
IF YOU DO GET ANY ACTION, WRAP THAT RASCAL. BEDELIA'S BEEN AROUND THE BLOCK A FEW HUNDRED TIMES, SO PLAY SAFE. I WOULDN'T WANT MY FAVORITE YOUNG TALENT TO SUCCUMB TO THE LATEST PLAGUE.
THAT'S A NICE THING TO INSINUATE ABOUT YOUR PAL MS. BRUNCH. BESIDES, I'M A FAITHFUL KIND OF GUY. I'M EVEN GOING RING SHOPPING TODAY. I WANNA PROPOSE TO SYLVIA ON NEW YEAR'S. ROMANTIC, HUH?
MY GOD, YOU'RE SUCH A CONVENTIONAL GUY. IT BEGGARS BELIEF THAT SOMEONE AS YOUNG AS YOU WOULD WANT TO SETTLE DOWN. ARE YOU THAT INSECURE? WHAT COULD POSSIBLY MOTIVATE SUCH A MONUMENTALLY PROSAIC DEED?
FEEL FREE TO POOP ALL OVER MY PARADE, ELVIS. I LOVE HER, THAT'S WHY.
HO HO HO! AAH, TO BE YOUNG AND STUPID. WELL, WHAT CAN I SAY? YOU WANT TO GET BETROTHED TO SOMEONE, GO AHEAD. HO HO HO, HOW JOCOSE!
I'M SO GLAD I TOLD YOU, REALLY I AM. JUST KEEP IT UNDER YOUR HAT, WOULDJA? AND SET ME UP WITH BEDELIA. TELL BRIAN I'M SORRY I MISSED HIM. LATER.
MAN, THAT GUY IS JADED AS SHIT. HE PRETENDS TO BE ALL LOVELESS AND APATHETIC, BUT ALL HIS WRITING IS FILLED WITH GOOEY NEEDINESS. BAH.
DING!
CHECK MY SEXY BINACAS!!!
BINACAS? ISN'T THAT A MOUTH WASH?
IS THAT A PUSSY OR A ROACH?
SNATCH!
SEXY SEX CREW

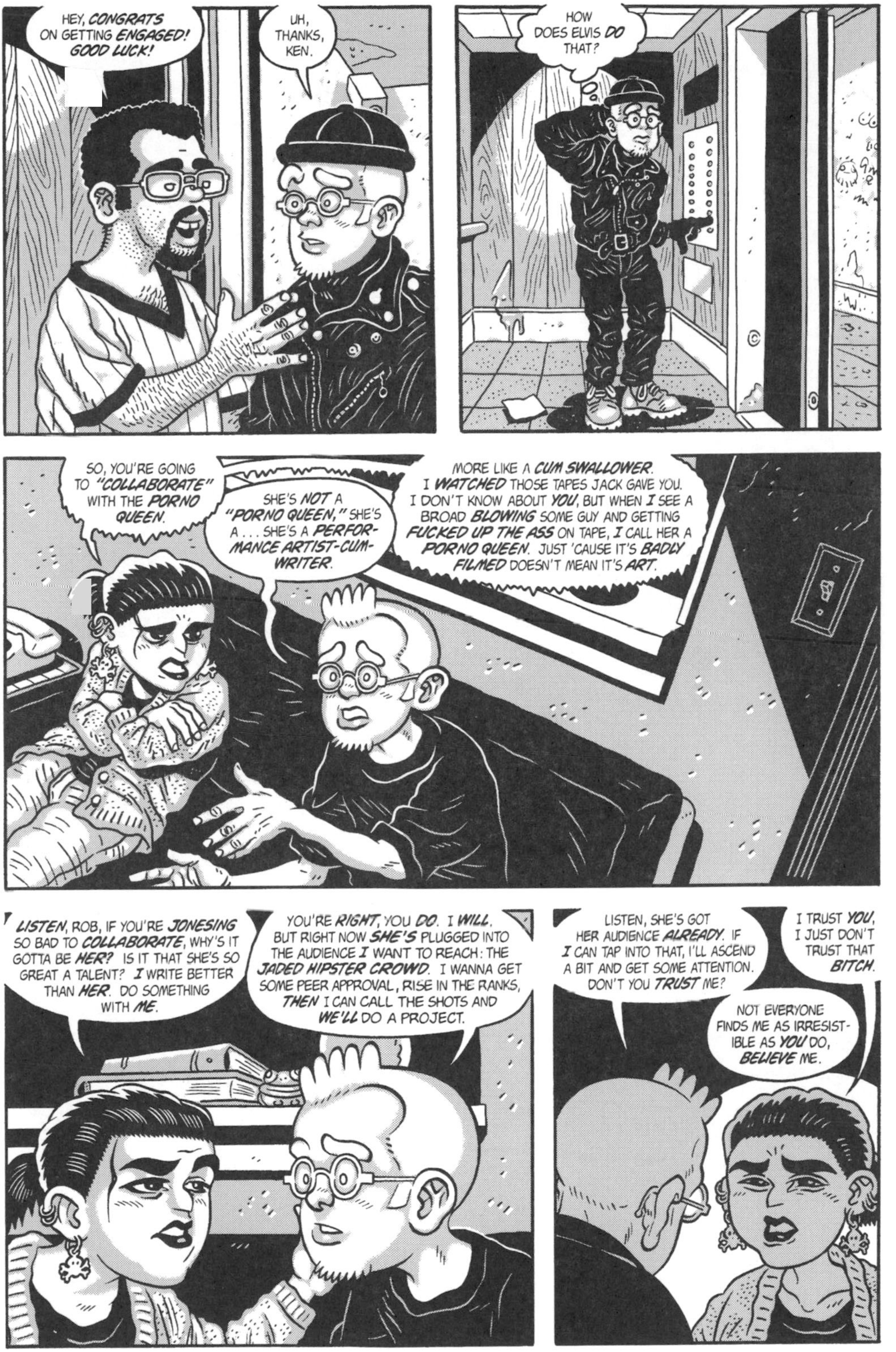
HEY, CONGRATS ON GETTING ENGAGED! GOOD LUCK!
UH, THANKS, KEN.
HOW DOES ELVIS DO THAT?
SO, YOU'RE GOING TO "COLLABORATE" WITH THE PORNO QUEEN.
SHE'S NOT A "PORNO QUEEN," SHE'S A . . . SHE'S A PERFORMANCE ARTIST-CUM-WRITER.
MORE LIKE A CUM SWALLOWER. I WATCHED THOSE TAPES JACK GAVE YOU. I DON'T KNOW ABOUT YOU, BUT WHEN I SEE A BROAD BLOWING SOME GUY AND GETTING FUCKED UP THE ASS ON TAPE, I CALL HER A PORNO QUEEN. JUST 'CAUSE IT'S BADLY FILMED DOESN'T MEAN IT'S ART.
LISTEN, ROB, IF YOU'RE JONESING SO BAD TO COLLABORATE, WHY'S IT GOTTA BE HER? IS IT THAT SHE'S SO GREAT A TALENT? I WRITE BETTER THAN HER. DO SOMETHING WITH ME.
YOU'RE RIGHT, YOU DO. I WILL. BUT RIGHT NOW SHE'S PLUGGED INTO THE AUDIENCE I WANT TO REACH: THE JADED HIPSTER CROWD. I WANNA GET SOME PEER APPROVAL, RISE IN THE RANKS, THEN I CAN CALL THE SHOTS AND WE'LL DO A PROJECT.
LISTEN, SHE'S GOT HER AUDIENCE ALREADY. IF I CAN TAP INTO THAT, I'LL ASCEND A BIT AND GET SOME ATTENTION. DON'T YOU TRUST ME?
I TRUST YOU, I JUST DON'T TRUST THAT BITCH.
NOT EVERYONE FINDS ME AS IRRESISTIBLE AS YOU DO, BELIEVE ME.

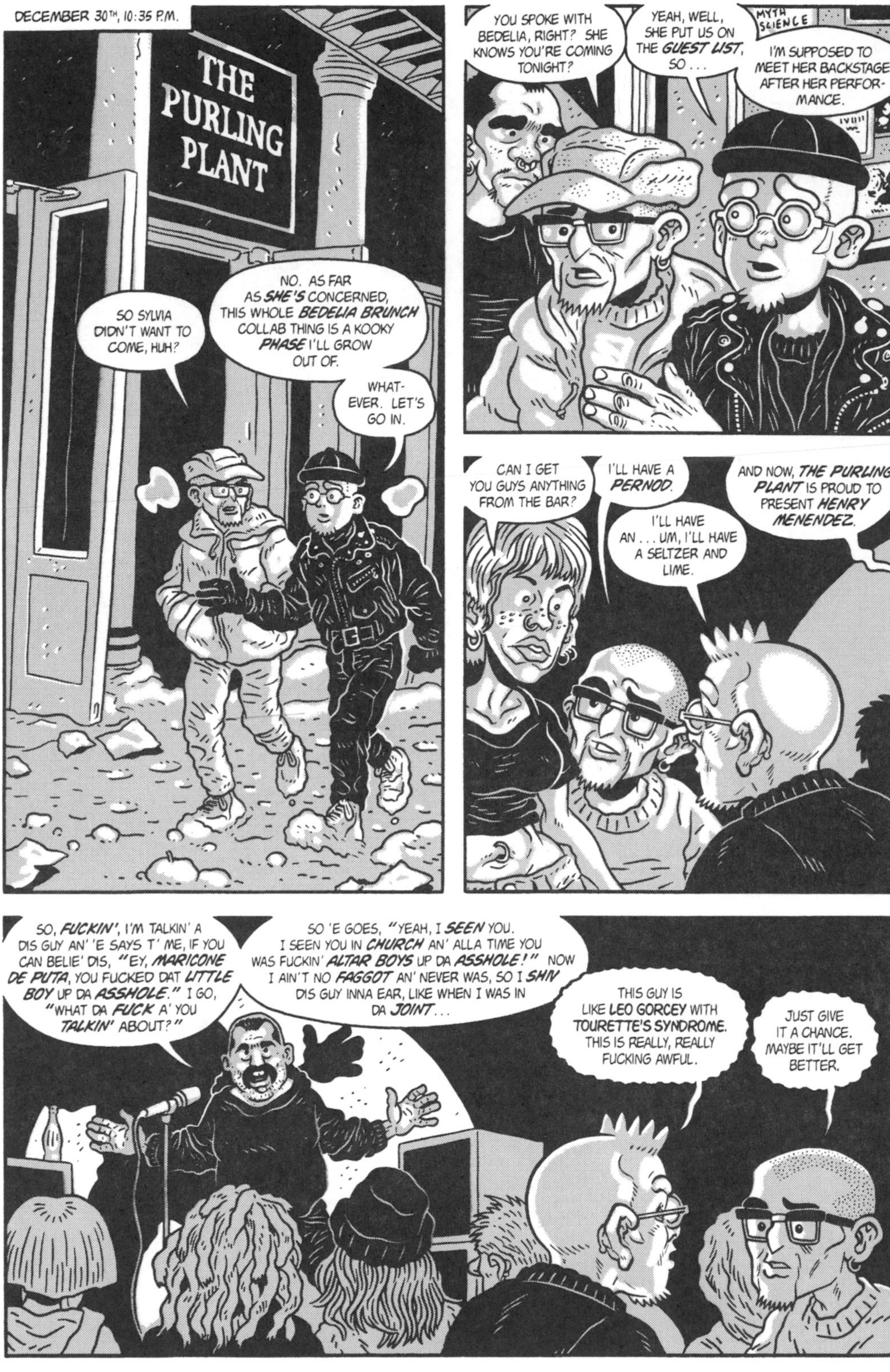
DECEMBER 30TH, 10:35 P.M.
THE PURLING PLANT
SO SYLVIA DIDN'T WANT TO COME, HUH?
NO. AS FAR AS SHE'S CONCERNED, THIS WHOLE BEDELIA BRUNCH COLLAB THING IS A KOOKY PHASE I'LL GROW OUT OF.
WHAT-EVER. LET'S GO IN.
YOU SPOKE WITH BEDELIA, RIGHT? SHE KNOWS YOU'RE COMING TONIGHT?
YEAH, WELL, SHE PUT US ON THE GUEST LIST, SO . . .
MYTH SCIENCE
I'M SUPPOSED TO MEET HER BACKSTAGE AFTER HER PERFOR-MANCE.
CAN I GET YOU GUYS ANYTHING FROM THE BAR?
I'LL HAVE A PERNOD.
I'LL HAVE AN . . . UM, I'LL HAVE A SELTZER AND LIME.
AND NOW, THE PURLING PLANT IS PROUD TO PRESENT HENRY MENENDEZ.
SO, FUCKIN', I'M TALKIN' A DIS GUY AN' 'E SAYS T' ME, IF YOU CAN BELIE' DIS, "EY, MARICONE DE PUTA, YOU FUCKED DAT LITTLE BOY UP DA ASSHOLE." I GO, "WHAT DA FUCK A' YOU TALKIN' ABOUT?"
SO 'E GOES, "YEAH, I SEEN YOU. I SEEN YOU IN CHURCH AN' ALLA TIME YOU WAS FUCKIN' ALTAR BOYS UP DA ASSHOLE!" NOW I AIN'T NO FAGGOT AN' NEVER WAS, SO I SHIV DIS GUY INNA EAR, LIKE WHEN I WAS IN DA JOINT . . .
THIS GUY IS LIKE LEO GORCEY WITH TOURETTE'S SYNDROME. THIS IS REALLY, REALLY FUCKING AWFUL.
JUST GIVE IT A CHANCE. MAYBE IT'LL GET BETTER.

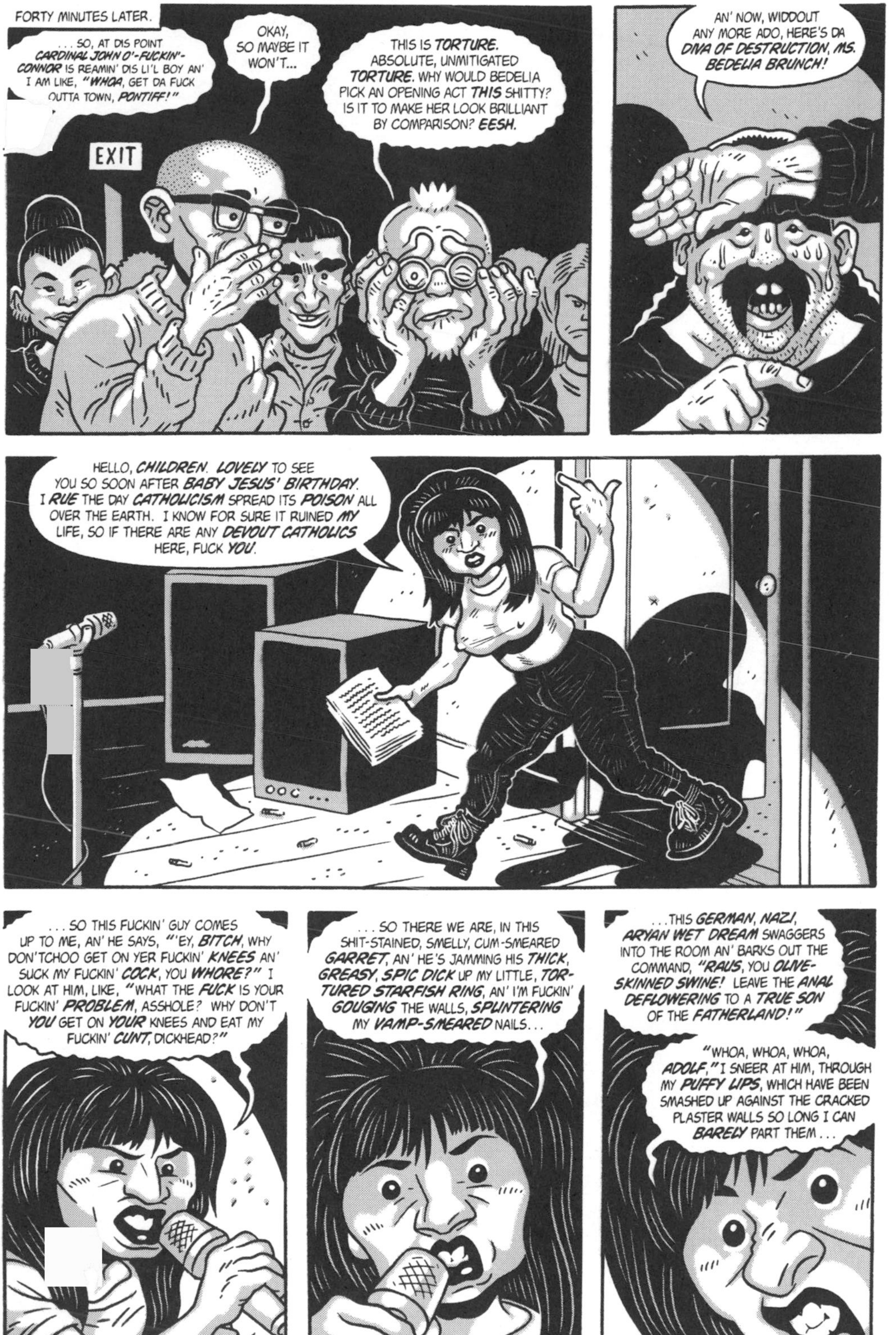
FORTY MINUTES LATER.
. . . SO, AT DIS POINT CARDINAL JOHN O'-FUCKIN'-CONNOR IS REAMIN' DIS LI'L BOY AN' I AM LIKE, "WHOA, GET DA FUCK OUTTA TOWN, PONTIFF!"
OKAY, SO MAYBE IT WON'T...
THIS IS TORTURE. ABSOLUTE, UNMITIGATED TORTURE. WHY WOULD BEDELIA PICK AN OPENING ACT THIS SHITTY? IS IT TO MAKE HER LOOK BRILLIANT BY COMPARISON? EESH.
EXIT
AN' NOW, WIDDOUT ANY MORE ADO, HERE'S DA DIVA OF DESTRUCTION, MS. BEDELIA BRUNCH!
HELLO, CHILDREN. LOVELY TO SEE YOU SO SOON AFTER BABY JESUS' BIRTHDAY. I RUE THE DAY CATHOLICISM SPREAD ITS POISON ALL OVER THE EARTH. I KNOW FOR SURE IT RUINED MY LIFE, SO IF THERE ARE ANY DEVOUT CATHOLICS HERE, FUCK YOU.
. . . SO THIS FUCKIN' GUY COMES UP TO ME, AN' HE SAYS, "'EY, BITCH, WHY DON'TCHOO GET ON YER FUCKIN' KNEES AN' SUCK MY FUCKIN' COCK, YOU WHORE?" I LOOK AT HIM, LIKE, "WHAT THE FUCK IS YOUR FUCKIN' PROBLEM, ASSHOLE? WHY DON'T YOU GET ON YOUR KNEES AND EAT MY FUCKIN' CUNT, DICKHEAD?"
. . . SO THERE WE ARE, IN THIS SHIT-STAINED, SMELLY, CUM-SMEARED GARRET, AN' HE'S JAMMING HIS THICK, GREASY, SPIC DICK UP MY LITTLE, TORTURED STARFISH RING, AN' I'M FUCKIN' GOUGING THE WALLS, SPLINTERING MY VAMP-SMEARED NAILS . . .
. . . THIS GERMAN, NAZI, ARYAN WET DREAM SWAGGERS INTO THE ROOM AN' BARKS OUT THE COMMAND, "RAUS, YOU OLIVE-SKINNED SWINE! LEAVE THE ANAL DEFLOWERING TO A TRUE SON OF THE FATHERLAND!"
"WHOA, WHOA, WHOA, ADOLF," I SNEER AT HIM, THROUGH MY PUFFY LIPS, WHICH HAVE BEEN SMASHED UP AGAINST THE CRACKED PLASTER WALLS SO LONG I CAN BARELY PART THEM . . .

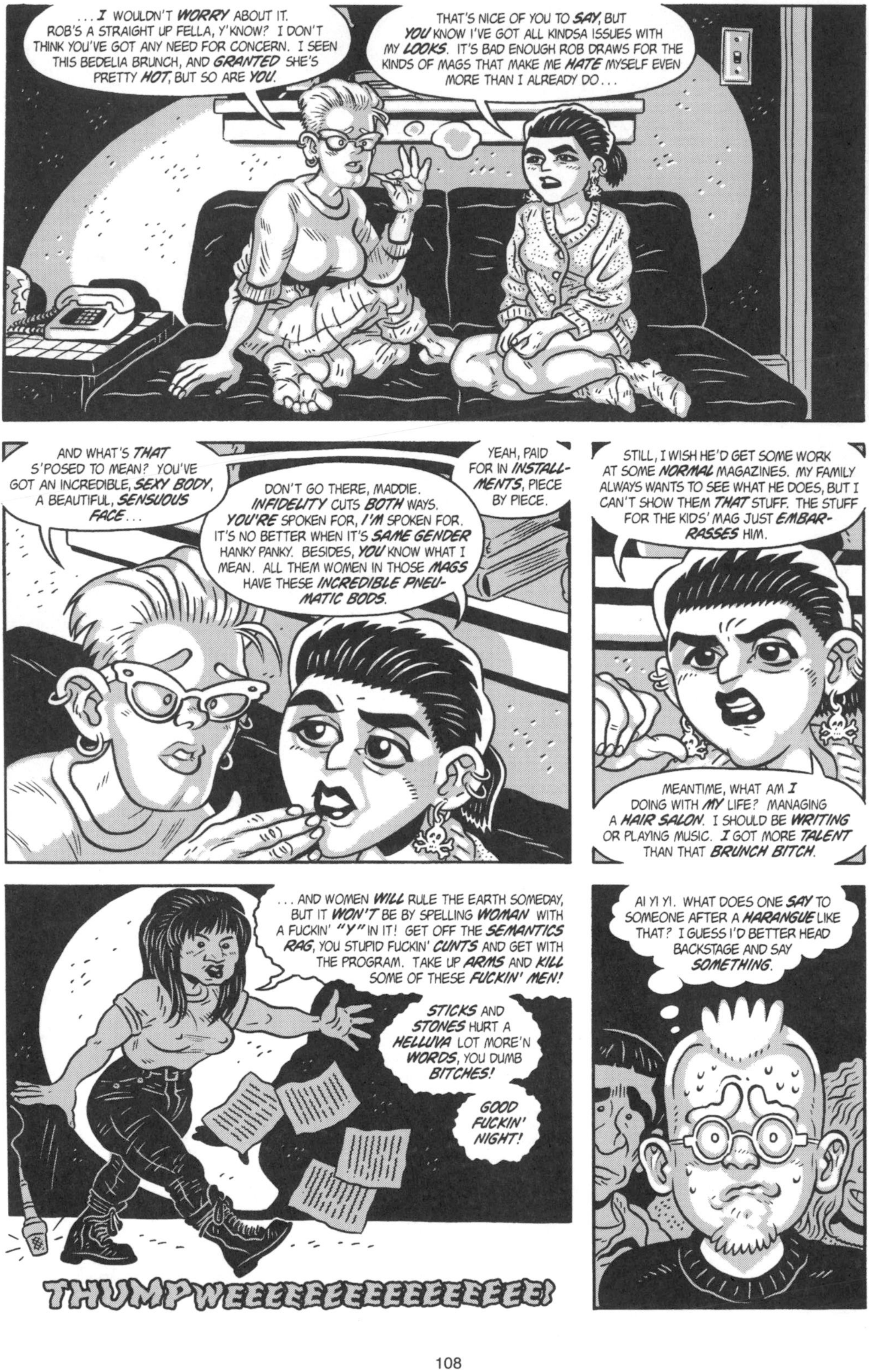

...I WOULDN'T WORRY ABOUT IT. ROB'S A STRAIGHT UP FELLA, Y'KNOW? I DON'T THINK YOU'VE GOT ANY NEED FOR CONCERN. I SEEN THIS BEDELIA BRUNCH, AND GRANTED SHE'S PRETTY HOT, BUT SO ARE YOU.
THAT'S NICE OF YOU TO SAY, BUT YOU KNOW I'VE GOT ALL KINDSA ISSUES WITH MY LOOKS. IT'S BAD ENOUGH ROB DRAWS FOR THE KINDS OF MAGS THAT MAKE ME HATE MYSELF EVEN MORE THAN I ALREADY DO...
AND WHAT'S THAT S'POSED TO MEAN? YOU'VE GOT AN INCREDIBLE, SEXY BODY, A BEAUTIFUL, SENSUOUS FACE...
YEAH, PAID FOR IN INSTALL-MENTS, PIECE BY PIECE.
DON'T GO THERE, MADDIE. INFIDELITY CUTS BOTH WAYS. YOU'RE SPOKEN FOR, I'M SPOKEN FOR. IT'S NO BETTER WHEN IT'S SAME GENDER HANKY PANKY. BESIDES, YOU KNOW WHAT I MEAN. ALL THEM WOMEN IN THOSE MAGS HAVE THESE INCREDIBLE PNEU-MATIC BODS.
STILL, I WISH HE'D GET SOME WORK AT SOME NORMAL MAGAZINES. MY FAMILY ALWAYS WANTS TO SEE WHAT HE DOES, BUT I CAN'T SHOW THEM THAT STUFF. THE STUFF FOR THE KIDS' MAG JUST EMBAR-RASSES HIM.
MEANTIME, WHAT AM I DOING WITH MY LIFE? MANAGING A HAIR SALON. I SHOULD BE WRITING OR PLAYING MUSIC. I GOT MORE TALENT THAN THAT BRUNCH BITCH.
...AND WOMEN WILL RULE THE EARTH SOMEDAY, BUT IT WON'T BE BY SPELLING WOMAN WITH A FUCKIN' "Y" IN IT! GET OFF THE SEMANTICS RAG, YOU STUPID FUCKIN' CUNTS AND GET WITH THE PROGRAM. TAKE UP ARMS AND KILL SOME OF THESE FUCKIN' MEN!
STICKS AND STONES HURT A HELLUVA LOT MORE'N WORDS, YOU DUMB BITCHES!
GOOD FUCKIN' NIGHT!
THUMPWEEEEEEEEEEEEEEEEE!
AI YI YI. WHAT DOES ONE SAY TO SOMEONE AFTER A HARANGUE LIKE THAT? I GUESS I'D BETTER HEAD BACKSTAGE AND SAY SOMETHING.

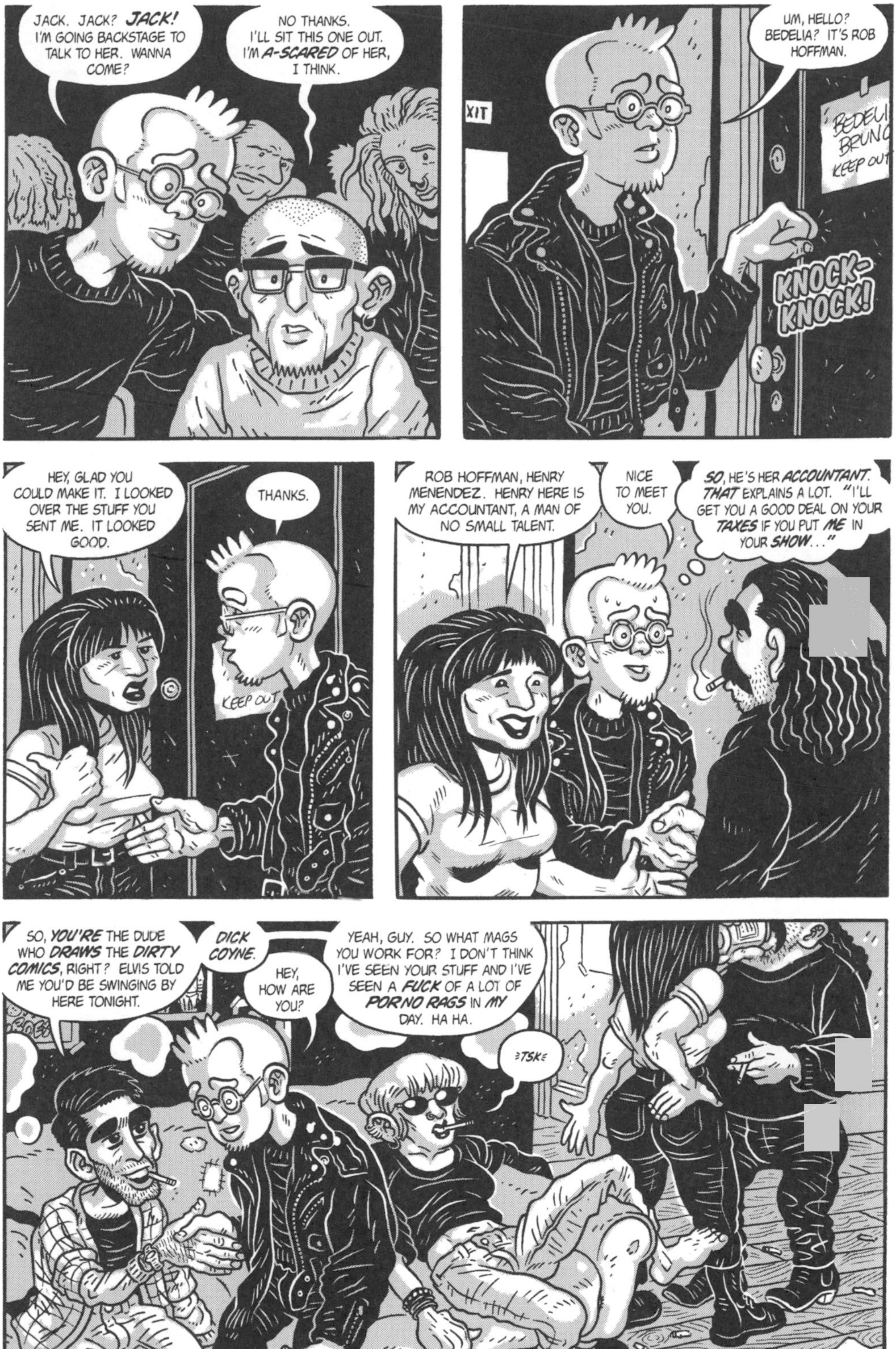
JACK. JACK? JACK! I'M GOING BACKSTAGE TO TALK TO HER. WANNA COME?
NO THANKS. I'LL SIT THIS ONE OUT. I'M A-SCARED OF HER, I THINK.
XIT
UM, HELLO? BEDELIA? IT'S ROB HOFFMAN.
KEEP OUT
KNOCK-KNOCK!
HEY, GLAD YOU COULD MAKE IT. I LOOKED OVER THE STUFF YOU SENT ME. IT LOOKED GOOD.
THANKS.
KEEP OUT
ROB HOFFMAN, HENRY MENENDEZ. HENRY HERE IS MY ACCOUNTANT, A MAN OF NO SMALL TALENT.
NICE TO MEET YOU.
SO, HE'S HER ACCOUNTANT. THAT EXPLAINS A LOT. "I'LL GET YOU A GOOD DEAL ON YOUR TAXES IF YOU PUT ME IN YOUR SHOW..."
SO, YOU'RE THE DUDE WHO DRAWS THE DIRTY COMICS, RIGHT? ELVIS TOLD ME YOU'D BE SWINGING BY HERE TONIGHT.
DICK COYNE.
HEY, HOW ARE YOU?
YEAH, GUY. SO WHAT MAGS YOU WORK FOR? I DON'T THINK I'VE SEEN YOUR STUFF AND I'VE SEEN A FUCK OF A LOT OF PORNO RAGS IN MY DAY. HA HA.
TSK

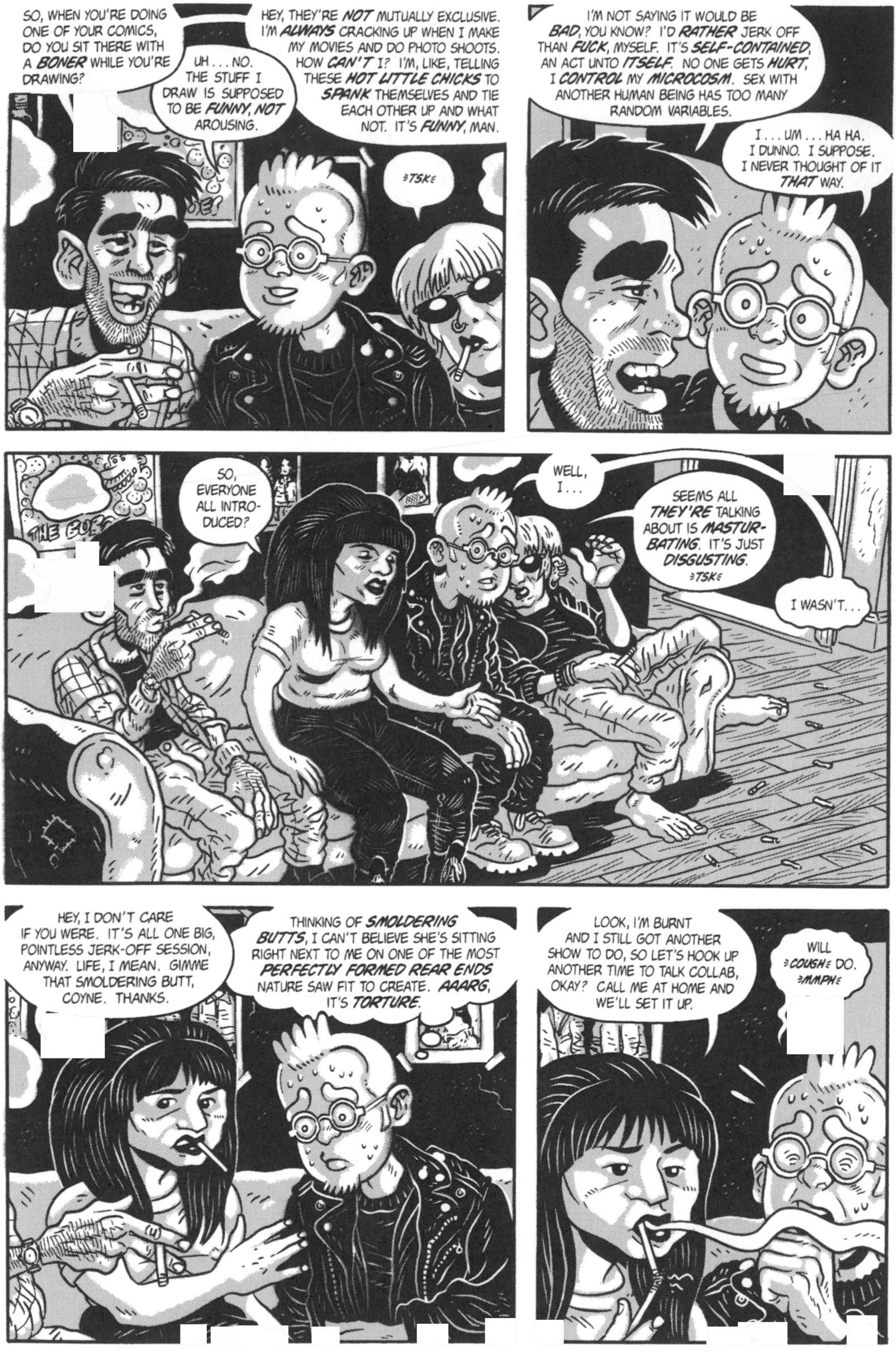

SO, WHEN YOU'RE DOING ONE OF YOUR COMICS, DO YOU SIT THERE WITH A BONER WHILE YOU'RE DRAWING?
UH . . . NO. THE STUFF I DRAW IS SUPPOSED TO BE FUNNY, NOT AROUSING.
HEY, THEY'RE NOT MUTUALLY EXCLUSIVE. I'M ALWAYS CRACKING UP WHEN I MAKE MY MOVIES AND DO PHOTO SHOOTS. HOW CAN'T I? I'M, LIKE, TELLING THESE HOT LITTLE CHICKS TO SPANK THEMSELVES AND TIE EACH OTHER UP AND WHAT NOT. IT'S FUNNY, MAN.
TSK
I'M NOT SAYING IT WOULD BE BAD, YOU KNOW? I'D RATHER JERK OFF THAN FUCK, MYSELF. IT'S SELF-CONTAINED, AN ACT UNTO ITSELF. NO ONE GETS HURT, I CONTROL MY MICROCOSM. SEX WITH ANOTHER HUMAN BEING HAS TOO MANY RANDOM VARIABLES.
I . . . UM . . . HA HA. I DUNNO. I SUPPOSE. I NEVER THOUGHT OF IT THAT WAY.
SO, EVERYONE ALL INTRO-DUCED?
WELL, I . . .
SEEMS ALL THEY'RE TALKING ABOUT IS MASTUR-BATING. IT'S JUST DISGUSTING.
TSK
I WASN'T. . .
HEY, I DON'T CARE IF YOU WERE. IT'S ALL ONE BIG, POINTLESS JERK-OFF SESSION, ANYWAY. LIFE, I MEAN. GIMME THAT SMOLDERING BUTT, COYNE. THANKS.
THINKING OF SMOLDERING BUTTS, I CAN'T BELIEVE SHE'S SITTING RIGHT NEXT TO ME ON ONE OF THE MOST PERFECTLY FORMED REAR ENDS NATURE SAW FIT TO CREATE. AAARG, IT'S TORTURE.
LOOK, I'M BURNT AND I STILL GOT ANOTHER SHOW TO DO, SO LET'S HOOK UP ANOTHER TIME TO TALK COLLAB, OKAY? CALL ME AT HOME AND WE'LL SET IT UP.
WILL COUGH DO.
MMPH

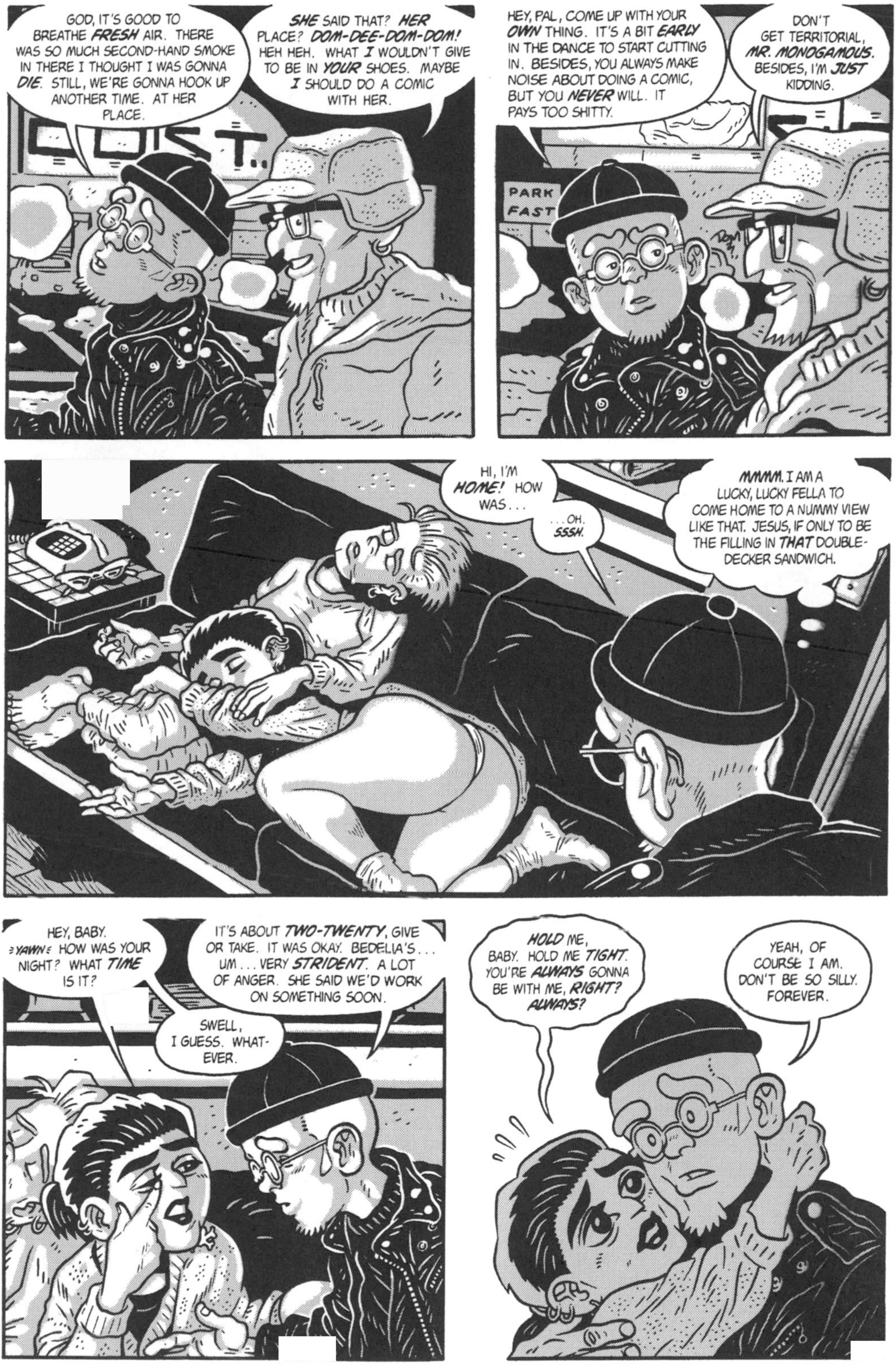
GOD, IT'S GOOD TO BREATHE FRESH AIR. THERE WAS SO MUCH SECOND-HAND SMOKE IN THERE I THOUGHT I WAS GONNA DIE. STILL, WE'RE GONNA HOOK UP ANOTHER TIME. AT HER PLACE.
SHE SAID THAT? HER PLACE? DOM-DEE-DOM-DOM! HEH HEH. WHAT I WOULDN'T GIVE TO BE IN YOUR SHOES. MAYBE I SHOULD DO A COMIC WITH HER.
HEY, PAL, COME UP WITH YOUR OWN THING. IT'S A BIT EARLY IN THE DANCE TO START CUTTING IN. BESIDES, YOU ALWAYS MAKE NOISE ABOUT DOING A COMIC, BUT YOU NEVER WILL. IT PAYS TOO SHITTY.
DON'T GET TERRITORIAL, MR. MONOGAMOUS. BESIDES, I'M JUST KIDDING.
PARK
FAST
HI, I'M HOME! HOW WAS...
...OH. SSSH.
MMMM. I AM A LUCKY, LUCKY FELLA TO COME HOME TO A NUMMY VIEW LIKE THAT. JESUS, IF ONLY TO BE THE FILLING IN THAT DOUBLE-DECKER SANDWICH.
HEY, BABY. ≡YAWN≡ HOW WAS YOUR NIGHT? WHAT TIME IS IT?
IT'S ABOUT TWO-TWENTY, GIVE OR TAKE. IT WAS OKAY. BEDELIA'S... UM... VERY STRIDENT. A LOT OF ANGER. SHE SAID WE'D WORK ON SOMETHING SOON.
SWELL, I GUESS. WHAT-EVER.
HOLD ME, BABY. HOLD ME TIGHT. YOU'RE ALWAYS GONNA BE WITH ME, RIGHT? ALWAYS?
YEAH, OF COURSE I AM. DON'T BE SO SILLY. FOREVER.

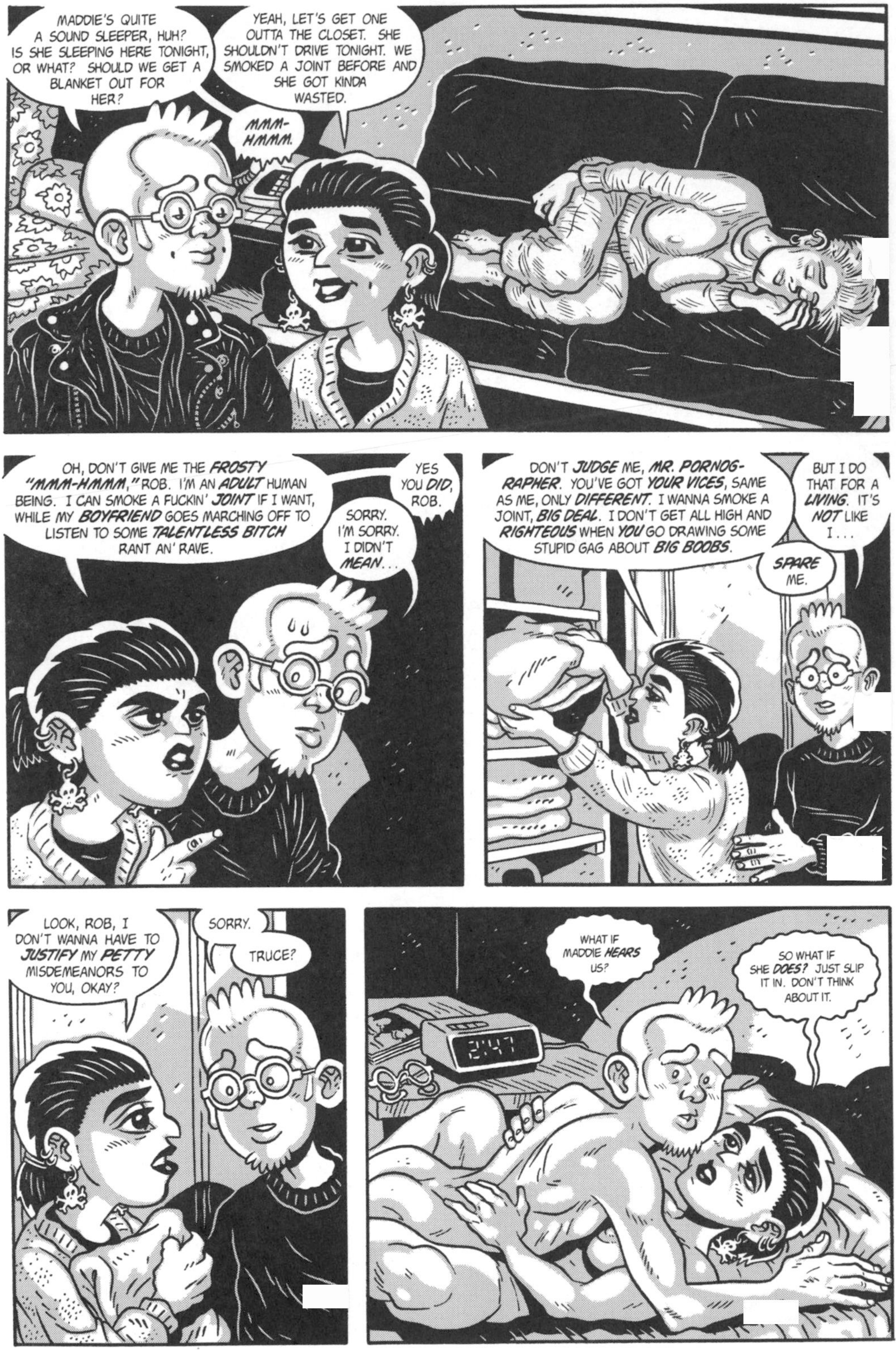
MADDIE'S QUITE A SOUND SLEEPER, HUH? IS SHE SLEEPING HERE TONIGHT, OR WHAT? SHOULD WE GET A BLANKET OUT FOR HER?
YEAH, LET'S GET ONE OUTTA THE CLOSET. SHE SHOULDN'T DRIVE TONIGHT. WE SMOKED A JOINT BEFORE AND SHE GOT KINDA WASTED.
MMM-HMMM.
OH, DON'T GIVE ME THE FROSTY "MMM-HMMM," ROB. I'M AN ADULT HUMAN BEING. I CAN SMOKE A FUCKIN' JOINT IF I WANT, WHILE MY BOYFRIEND GOES MARCHING OFF TO LISTEN TO SOME TALENTLESS BITCH RANT AN' RAVE.
SORRY. I'M SORRY. I DIDN'T MEAN...
YES YOU DID, ROB.
DON'T JUDGE ME, MR. PORNOG-RAPHER. YOU'VE GOT YOUR VICES, SAME AS ME, ONLY DIFFERENT. I WANNA SMOKE A JOINT, BIG DEAL. I DON'T GET ALL HIGH AND RIGHTEOUS WHEN YOU GO DRAWING SOME STUPID GAG ABOUT BIG BOOBS.
BUT I DO THAT FOR A LIVING. IT'S NOT LIKE I...
SPARE ME.
LOOK, ROB, I DON'T WANNA HAVE TO JUSTIFY MY PETTY MISDEMEANORS TO YOU, OKAY?
SORRY.
TRUCE?
WHAT IF MADDIE HEARS US?
SO WHAT IF SHE DOES? JUST SLIP IT IN. DON'T THINK ABOUT IT.

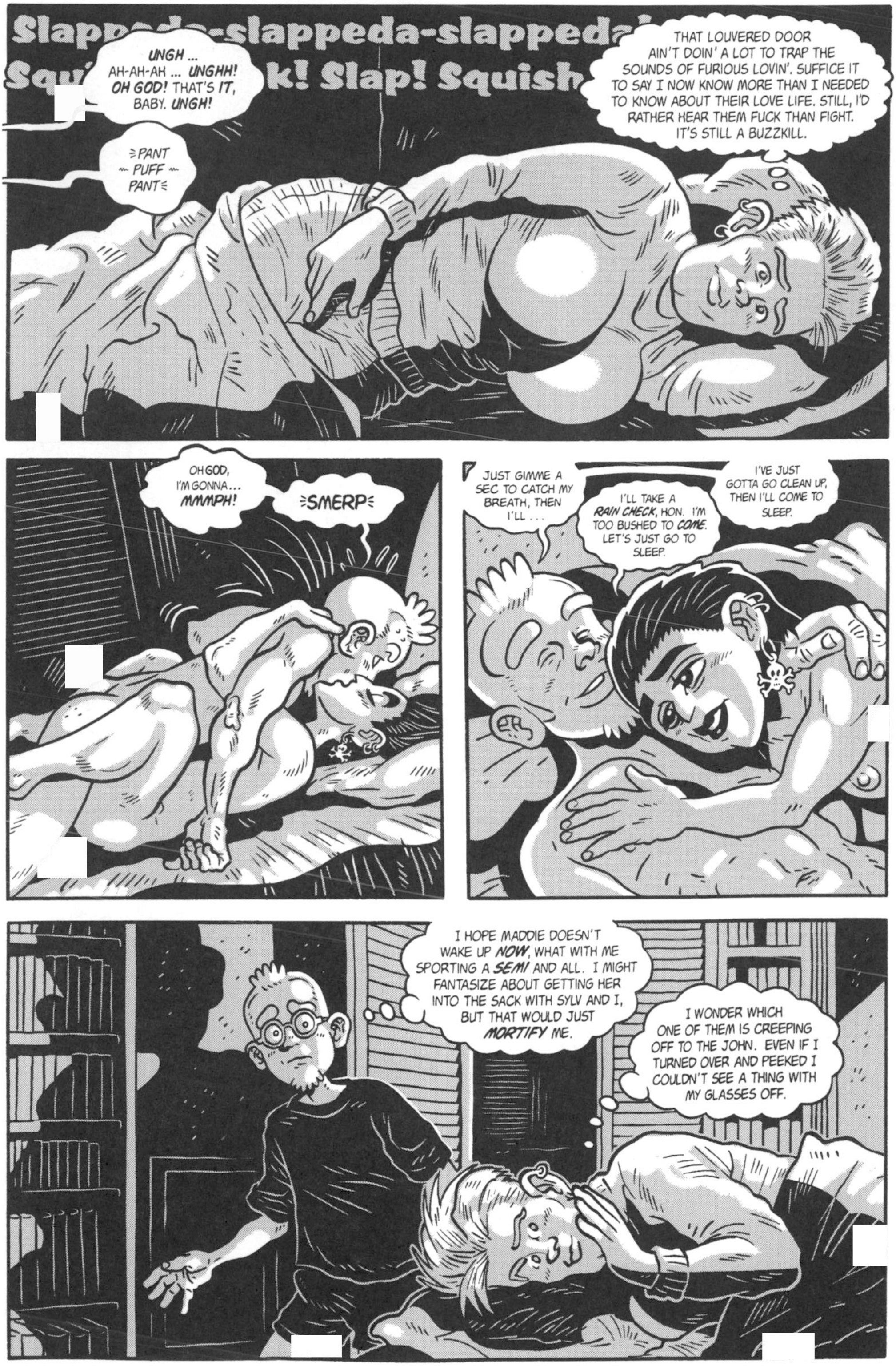
Slappeda-slappeda-slappeda
k! Slap! Squish
UNGH ... AH-AH-AH ... UNGHH! OH GOD! THAT'S IT, BABY. UNGH!
PANT ~ PUFF ~ PANT
THAT LOUVERED DOOR AIN'T DOIN' A LOT TO TRAP THE SOUNDS OF FURIOUS LOVIN'. SUFFICE IT TO SAY I NOW KNOW MORE THAN I NEEDED TO KNOW ABOUT THEIR LOVE LIFE. STILL, I'D RATHER HEAR THEM FUCK THAN FIGHT. IT'S STILL A BUZZKILL.
OH GOD, I'M GONNA... MMMPH!
SMERP
JUST GIMME A SEC TO CATCH MY BREATH, THEN I'LL . . .
I'LL TAKE A RAIN CHECK, HON. I'M TOO BUSHED TO COME. LET'S JUST GO TO SLEEP.
I'VE JUST GOTTA GO CLEAN UP, THEN I'LL COME TO SLEEP.
I HOPE MADDIE DOESN'T WAKE UP NOW, WHAT WITH ME SPORTING A SEMI AND ALL. I MIGHT FANTASIZE ABOUT GETTING HER INTO THE SACK WITH SYLV AND I, BUT THAT WOULD JUST MORTIFY ME.
I WONDER WHICH ONE OF THEM IS CREEPING OFF TO THE JOHN. EVEN IF I TURNED OVER AND PEEKED I COULDN'T SEE A THING WITH MY GLASSES OFF.

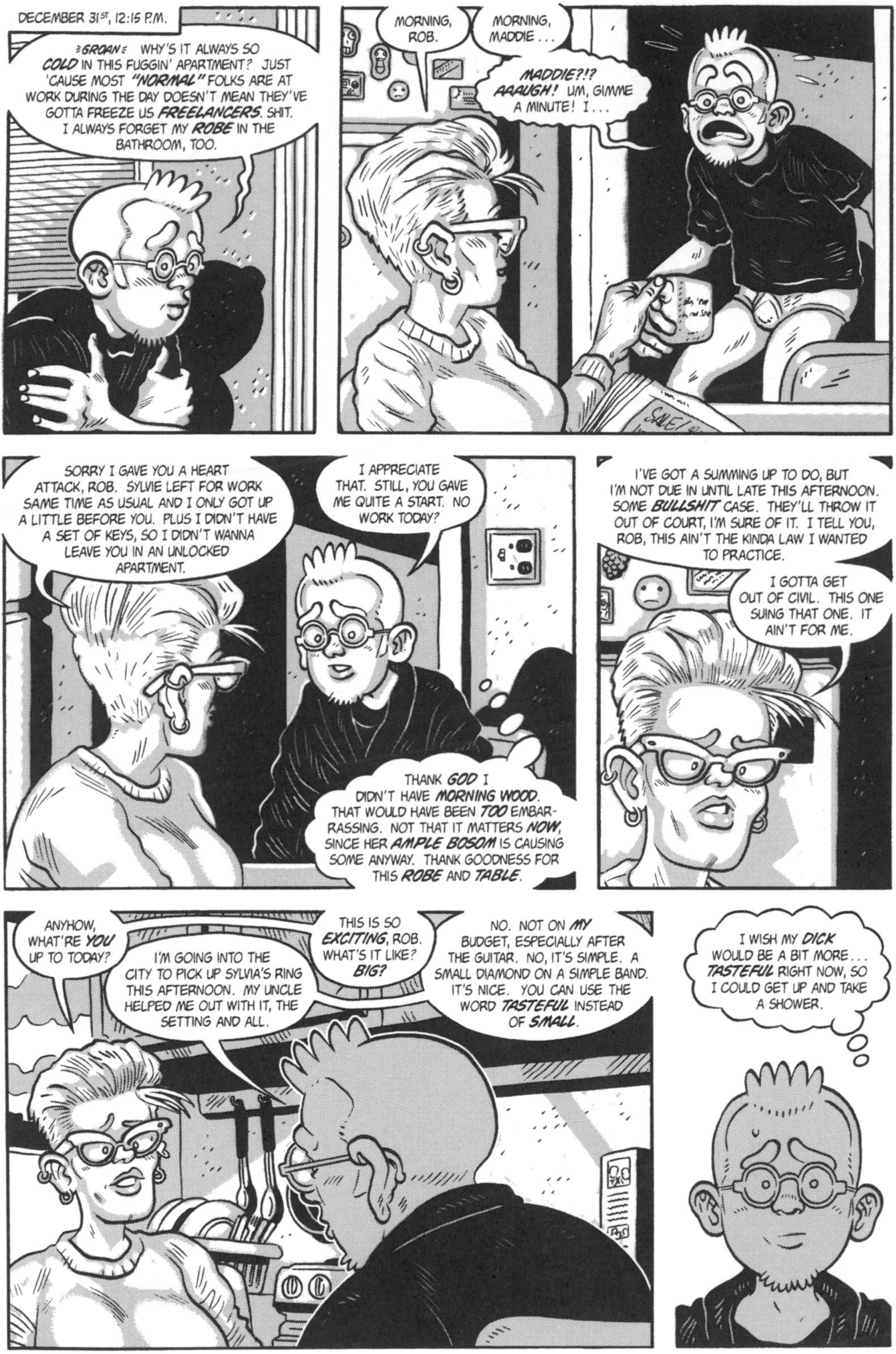
DECEMBER 31ST, 12:15 P.M.
≥GROAN≤ WHY'S IT ALWAYS SO COLD IN THIS FUGGIN' APARTMENT? JUST 'CAUSE MOST "NORMAL" FOLKS ARE AT WORK DURING THE DAY DOESN'T MEAN THEY'VE GOTTA FREEZE US FREELANCERS. SHIT. I ALWAYS FORGET MY ROBE IN THE BATHROOM, TOO.
MORNING, ROB.
MORNING, MADDIE . . .
MADDIE?!? AAAUGH! UM, GIMME A MINUTE! I . . .
SORRY I GAVE YOU A HEART ATTACK, ROB. SYLVIE LEFT FOR WORK SAME TIME AS USUAL AND I ONLY GOT UP A LITTLE BEFORE YOU. PLUS I DIDN'T HAVE A SET OF KEYS, SO I DIDN'T WANNA LEAVE YOU IN AN UNLOCKED APARTMENT.
I APPRECIATE THAT. STILL, YOU GAVE ME QUITE A START. NO WORK TODAY?
THANK GOD I DIDN'T HAVE MORNING WOOD. THAT WOULD HAVE BEEN TOO EMBARRASSING. NOT THAT IT MATTERS NOW, SINCE HER AMPLE BOSOM IS CAUSING SOME ANYWAY. THANK GOODNESS FOR THIS ROBE AND TABLE.
I'VE GOT A SUMMING UP TO DO, BUT I'M NOT DUE IN UNTIL LATE THIS AFTERNOON. SOME BULLSHIT CASE. THEY'LL THROW IT OUT OF COURT, I'M SURE OF IT. I TELL YOU, ROB, THIS AIN'T THE KINDA LAW I WANTED TO PRACTICE.
I GOTTA GET OUT OF CIVIL. THIS ONE SUING THAT ONE. IT AIN'T FOR ME.
ANYHOW, WHAT'RE YOU UP TO TODAY?
I'M GOING INTO THE CITY TO PICK UP SYLVIA'S RING THIS AFTERNOON. MY UNCLE HELPED ME OUT WITH IT, THE SETTING AND ALL.
THIS IS SO EXCITING, ROB. WHAT'S IT LIKE? BIG?
NO. NOT ON MY BUDGET, ESPECIALLY AFTER THE GUITAR. NO, IT'S SIMPLE. A SMALL DIAMOND ON A SIMPLE BAND. IT'S NICE. YOU CAN USE THE WORD TASTEFUL INSTEAD OF SMALL.
I WISH MY DICK WOULD BE A BIT MORE . . . TASTEFUL RIGHT NOW, SO I COULD GET UP AND TAKE A SHOWER.

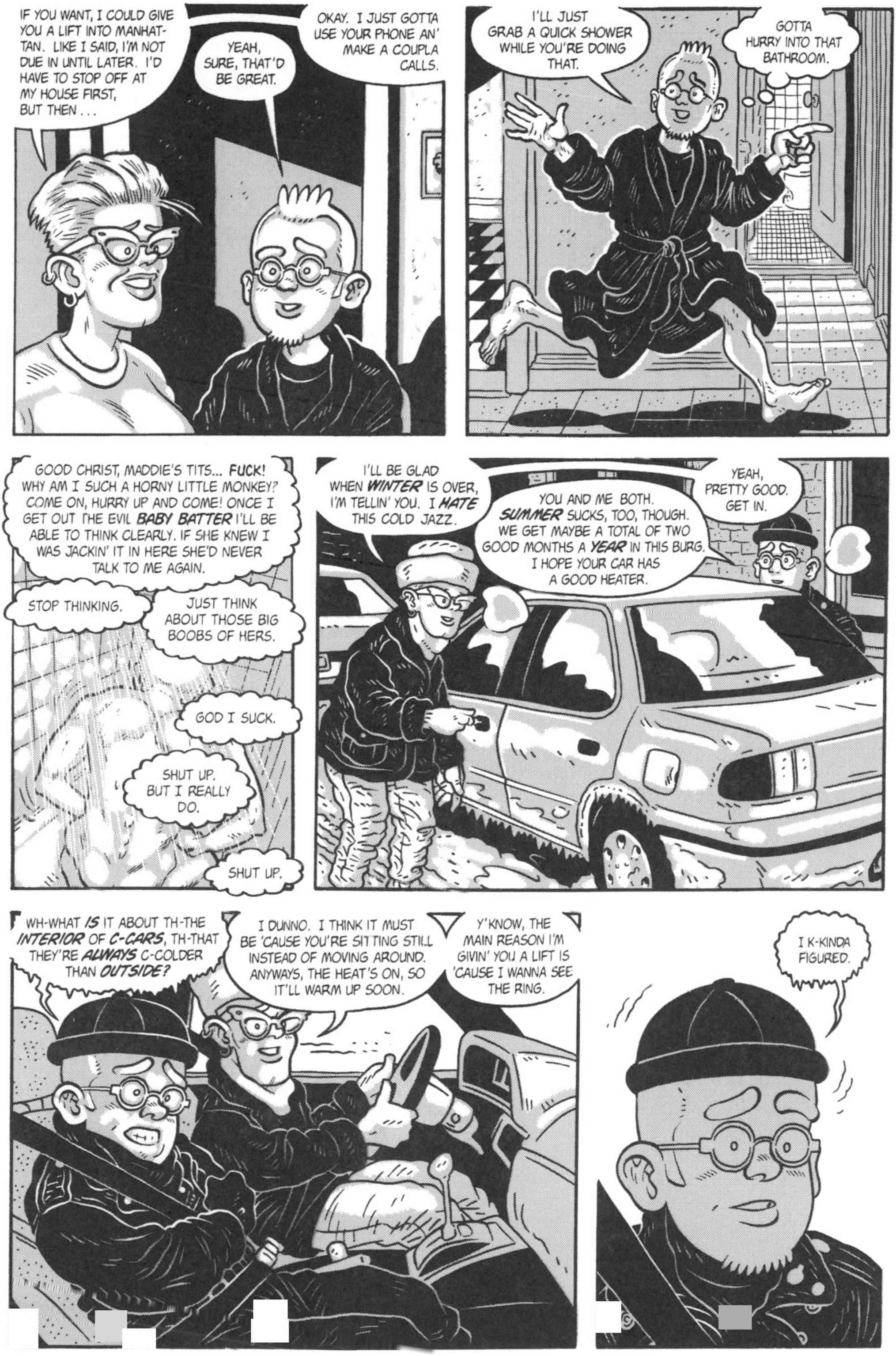
IF YOU WANT, I COULD GIVE YOU A LIFT INTO MANHATTAN. LIKE I SAID, I'M NOT DUE IN UNTIL LATER. I'D HAVE TO STOP OFF AT MY HOUSE FIRST, BUT THEN . . .
YEAH, SURE, THAT'D BE GREAT.
OKAY. I JUST GOTTA USE YOUR PHONE AN' MAKE A COUPLA CALLS.
I'LL JUST GRAB A QUICK SHOWER WHILE YOU'RE DOING THAT.
GOTTA HURRY INTO THAT BATHROOM.
GOOD CHRIST, MADDIE'S TITS... FUCK! WHY AM I SUCH A HORNY LITTLE MONKEY? COME ON, HURRY UP AND COME! ONCE I GET OUT THE EVIL BABY BATTER I'LL BE ABLE TO THINK CLEARLY. IF SHE KNEW I WAS JACKIN' IT IN HERE SHE'D NEVER TALK TO ME AGAIN.
STOP THINKING.
JUST THINK ABOUT THOSE BIG BOOBS OF HERS.
GOD I SUCK.
SHUT UP. BUT I REALLY DO.
SHUT UP.
I'LL BE GLAD WHEN WINTER IS OVER, I'M TELLIN' YOU. I HATE THIS COLD JAZZ.
YOU AND ME BOTH. SUMMER SUCKS, TOO, THOUGH. WE GET MAYBE A TOTAL OF TWO GOOD MONTHS A YEAR IN THIS BURG. I HOPE YOUR CAR HAS A GOOD HEATER.
YEAH, PRETTY GOOD. GET IN.
WH-WHAT IS IT ABOUT TH-THE INTERIOR OF C-CARS, TH-THAT THEY'RE ALWAYS C-COLDER THAN OUTSIDE?
I DUNNO. I THINK IT MUST BE 'CAUSE YOU'RE SITTING STILL INSTEAD OF MOVING AROUND. ANYWAYS, THE HEAT'S ON, SO IT'LL WARM UP SOON.
Y'KNOW, THE MAIN REASON I'M GIVIN' YOU A LIFT IS 'CAUSE I WANNA SEE THE RING.
I K-KINDA FIGURED.

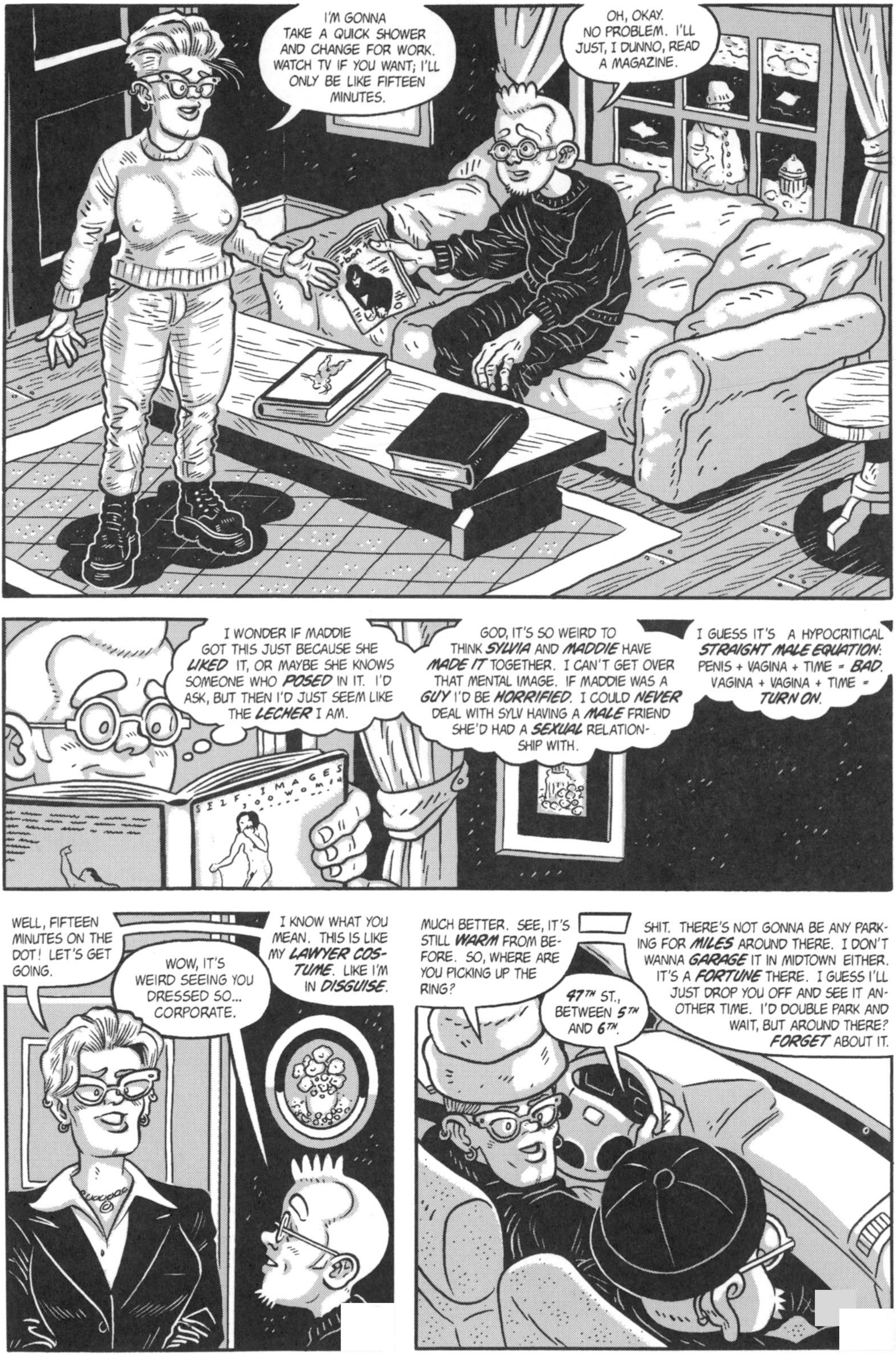
I'M GONNA TAKE A QUICK SHOWER AND CHANGE FOR WORK. WATCH TV IF YOU WANT; I'LL ONLY BE LIKE FIFTEEN MINUTES.
OH, OKAY. NO PROBLEM. I'LL JUST, I DUNNO, READ A MAGAZINE.
I WONDER IF MADDIE GOT THIS JUST BECAUSE SHE LIKED IT, OR MAYBE SHE KNOWS SOMEONE WHO POSED IN IT. I'D ASK, BUT THEN I'D JUST SEEM LIKE THE LECHER I AM.
GOD, IT'S SO WEIRD TO THINK SYLVIA AND MADDIE HAVE MADE IT TOGETHER. I CAN'T GET OVER THAT MENTAL IMAGE. IF MADDIE WAS A GUY I'D BE HORRIFIED. I COULD NEVER DEAL WITH SYLV HAVING A MALE FRIEND SHE'D HAD A SEXUAL RELATIONSHIP WITH.
I GUESS IT'S A HYPOCRITICAL STRAIGHT MALE EQUATION: PENIS + VAGINA + TIME = BAD. VAGINA + VAGINA + TIME = TURN ON.
WELL, FIFTEEN MINUTES ON THE DOT! LET'S GET GOING.
WOW, IT'S WEIRD SEEING YOU DRESSED SO... CORPORATE.
I KNOW WHAT YOU MEAN. THIS IS LIKE MY LAWYER COSTUME. LIKE I'M IN DISGUISE.
MUCH BETTER. SEE, IT'S STILL WARM FROM BEFORE. SO, WHERE ARE YOU PICKING UP THE RING?
47TH ST., BETWEEN 5TH AND 6TH.
SHIT. THERE'S NOT GONNA BE ANY PARKING FOR MILES AROUND THERE. I DON'T WANNA GARAGE IT IN MIDTOWN EITHER. IT'S A FORTUNE THERE. I GUESS I'LL JUST DROP YOU OFF AND SEE IT ANOTHER TIME. I'D DOUBLE PARK AND WAIT, BUT AROUND THERE? FORGET ABOUT IT.

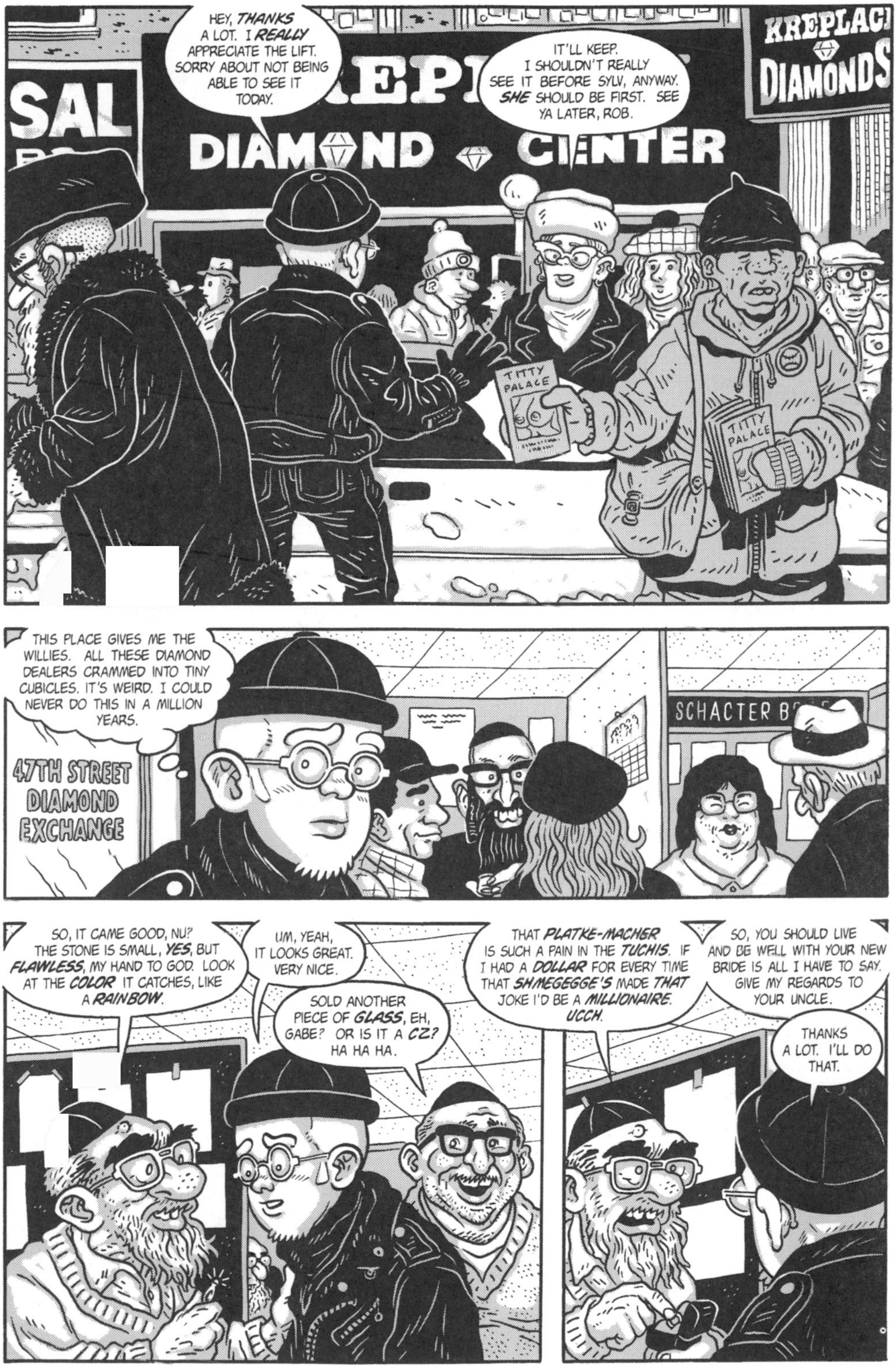
HEY, THANKS A LOT. I REALLY APPRECIATE THE LIFT. SORRY ABOUT NOT BEING ABLE TO SEE IT TODAY.
IT'LL KEEP. I SHOULDN'T REALLY SEE IT BEFORE SYLV, ANYWAY. SHE SHOULD BE FIRST. SEE YA LATER, ROB.
DIAMOND CENTER
KREPLACH DIAMONDS
SAL
TITTY PALACE
THIS PLACE GIVES ME THE WILLIES. ALL THESE DIAMOND DEALERS CRAMMED INTO TINY CUBICLES. IT'S WEIRD. I COULD NEVER DO THIS IN A MILLION YEARS.
47TH STREET DIAMOND EXCHANGE
SCHACTER BR
SO, IT CAME GOOD, NU? THE STONE IS SMALL, YES, BUT FLAWLESS, MY HAND TO GOD. LOOK AT THE COLOR IT CATCHES, LIKE A RAINBOW.
UM, YEAH, IT LOOKS GREAT. VERY NICE.
SOLD ANOTHER PIECE OF GLASS, EH, GABE? OR IS IT A CZ? HA HA HA.
THAT PLATKE-MACHER IS SUCH A PAIN IN THE TUCHIS. IF I HAD A DOLLAR FOR EVERY TIME THAT SHMEGEGGE'S MADE THAT JOKE I'D BE A MILLIONAIRE. UCCH.
SO, YOU SHOULD LIVE AND BE WELL WITH YOUR NEW BRIDE IS ALL I HAVE TO SAY. GIVE MY REGARDS TO YOUR UNCLE.
THANKS A LOT. I'LL DO THAT.

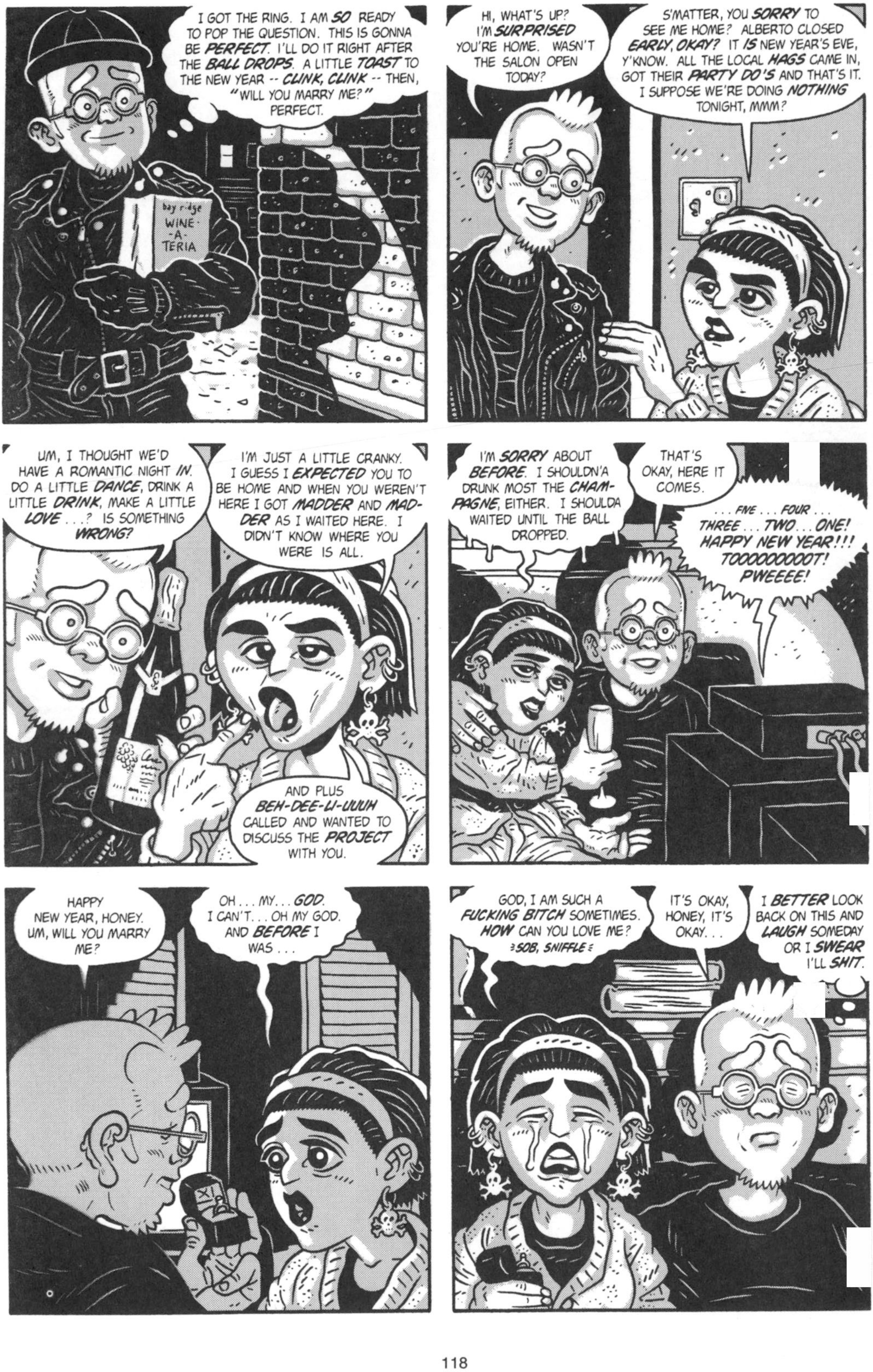
I GOT THE RING. I AM SO READY TO POP THE QUESTION. THIS IS GONNA BE PERFECT. I'LL DO IT RIGHT AFTER THE BALL DROPS. A LITTLE TOAST TO THE NEW YEAR -- CLINK, CLINK -- THEN, "WILL YOU MARRY ME?" PERFECT.
bay ridge WINE-A-TERIA
HI, WHAT'S UP? I'M SURPRISED YOU'RE HOME. WASN'T THE SALON OPEN TODAY?
S'MATTER, YOU SORRY TO SEE ME HOME? ALBERTO CLOSED EARLY, OKAY? IT IS NEW YEAR'S EVE, Y'KNOW. ALL THE LOCAL HAGS CAME IN, GOT THEIR PARTY DO'S AND THAT'S IT. I SUPPOSE WE'RE DOING NOTHING TONIGHT, MMM?
UM, I THOUGHT WE'D HAVE A ROMANTIC NIGHT IN. DO A LITTLE DANCE, DRINK A LITTLE DRINK, MAKE A LITTLE LOVE . . .? IS SOMETHING WRONG?
I'M JUST A LITTLE CRANKY. I GUESS I EXPECTED YOU TO BE HOME AND WHEN YOU WEREN'T HERE I GOT MADDER AND MADDER AS I WAITED HERE. I DIDN'T KNOW WHERE YOU WERE IS ALL.
AND PLUS BEH-DEE-LI-UUUH CALLED AND WANTED TO DISCUSS THE PROJECT WITH YOU.
I'M SORRY ABOUT BEFORE. I SHOULDN'A DRUNK MOST THE CHAMPAGNE, EITHER. I SHOULDA WAITED UNTIL THE BALL DROPPED.
THAT'S OKAY, HERE IT COMES.
. . . FIVE . . . FOUR . . . THREE . . . TWO . . . ONE! HAPPY NEW YEAR!!! TOOOOOOOOOT! PWEEEE!
HAPPY NEW YEAR, HONEY. UM, WILL YOU MARRY ME?
OH . . . MY . . . GOD. I CAN'T . . . OH MY GOD. AND BEFORE I WAS . . .
GOD, I AM SUCH A FUCKING BITCH SOMETIMES. HOW CAN YOU LOVE ME? SOB, SNIFFLE
IT'S OKAY, HONEY, IT'S OKAY . . .
I BETTER LOOK BACK ON THIS AND LAUGH SOMEDAY OR I SWEAR I'LL SHIT.

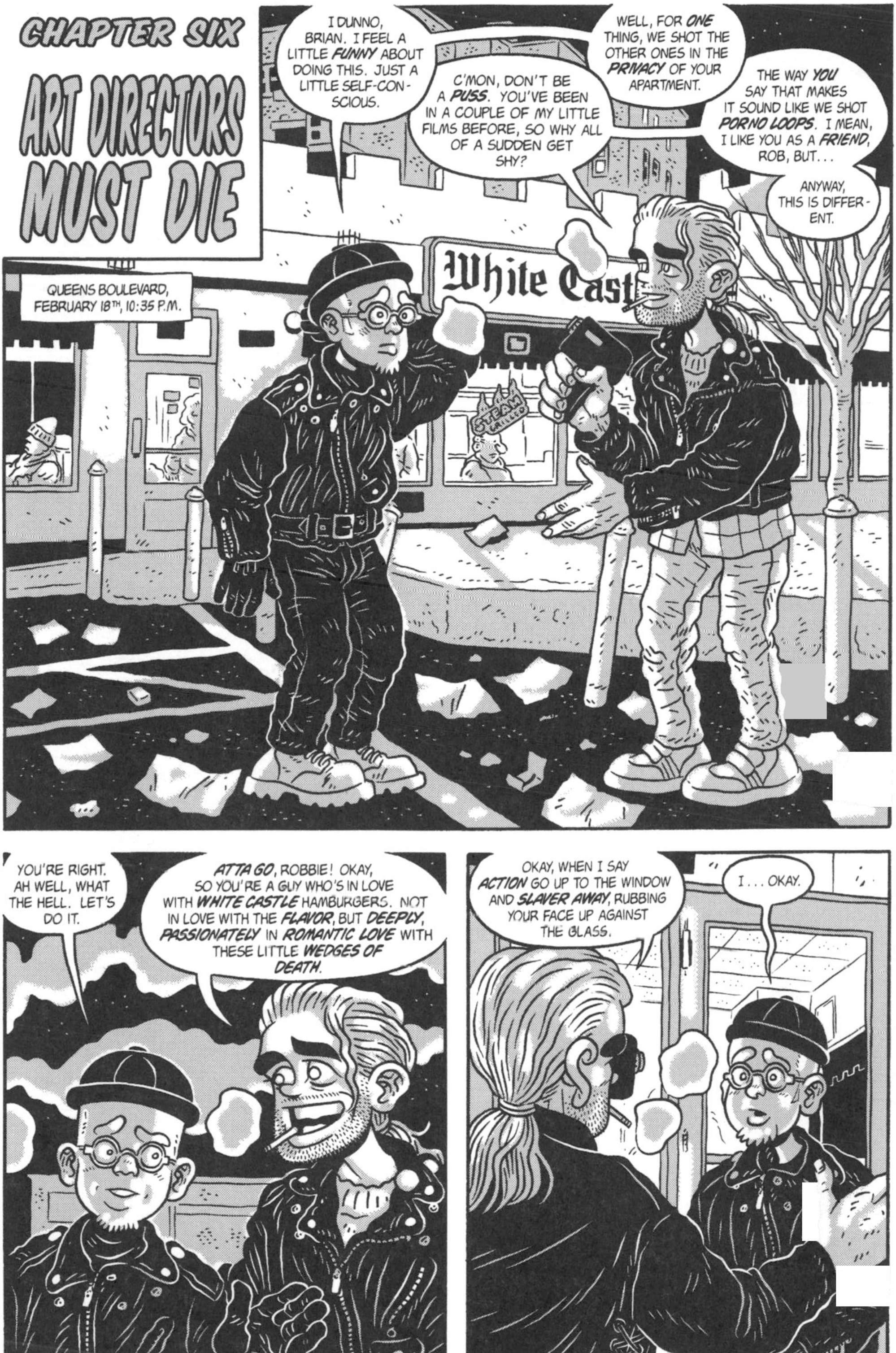
CHAPTER SIX
ART DIRECTORS MUST DIE
I DUNNO, BRIAN. I FEEL A LITTLE FUNNY ABOUT DOING THIS. JUST A LITTLE SELF-CONSCIOUS.
C'MON, DON'T BE A PUSS. YOU'VE BEEN IN A COUPLE OF MY LITTLE FILMS BEFORE, SO WHY ALL OF A SUDDEN GET SHY?
WELL, FOR ONE THING, WE SHOT THE OTHER ONES IN THE PRIVACY OF YOUR APARTMENT.
THE WAY YOU SAY THAT MAKES IT SOUND LIKE WE SHOT PORNO LOOPS. I MEAN, I LIKE YOU AS A FRIEND, ROB, BUT...
ANYWAY, THIS IS DIFFERENT.
QUEENS BOULEVARD, FEBRUARY 18TH, 10:35 P.M.
White Cast
STEAM GRILLED
YOU'RE RIGHT. AH WELL, WHAT THE HELL. LET'S DO IT.
ATTA GO, ROBBIE! OKAY, SO YOU'RE A GUY WHO'S IN LOVE WITH WHITE CASTLE HAMBURGERS. NOT IN LOVE WITH THE FLAVOR, BUT DEEPLY, PASSIONATELY IN ROMANTIC LOVE WITH THESE LITTLE WEDGES OF DEATH.
OKAY, WHEN I SAY ACTION GO UP TO THE WINDOW AND SLAVER AWAY, RUBBING YOUR FACE UP AGAINST THE GLASS.
I... OKAY.

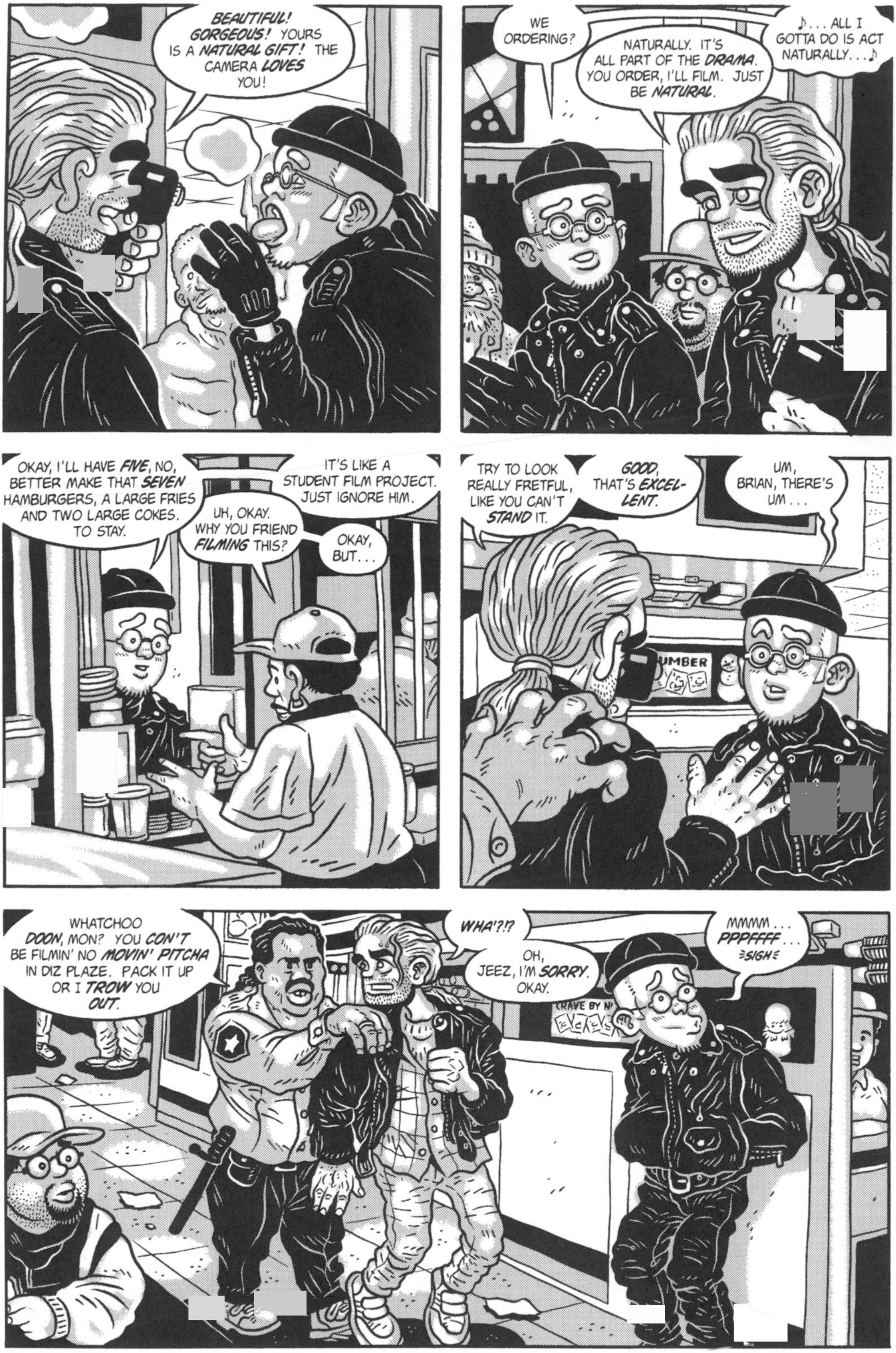
BEAUTIFUL! GORGEOUS! YOURS IS A NATURAL GIFT! THE CAMERA LOVES YOU!
WE ORDERING?
NATURALLY. IT'S ALL PART OF THE DRAMA. YOU ORDER, I'LL FILM. JUST BE NATURAL.
♪... ALL I GOTTA DO IS ACT NATURALLY...♪
OKAY, I'LL HAVE FIVE, NO, BETTER MAKE THAT SEVEN HAMBURGERS, A LARGE FRIES AND TWO LARGE COKES. TO STAY.
UH, OKAY. WHY YOU FRIEND FILMING THIS?
IT'S LIKE A STUDENT FILM PROJECT. JUST IGNORE HIM.
OKAY, BUT...
TRY TO LOOK REALLY FRETFUL, LIKE YOU CAN'T STAND IT.
GOOD, THAT'S EXCEL-LENT.
UM, BRIAN, THERE'S UM...
WHATCHOO DOON, MON? YOU CON'T BE FILMIN' NO MOVIN' PITCHA IN DIZ PLAZE. PACK IT UP OR I TROW YOU OUT.
WHA'?!?
OH, JEEZ, I'M SORRY. OKAY.
MMMM... PPPFFFF... SIGH

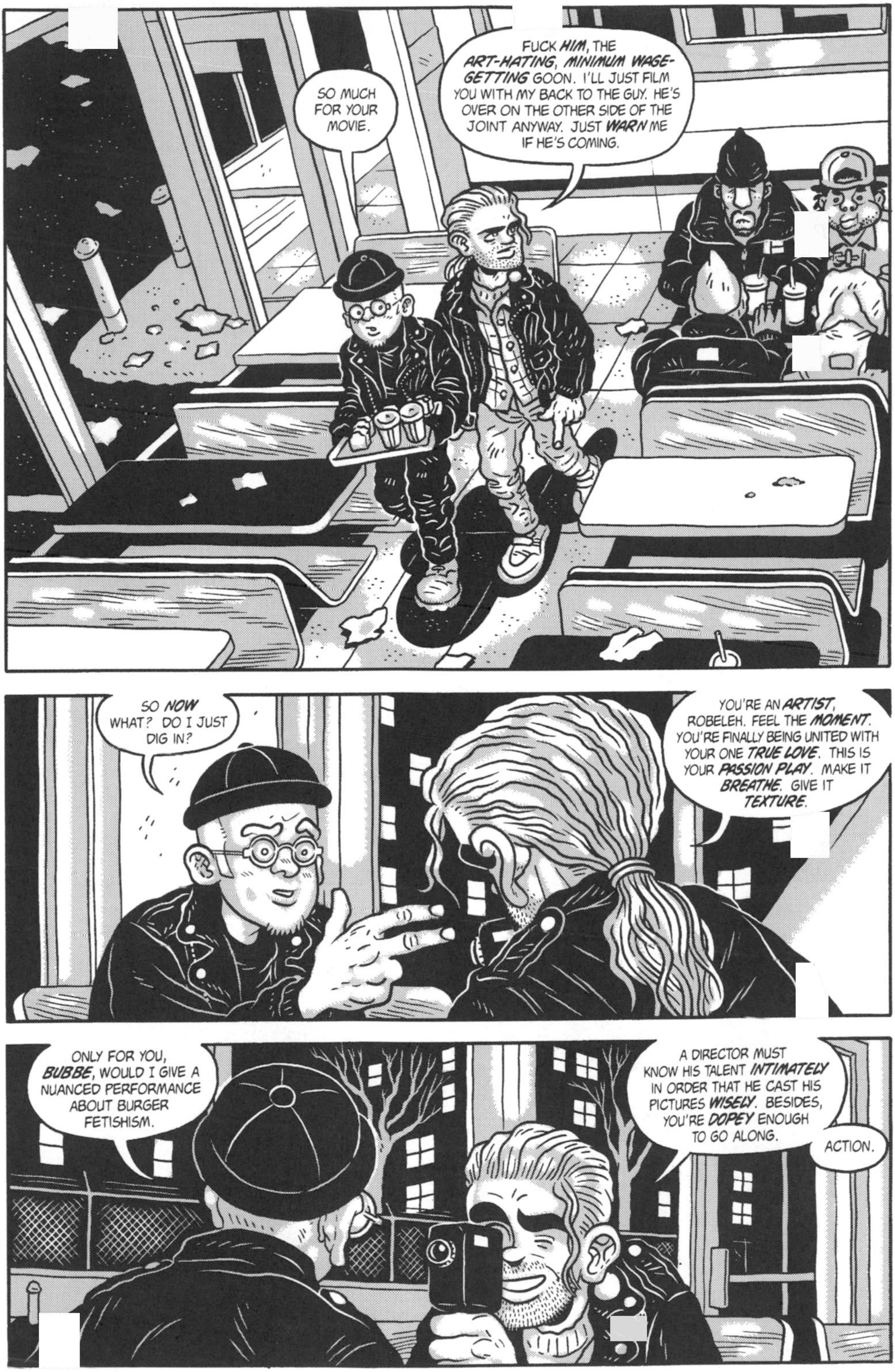
SO MUCH FOR YOUR MOVIE.
FUCK HIM, THE ART-HATING, MINIMUM WAGE-GETTING GOON. I'LL JUST FILM YOU WITH MY BACK TO THE GUY. HE'S OVER ON THE OTHER SIDE OF THE JOINT ANYWAY. JUST WARN ME IF HE'S COMING.
SO NOW WHAT? DO I JUST DIG IN?
YOU'RE AN ARTIST, ROBELEH. FEEL THE MOMENT. YOU'RE FINALLY BEING UNITED WITH YOUR ONE TRUE LOVE. THIS IS YOUR PASSION PLAY. MAKE IT BREATHE. GIVE IT TEXTURE.
ONLY FOR YOU, BUBBE, WOULD I GIVE A NUANCED PERFORMANCE ABOUT BURGER FETISHISM.
A DIRECTOR MUST KNOW HIS TALENT INTIMATELY IN ORDER THAT HE CAST HIS PICTURES WISELY. BESIDES, YOU'RE DOPEY ENOUGH TO GO ALONG.
ACTION.

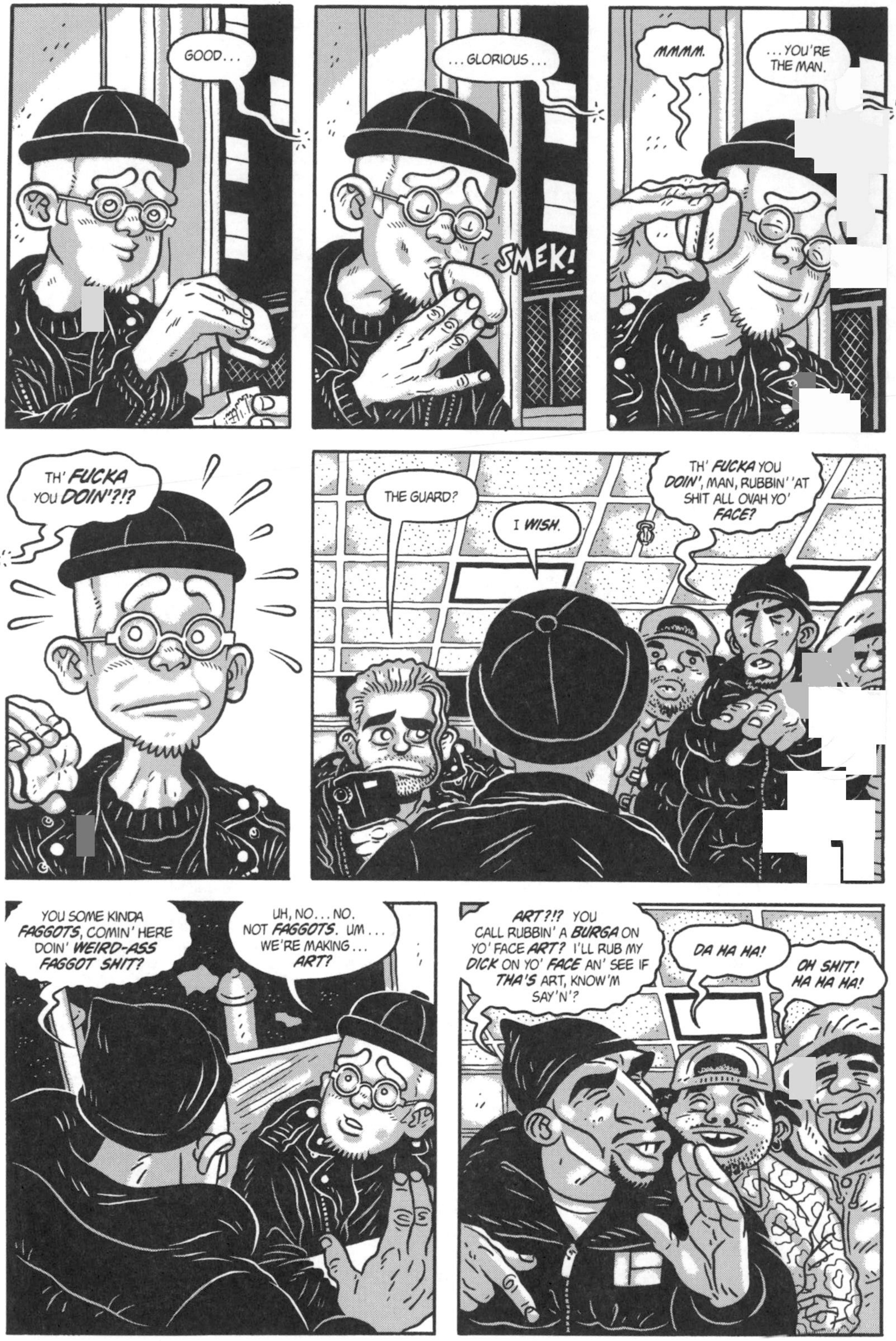
GOOD...
...GLORIOUS...
SMEK!
MMMM.
...YOU'RE THE MAN.
TH' FUCKA YOU DOIN'?!?
THE GUARD?
I WISH.
TH' FUCKA YOU DOIN', MAN, RUBBIN' 'AT SHIT ALL OVAH YO' FACE?
YOU SOME KINDA FAGGOTS, COMIN' HERE DOIN' WEIRD-ASS FAGGOT SHIT?
UH, NO... NO. NOT FAGGOTS. UM... WE'RE MAKING... ART?
ART?!? YOU CALL RUBBIN' A BURGA ON YO' FACE ART? I'LL RUB MY DICK ON YO' FACE AN' SEE IF THA'S ART, KNOW'M SAY'N'?
DA HA HA!
OH SHIT! HA HA HA!

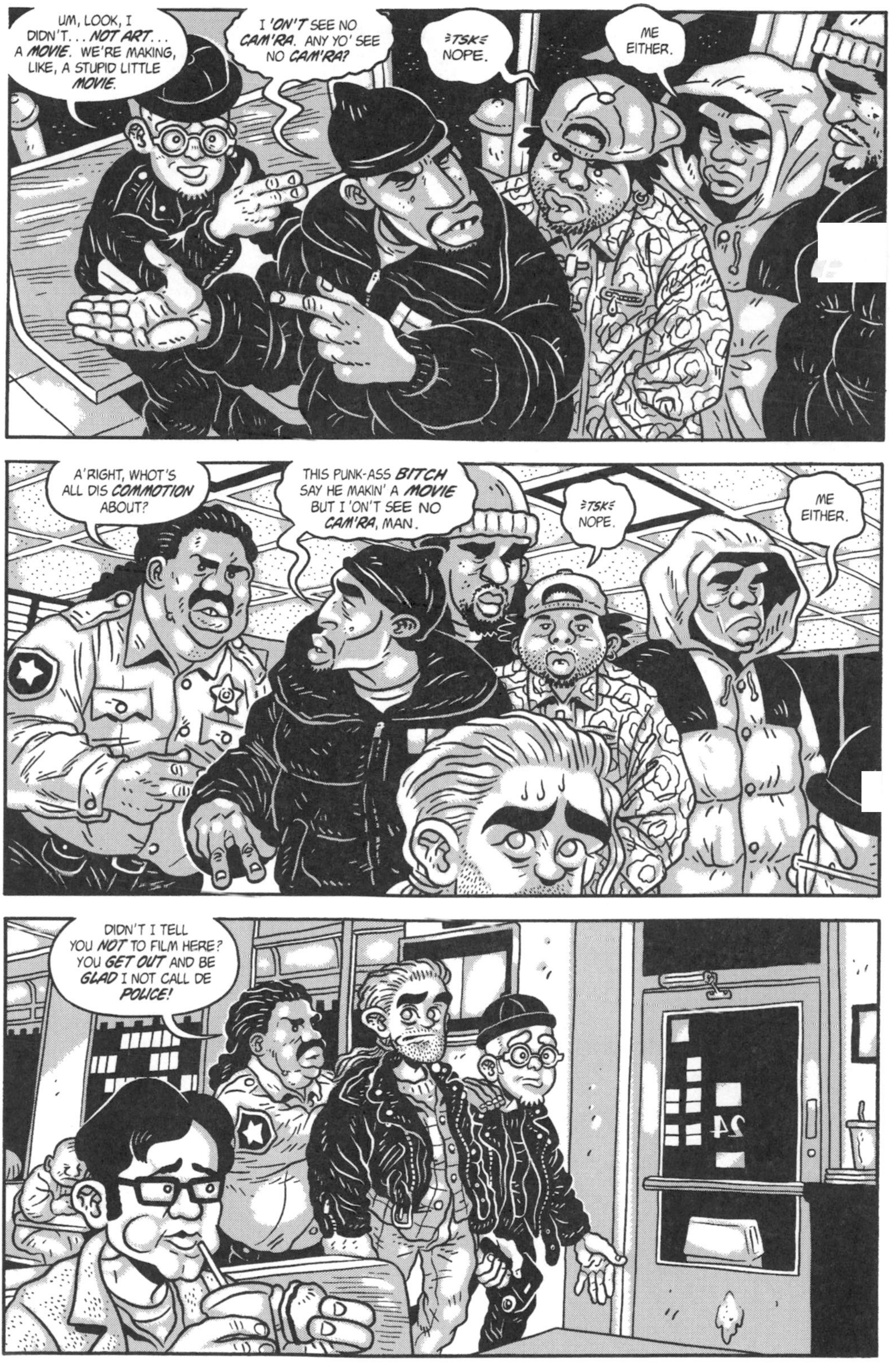
UM, LOOK, I DIDN'T... NOT ART... A MOVIE. WE'RE MAKING, LIKE, A STUPID LITTLE MOVIE.
I 'ON'T SEE NO CAM'RA. ANY YO' SEE NO CAM'RA?
TSK NOPE.
ME EITHER.
A'RIGHT, WHOT'S ALL DIS COMMOTION ABOUT?
THIS PUNK-ASS BITCH SAY HE MAKIN' A MOVIE BUT I 'ON'T SEE NO CAM'RA, MAN.
TSK NOPE.
ME EITHER.
DIDN'T I TELL YOU NOT TO FILM HERE? YOU GET OUT AND BE GLAD I NOT CALL DE POLICE!
24

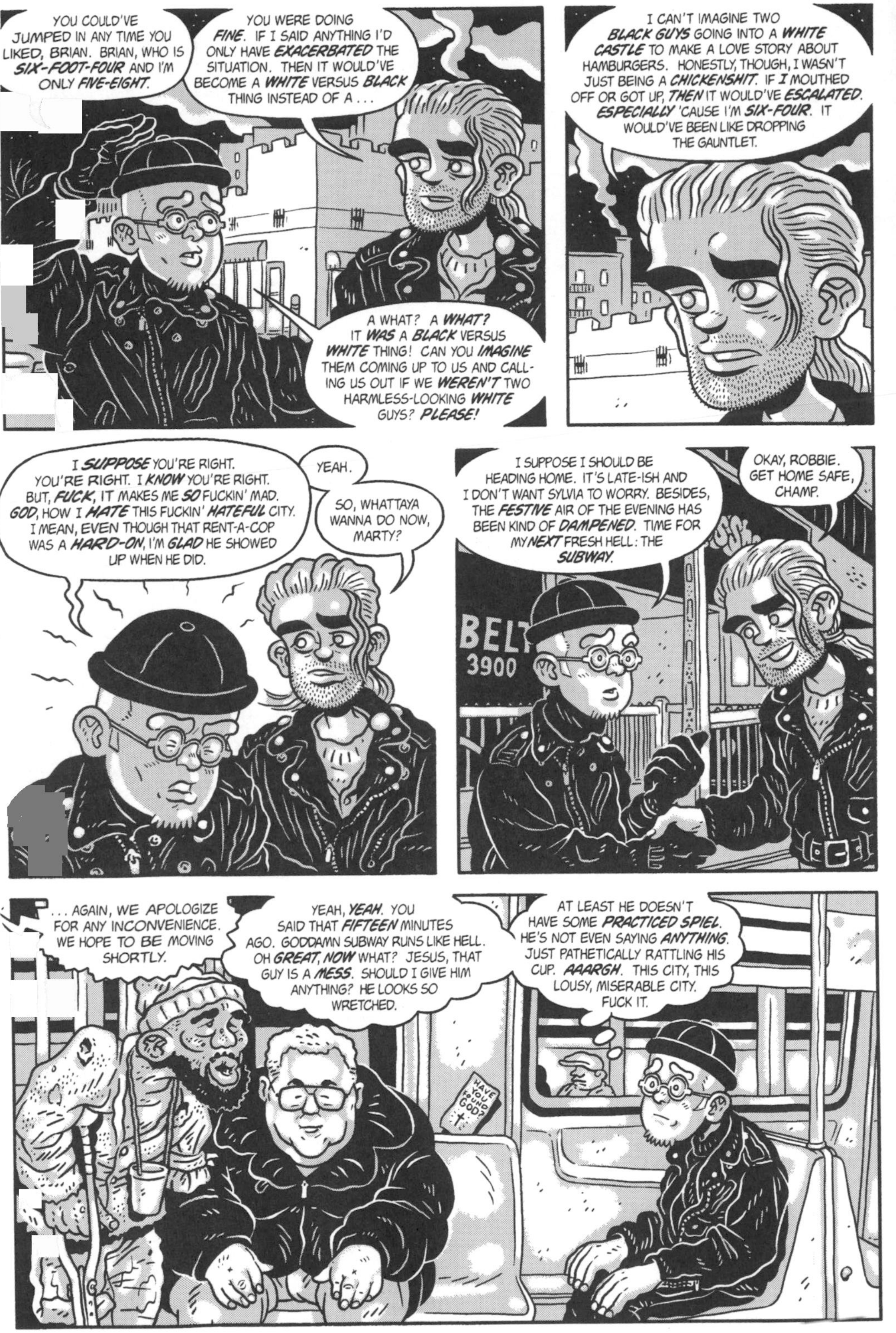
YOU COULD'VE JUMPED IN ANY TIME YOU LIKED, BRIAN. BRIAN, WHO IS SIX-FOOT-FOUR AND I'M ONLY FIVE-EIGHT.
YOU WERE DOING FINE. IF I SAID ANYTHING I'D ONLY HAVE EXACERBATED THE SITUATION. THEN IT WOULD'VE BECOME A WHITE VERSUS BLACK THING INSTEAD OF A . . .
A WHAT? A WHAT? IT WAS A BLACK VERSUS WHITE THING! CAN YOU IMAGINE THEM COMING UP TO US AND CALLING US OUT IF WE WEREN'T TWO HARMLESS-LOOKING WHITE GUYS? PLEASE!
I CAN'T IMAGINE TWO BLACK GUYS GOING INTO A WHITE CASTLE TO MAKE A LOVE STORY ABOUT HAMBURGERS. HONESTLY, THOUGH, I WASN'T JUST BEING A CHICKENSHIT. IF I MOUTHED OFF OR GOT UP, THEN IT WOULD'VE ESCALATED. ESPECIALLY 'CAUSE I'M SIX-FOUR. IT WOULD'VE BEEN LIKE DROPPING THE GAUNTLET.
I SUPPOSE YOU'RE RIGHT. YOU'RE RIGHT. I KNOW YOU'RE RIGHT. BUT, FUCK, IT MAKES ME SO FUCKIN' MAD. GOD, HOW I HATE THIS FUCKIN' HATEFUL CITY. I MEAN, EVEN THOUGH THAT RENT-A-COP WAS A HARD-ON, I'M GLAD HE SHOWED UP WHEN HE DID.
YEAH.
SO, WHATTAYA WANNA DO NOW, MARTY?
I SUPPOSE I SHOULD BE HEADING HOME. IT'S LATE-ISH AND I DON'T WANT SYLVIA TO WORRY. BESIDES, THE FESTIVE AIR OF THE EVENING HAS BEEN KIND OF DAMPENED. TIME FOR MY NEXT FRESH HELL: THE SUBWAY.
OKAY, ROBBIE. GET HOME SAFE, CHAMP.
BELT
3900
. . . AGAIN, WE APOLOGIZE FOR ANY INCONVENIENCE. WE HOPE TO BE MOVING SHORTLY.
YEAH, YEAH. YOU SAID THAT FIFTEEN MINUTES AGO. GODDAMN SUBWAY RUNS LIKE HELL. OH GREAT, NOW WHAT? JESUS, THAT GUY IS A MESS. SHOULD I GIVE HIM ANYTHING? HE LOOKS SO WRETCHED.
AT LEAST HE DOESN'T HAVE SOME PRACTICED SPIEL. HE'S NOT EVEN SAYING ANYTHING. JUST PATHETICALLY RATTLING HIS CUP. AAARGH. THIS CITY, THIS LOUSY, MISERABLE CITY. FUCK IT.
HAVE YOU FOUND GOD?

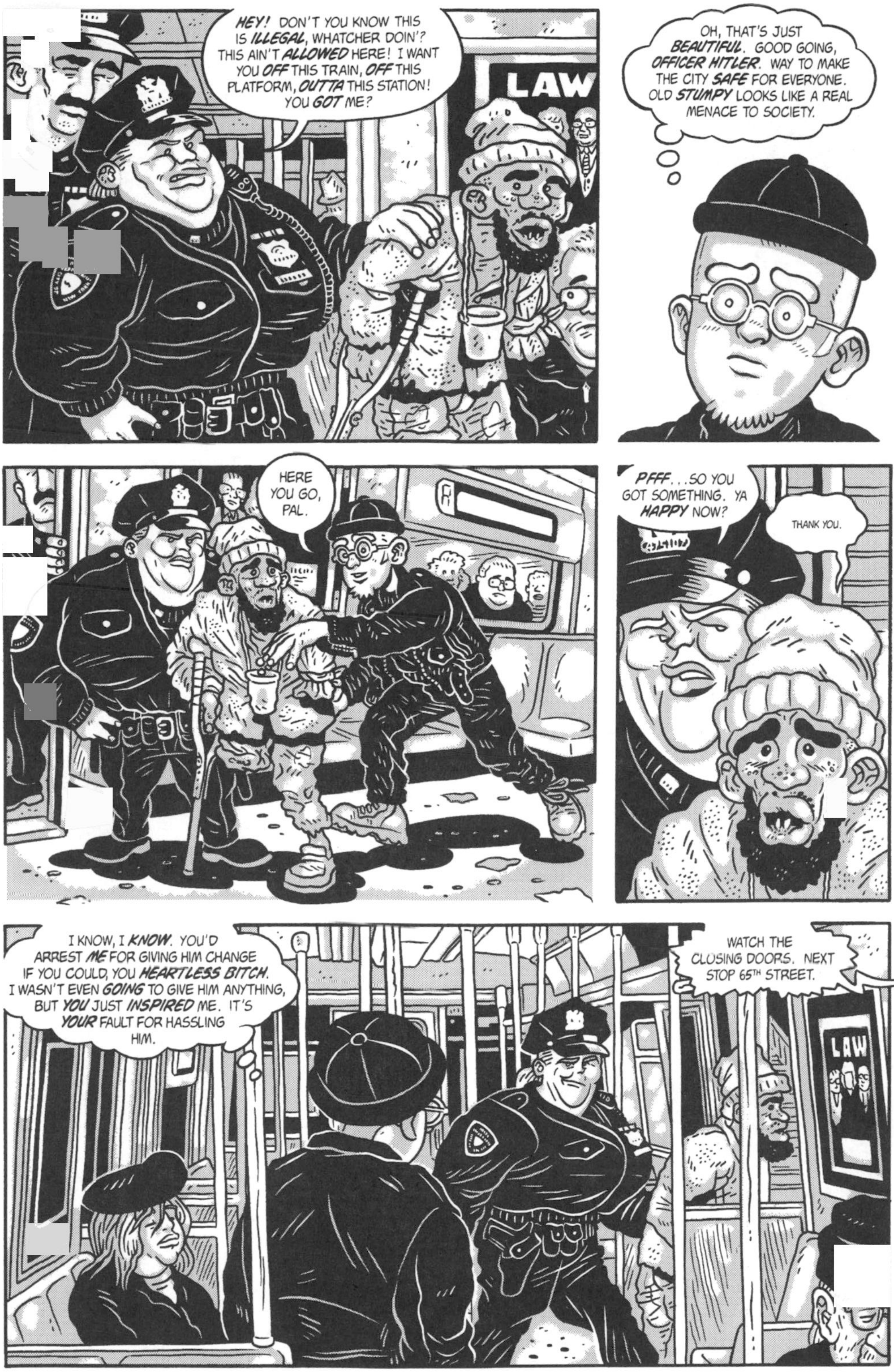
HEY! DON'T YOU KNOW THIS IS ILLEGAL, WHATCHER DOIN'? THIS AIN'T ALLOWED HERE! I WANT YOU OFF THIS TRAIN, OFF THIS PLATFORM, OUTTA THIS STATION! YOU GOT ME?
LAW
OH, THAT'S JUST BEAUTIFUL. GOOD GOING, OFFICER HITLER. WAY TO MAKE THE CITY SAFE FOR EVERYONE. OLD STUMPY LOOKS LIKE A REAL MENACE TO SOCIETY.
HERE YOU GO, PAL.
PFFF. . . SO YOU GOT SOMETHING. YA HAPPY NOW?
THANK YOU.
I KNOW, I KNOW. YOU'D ARREST ME FOR GIVING HIM CHANGE IF YOU COULD, YOU HEARTLESS BITCH. I WASN'T EVEN GOING TO GIVE HIM ANYTHING, BUT YOU JUST INSPIRED ME. IT'S YOUR FAULT FOR HASSLING HIM.
WATCH THE CLOSING DOORS. NEXT STOP 65TH STREET.
LAW

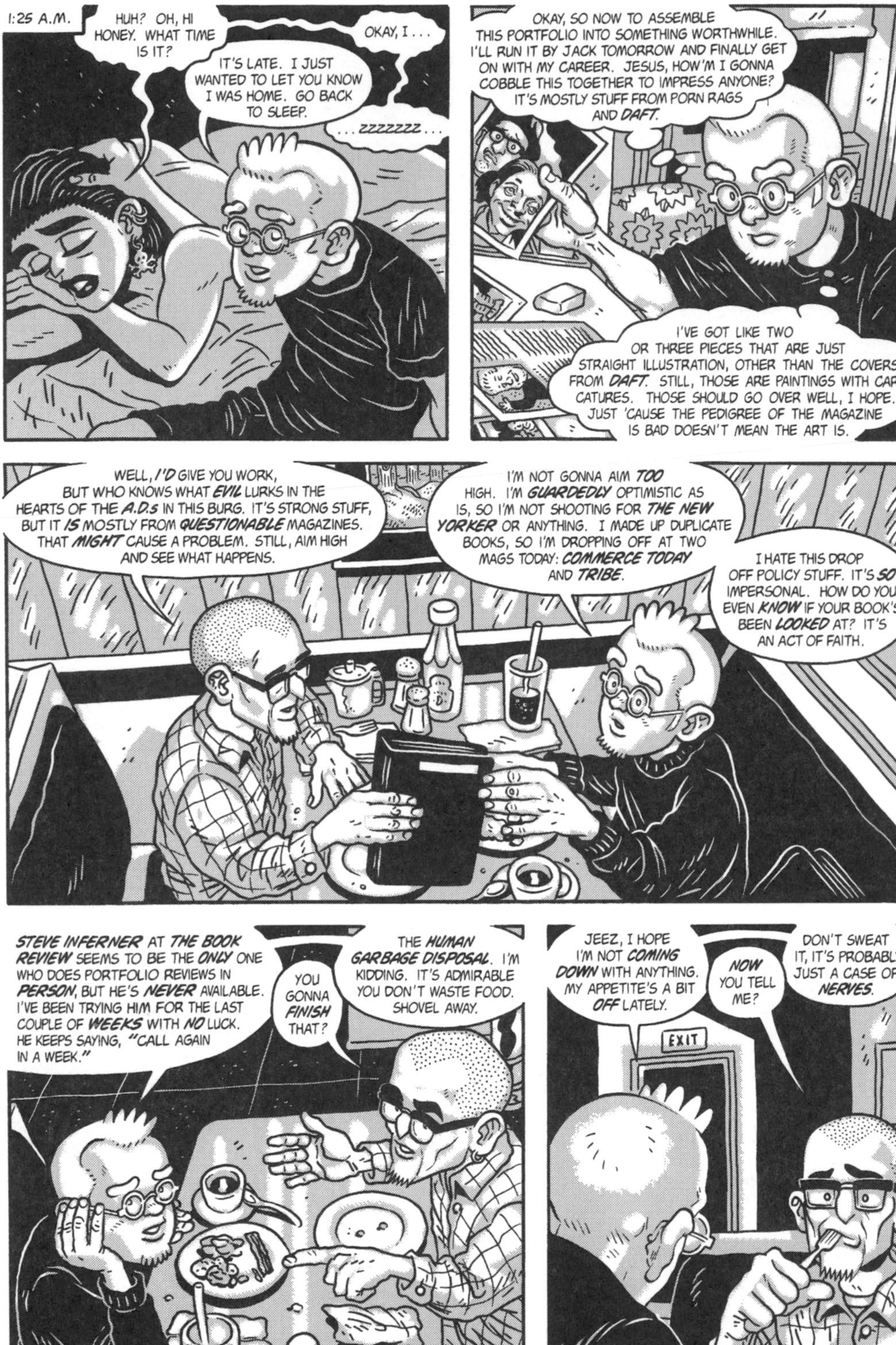
1:25 A.M.
HUH? OH, HI HONEY. WHAT TIME IS IT?
IT'S LATE. I JUST WANTED TO LET YOU KNOW I WAS HOME. GO BACK TO SLEEP.
OKAY, I . . .
. . . ZZZZZZZ . . .
OKAY, SO NOW TO ASSEMBLE THIS PORTFOLIO INTO SOMETHING WORTHWHILE. I'LL RUN IT BY JACK TOMORROW AND FINALLY GET ON WITH MY CAREER. JESUS, HOW'M I GONNA COBBLE THIS TOGETHER TO IMPRESS ANYONE? IT'S MOSTLY STUFF FROM PORN RAGS AND DAFT.
I'VE GOT LIKE TWO OR THREE PIECES THAT ARE JUST STRAIGHT ILLUSTRATION, OTHER THAN THE COVERS FROM DAFT. STILL, THOSE ARE PAINTINGS WITH CARICATURES. THOSE SHOULD GO OVER WELL, I HOPE. JUST 'CAUSE THE PEDIGREE OF THE MAGAZINE IS BAD DOESN'T MEAN THE ART IS.
WELL, I'D GIVE YOU WORK, BUT WHO KNOWS WHAT EVIL LURKS IN THE HEARTS OF THE A.D.s IN THIS BURG. IT'S STRONG STUFF, BUT IT IS MOSTLY FROM QUESTIONABLE MAGAZINES. THAT MIGHT CAUSE A PROBLEM. STILL, AIM HIGH AND SEE WHAT HAPPENS.
I'M NOT GONNA AIM TOO HIGH. I'M GUARDEDLY OPTIMISTIC AS IS, SO I'M NOT SHOOTING FOR THE NEW YORKER OR ANYTHING. I MADE UP DUPLICATE BOOKS, SO I'M DROPPING OFF AT TWO MAGS TODAY: COMMERCE TODAY AND TRIBE.
I HATE THIS DROP OFF POLICY STUFF. IT'S SO IMPERSONAL. HOW DO YOU EVEN KNOW IF YOUR BOOK'S BEEN LOOKED AT? IT'S AN ACT OF FAITH.
STEVE INFERNER AT THE BOOK REVIEW SEEMS TO BE THE ONLY ONE WHO DOES PORTFOLIO REVIEWS IN PERSON, BUT HE'S NEVER AVAILABLE. I'VE BEEN TRYING HIM FOR THE LAST COUPLE OF WEEKS WITH NO LUCK. HE KEEPS SAYING, "CALL AGAIN IN A WEEK."
YOU GONNA FINISH THAT?
THE HUMAN GARBAGE DISPOSAL. I'M KIDDING. IT'S ADMIRABLE YOU DON'T WASTE FOOD. SHOVEL AWAY.
JEEZ, I HOPE I'M NOT COMING DOWN WITH ANYTHING. MY APPETITE'S A BIT OFF LATELY.
NOW YOU TELL ME?
DON'T SWEAT IT, IT'S PROBABLY JUST A CASE OF NERVES.
EXIT

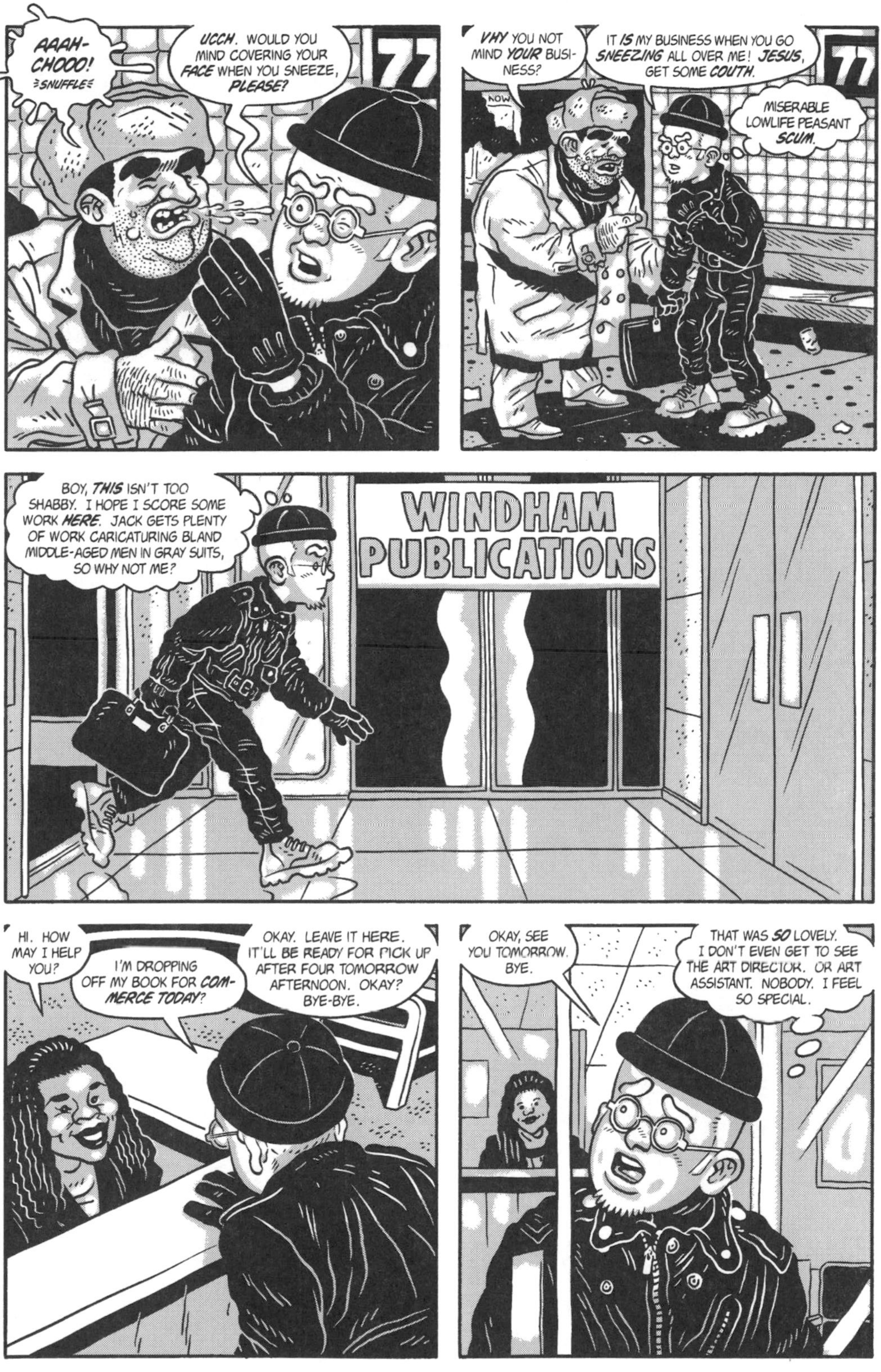
AAAH-CHOOO! ≡SNUFFLE≡
UCCH. WOULD YOU MIND COVERING YOUR FACE WHEN YOU SNEEZE, PLEASE?
77
VHY YOU NOT MIND YOUR BUSINESS?
IT IS MY BUSINESS WHEN YOU GO SNEEZING ALL OVER ME! JESUS, GET SOME COUTH.
MISERABLE LOWLIFE PEASANT SCUM.
77
BOY, THIS ISN'T TOO SHABBY. I HOPE I SCORE SOME WORK HERE. JACK GETS PLENTY OF WORK CARICATURING BLAND MIDDLE-AGED MEN IN GRAY SUITS, SO WHY NOT ME?
WINDHAM PUBLICATIONS
HI. HOW MAY I HELP YOU?
I'M DROPPING OFF MY BOOK FOR COMMERCE TODAY?
OKAY. LEAVE IT HERE. IT'LL BE READY FOR PICK UP AFTER FOUR TOMORROW AFTERNOON. OKAY? BYE-BYE.
OKAY, SEE YOU TOMORROW. BYE.
THAT WAS SO LOVELY. I DON'T EVEN GET TO SEE THE ART DIRECTOR. OR ART ASSISTANT. NOBODY. I FEEL SO SPECIAL.

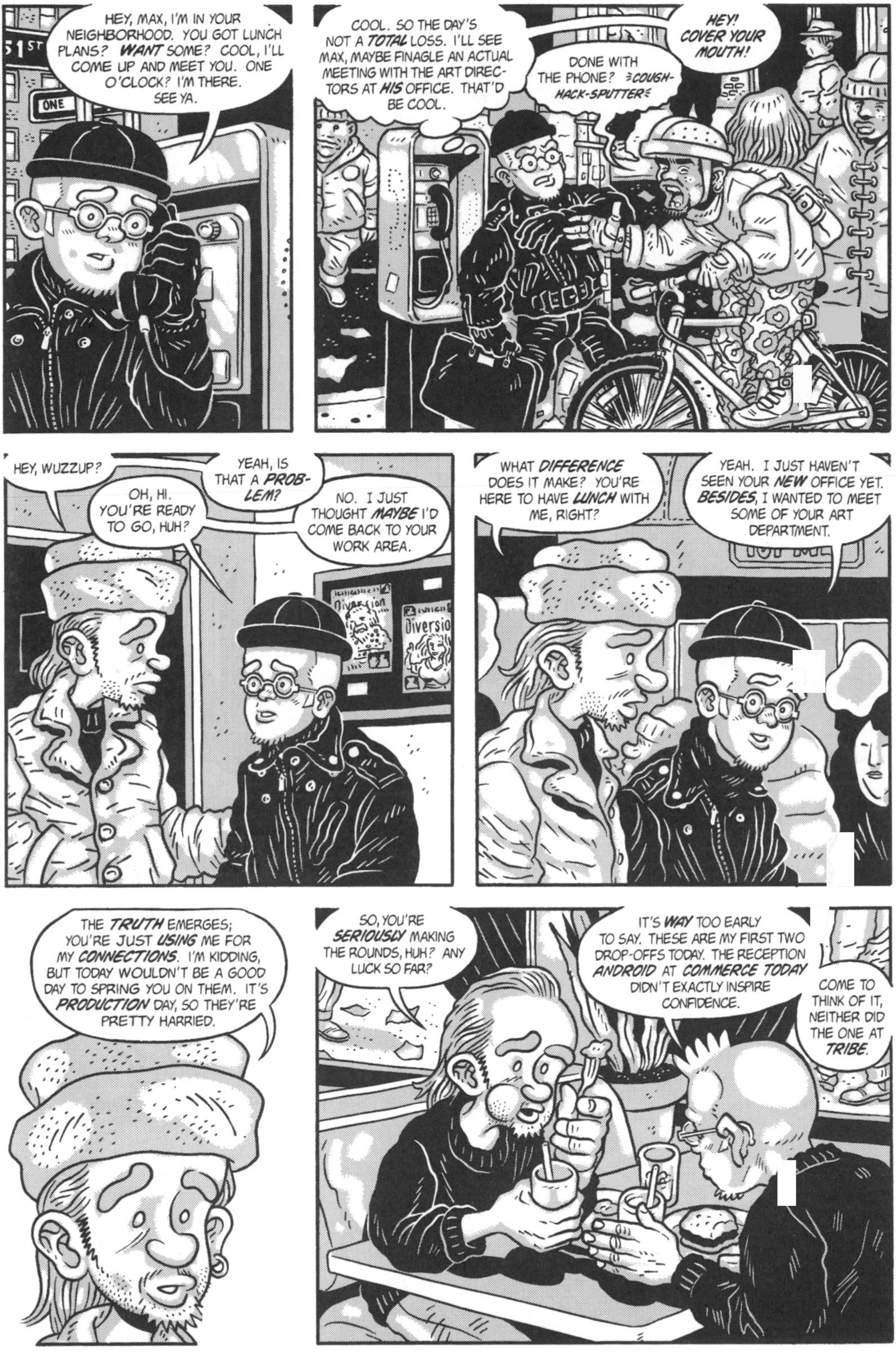
51ST
ONE
HEY, MAX, I'M IN YOUR NEIGHBORHOOD. YOU GOT LUNCH PLANS? WANT SOME? COOL, I'LL COME UP AND MEET YOU. ONE O'CLOCK? I'M THERE. SEE YA.
COOL. SO THE DAY'S NOT A TOTAL LOSS. I'LL SEE MAX, MAYBE FINAGLE AN ACTUAL MEETING WITH THE ART DIRECTORS AT HIS OFFICE. THAT'D BE COOL.
DONE WITH THE PHONE? ≷COUGH-HACK-SPUTTER≶
HEY! COVER YOUR MOUTH!
HEY, WUZZUP?
OH, HI. YOU'RE READY TO GO, HUH?
YEAH, IS THAT A PROBLEM?
NO. I JUST THOUGHT MAYBE I'D COME BACK TO YOUR WORK AREA.
WHAT DIFFERENCE DOES IT MAKE? YOU'RE HERE TO HAVE LUNCH WITH ME, RIGHT?
YEAH. I JUST HAVEN'T SEEN YOUR NEW OFFICE YET. BESIDES, I WANTED TO MEET SOME OF YOUR ART DEPARTMENT.
THE TRUTH EMERGES; YOU'RE JUST USING ME FOR MY CONNECTIONS. I'M KIDDING, BUT TODAY WOULDN'T BE A GOOD DAY TO SPRING YOU ON THEM. IT'S PRODUCTION DAY, SO THEY'RE PRETTY HARRIED.
SO, YOU'RE SERIOUSLY MAKING THE ROUNDS, HUH? ANY LUCK SO FAR?
IT'S WAY TOO EARLY TO SAY. THESE ARE MY FIRST TWO DROP-OFFS TODAY. THE RECEPTION ANDROID AT COMMERCE TODAY DIDN'T EXACTLY INSPIRE CONFIDENCE.
COME TO THINK OF IT, NEITHER DID THE ONE AT TRIBE.

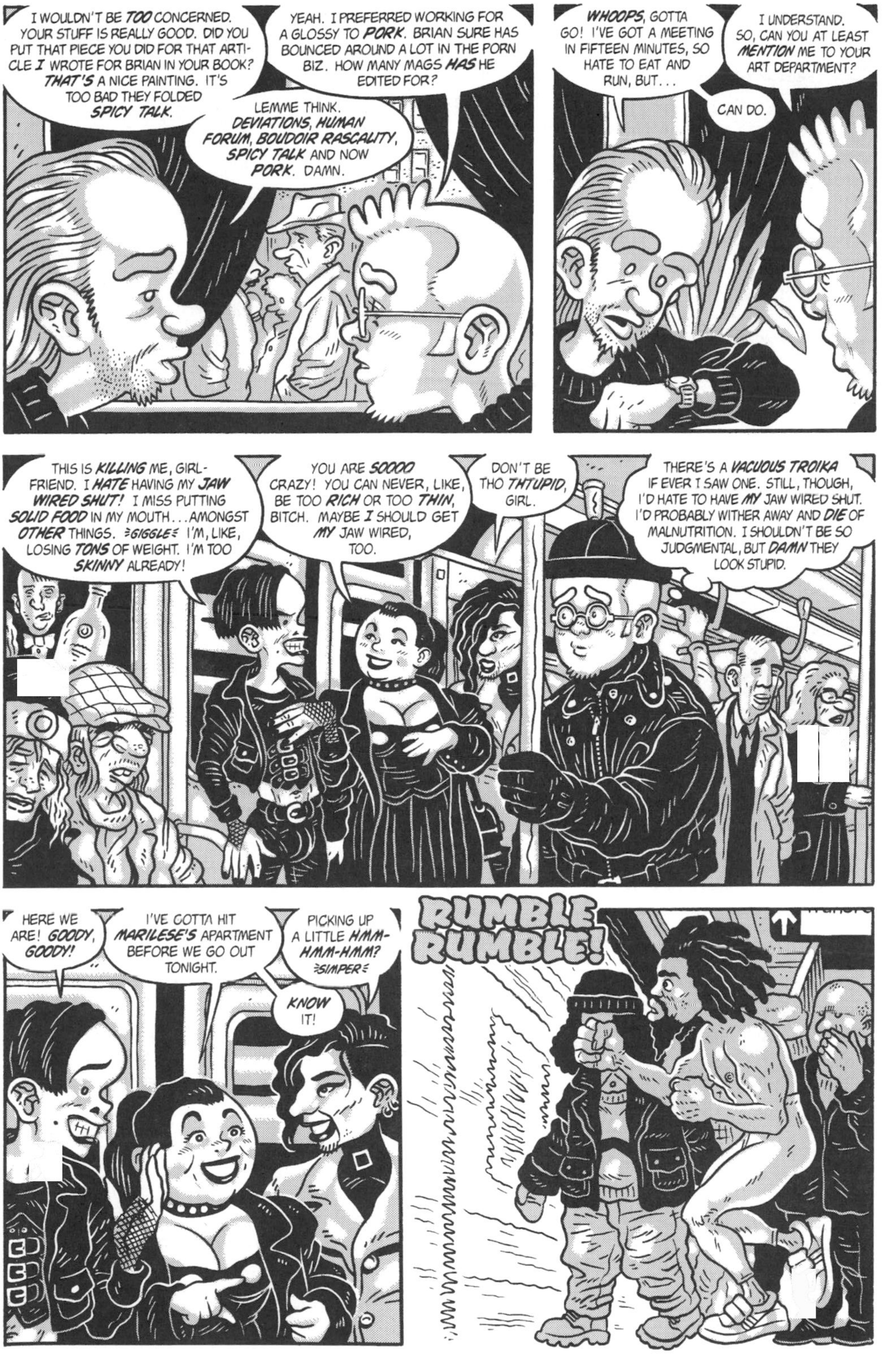
I WOULDN'T BE TOO CONCERNED. YOUR STUFF IS REALLY GOOD. DID YOU PUT THAT PIECE YOU DID FOR THAT ARTICLE I WROTE FOR BRIAN IN YOUR BOOK? THAT'S A NICE PAINTING. IT'S TOO BAD THEY FOLDED SPICY TALK.
YEAH. I PREFERRED WORKING FOR A GLOSSY TO PORK. BRIAN SURE HAS BOUNCED AROUND A LOT IN THE PORN BIZ. HOW MANY MAGS HAS HE EDITED FOR?
LEMME THINK. DEVIATIONS, HUMAN FORUM, BOUDOIR RASCALITY, SPICY TALK AND NOW PORK. DAMN.
WHOOPS, GOTTA GO! I'VE GOT A MEETING IN FIFTEEN MINUTES, SO HATE TO EAT AND RUN, BUT...
I UNDERSTAND. SO, CAN YOU AT LEAST MENTION ME TO YOUR ART DEPARTMENT?
CAN DO.
THIS IS KILLING ME, GIRLFRIEND. I HATE HAVING MY JAW WIRED SHUT! I MISS PUTTING SOLID FOOD IN MY MOUTH...AMONGST OTHER THINGS. ≡GIGGLE≡ I'M, LIKE, LOSING TONS OF WEIGHT. I'M TOO SKINNY ALREADY!
YOU ARE SOOOO CRAZY! YOU CAN NEVER, LIKE, BE TOO RICH OR TOO THIN, BITCH. MAYBE I SHOULD GET MY JAW WIRED, TOO.
DON'T BE THO THTUPID, GIRL.
THERE'S A VACUOUS TROIKA IF EVER I SAW ONE. STILL, THOUGH, I'D HATE TO HAVE MY JAW WIRED SHUT. I'D PROBABLY WITHER AWAY AND DIE OF MALNUTRITION. I SHOULDN'T BE SO JUDGMENTAL, BUT DAMN THEY LOOK STUPID.
HERE WE ARE! GOODY, GOODY!
I'VE GOTTA HIT MARILESE'S APARTMENT BEFORE WE GO OUT TONIGHT.
PICKING UP A LITTLE HMM-HMM-HMM? ≡SIMPER≡
KNOW IT!
RUMBLE RUMBLE!

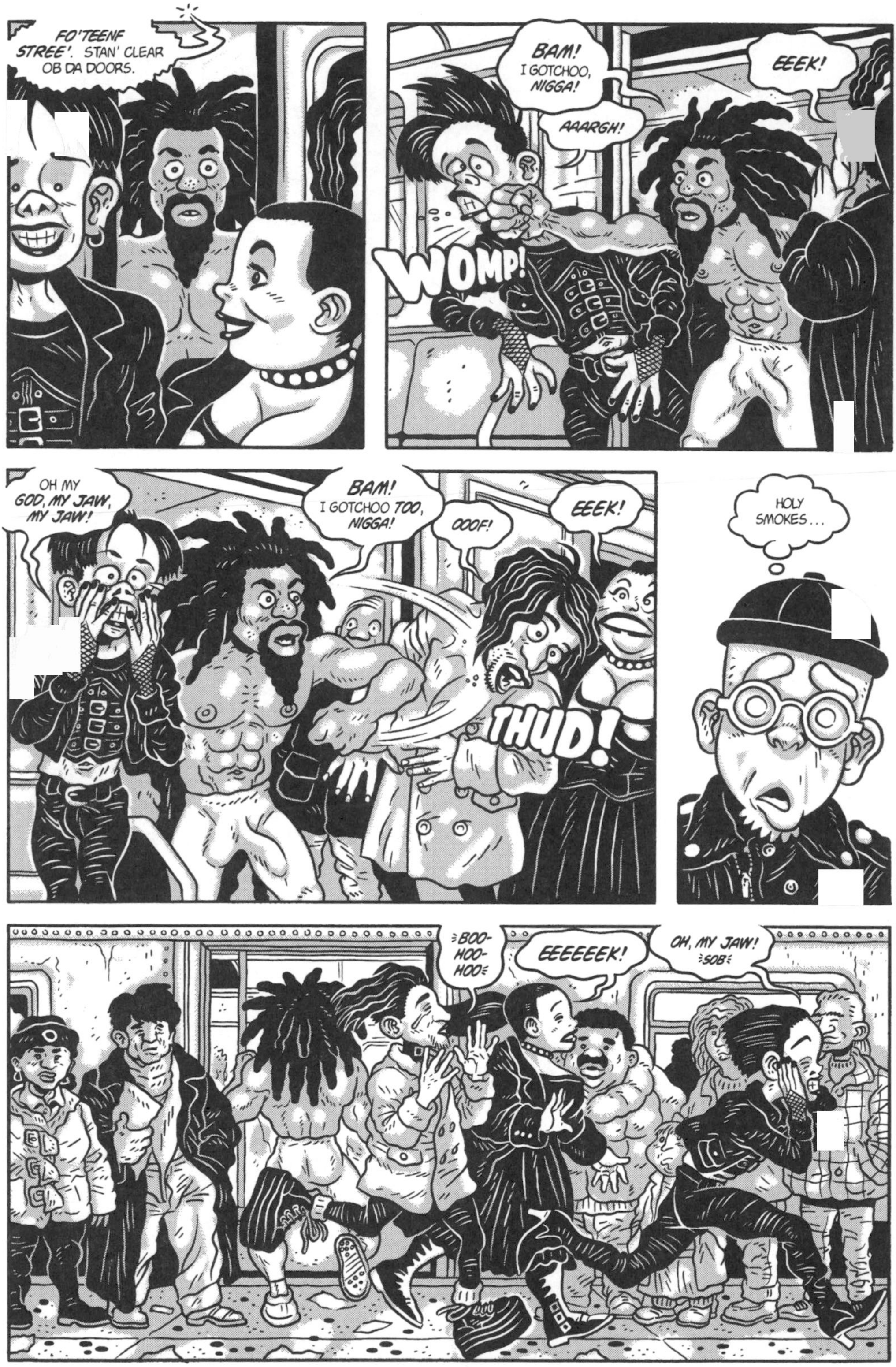
FO'TEENF STREE'. STAN' CLEAR OB DA DOORS.
BAM! I GOTCHOO, NIGGA!
AAARGH!
EEEK!
WOMP!
OH MY GOD, MY JAW, MY JAW!
BAM! I GOTCHOO TOO, NIGGA!
OOOF!
EEEK!
THUD!
HOLY SMOKES...
BOO-HOO-HOO
EEEEEEK!
OH, MY JAW!
SOB

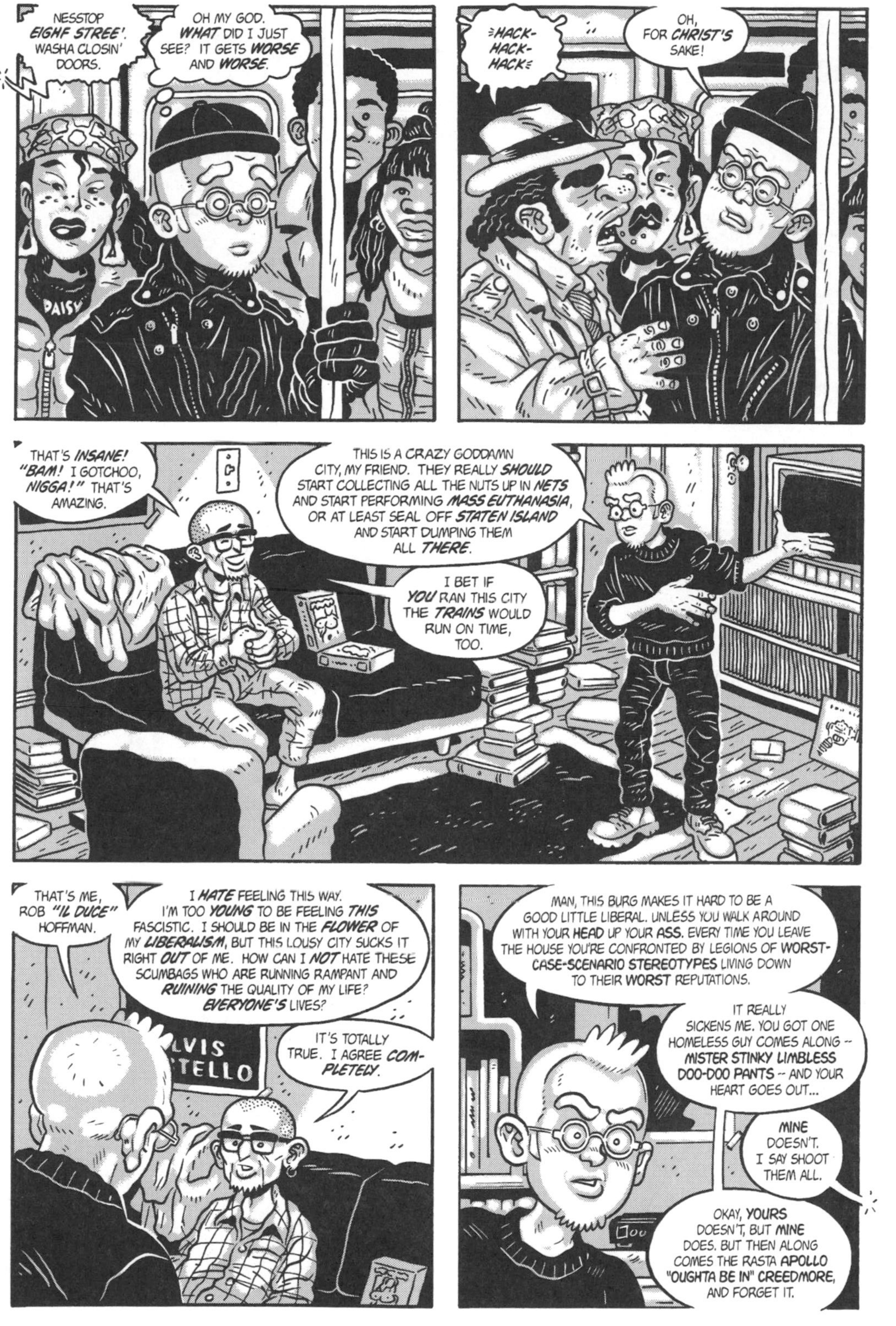
NESSTOP EIGHF STREE'. WASHA CLOSIN' DOORS.
OH MY GOD. WHAT DID I JUST SEE? IT GETS WORSE AND WORSE.
DAISY
HACK-HACK-HACK
OH, FOR CHRIST'S SAKE!
THAT'S INSANE! "BAM! I GOTCHOO, NIGGA!" THAT'S AMAZING.
THIS IS A CRAZY GODDAMN CITY, MY FRIEND. THEY REALLY SHOULD START COLLECTING ALL THE NUTS UP IN NETS AND START PERFORMING MASS EUTHANASIA, OR AT LEAST SEAL OFF STATEN ISLAND AND START DUMPING THEM ALL THERE.
I BET IF YOU RAN THIS CITY THE TRAINS WOULD RUN ON TIME, TOO.
THAT'S ME, ROB "IL DUCE" HOFFMAN.
I HATE FEELING THIS WAY. I'M TOO YOUNG TO BE FEELING THIS FASCISTIC. I SHOULD BE IN THE FLOWER OF MY LIBERALISM, BUT THIS LOUSY CITY SUCKS IT RIGHT OUT OF ME. HOW CAN I NOT HATE THESE SCUMBAGS WHO ARE RUNNING RAMPANT AND RUINING THE QUALITY OF MY LIFE? EVERYONE'S LIVES?
IT'S TOTALLY TRUE. I AGREE COMPLETELY.
MAN, THIS BURG MAKES IT HARD TO BE A GOOD LITTLE LIBERAL. UNLESS YOU WALK AROUND WITH YOUR HEAD UP YOUR ASS. EVERY TIME YOU LEAVE THE HOUSE YOU'RE CONFRONTED BY LEGIONS OF WORST-CASE-SCENARIO STEREOTYPES LIVING DOWN TO THEIR WORST REPUTATIONS.
IT REALLY SICKENS ME. YOU GOT ONE HOMELESS GUY COMES ALONG -- MISTER STINKY LIMBLESS DOO-DOO PANTS -- AND YOUR HEART GOES OUT...
MINE DOESN'T. I SAY SHOOT THEM ALL.
OKAY, YOURS DOESN'T, BUT MINE DOES. BUT THEN ALONG COMES THE RASTA APOLLO "OUGHTA BE IN" CREEDMORE, AND FORGET IT.

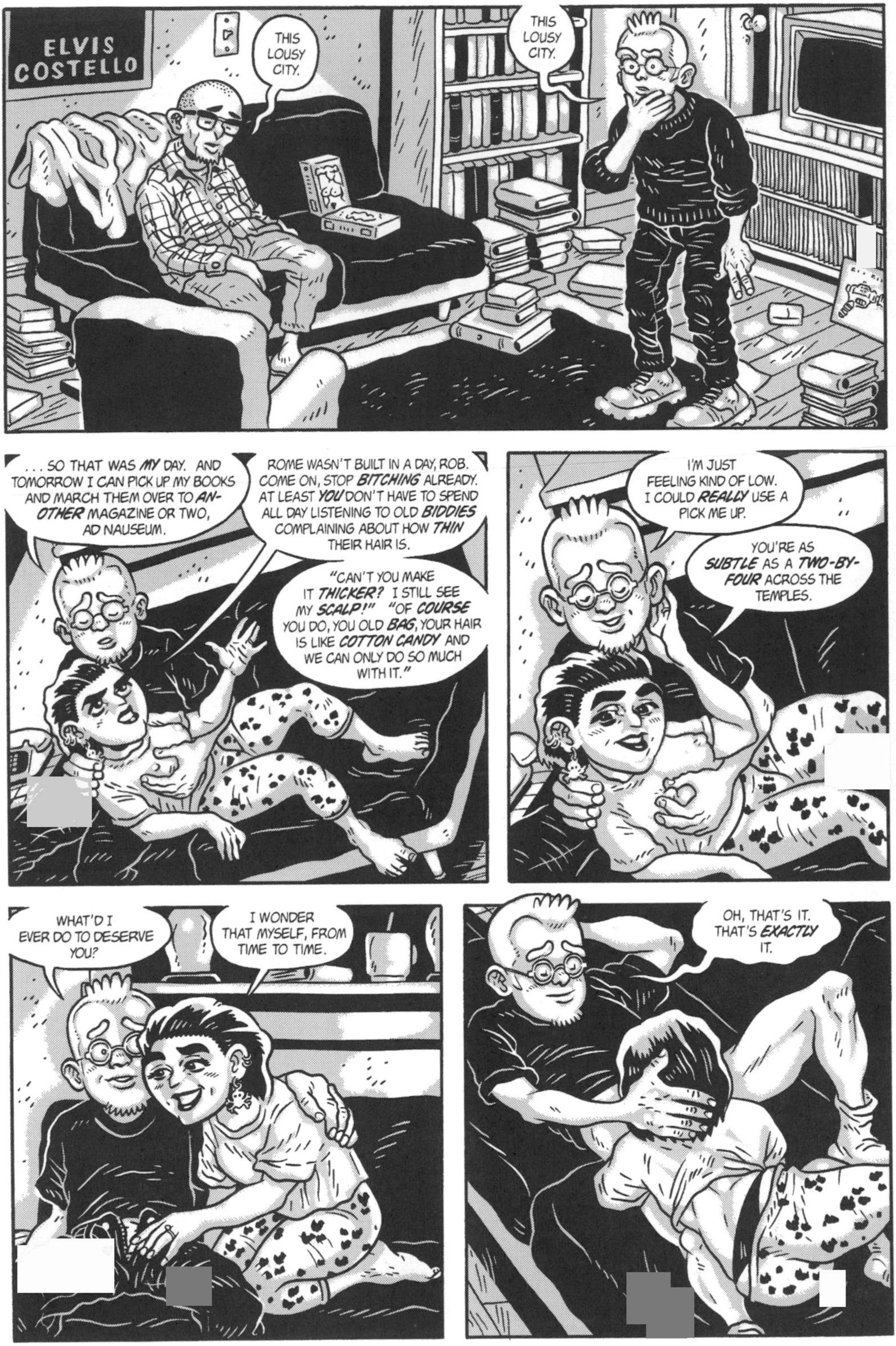
ELVIS COSTELLO
THIS LOUSY CITY.
THIS LOUSY CITY.
. . . SO THAT WAS MY DAY. AND TOMORROW I CAN PICK UP MY BOOKS AND MARCH THEM OVER TO AN-OTHER MAGAZINE OR TWO, AD NAUSEUM.
ROME WASN'T BUILT IN A DAY, ROB. COME ON, STOP BITCHING ALREADY. AT LEAST YOU DON'T HAVE TO SPEND ALL DAY LISTENING TO OLD BIDDIES COMPLAINING ABOUT HOW THIN THEIR HAIR IS.
"CAN'T YOU MAKE IT THICKER? I STILL SEE MY SCALP!" "OF COURSE YOU DO, YOU OLD BAG, YOUR HAIR IS LIKE COTTON CANDY AND WE CAN ONLY DO SO MUCH WITH IT."
I'M JUST FEELING KIND OF LOW. I COULD REALLY USE A PICK ME UP.
YOU'RE AS SUBTLE AS A TWO-BY-FOUR ACROSS THE TEMPLES.
WHAT'D I EVER DO TO DESERVE YOU?
I WONDER THAT MYSELF, FROM TIME TO TIME.
OH, THAT'S IT. THAT'S EXACTLY IT.

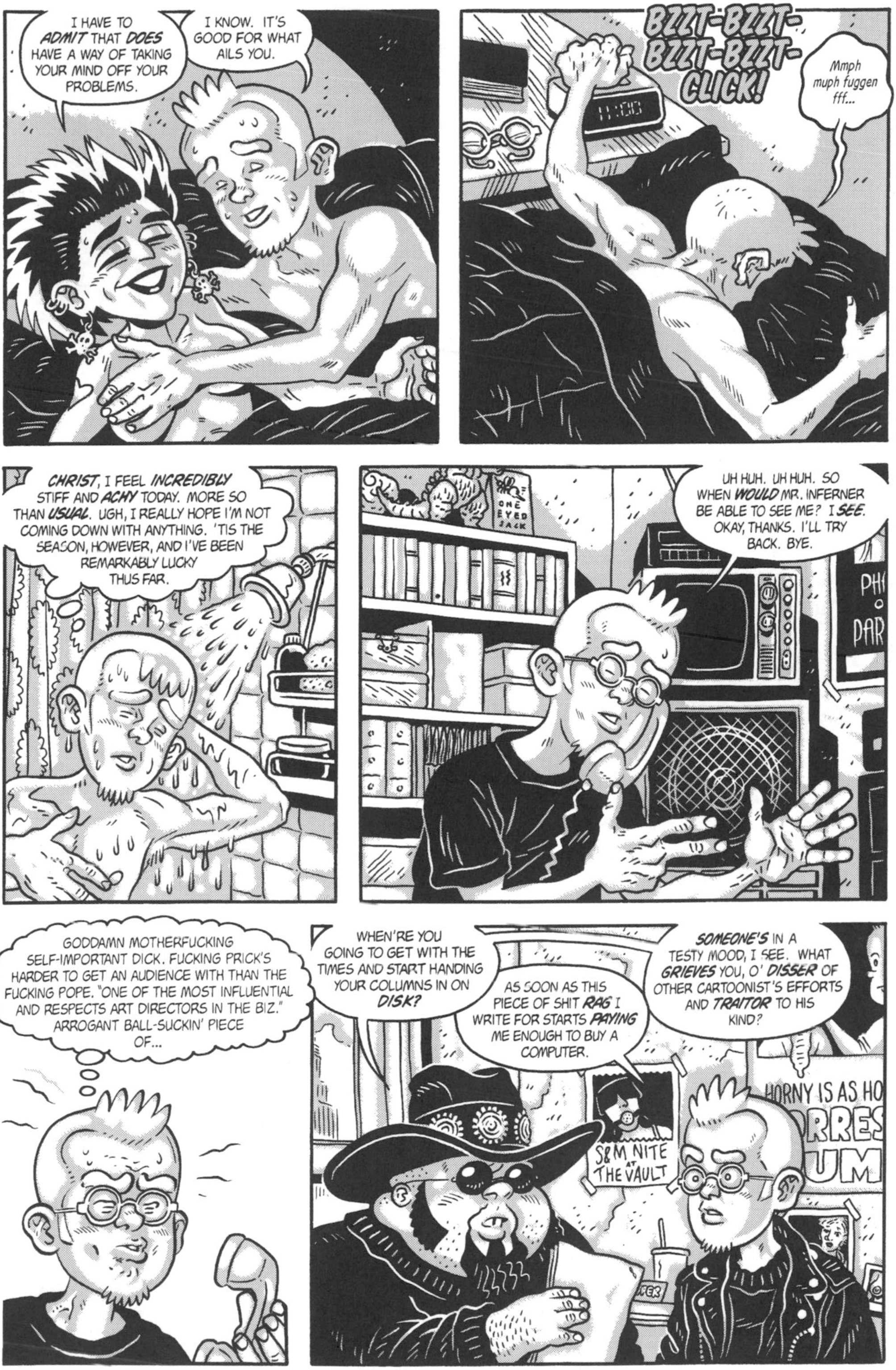
I HAVE TO ADMIT THAT DOES HAVE A WAY OF TAKING YOUR MIND OFF YOUR PROBLEMS.
I KNOW. IT'S GOOD FOR WHAT AILS YOU.
BZZT-BZZT-BZZT-BZZT-CLICK!
Mmph muph fuggen fff...
CHRIST, I FEEL INCREDIBLY STIFF AND ACHY TODAY. MORE SO THAN USUAL. UGH, I REALLY HOPE I'M NOT COMING DOWN WITH ANYTHING. 'TIS THE SEASON, HOWEVER, AND I'VE BEEN REMARKABLY LUCKY THUS FAR.
ONE EYED JACK
UH HUH. UH HUH. SO WHEN WOULD MR. INFERNER BE ABLE TO SEE ME? I SEE. OKAY, THANKS. I'LL TRY BACK. BYE.
GODDAMN MOTHERFUCKING SELF-IMPORTANT DICK. FUCKING PRICK'S HARDER TO GET AN AUDIENCE WITH THAN THE FUCKING POPE. "ONE OF THE MOST INFLUENTIAL AND RESPECTS ART DIRECTORS IN THE BIZ." ARROGANT BALL-SUCKIN' PIECE OF...
WHEN'RE YOU GOING TO GET WITH THE TIMES AND START HANDING YOUR COLUMNS IN ON DISK?
AS SOON AS THIS PIECE OF SHIT RAG I WRITE FOR STARTS PAYING ME ENOUGH TO BUY A COMPUTER.
SOMEONE'S IN A TESTY MOOD, I SEE. WHAT GRIEVES YOU, O' DISSER OF OTHER CARTOONIST'S EFFORTS AND TRAITOR TO HIS KIND?
S&M NITE AT THE VAULT
HORNY IS AS HO

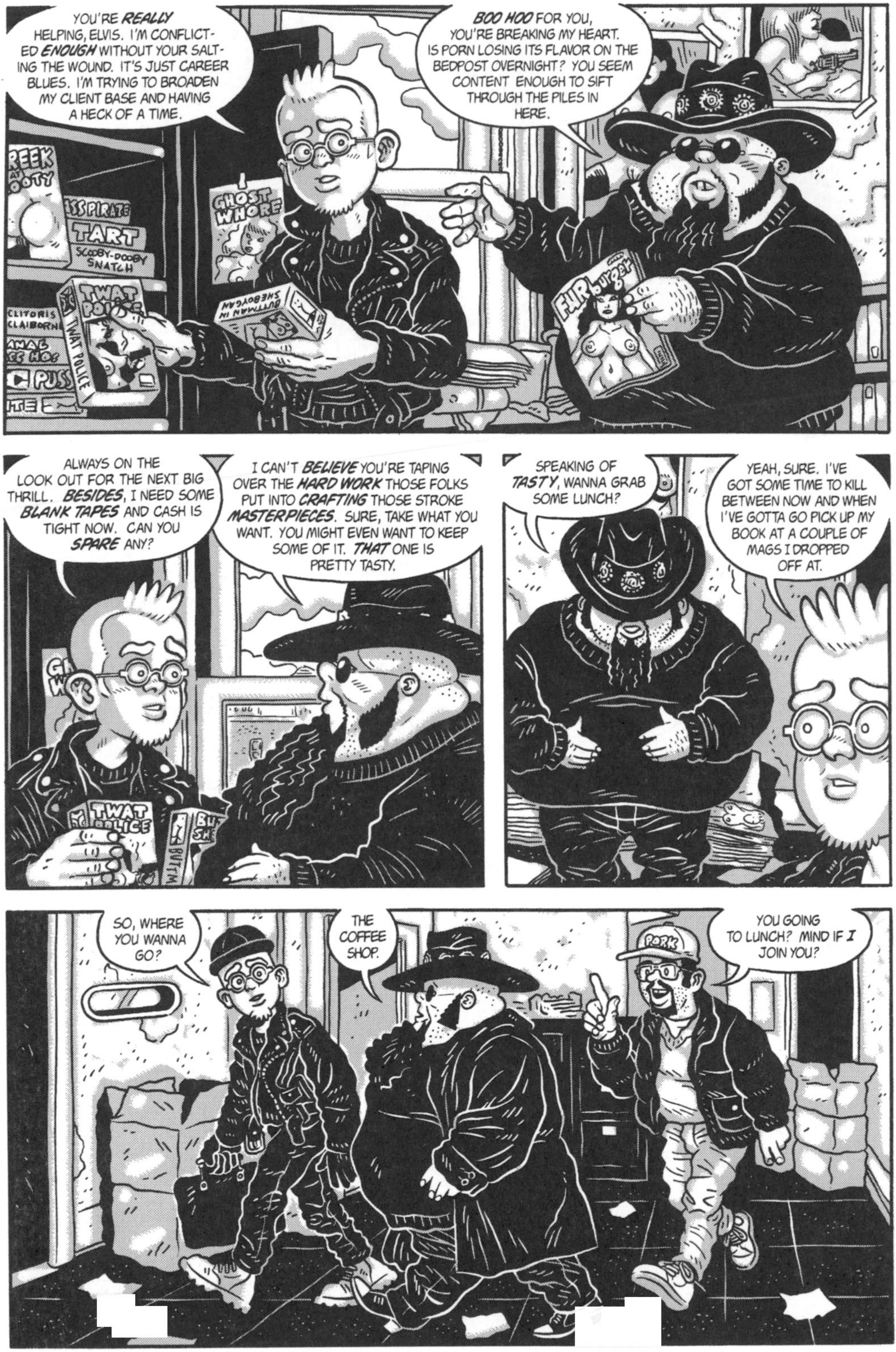
YOU'RE REALLY HELPING, ELVIS. I'M CONFLICTED ENOUGH WITHOUT YOUR SALTING THE WOUND. IT'S JUST CAREER BLUES. I'M TRYING TO BROADEN MY CLIENT BASE AND HAVING A HECK OF A TIME.
BOO HOO FOR YOU, YOU'RE BREAKING MY HEART. IS PORN LOSING ITS FLAVOR ON THE BEDPOST OVERNIGHT? YOU SEEM CONTENT ENOUGH TO SIFT THROUGH THE PILES IN HERE.
TART
SCOOBY-DOOBY SNATCH
GHOST WHORE
TWAT POLICE
CLITORIS CLAIBORNE
BUTTMAN IN SHEBOYGAN
FURburger
ALWAYS ON THE LOOK OUT FOR THE NEXT BIG THRILL. BESIDES, I NEED SOME BLANK TAPES AND CASH IS TIGHT NOW. CAN YOU SPARE ANY?
I CAN'T BELIEVE YOU'RE TAPING OVER THE HARD WORK THOSE FOLKS PUT INTO CRAFTING THOSE STROKE MASTERPIECES. SURE, TAKE WHAT YOU WANT. YOU MIGHT EVEN WANT TO KEEP SOME OF IT. THAT ONE IS PRETTY TASTY.
SPEAKING OF TASTY, WANNA GRAB SOME LUNCH?
YEAH, SURE. I'VE GOT SOME TIME TO KILL BETWEEN NOW AND WHEN I'VE GOTTA GO PICK UP MY BOOK AT A COUPLE OF MAGS I DROPPED OFF AT.
SO, WHERE YOU WANNA GO?
THE COFFEE SHOP.
YOU GOING TO LUNCH? MIND IF I JOIN YOU?
PORK

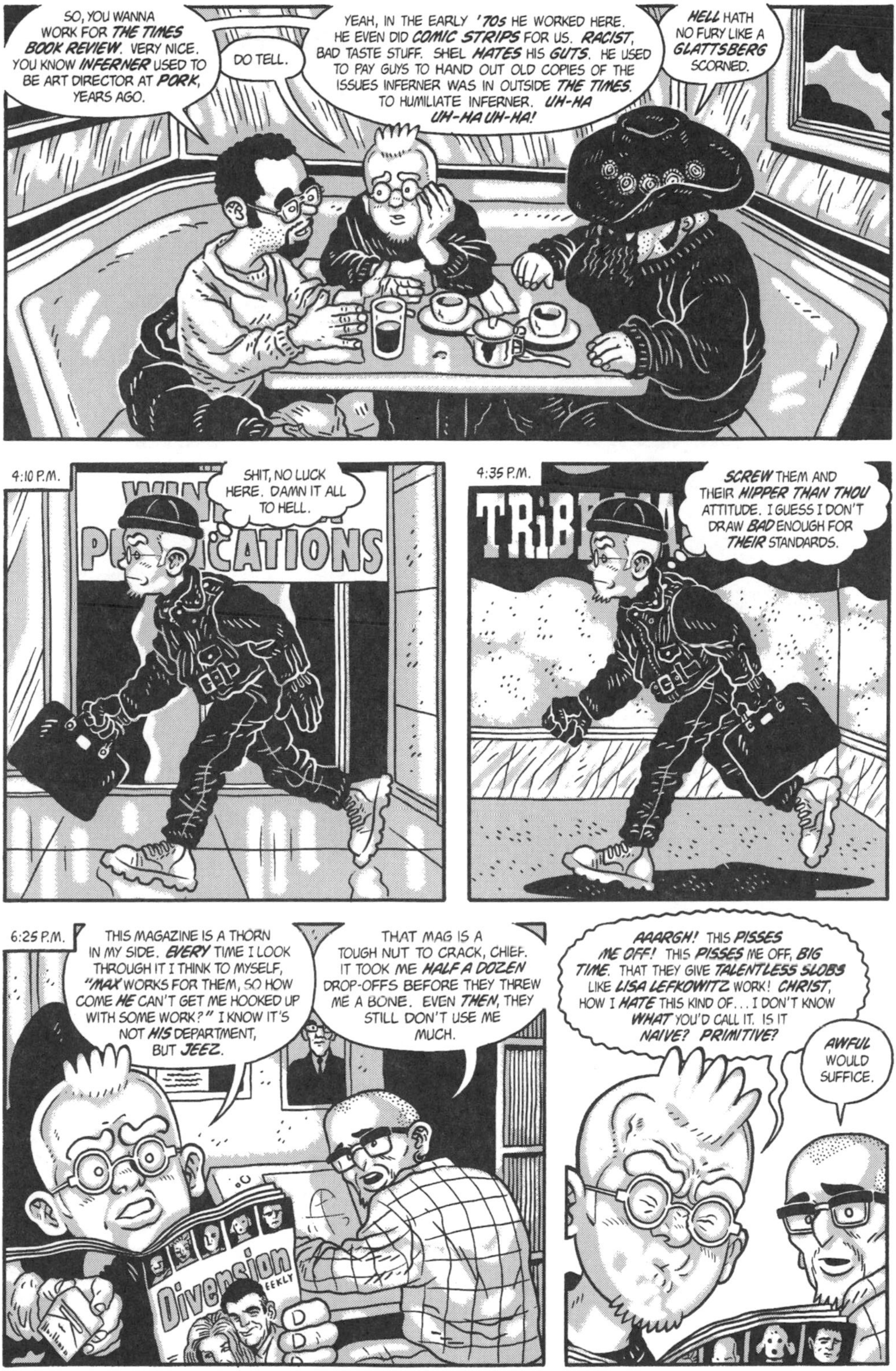
SO, YOU WANNA WORK FOR THE TIMES BOOK REVIEW. VERY NICE. YOU KNOW INFERNER USED TO BE ART DIRECTOR AT PORK, YEARS AGO.
DO TELL.
YEAH, IN THE EARLY '70s HE WORKED HERE. HE EVEN DID COMIC STRIPS FOR US. RACIST, BAD TASTE STUFF. SHEL HATES HIS GUTS. HE USED TO PAY GUYS TO HAND OUT OLD COPIES OF THE ISSUES INFERNER WAS IN OUTSIDE THE TIMES. TO HUMILIATE INFERNER. UH-HA UH-HA UH-HA!
HELL HATH NO FURY LIKE A GLATTSBERG SCORNED.
4:10 P.M.
SHIT, NO LUCK HERE. DAMN IT ALL TO HELL.
4:35 P.M.
SCREW THEM AND THEIR HIPPER THAN THOU ATTITUDE. I GUESS I DON'T DRAW BAD ENOUGH FOR THEIR STANDARDS.
6:25 P.M.
THIS MAGAZINE IS A THORN IN MY SIDE. EVERY TIME I LOOK THROUGH IT I THINK TO MYSELF, "MAX WORKS FOR THEM, SO HOW COME HE CAN'T GET ME HOOKED UP WITH SOME WORK?" I KNOW IT'S NOT HIS DEPARTMENT, BUT JEEZ.
THAT MAG IS A TOUGH NUT TO CRACK, CHIEF. IT TOOK ME HALF A DOZEN DROP-OFFS BEFORE THEY THREW ME A BONE. EVEN THEN, THEY STILL DON'T USE ME MUCH.
Diversion
AAARGH! THIS PISSES ME OFF! THIS PISSES ME OFF, BIG TIME. THAT THEY GIVE TALENTLESS SLOBS LIKE LISA LEFKOWITZ WORK! CHRIST, HOW I HATE THIS KIND OF... I DON'T KNOW WHAT YOU'D CALL IT. IS IT NAIVE? PRIMITIVE?
AWFUL WOULD SUFFICE.

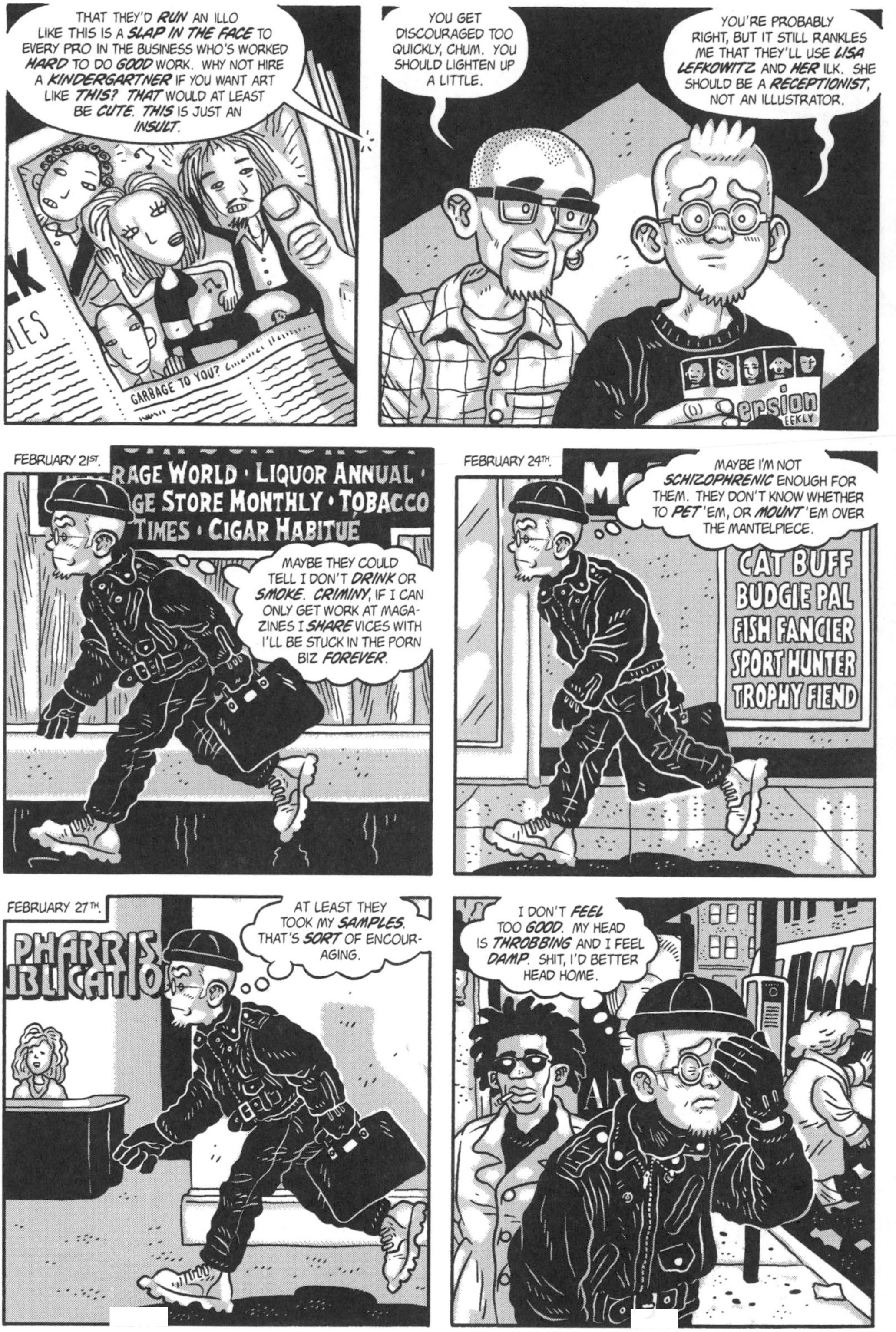
THAT THEY'D RUN AN ILLO LIKE THIS IS A SLAP IN THE FACE TO EVERY PRO IN THE BUSINESS WHO'S WORKED HARD TO DO GOOD WORK. WHY NOT HIRE A KINDERGARTNER IF YOU WANT ART LIKE THIS? THAT WOULD AT LEAST BE CUTE. THIS IS JUST AN INSULT.
GARBAGE TO YOU?
YOU GET DISCOURAGED TOO QUICKLY, CHUM. YOU SHOULD LIGHTEN UP A LITTLE.
YOU'RE PROBABLY RIGHT, BUT IT STILL RANKLES ME THAT THEY'LL USE LISA LEFKOWITZ AND HER ILK. SHE SHOULD BE A RECEPTIONIST, NOT AN ILLUSTRATOR.
FEBRUARY 21ST.
RAGE WORLD · LIQUOR ANNUAL ·
GE STORE MONTHLY · TOBACCO
TIMES · CIGAR HABITUÉ
MAYBE THEY COULD TELL I DON'T DRINK OR SMOKE. CRIMINY, IF I CAN ONLY GET WORK AT MAGAZINES I SHARE VICES WITH I'LL BE STUCK IN THE PORN BIZ FOREVER.
FEBRUARY 24TH.
MAYBE I'M NOT SCHIZOPHRENIC ENOUGH FOR THEM. THEY DON'T KNOW WHETHER TO PET 'EM, OR MOUNT 'EM OVER THE MANTELPIECE.
CAT BUFF
BUDGIE PAL
FISH FANCIER
SPORT HUNTER
TROPHY FIEND
FEBRUARY 27TH.
PHARRIS
JBLICATIO
AT LEAST THEY TOOK MY SAMPLES. THAT'S SORT OF ENCOURAGING.
I DON'T FEEL TOO GOOD. MY HEAD IS THROBBING AND I FEEL DAMP. SHIT, I'D BETTER HEAD HOME.

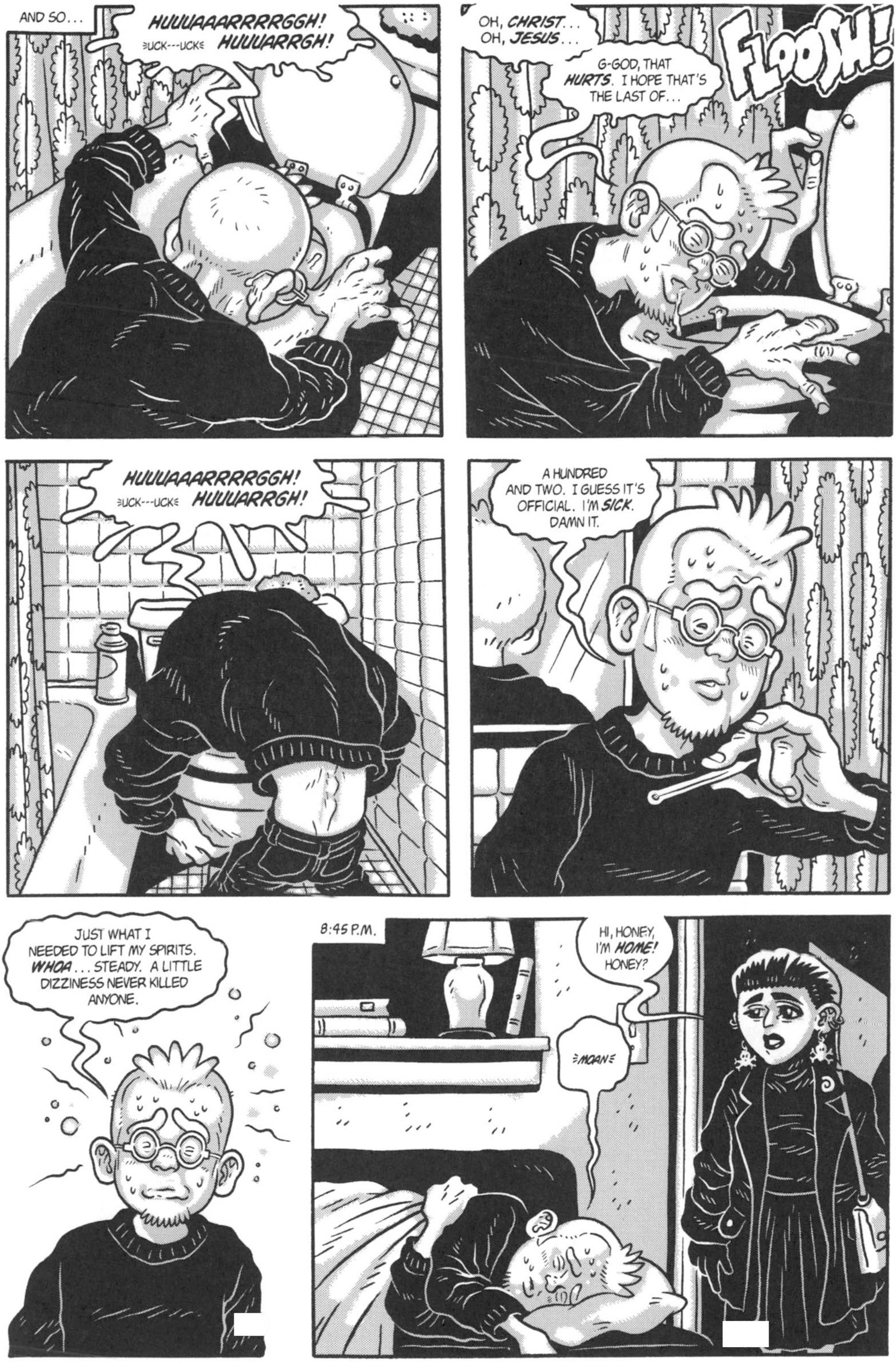
AND SO...
HUUUAAARRRRGGH! ≡UCK---UCK≡ HUUUARRGH!
OH, CHRIST... OH, JESUS...
G-GOD, THAT HURTS. I HOPE THAT'S THE LAST OF...
FLOOSH!
HUUUAAARRRRGGH! ≡UCK---UCK≡ HUUUARRGH!
A HUNDRED AND TWO. I GUESS IT'S OFFICIAL. I'M SICK. DAMN IT.
JUST WHAT I NEEDED TO LIFT MY SPIRITS. WHOA... STEADY. A LITTLE DIZZINESS NEVER KILLED ANYONE.
8:45 P.M.
HI, HONEY, I'M HOME! HONEY?
≡MOAN≡

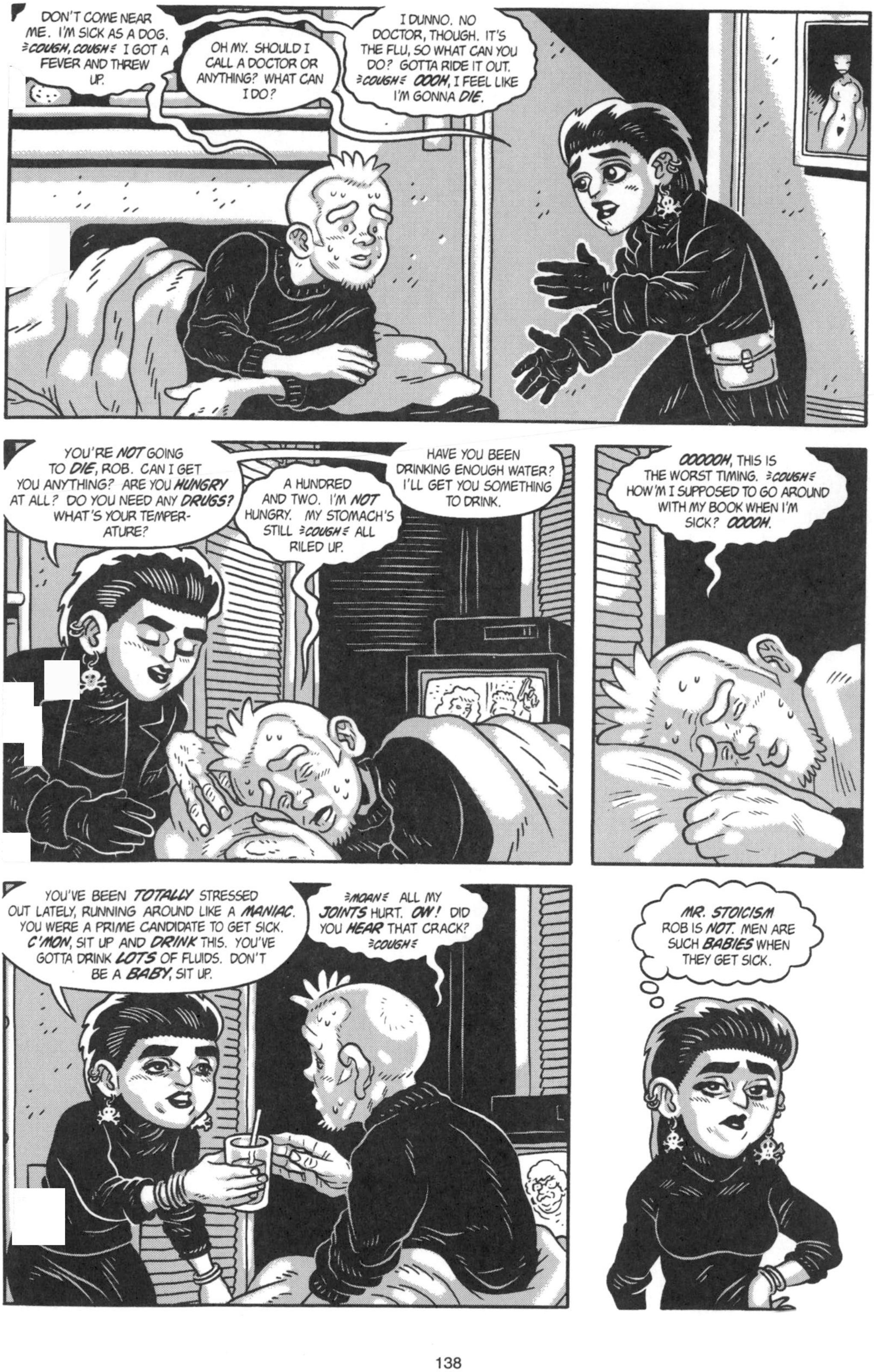
DON'T COME NEAR ME. I'M SICK AS A DOG. ≡COUGH, COUGH≡ I GOT A FEVER AND THREW UP.
OH MY. SHOULD I CALL A DOCTOR OR ANYTHING? WHAT CAN I DO?
I DUNNO. NO DOCTOR, THOUGH. IT'S THE FLU, SO WHAT CAN YOU DO? GOTTA RIDE IT OUT. ≡COUGH≡ OOOH, I FEEL LIKE I'M GONNA DIE.
YOU'RE NOT GOING TO DIE, ROB. CAN I GET YOU ANYTHING? ARE YOU HUNGRY AT ALL? DO YOU NEED ANY DRUGS? WHAT'S YOUR TEMPERATURE?
A HUNDRED AND TWO. I'M NOT HUNGRY. MY STOMACH'S STILL ≡COUGH≡ ALL RILED UP.
HAVE YOU BEEN DRINKING ENOUGH WATER? I'LL GET YOU SOMETHING TO DRINK.
OOOOOH, THIS IS THE WORST TIMING. ≡COUGH≡ HOW'M I SUPPOSED TO GO AROUND WITH MY BOOK WHEN I'M SICK? OOOOH.
YOU'VE BEEN TOTALLY STRESSED OUT LATELY, RUNNING AROUND LIKE A MANIAC. YOU WERE A PRIME CANDIDATE TO GET SICK. C'MON, SIT UP AND DRINK THIS. YOU'VE GOTTA DRINK LOTS OF FLUIDS. DON'T BE A BABY, SIT UP.
≡MOAN≡ ALL MY JOINTS HURT. OW! DID YOU HEAR THAT CRACK? ≡COUGH≡
MR. STOICISM ROB IS NOT. MEN ARE SUCH BABIES WHEN THEY GET SICK.

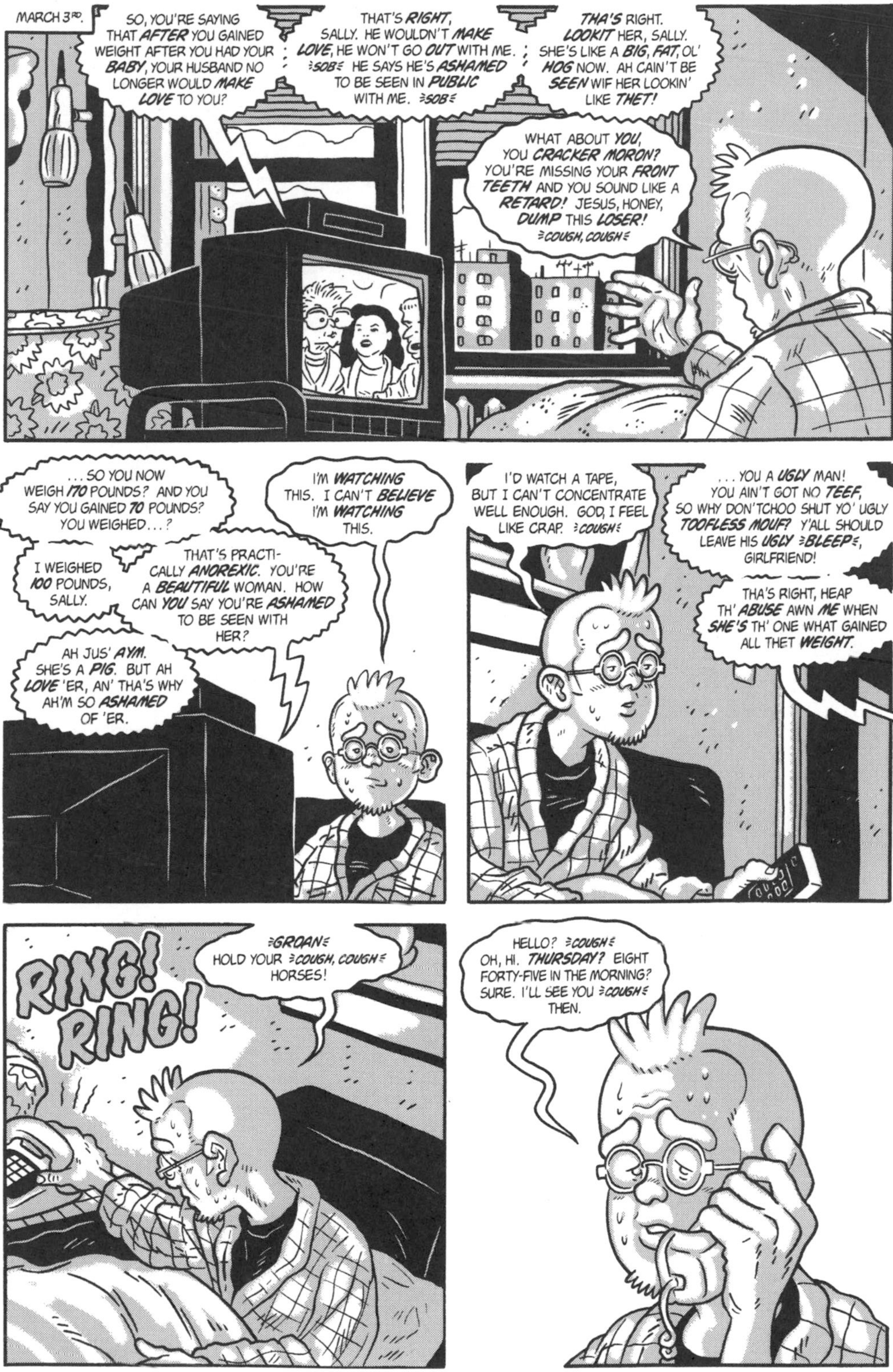
MARCH 3RD.
SO, YOU'RE SAYING THAT AFTER YOU GAINED WEIGHT AFTER YOU HAD YOUR BABY, YOUR HUSBAND NO LONGER WOULD MAKE LOVE TO YOU?
THAT'S RIGHT, SALLY. HE WOULDN'T MAKE LOVE, HE WON'T GO OUT WITH ME. ≶SOB≶ HE SAYS HE'S ASHAMED TO BE SEEN IN PUBLIC WITH ME. ≶SOB≶
THA'S RIGHT. LOOKIT HER, SALLY. SHE'S LIKE A BIG, FAT, OL' HOG NOW. AH CAIN'T BE SEEN WIF HER LOOKIN' LIKE THET!
WHAT ABOUT YOU, YOU CRACKER MORON? YOU'RE MISSING YOUR FRONT TEETH AND YOU SOUND LIKE A RETARD! JESUS, HONEY, DUMP THIS LOSER! ≶COUGH, COUGH≶
...SO YOU NOW WEIGH 170 POUNDS? AND YOU SAY YOU GAINED 70 POUNDS? YOU WEIGHED...?
I WEIGHED 100 POUNDS, SALLY.
THAT'S PRACTI-CALLY ANOREXIC. YOU'RE A BEAUTIFUL WOMAN. HOW CAN YOU SAY YOU'RE ASHAMED TO BE SEEN WITH HER?
AH JUS' AYM. SHE'S A PIG. BUT AH LOVE 'ER, AN' THA'S WHY AH'M SO ASHAMED OF 'ER.
I'M WATCHING THIS. I CAN'T BELIEVE I'M WATCHING THIS.
I'D WATCH A TAPE, BUT I CAN'T CONCENTRATE WELL ENOUGH. GOD, I FEEL LIKE CRAP. ≶COUGH≶
...YOU A UGLY MAN! YOU AIN'T GOT NO TEEF, SO WHY DON'TCHOO SHUT YO' UGLY TOOFLESS MOUF? Y'ALL SHOULD LEAVE HIS UGLY ≶BLEEP≶, GIRLFRIEND!
THA'S RIGHT, HEAP TH' ABUSE AWN ME WHEN SHE'S TH' ONE WHAT GAINED ALL THET WEIGHT.
RING! RING!
≶GROAN≶ HOLD YOUR ≶COUGH, COUGH≶ HORSES!
HELLO? ≶COUGH≶ OH, HI. THURSDAY? EIGHT FORTY-FIVE IN THE MORNING? SURE. I'LL SEE YOU ≶COUGH≶ THEN.

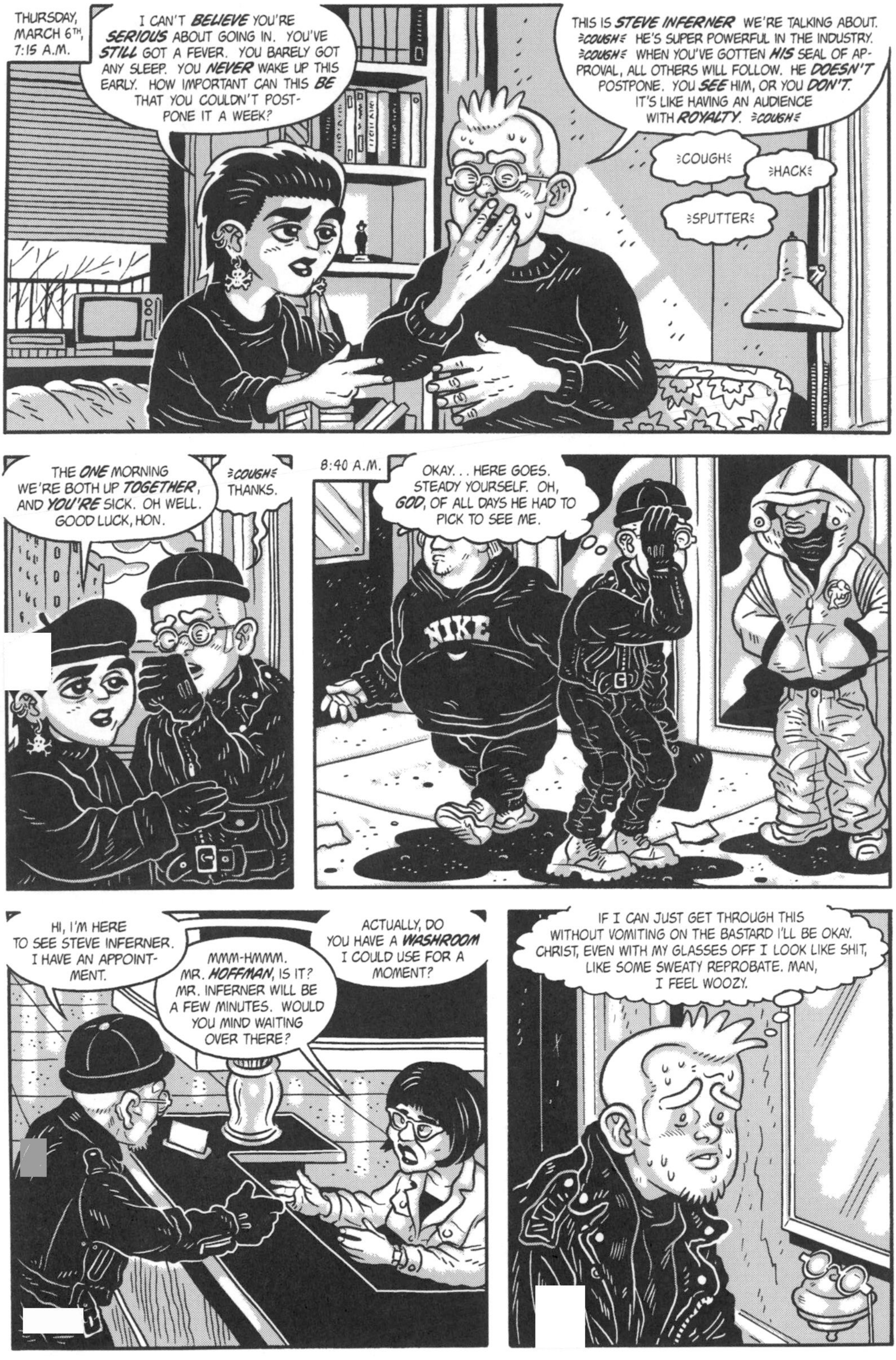
THURSDAY, MARCH 6TH, 7:15 A.M.
I CAN'T BELIEVE YOU'RE SERIOUS ABOUT GOING IN. YOU'VE STILL GOT A FEVER. YOU BARELY GOT ANY SLEEP. YOU NEVER WAKE UP THIS EARLY. HOW IMPORTANT CAN THIS BE THAT YOU COULDN'T POSTPONE IT A WEEK?
THIS IS STEVE INFERNER WE'RE TALKING ABOUT. ≥COUGH≤ HE'S SUPER POWERFUL IN THE INDUSTRY. ≥COUGH≤ WHEN YOU'VE GOTTEN HIS SEAL OF APPROVAL, ALL OTHERS WILL FOLLOW. HE DOESN'T POSTPONE. YOU SEE HIM, OR YOU DON'T. IT'S LIKE HAVING AN AUDIENCE WITH ROYALTY. ≥COUGH≤
≥COUGH≤
≥HACK≤
≥SPUTTER≤
THE ONE MORNING WE'RE BOTH UP TOGETHER, AND YOU'RE SICK. OH WELL. GOOD LUCK, HON.
≥COUGH≤ THANKS.
8:40 A.M.
OKAY... HERE GOES. STEADY YOURSELF. OH, GOD, OF ALL DAYS HE HAD TO PICK TO SEE ME.
NIKE
HI, I'M HERE TO SEE STEVE INFERNER. I HAVE AN APPOINTMENT.
MMM-HMMM. MR. HOFFMAN, IS IT? MR. INFERNER WILL BE A FEW MINUTES. WOULD YOU MIND WAITING OVER THERE?
ACTUALLY, DO YOU HAVE A WASHROOM I COULD USE FOR A MOMENT?
IF I CAN JUST GET THROUGH THIS WITHOUT VOMITING ON THE BASTARD I'LL BE OKAY. CHRIST, EVEN WITH MY GLASSES OFF I LOOK LIKE SHIT, LIKE SOME SWEATY REPROBATE. MAN, I FEEL WOOZY.

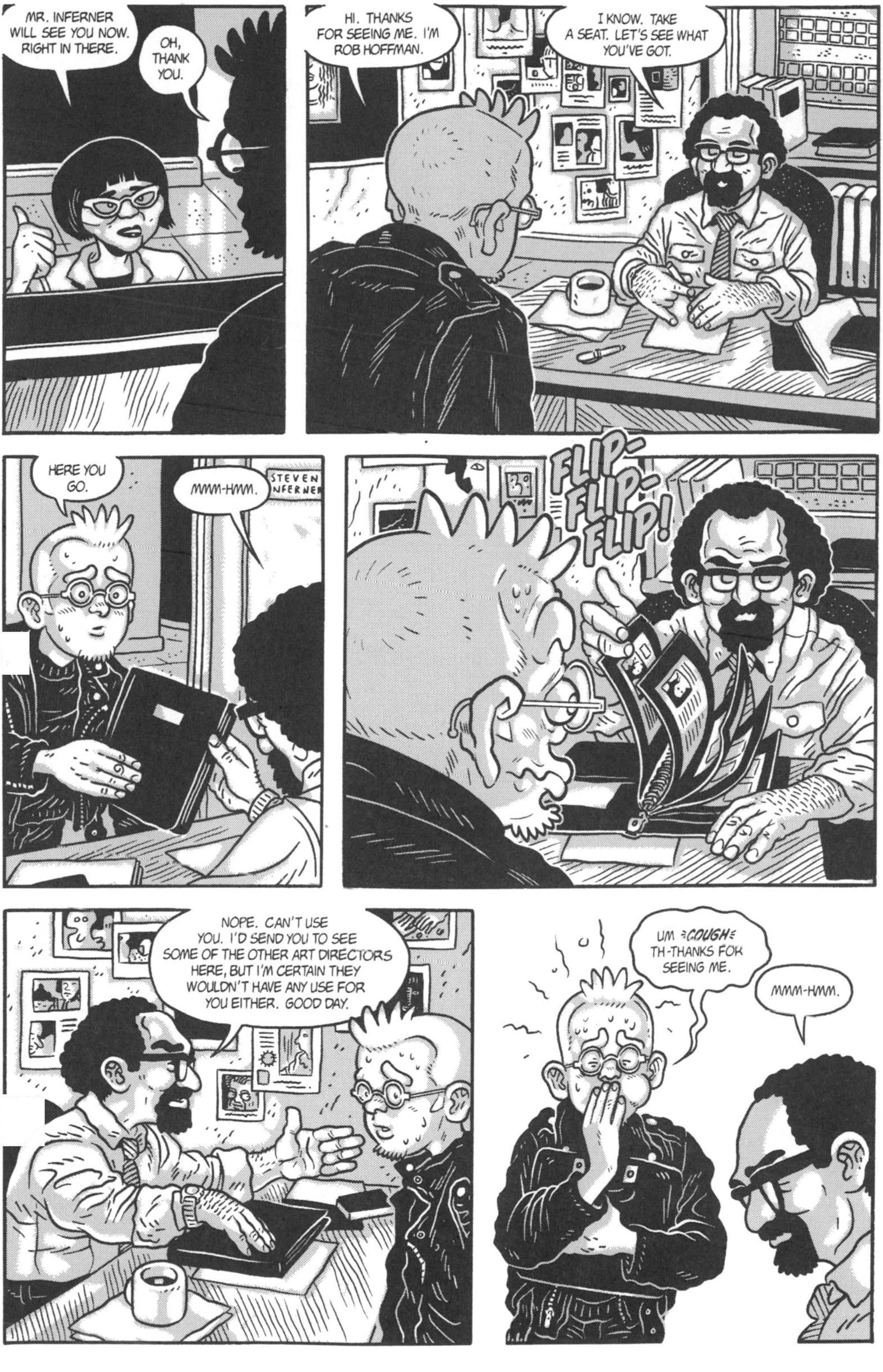
MR. INFERNER WILL SEE YOU NOW. RIGHT IN THERE.
OH, THANK YOU.
HI. THANKS FOR SEEING ME. I'M ROB HOFFMAN.
I KNOW. TAKE A SEAT. LET'S SEE WHAT YOU'VE GOT.
HERE YOU GO.
MMM-HMM.
STEVEN INFERNER
FLIP-FLIP-FLIP!
NOPE. CAN'T USE YOU. I'D SEND YOU TO SEE SOME OF THE OTHER ART DIRECTORS HERE, BUT I'M CERTAIN THEY WOULDN'T HAVE ANY USE FOR YOU EITHER. GOOD DAY.
UM COUGH TH-THANKS FOR SEEING ME.
MMM-HMM.

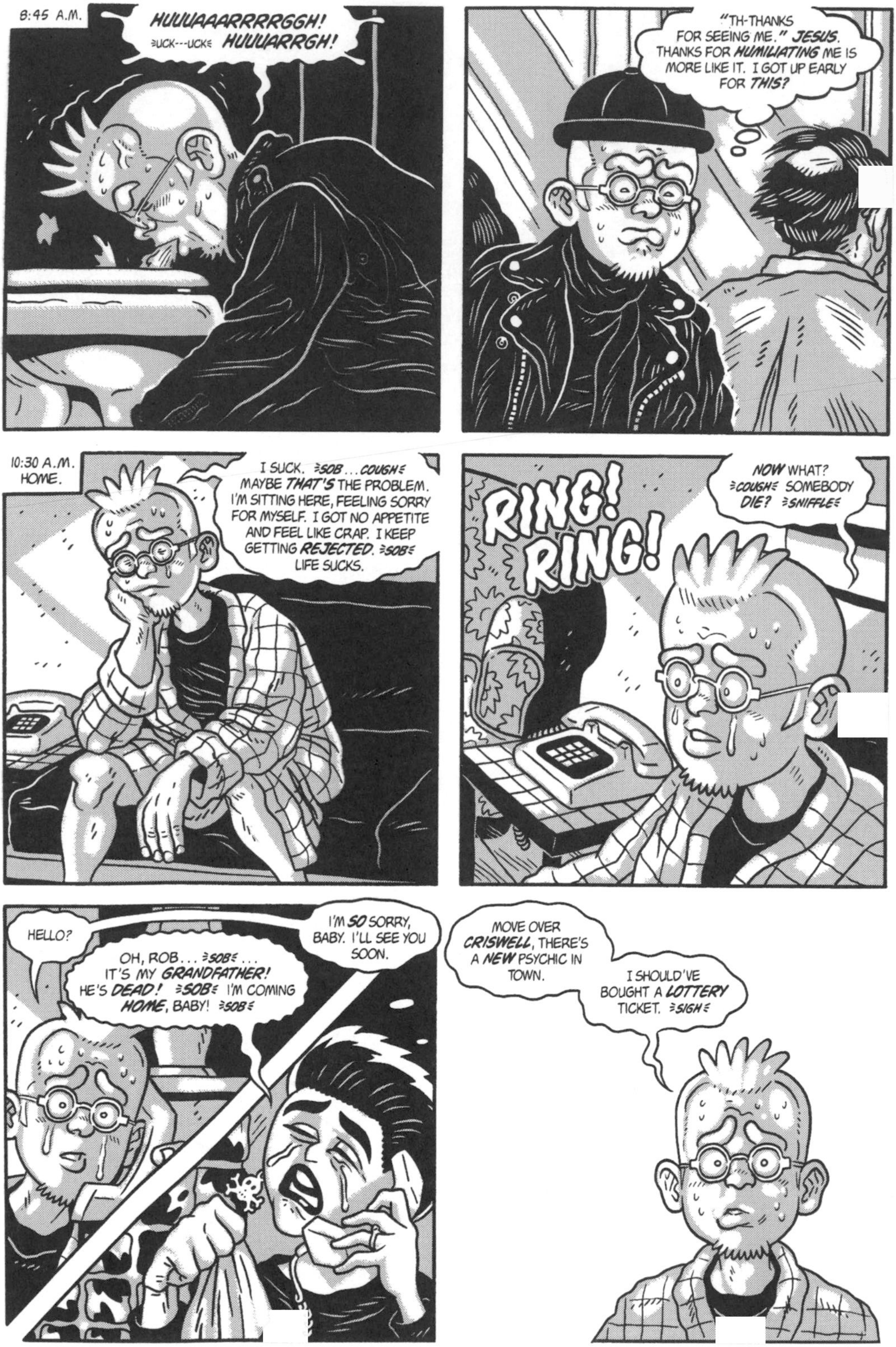
8:45 A.M.
HUUUAAARRRRGGH! ≡UCK---UCK≡ HUUUARRGH!
"TH-THANKS FOR SEEING ME." JESUS. THANKS FOR HUMILIATING ME IS MORE LIKE IT. I GOT UP EARLY FOR THIS?
10:30 A.M. HOME.
I SUCK. ≡SOB≡ ... COUGH≡ MAYBE THAT'S THE PROBLEM. I'M SITTING HERE, FEELING SORRY FOR MYSELF. I GOT NO APPETITE AND FEEL LIKE CRAP. I KEEP GETTING REJECTED. ≡SOB≡ LIFE SUCKS.
RING! RING!
NOW WHAT? ≡COUGH≡ SOMEBODY DIE? ≡SNIFFLE≡
HELLO?
OH, ROB... ≡SOB≡ ... IT'S MY GRANDFATHER! HE'S DEAD! ≡SOB≡ I'M COMING HOME, BABY! ≡SOB≡
I'M SO SORRY, BABY. I'LL SEE YOU SOON.
MOVE OVER CRISWELL, THERE'S A NEW PSYCHIC IN TOWN.
I SHOULD'VE BOUGHT A LOTTERY TICKET. ≡SIGH≡

# CHAPTER SEVEN

# BRIDGE WATCHING

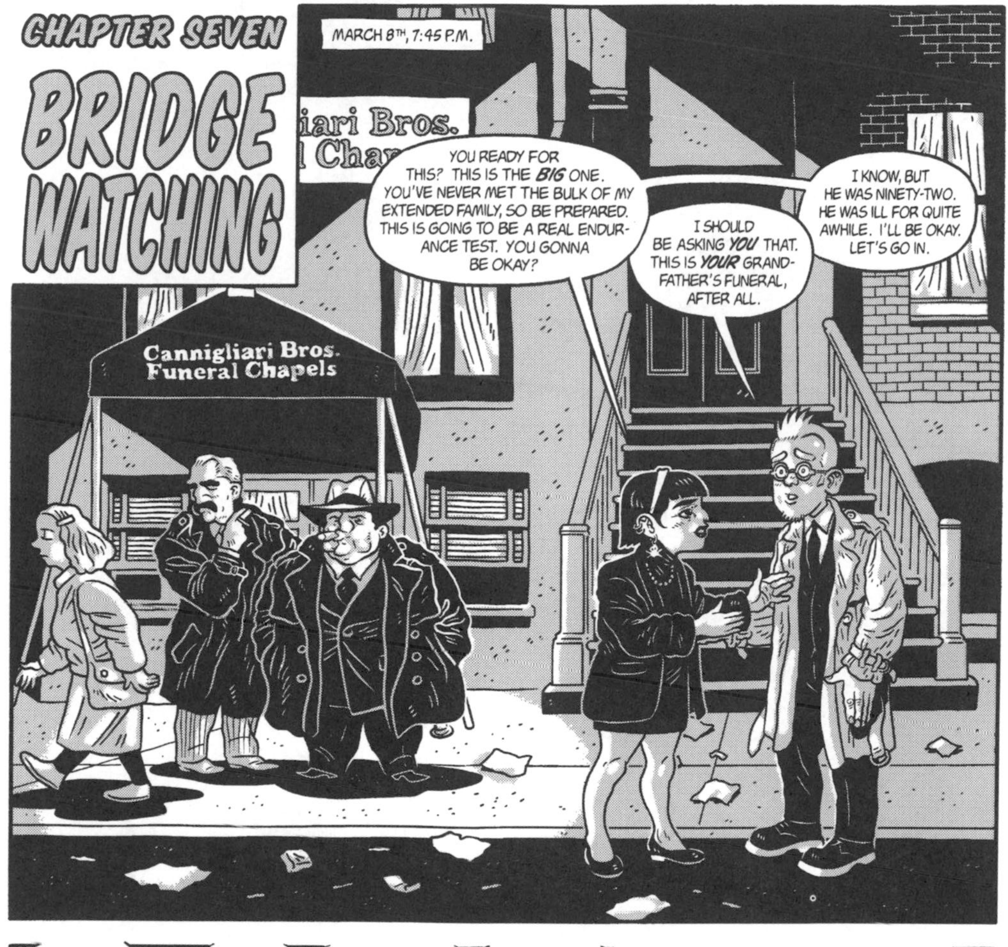
MARCH 8TH, 7:45 P.M.
Cannigliari Bros. Funeral Chapels
YOU READY FOR THIS? THIS IS THE BIG ONE. YOU'VE NEVER MET THE BULK OF MY EXTENDED FAMILY, SO BE PREPARED. THIS IS GOING TO BE A REAL ENDURANCE TEST. YOU GONNA BE OKAY?
I SHOULD BE ASKING YOU THAT. THIS IS YOUR GRANDFATHER'S FUNERAL, AFTER ALL.
I KNOW, BUT HE WAS NINETY-TWO. HE WAS ILL FOR QUITE AWHILE. I'LL BE OKAY. LET'S GO IN.

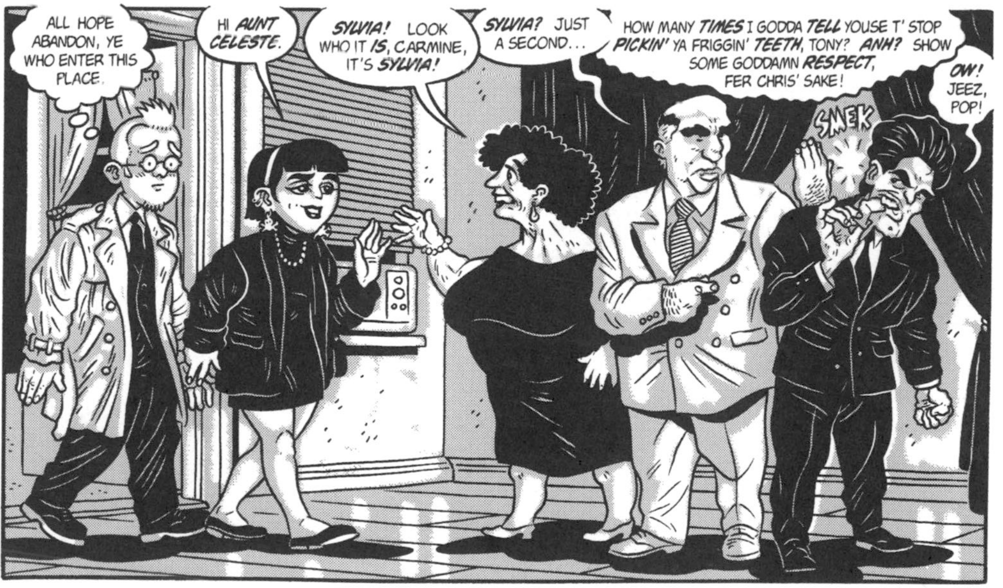
ALL HOPE ABANDON, YE WHO ENTER THIS PLACE.
HI AUNT CELESTE.
SYLVIA! LOOK WHO IT IS, CARMINE, IT'S SYLVIA!
SYLVIA? JUST A SECOND...
HOW MANY TIMES I GODDA TELL YOUSE T' STOP PICKIN' YA FRIGGIN' TEETH, TONY? ANH? SHOW SOME GODDAMN RESPECT, FER CHRIS' SAKE!
SMEK
OW! JEEZ, POP!

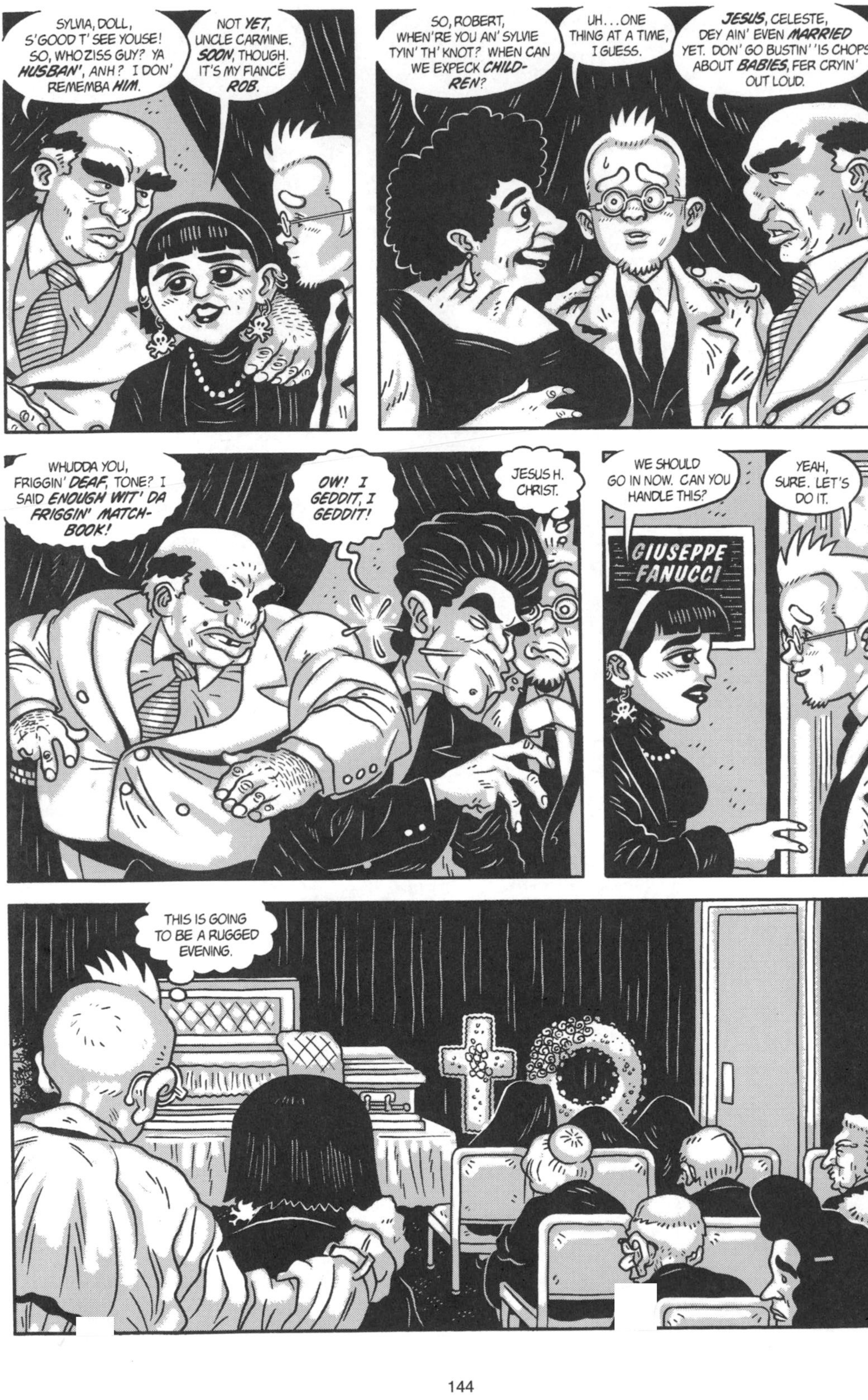
SYLVIA, DOLL, S'GOOD T' SEE YOUSE! SO, WHOZISS GUY? YA HUSBAN', ANH? I DON' REMEMBA HIM.
NOT YET, UNCLE CARMINE. SOON, THOUGH. IT'S MY FIANCÉ ROB.
SO, ROBERT, WHEN'RE YOU AN' SYLVIE TYIN' TH' KNOT? WHEN CAN WE EXPECK CHILD-REN?
UH...ONE THING AT A TIME, I GUESS.
JESUS, CELESTE, DEY AIN' EVEN MARRIED YET. DON' GO BUSTIN' 'IS CHOPS ABOUT BABIES, FER CRYIN' OUT LOUD.
WHUDDA YOU, FRIGGIN' DEAF, TONE? I SAID ENOUGH WIT' DA FRIGGIN' MATCH-BOOK!
OW! I GEDDIT, I GEDDIT!
JESUS H. CHRIST.
WE SHOULD GO IN NOW. CAN YOU HANDLE THIS?
GIUSEPPE FANUCCI
YEAH, SURE. LET'S DO IT.
THIS IS GOING TO BE A RUGGED EVENING.

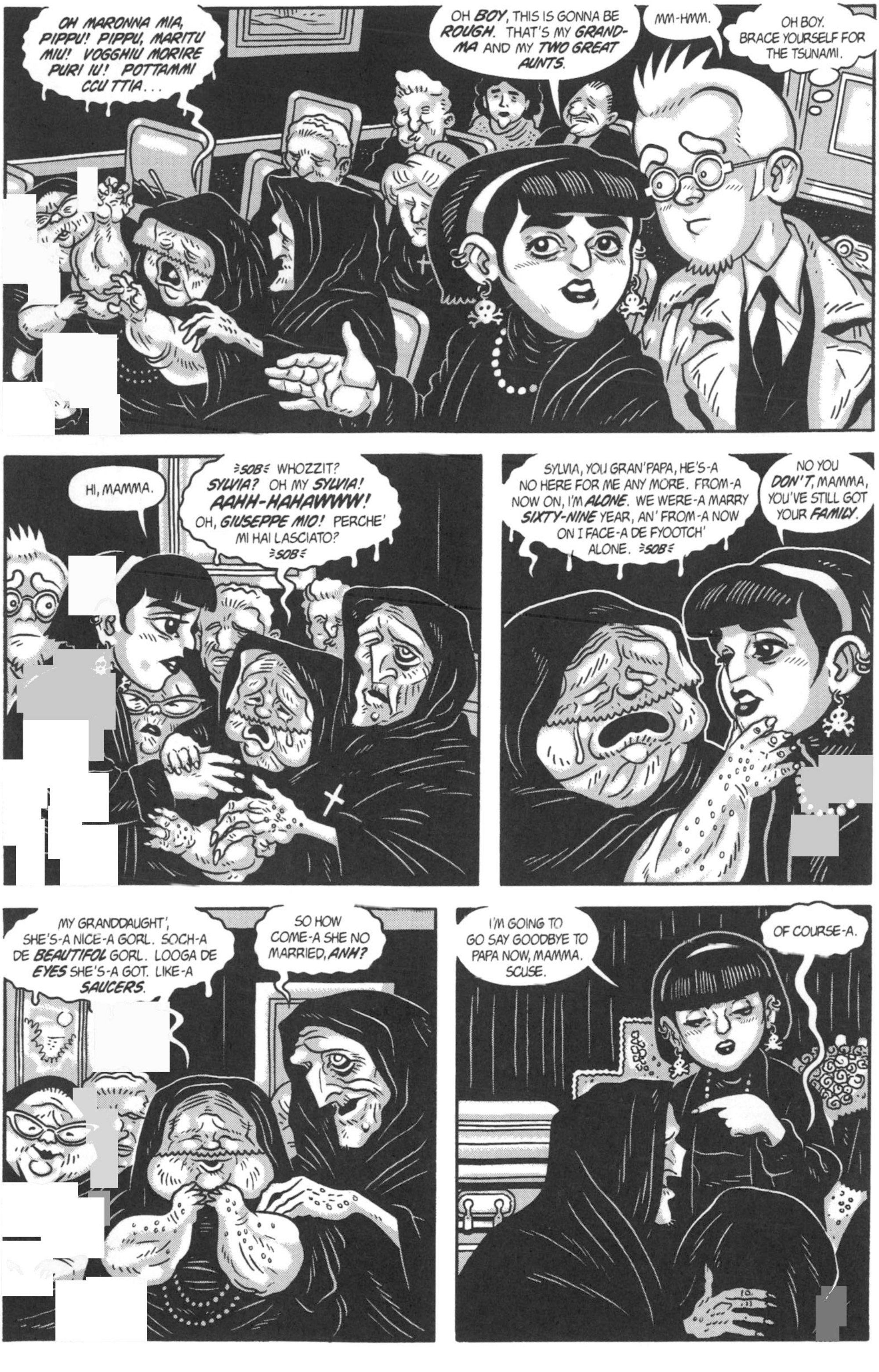
OH MARONNA MIA, PIPPU! PIPPU, MARITU MIU! VOGGHIU MORIRE PURI IU! POTTAMMI CCU TTIA...
OH BOY, THIS IS GONNA BE ROUGH. THAT'S MY GRANDMA AND MY TWO GREAT AUNTS.
MM-HMM.
OH BOY. BRACE YOURSELF FOR THE TSUNAMI.
HI, MAMMA.
SOB WHOZZIT? SYLVIA? OH MY SYLVIA! AAHH-HAHAWWW! OH, GIUSEPPE MIO! PERCHE' MI HAI LASCIATO? SOB
SYLVIA, YOU GRAN'PAPA, HE'S-A NO HERE FOR ME ANY MORE. FROM-A NOW ON, I'M ALONE. WE WERE-A MARRY SIXTY-NINE YEAR, AN' FROM-A NOW ON I FACE-A DE FYOOTCH' ALONE. SOB
NO YOU DON'T, MAMMA, YOU'VE STILL GOT YOUR FAMILY.
MY GRANDDAUGHT', SHE'S-A NICE-A GORL. SOCH-A DE BEAUTIFOL GORL. LOOGA DE EYES SHE'S-A GOT. LIKE-A SAUCERS.
SO HOW COME-A SHE NO MARRIED, ANH?
I'M GOING TO GO SAY GOODBYE TO PAPA NOW, MAMMA. SCUSE.
OF COURSE-A.

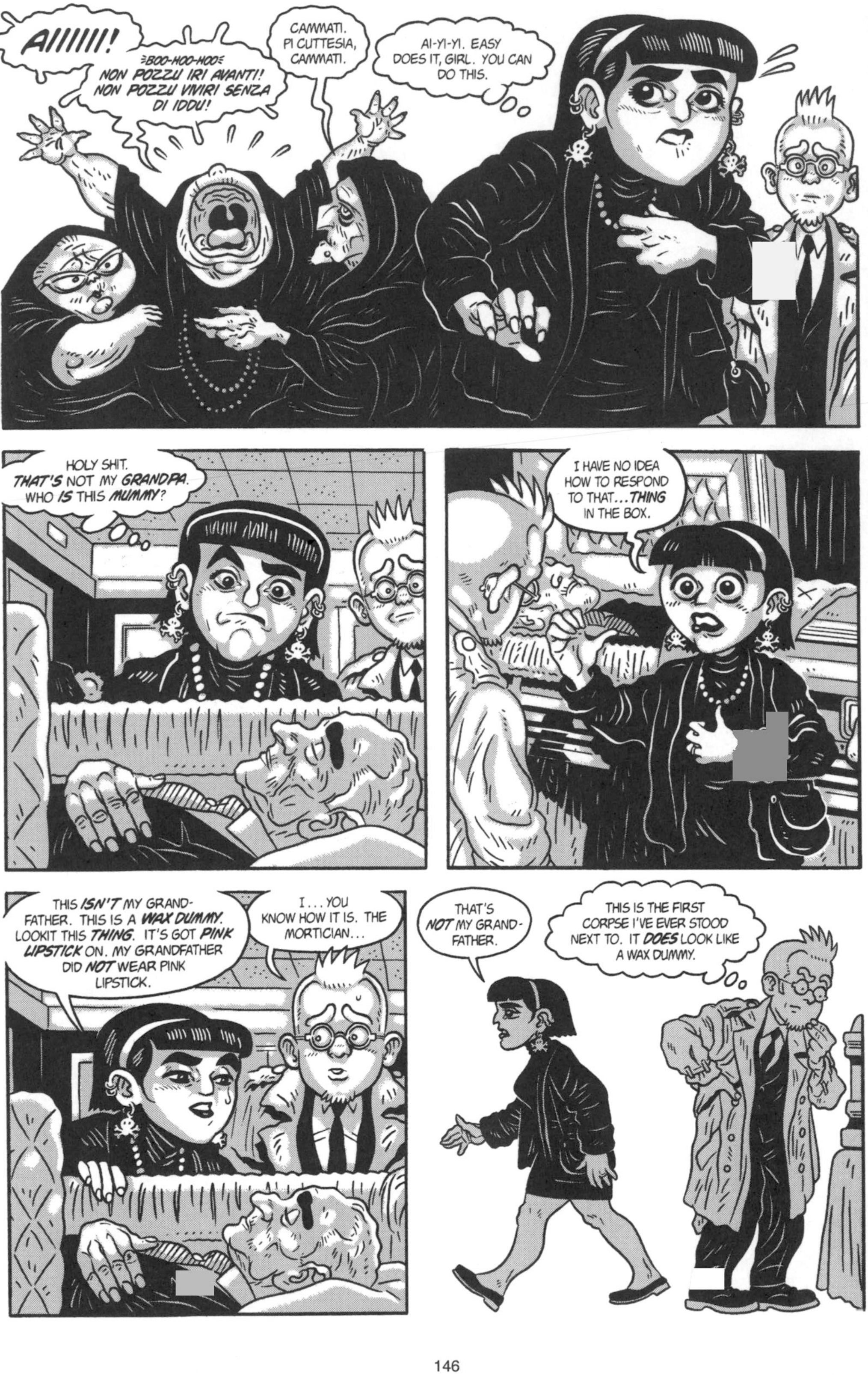
AIIIIII!
BOO-HOO-HOO
NON POZZU IRI AVANTI! NON POZZU VIVIRI SENZA DI IDDU!
CAMMATI. PI CUTTESIA, CAMMATI.
AI-YI-YI. EASY DOES IT, GIRL. YOU CAN DO THIS.
HOLY SHIT. THAT'S NOT MY GRANDPA. WHO IS THIS MUMMY?
I HAVE NO IDEA HOW TO RESPOND TO THAT... THING IN THE BOX.
THIS ISN'T MY GRAND-FATHER. THIS IS A WAX DUMMY. LOOKIT THIS THING. IT'S GOT PINK LIPSTICK ON. MY GRANDFATHER DID NOT WEAR PINK LIPSTICK.
I... YOU KNOW HOW IT IS. THE MORTICIAN...
THAT'S NOT MY GRAND-FATHER.
THIS IS THE FIRST CORPSE I'VE EVER STOOD NEXT TO. IT DOES LOOK LIKE A WAX DUMMY.

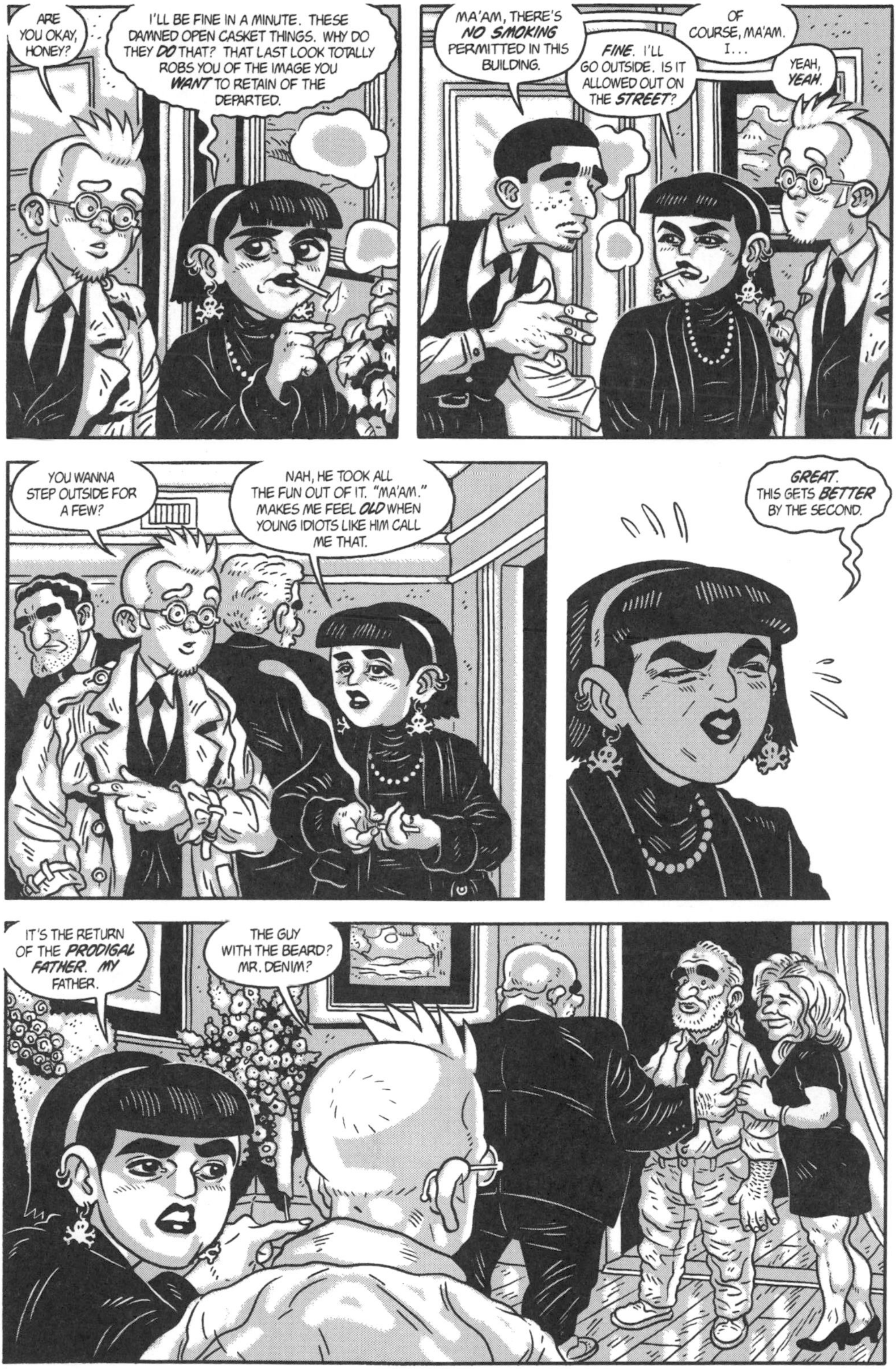
ARE YOU OKAY, HONEY?
I'LL BE FINE IN A MINUTE. THESE DAMNED OPEN CASKET THINGS. WHY DO THEY DO THAT? THAT LAST LOOK TOTALLY ROBS YOU OF THE IMAGE YOU WANT TO RETAIN OF THE DEPARTED.
MA'AM, THERE'S NO SMOKING PERMITTED IN THIS BUILDING.
FINE. I'LL GO OUTSIDE. IS IT ALLOWED OUT ON THE STREET?
OF COURSE, MA'AM. I...
YEAH, YEAH.
YOU WANNA STEP OUTSIDE FOR A FEW?
NAH, HE TOOK ALL THE FUN OUT OF IT. "MA'AM." MAKES ME FEEL OLD WHEN YOUNG IDIOTS LIKE HIM CALL ME THAT.
GREAT. THIS GETS BETTER BY THE SECOND.
IT'S THE RETURN OF THE PRODIGAL FATHER. MY FATHER.
THE GUY WITH THE BEARD? MR. DENIM?

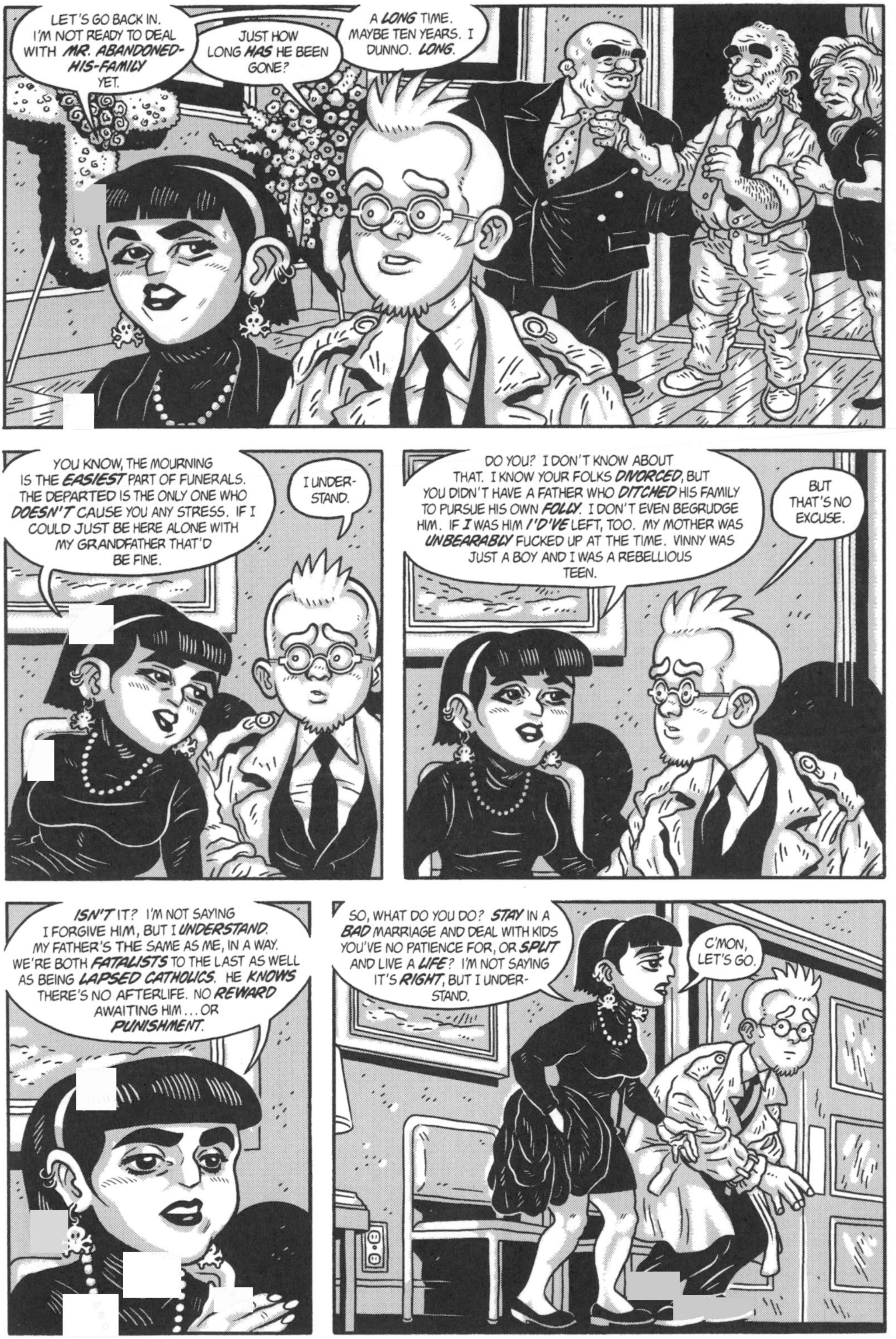
LET'S GO BACK IN. I'M NOT READY TO DEAL WITH MR. ABANDONED-HIS-FAMILY YET.
JUST HOW LONG HAS HE BEEN GONE?
A LONG TIME. MAYBE TEN YEARS. I DUNNO. LONG.
YOU KNOW, THE MOURNING IS THE EASIEST PART OF FUNERALS. THE DEPARTED IS THE ONLY ONE WHO DOESN'T CAUSE YOU ANY STRESS. IF I COULD JUST BE HERE ALONE WITH MY GRANDFATHER THAT'D BE FINE.
I UNDER-STAND.
DO YOU? I DON'T KNOW ABOUT THAT. I KNOW YOUR FOLKS DIVORCED, BUT YOU DIDN'T HAVE A FATHER WHO DITCHED HIS FAMILY TO PURSUE HIS OWN FOLLY. I DON'T EVEN BEGRUDGE HIM. IF I WAS HIM I'D'VE LEFT, TOO. MY MOTHER WAS UNBEARABLY FUCKED UP AT THE TIME. VINNY WAS JUST A BOY AND I WAS A REBELLIOUS TEEN.
BUT THAT'S NO EXCUSE.
ISN'T IT? I'M NOT SAYING I FORGIVE HIM, BUT I UNDERSTAND. MY FATHER'S THE SAME AS ME, IN A WAY. WE'RE BOTH FATALISTS TO THE LAST AS WELL AS BEING LAPSED CATHOLICS. HE KNOWS THERE'S NO AFTERLIFE. NO REWARD AWAITING HIM ... OR PUNISHMENT.
SO, WHAT DO YOU DO? STAY IN A BAD MARRIAGE AND DEAL WITH KIDS YOU'VE NO PATIENCE FOR, OR SPLIT AND LIVE A LIFE? I'M NOT SAYING IT'S RIGHT, BUT I UNDER-STAND.
C'MON, LET'S GO.

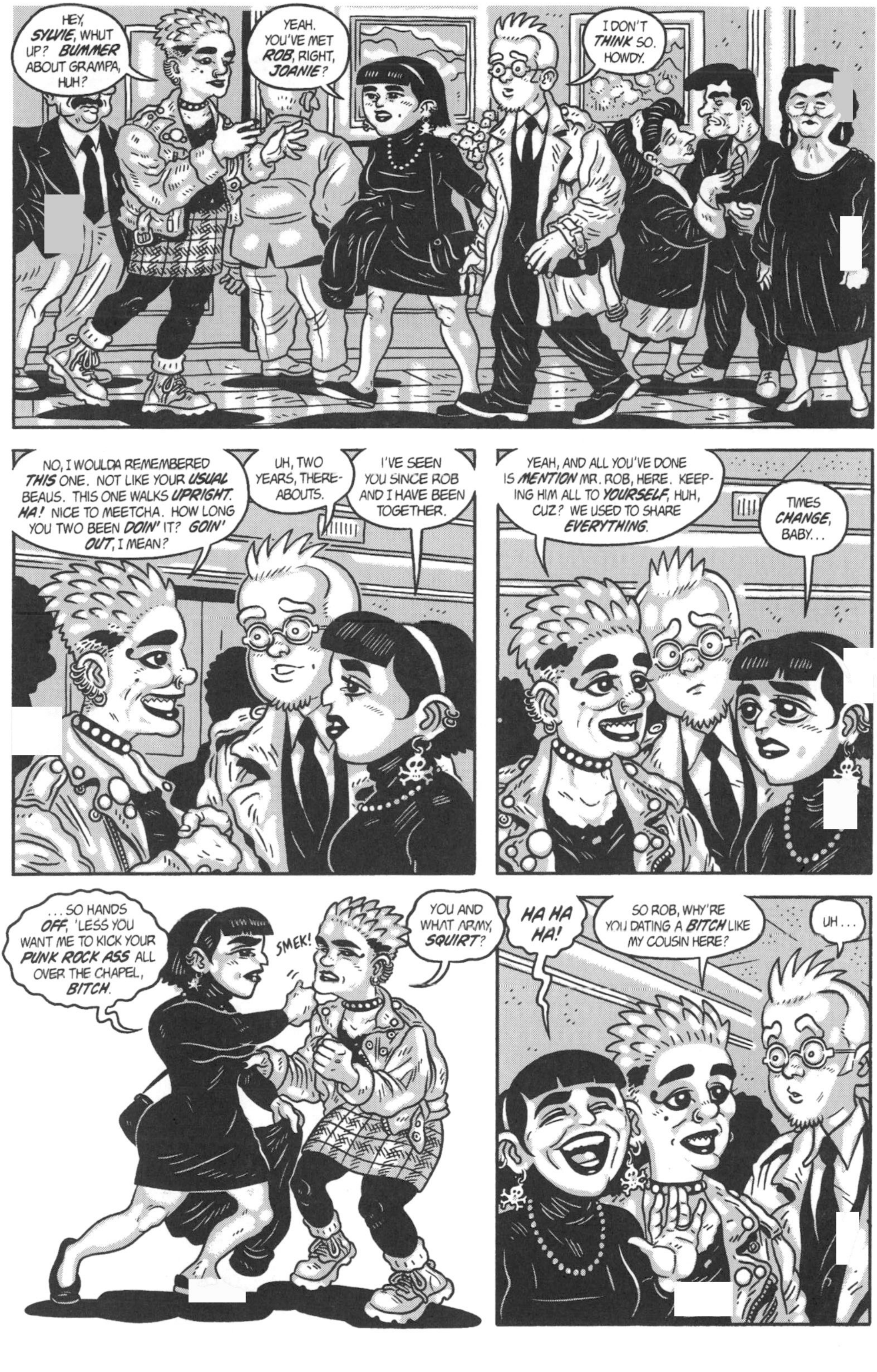
HEY, SYLVIE, WHUT UP? BUMMER ABOUT GRAMPA, HUH?
YEAH. YOU'VE MET ROB, RIGHT, JOANIE?
I DON'T THINK SO. HOWDY.
NO, I WOULDA REMEMBERED THIS ONE. NOT LIKE YOUR USUAL BEAUS. THIS ONE WALKS UPRIGHT. HA! NICE TO MEETCHA. HOW LONG YOU TWO BEEN DOIN' IT? GOIN' OUT, I MEAN?
UH, TWO YEARS, THERE-ABOUTS.
I'VE SEEN YOU SINCE ROB AND I HAVE BEEN TOGETHER.
YEAH, AND ALL YOU'VE DONE IS MENTION MR. ROB, HERE. KEEP-ING HIM ALL TO YOURSELF, HUH, CUZ? WE USED TO SHARE EVERYTHING.
TIMES CHANGE, BABY...
...SO HANDS OFF, 'LESS YOU WANT ME TO KICK YOUR PUNK ROCK ASS ALL OVER THE CHAPEL, BITCH.
SMEK!
YOU AND WHAT ARMY, SQUIRT?
HA HA HA!
SO ROB, WHY'RE YOU DATING A BITCH LIKE MY COUSIN HERE?
UH...

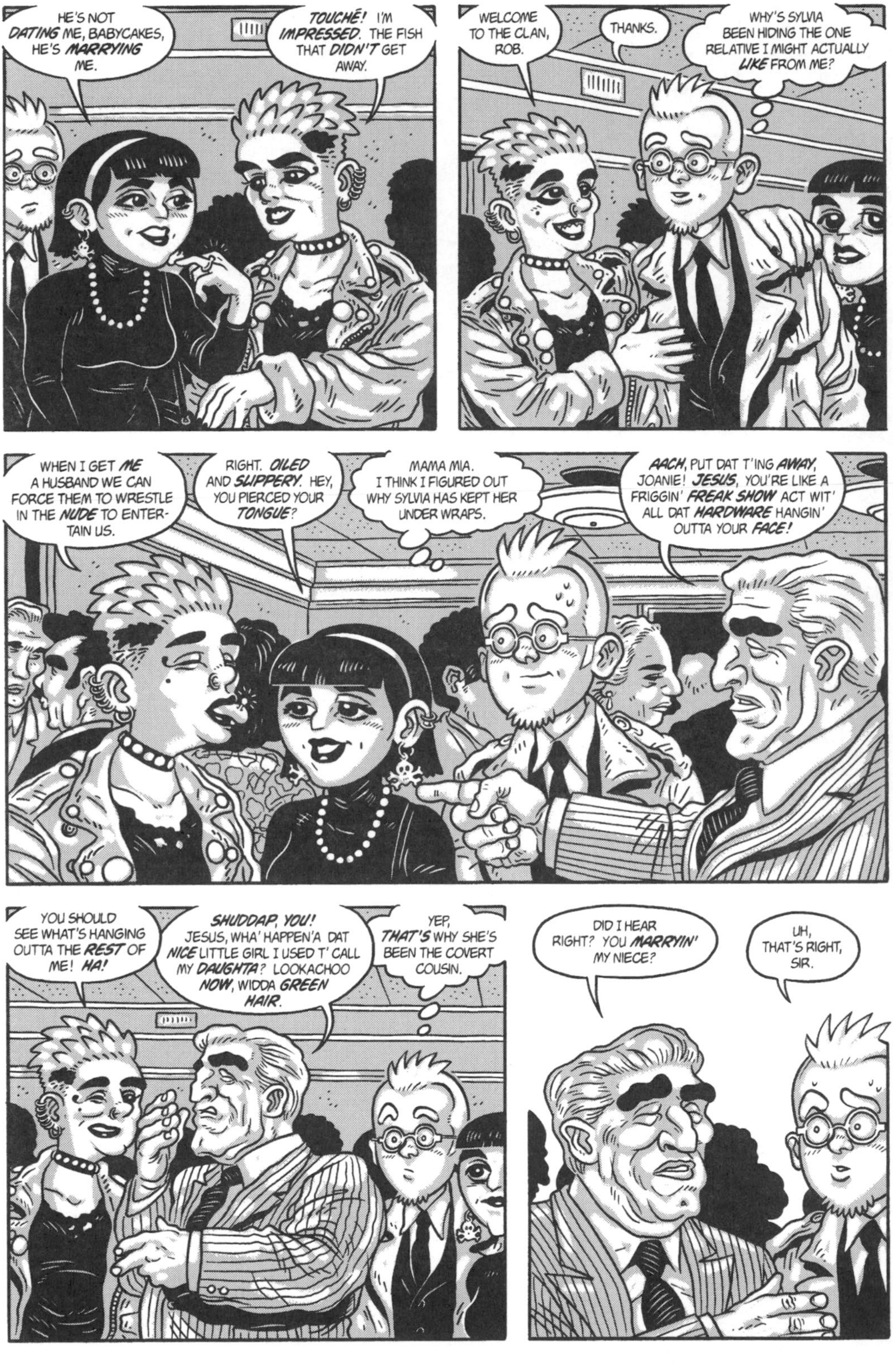
HE'S NOT DATING ME, BABYCAKES, HE'S MARRYING ME.
TOUCHÉ! I'M IMPRESSED. THE FISH THAT DIDN'T GET AWAY.
WELCOME TO THE CLAN, ROB.
THANKS.
WHY'S SYLVIA BEEN HIDING THE ONE RELATIVE I MIGHT ACTUALLY LIKE FROM ME?
WHEN I GET ME A HUSBAND WE CAN FORCE THEM TO WRESTLE IN THE NUDE TO ENTER-TAIN US.
RIGHT. OILED AND SLIPPERY. HEY, YOU PIERCED YOUR TONGUE?
MAMA MIA. I THINK I FIGURED OUT WHY SYLVIA HAS KEPT HER UNDER WRAPS.
AACH, PUT DAT T'ING AWAY, JOANIE! JESUS, YOU'RE LIKE A FRIGGIN' FREAK SHOW ACT WIT' ALL DAT HARDWARE HANGIN' OUTTA YOUR FACE!
YOU SHOULD SEE WHAT'S HANGING OUTTA THE REST OF ME! HA!
SHUDDAP, YOU! JESUS, WHA' HAPPEN'A DAT NICE LITTLE GIRL I USED T' CALL MY DAUGHTA? LOOKACHOO NOW, WIDDA GREEN HAIR.
YEP, THAT'S WHY SHE'S BEEN THE COVERT COUSIN.
DID I HEAR RIGHT? YOU MARRYIN' MY NIECE?
UH, THAT'S RIGHT, SIR.

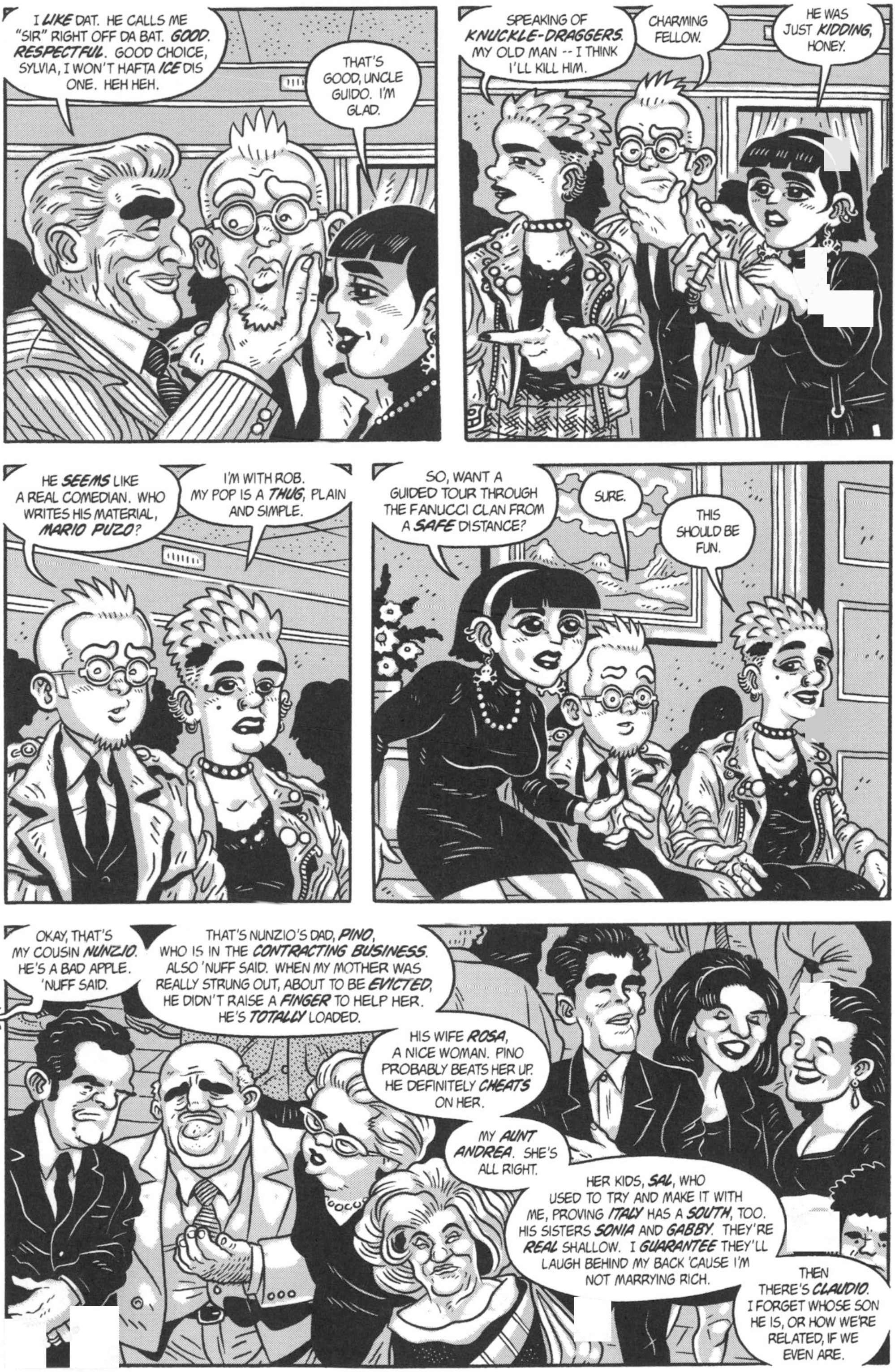
I LIKE DAT. HE CALLS ME "SIR" RIGHT OFF DA BAT. GOOD. RESPECTFUL. GOOD CHOICE, SYLVIA, I WON'T HAFTA ICE DIS ONE. HEH HEH.
THAT'S GOOD, UNCLE GUIDO. I'M GLAD.
SPEAKING OF KNUCKLE-DRAGGERS. MY OLD MAN -- I THINK I'LL KILL HIM.
CHARMING FELLOW.
HE WAS JUST KIDDING, HONEY.
HE SEEMS LIKE A REAL COMEDIAN. WHO WRITES HIS MATERIAL, MARIO PUZO?
I'M WITH ROB. MY POP IS A THUG, PLAIN AND SIMPLE.
SO, WANT A GUIDED TOUR THROUGH THE FANUCCI CLAN FROM A SAFE DISTANCE?
SURE.
THIS SHOULD BE FUN.
OKAY, THAT'S MY COUSIN NUNZIO. HE'S A BAD APPLE. 'NUFF SAID.
THAT'S NUNZIO'S DAD, PINO, WHO IS IN THE CONTRACTING BUSINESS. ALSO 'NUFF SAID. WHEN MY MOTHER WAS REALLY STRUNG OUT, ABOUT TO BE EVICTED, HE DIDN'T RAISE A FINGER TO HELP HER. HE'S TOTALLY LOADED.
HIS WIFE ROSA, A NICE WOMAN. PINO PROBABLY BEATS HER UP. HE DEFINITELY CHEATS ON HER.
MY AUNT ANDREA. SHE'S ALL RIGHT.
HER KIDS, SAL, WHO USED TO TRY AND MAKE IT WITH ME, PROVING ITALY HAS A SOUTH, TOO. HIS SISTERS SONIA AND GABBY. THEY'RE REAL SHALLOW. I GUARANTEE THEY'LL LAUGH BEHIND MY BACK 'CAUSE I'M NOT MARRYING RICH.
THEN THERE'S CLAUDIO. I FORGET WHOSE SON HE IS, OR HOW WE'RE RELATED, IF WE EVEN ARE.

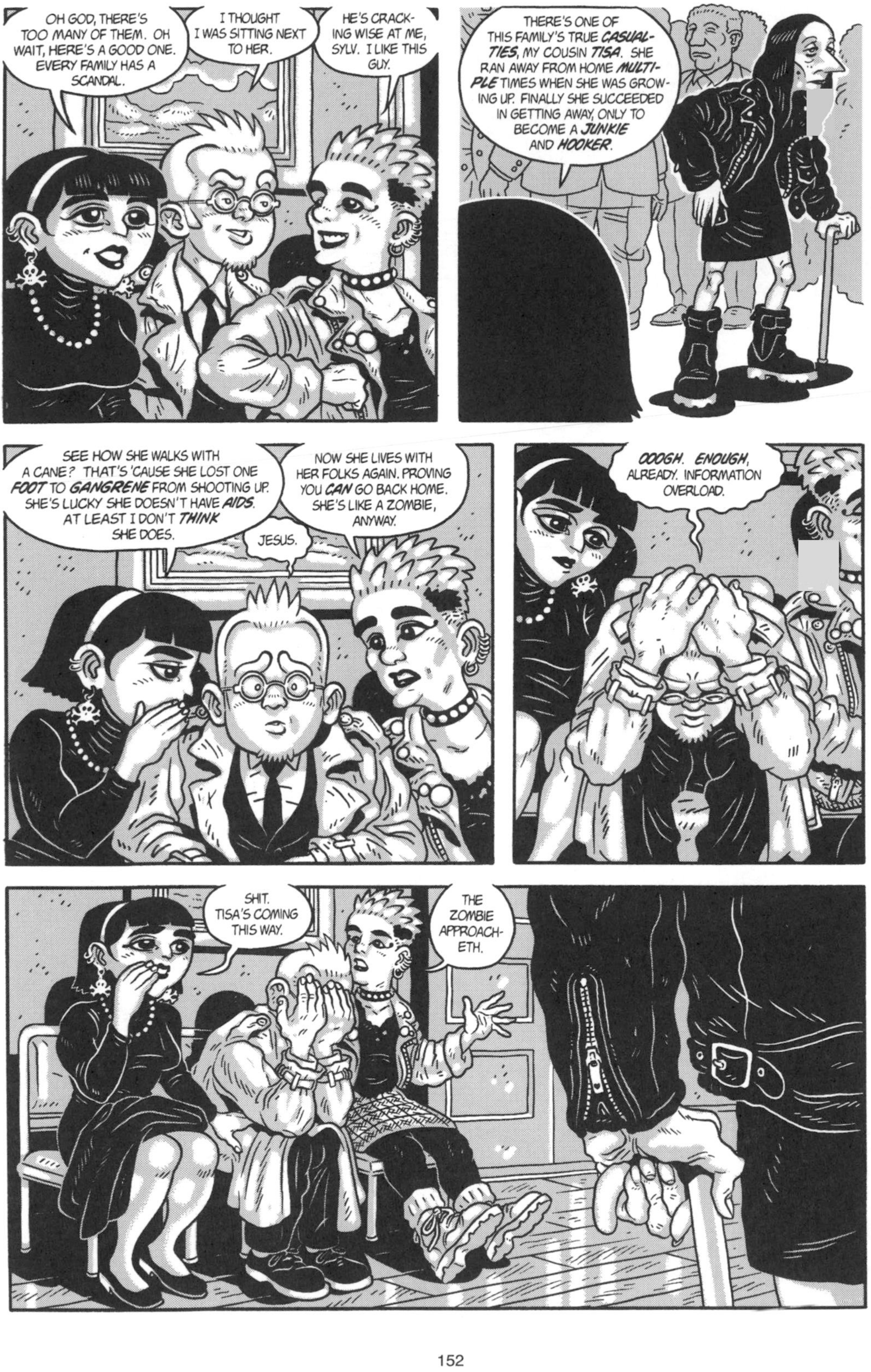
OH GOD, THERE'S TOO MANY OF THEM. OH WAIT, HERE'S A GOOD ONE. EVERY FAMILY HAS A SCANDAL.
I THOUGHT I WAS SITTING NEXT TO HER.
HE'S CRACKING WISE AT ME, SYLV. I LIKE THIS GUY.
THERE'S ONE OF THIS FAMILY'S TRUE CASUALTIES, MY COUSIN TISA. SHE RAN AWAY FROM HOME MULTIPLE TIMES WHEN SHE WAS GROWING UP. FINALLY SHE SUCCEEDED IN GETTING AWAY, ONLY TO BECOME A JUNKIE AND HOOKER.
SEE HOW SHE WALKS WITH A CANE? THAT'S 'CAUSE SHE LOST ONE FOOT TO GANGRENE FROM SHOOTING UP. SHE'S LUCKY SHE DOESN'T HAVE AIDS. AT LEAST I DON'T THINK SHE DOES.
JESUS.
NOW SHE LIVES WITH HER FOLKS AGAIN. PROVING YOU CAN GO BACK HOME. SHE'S LIKE A ZOMBIE, ANYWAY.
OOOGH. ENOUGH, ALREADY. INFORMATION OVERLOAD.
SHIT. TISA'S COMING THIS WAY.
THE ZOMBIE APPROACHETH.

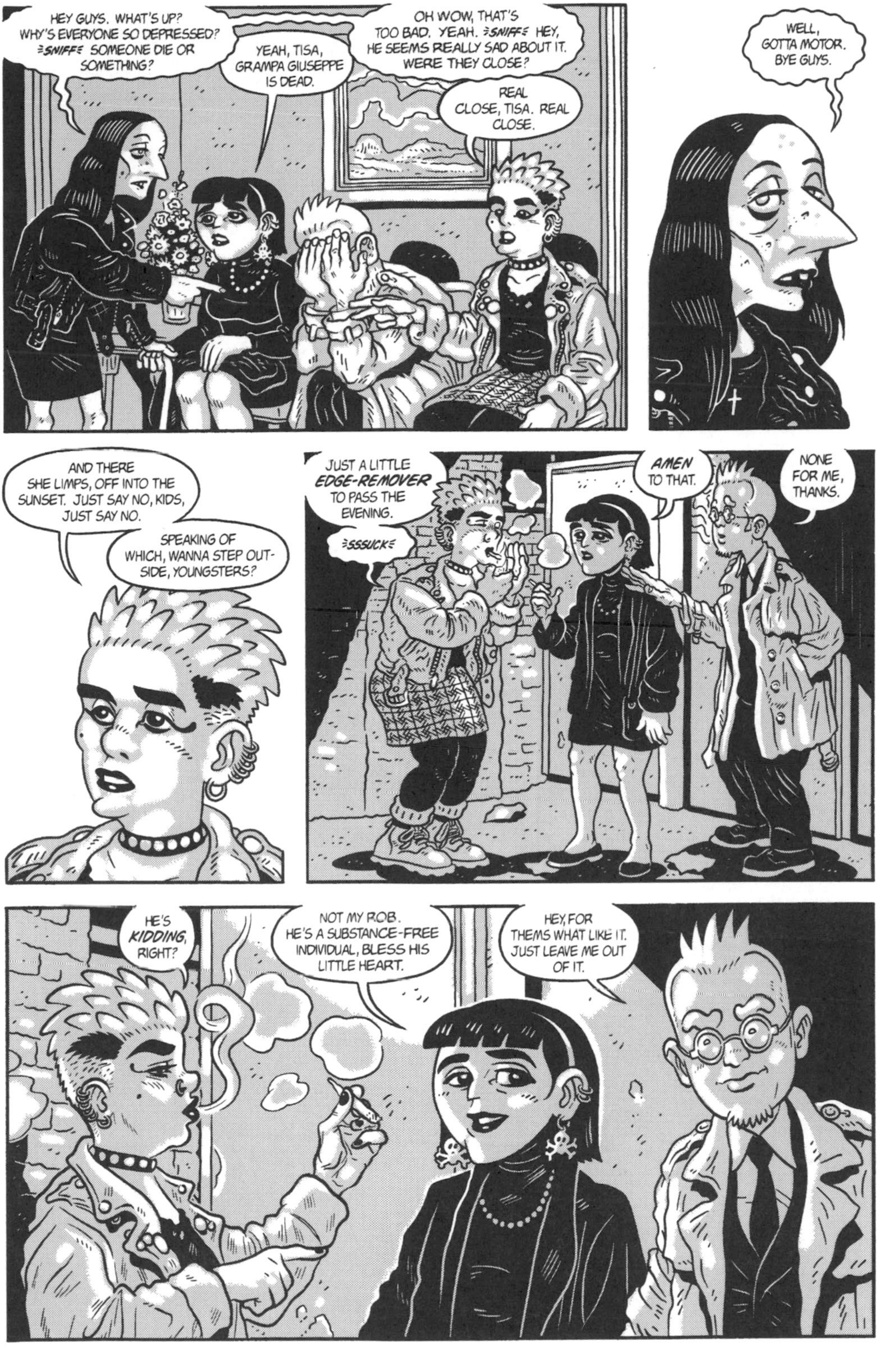
HEY GUYS. WHAT'S UP? WHY'S EVERYONE SO DEPRESSED? ≡SNIFF≡ SOMEONE DIE OR SOMETHING?
YEAH, TISA, GRAMPA GIUSEPPE IS DEAD.
OH WOW, THAT'S TOO BAD. YEAH. ≡SNIFF≡ HEY, HE SEEMS REALLY SAD ABOUT IT. WERE THEY CLOSE?
REAL CLOSE, TISA. REAL CLOSE.
WELL, GOTTA MOTOR. BYE GUYS.
AND THERE SHE LIMPS, OFF INTO THE SUNSET. JUST SAY NO, KIDS, JUST SAY NO.
SPEAKING OF WHICH, WANNA STEP OUTSIDE, YOUNGSTERS?
JUST A LITTLE EDGE-REMOVER TO PASS THE EVENING.
≡SSSUCK≡
AMEN TO THAT.
NONE FOR ME, THANKS.
HE'S KIDDING, RIGHT?
NOT MY ROB. HE'S A SUBSTANCE-FREE INDIVIDUAL, BLESS HIS LITTLE HEART.
HEY, FOR THEMS WHAT LIKE IT. JUST LEAVE ME OUT OF IT.

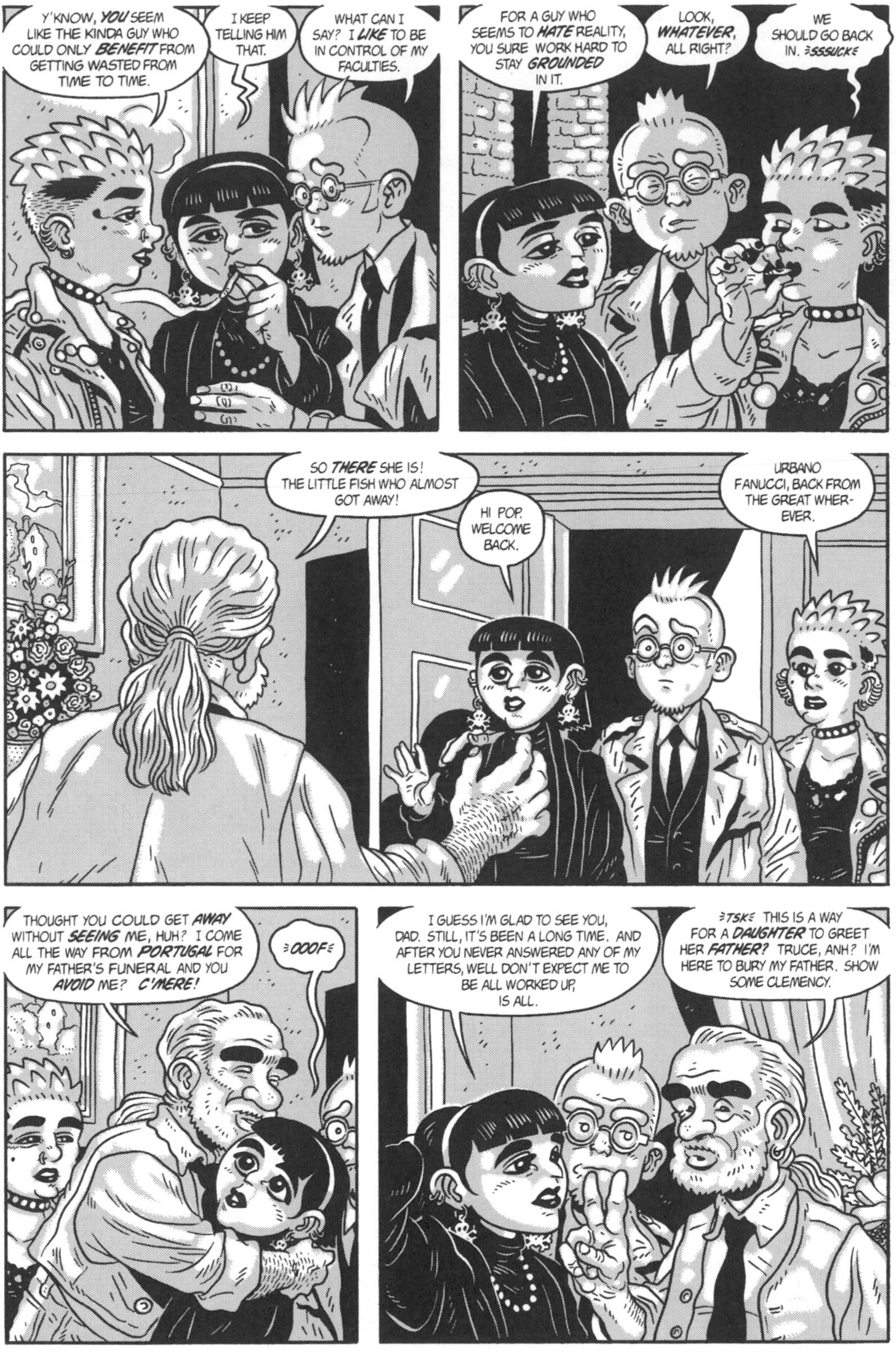

Y'KNOW, YOU SEEM LIKE THE KINDA GUY WHO COULD ONLY BENEFIT FROM GETTING WASTED FROM TIME TO TIME.
I KEEP TELLING HIM THAT.
WHAT CAN I SAY? I LIKE TO BE IN CONTROL OF MY FACULTIES.
FOR A GUY WHO SEEMS TO HATE REALITY, YOU SURE WORK HARD TO STAY GROUNDED IN IT.
LOOK, WHATEVER, ALL RIGHT?
WE SHOULD GO BACK IN. ≶SSSUCK≶
SO THERE SHE IS! THE LITTLE FISH WHO ALMOST GOT AWAY!
HI POP. WELCOME BACK.
URBANO FANUCCI, BACK FROM THE GREAT WHER-EVER.
THOUGHT YOU COULD GET AWAY WITHOUT SEEING ME, HUH? I COME ALL THE WAY FROM PORTUGAL FOR MY FATHER'S FUNERAL AND YOU AVOID ME? C'MERE!
≶OOOF≶
I GUESS I'M GLAD TO SEE YOU, DAD. STILL, IT'S BEEN A LONG TIME. AND AFTER YOU NEVER ANSWERED ANY OF MY LETTERS, WELL DON'T EXPECT ME TO BE ALL WORKED UP, IS ALL.
≶TSK≶ THIS IS A WAY FOR A DAUGHTER TO GREET HER FATHER? TRUCE, ANH? I'M HERE TO BURY MY FATHER. SHOW SOME CLEMENCY.

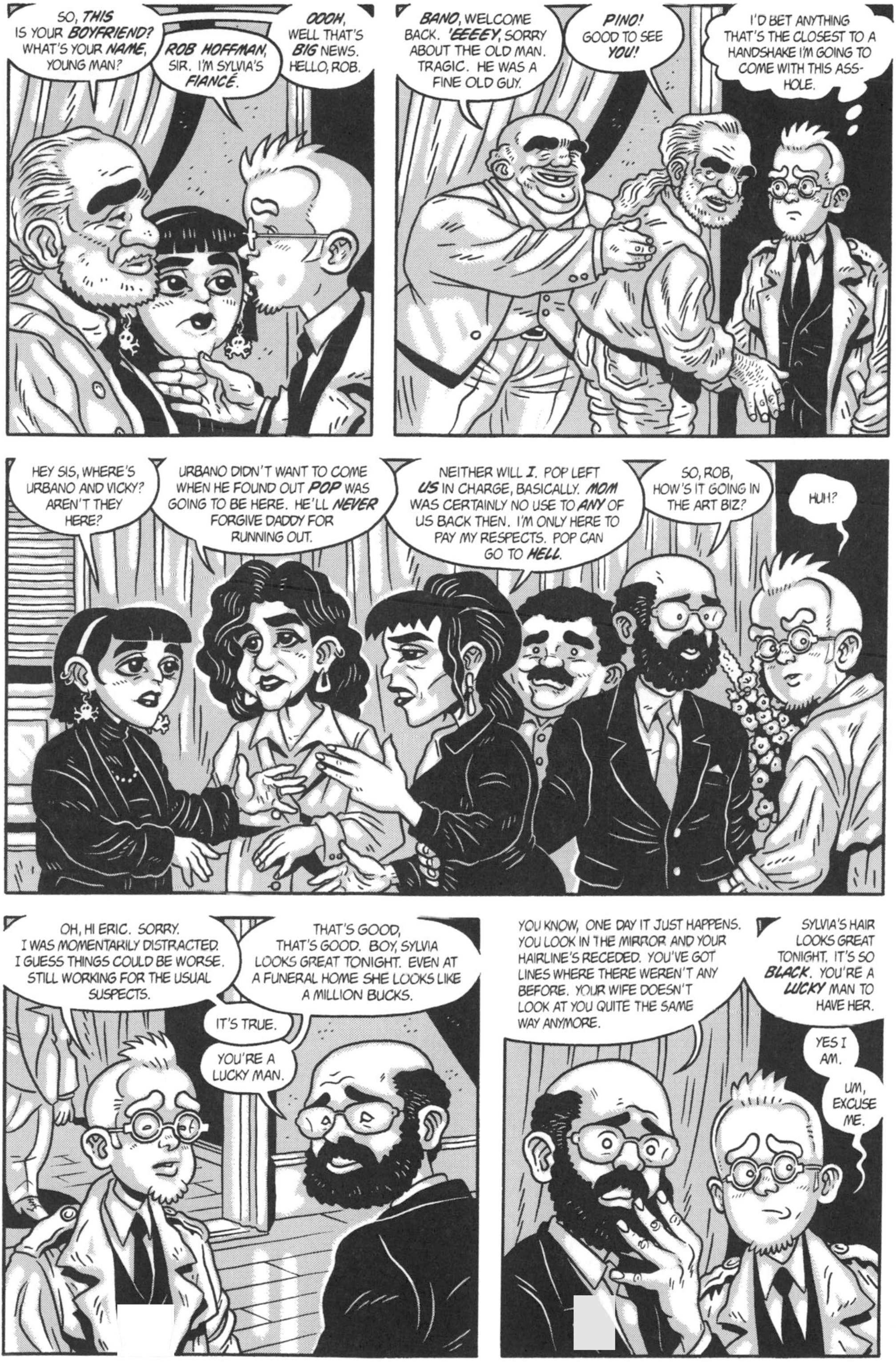
SO, THIS IS YOUR BOYFRIEND? WHAT'S YOUR NAME, YOUNG MAN?
ROB HOFFMAN, SIR. I'M SYLVIA'S FIANCÉ.
OOOH, WELL THAT'S BIG NEWS. HELLO, ROB.
BANO, WELCOME BACK. 'EEEEY, SORRY ABOUT THE OLD MAN. TRAGIC. HE WAS A FINE OLD GUY.
PINO! GOOD TO SEE YOU!
I'D BET ANYTHING THAT'S THE CLOSEST TO A HANDSHAKE I'M GOING TO COME WITH THIS ASS-HOLE.
HEY SIS, WHERE'S URBANO AND VICKY? AREN'T THEY HERE?
URBANO DIDN'T WANT TO COME WHEN HE FOUND OUT POP WAS GOING TO BE HERE. HE'LL NEVER FORGIVE DADDY FOR RUNNING OUT.
NEITHER WILL I. POP LEFT US IN CHARGE, BASICALLY. MOM WAS CERTAINLY NO USE TO ANY OF US BACK THEN. I'M ONLY HERE TO PAY MY RESPECTS. POP CAN GO TO HELL.
SO, ROB, HOW'S IT GOING IN THE ART BIZ?
HUH?
OH, HI ERIC. SORRY. I WAS MOMENTARILY DISTRACTED. I GUESS THINGS COULD BE WORSE. STILL WORKING FOR THE USUAL SUSPECTS.
THAT'S GOOD, THAT'S GOOD. BOY, SYLVIA LOOKS GREAT TONIGHT. EVEN AT A FUNERAL HOME SHE LOOKS LIKE A MILLION BUCKS.
IT'S TRUE.
YOU'RE A LUCKY MAN.
YOU KNOW, ONE DAY IT JUST HAPPENS. YOU LOOK IN THE MIRROR AND YOUR HAIRLINE'S RECEDED. YOU'VE GOT LINES WHERE THERE WEREN'T ANY BEFORE. YOUR WIFE DOESN'T LOOK AT YOU QUITE THE SAME WAY ANYMORE.
SYLVIA'S HAIR LOOKS GREAT TONIGHT. IT'S SO BLACK. YOU'RE A LUCKY MAN TO HAVE HER.
YES I AM.
UM, EXCUSE ME.

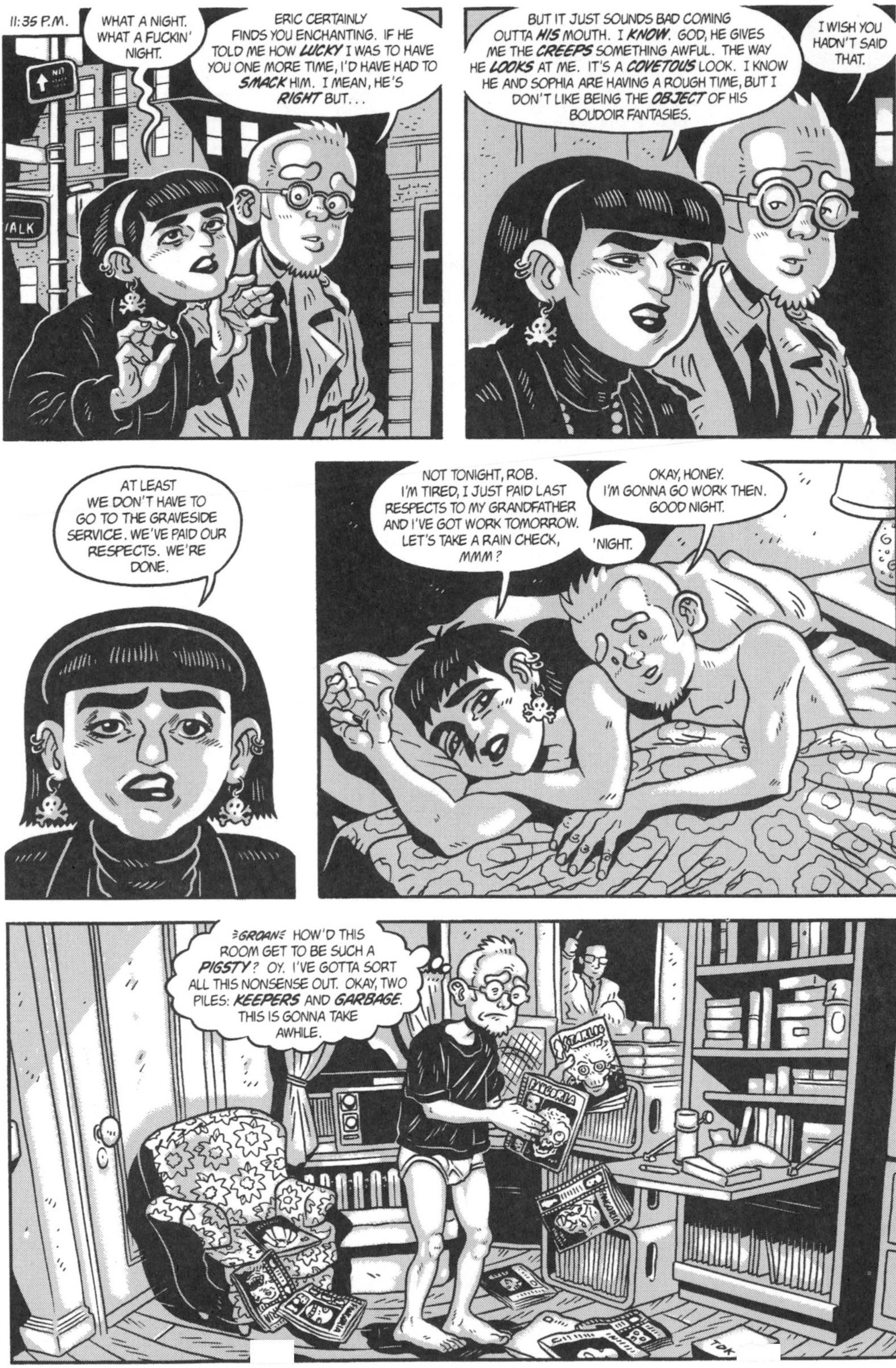
11:35 P.M.
WHAT A NIGHT. WHAT A FUCKIN' NIGHT.
ERIC CERTAINLY FINDS YOU ENCHANTING. IF HE TOLD ME HOW LUCKY I WAS TO HAVE YOU ONE MORE TIME, I'D HAVE HAD TO SMACK HIM. I MEAN, HE'S RIGHT BUT...
WALK
BUT IT JUST SOUNDS BAD COMING OUTTA HIS MOUTH. I KNOW. GOD, HE GIVES ME THE CREEPS SOMETHING AWFUL. THE WAY HE LOOKS AT ME. IT'S A COVETOUS LOOK. I KNOW HE AND SOPHIA ARE HAVING A ROUGH TIME, BUT I DON'T LIKE BEING THE OBJECT OF HIS BOUDOIR FANTASIES.
I WISH YOU HADN'T SAID THAT.
AT LEAST WE DON'T HAVE TO GO TO THE GRAVESIDE SERVICE. WE'VE PAID OUR RESPECTS. WE'RE DONE.
NOT TONIGHT, ROB. I'M TIRED, I JUST PAID LAST RESPECTS TO MY GRANDFATHER AND I'VE GOT WORK TOMORROW. LET'S TAKE A RAIN CHECK, MMM?
OKAY, HONEY. I'M GONNA GO WORK THEN. GOOD NIGHT.
'NIGHT.
GROAN HOW'D THIS ROOM GET TO BE SUCH A PIGSTY? OY. I'VE GOTTA SORT ALL THIS NONSENSE OUT. OKAY, TWO PILES: KEEPERS AND GARBAGE. THIS IS GONNA TAKE AWHILE.
TOK

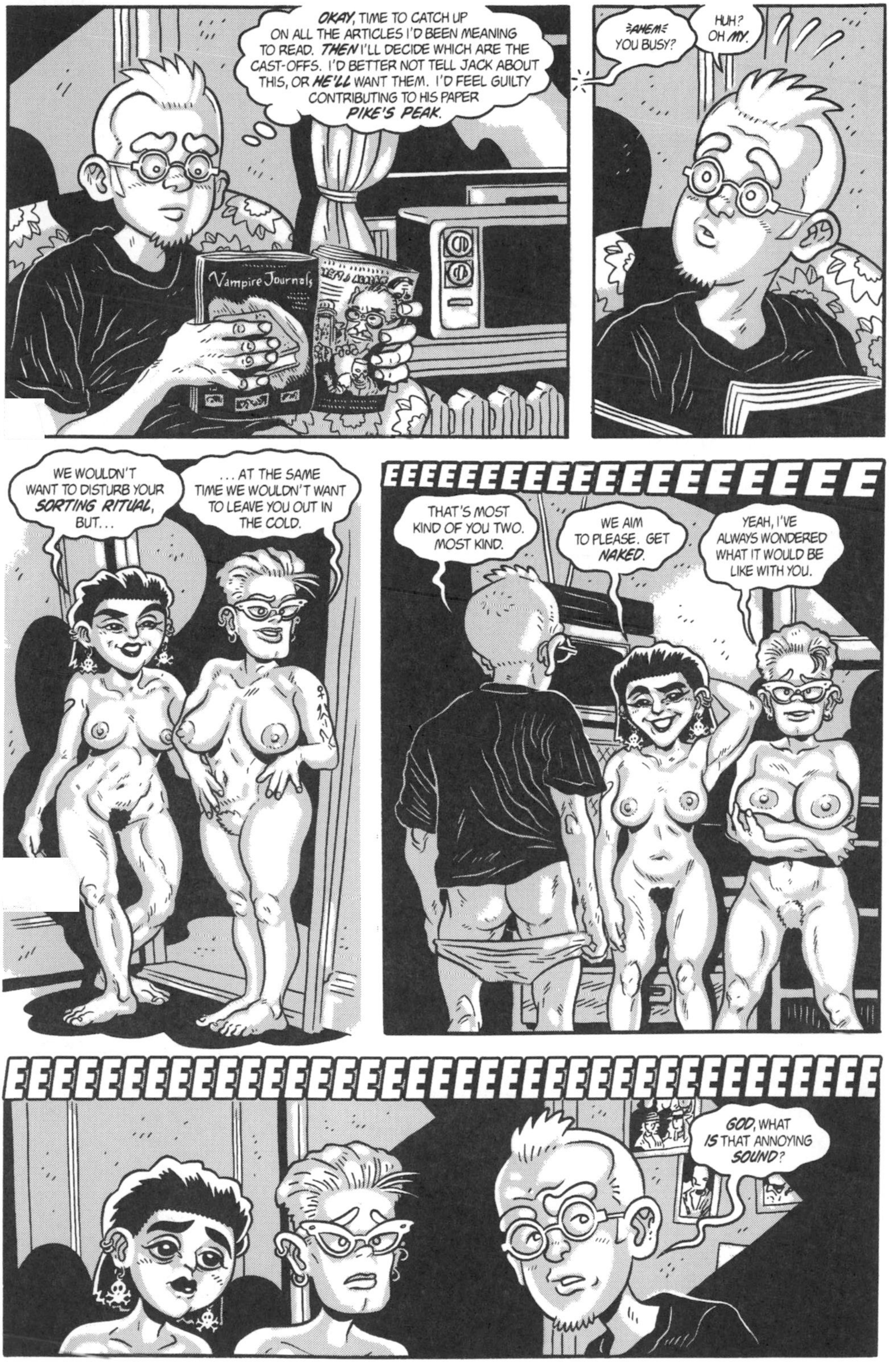
OKAY, TIME TO CATCH UP ON ALL THE ARTICLES I'D BEEN MEANING TO READ. THEN I'LL DECIDE WHICH ARE THE CAST-OFFS. I'D BETTER NOT TELL JACK ABOUT THIS, OR HE'LL WANT THEM. I'D FEEL GUILTY CONTRIBUTING TO HIS PAPER PIKE'S PEAK.
Vampire Journals
AHEM YOU BUSY?
HUH? OH MY.
WE WOULDN'T WANT TO DISTURB YOUR SORTING RITUAL, BUT...
...AT THE SAME TIME WE WOULDN'T WANT TO LEAVE YOU OUT IN THE COLD.
EEEEEEEEEEEEEEEEEEEEE
THAT'S MOST KIND OF YOU TWO. MOST KIND.
WE AIM TO PLEASE. GET NAKED.
YEAH, I'VE ALWAYS WONDERED WHAT IT WOULD BE LIKE WITH YOU.
EEEEEEEEEEEEEEEEEEEEEEEEEEEEEEEEEEEE
GOD, WHAT IS THAT ANNOYING SOUND?

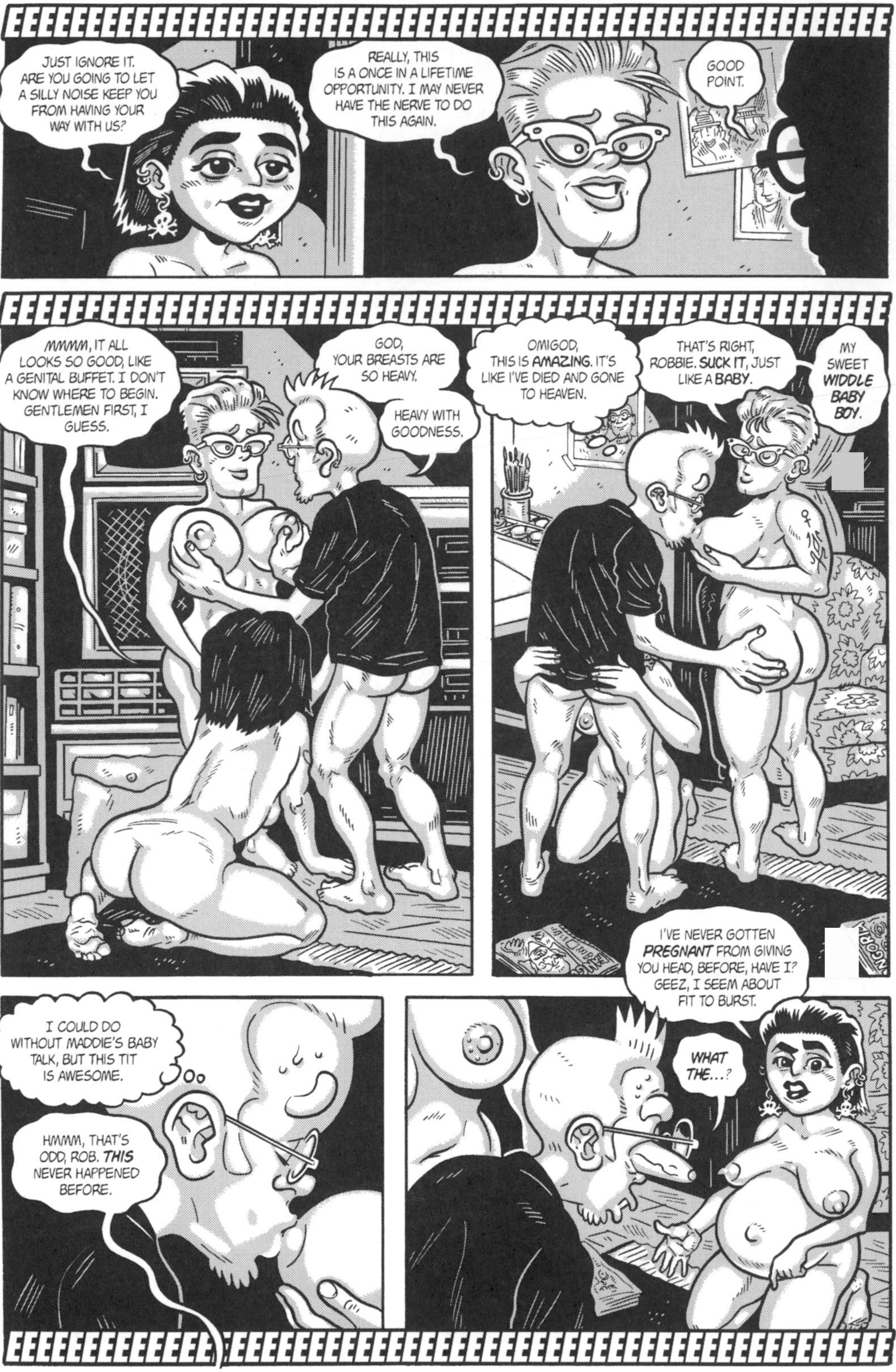
JUST IGNORE IT. ARE YOU GOING TO LET A SILLY NOISE KEEP YOU FROM HAVING YOUR WAY WITH US?
REALLY, THIS IS A ONCE IN A LIFETIME OPPORTUNITY. I MAY NEVER HAVE THE NERVE TO DO THIS AGAIN.
GOOD POINT.
MMMM, IT ALL LOOKS SO GOOD, LIKE A GENITAL BUFFET. I DON'T KNOW WHERE TO BEGIN. GENTLEMEN FIRST, I GUESS.
GOD, YOUR BREASTS ARE SO HEAVY.
HEAVY WITH GOODNESS.
OMIGOD, THIS IS AMAZING. IT'S LIKE I'VE DIED AND GONE TO HEAVEN.
THAT'S RIGHT, ROBBIE. SUCK IT, JUST LIKE A BABY.
MY SWEET WIDDLE BABY BOY.
I COULD DO WITHOUT MADDIE'S BABY TALK, BUT THIS TIT IS AWESOME.
HMMM, THAT'S ODD, ROB. THIS NEVER HAPPENED BEFORE.
I'VE NEVER GOTTEN PREGNANT FROM GIVING YOU HEAD, BEFORE, HAVE I? GEEZ, I SEEM ABOUT FIT TO BURST.
WHAT THE...?

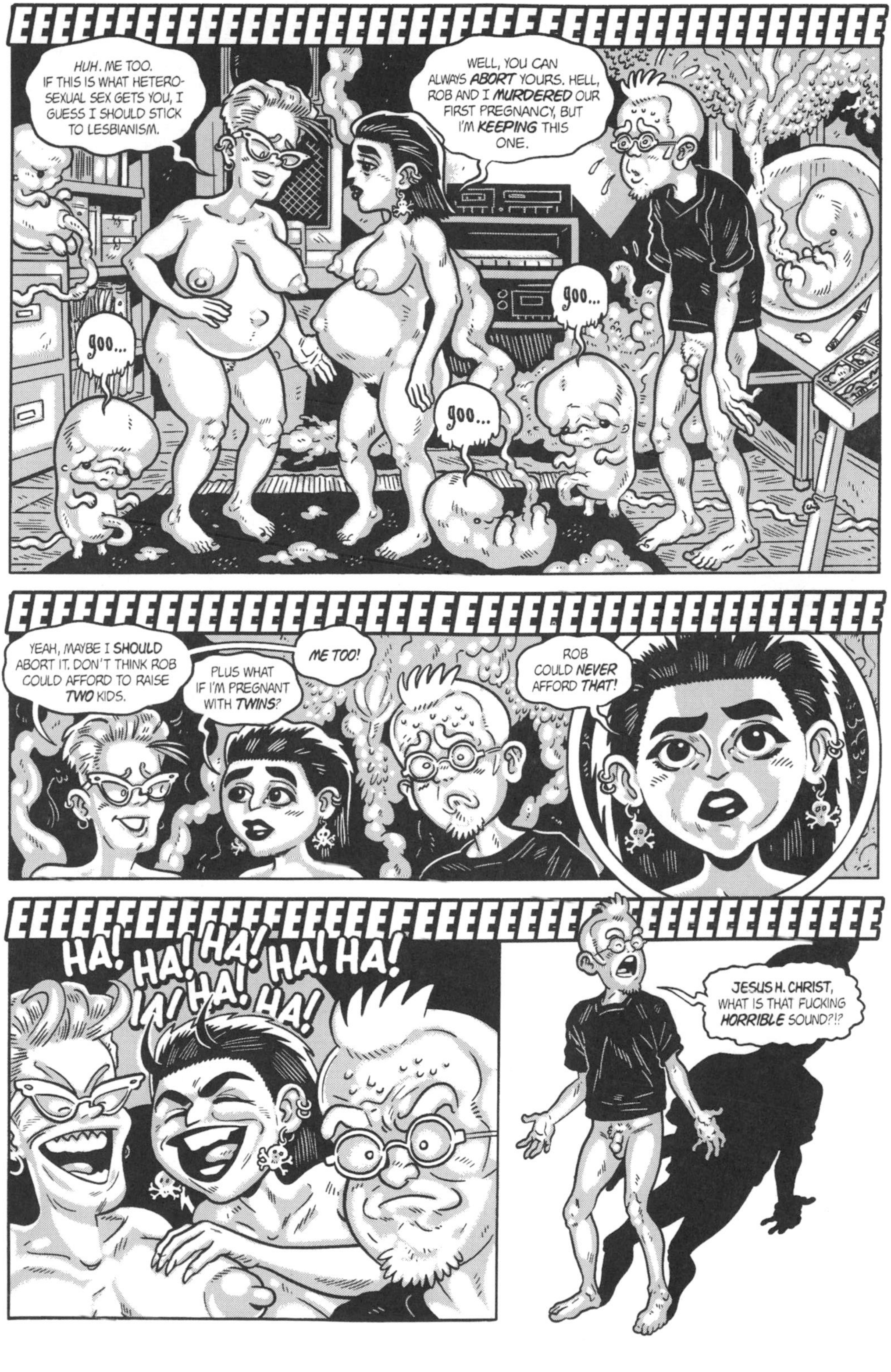
EEEEEEEEEEEEEEEEEEEEEEEEEEEEEEEEEEEEEEEEEEEEE
HUH. ME TOO. IF THIS IS WHAT HETERO-SEXUAL SEX GETS YOU, I GUESS I SHOULD STICK TO LESBIANISM.
WELL, YOU CAN ALWAYS ABORT YOURS. HELL, ROB AND I MURDERED OUR FIRST PREGNANCY, BUT I'M KEEPING THIS ONE.
goo...
goo...
goo...
EEEEEEEEEEEEEEEEEEEEEEEEEEEEEEEEEEEEEEEEEEEEE
YEAH, MAYBE I SHOULD ABORT IT. DON'T THINK ROB COULD AFFORD TO RAISE TWO KIDS.
PLUS WHAT IF I'M PREGNANT WITH TWINS?
ME TOO!
ROB COULD NEVER AFFORD THAT!
EEEEEEEEEEEEEEEEEEEEEEEEEEEEEEEEEEEEEEEEEEEEE
HA! HA! HA! HA! HA! HA! HA! HA!
JESUS H. CHRIST, WHAT IS THAT FUCKING HORRIBLE SOUND?!?

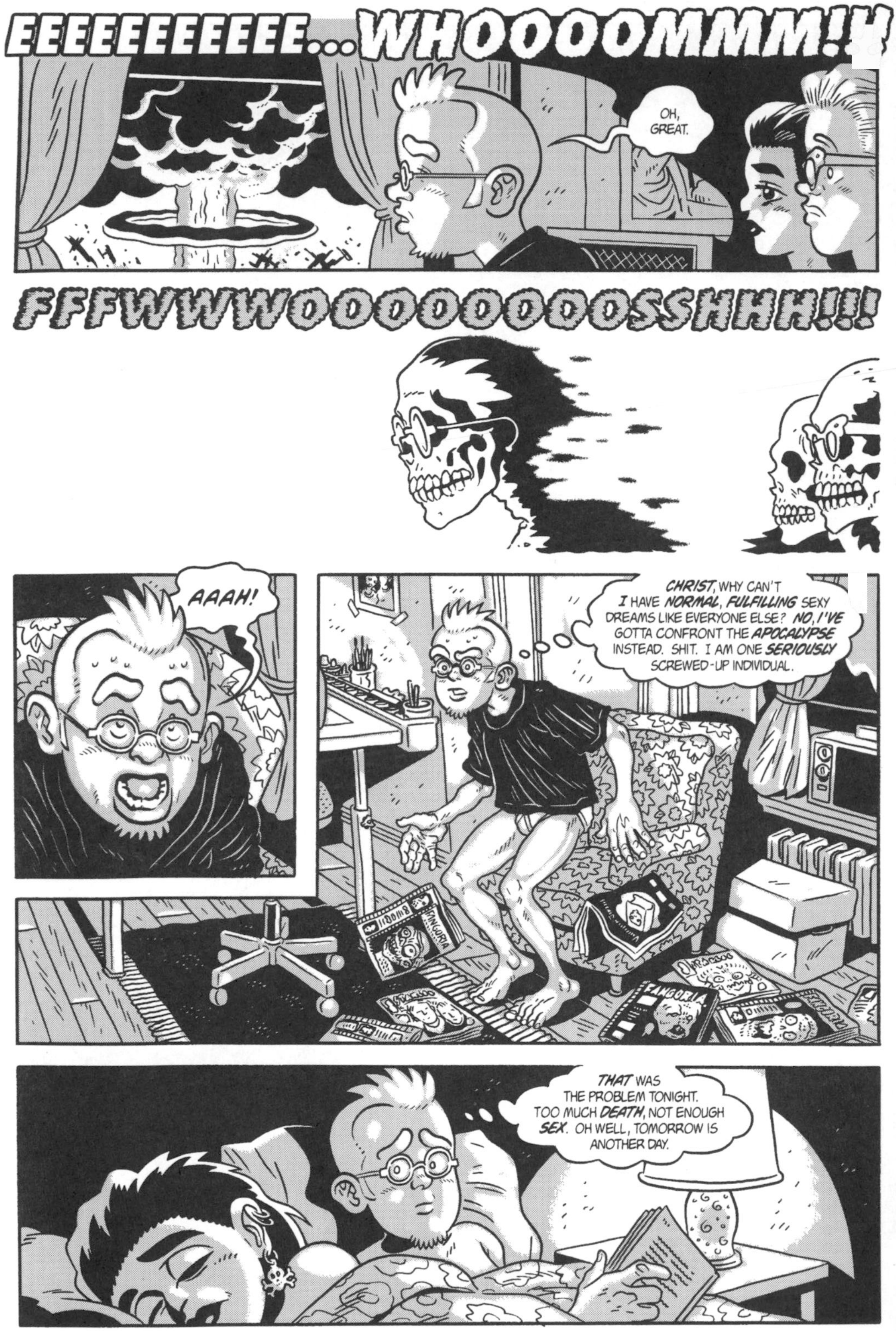
EEEEEEEEEEE...WHOOOOMMMM!!!
OH, GREAT.
FFFWWWOOOOOOOOOOSSHHH!!!
AAAH!
CHRIST, WHY CAN'T I HAVE NORMAL, FULFILLING SEXY DREAMS LIKE EVERYONE ELSE? NO, I'VE GOTTA CONFRONT THE APOCALYPSE INSTEAD. SHIT. I AM ONE SERIOUSLY SCREWED-UP INDIVIDUAL.
FANGORIA
THAT WAS THE PROBLEM TONIGHT. TOO MUCH DEATH, NOT ENOUGH SEX. OH WELL, TOMORROW IS ANOTHER DAY.

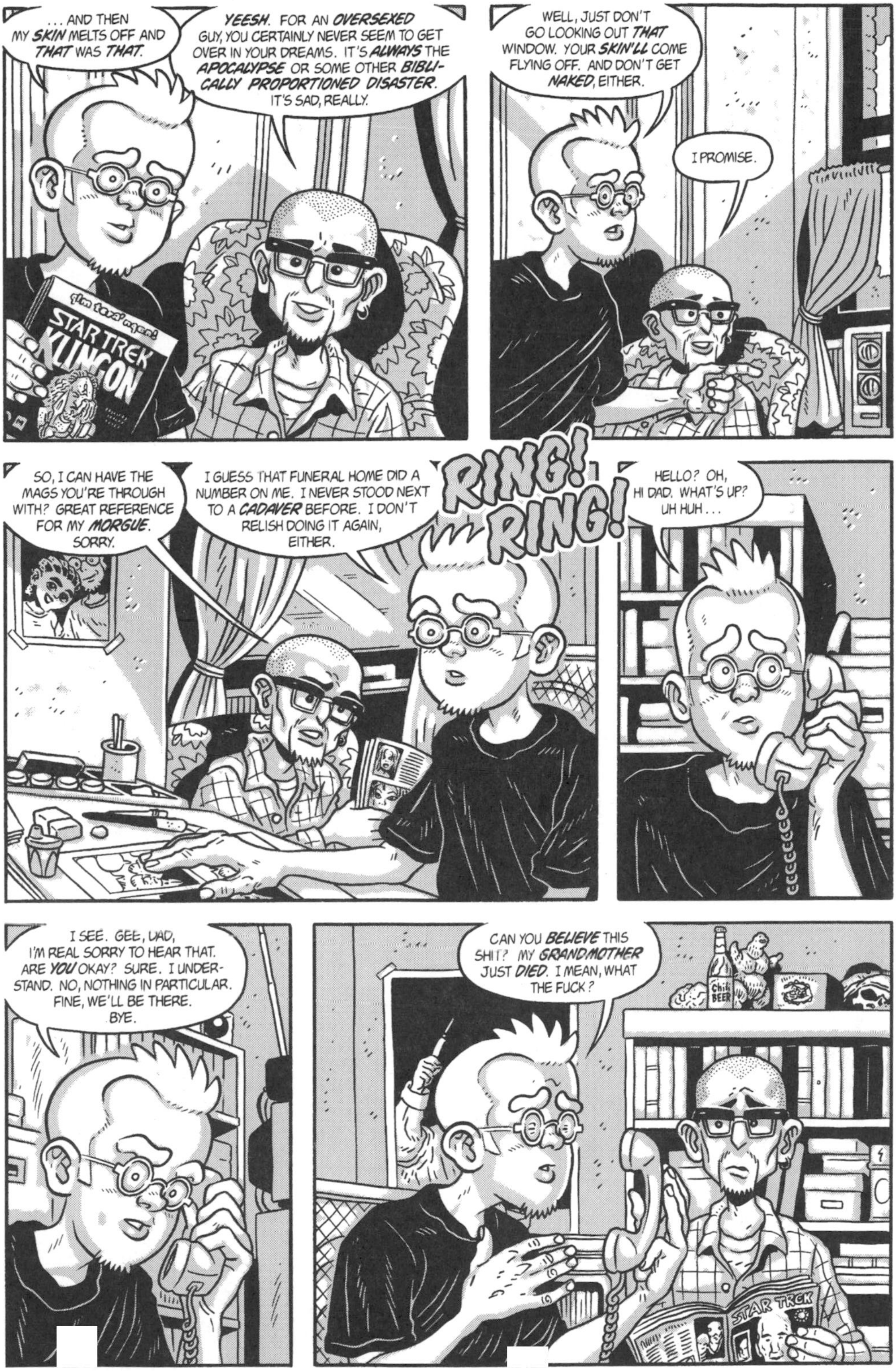
... AND THEN MY SKIN MELTS OFF AND THAT WAS THAT.
YEESH. FOR AN OVERSEXED GUY, YOU CERTAINLY NEVER SEEM TO GET OVER IN YOUR DREAMS. IT'S ALWAYS THE APOCALYPSE OR SOME OTHER BIBLICALLY PROPORTIONED DISASTER. IT'S SAD, REALLY.
STAR TREK KLINGON
WELL, JUST DON'T GO LOOKING OUT THAT WINDOW. YOUR SKIN'LL COME FLYING OFF. AND DON'T GET NAKED, EITHER.
I PROMISE.
SO, I CAN HAVE THE MAGS YOU'RE THROUGH WITH? GREAT REFERENCE FOR MY MORGUE. SORRY.
I GUESS THAT FUNERAL HOME DID A NUMBER ON ME. I NEVER STOOD NEXT TO A CADAVER BEFORE. I DON'T RELISH DOING IT AGAIN, EITHER.
RING! RING!
HELLO? OH, HI DAD. WHAT'S UP? UH HUH ...
I SEE. GEE, DAD, I'M REAL SORRY TO HEAR THAT. ARE YOU OKAY? SURE. I UNDERSTAND. NO, NOTHING IN PARTICULAR. FINE, WE'LL BE THERE. BYE.
CAN YOU BELIEVE THIS SHIT? MY GRANDMOTHER JUST DIED. I MEAN, WHAT THE FUCK?
Chili BEER
STAR TREK

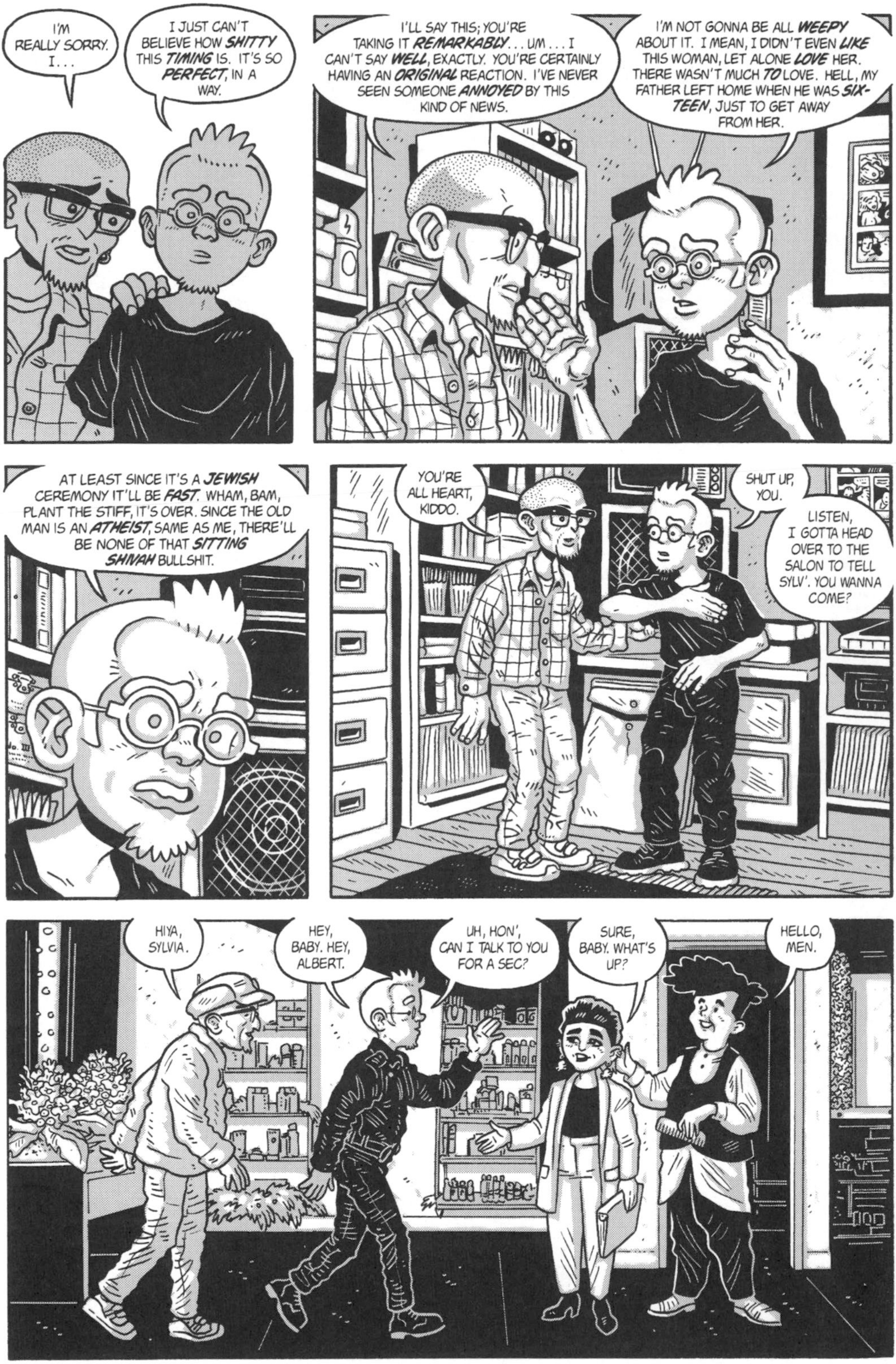
I'M REALLY SORRY. I...
I JUST CAN'T BELIEVE HOW SHITTY THIS TIMING IS. IT'S SO PERFECT, IN A WAY.
I'LL SAY THIS; YOU'RE TAKING IT REMARKABLY... UM... I CAN'T SAY WELL, EXACTLY. YOU'RE CERTAINLY HAVING AN ORIGINAL REACTION. I'VE NEVER SEEN SOMEONE ANNOYED BY THIS KIND OF NEWS.
I'M NOT GONNA BE ALL WEEPY ABOUT IT. I MEAN, I DIDN'T EVEN LIKE THIS WOMAN, LET ALONE LOVE HER. THERE WASN'T MUCH TO LOVE. HELL, MY FATHER LEFT HOME WHEN HE WAS SIX-TEEN, JUST TO GET AWAY FROM HER.
AT LEAST SINCE IT'S A JEWISH CEREMONY IT'LL BE FAST. WHAM, BAM, PLANT THE STIFF, IT'S OVER. SINCE THE OLD MAN IS AN ATHEIST, SAME AS ME, THERE'LL BE NONE OF THAT SITTING SHIVAH BULLSHIT.
YOU'RE ALL HEART, KIDDO.
SHUT UP, YOU.
LISTEN, I GOTTA HEAD OVER TO THE SALON TO TELL SYLV'. YOU WANNA COME?
HIYA, SYLVIA.
HEY, BABY. HEY, ALBERT.
UH, HON', CAN I TALK TO YOU FOR A SEC?
SURE, BABY. WHAT'S UP?
HELLO, MEN.

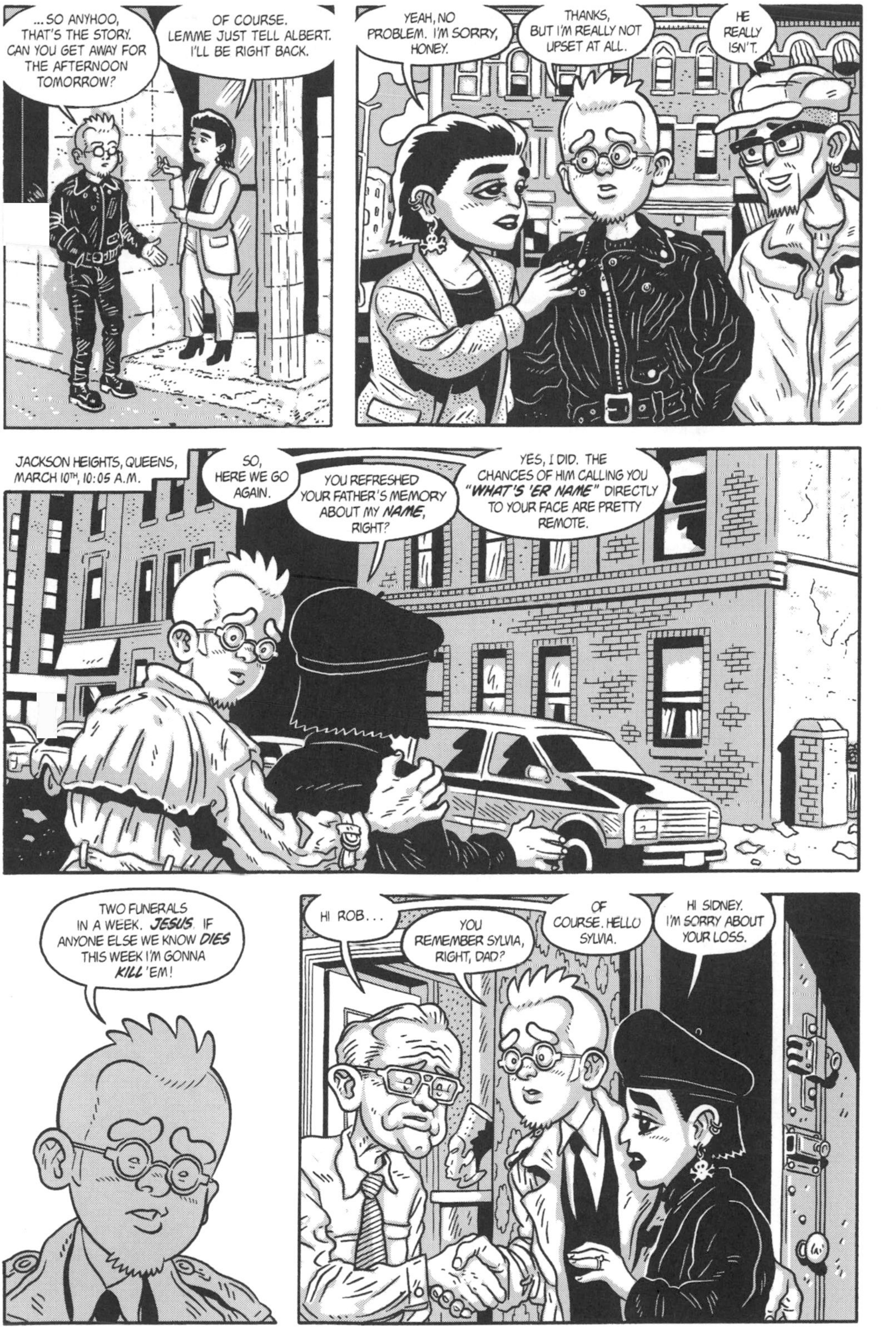
...SO ANYHOO, THAT'S THE STORY. CAN YOU GET AWAY FOR THE AFTERNOON TOMORROW?
OF COURSE. LEMME JUST TELL ALBERT. I'LL BE RIGHT BACK.
YEAH, NO PROBLEM. I'M SORRY, HONEY.
THANKS, BUT I'M REALLY NOT UPSET AT ALL.
HE REALLY ISN'T.
JACKSON HEIGHTS, QUEENS, MARCH 10TH, 10:05 A.M.
SO, HERE WE GO AGAIN.
YOU REFRESHED YOUR FATHER'S MEMORY ABOUT MY NAME, RIGHT?
YES, I DID. THE CHANCES OF HIM CALLING YOU "WHAT'S 'ER NAME" DIRECTLY TO YOUR FACE ARE PRETTY REMOTE.
TWO FUNERALS IN A WEEK. JESUS. IF ANYONE ELSE WE KNOW DIES THIS WEEK I'M GONNA KILL 'EM!
HI ROB...
YOU REMEMBER SYLVIA, RIGHT, DAD?
OF COURSE. HELLO SYLVIA.
HI SIDNEY. I'M SORRY ABOUT YOUR LOSS.

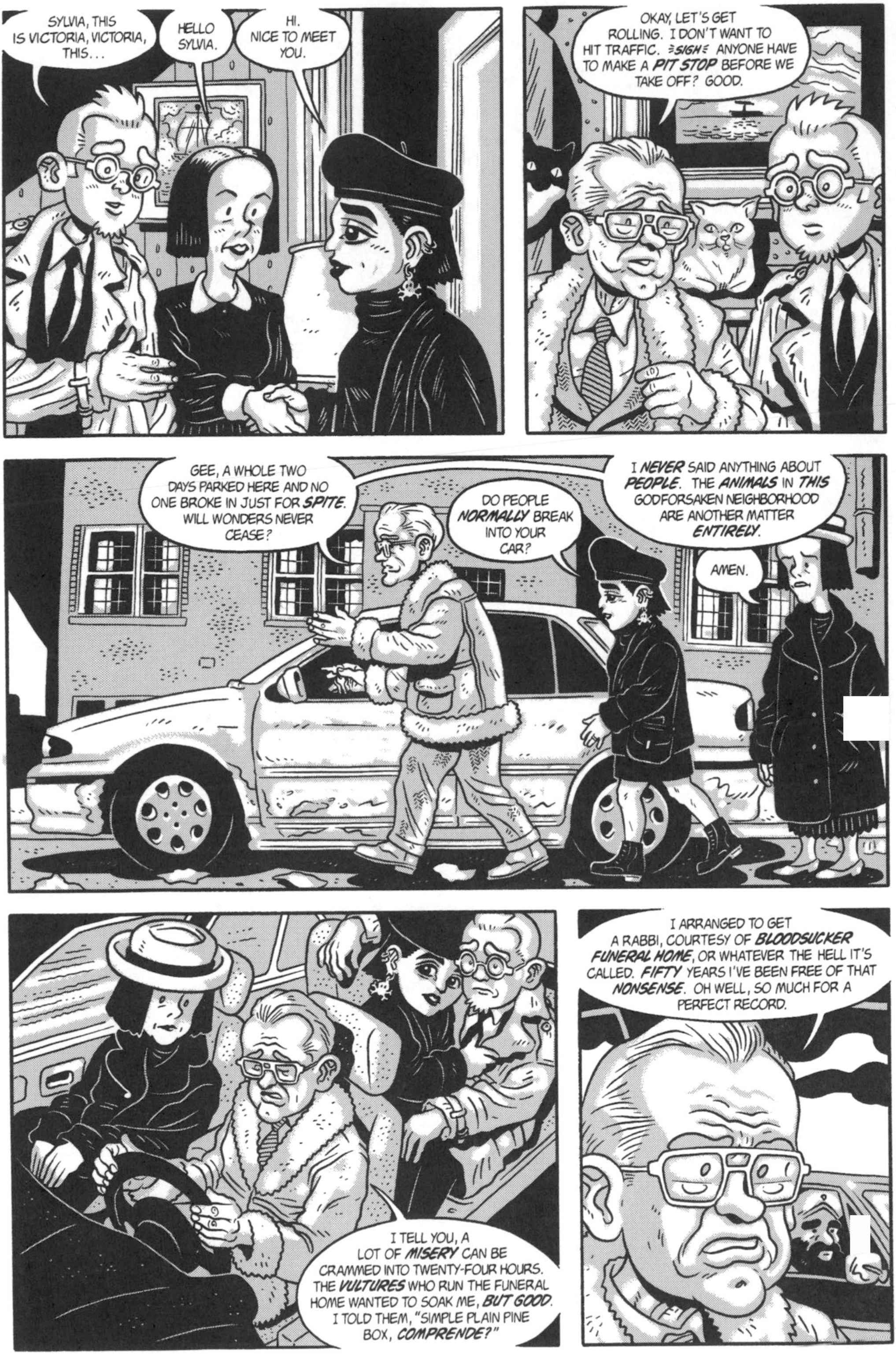
SYLVIA, THIS IS VICTORIA, VICTORIA, THIS...
HELLO SYLVIA.
HI. NICE TO MEET YOU.
OKAY, LET'S GET ROLLING. I DON'T WANT TO HIT TRAFFIC. *SIGH* ANYONE HAVE TO MAKE A PIT STOP BEFORE WE TAKE OFF? GOOD.
GEE, A WHOLE TWO DAYS PARKED HERE AND NO ONE BROKE IN JUST FOR SPITE. WILL WONDERS NEVER CEASE?
DO PEOPLE NORMALLY BREAK INTO YOUR CAR?
I NEVER SAID ANYTHING ABOUT PEOPLE. THE ANIMALS IN THIS GODFORSAKEN NEIGHBORHOOD ARE ANOTHER MATTER ENTIRELY.
AMEN.
I TELL YOU, A LOT OF MISERY CAN BE CRAMMED INTO TWENTY-FOUR HOURS. THE VULTURES WHO RUN THE FUNERAL HOME WANTED TO SOAK ME, BUT GOOD. I TOLD THEM, "SIMPLE PLAIN PINE BOX, COMPRENDE?"
I ARRANGED TO GET A RABBI, COURTESY OF BLOODSUCKER FUNERAL HOME, OR WHATEVER THE HELL IT'S CALLED. FIFTY YEARS I'VE BEEN FREE OF THAT NONSENSE. OH WELL, SO MUCH FOR A PERFECT RECORD.

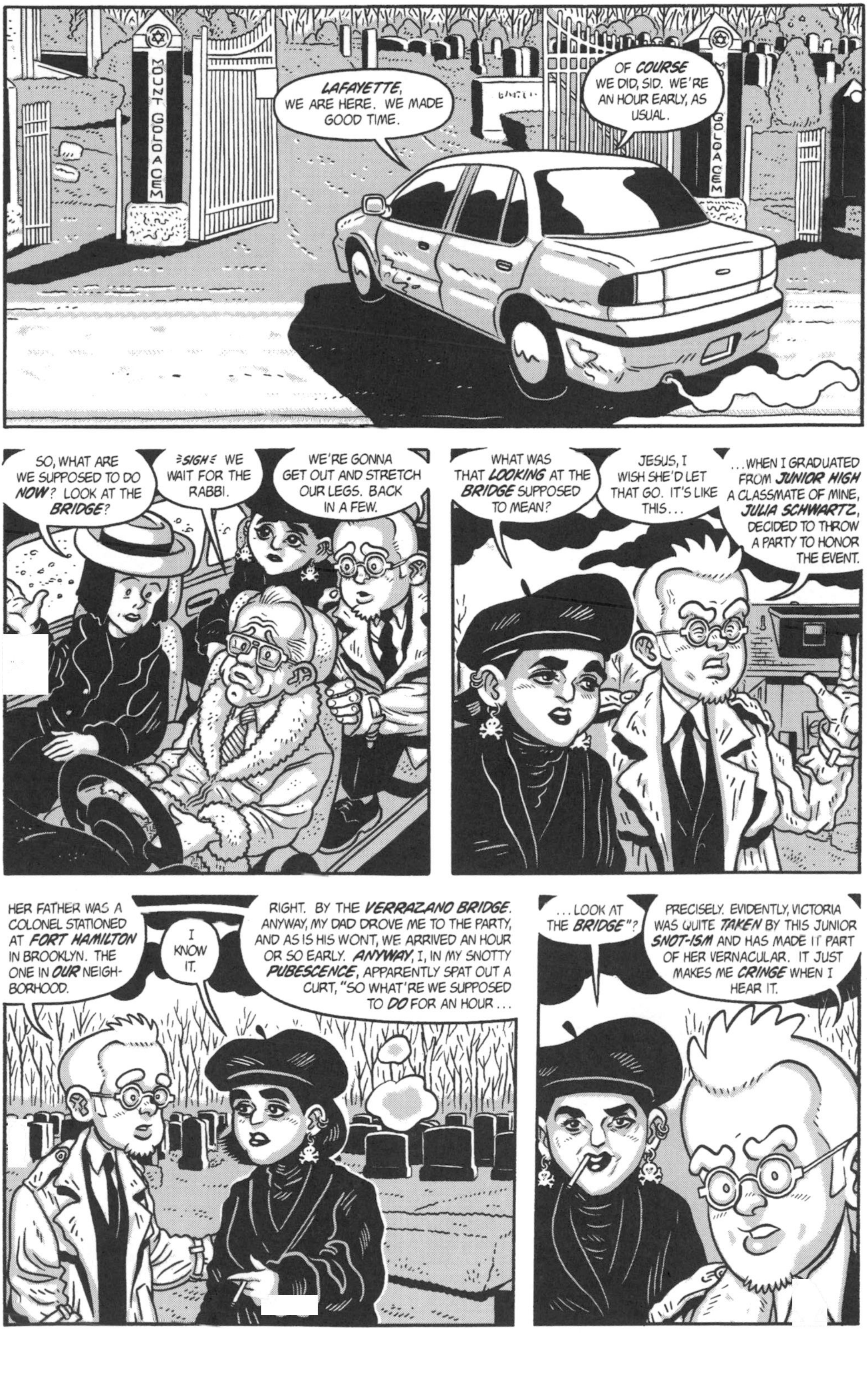

LAFAYETTE, WE ARE HERE. WE MADE GOOD TIME.
OF COURSE WE DID, SID. WE'RE AN HOUR EARLY, AS USUAL.
SO, WHAT ARE WE SUPPOSED TO DO NOW? LOOK AT THE BRIDGE?
≡SIGH≡ WE WAIT FOR THE RABBI.
WE'RE GONNA GET OUT AND STRETCH OUR LEGS. BACK IN A FEW.
WHAT WAS THAT LOOKING AT THE BRIDGE SUPPOSED TO MEAN?
JESUS, I WISH SHE'D LET THAT GO. IT'S LIKE THIS...
...WHEN I GRADUATED FROM JUNIOR HIGH A CLASSMATE OF MINE, JULIA SCHWARTZ, DECIDED TO THROW A PARTY TO HONOR THE EVENT.
HER FATHER WAS A COLONEL STATIONED AT FORT HAMILTON IN BROOKLYN. THE ONE IN OUR NEIGHBORHOOD.
I KNOW IT.
RIGHT. BY THE VERRAZANO BRIDGE. ANYWAY, MY DAD DROVE ME TO THE PARTY, AND AS IS HIS WONT, WE ARRIVED AN HOUR OR SO EARLY. ANYWAY, I, IN MY SNOTTY PUBESCENCE, APPARENTLY SPAT OUT A CURT, "SO WHAT'RE WE SUPPOSED TO DO FOR AN HOUR...
...LOOK AT THE BRIDGE"?
PRECISELY. EVIDENTLY, VICTORIA WAS QUITE TAKEN BY THIS JUNIOR SNOT-ISM AND HAS MADE IT PART OF HER VERNACULAR. IT JUST MAKES ME CRINGE WHEN I HEAR IT.

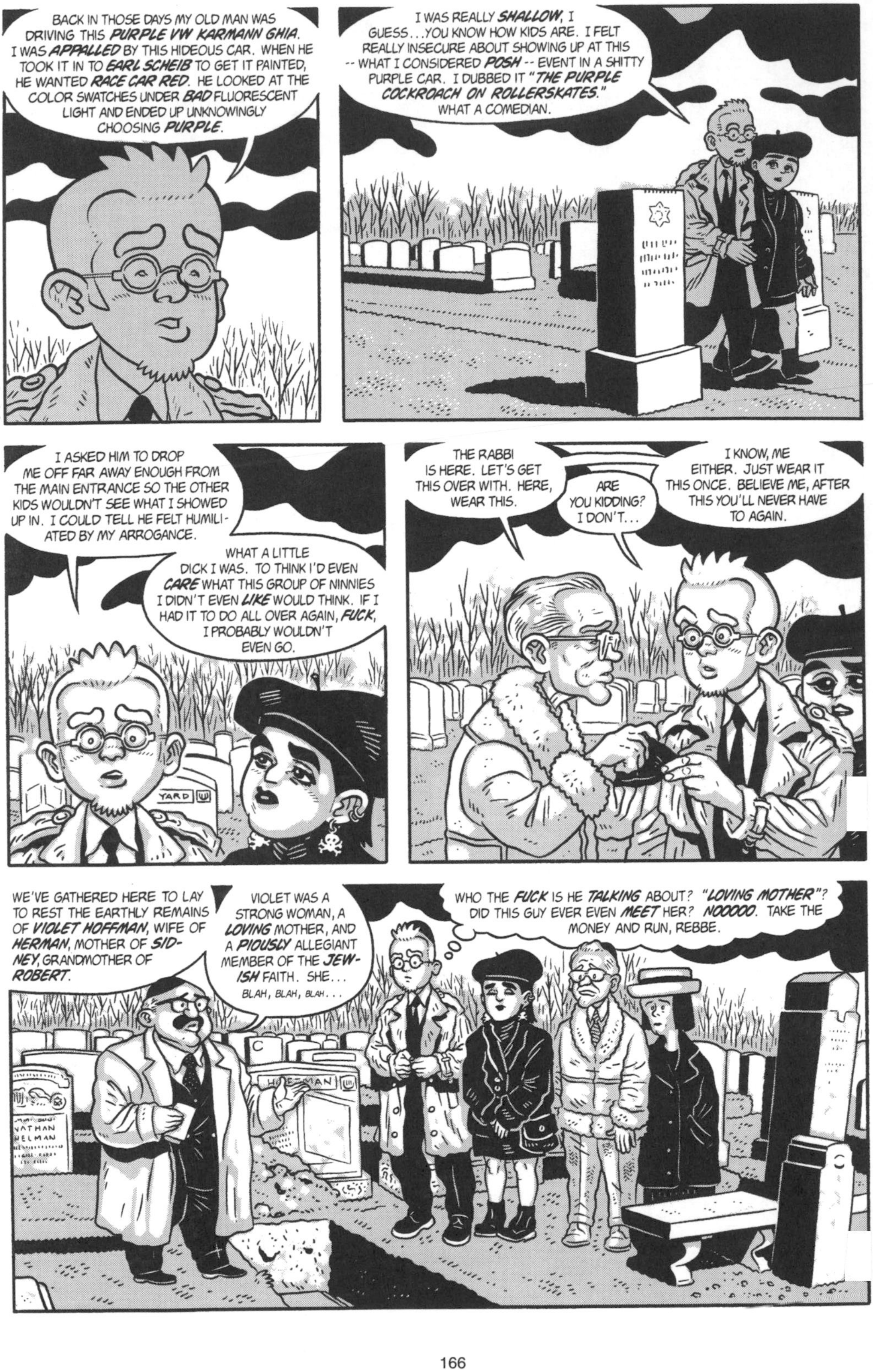
BACK IN THOSE DAYS MY OLD MAN WAS DRIVING THIS PURPLE VW KARMANN GHIA. I WAS APPALLED BY THIS HIDEOUS CAR. WHEN HE TOOK IT IN TO EARL SCHEIB TO GET IT PAINTED, HE WANTED RACE CAR RED. HE LOOKED AT THE COLOR SWATCHES UNDER BAD FLUORESCENT LIGHT AND ENDED UP UNKNOWINGLY CHOOSING PURPLE.
I WAS REALLY SHALLOW, I GUESS...YOU KNOW HOW KIDS ARE. I FELT REALLY INSECURE ABOUT SHOWING UP AT THIS -- WHAT I CONSIDERED POSH -- EVENT IN A SHITTY PURPLE CAR. I DUBBED IT "THE PURPLE COCKROACH ON ROLLERSKATES." WHAT A COMEDIAN.
I ASKED HIM TO DROP ME OFF FAR AWAY ENOUGH FROM THE MAIN ENTRANCE SO THE OTHER KIDS WOULDN'T SEE WHAT I SHOWED UP IN. I COULD TELL HE FELT HUMILIATED BY MY ARROGANCE.
WHAT A LITTLE DICK I WAS. TO THINK I'D EVEN CARE WHAT THIS GROUP OF NINNIES I DIDN'T EVEN LIKE WOULD THINK. IF I HAD IT TO DO ALL OVER AGAIN, FUCK, I PROBABLY WOULDN'T EVEN GO.
YARD
THE RABBI IS HERE. LET'S GET THIS OVER WITH. HERE, WEAR THIS.
ARE YOU KIDDING? I DON'T...
I KNOW, ME EITHER. JUST WEAR IT THIS ONCE. BELIEVE ME, AFTER THIS YOU'LL NEVER HAVE TO AGAIN.
WE'VE GATHERED HERE TO LAY TO REST THE EARTHLY REMAINS OF VIOLET HOFFMAN, WIFE OF HERMAN, MOTHER OF SIDNEY, GRANDMOTHER OF ROBERT.
VIOLET WAS A STRONG WOMAN, A LOVING MOTHER, AND A PIOUSLY ALLEGIANT MEMBER OF THE JEWISH FAITH. SHE... BLAH, BLAH, BLAH...
WHO THE FUCK IS HE TALKING ABOUT? "LOVING MOTHER"? DID THIS GUY EVER EVEN MEET HER? NOOOOO. TAKE THE MONEY AND RUN, REBBE.
NATHAN HELMAN

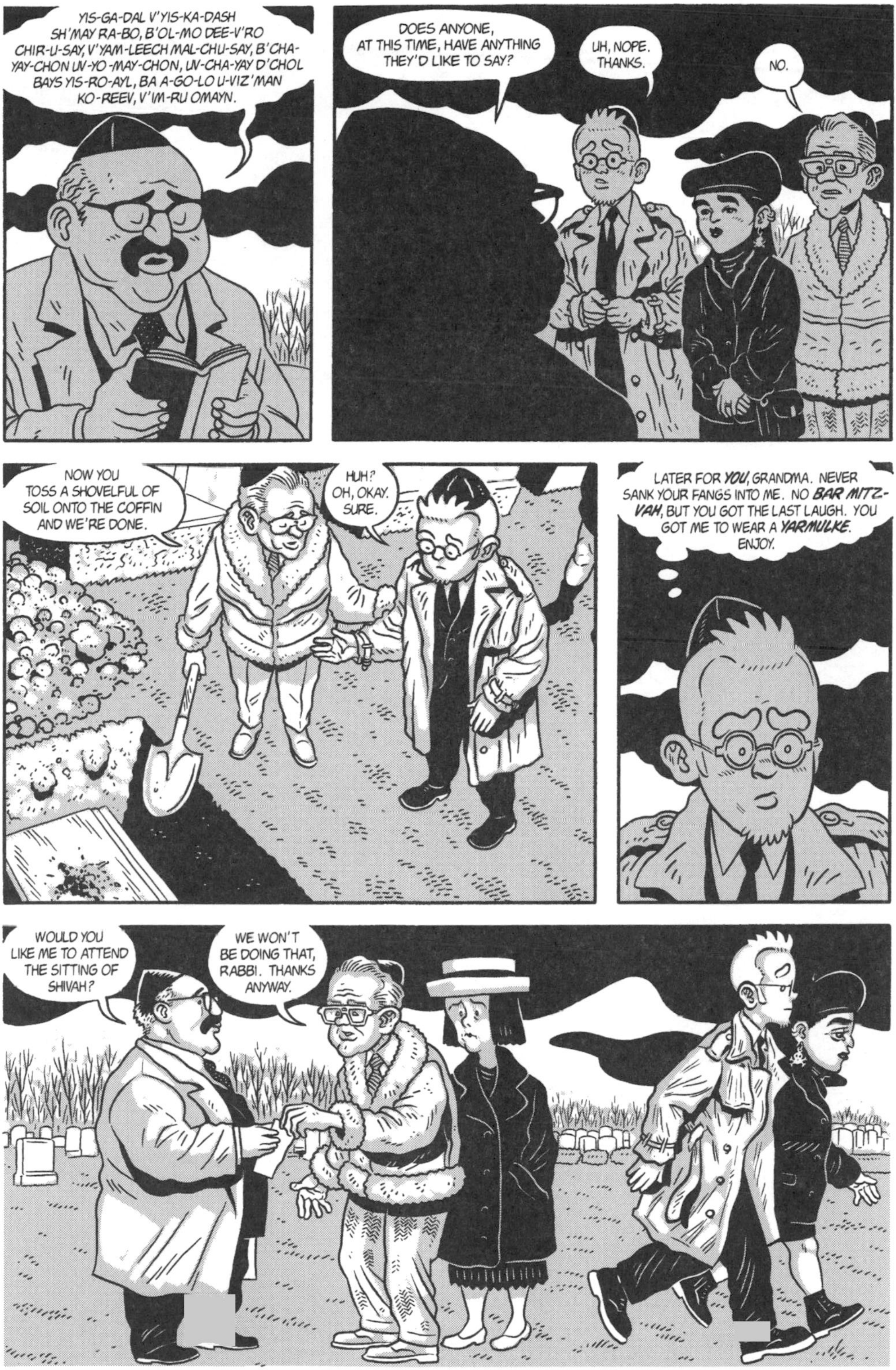
YIS-GA-DAL V'YIS-KA-DASH SH'MAY RA-BO, B'OL-MO DEE-V'RO CHIR-U-SAY, V'YAM-LEECH MAL-CHU-SAY, B'CHA-YAY-CHON UV-YO-MAY-CHON, UV-CHA-YAY D'CHOL BAYS YIS-RO-AYL, BA A-GO-LO U-VIZ'MAN KO-REEV, V'IM-RU OMAYN.
DOES ANYONE, AT THIS TIME, HAVE ANYTHING THEY'D LIKE TO SAY?
UH, NOPE. THANKS.
NO.
NOW YOU TOSS A SHOVELFUL OF SOIL ONTO THE COFFIN AND WE'RE DONE.
HUH? OH, OKAY. SURE.
LATER FOR YOU, GRANDMA. NEVER SANK YOUR FANGS INTO ME. NO BAR MITZ-VAH, BUT YOU GOT THE LAST LAUGH. YOU GOT ME TO WEAR A YARMULKE. ENJOY.
WOULD YOU LIKE ME TO ATTEND THE SITTING OF SHIVAH?
WE WON'T BE DOING THAT, RABBI. THANKS ANYWAY.

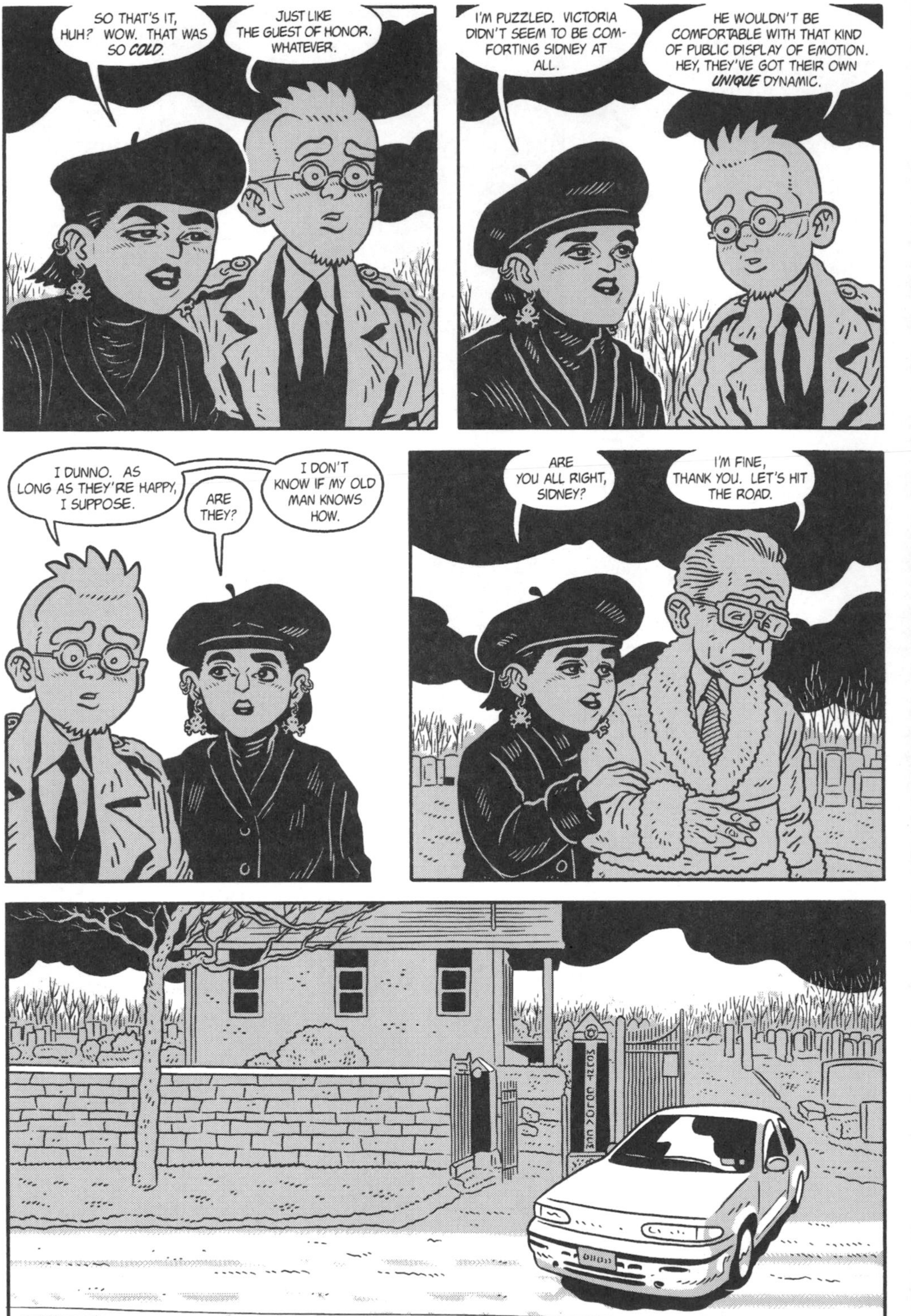
SO THAT'S IT, HUH? WOW. THAT WAS SO COLD.
JUST LIKE THE GUEST OF HONOR. WHATEVER.
I'M PUZZLED. VICTORIA DIDN'T SEEM TO BE COMFORTING SIDNEY AT ALL.
HE WOULDN'T BE COMFORTABLE WITH THAT KIND OF PUBLIC DISPLAY OF EMOTION. HEY, THEY'VE GOT THEIR OWN UNIQUE DYNAMIC.
I DUNNO. AS LONG AS THEY'RE HAPPY, I SUPPOSE.
ARE THEY?
I DON'T KNOW IF MY OLD MAN KNOWS HOW.
ARE YOU ALL RIGHT, SIDNEY?
I'M FINE, THANK YOU. LET'S HIT THE ROAD.

# CHAPTER EIGHT

# HOMO ERRATA

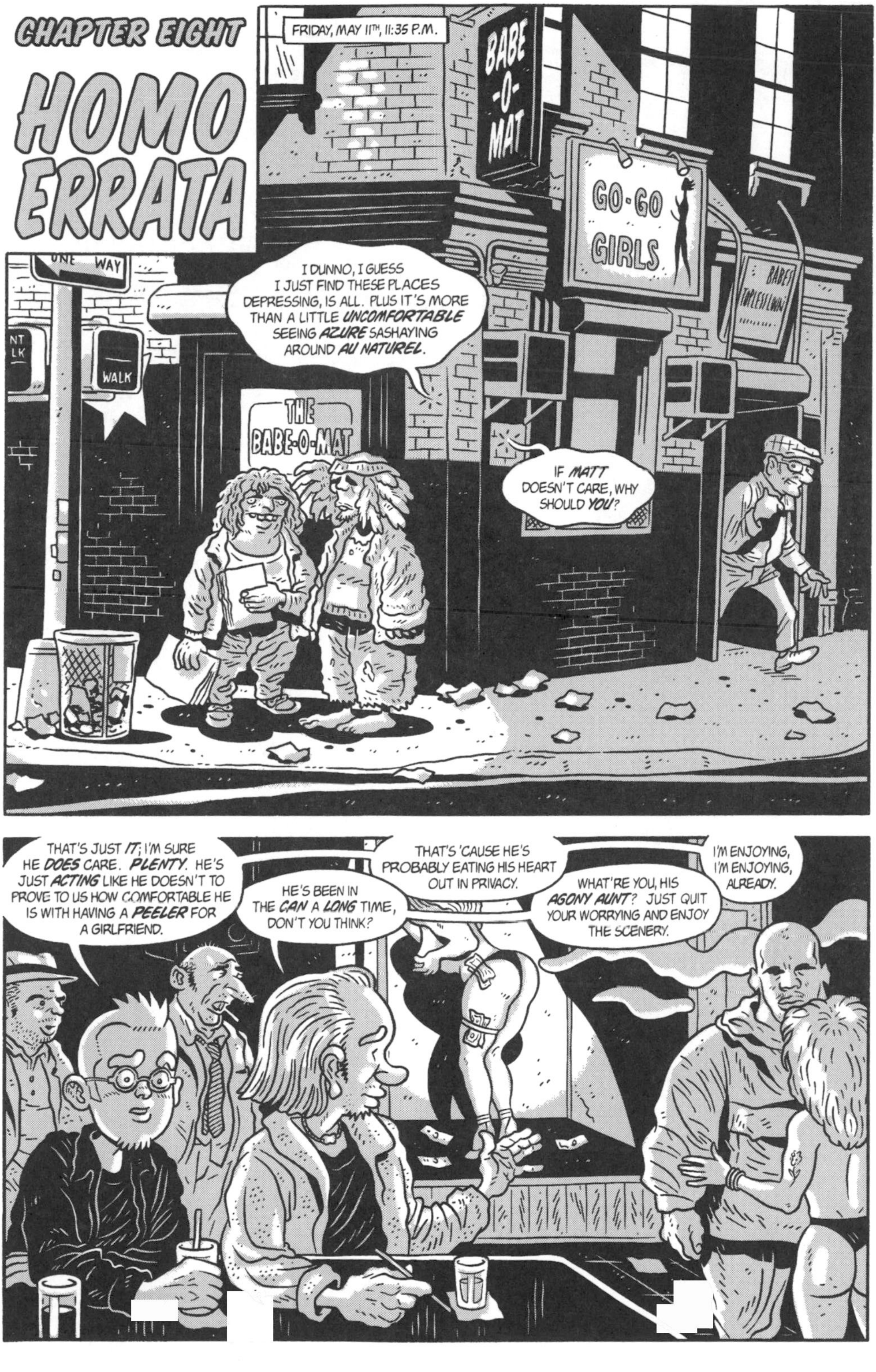

FRIDAY, MAY 11TH, 11:35 P.M.
BABE -O- MAT
GO-GO GIRLS
ONE WAY
WALK
THE BABE-O-MAT
I DUNNO, I GUESS I JUST FIND THESE PLACES DEPRESSING, IS ALL. PLUS IT'S MORE THAN A LITTLE **UNCOMFORTABLE** SEEING **AZURE** SASHAYING AROUND **AU NATUREL**.
IF **MATT** DOESN'T CARE, WHY SHOULD **YOU**?
THAT'S JUST **IT**; I'M SURE HE **DOES** CARE. **PLENTY**. HE'S JUST **ACTING** LIKE HE DOESN'T TO PROVE TO US HOW COMFORTABLE HE IS WITH HAVING A **PEELER** FOR A GIRLFRIEND.
HE'S BEEN IN THE **CAN** A **LONG** TIME, DON'T YOU THINK?
THAT'S 'CAUSE HE'S PROBABLY EATING HIS HEART OUT IN PRIVACY.
WHAT'RE YOU, HIS **AGONY AUNT**? JUST QUIT YOUR WORRYING AND ENJOY THE SCENERY.
I'M ENJOYING, I'M ENJOYING, ALREADY.

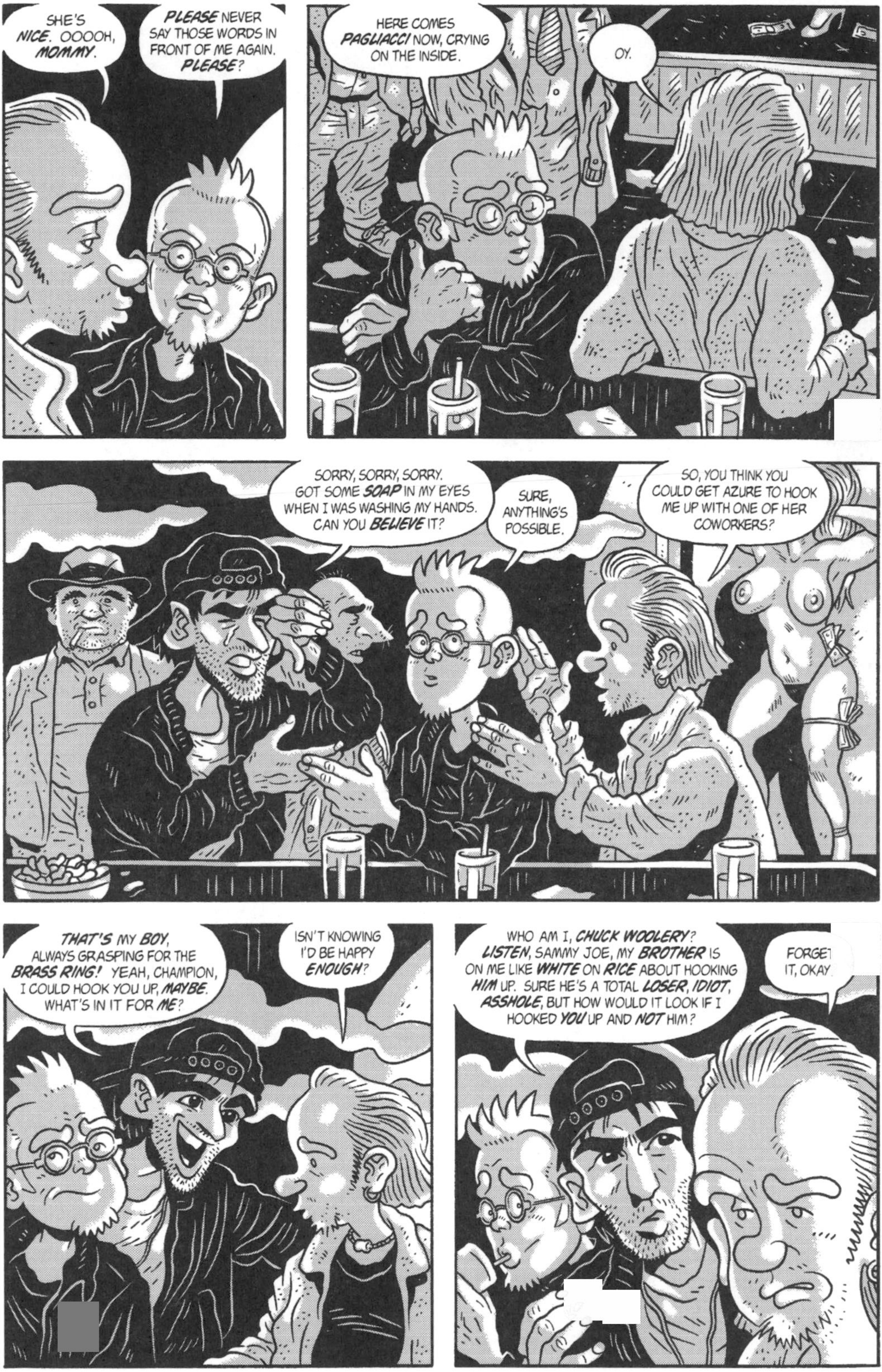
SHE'S NICE. OOOOH, MOMMY.
PLEASE NEVER SAY THOSE WORDS IN FRONT OF ME AGAIN. PLEASE?
HERE COMES PAGLIACCI NOW, CRYING ON THE INSIDE.
OY.
SORRY, SORRY, SORRY. GOT SOME SOAP IN MY EYES WHEN I WAS WASHING MY HANDS. CAN YOU BELIEVE IT?
SURE, ANYTHING'S POSSIBLE.
SO, YOU THINK YOU COULD GET AZURE TO HOOK ME UP WITH ONE OF HER COWORKERS?
THAT'S MY BOY, ALWAYS GRASPING FOR THE BRASS RING! YEAH, CHAMPION, I COULD HOOK YOU UP, MAYBE. WHAT'S IN IT FOR ME?
ISN'T KNOWING I'D BE HAPPY ENOUGH?
WHO AM I, CHUCK WOOLERY? LISTEN, SAMMY JOE, MY BROTHER IS ON ME LIKE WHITE ON RICE ABOUT HOOKING HIM UP. SURE HE'S A TOTAL LOSER, IDIOT, ASSHOLE, BUT HOW WOULD IT LOOK IF I HOOKED YOU UP AND NOT HIM?
FORGET IT, OKAY

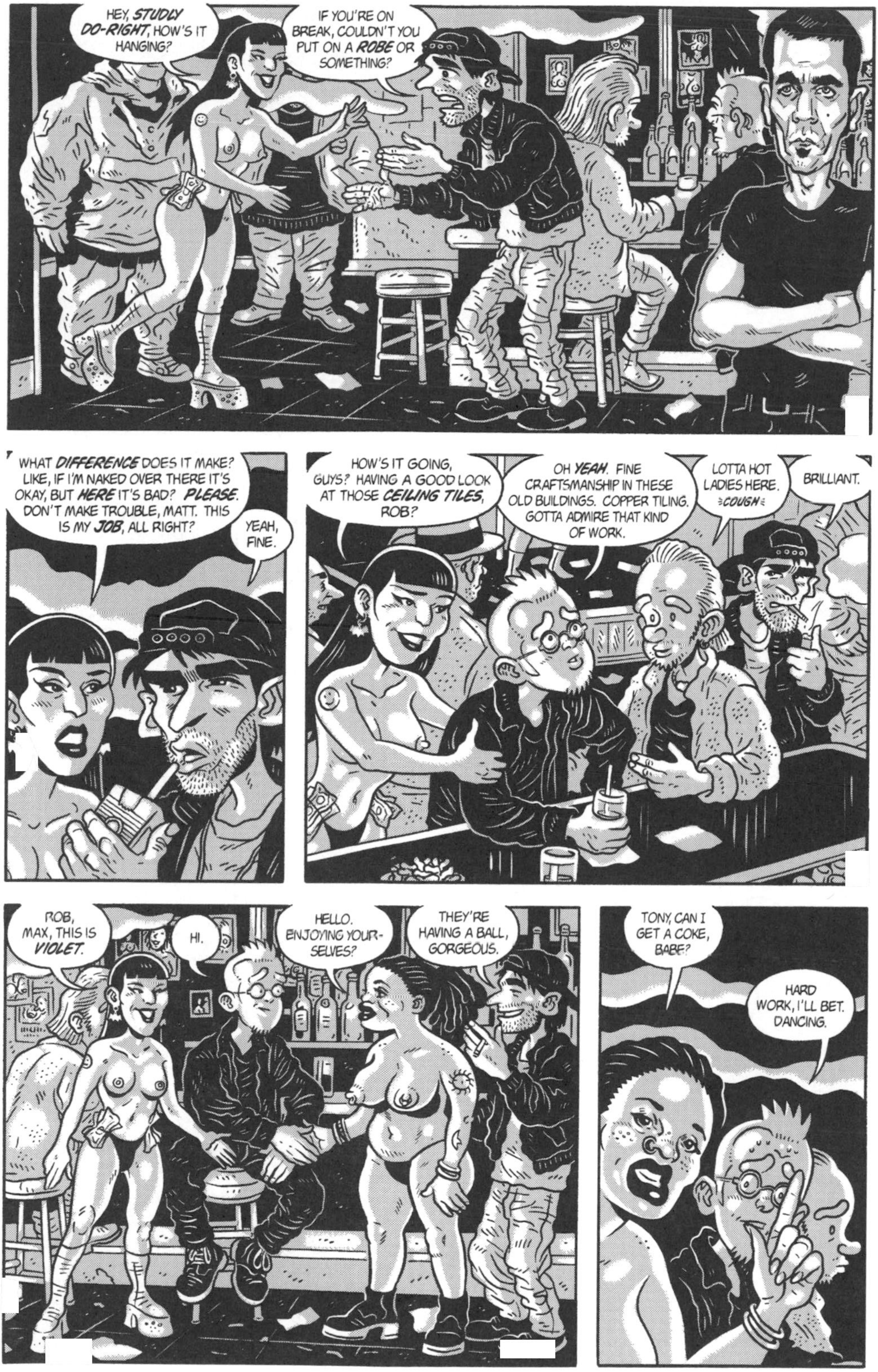
HEY, STUDLY DO-RIGHT, HOW'S IT HANGING?
IF YOU'RE ON BREAK, COULDN'T YOU PUT ON A ROBE OR SOMETHING?
WHAT DIFFERENCE DOES IT MAKE? LIKE, IF I'M NAKED OVER THERE IT'S OKAY, BUT HERE IT'S BAD? PLEASE. DON'T MAKE TROUBLE, MATT. THIS IS MY JOB, ALL RIGHT?
YEAH, FINE.
HOW'S IT GOING, GUYS? HAVING A GOOD LOOK AT THOSE CEILING TILES, ROB?
OH YEAH. FINE CRAFTSMANSHIP IN THESE OLD BUILDINGS. COPPER TILING. GOTTA ADMIRE THAT KIND OF WORK.
LOTTA HOT LADIES HERE. *COUGH*
BRILLIANT.
ROB, MAX, THIS IS VIOLET.
HI.
HELLO. ENJOYING YOURSELVES?
THEY'RE HAVING A BALL, GORGEOUS.
TONY, CAN I GET A COKE, BABE?
HARD WORK, I'LL BET. DANCING.

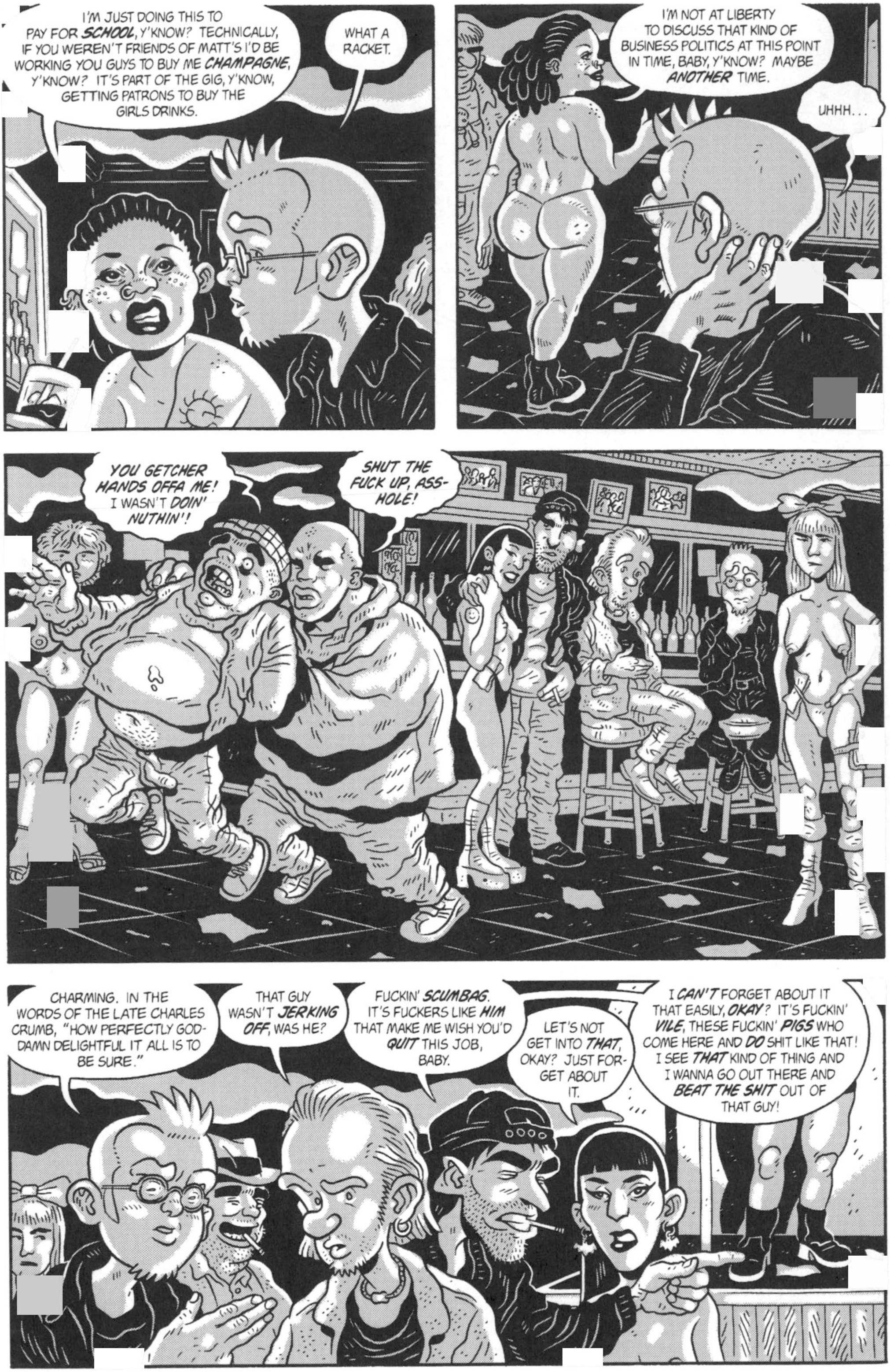

I'M JUST DOING THIS TO PAY FOR SCHOOL, Y'KNOW? TECHNICALLY, IF YOU WEREN'T FRIENDS OF MATT'S I'D BE WORKING YOU GUYS TO BUY ME CHAMPAGNE, Y'KNOW? IT'S PART OF THE GIG, Y'KNOW, GETTING PATRONS TO BUY THE GIRLS DRINKS.
WHAT A RACKET.
I'M NOT AT LIBERTY TO DISCUSS THAT KIND OF BUSINESS POLITICS AT THIS POINT IN TIME, BABY, Y'KNOW? MAYBE ANOTHER TIME.
UHHH...
YOU GETCHER HANDS OFFA ME! I WASN'T DOIN' NUTHIN'!
SHUT THE FUCK UP, ASS-HOLE!
CHARMING. IN THE WORDS OF THE LATE CHARLES CRUMB, "HOW PERFECTLY GOD-DAMN DELIGHTFUL IT ALL IS TO BE SURE."
THAT GUY WASN'T JERKING OFF, WAS HE?
FUCKIN' SCUMBAG. IT'S FUCKERS LIKE HIM THAT MAKE ME WISH YOU'D QUIT THIS JOB, BABY.
LET'S NOT GET INTO THAT, OKAY? JUST FOR-GET ABOUT IT.
I CAN'T FORGET ABOUT IT THAT EASILY, OKAY? IT'S FUCKIN' VILE, THESE FUCKIN' PIGS WHO COME HERE AND DO SHIT LIKE THAT! I SEE THAT KIND OF THING AND I WANNA GO OUT THERE AND BEAT THE SHIT OUT OF THAT GUY!

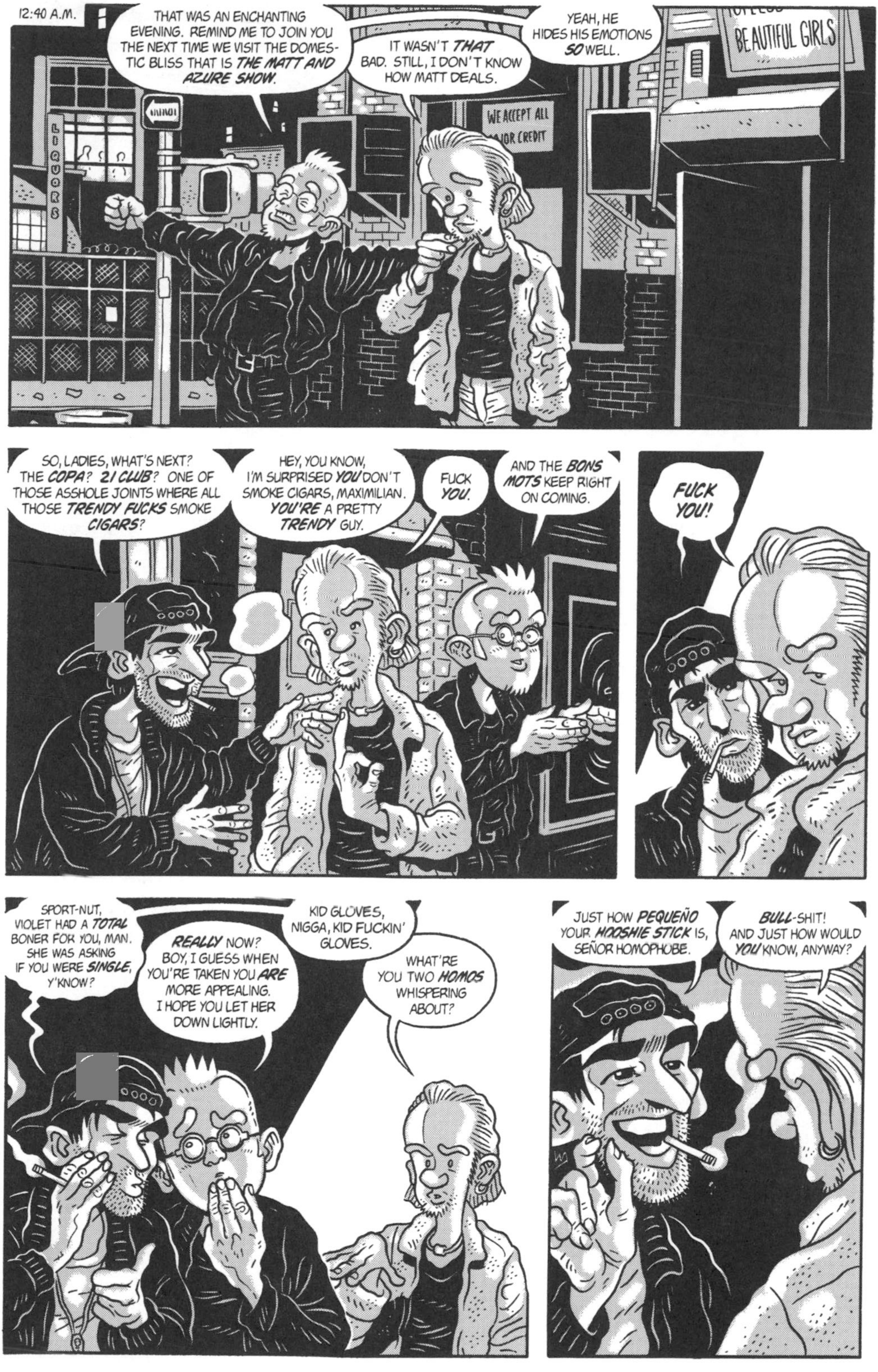
12:40 A.M.
THAT WAS AN ENCHANTING EVENING. REMIND ME TO JOIN YOU THE NEXT TIME WE VISIT THE DOMESTIC BLISS THAT IS THE MATT AND AZURE SHOW.
IT WASN'T THAT BAD. STILL, I DON'T KNOW HOW MATT DEALS.
YEAH, HE HIDES HIS EMOTIONS SO WELL.
BEAUTIFUL GIRLS
LIQUORS
SO, LADIES, WHAT'S NEXT? THE COPA? 21 CLUB? ONE OF THOSE ASSHOLE JOINTS WHERE ALL THOSE TRENDY FUCKS SMOKE CIGARS?
HEY, YOU KNOW, I'M SURPRISED YOU DON'T SMOKE CIGARS, MAXIMILIAN. YOU'RE A PRETTY TRENDY GUY.
FUCK YOU.
AND THE BONS MOTS KEEP RIGHT ON COMING.
FUCK YOU!
SPORT-NUT, VIOLET HAD A TOTAL BONER FOR YOU, MAN. SHE WAS ASKING IF YOU WERE SINGLE, Y'KNOW?
REALLY NOW? BOY, I GUESS WHEN YOU'RE TAKEN YOU ARE MORE APPEALING. I HOPE YOU LET HER DOWN LIGHTLY.
KID GLOVES, NIGGA, KID FUCKIN' GLOVES.
WHAT'RE YOU TWO HOMOS WHISPERING ABOUT?
JUST HOW PEQUEÑO YOUR HOOSHIE STICK IS, SEÑOR HOMOPHOBE.
BULL-SHIT! AND JUST HOW WOULD YOU KNOW, ANYWAY?

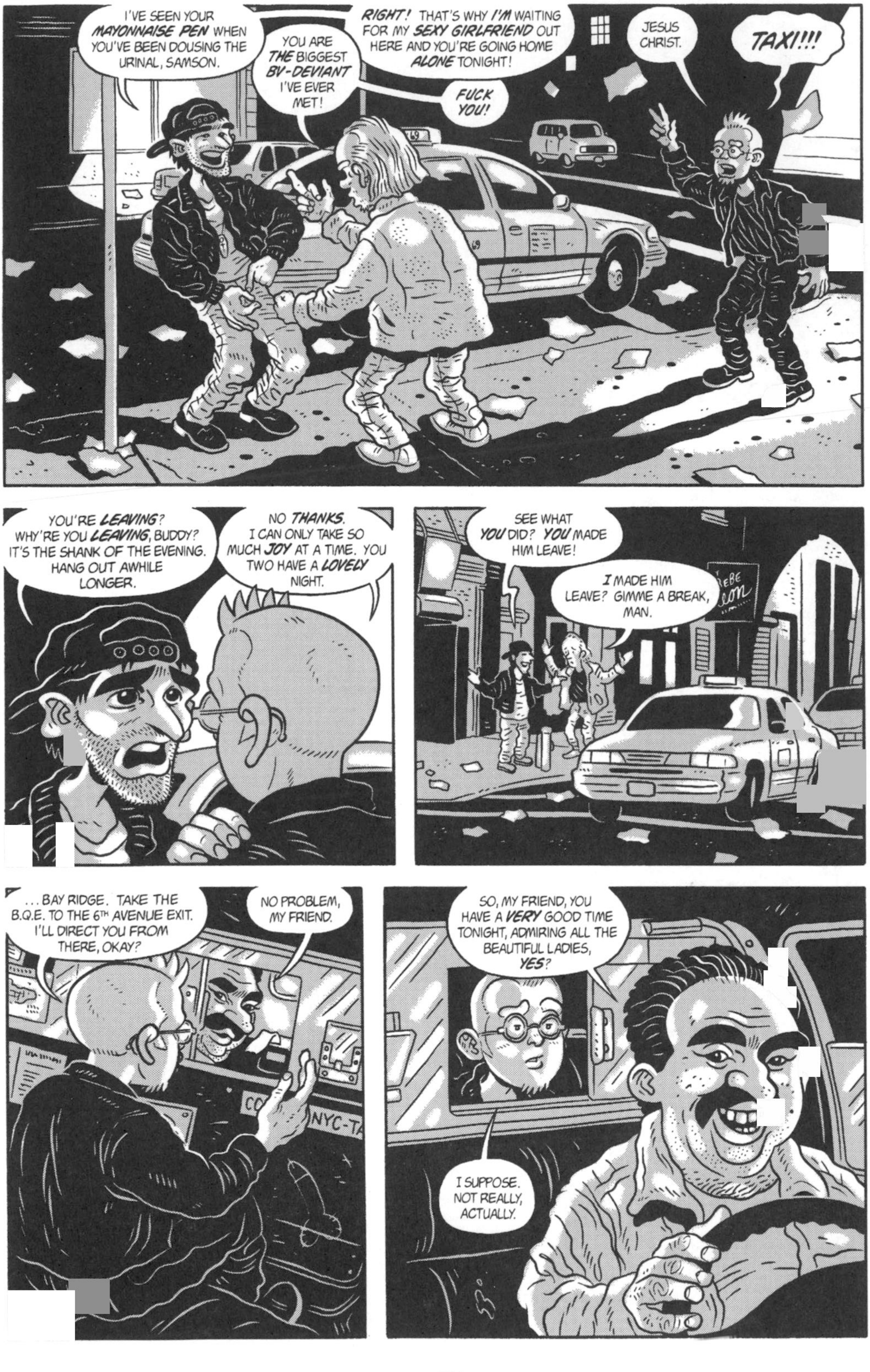
I'VE SEEN YOUR MAYONNAISE PEN WHEN YOU'VE BEEN DOUSING THE URINAL, SAMSON.
YOU ARE THE BIGGEST BV-DEVIANT I'VE EVER MET!
RIGHT! THAT'S WHY I'M WAITING FOR MY SEXY GIRLFRIEND OUT HERE AND YOU'RE GOING HOME ALONE TONIGHT!
FUCK YOU!
JESUS CHRIST.
TAXI!!!
YOU'RE LEAVING? WHY'RE YOU LEAVING, BUDDY? IT'S THE SHANK OF THE EVENING. HANG OUT AWHILE LONGER.
NO THANKS. I CAN ONLY TAKE SO MUCH JOY AT A TIME. YOU TWO HAVE A LOVELY NIGHT.
SEE WHAT YOU DID? YOU MADE HIM LEAVE!
I MADE HIM LEAVE? GIMME A BREAK, MAN.
... BAY RIDGE. TAKE THE B.Q.E. TO THE 6TH AVENUE EXIT. I'LL DIRECT YOU FROM THERE, OKAY?
NO PROBLEM, MY FRIEND.
NYC-TA
SO, MY FRIEND, YOU HAVE A VERY GOOD TIME TONIGHT, ADMIRING ALL THE BEAUTIFUL LADIES, YES?
I SUPPOSE. NOT REALLY, ACTUALLY.

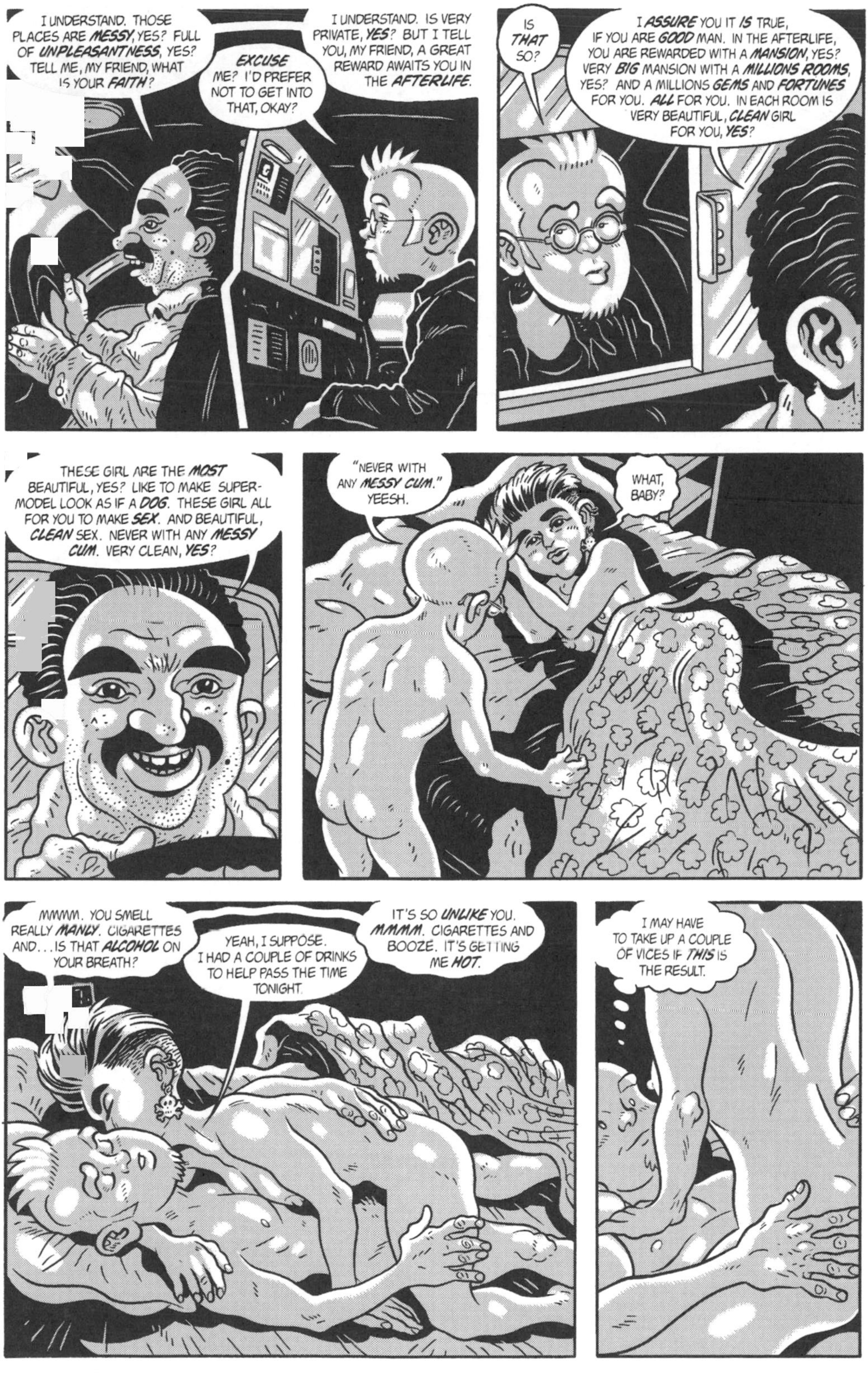
I UNDERSTAND. THOSE PLACES ARE MESSY, YES? FULL OF UNPLEASANTNESS, YES? TELL ME, MY FRIEND, WHAT IS YOUR FAITH?
EXCUSE ME? I'D PREFER NOT TO GET INTO THAT, OKAY?
I UNDERSTAND. IS VERY PRIVATE, YES? BUT I TELL YOU, MY FRIEND, A GREAT REWARD AWAITS YOU IN THE AFTERLIFE.
IS THAT SO?
I ASSURE YOU IT IS TRUE, IF YOU ARE GOOD MAN. IN THE AFTERLIFE, YOU ARE REWARDED WITH A MANSION, YES? VERY BIG MANSION WITH A MILLIONS ROOMS, YES? AND A MILLIONS GEMS AND FORTUNES FOR YOU. ALL FOR YOU. IN EACH ROOM IS VERY BEAUTIFUL, CLEAN GIRL FOR YOU, YES?
THESE GIRL ARE THE MOST BEAUTIFUL, YES? LIKE TO MAKE SUPER-MODEL LOOK AS IF A DOG. THESE GIRL ALL FOR YOU TO MAKE SEX. AND BEAUTIFUL, CLEAN SEX. NEVER WITH ANY MESSY CUM. VERY CLEAN, YES?
"NEVER WITH ANY MESSY CUM." YEESH.
WHAT, BABY?
MMMM. YOU SMELL REALLY MANLY. CIGARETTES AND... IS THAT ALCOHOL ON YOUR BREATH?
YEAH, I SUPPOSE. I HAD A COUPLE OF DRINKS TO HELP PASS THE TIME TONIGHT.
IT'S SO UNLIKE YOU. MMMM. CIGARETTES AND BOOZE. IT'S GETTING ME HOT.
I MAY HAVE TO TAKE UP A COUPLE OF VICES IF THIS IS THE RESULT.

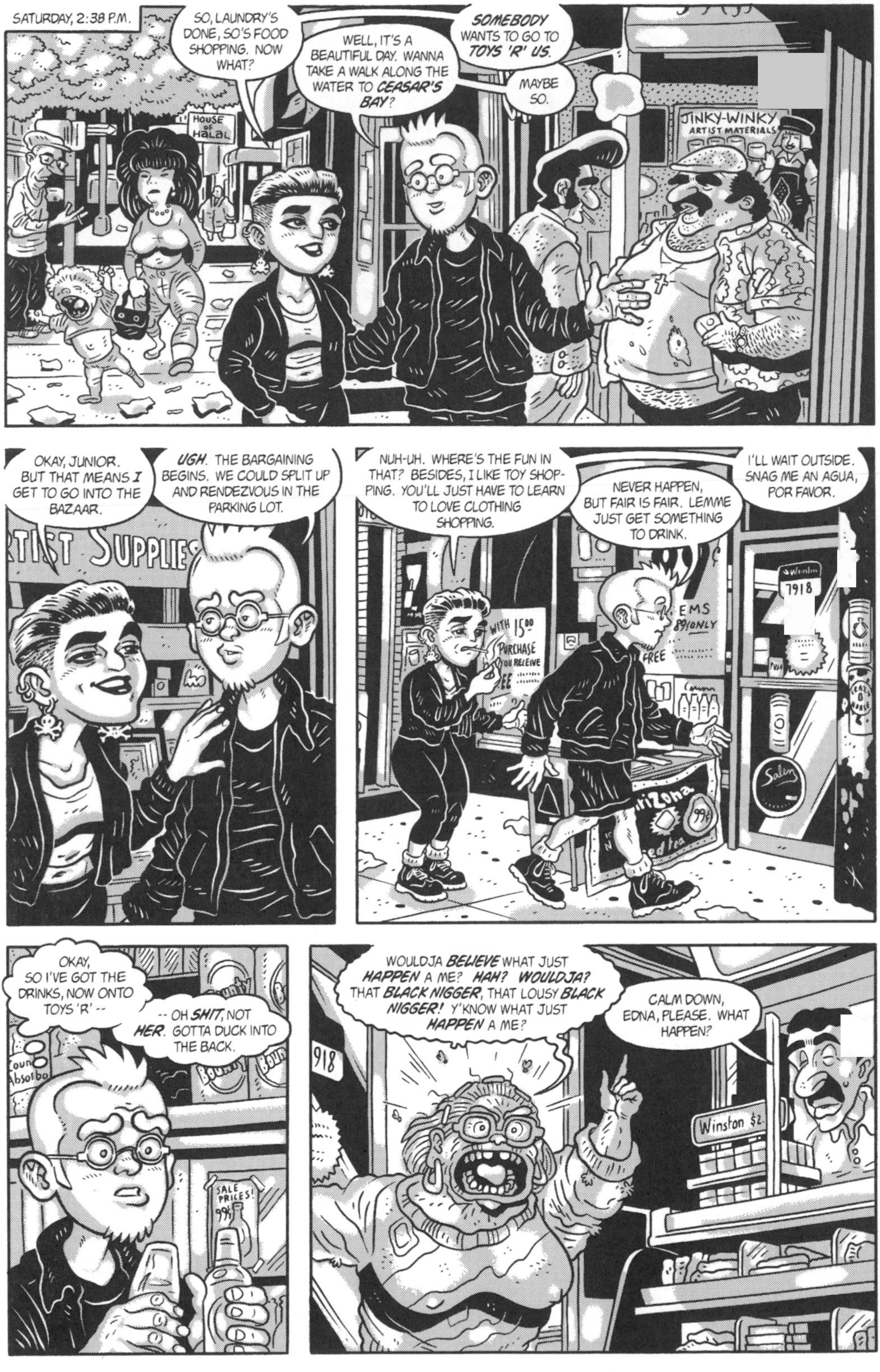

SATURDAY, 2:38 P.M.
SO, LAUNDRY'S DONE, SO'S FOOD SHOPPING. NOW WHAT?
WELL, IT'S A BEAUTIFUL DAY. WANNA TAKE A WALK ALONG THE WATER TO **CEASAR'S BAY**?
**SOMEBODY** WANTS TO GO TO **TOYS 'R' US**.
MAYBE SO.
HOUSE of HALAL
JINKY-WINKY ARTIST MATERIALS
OKAY, JUNIOR. BUT THAT MEANS *I* GET TO GO INTO THE BAZAAR.
**UGH**. THE BARGAINING BEGINS. WE COULD SPLIT UP AND RENDEZVOUS IN THE PARKING LOT.
NUH-UH. WHERE'S THE FUN IN THAT? BESIDES, I LIKE TOY SHOPPING. YOU'LL JUST HAVE TO LEARN TO LOVE CLOTHING SHOPPING.
NEVER HAPPEN, BUT FAIR IS FAIR. LEMME JUST GET SOMETHING TO DRINK.
I'LL WAIT OUTSIDE. SNAG ME AN AGUA, POR FAVOR.
WITH 15.00 PURCHASE YOU RECEIVE
7918
OKAY, SO I'VE GOT THE DRINKS, NOW ONTO TOYS 'R' --
-- OH **SHIT**, NOT **HER**. GOTTA DUCK INTO THE BACK.
SALE PRICES! 99¢
WOULDJA **BELIEVE** WHAT JUST **HAPPEN** A ME? **HAH? WOULDJA?** THAT **BLACK NIGGER**, THAT LOUSY **BLACK NIGGER!** Y'KNOW WHAT JUST **HAPPEN** A ME?
CALM DOWN, EDNA, PLEASE. WHAT HAPPEN?
Winston $2.

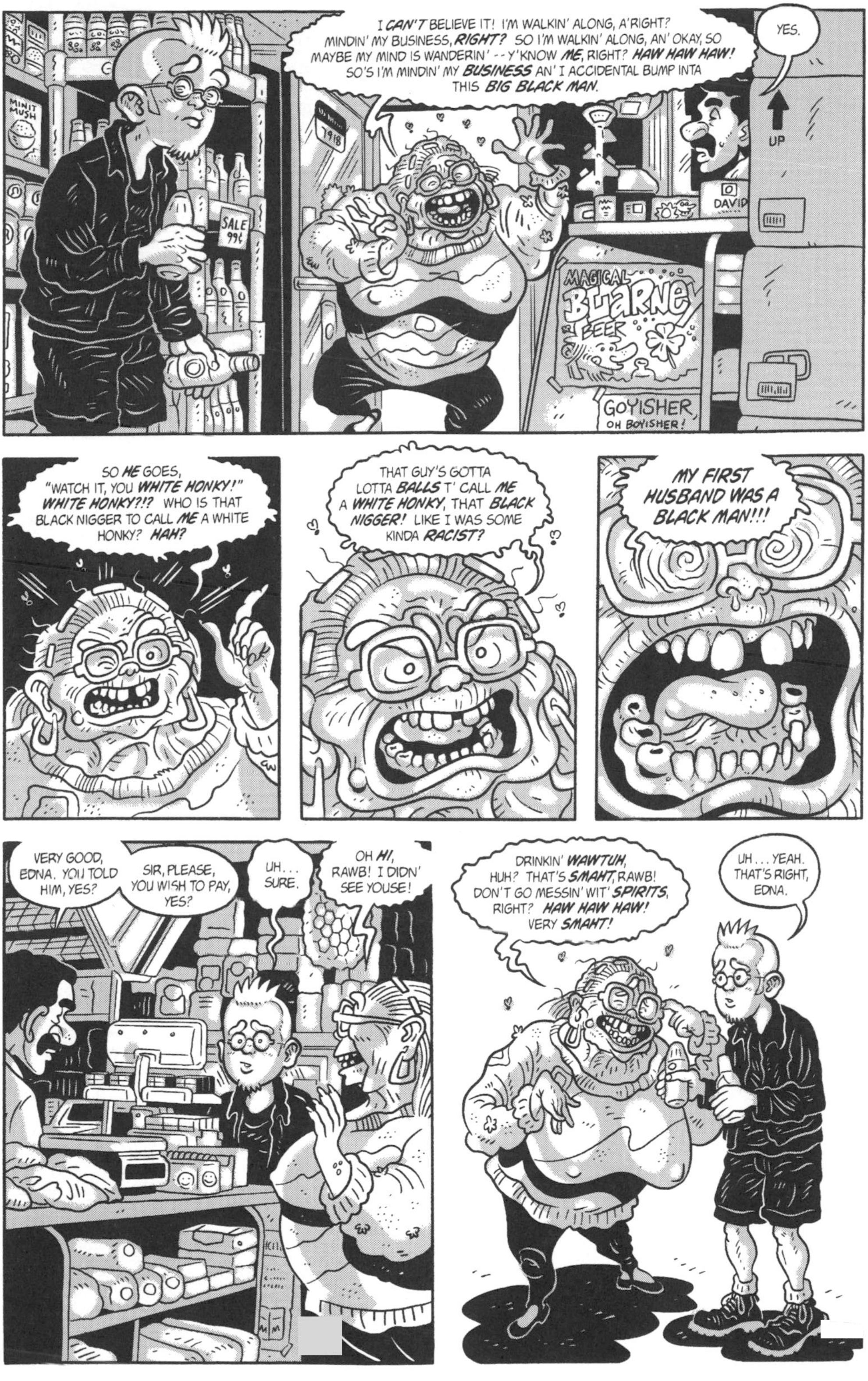
I CAN'T BELIEVE IT! I'M WALKIN' ALONG, A'RIGHT? MINDIN' MY BUSINESS, RIGHT? SO I'M WALKIN' ALONG, AN' OKAY, SO MAYBE MY MIND IS WANDERIN' --Y'KNOW ME, RIGHT? HAW HAW HAW! SO'S I'M MINDIN' MY BUSINESS AN' I ACCIDENTAL BUMP INTA THIS BIG BLACK MAN.
YES.
MINIT MUSH
SALE 99¢
1918
UP
DAVID
MAGICAL BLARNEY BEER
GOYISHER OH BOYISHER!
SO HE GOES, "WATCH IT, YOU WHITE HONKY!" WHITE HONKY?!? WHO IS THAT BLACK NIGGER TO CALL ME A WHITE HONKY? HAH?
THAT GUY'S GOTTA LOTTA BALLS T' CALL ME A WHITE HONKY, THAT BLACK NIGGER! LIKE I WAS SOME KINDA RACIST?
MY FIRST HUSBAND WAS A BLACK MAN!!!
VERY GOOD, EDNA. YOU TOLD HIM, YES?
SIR, PLEASE, YOU WISH TO PAY, YES?
UH... SURE.
OH HI, RAWB! I DIDN' SEE YOUSE!
DRINKIN' WAWTUH, HUH? THAT'S SMAHT, RAWB! DON'T GO MESSIN' WIT' SPIRITS, RIGHT? HAW HAW HAW! VERY SMAHT!
UH... YEAH. THAT'S RIGHT, EDNA.

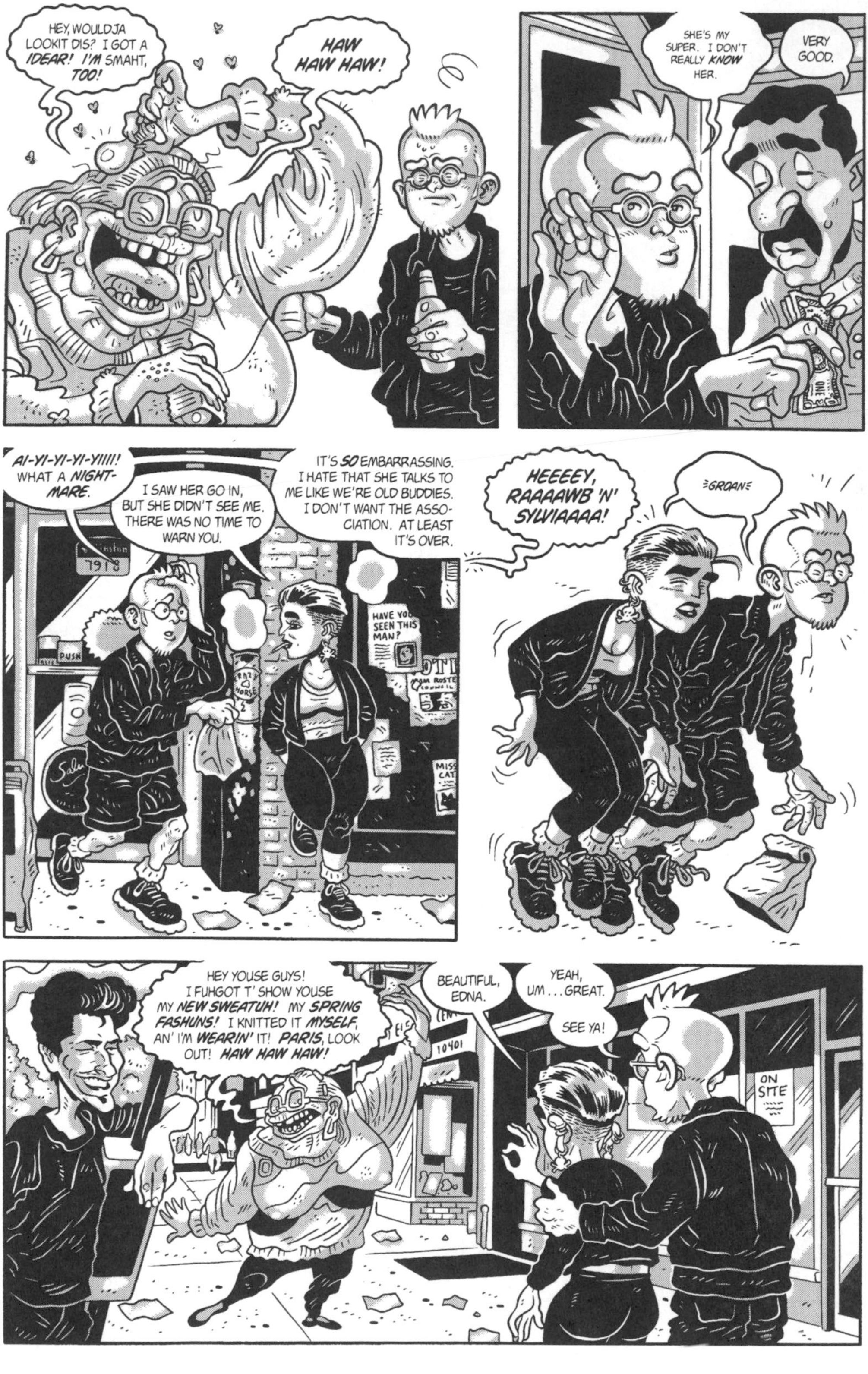
HEY, WOULDJA LOOKIT DIS? I GOT A IDEAR! I'M SMAHT, TOO!
HAW HAW HAW!
SHE'S MY SUPER. I DON'T REALLY KNOW HER.
VERY GOOD.
AI-YI-YI-YI-YIIII! WHAT A NIGHTMARE.
I SAW HER GO IN, BUT SHE DIDN'T SEE ME. THERE WAS NO TIME TO WARN YOU.
IT'S SO EMBARRASSING. I HATE THAT SHE TALKS TO ME LIKE WE'RE OLD BUDDIES. I DON'T WANT THE ASSOCIATION. AT LEAST IT'S OVER.
HAVE YOU SEEN THIS MAN?
HEEEEY, RAAAAWB 'N' SYLVIAAAA!
GROAN
HEY YOUSE GUYS! I FUHGOT T' SHOW YOUSE MY NEW SWEATUH! MY SPRING FASHUNS! I KNITTED IT MYSELF, AN' I'M WEARIN' IT! PARIS, LOOK OUT! HAW HAW HAW!
BEAUTIFUL, EDNA.
YEAH, UM... GREAT.
SEE YA!
ON SITE

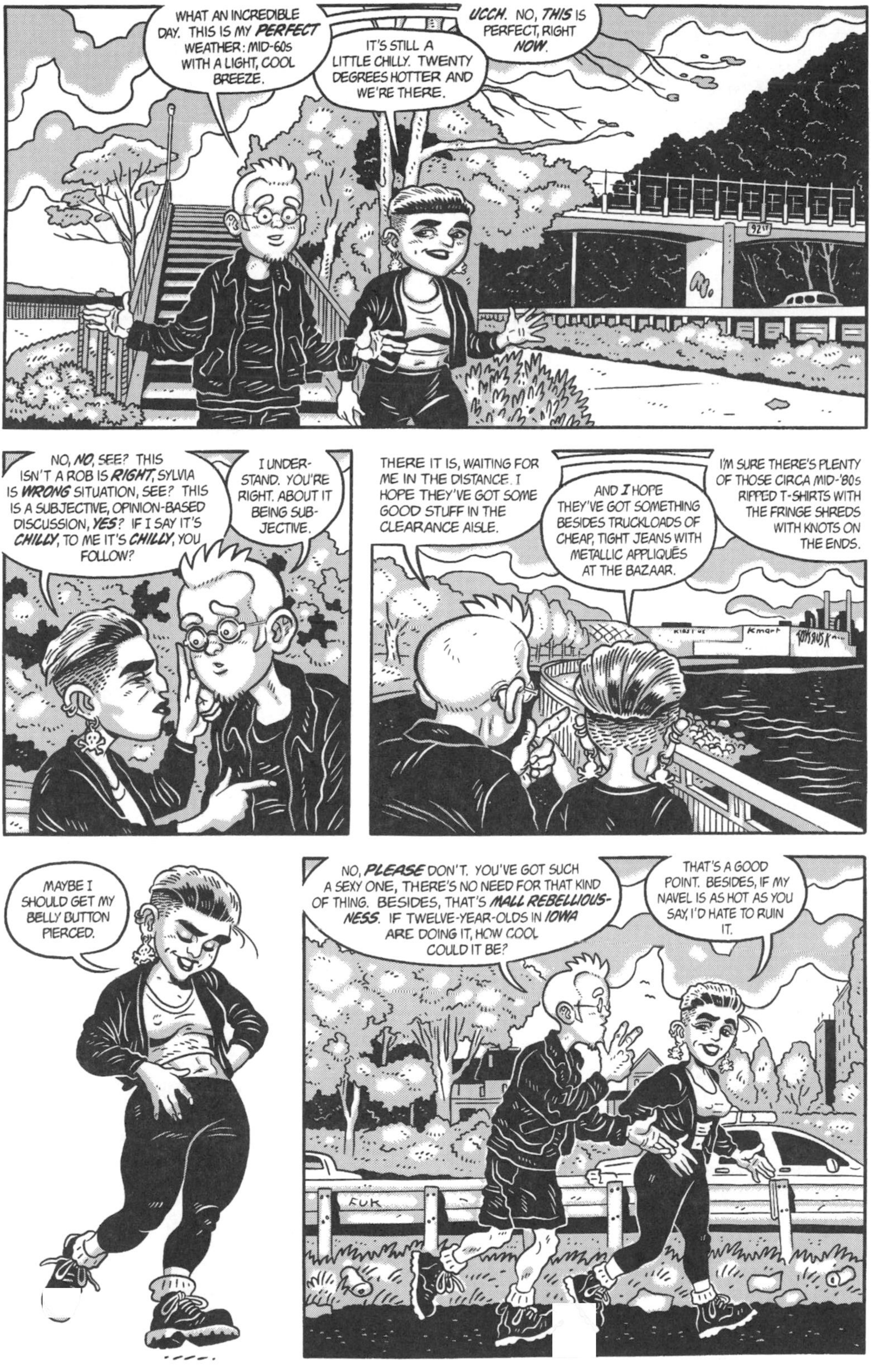
WHAT AN INCREDIBLE DAY. THIS IS MY PERFECT WEATHER: MID-60s WITH A LIGHT, COOL BREEZE.
IT'S STILL A LITTLE CHILLY. TWENTY DEGREES HOTTER AND WE'RE THERE.
UCCH. NO, THIS IS PERFECT, RIGHT NOW.
NO, NO, SEE? THIS ISN'T A ROB IS RIGHT, SYLVIA IS WRONG SITUATION, SEE? THIS IS A SUBJECTIVE, OPINION-BASED DISCUSSION, YES? IF I SAY IT'S CHILLY, TO ME IT'S CHILLY, YOU FOLLOW?
I UNDERSTAND. YOU'RE RIGHT. ABOUT IT BEING SUBJECTIVE.
THERE IT IS, WAITING FOR ME IN THE DISTANCE. I HOPE THEY'VE GOT SOME GOOD STUFF IN THE CLEARANCE AISLE.
AND I HOPE THEY'VE GOT SOMETHING BESIDES TRUCKLOADS OF CHEAP, TIGHT JEANS WITH METALLIC APPLIQUÉS AT THE BAZAAR.
I'M SURE THERE'S PLENTY OF THOSE CIRCA MID-'80s RIPPED T-SHIRTS WITH THE FRINGE SHREDS WITH KNOTS ON THE ENDS.
Kmart
MAYBE I SHOULD GET MY BELLY BUTTON PIERCED.
NO, PLEASE DON'T. YOU'VE GOT SUCH A SEXY ONE, THERE'S NO NEED FOR THAT KIND OF THING. BESIDES, THAT'S MALL REBELLIOUSNESS. IF TWELVE-YEAR-OLDS IN IOWA ARE DOING IT, HOW COOL COULD IT BE?
THAT'S A GOOD POINT. BESIDES, IF MY NAVEL IS AS HOT AS YOU SAY, I'D HATE TO RUIN IT.
FUK

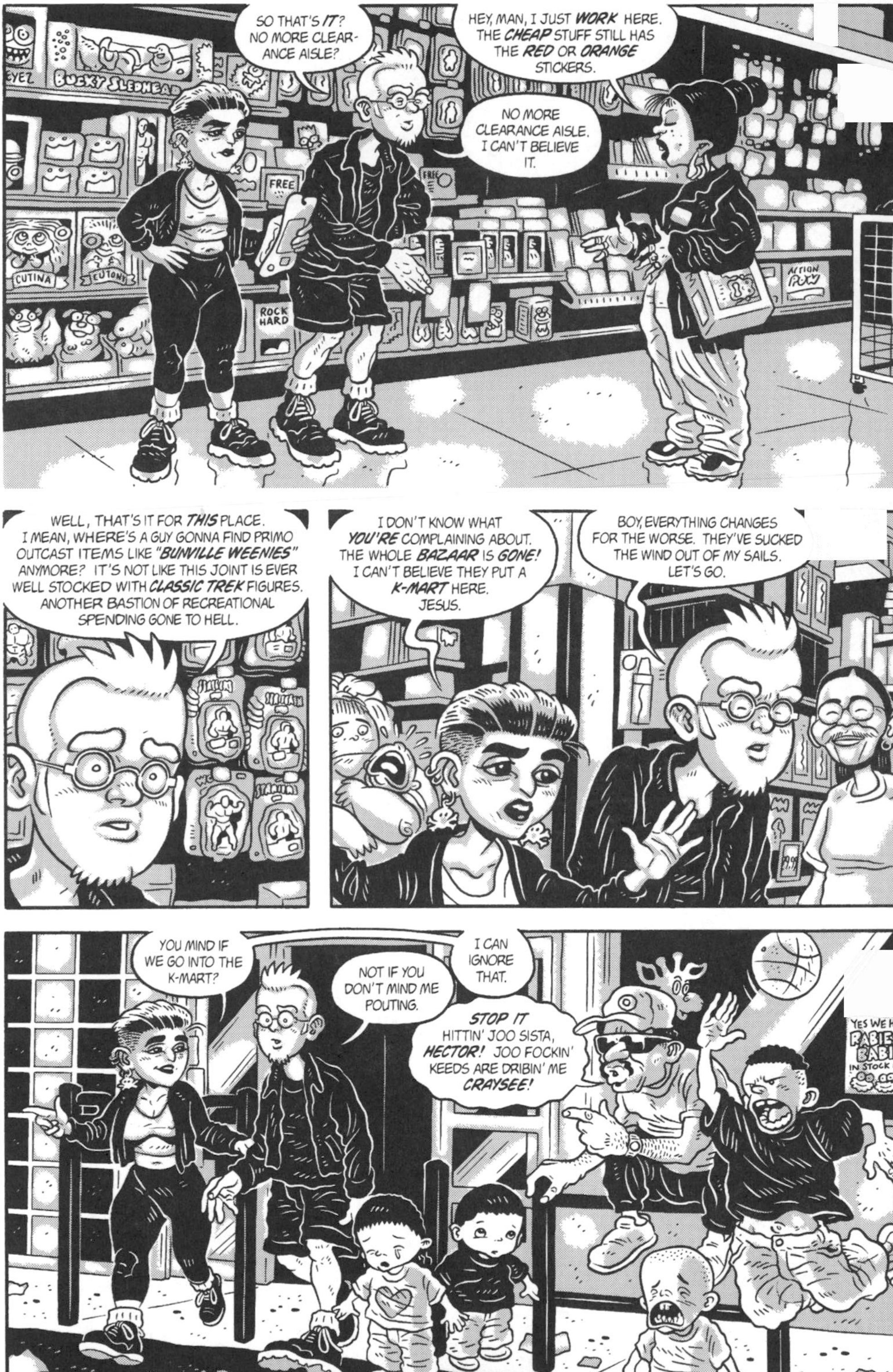
SO THAT'S *IT*? NO MORE CLEAR- ANCE AISLE?
HEY, MAN, I JUST *WORK* HERE. THE *CHEAP* STUFF STILL HAS THE *RED* OR *ORANGE* STICKERS.
NO MORE CLEARANCE AISLE. I CAN'T BELIEVE IT.
WELL, THAT'S IT FOR *THIS* PLACE. I MEAN, WHERE'S A GUY GONNA FIND PRIMO OUTCAST ITEMS LIKE *"BUNVILLE WEENIES"* ANYMORE? IT'S NOT LIKE THIS JOINT IS EVER WELL STOCKED WITH *CLASSIC TREK* FIGURES. ANOTHER BASTION OF RECREATIONAL SPENDING GONE TO HELL.
I DON'T KNOW WHAT *YOU'RE* COMPLAINING ABOUT. THE WHOLE *BAZAAR* IS *GONE!* I CAN'T BELIEVE THEY PUT A *K-MART* HERE. JESUS.
BOY, EVERYTHING CHANGES FOR THE WORSE. THEY'VE SUCKED THE WIND OUT OF MY SAILS. LET'S GO.
YOU MIND IF WE GO INTO THE K-MART?
NOT IF YOU DON'T MIND ME POUTING.
I CAN IGNORE THAT.
*STOP IT* HITTIN' JOO SISTA, *HECTOR!* JOO FOCKIN' KEEDS ARE DRIBIN' ME *CRAYSEE!*

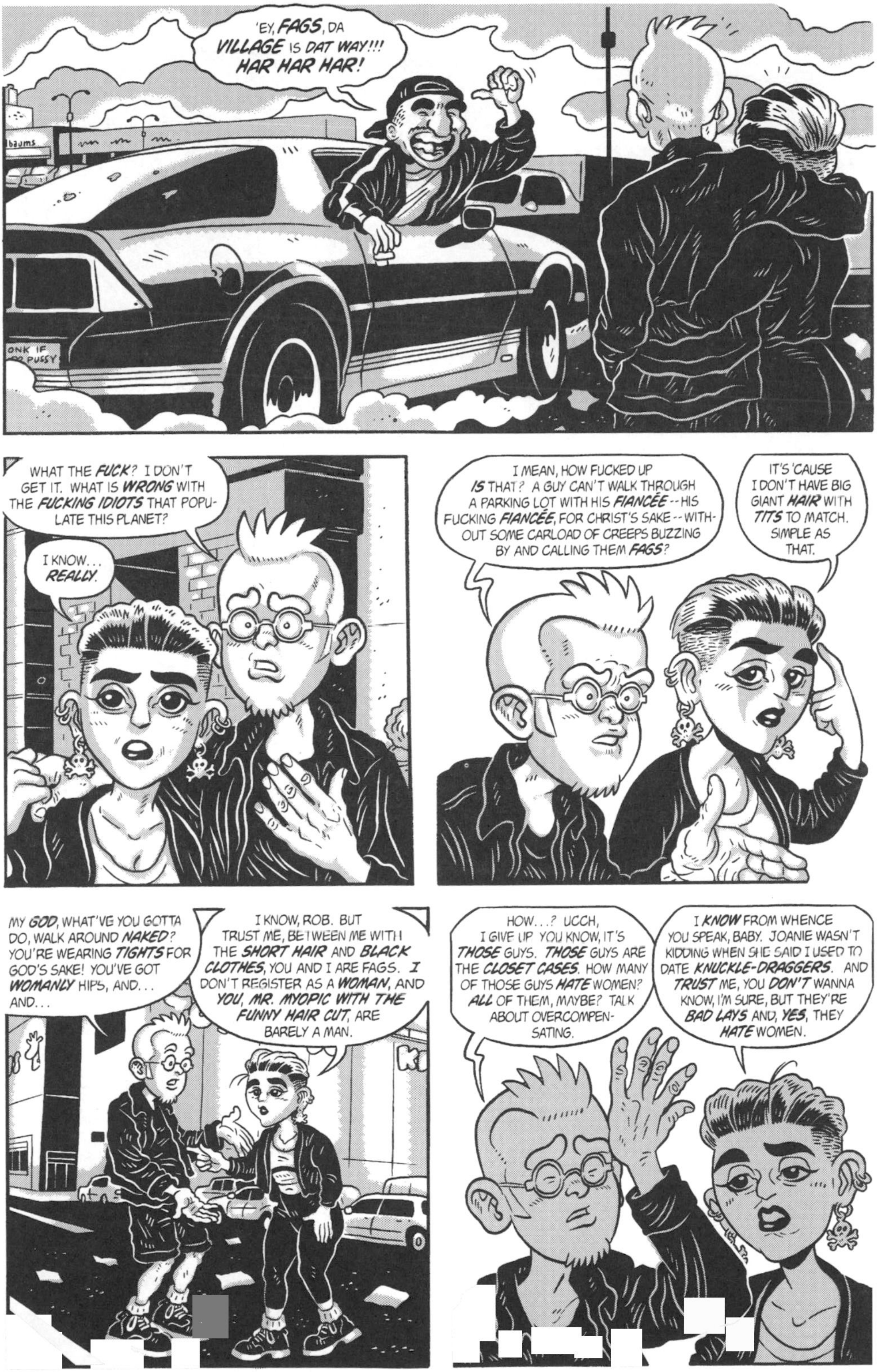

'EY, FAGS, DA VILLAGE IS DAT WAY!!! HAR HAR HAR!
WHAT THE FUCK? I DON'T GET IT. WHAT IS WRONG WITH THE FUCKING IDIOTS THAT POPULATE THIS PLANET?
I KNOW... REALLY.
I MEAN, HOW FUCKED UP IS THAT? A GUY CAN'T WALK THROUGH A PARKING LOT WITH HIS FIANCÉE -- HIS FUCKING FIANCÉE, FOR CHRIST'S SAKE -- WITHOUT SOME CARLOAD OF CREEPS BUZZING BY AND CALLING THEM FAGS?
IT'S 'CAUSE I DON'T HAVE BIG GIANT HAIR WITH TITS TO MATCH. SIMPLE AS THAT.
MY GOD, WHAT'VE YOU GOTTA DO, WALK AROUND NAKED? YOU'RE WEARING TIGHTS FOR GOD'S SAKE! YOU'VE GOT WOMANLY HIPS, AND... AND...
I KNOW, ROB. BUT TRUST ME, BETWEEN ME WITH THE SHORT HAIR AND BLACK CLOTHES, YOU AND I ARE FAGS. I DON'T REGISTER AS A WOMAN, AND YOU, MR. MYOPIC WITH THE FUNNY HAIR CUT, ARE BARELY A MAN.
HOW...? UCCH, I GIVE UP. YOU KNOW, IT'S THOSE GUYS. THOSE GUYS ARE THE CLOSET CASES. HOW MANY OF THOSE GUYS HATE WOMEN? ALL OF THEM, MAYBE? TALK ABOUT OVERCOMPENSATING.
I KNOW FROM WHENCE YOU SPEAK, BABY. JOANIE WASN'T KIDDING WHEN SHE SAID I USED TO DATE KNUCKLE-DRAGGERS. AND TRUST ME, YOU DON'T WANNA KNOW, I'M SURE, BUT THEY'RE BAD LAYS AND, YES, THEY HATE WOMEN.

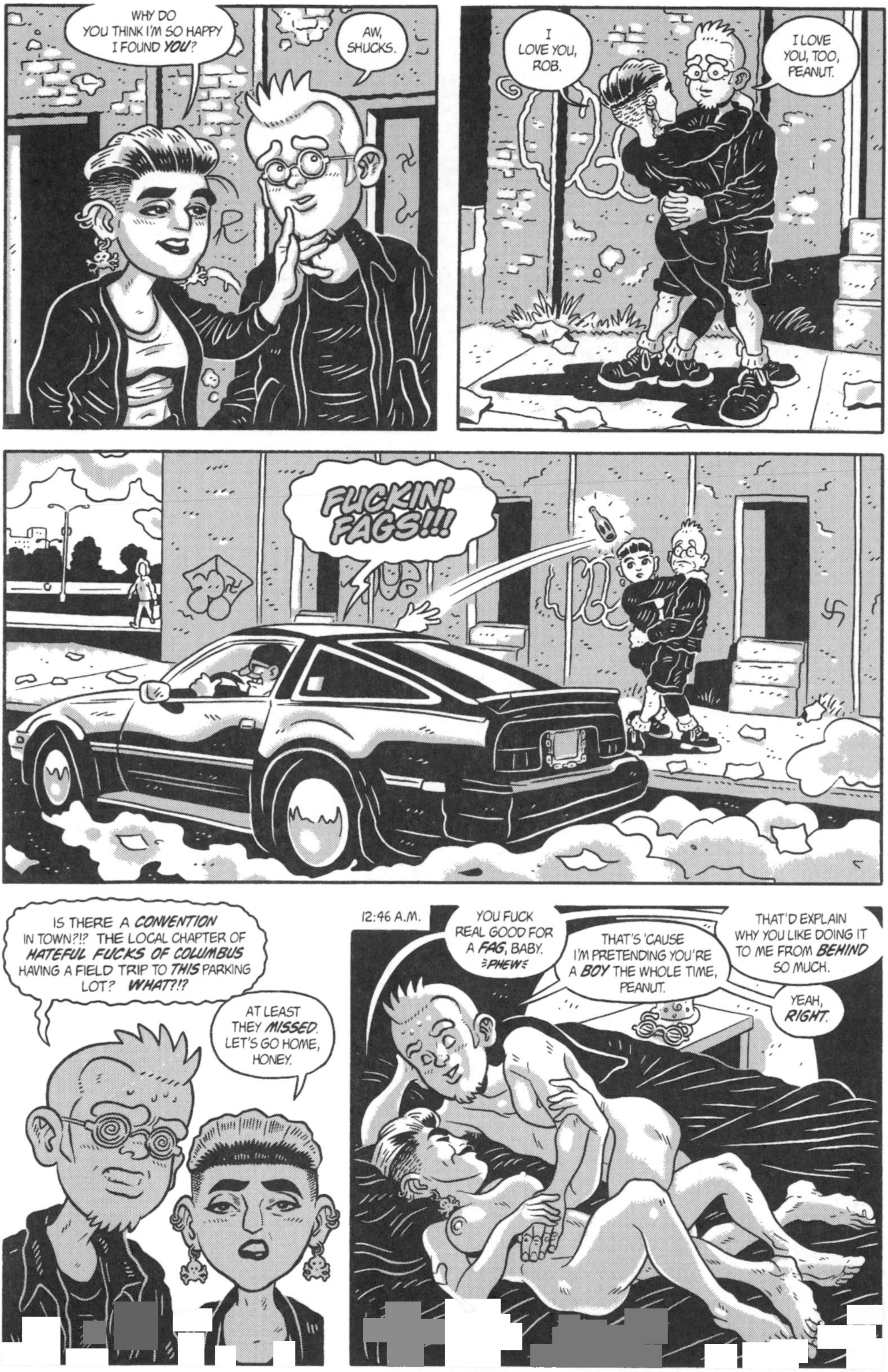
WHY DO YOU THINK I'M SO HAPPY I FOUND YOU?
AW, SHUCKS.
I LOVE YOU, ROB.
I LOVE YOU, TOO, PEANUT.
FUCKIN' FAGS!!!
IS THERE A CONVENTION IN TOWN?!? THE LOCAL CHAPTER OF HATEFUL FUCKS OF COLUMBUS HAVING A FIELD TRIP TO THIS PARKING LOT? WHAT?!?
AT LEAST THEY MISSED. LET'S GO HOME, HONEY.
12:46 A.M.
YOU FUCK REAL GOOD FOR A FAG, BABY. PHEW
THAT'S 'CAUSE I'M PRETENDING YOU'RE A BOY THE WHOLE TIME, PEANUT.
THAT'D EXPLAIN WHY YOU LIKE DOING IT TO ME FROM BEHIND SO MUCH.
YEAH, RIGHT.

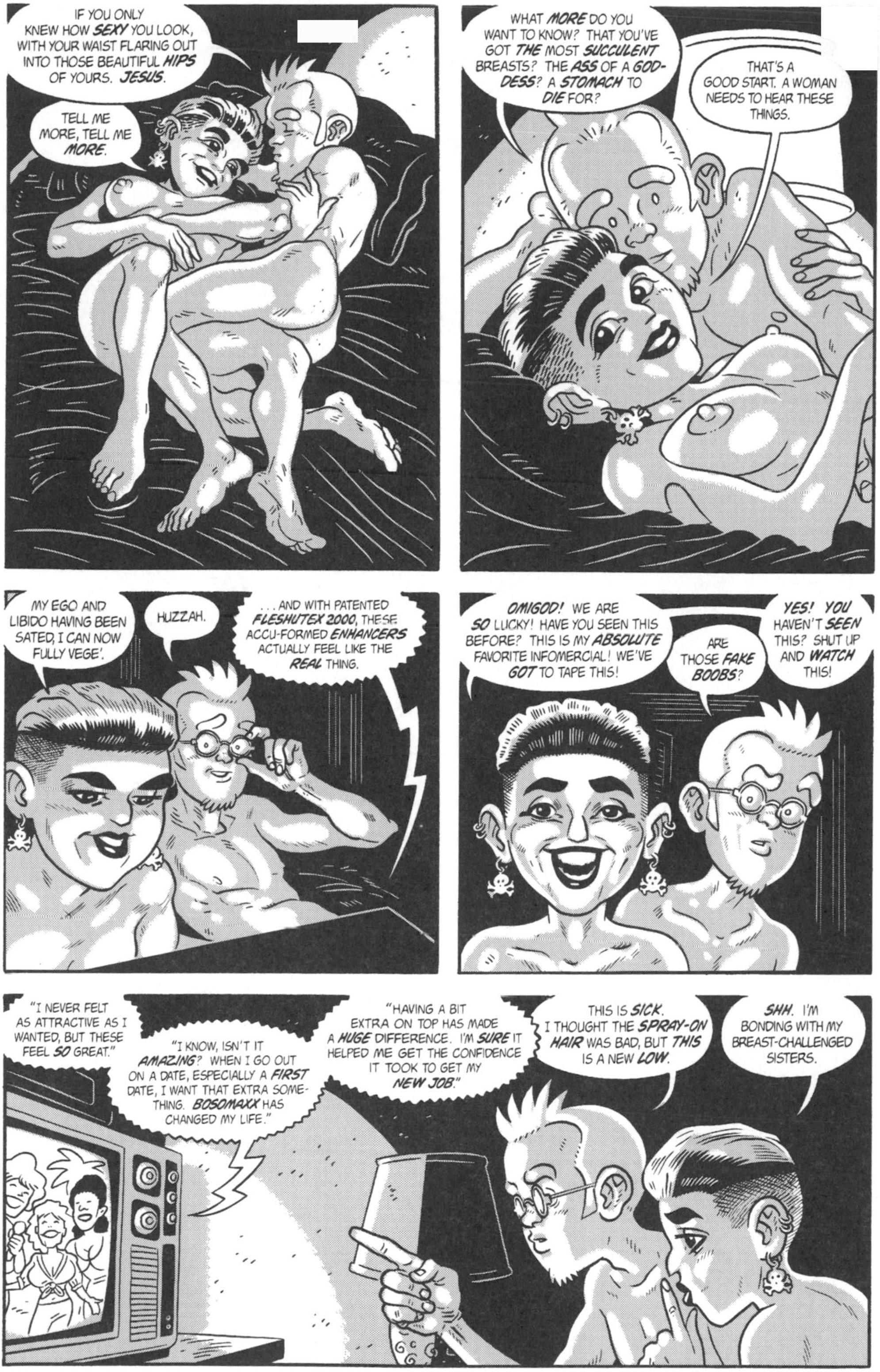
IF YOU ONLY KNEW HOW SEXY YOU LOOK, WITH YOUR WAIST FLARING OUT INTO THOSE BEAUTIFUL HIPS OF YOURS. JESUS.
TELL ME MORE, TELL ME MORE.
WHAT MORE DO YOU WANT TO KNOW? THAT YOU'VE GOT THE MOST SUCCULENT BREASTS? THE ASS OF A GOD-DESS? A STOMACH TO DIE FOR?
THAT'S A GOOD START. A WOMAN NEEDS TO HEAR THESE THINGS.
MY EGO AND LIBIDO HAVING BEEN SATED, I CAN NOW FULLY VEGE'.
HUZZAH.
. . . AND WITH PATENTED FLESHUTEX 2000, THESE ACCU-FORMED ENHANCERS ACTUALLY FEEL LIKE THE REAL THING.
OMIGOD! WE ARE SO LUCKY! HAVE YOU SEEN THIS BEFORE? THIS IS MY ABSOLUTE FAVORITE INFOMERCIAL! WE'VE GOT TO TAPE THIS!
ARE THOSE FAKE BOOBS?
YES! YOU HAVEN'T SEEN THIS? SHUT UP AND WATCH THIS!
"I NEVER FELT AS ATTRACTIVE AS I WANTED, BUT THESE FEEL SO GREAT."
"I KNOW, ISN'T IT AMAZING? WHEN I GO OUT ON A DATE, ESPECIALLY A FIRST DATE, I WANT THAT EXTRA SOME-THING. BOSOMAXX HAS CHANGED MY LIFE."
"HAVING A BIT EXTRA ON TOP HAS MADE A HUGE DIFFERENCE. I'M SURE IT HELPED ME GET THE CONFIDENCE IT TOOK TO GET MY NEW JOB."
THIS IS SICK. I THOUGHT THE SPRAY-ON HAIR WAS BAD, BUT THIS IS A NEW LOW.
SHH. I'M BONDING WITH MY BREAST-CHALLENGED SISTERS.

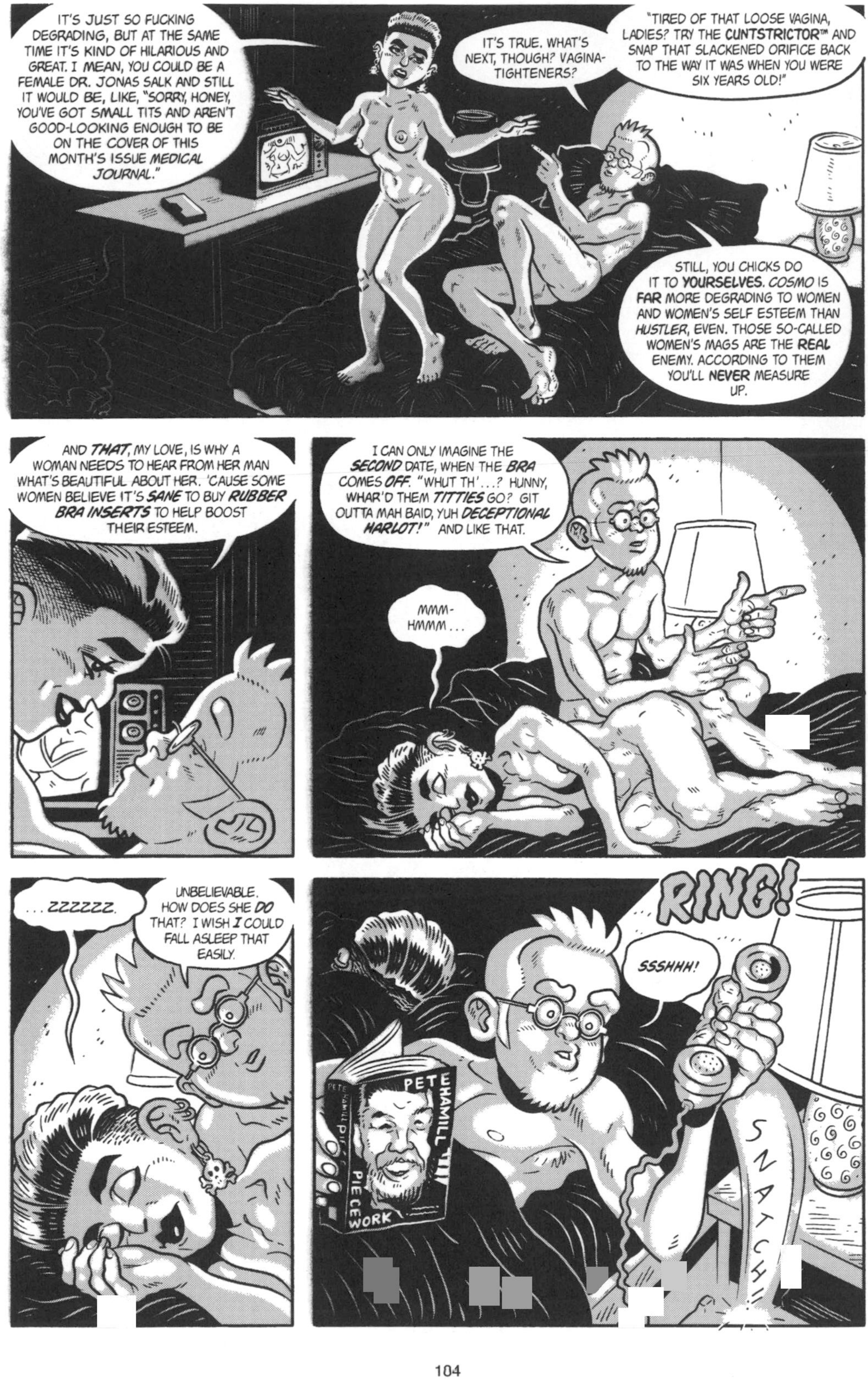
IT'S JUST SO FUCKING DEGRADING, BUT AT THE SAME TIME IT'S KIND OF HILARIOUS AND GREAT. I MEAN, YOU COULD BE A FEMALE DR. JONAS SALK AND STILL IT WOULD BE, LIKE, "SORRY, HONEY, YOU'VE GOT SMALL TITS AND AREN'T GOOD-LOOKING ENOUGH TO BE ON THE COVER OF THIS MONTH'S ISSUE MEDICAL JOURNAL."
IT'S TRUE. WHAT'S NEXT, THOUGH? VAGINA-TIGHTENERS?
"TIRED OF THAT LOOSE VAGINA, LADIES? TRY THE CUNTSTRICTOR™ AND SNAP THAT SLACKENED ORIFICE BACK TO THE WAY IT WAS WHEN YOU WERE SIX YEARS OLD!"
. . .
STILL, YOU CHICKS DO IT TO YOURSELVES. COSMO IS FAR MORE DEGRADING TO WOMEN AND WOMEN'S SELF ESTEEM THAN HUSTLER, EVEN. THOSE SO-CALLED WOMEN'S MAGS ARE THE REAL ENEMY. ACCORDING TO THEM YOU'LL NEVER MEASURE UP.
AND THAT, MY LOVE, IS WHY A WOMAN NEEDS TO HEAR FROM HER MAN WHAT'S BEAUTIFUL ABOUT HER. 'CAUSE SOME WOMEN BELIEVE IT'S SANE TO BUY RUBBER BRA INSERTS TO HELP BOOST THEIR ESTEEM.
I CAN ONLY IMAGINE THE SECOND DATE, WHEN THE BRA COMES OFF. "WHUT TH'...? HUNNY, WHAR'D THEM TITTIES GO? GIT OUTTA MAH BAID, YUH DECEPTIONAL HARLOT!" AND LIKE THAT.
MMM-HMMM . . .
. . . ZZZZZZ.
UNBELIEVABLE. HOW DOES SHE DO THAT? I WISH I COULD FALL ASLEEP THAT EASILY.
RING!
SSSHHH!
PETE HAMILL
PIECEWORK
SNATCH!

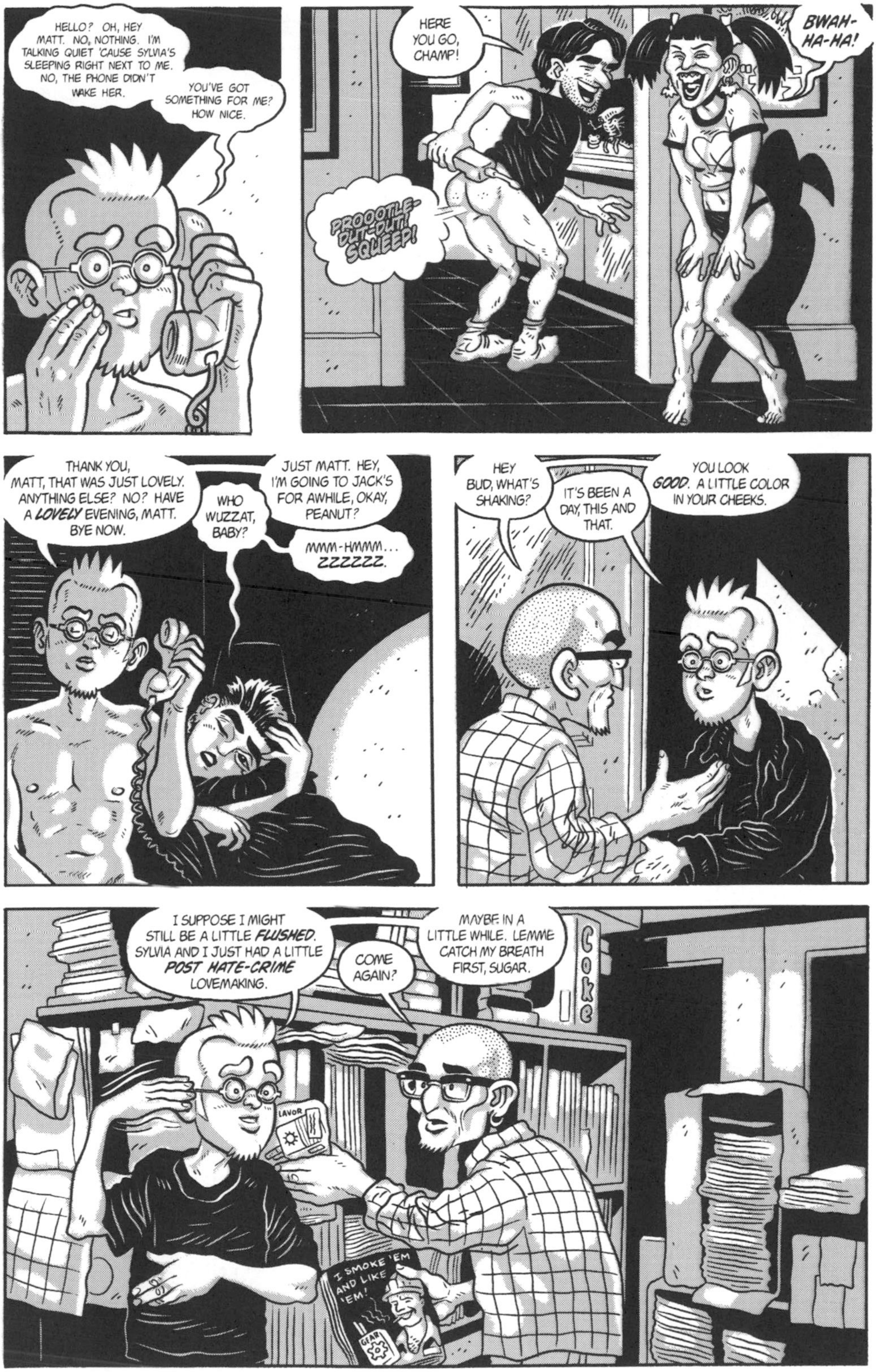
HELLO? OH, HEY MATT. NO, NOTHING. I'M TALKING QUIET 'CAUSE SYLVIA'S SLEEPING RIGHT NEXT TO ME. NO, THE PHONE DIDN'T WAKE HER.
YOU'VE GOT SOMETHING FOR ME? HOW NICE.
HERE YOU GO, CHAMP!
PROOOTLE-DUT-DUT! SQUEEP!
BWAH-HA-HA!
THANK YOU, MATT, THAT WAS JUST LOVELY. ANYTHING ELSE? NO? HAVE A LOVELY EVENING, MATT. BYE NOW.
WHO WUZZAT, BABY?
JUST MATT. HEY, I'M GOING TO JACK'S FOR AWHILE, OKAY, PEANUT?
MMM-HMMM... ZZZZZZ.
HEY BUD, WHAT'S SHAKING?
IT'S BEEN A DAY, THIS AND THAT.
YOU LOOK GOOD. A LITTLE COLOR IN YOUR CHEEKS.
I SUPPOSE I MIGHT STILL BE A LITTLE FLUSHED. SYLVIA AND I JUST HAD A LITTLE POST HATE-CRIME LOVEMAKING.
COME AGAIN?
MAYBE IN A LITTLE WHILE. LEMME CATCH MY BREATH FIRST, SUGAR.
Coke
I SMOKE 'EM AND LIKE 'EM!

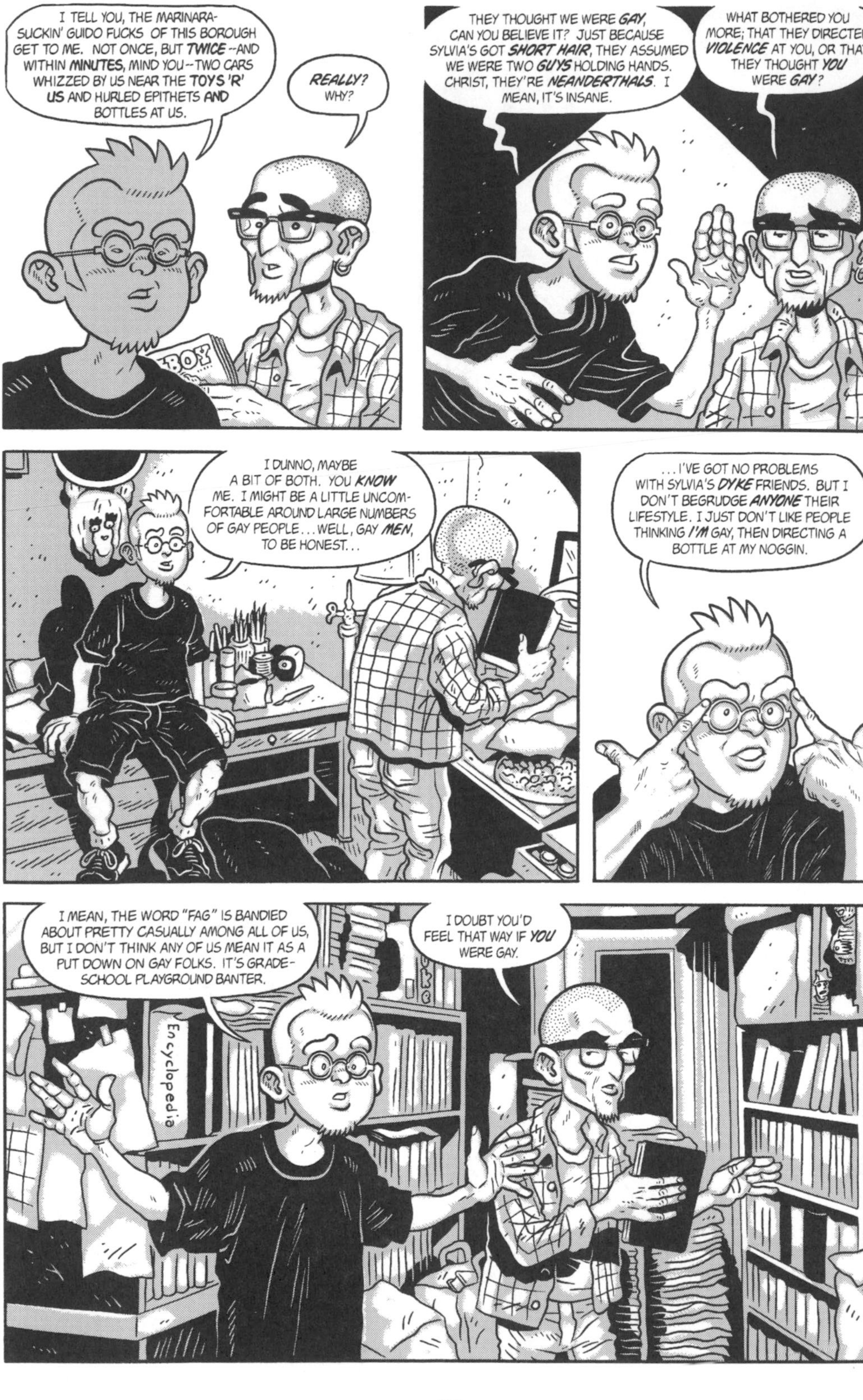
I TELL YOU, THE MARINARA-SUCKIN' GUIDO FUCKS OF THIS BOROUGH GET TO ME. NOT ONCE, BUT TWICE--AND WITHIN MINUTES, MIND YOU--TWO CARS WHIZZED BY US NEAR THE TOYS 'R' US AND HURLED EPITHETS AND BOTTLES AT US.
REALLY? WHY?
THEY THOUGHT WE WERE GAY, CAN YOU BELIEVE IT? JUST BECAUSE SYLVIA'S GOT SHORT HAIR, THEY ASSUMED WE WERE TWO GUYS HOLDING HANDS. CHRIST, THEY'RE NEANDERTHALS. I MEAN, IT'S INSANE.
WHAT BOTHERED YOU MORE; THAT THEY DIRECTED VIOLENCE AT YOU, OR THAT THEY THOUGHT YOU WERE GAY?
I DUNNO, MAYBE A BIT OF BOTH. YOU KNOW ME. I MIGHT BE A LITTLE UNCOMFORTABLE AROUND LARGE NUMBERS OF GAY PEOPLE...WELL, GAY MEN, TO BE HONEST...
...I'VE GOT NO PROBLEMS WITH SYLVIA'S DYKE FRIENDS. BUT I DON'T BEGRUDGE ANYONE THEIR LIFESTYLE. I JUST DON'T LIKE PEOPLE THINKING I'M GAY, THEN DIRECTING A BOTTLE AT MY NOGGIN.
I MEAN, THE WORD "FAG" IS BANDIED ABOUT PRETTY CASUALLY AMONG ALL OF US, BUT I DON'T THINK ANY OF US MEAN IT AS A PUT DOWN ON GAY FOLKS. IT'S GRADE-SCHOOL PLAYGROUND BANTER.
I DOUBT YOU'D FEEL THAT WAY IF YOU WERE GAY.
Encyclopedia

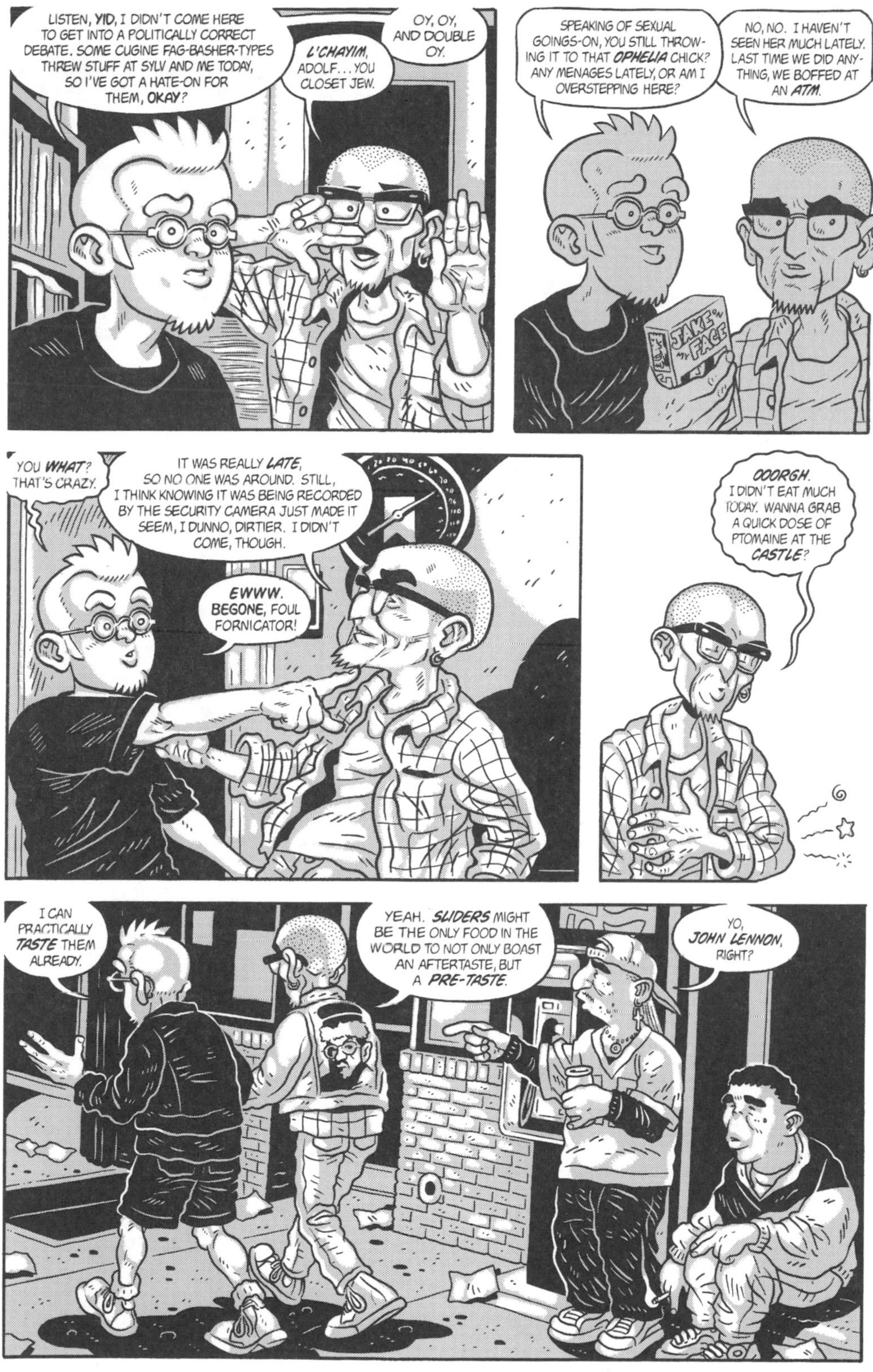
LISTEN, YID, I DIDN'T COME HERE TO GET INTO A POLITICALLY CORRECT DEBATE. SOME CUGINE FAG-BASHER-TYPES THREW STUFF AT SYLV AND ME TODAY, SO I'VE GOT A HATE-ON FOR THEM, OKAY?
OY, OY, AND DOUBLE OY.
L'CHAYIM, ADOLF... YOU CLOSET JEW.
SPEAKING OF SEXUAL GOINGS-ON, YOU STILL THROWING IT TO THAT OPHELIA CHICK? ANY MENAGES LATELY, OR AM I OVERSTEPPING HERE?
NO, NO. I HAVEN'T SEEN HER MUCH LATELY. LAST TIME WE DID ANYTHING, WE BOFFED AT AN ATM.
JAKE ON MY FACE
YOU WHAT? THAT'S CRAZY.
IT WAS REALLY LATE, SO NO ONE WAS AROUND. STILL, I THINK KNOWING IT WAS BEING RECORDED BY THE SECURITY CAMERA JUST MADE IT SEEM, I DUNNO, DIRTIER. I DIDN'T COME, THOUGH.
EWWW. BEGONE, FOUL FORNICATOR!
OOORGH. I DIDN'T EAT MUCH TODAY. WANNA GRAB A QUICK DOSE OF PTOMAINE AT THE CASTLE?
I CAN PRACTICALLY TASTE THEM ALREADY.
YEAH. SLIDERS MIGHT BE THE ONLY FOOD IN THE WORLD TO NOT ONLY BOAST AN AFTERTASTE, BUT A PRE-TASTE.
YO, JOHN LENNON, RIGHT?

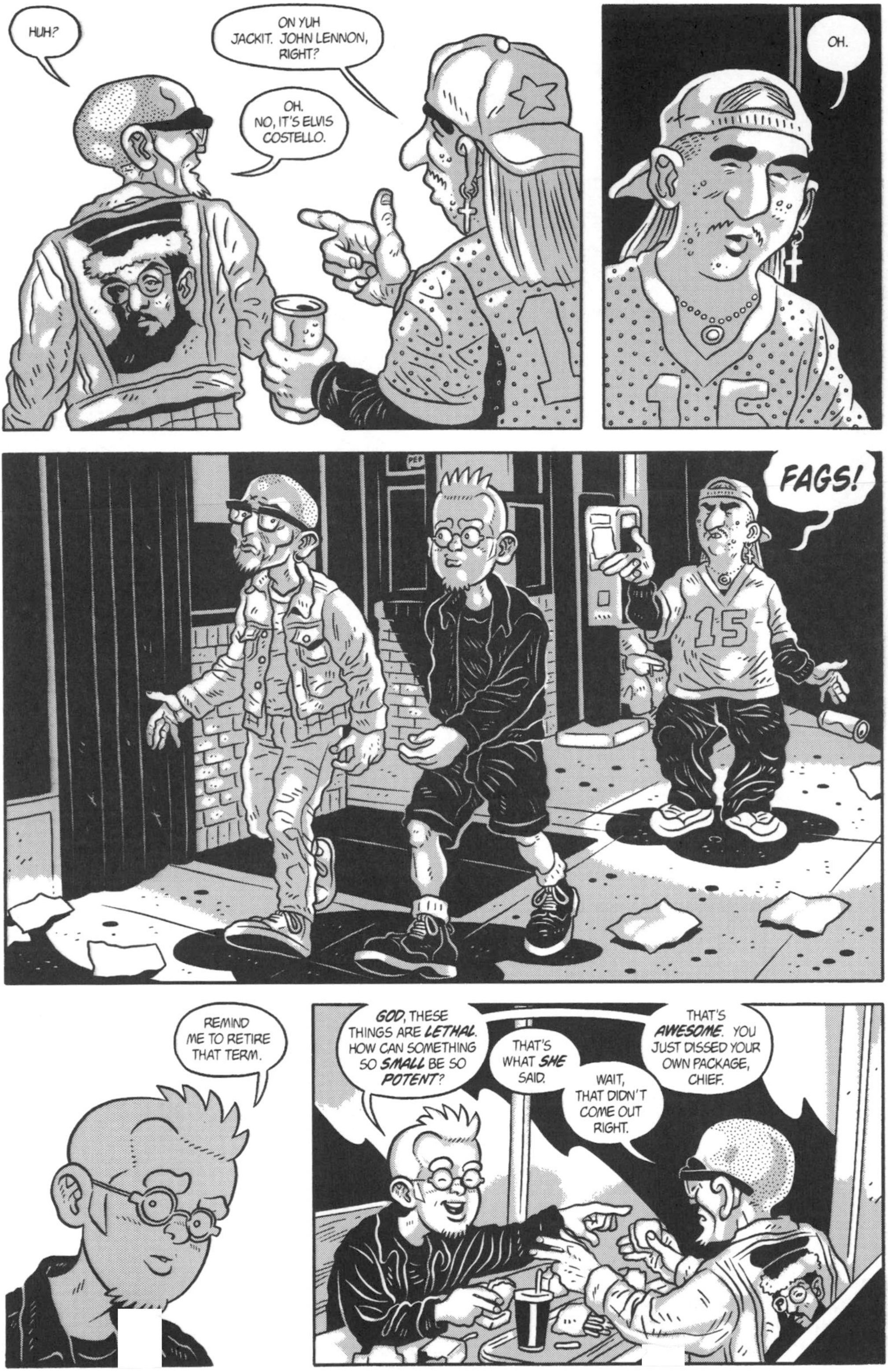
HUH?
ON YUH JACKIT. JOHN LENNON, RIGHT?
OH. NO, IT'S ELVIS COSTELLO.
OH.
FAGS!
REMIND ME TO RETIRE THAT TERM.
GOD, THESE THINGS ARE LETHAL. HOW CAN SOMETHING SO SMALL BE SO POTENT?
THAT'S WHAT SHE SAID.
WAIT, THAT DIDN'T COME OUT RIGHT.
THAT'S AWESOME. YOU JUST DISSED YOUR OWN PACKAGE, CHIEF.

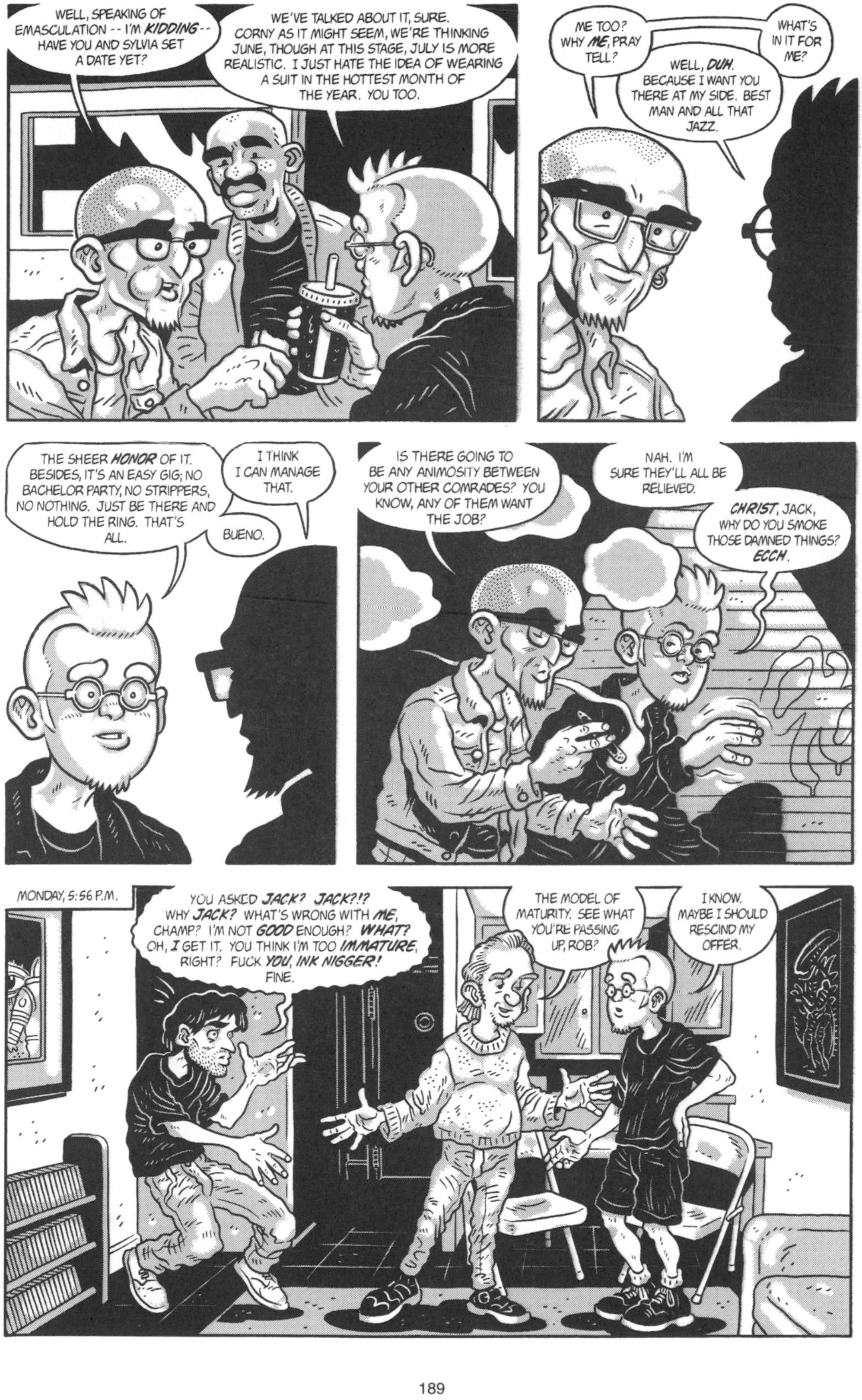
WELL, SPEAKING OF EMASCULATION -- I'M KIDDING -- HAVE YOU AND SYLVIA SET A DATE YET?
WE'VE TALKED ABOUT IT, SURE. CORNY AS IT MIGHT SEEM, WE'RE THINKING JUNE, THOUGH AT THIS STAGE, JULY IS MORE REALISTIC. I JUST HATE THE IDEA OF WEARING A SUIT IN THE HOTTEST MONTH OF THE YEAR. YOU TOO.
ME TOO? WHY ME, PRAY TELL?
WHAT'S IN IT FOR ME?
WELL, DUH. BECAUSE I WANT YOU THERE AT MY SIDE. BEST MAN AND ALL THAT JAZZ.
THE SHEER HONOR OF IT. BESIDES, IT'S AN EASY GIG; NO BACHELOR PARTY, NO STRIPPERS, NO NOTHING. JUST BE THERE AND HOLD THE RING. THAT'S ALL.
I THINK I CAN MANAGE THAT.
BUENO.
IS THERE GOING TO BE ANY ANIMOSITY BETWEEN YOUR OTHER COMRADES? YOU KNOW, ANY OF THEM WANT THE JOB?
NAH. I'M SURE THEY'LL ALL BE RELIEVED.
CHRIST, JACK, WHY DO YOU SMOKE THOSE DAMNED THINGS? ECCH.
MONDAY, 5:56 P.M.
YOU ASKED JACK? JACK?!? WHY JACK? WHAT'S WRONG WITH ME, CHAMP? I'M NOT GOOD ENOUGH? WHAT? OH, I GET IT. YOU THINK I'M TOO IMMATURE, RIGHT? FUCK YOU, INK NIGGER! FINE.
THE MODEL OF MATURITY. SEE WHAT YOU'RE PASSING UP, ROB?
I KNOW. MAYBE I SHOULD RESCIND MY OFFER.

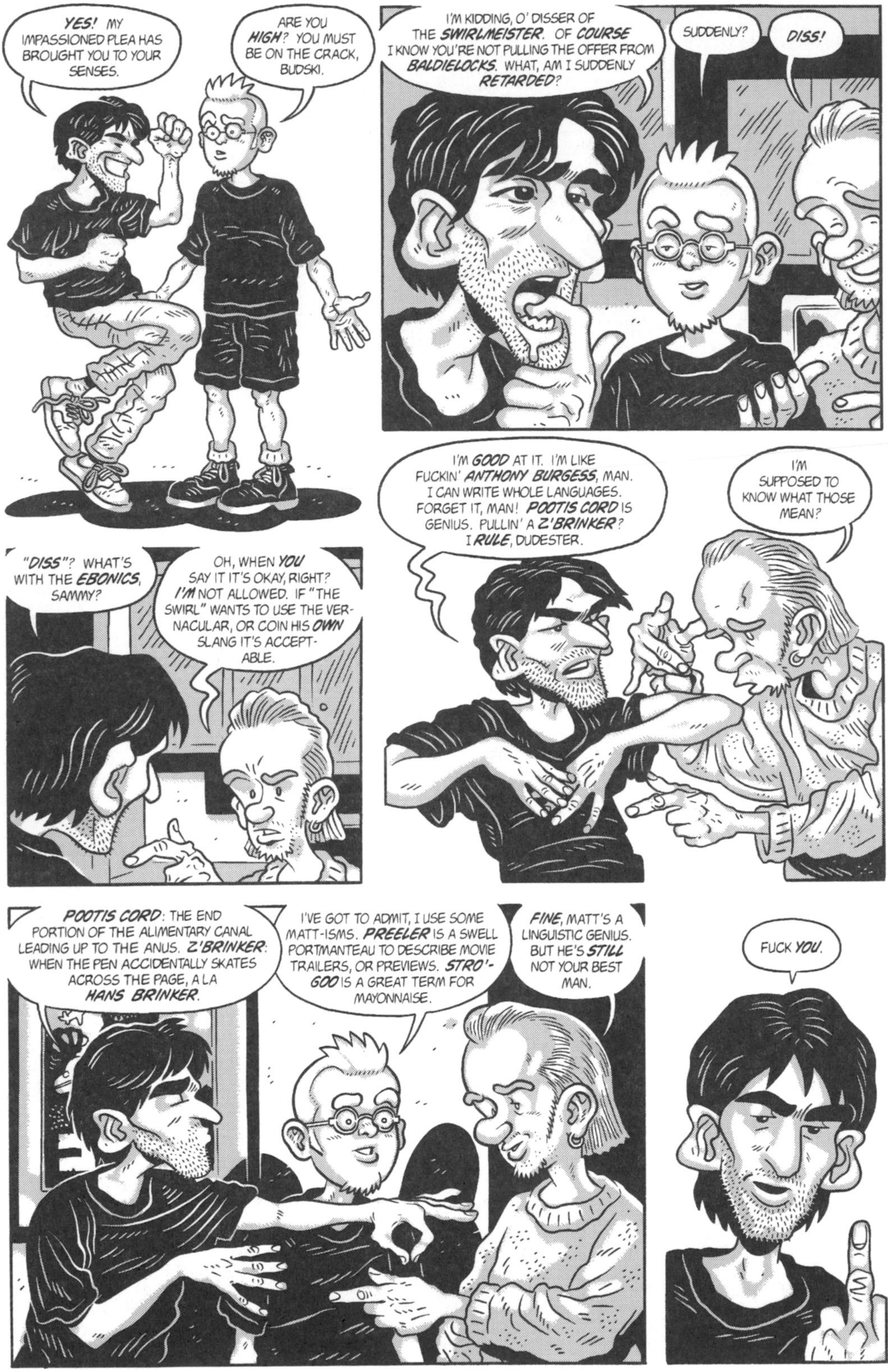
YES! MY IMPASSIONED PLEA HAS BROUGHT YOU TO YOUR SENSES.
ARE YOU HIGH? YOU MUST BE ON THE CRACK, BUDSKI.
I'M KIDDING, O' DISSER OF THE SWIRLMEISTER. OF COURSE I KNOW YOU'RE NOT PULLING THE OFFER FROM BALDIELOCKS. WHAT, AM I SUDDENLY RETARDED?
SUDDENLY?
DISS!
"DISS"? WHAT'S WITH THE EBONICS, SAMMY?
OH, WHEN YOU SAY IT IT'S OKAY, RIGHT? I'M NOT ALLOWED. IF "THE SWIRL" WANTS TO USE THE VERNACULAR, OR COIN HIS OWN SLANG IT'S ACCEPTABLE.
I'M GOOD AT IT. I'M LIKE FUCKIN' ANTHONY BURGESS, MAN. I CAN WRITE WHOLE LANGUAGES. FORGET IT, MAN! POOTIS CORD IS GENIUS. PULLIN' A Z'BRINKER? I RULE, DUDESTER.
I'M SUPPOSED TO KNOW WHAT THOSE MEAN?
POOTIS CORD: THE END PORTION OF THE ALIMENTARY CANAL LEADING UP TO THE ANUS. Z'BRINKER: WHEN THE PEN ACCIDENTALLY SKATES ACROSS THE PAGE, A LA HANS BRINKER.
I'VE GOT TO ADMIT, I USE SOME MATT-ISMS. PREELER IS A SWELL PORTMANTEAU TO DESCRIBE MOVIE TRAILERS, OR PREVIEWS. STRO'-GOO IS A GREAT TERM FOR MAYONNAISE.
FINE, MATT'S A LINGUISTIC GENIUS. BUT HE'S STILL NOT YOUR BEST MAN.
FUCK YOU.

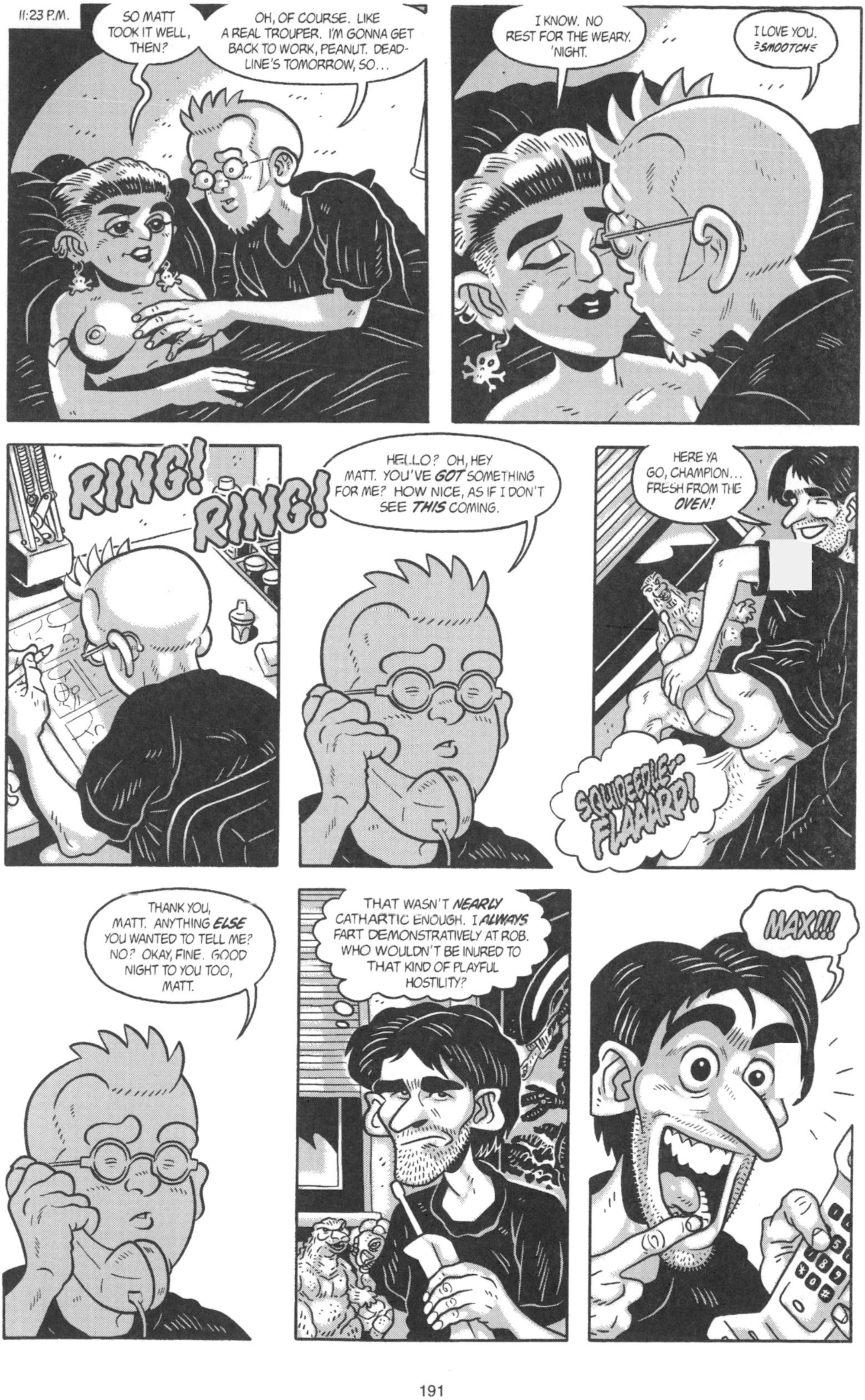
11:23 P.M.
SO MATT TOOK IT WELL, THEN?
OH, OF COURSE. LIKE A REAL TROUPER. I'M GONNA GET BACK TO WORK, PEANUT. DEADLINE'S TOMORROW, SO...
I KNOW. NO REST FOR THE WEARY. 'NIGHT.
I LOVE YOU.
SMOOTCH
RING! RING!
HELLO? OH, HEY MATT. YOU'VE GOT SOMETHING FOR ME? HOW NICE, AS IF I DON'T SEE THIS COMING.
HERE YA GO, CHAMPION... FRESH FROM THE OVEN!
SQUIDEEDLE-FLAAARD!
THANK YOU, MATT. ANYTHING ELSE YOU WANTED TO TELL ME? NO? OKAY, FINE. GOOD NIGHT TO YOU TOO, MATT.
THAT WASN'T NEARLY CATHARTIC ENOUGH. I ALWAYS FART DEMONSTRATIVELY AT ROB. WHO WOULDN'T BE INURED TO THAT KIND OF PLAYFUL HOSTILITY?
MAX!!!

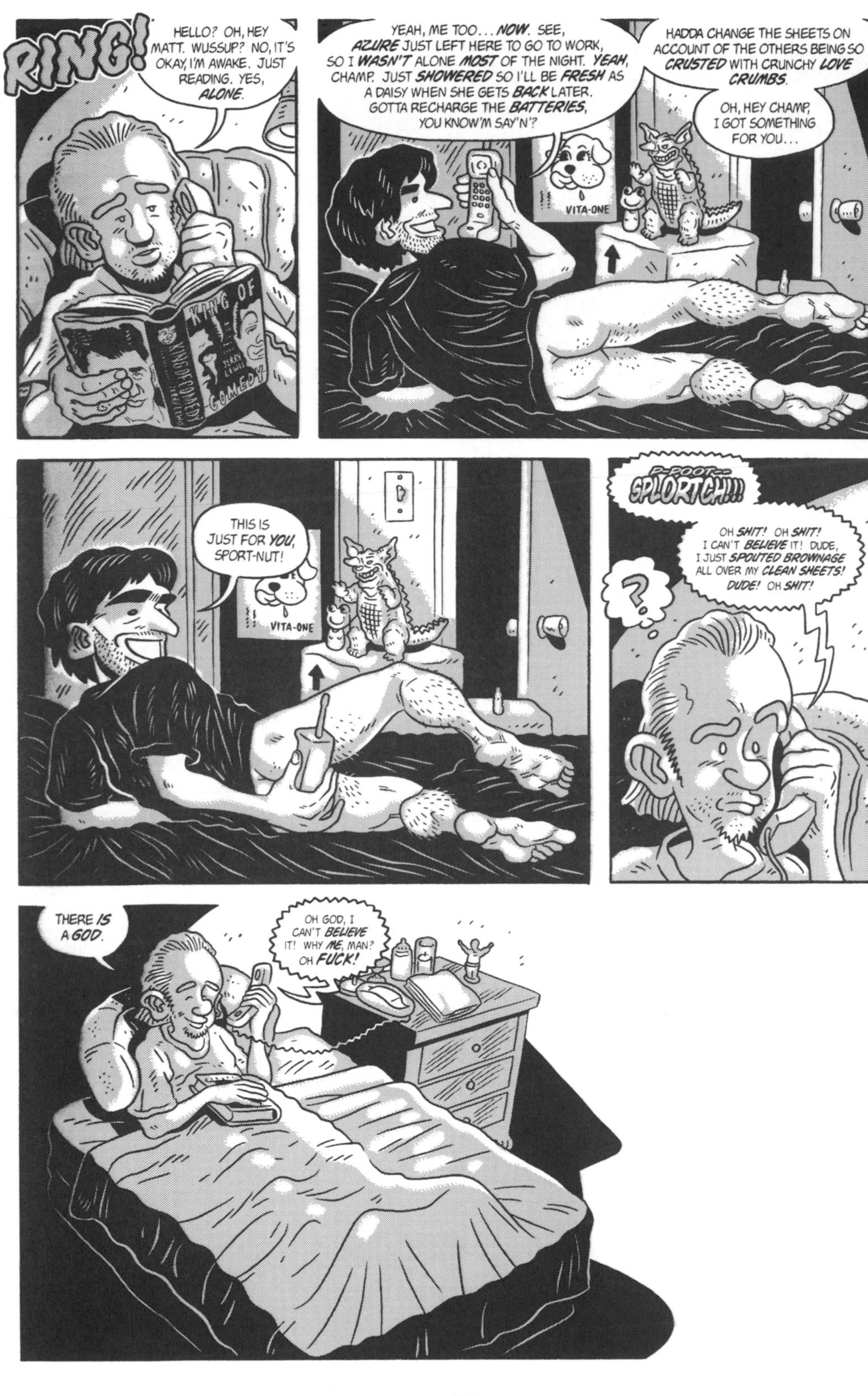
RING!
HELLO? OH, HEY MATT. WUSSUP? NO, IT'S OKAY, I'M AWAKE. JUST READING. YES, ALONE.
KING OF COMEDY
JERRY LEWIS
YEAH, ME TOO... NOW. SEE, AZURE JUST LEFT HERE TO GO TO WORK, SO I WASN'T ALONE MOST OF THE NIGHT. YEAH, CHAMP. JUST SHOWERED SO I'LL BE FRESH AS A DAISY WHEN SHE GETS BACK LATER. GOTTA RECHARGE THE BATTERIES, YOU KNOW'M SAY'N'?
VITA-ONE
HADDA CHANGE THE SHEETS ON ACCOUNT OF THE OTHERS BEING SO CRUSTED WITH CRUNCHY LOVE CRUMBS.
OH, HEY CHAMP, I GOT SOMETHING FOR YOU...
THIS IS JUST FOR YOU, SPORT-NUT!
VITA-ONE
P-POOT--
SPLORTCH!!!
?
OH SHIT! OH SHIT! I CAN'T BELIEVE IT! DUDE, I JUST SPOUTED BROWNAGE ALL OVER MY CLEAN SHEETS! DUDE! OH SHIT!
THERE IS A GOD.
OH GOD, I CAN'T BELIEVE IT! WHY ME, MAN? OH FUCK!

# CHAPTER NINE

# ECCH LIBRIS

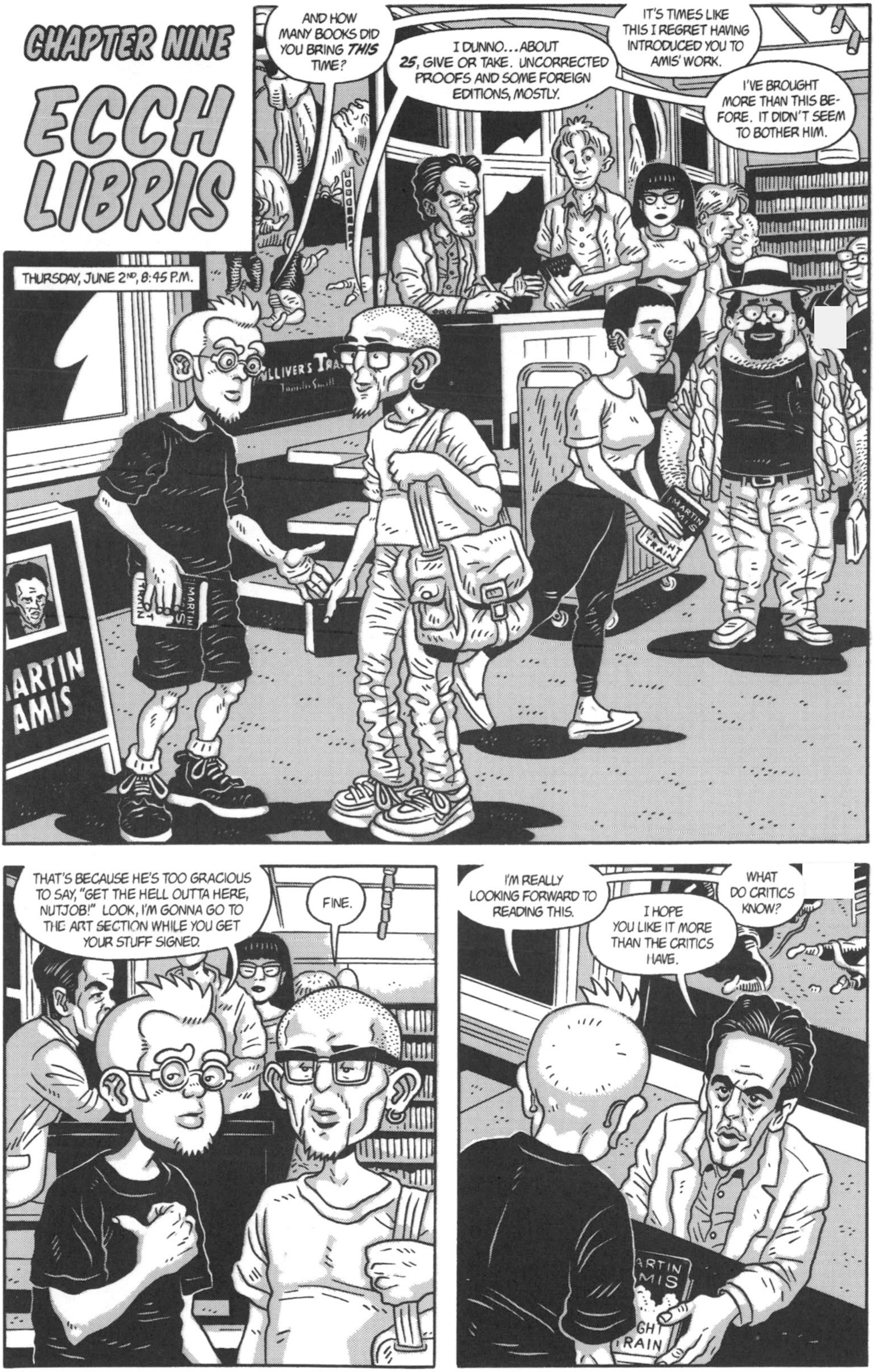
AND HOW MANY BOOKS DID YOU BRING THIS TIME?
I DUNNO... ABOUT 25, GIVE OR TAKE. UNCORRECTED PROOFS AND SOME FOREIGN EDITIONS, MOSTLY.
IT'S TIMES LIKE THIS I REGRET HAVING INTRODUCED YOU TO AMIS' WORK.
I'VE BROUGHT MORE THAN THIS BEFORE. IT DIDN'T SEEM TO BOTHER HIM.
THURSDAY, JUNE 2ND, 8:45 P.M.
GULLIVER'S TRA
MARTIN AMIS
NIGHT TRAIN
THAT'S BECAUSE HE'S TOO GRACIOUS TO SAY, "GET THE HELL OUTTA HERE, NUTJOB!" LOOK, I'M GONNA GO TO THE ART SECTION WHILE YOU GET YOUR STUFF SIGNED.
FINE.
I'M REALLY LOOKING FORWARD TO READING THIS.
I HOPE YOU LIKE IT MORE THAN THE CRITICS HAVE.
WHAT DO CRITICS KNOW?

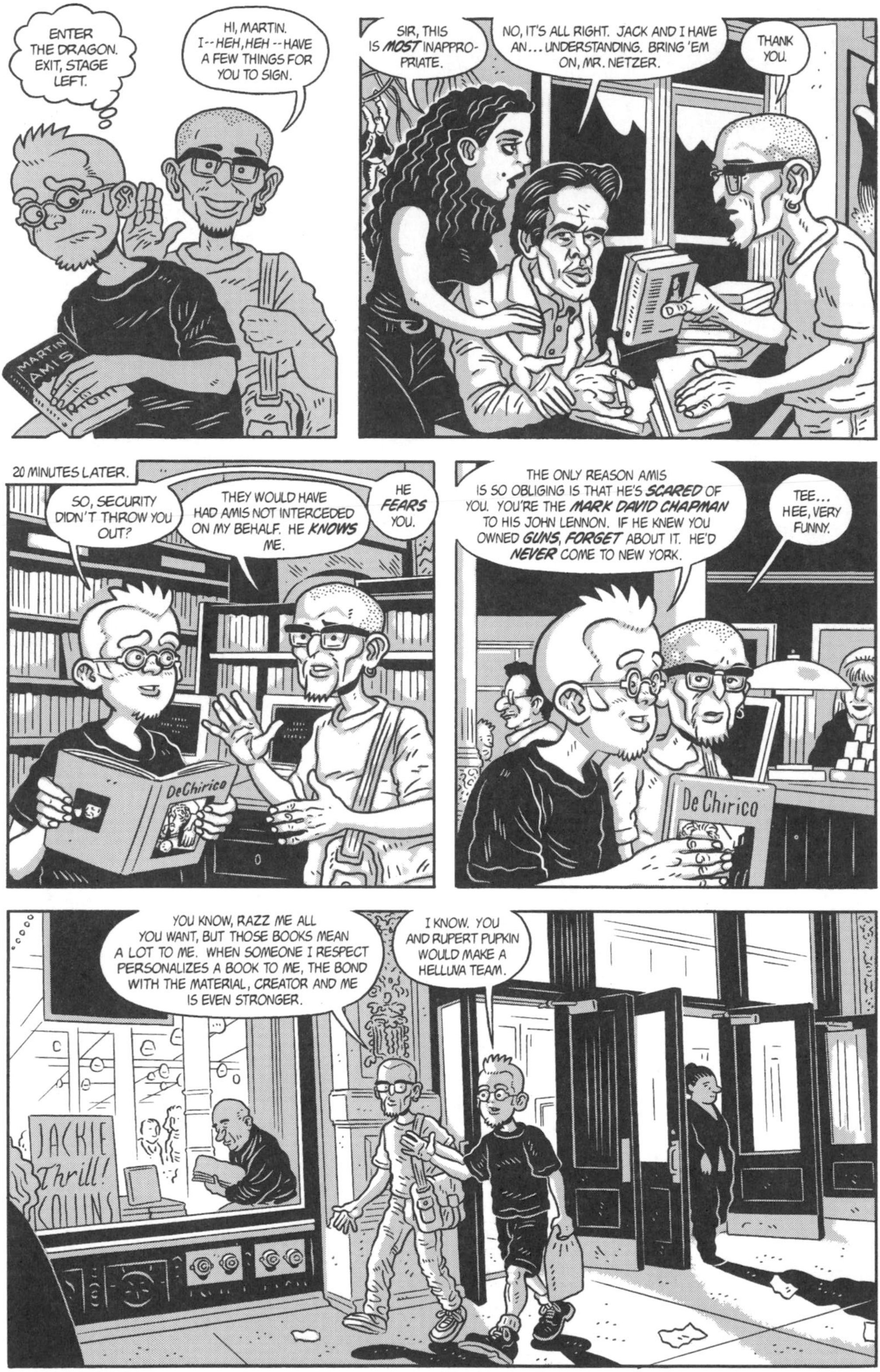
ENTER THE DRAGON. EXIT, STAGE LEFT.
HI, MARTIN. I-- HEH, HEH -- HAVE A FEW THINGS FOR YOU TO SIGN.
MARTIN AMIS
SIR, THIS IS MOST INAPPROPRIATE.
NO, IT'S ALL RIGHT. JACK AND I HAVE AN... UNDERSTANDING. BRING 'EM ON, MR. NETZER.
THANK YOU.
20 MINUTES LATER.
SO, SECURITY DIDN'T THROW YOU OUT?
THEY WOULD HAVE HAD AMIS NOT INTERCEDED ON MY BEHALF. HE KNOWS ME.
HE FEARS YOU.
DeChirico
THE ONLY REASON AMIS IS SO OBLIGING IS THAT HE'S SCARED OF YOU. YOU'RE THE MARK DAVID CHAPMAN TO HIS JOHN LENNON. IF HE KNEW YOU OWNED GUNS, FORGET ABOUT IT. HE'D NEVER COME TO NEW YORK.
TEE... HEE, VERY FUNNY.
De Chirico
YOU KNOW, RAZZ ME ALL YOU WANT, BUT THOSE BOOKS MEAN A LOT TO ME. WHEN SOMEONE I RESPECT PERSONALIZES A BOOK TO ME, THE BOND WITH THE MATERIAL, CREATOR AND ME IS EVEN STRONGER.
I KNOW. YOU AND RUPERT PUPKIN WOULD MAKE A HELLUVA TEAM.
JACKIE Thrill! COLLINS

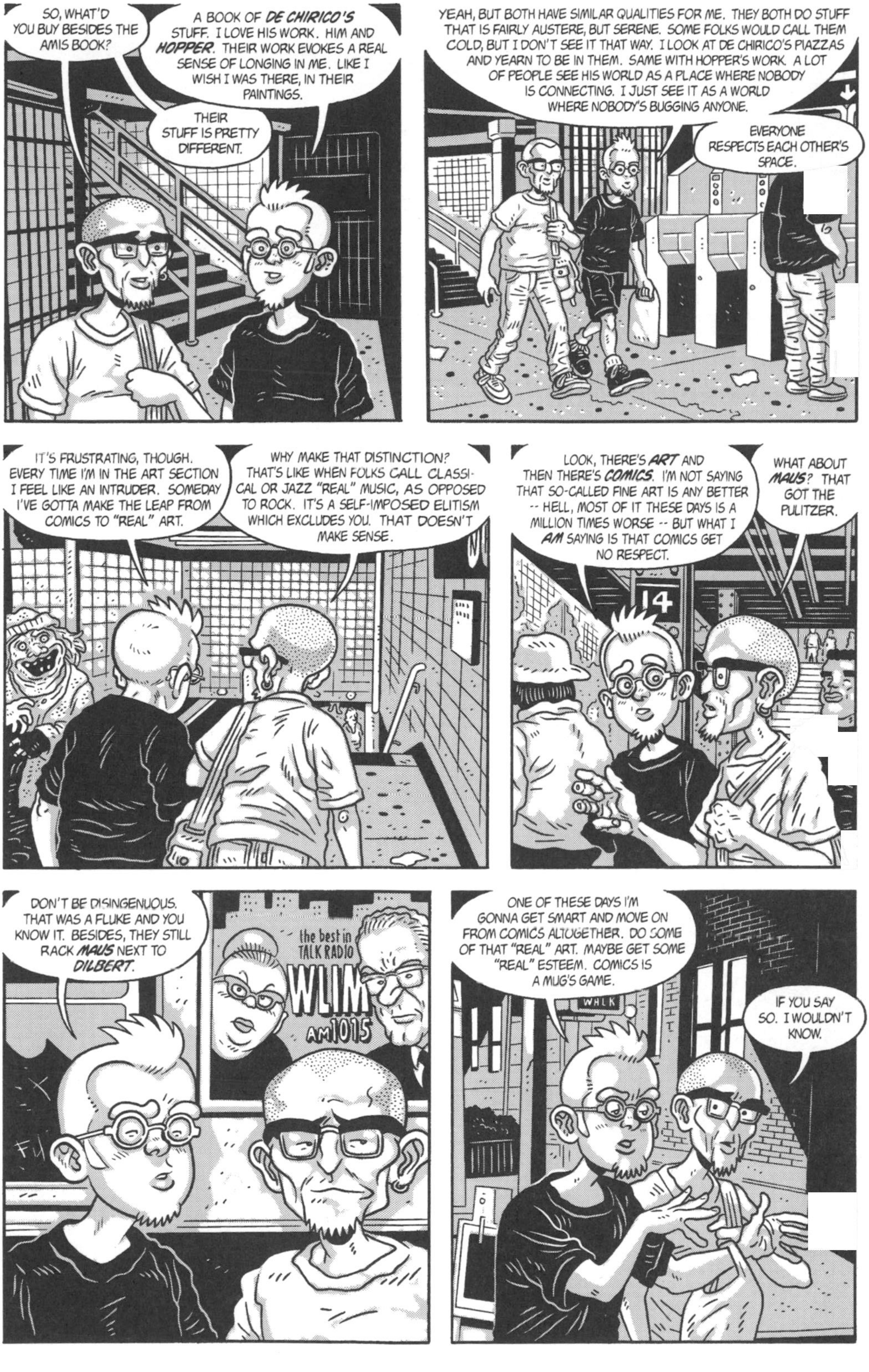
SO, WHAT'D YOU BUY BESIDES THE AMIS BOOK?
A BOOK OF DE CHIRICO'S STUFF. I LOVE HIS WORK. HIM AND HOPPER. THEIR WORK EVOKES A REAL SENSE OF LONGING IN ME. LIKE I WISH I WAS THERE, IN THEIR PAINTINGS.
THEIR STUFF IS PRETTY DIFFERENT.
YEAH, BUT BOTH HAVE SIMILAR QUALITIES FOR ME. THEY BOTH DO STUFF THAT IS FAIRLY AUSTERE, BUT SERENE. SOME FOLKS WOULD CALL THEM COLD, BUT I DON'T SEE IT THAT WAY. I LOOK AT DE CHIRICO'S PIAZZAS AND YEARN TO BE IN THEM. SAME WITH HOPPER'S WORK. A LOT OF PEOPLE SEE HIS WORLD AS A PLACE WHERE NOBODY IS CONNECTING. I JUST SEE IT AS A WORLD WHERE NOBODY'S BUGGING ANYONE.
EVERYONE RESPECTS EACH OTHER'S SPACE.
IT'S FRUSTRATING, THOUGH. EVERY TIME I'M IN THE ART SECTION I FEEL LIKE AN INTRUDER. SOMEDAY I'VE GOTTA MAKE THE LEAP FROM COMICS TO "REAL" ART.
WHY MAKE THAT DISTINCTION? THAT'S LIKE WHEN FOLKS CALL CLASSICAL OR JAZZ "REAL" MUSIC, AS OPPOSED TO ROCK. IT'S A SELF-IMPOSED ELITISM WHICH EXCLUDES YOU. THAT DOESN'T MAKE SENSE.
LOOK, THERE'S ART AND THEN THERE'S COMICS. I'M NOT SAYING THAT SO-CALLED FINE ART IS ANY BETTER -- HELL, MOST OF IT THESE DAYS IS A MILLION TIMES WORSE -- BUT WHAT I AM SAYING IS THAT COMICS GET NO RESPECT.
14
WHAT ABOUT MAUS? THAT GOT THE PULITZER.
DON'T BE DISINGENUOUS. THAT WAS A FLUKE AND YOU KNOW IT. BESIDES, THEY STILL RACK MAUS NEXT TO DILBERT.
the best in TALK RADIO
WLIM
AM1015
ONE OF THESE DAYS I'M GONNA GET SMART AND MOVE ON FROM COMICS ALTOGETHER. DO SOME OF THAT "REAL" ART. MAYBE GET SOME "REAL" ESTEEM. COMICS IS A MUG'S GAME.
WALK
IF YOU SAY SO. I WOULDN'T KNOW.

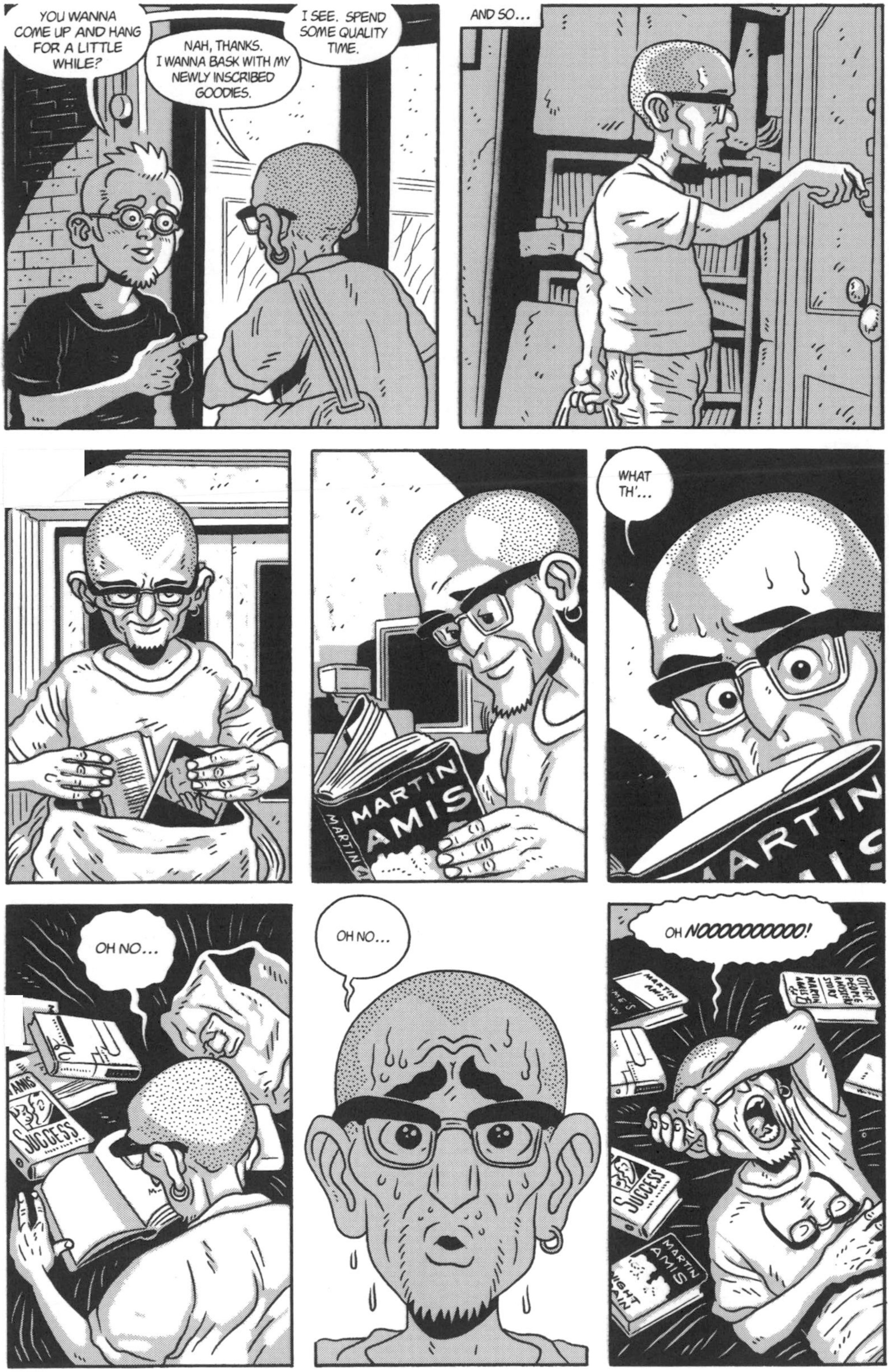
YOU WANNA COME UP AND HANG FOR A LITTLE WHILE?
NAH, THANKS. I WANNA BASK WITH MY NEWLY INSCRIBED GOODIES.
I SEE. SPEND SOME QUALITY TIME.
AND SO...
MARTIN AMIS
MARTIN
WHAT TH'...
MARTIN
OH NO...
SUCCESS
OH NO...
OH NOOOOOOOOOO!
MARTIN AMIS
OTHER PEOPLE
SUCCESS
MARTIN AMIS

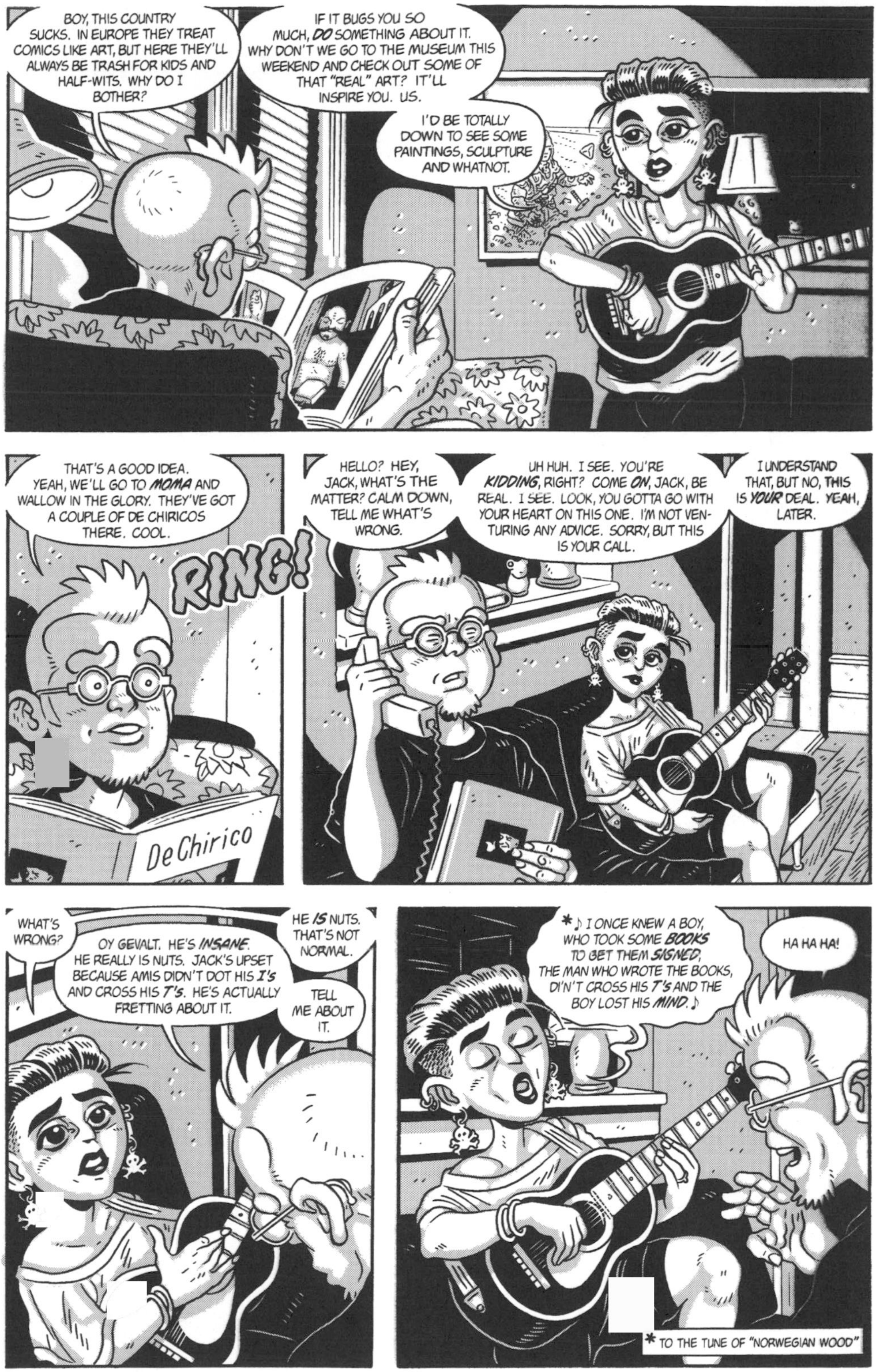
BOY, THIS COUNTRY SUCKS. IN EUROPE THEY TREAT COMICS LIKE ART, BUT HERE THEY'LL ALWAYS BE TRASH FOR KIDS AND HALF-WITS. WHY DO I BOTHER?
IF IT BUGS YOU SO MUCH, DO SOMETHING ABOUT IT. WHY DON'T WE GO TO THE MUSEUM THIS WEEKEND AND CHECK OUT SOME OF THAT "REAL" ART? IT'LL INSPIRE YOU. US.
I'D BE TOTALLY DOWN TO SEE SOME PAINTINGS, SCULPTURE AND WHATNOT.
THAT'S A GOOD IDEA. YEAH, WE'LL GO TO MOMA AND WALLOW IN THE GLORY. THEY'VE GOT A COUPLE OF DE CHIRICOS THERE. COOL.
RING!
DeChirico
HELLO? HEY, JACK, WHAT'S THE MATTER? CALM DOWN, TELL ME WHAT'S WRONG.
UH HUH. I SEE. YOU'RE KIDDING, RIGHT? COME ON, JACK, BE REAL. I SEE. LOOK, YOU GOTTA GO WITH YOUR HEART ON THIS ONE. I'M NOT VENTURING ANY ADVICE. SORRY, BUT THIS IS YOUR CALL.
I UNDERSTAND THAT, BUT NO, THIS IS YOUR DEAL. YEAH, LATER.
WHAT'S WRONG?
OY GEVALT. HE'S INSANE. HE REALLY IS NUTS. JACK'S UPSET BECAUSE AMIS DIDN'T DOT HIS I'S AND CROSS HIS T'S. HE'S ACTUALLY FRETTING ABOUT IT.
HE IS NUTS. THAT'S NOT NORMAL.
TELL ME ABOUT IT.
*♪ I ONCE KNEW A BOY, WHO TOOK SOME BOOKS TO GET THEM SIGNED, THE MAN WHO WROTE THE BOOKS, DI'N'T CROSS HIS T'S AND THE BOY LOST HIS MIND.♪
HA HA HA!
* TO THE TUNE OF "NORWEGIAN WOOD"

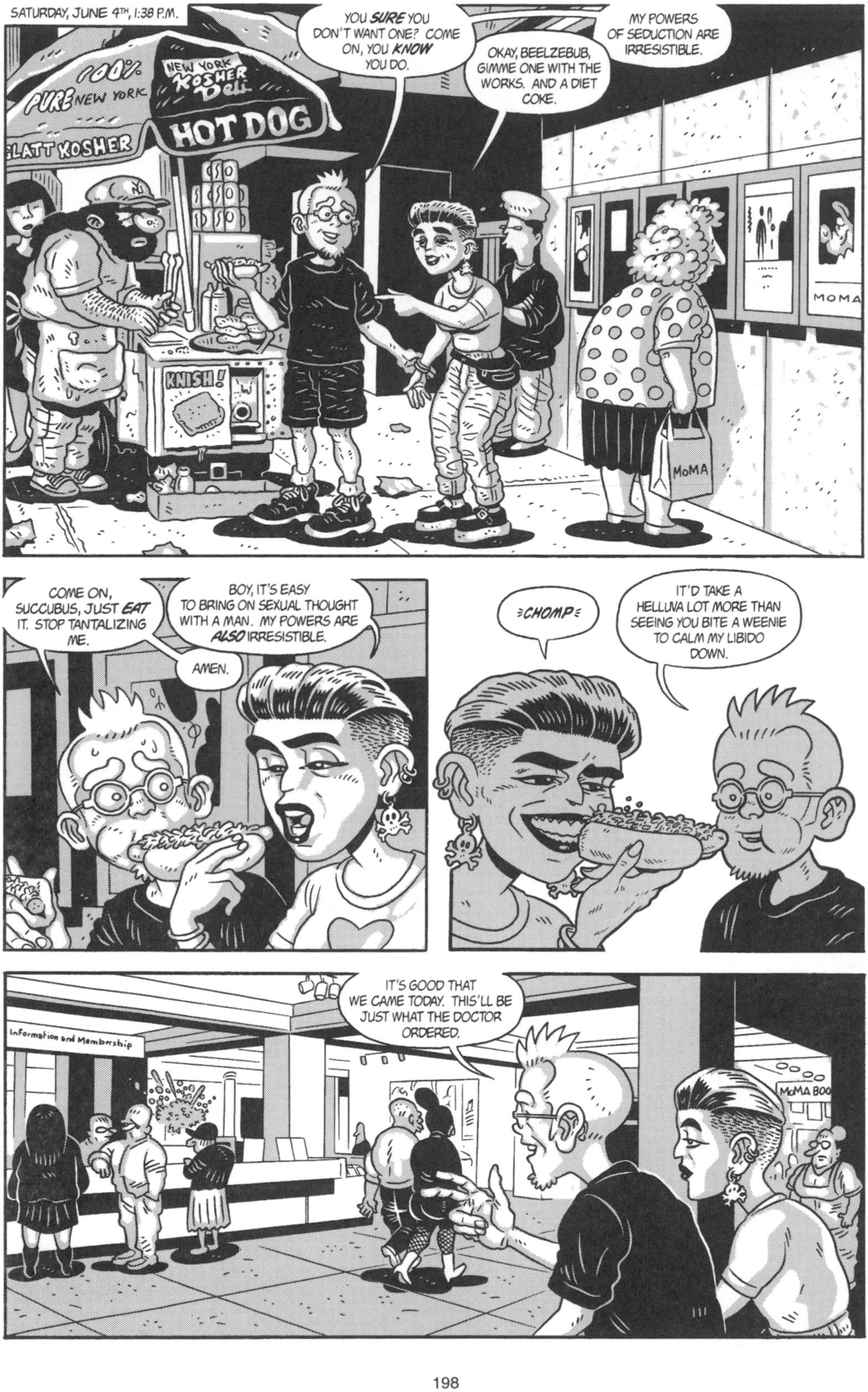
SATURDAY, JUNE 4TH, 1:38 P.M.
YOU SURE YOU DON'T WANT ONE? COME ON, YOU KNOW YOU DO.
OKAY, BEELZEBUB, GIMME ONE WITH THE WORKS. AND A DIET COKE.
MY POWERS OF SEDUCTION ARE IRRESISTIBLE.
100% PURE NEW YORK
NEW YORK KOSHER Deli
HOT DOG
GLATT KOSHER
KNISH!
MOMA
MoMA
COME ON, SUCCUBUS, JUST EAT IT. STOP TANTALIZING ME.
BOY, IT'S EASY TO BRING ON SEXUAL THOUGHT WITH A MAN. MY POWERS ARE ALSO IRRESISTIBLE.
AMEN.
CHOMP
IT'D TAKE A HELLUVA LOT MORE THAN SEEING YOU BITE A WEENIE TO CALM MY LIBIDO DOWN.
IT'S GOOD THAT WE CAME TODAY. THIS'LL BE JUST WHAT THE DOCTOR ORDERED.
Information and Membership
MoMA BOO

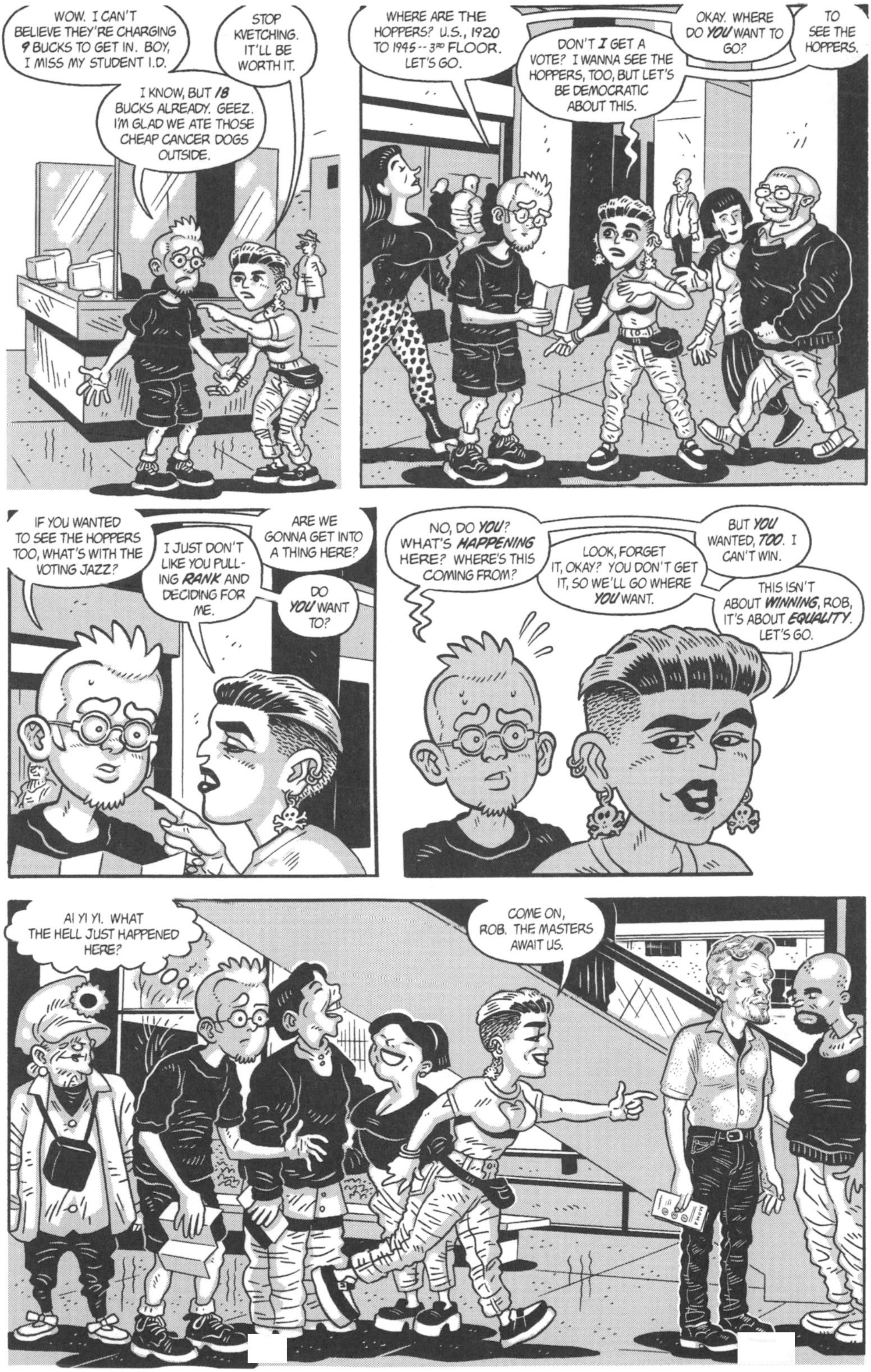
WOW. I CAN'T BELIEVE THEY'RE CHARGING 9 BUCKS TO GET IN. BOY, I MISS MY STUDENT I.D.
STOP KVETCHING. IT'LL BE WORTH IT.
I KNOW, BUT 18 BUCKS ALREADY. GEEZ. I'M GLAD WE ATE THOSE CHEAP CANCER DOGS OUTSIDE.
WHERE ARE THE HOPPERS? U.S., 1920 TO 1945 -- 3RD FLOOR. LET'S GO.
DON'T I GET A VOTE? I WANNA SEE THE HOPPERS, TOO, BUT LET'S BE DEMOCRATIC ABOUT THIS.
OKAY. WHERE DO YOU WANT TO GO?
TO SEE THE HOPPERS.
IF YOU WANTED TO SEE THE HOPPERS TOO, WHAT'S WITH THE VOTING JAZZ?
I JUST DON'T LIKE YOU PULLING RANK AND DECIDING FOR ME.
ARE WE GONNA GET INTO A THING HERE?
DO YOU WANT TO?
NO, DO YOU? WHAT'S HAPPENING HERE? WHERE'S THIS COMING FROM?
LOOK, FORGET IT, OKAY? YOU DON'T GET IT, SO WE'LL GO WHERE YOU WANT.
BUT YOU WANTED, TOO. I CAN'T WIN.
THIS ISN'T ABOUT WINNING, ROB, IT'S ABOUT EQUALITY. LET'S GO.
AI YI YI. WHAT THE HELL JUST HAPPENED HERE?
COME ON, ROB. THE MASTERS AWAIT US.

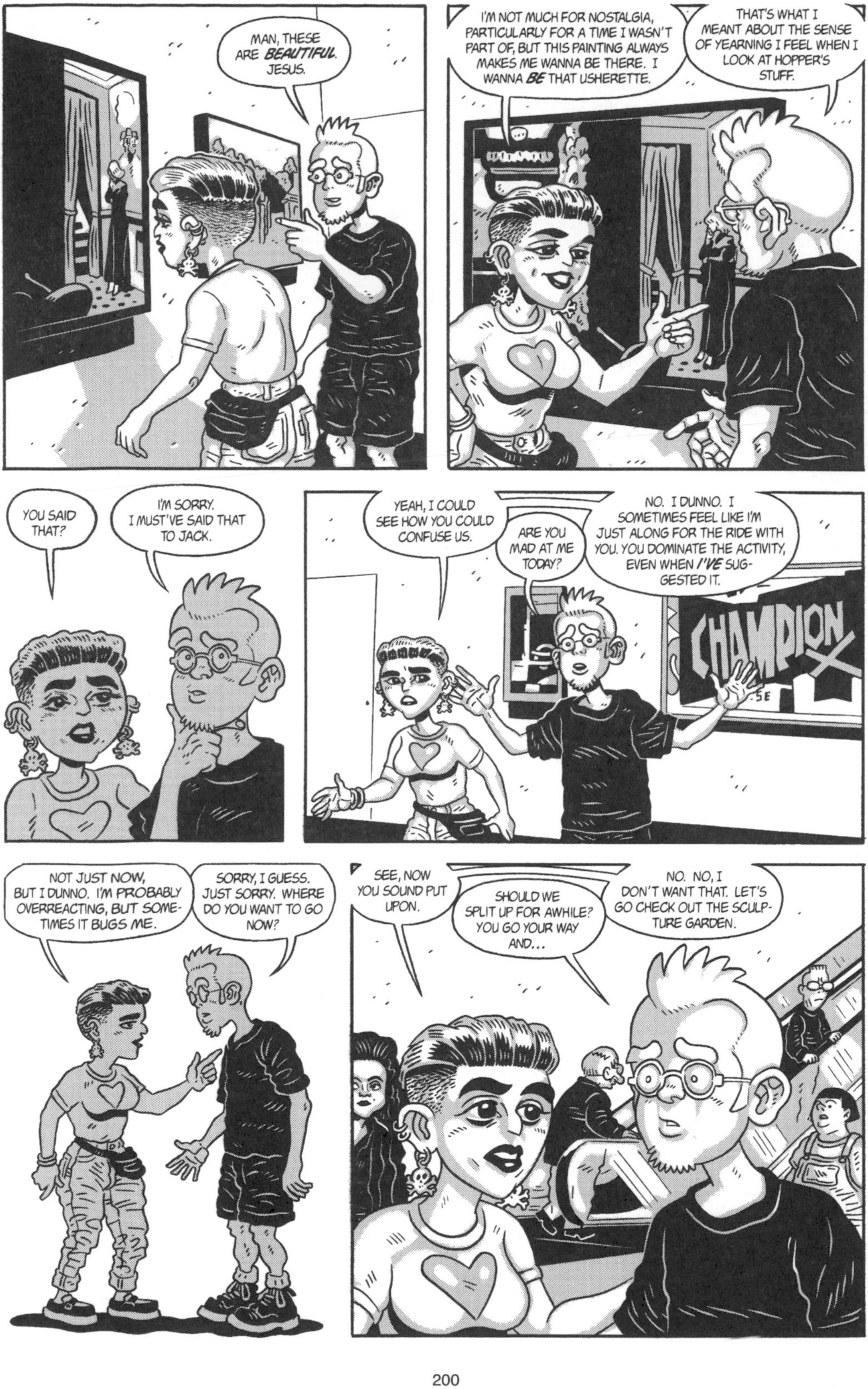
MAN, THESE ARE BEAUTIFUL. JESUS.
I'M NOT MUCH FOR NOSTALGIA, PARTICULARLY FOR A TIME I WASN'T PART OF, BUT THIS PAINTING ALWAYS MAKES ME WANNA BE THERE. I WANNA BE THAT USHERETTE.
THAT'S WHAT I MEANT ABOUT THE SENSE OF YEARNING I FEEL WHEN I LOOK AT HOPPER'S STUFF.
YOU SAID THAT?
I'M SORRY. I MUST'VE SAID THAT TO JACK.
YEAH, I COULD SEE HOW YOU COULD CONFUSE US.
ARE YOU MAD AT ME TODAY?
NO. I DUNNO. I SOMETIMES FEEL LIKE I'M JUST ALONG FOR THE RIDE WITH YOU. YOU DOMINATE THE ACTIVITY, EVEN WHEN I'VE SUGGESTED IT.
CHAMPION
NOT JUST NOW, BUT I DUNNO. I'M PROBABLY OVERREACTING, BUT SOMETIMES IT BUGS ME.
SORRY, I GUESS. JUST SORRY. WHERE DO YOU WANT TO GO NOW?
SEE, NOW YOU SOUND PUT UPON.
SHOULD WE SPLIT UP FOR AWHILE? YOU GO YOUR WAY AND...
NO. NO, I DON'T WANT THAT. LET'S GO CHECK OUT THE SCULPTURE GARDEN.

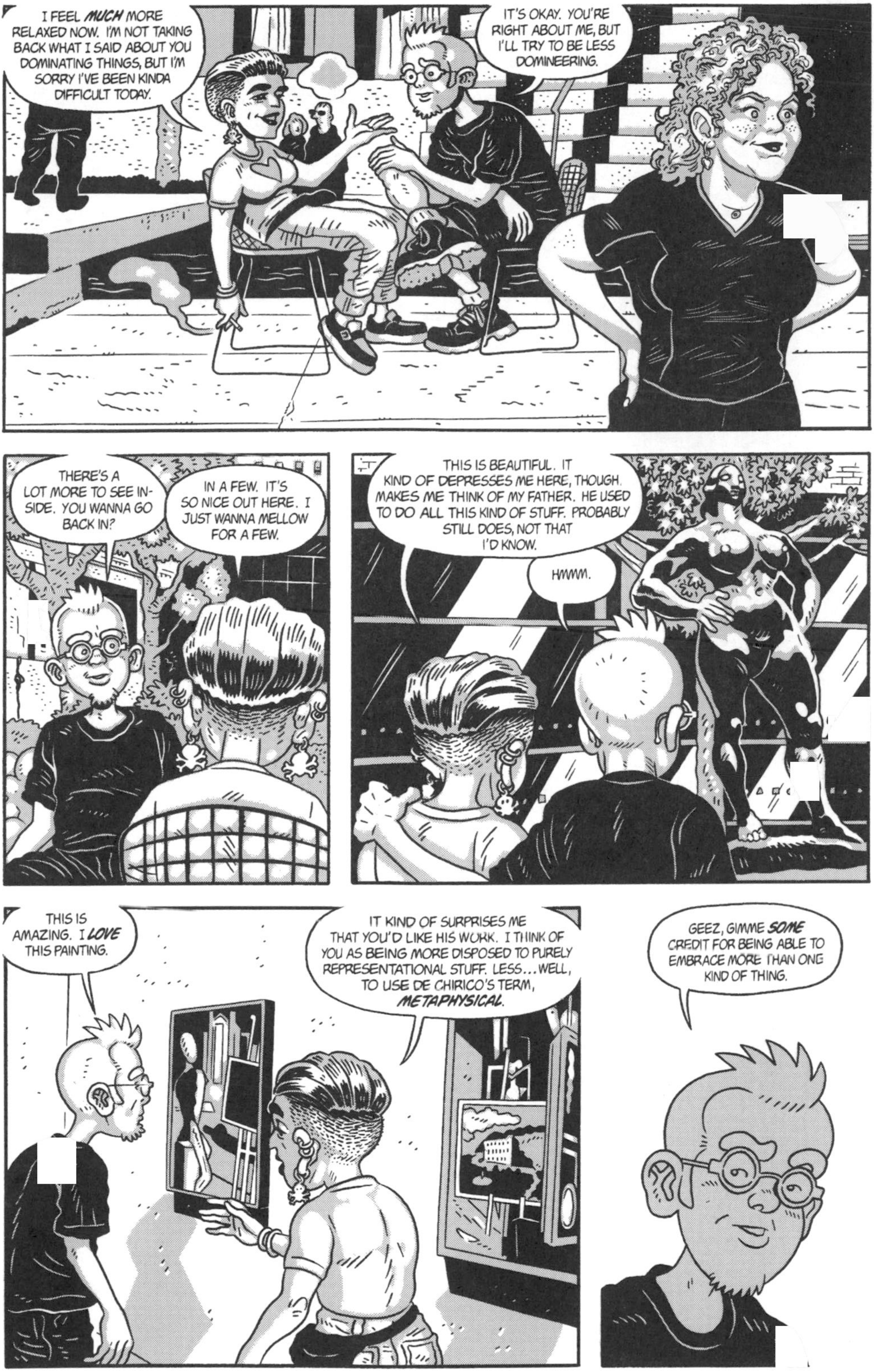
I FEEL MUCH MORE RELAXED NOW. I'M NOT TAKING BACK WHAT I SAID ABOUT YOU DOMINATING THINGS, BUT I'M SORRY I'VE BEEN KINDA DIFFICULT TODAY.
IT'S OKAY. YOU'RE RIGHT ABOUT ME, BUT I'LL TRY TO BE LESS DOMINEERING.
THERE'S A LOT MORE TO SEE INSIDE. YOU WANNA GO BACK IN?
IN A FEW. IT'S SO NICE OUT HERE. I JUST WANNA MELLOW FOR A FEW.
THIS IS BEAUTIFUL. IT KIND OF DEPRESSES ME HERE, THOUGH. MAKES ME THINK OF MY FATHER. HE USED TO DO ALL THIS KIND OF STUFF. PROBABLY STILL DOES, NOT THAT I'D KNOW.
HMMM.
THIS IS AMAZING. I LOVE THIS PAINTING.
IT KIND OF SURPRISES ME THAT YOU'D LIKE HIS WORK. I THINK OF YOU AS BEING MORE DISPOSED TO PURELY REPRESENTATIONAL STUFF. LESS... WELL, TO USE DE CHIRICO'S TERM, METAPHYSICAL.
GEEZ, GIMME SOME CREDIT FOR BEING ABLE TO EMBRACE MORE THAN ONE KIND OF THING.

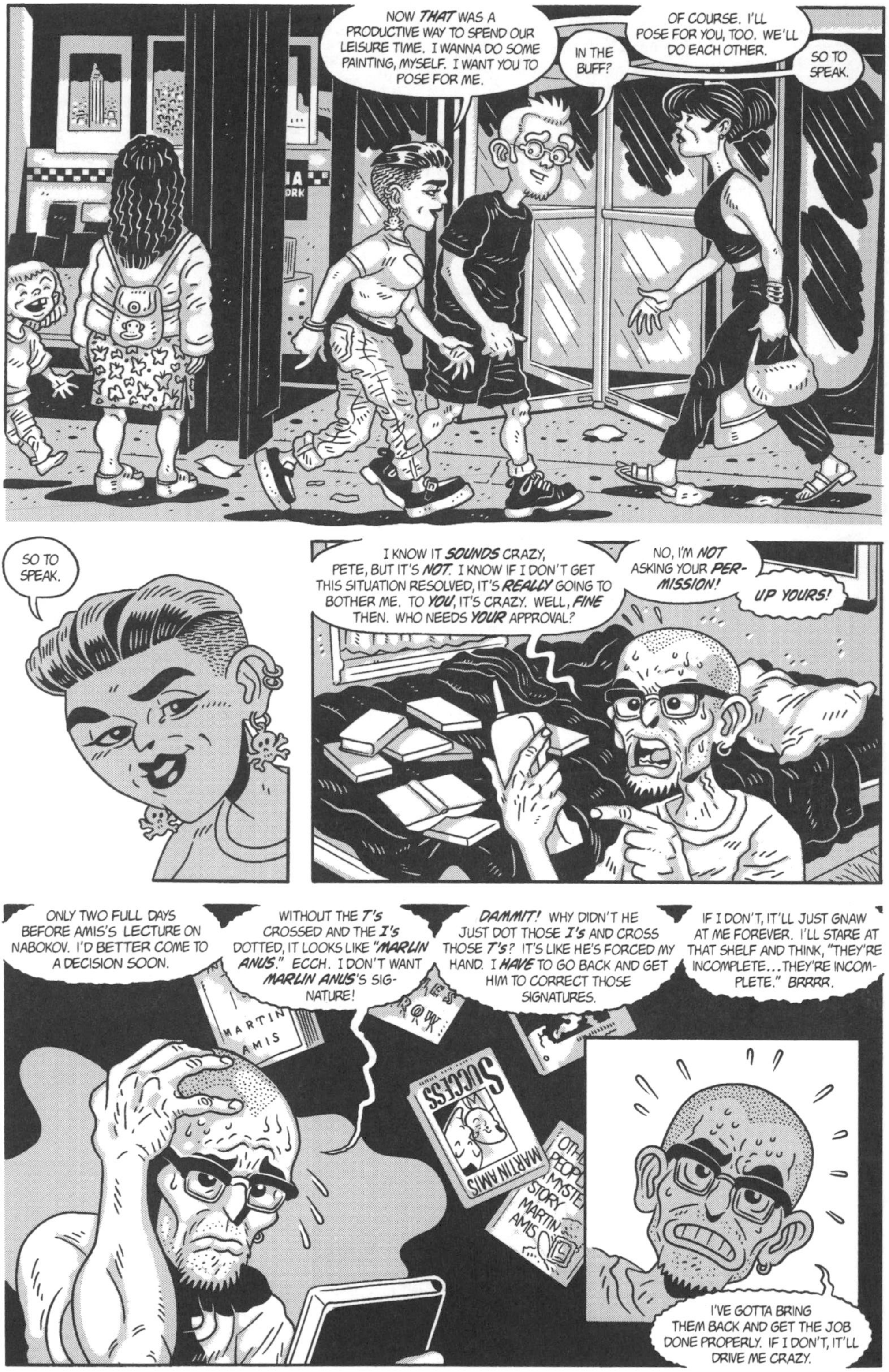
NOW *THAT* WAS A PRODUCTIVE WAY TO SPEND OUR LEISURE TIME. I WANNA DO SOME PAINTING, MYSELF. I WANT YOU TO POSE FOR ME.
IN THE BUFF?
OF COURSE. I'LL POSE FOR YOU, TOO. WE'LL DO EACH OTHER.
SO TO SPEAK.
SO TO SPEAK.
I KNOW IT *SOUNDS* CRAZY, PETE, BUT IT'S *NOT*. I KNOW IF I DON'T GET THIS SITUATION RESOLVED, IT'S *REALLY* GOING TO BOTHER ME. TO *YOU*, IT'S CRAZY. WELL, *FINE* THEN. WHO NEEDS *YOUR* APPROVAL?
NO, I'M *NOT* ASKING YOUR *PERMISSION!*
*UP YOURS!*
ONLY TWO FULL DAYS BEFORE AMIS'S LECTURE ON NABOKOV. I'D BETTER COME TO A DECISION SOON.
WITHOUT THE *T's* CROSSED AND THE *I's* DOTTED, IT LOOKS LIKE *"MARLIN ANUS."* ECCH. I DON'T WANT *MARLIN ANUS*'S SIGNATURE!
*DAMMIT!* WHY DIDN'T HE JUST DOT THOSE *I's* AND CROSS THOSE *T's*? IT'S LIKE HE'S FORCED MY HAND. I *HAVE* TO GO BACK AND GET HIM TO CORRECT THOSE SIGNATURES.
IF I DON'T, IT'LL JUST GNAW AT ME FOREVER. I'LL STARE AT THAT SHELF AND THINK, "THEY'RE INCOMPLETE... THEY'RE INCOMPLETE." *BRRRR.*
MARTIN AMIS
SUCCESS
MARTIN AMIS
STORY
MARTIN AMIS
I'VE GOTTA BRING THEM BACK AND GET THE JOB DONE PROPERLY. IF I DON'T, IT'LL DRIVE ME CRAZY.

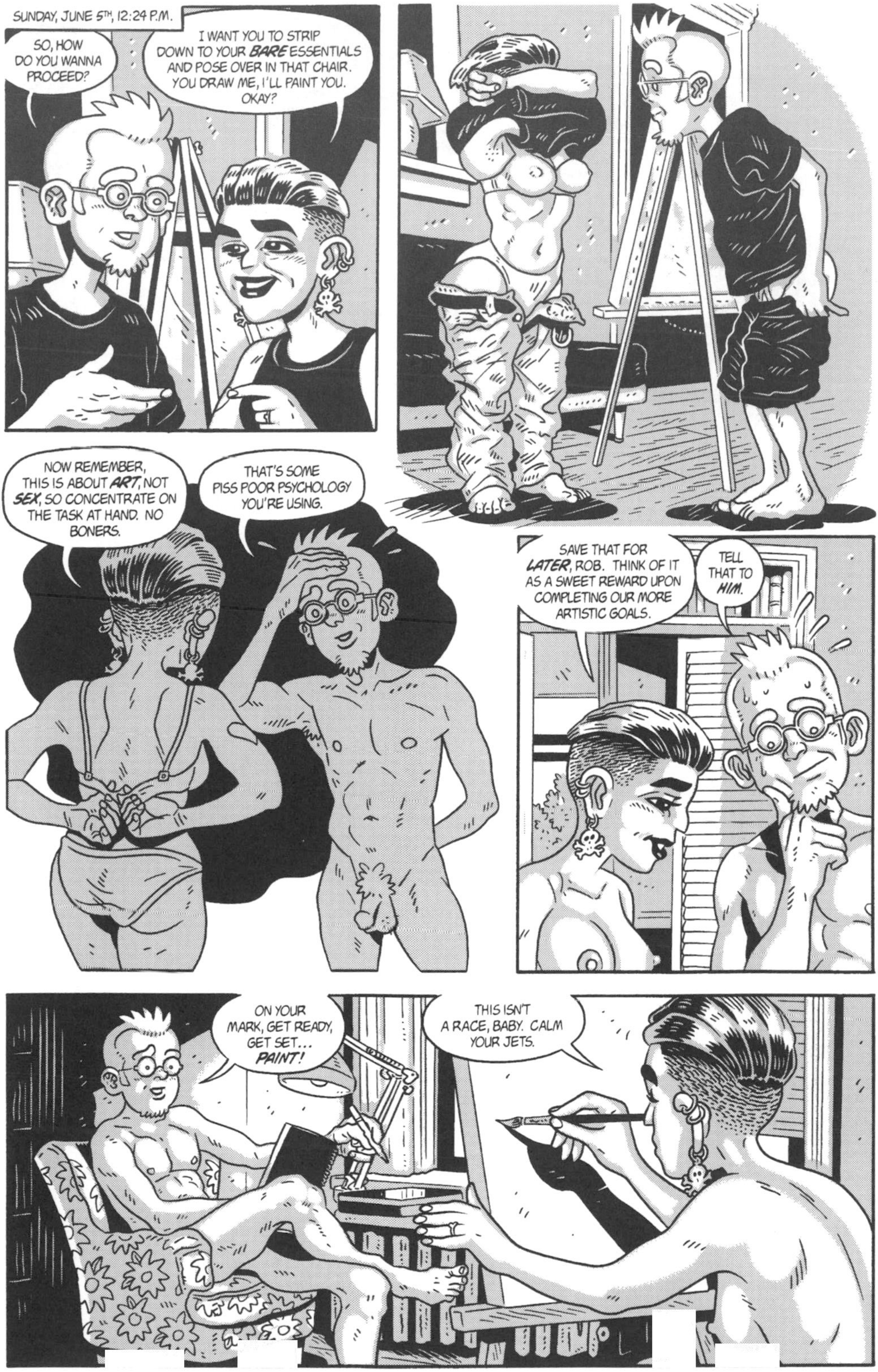

SUNDAY, JUNE 5TH, 12:24 P.M.
SO, HOW DO YOU WANNA PROCEED?
I WANT YOU TO STRIP DOWN TO YOUR BARE ESSENTIALS AND POSE OVER IN THAT CHAIR. YOU DRAW ME, I'LL PAINT YOU. OKAY?
NOW REMEMBER, THIS IS ABOUT ART, NOT SEX, SO CONCENTRATE ON THE TASK AT HAND. NO BONERS.
THAT'S SOME PISS POOR PSYCHOLOGY YOU'RE USING.
SAVE THAT FOR LATER, ROB. THINK OF IT AS A SWEET REWARD UPON COMPLETING OUR MORE ARTISTIC GOALS.
TELL THAT TO HIM.
ON YOUR MARK, GET READY, GET SET... PAINT!
THIS ISN'T A RACE, BABY. CALM YOUR JETS.

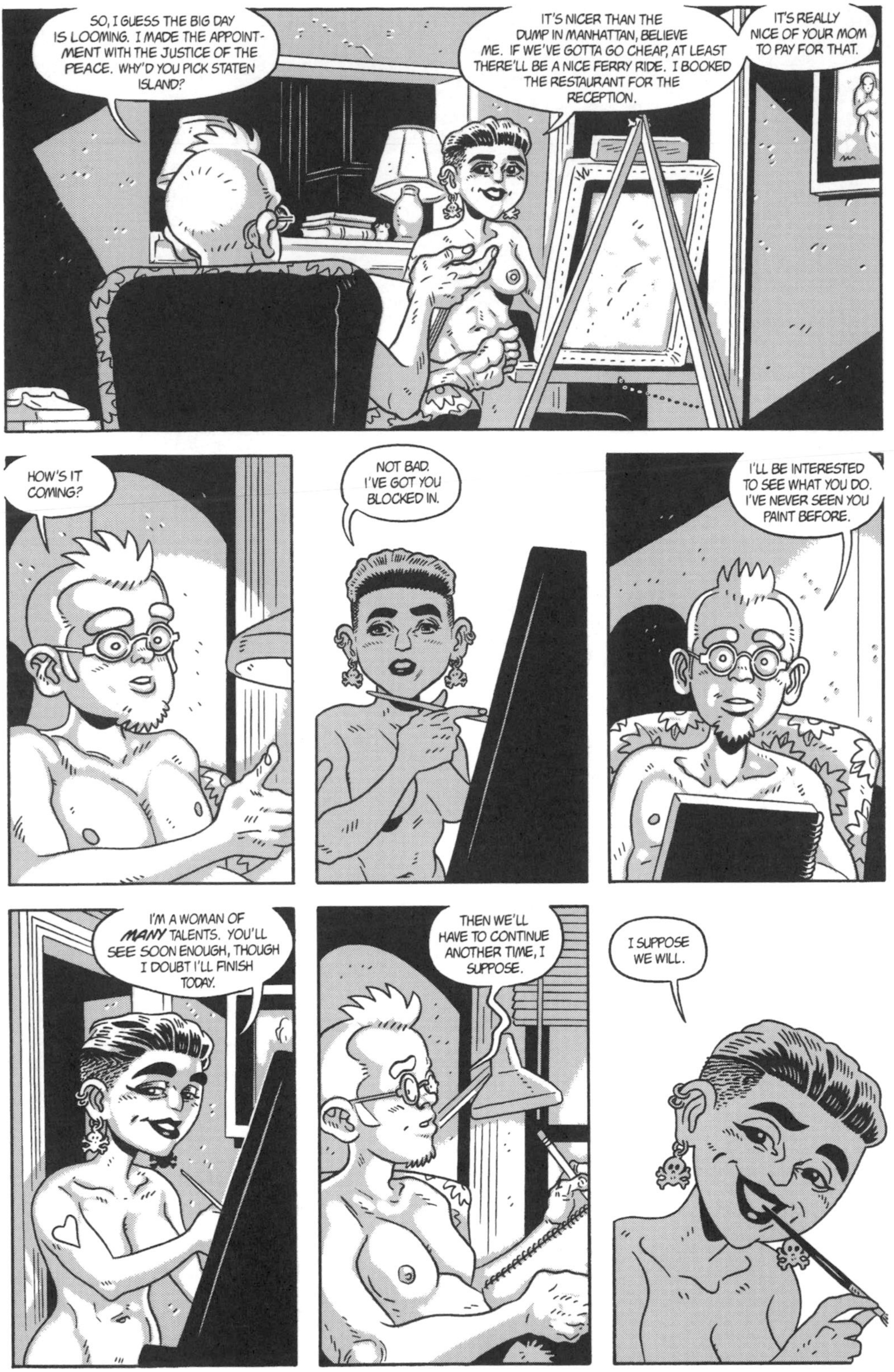
SO, I GUESS THE BIG DAY IS LOOMING. I MADE THE APPOINTMENT WITH THE JUSTICE OF THE PEACE. WHY'D YOU PICK STATEN ISLAND?
IT'S NICER THAN THE DUMP IN MANHATTAN, BELIEVE ME. IF WE'VE GOTTA GO CHEAP, AT LEAST THERE'LL BE A NICE FERRY RIDE. I BOOKED THE RESTAURANT FOR THE RECEPTION.
IT'S REALLY NICE OF YOUR MOM TO PAY FOR THAT.
HOW'S IT COMING?
NOT BAD. I'VE GOT YOU BLOCKED IN.
I'LL BE INTERESTED TO SEE WHAT YOU DO. I'VE NEVER SEEN YOU PAINT BEFORE.
I'M A WOMAN OF *MANY* TALENTS. YOU'LL SEE SOON ENOUGH, THOUGH I DOUBT I'LL FINISH TODAY.
THEN WE'LL HAVE TO CONTINUE ANOTHER TIME, I SUPPOSE.
I SUPPOSE WE WILL.

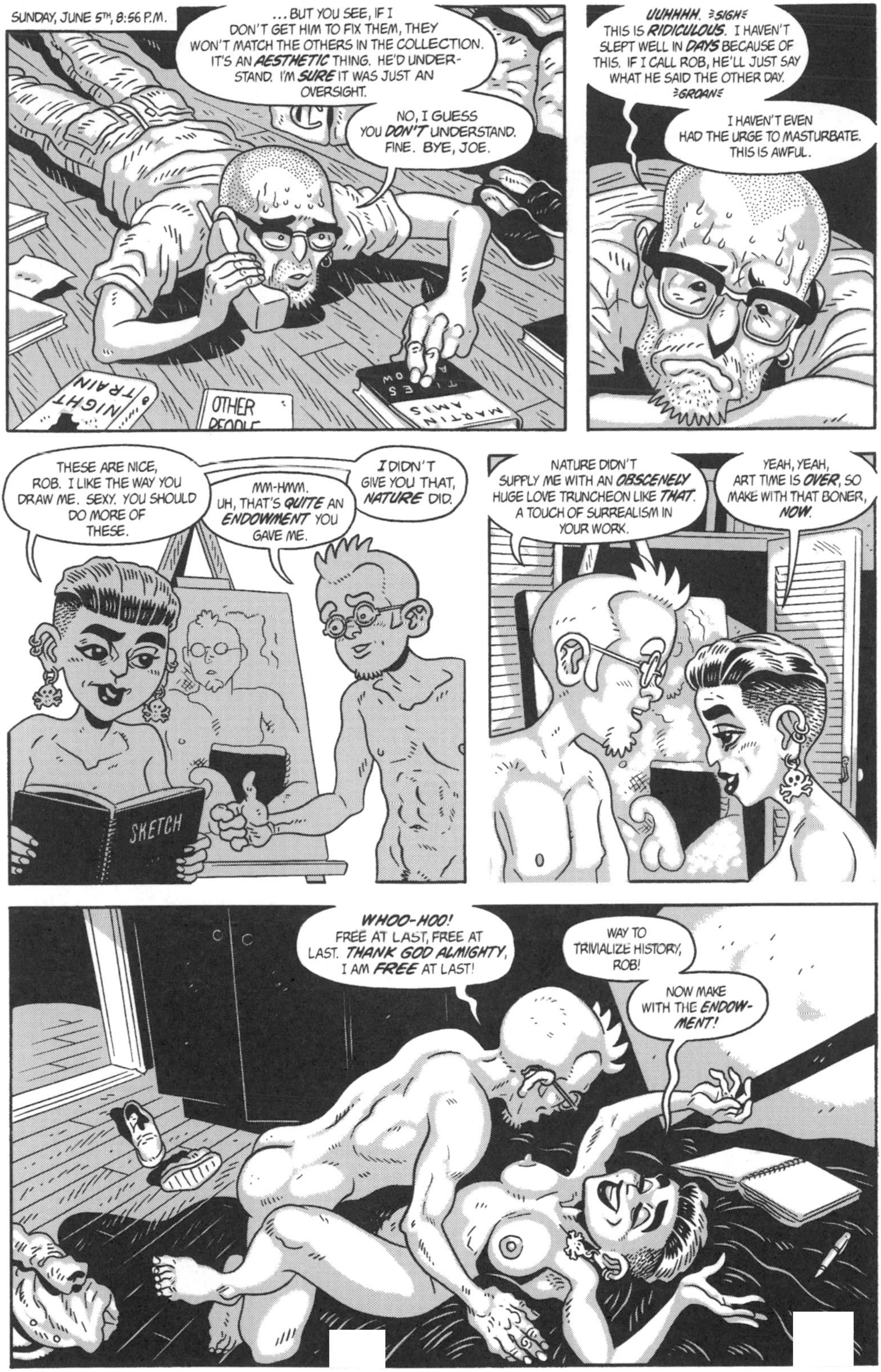
SUNDAY, JUNE 5TH, 8:56 P.M.
...BUT YOU SEE, IF I DON'T GET HIM TO FIX THEM, THEY WON'T MATCH THE OTHERS IN THE COLLECTION. IT'S AN AESTHETIC THING. HE'D UNDERSTAND. I'M SURE IT WAS JUST AN OVERSIGHT.
NO, I GUESS YOU DON'T UNDERSTAND. FINE. BYE, JOE.
NIGHT TRAIN
OTHER
MARTIN AMIS
UUHHHH. SIGH THIS IS RIDICULOUS. I HAVEN'T SLEPT WELL IN DAYS BECAUSE OF THIS. IF I CALL ROB, HE'LL JUST SAY WHAT HE SAID THE OTHER DAY. GROAN
I HAVEN'T EVEN HAD THE URGE TO MASTURBATE. THIS IS AWFUL.
THESE ARE NICE, ROB. I LIKE THE WAY YOU DRAW ME. SEXY. YOU SHOULD DO MORE OF THESE.
MM-HMM. UH, THAT'S QUITE AN ENDOWMENT YOU GAVE ME.
I DIDN'T GIVE YOU THAT, NATURE DID.
SKETCH
NATURE DIDN'T SUPPLY ME WITH AN OBSCENELY HUGE LOVE TRUNCHEON LIKE THAT. A TOUCH OF SURREALISM IN YOUR WORK.
YEAH, YEAH, ART TIME IS OVER, SO MAKE WITH THAT BONER, NOW.
WHOO-HOO! FREE AT LAST, FREE AT LAST. THANK GOD ALMIGHTY, I AM FREE AT LAST!
WAY TO TRIVIALIZE HISTORY, ROB!
NOW MAKE WITH THE ENDOWMENT!

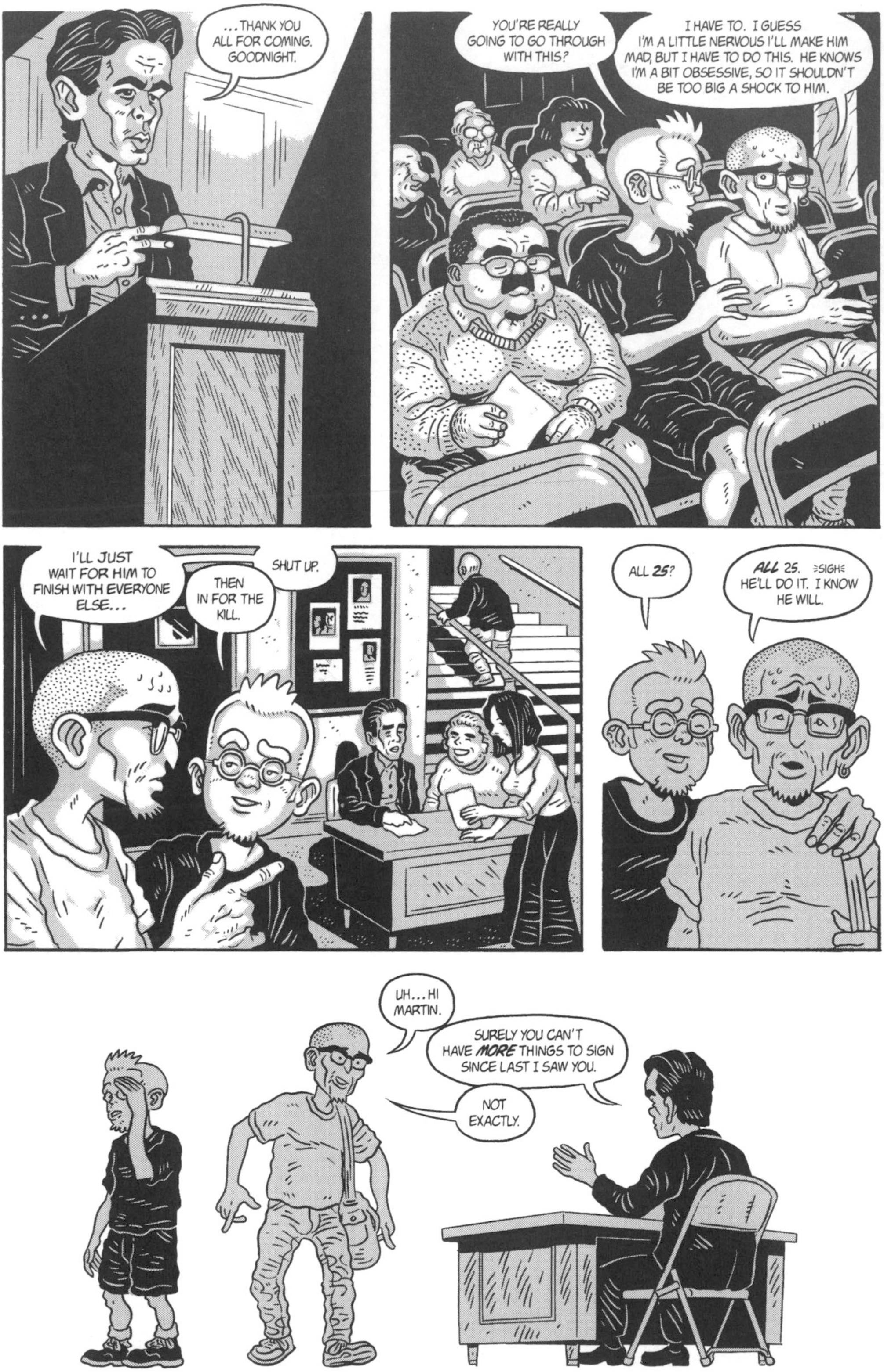
...THANK YOU ALL FOR COMING. GOODNIGHT.
YOU'RE REALLY GOING TO GO THROUGH WITH THIS?
I HAVE TO. I GUESS I'M A LITTLE NERVOUS I'LL MAKE HIM MAD, BUT I HAVE TO DO THIS. HE KNOWS I'M A BIT OBSESSIVE, SO IT SHOULDN'T BE TOO BIG A SHOCK TO HIM.
I'LL JUST WAIT FOR HIM TO FINISH WITH EVERYONE ELSE...
THEN IN FOR THE KILL.
SHUT UP.
ALL 25?
ALL 25. SIGH HE'LL DO IT. I KNOW HE WILL.
UH...HI MARTIN.
SURELY YOU CAN'T HAVE MORE THINGS TO SIGN SINCE LAST I SAW YOU.
NOT EXACTLY.

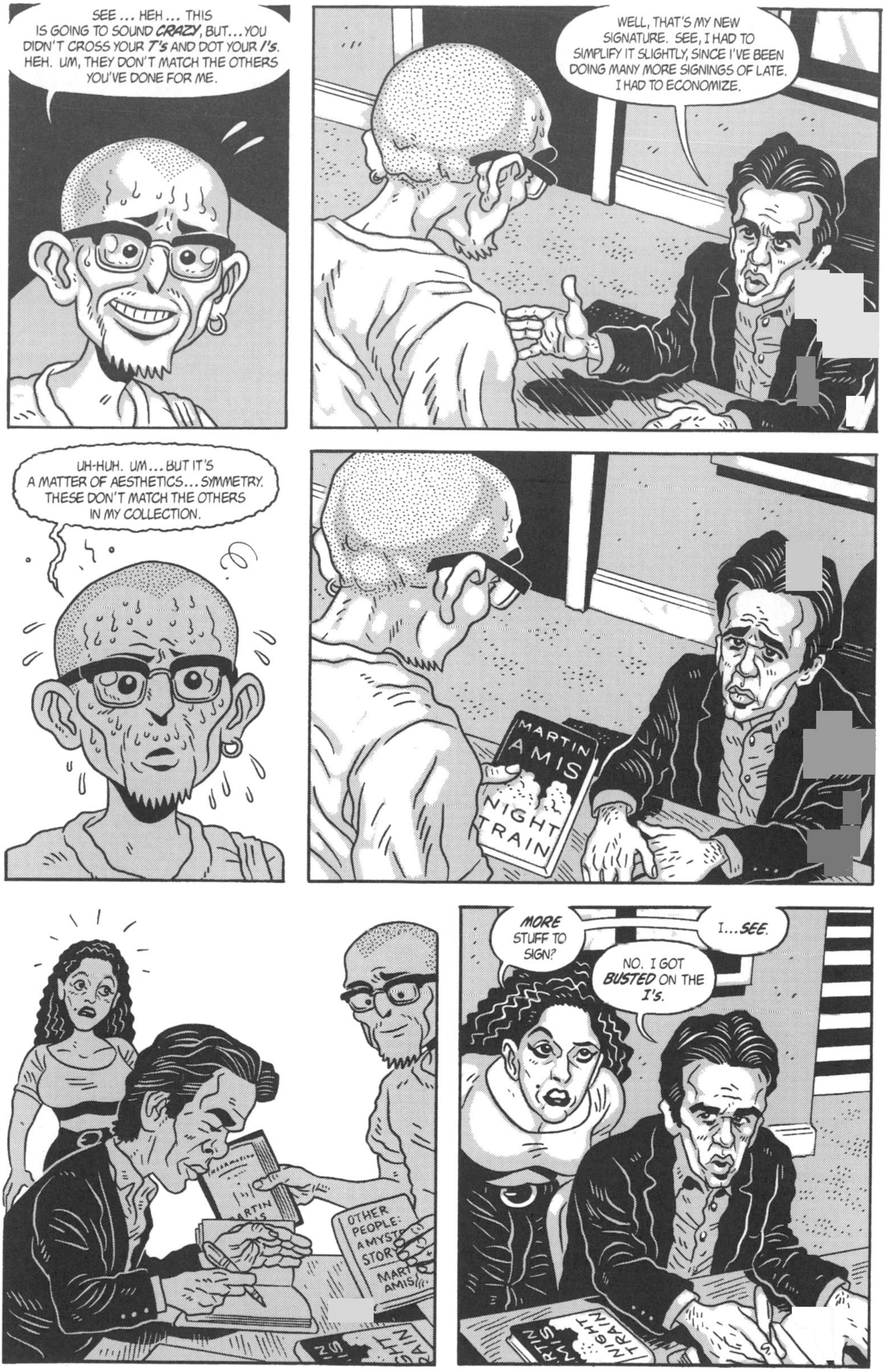
SEE ... HEH ... THIS IS GOING TO SOUND CRAZY, BUT... YOU DIDN'T CROSS YOUR T's AND DOT YOUR I's. HEH. UM, THEY DON'T MATCH THE OTHERS YOU'VE DONE FOR ME.
WELL, THAT'S MY NEW SIGNATURE. SEE, I HAD TO SIMPLIFY IT SLIGHTLY, SINCE I'VE BEEN DOING MANY MORE SIGNINGS OF LATE. I HAD TO ECONOMIZE.
UH-HUH. UM... BUT IT'S A MATTER OF AESTHETICS... SYMMETRY. THESE DON'T MATCH THE OTHERS IN MY COLLECTION.
MARTIN AMIS
NIGHT TRAIN
OTHER PEOPLE: A MYSTE STORY
MARTI AMIS
MORE STUFF TO SIGN?
I... SEE.
NO. I GOT BUSTED ON THE I's.

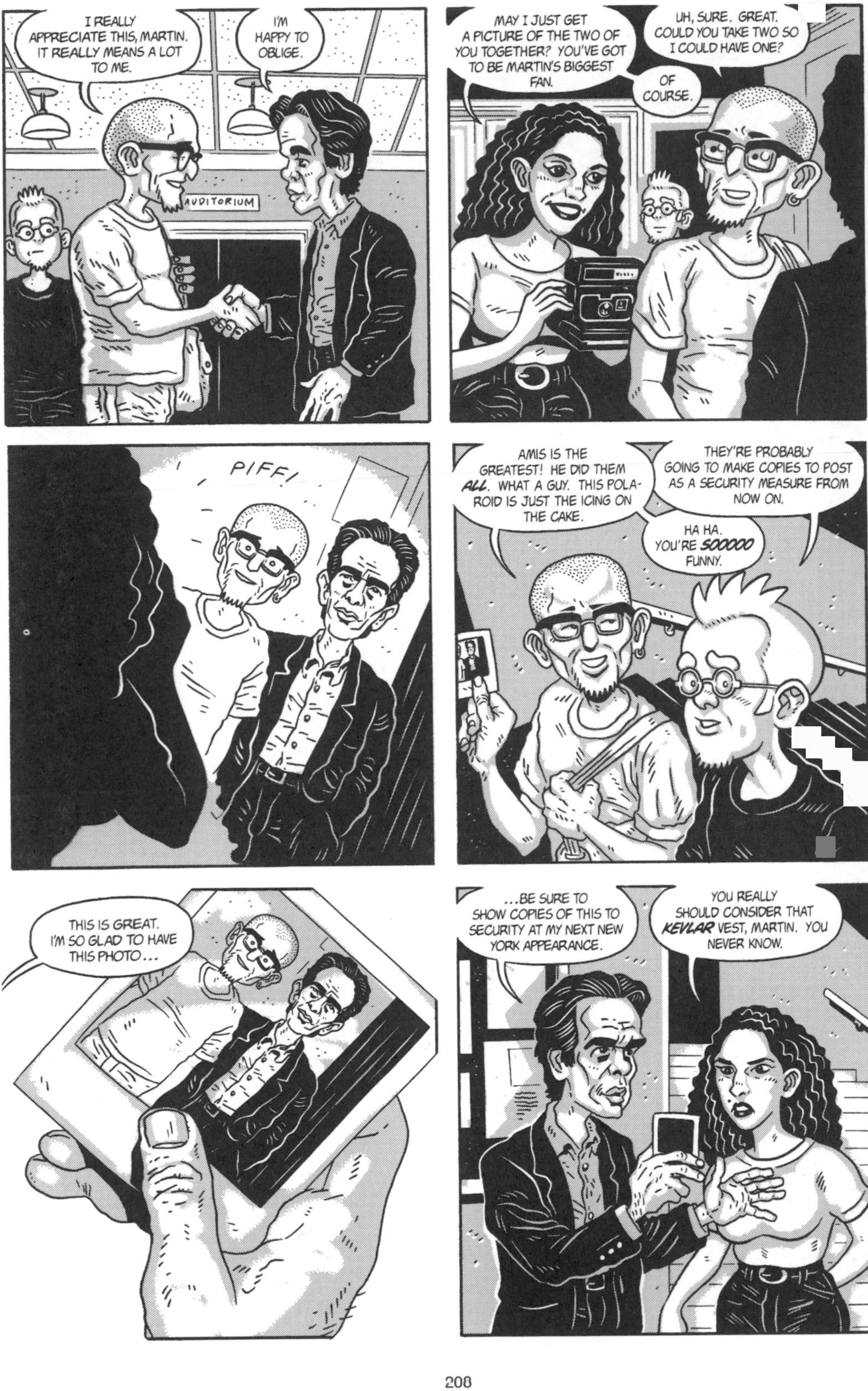
I REALLY APPRECIATE THIS, MARTIN. IT REALLY MEANS A LOT TO ME.
I'M HAPPY TO OBLIGE.
AUDITORIUM
MAY I JUST GET A PICTURE OF THE TWO OF YOU TOGETHER? YOU'VE GOT TO BE MARTIN'S BIGGEST FAN.
UH, SURE. GREAT. COULD YOU TAKE TWO SO I COULD HAVE ONE?
OF COURSE.
PIFF!
AMIS IS THE GREATEST! HE DID THEM ALL. WHAT A GUY. THIS POLAROID IS JUST THE ICING ON THE CAKE.
THEY'RE PROBABLY GOING TO MAKE COPIES TO POST AS A SECURITY MEASURE FROM NOW ON.
HA HA. YOU'RE SOOOOO FUNNY.
THIS IS GREAT. I'M SO GLAD TO HAVE THIS PHOTO...
...BE SURE TO SHOW COPIES OF THIS TO SECURITY AT MY NEXT NEW YORK APPEARANCE.
YOU REALLY SHOULD CONSIDER THAT KEVLAR VEST, MARTIN. YOU NEVER KNOW.

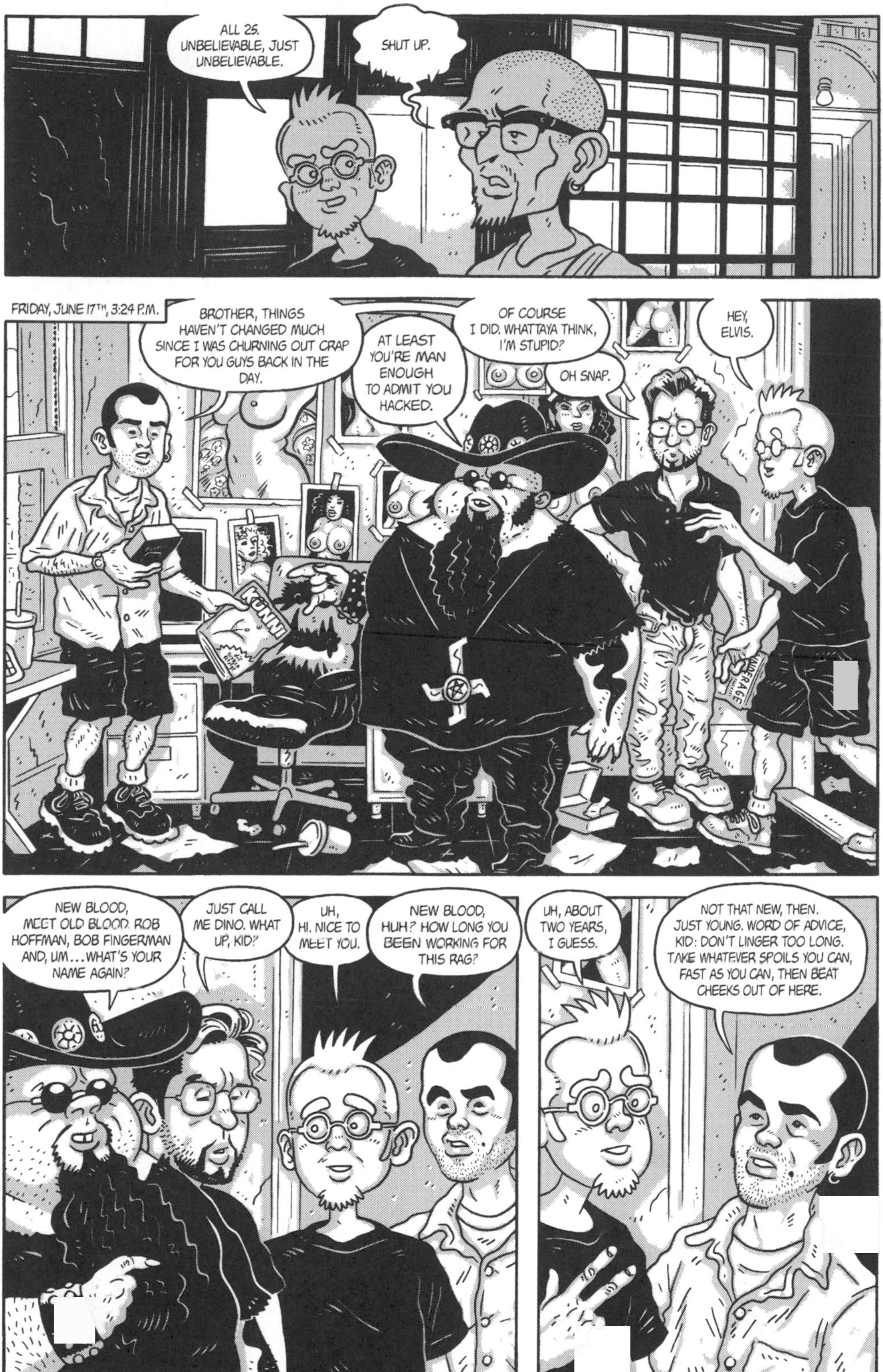
ALL 25. UNBELIEVABLE, JUST UNBELIEVABLE.
SHUT UP.
FRIDAY, JUNE 17TH, 3:24 P.M.
BROTHER, THINGS HAVEN'T CHANGED MUCH SINCE I WAS CHURNING OUT CRAP FOR YOU GUYS BACK IN THE DAY.
AT LEAST YOU'RE MAN ENOUGH TO ADMIT YOU HACKED.
OF COURSE I DID. WHATTAYA THINK, I'M STUPID?
OH SNAP.
HEY, ELVIS.
NEW BLOOD, MEET OLD BLOOD. ROB HOFFMAN, BOB FINGERMAN AND, UM...WHAT'S YOUR NAME AGAIN?
JUST CALL ME DINO. WHAT UP, KID?
UH, HI. NICE TO MEET YOU.
NEW BLOOD, HUH? HOW LONG YOU BEEN WORKING FOR THIS RAG?
UH, ABOUT TWO YEARS, I GUESS.
NOT THAT NEW, THEN. JUST YOUNG. WORD OF ADVICE, KID: DON'T LINGER TOO LONG. TAKE WHATEVER SPOILS YOU CAN, FAST AS YOU CAN, THEN BEAT CHEEKS OUT OF HERE.

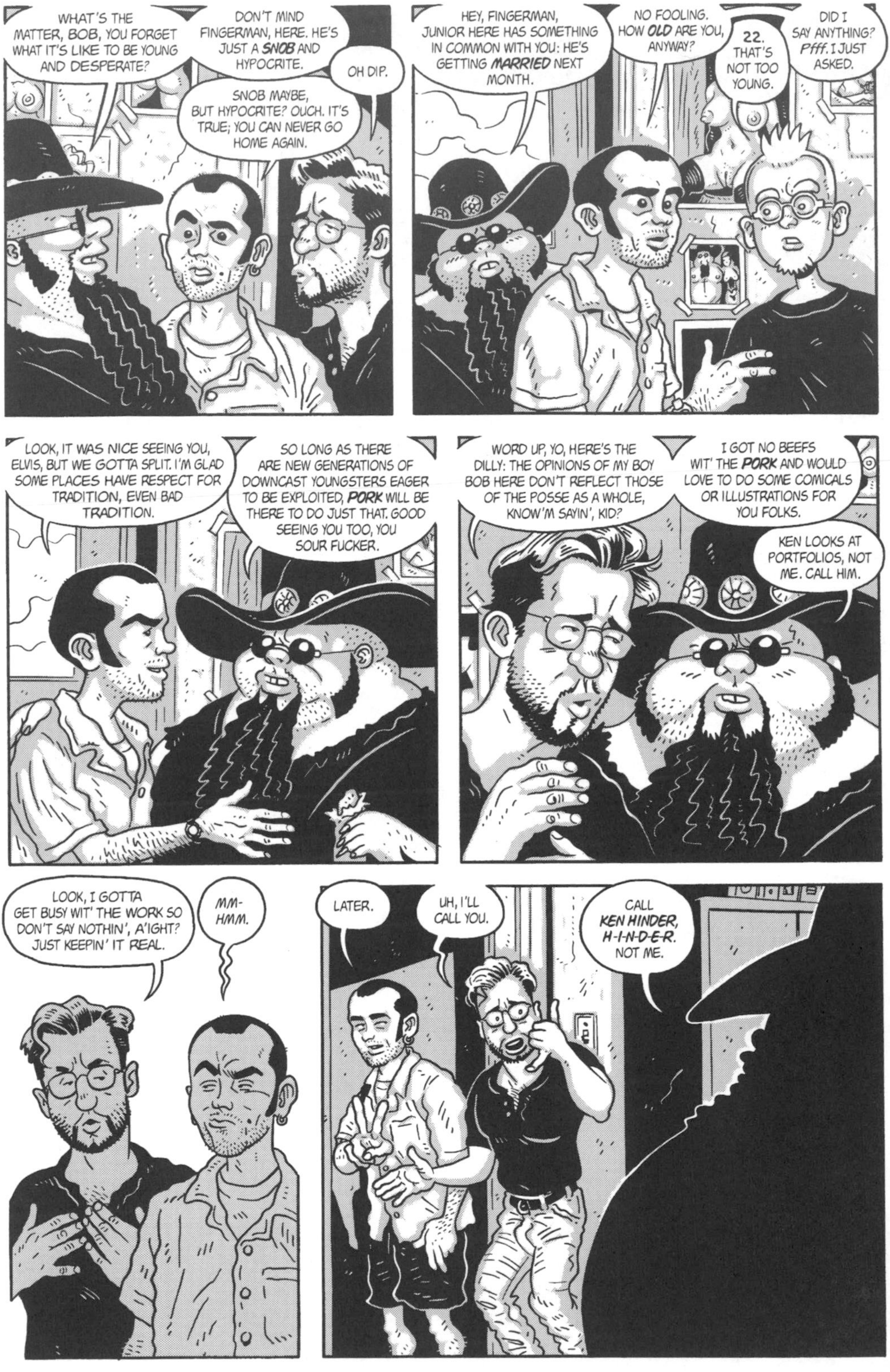

WHAT'S THE MATTER, BOB, YOU FORGET WHAT IT'S LIKE TO BE YOUNG AND DESPERATE?
DON'T MIND FINGERMAN, HERE. HE'S JUST A SNOB AND HYPOCRITE.
OH DIP.
SNOB MAYBE, BUT HYPOCRITE? OUCH. IT'S TRUE; YOU CAN NEVER GO HOME AGAIN.
HEY, FINGERMAN, JUNIOR HERE HAS SOMETHING IN COMMON WITH YOU: HE'S GETTING MARRIED NEXT MONTH.
NO FOOLING. HOW OLD ARE YOU, ANYWAY?
22. THAT'S NOT TOO YOUNG.
DID I SAY ANYTHING? Pfff. I JUST ASKED.
LOOK, IT WAS NICE SEEING YOU, ELVIS, BUT WE GOTTA SPLIT. I'M GLAD SOME PLACES HAVE RESPECT FOR TRADITION, EVEN BAD TRADITION.
SO LONG AS THERE ARE NEW GENERATIONS OF DOWNCAST YOUNGSTERS EAGER TO BE EXPLOITED, PORK WILL BE THERE TO DO JUST THAT. GOOD SEEING YOU TOO, YOU SOUR FUCKER.
WORD UP, YO, HERE'S THE DILLY: THE OPINIONS OF MY BOY BOB HERE DON'T REFLECT THOSE OF THE POSSE AS A WHOLE, KNOW'M SAYIN', KID?
I GOT NO BEEFS WIT' THE PORK AND WOULD LOVE TO DO SOME COMICALS OR ILLUSTRATIONS FOR YOU FOLKS.
KEN LOOKS AT PORTFOLIOS, NOT ME. CALL HIM.
LOOK, I GOTTA GET BUSY WIT' THE WORK SO DON'T SAY NOTHIN', A'IGHT? JUST KEEPIN' IT REAL.
MM-HMM.
LATER.
UH, I'LL CALL YOU.
CALL KEN HINDER, H-I-N-D-E-R. NOT ME.

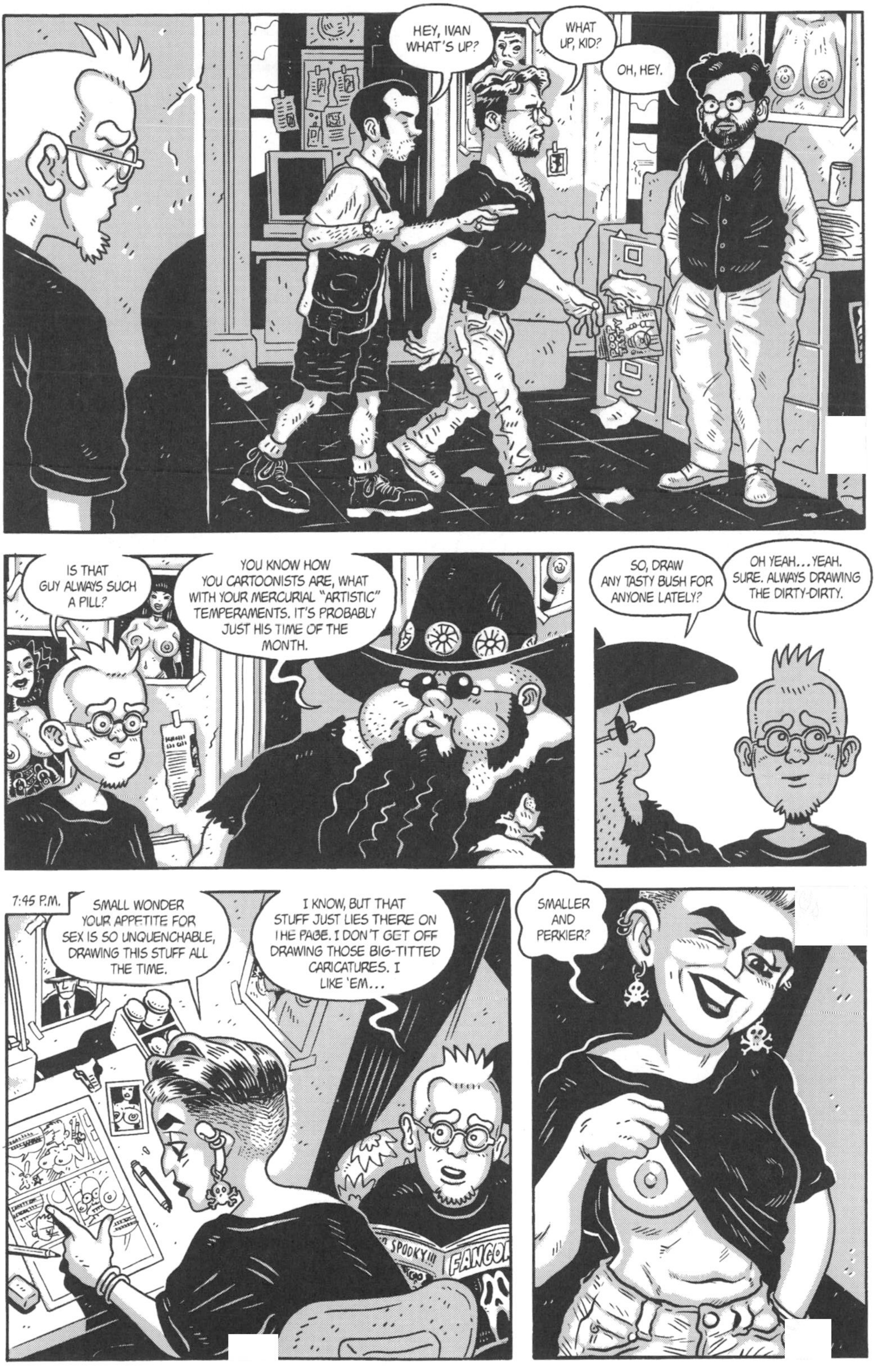
HEY, IVAN WHAT'S UP?
WHAT UP, KID?
OH, HEY.
IS THAT GUY ALWAYS SUCH A PILL?
YOU KNOW HOW YOU CARTOONISTS ARE, WHAT WITH YOUR MERCURIAL "ARTISTIC" TEMPERAMENTS. IT'S PROBABLY JUST HIS TIME OF THE MONTH.
SO, DRAW ANY TASTY BUSH FOR ANYONE LATELY?
OH YEAH... YEAH. SURE. ALWAYS DRAWING THE DIRTY-DIRTY.
7:45 P.M.
SMALL WONDER YOUR APPETITE FOR SEX IS SO UNQUENCHABLE, DRAWING THIS STUFF ALL THE TIME.
I KNOW, BUT THAT STUFF JUST LIES THERE ON THE PAGE. I DON'T GET OFF DRAWING THOSE BIG-TITTED CARICATURES. I LIKE 'EM...
SMALLER AND PERKIER?

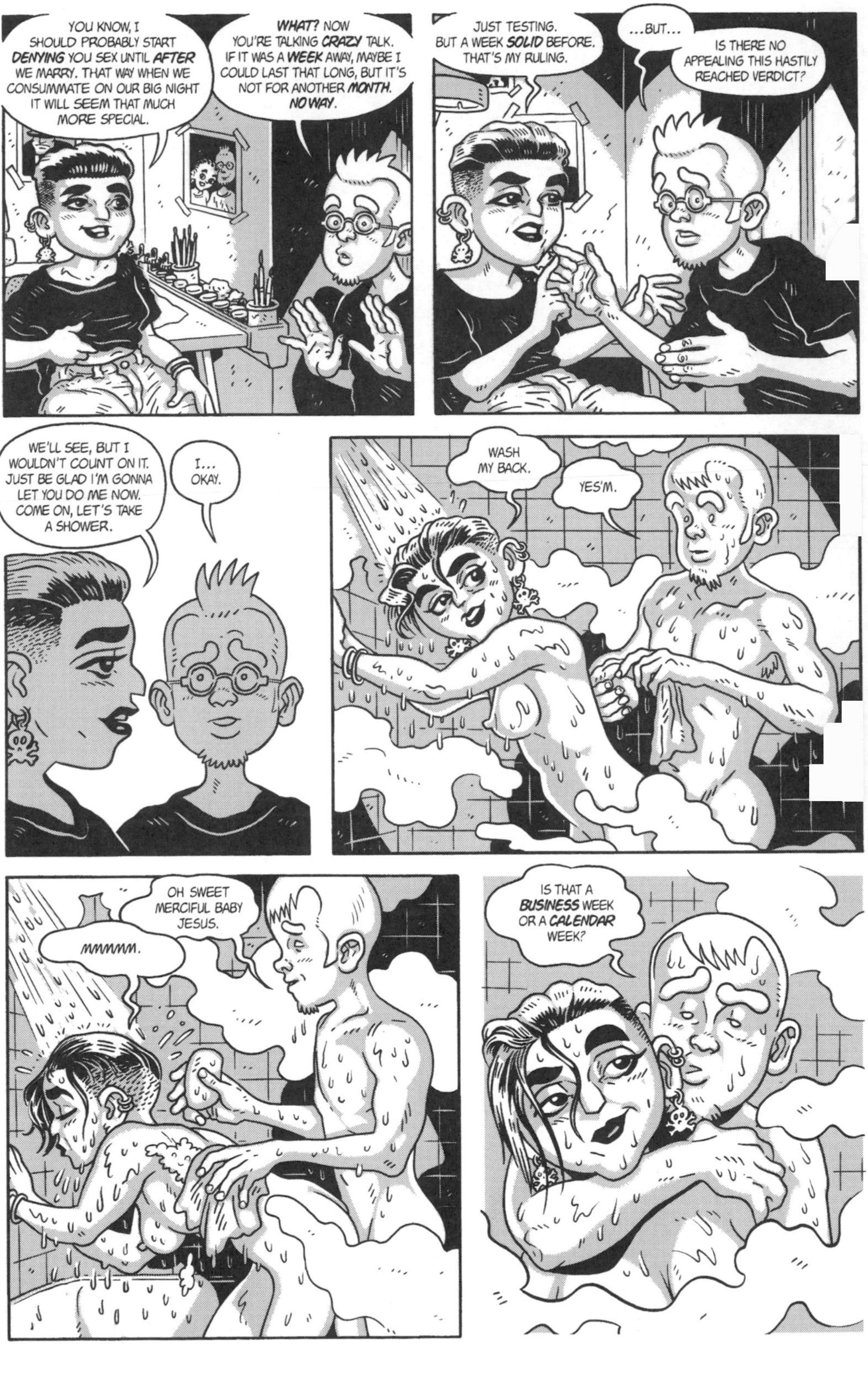
YOU KNOW, I SHOULD PROBABLY START DENYING YOU SEX UNTIL AFTER WE MARRY. THAT WAY WHEN WE CONSUMMATE ON OUR BIG NIGHT IT WILL SEEM THAT MUCH MORE SPECIAL.
WHAT? NOW YOU'RE TALKING CRAZY TALK. IF IT WAS A WEEK AWAY, MAYBE I COULD LAST THAT LONG, BUT IT'S NOT FOR ANOTHER MONTH. NO WAY.
JUST TESTING. BUT A WEEK SOLID BEFORE. THAT'S MY RULING.
...BUT...
IS THERE NO APPEALING THIS HASTILY REACHED VERDICT?
WE'LL SEE, BUT I WOULDN'T COUNT ON IT. JUST BE GLAD I'M GONNA LET YOU DO ME NOW. COME ON, LET'S TAKE A SHOWER.
I... OKAY.
WASH MY BACK.
YES'M.
MMMMM.
OH SWEET MERCIFUL BABY JESUS.
IS THAT A BUSINESS WEEK OR A CALENDAR WEEK?

# CHAPTER 10

# WEDLOCKED & LOADED

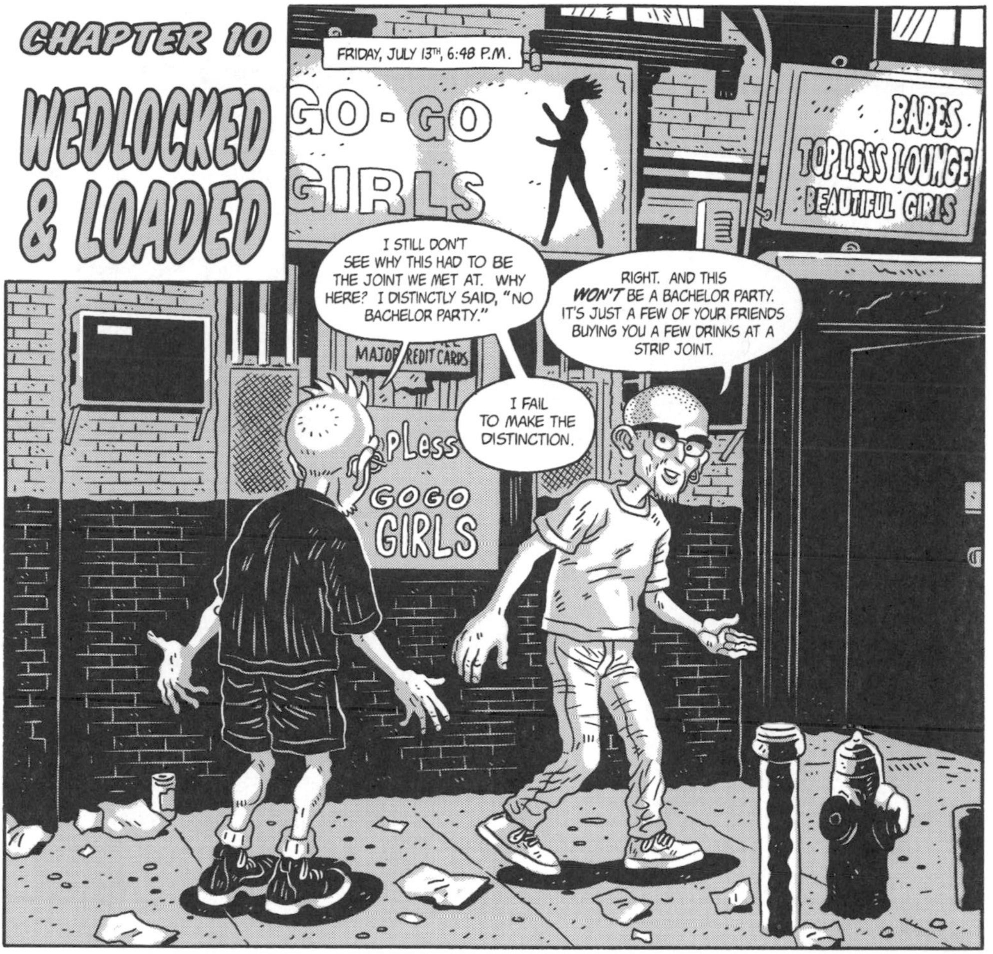
FRIDAY, JULY 13TH, 6:48 P.M.
GO-GO GIRLS
BABES TOPLESS LOUNGE BEAUTIFUL GIRLS
I STILL DON'T SEE WHY THIS HAD TO BE THE JOINT WE MET AT. WHY HERE? I DISTINCTLY SAID, "NO BACHELOR PARTY."
RIGHT. AND THIS *WON'T* BE A BACHELOR PARTY. IT'S JUST A FEW OF YOUR FRIENDS BUYING YOU A FEW DRINKS AT A STRIP JOINT.
MAJOR REDIT CARDS
I FAIL TO MAKE THE DISTINCTION.
pLess
GOGO GIRLS

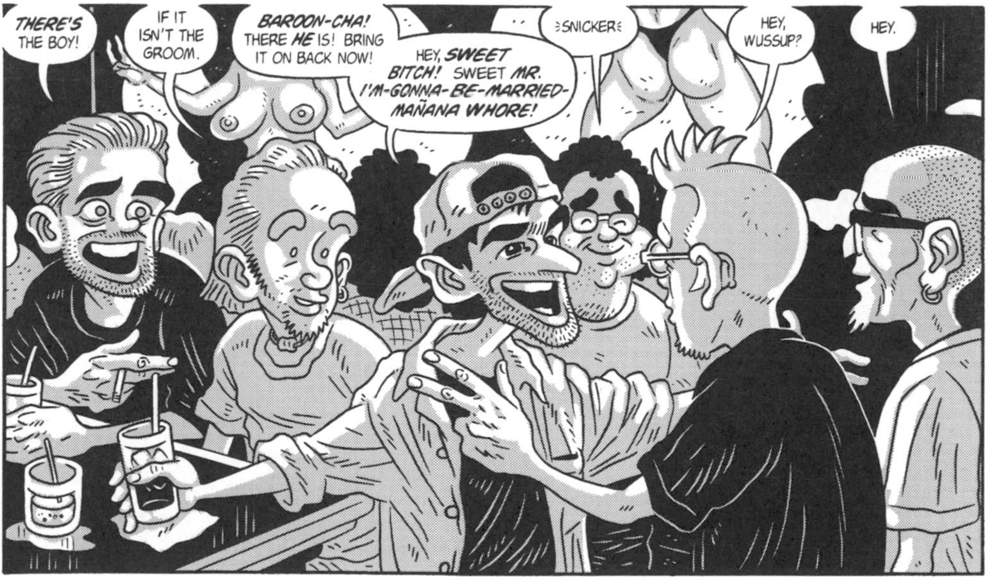
*THERE'S* THE BOY!
IF IT ISN'T THE GROOM.
*BAROON-CHA!* THERE *HE* IS! BRING IT ON BACK NOW!
HEY, *SWEET BITCH!* SWEET *MR. I'M-GONNA-BE-MARRIED-MAÑANA WHORE!*
..
SNICKER
HEY, WUSSUP?
HEY.

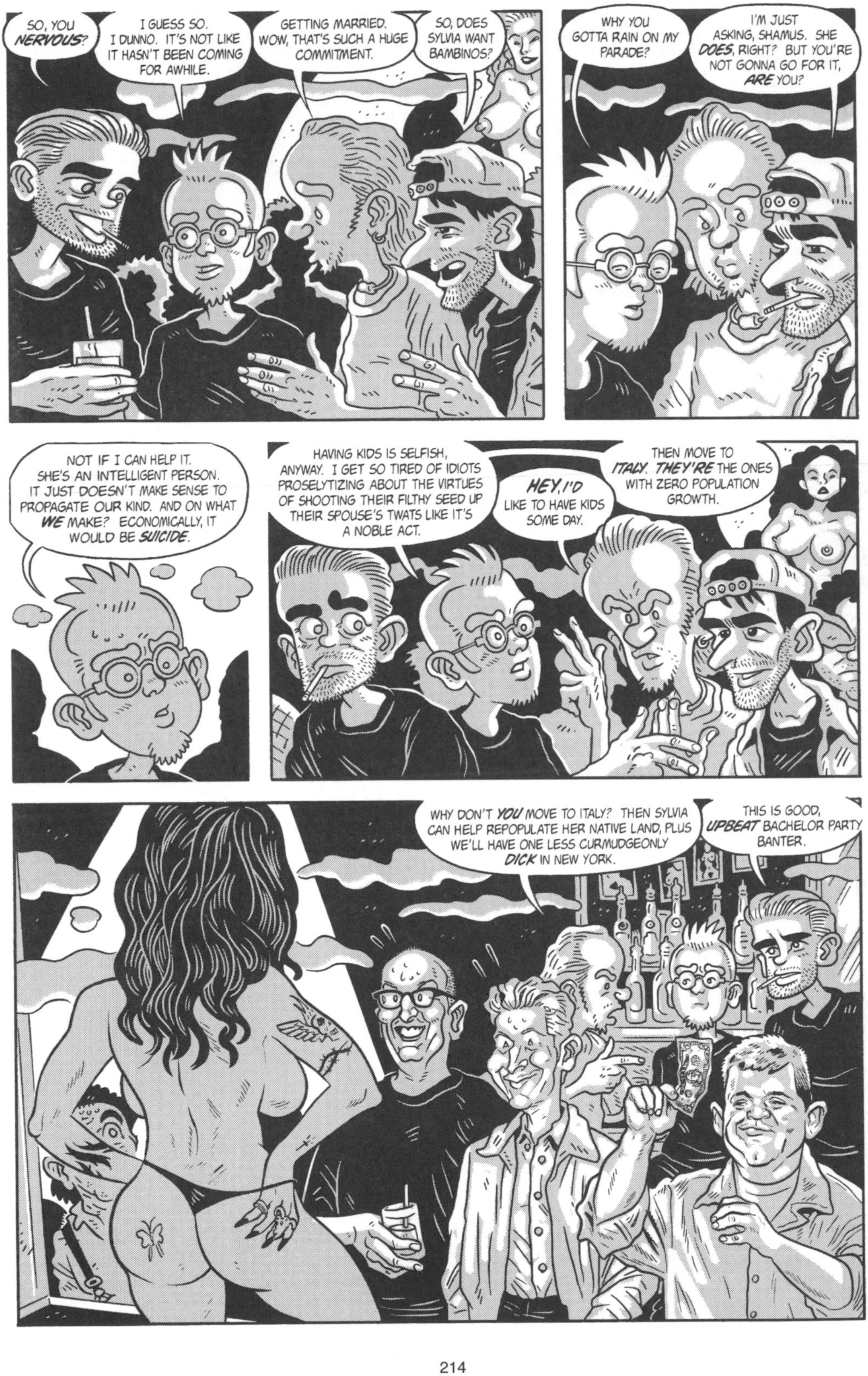
SO, YOU NERVOUS?
I GUESS SO. I DUNNO. IT'S NOT LIKE IT HASN'T BEEN COMING FOR AWHILE.
GETTING MARRIED. WOW, THAT'S SUCH A HUGE COMMITMENT.
SO, DOES SYLVIA WANT BAMBINOS?
WHY YOU GOTTA RAIN ON MY PARADE?
I'M JUST ASKING, SHAMUS. SHE DOES, RIGHT? BUT YOU'RE NOT GONNA GO FOR IT, ARE YOU?
NOT IF I CAN HELP IT. SHE'S AN INTELLIGENT PERSON. IT JUST DOESN'T MAKE SENSE TO PROPAGATE OUR KIND. AND ON WHAT WE MAKE? ECONOMICALLY, IT WOULD BE SUICIDE.
HAVING KIDS IS SELFISH, ANYWAY. I GET SO TIRED OF IDIOTS PROSELYTIZING ABOUT THE VIRTUES OF SHOOTING THEIR FILTHY SEED UP THEIR SPOUSE'S TWATS LIKE IT'S A NOBLE ACT.
HEY, I'D LIKE TO HAVE KIDS SOME DAY.
THEN MOVE TO ITALY. THEY'RE THE ONES WITH ZERO POPULATION GROWTH.
WHY DON'T YOU MOVE TO ITALY? THEN SYLVIA CAN HELP REPOPULATE HER NATIVE LAND, PLUS WE'LL HAVE ONE LESS CURMUDGEONLY DICK IN NEW YORK.
THIS IS GOOD, UPBEAT BACHELOR PARTY BANTER.

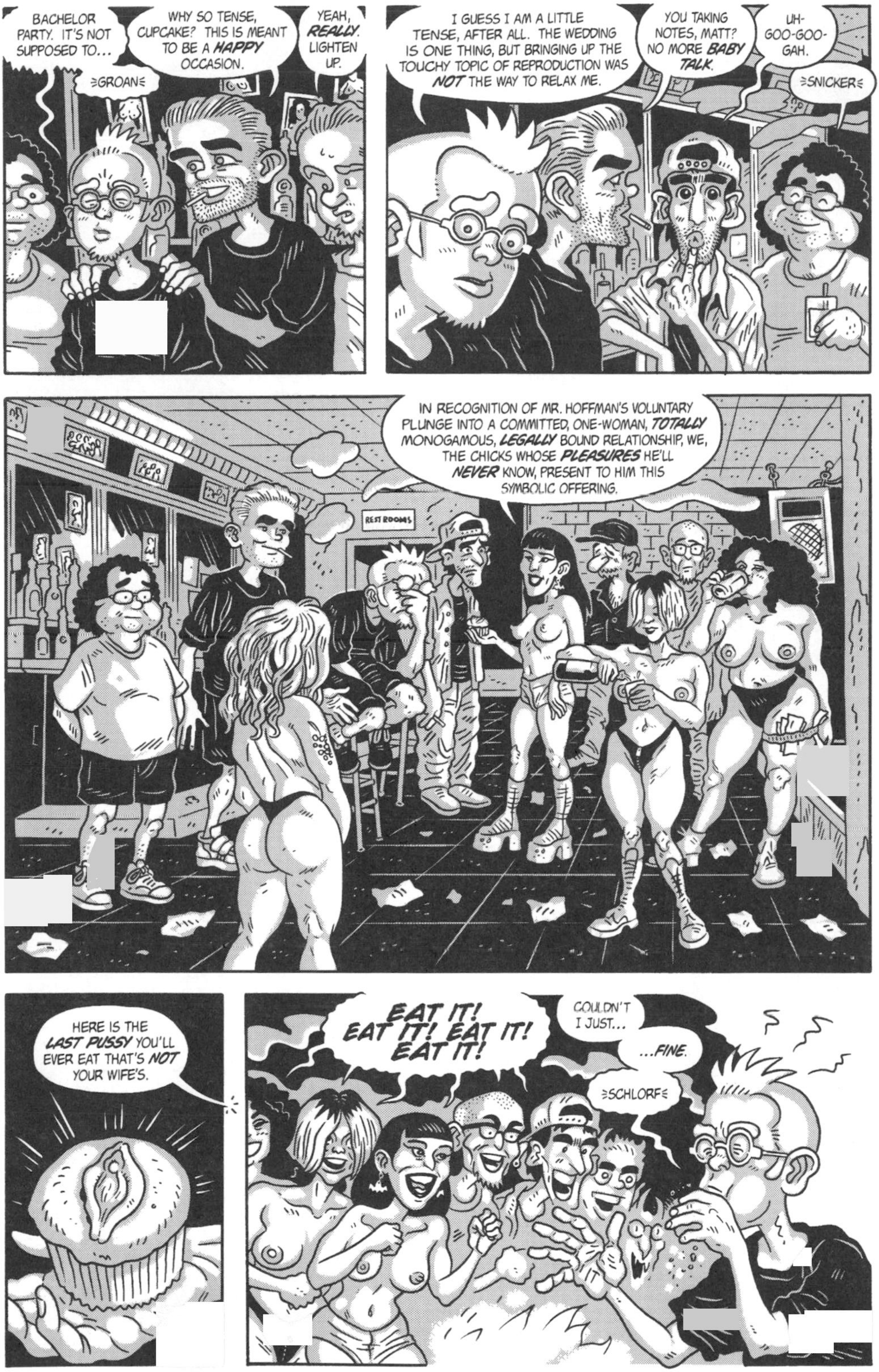
BACHELOR PARTY. IT'S NOT SUPPOSED TO...
≷GROAN≶
WHY SO TENSE, CUPCAKE? THIS IS MEANT TO BE A *HAPPY* OCCASION.
YEAH, *REALLY*. LIGHTEN UP.
I GUESS I AM A LITTLE TENSE, AFTER ALL. THE WEDDING IS ONE THING, BUT BRINGING UP THE TOUCHY TOPIC OF REPRODUCTION WAS *NOT* THE WAY TO RELAX ME.
YOU TAKING NOTES, MATT? NO MORE *BABY TALK*.
UH-GOO-GOO-GAH.
≷SNICKER≶
IN RECOGNITION OF MR. HOFFMAN'S VOLUNTARY PLUNGE INTO A COMMITTED, ONE-WOMAN, *TOTALLY* MONOGAMOUS, *LEGALLY* BOUND RELATIONSHIP, WE, THE CHICKS WHOSE *PLEASURES* HE'LL *NEVER* KNOW, PRESENT TO HIM THIS SYMBOLIC OFFERING.
REST ROOMS
HERE IS THE *LAST PUSSY* YOU'LL EVER EAT THAT'S *NOT* YOUR WIFE'S.
EAT IT! EAT IT! EAT IT! EAT IT!
COULDN'T I JUST...
...*FINE*.
≷SCHLORF≶

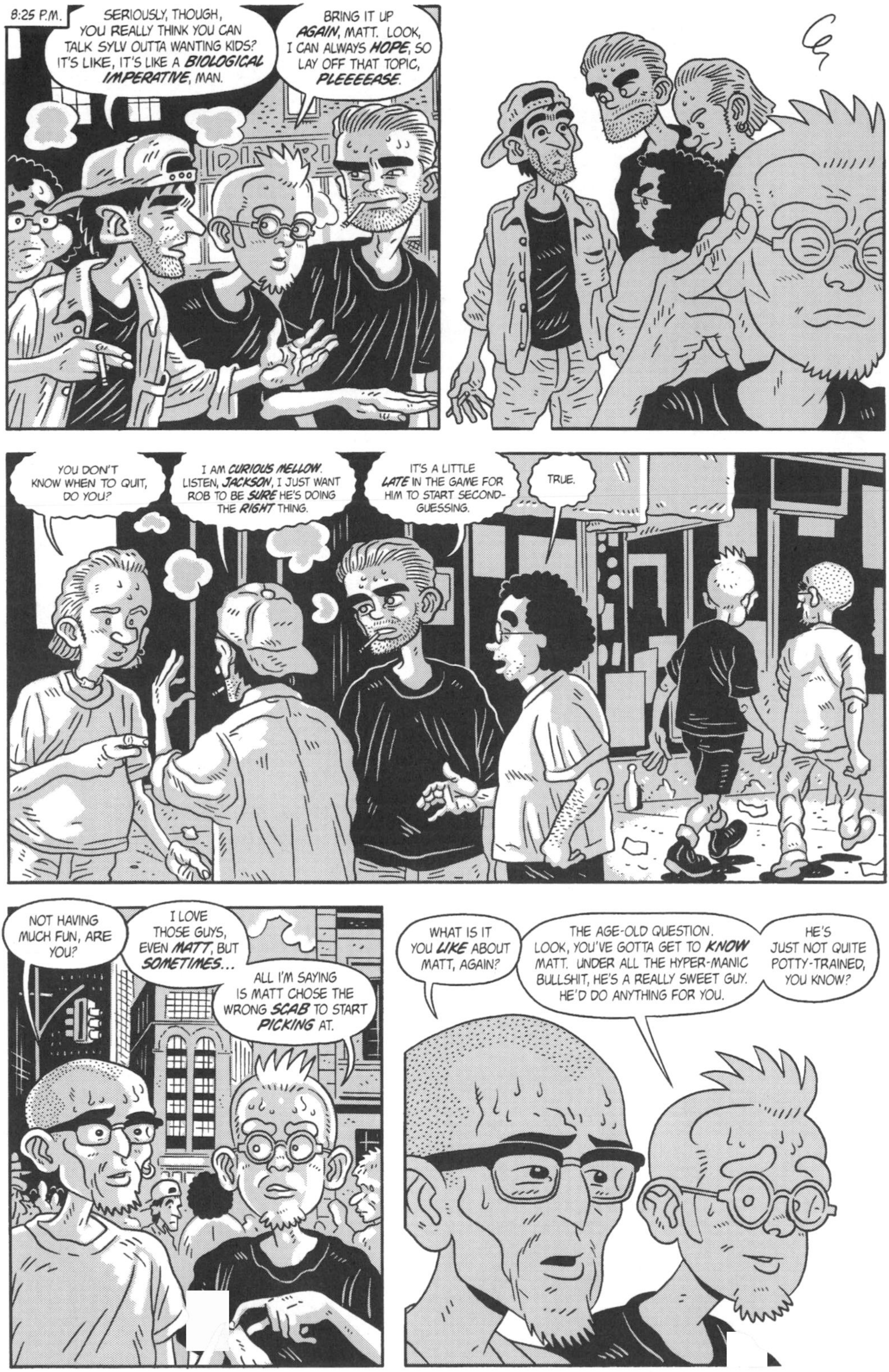
8:25 P.M.
SERIOUSLY, THOUGH, YOU REALLY THINK YOU CAN TALK SYLV OUTTA WANTING KIDS? IT'S LIKE, IT'S LIKE A BIOLOGICAL IMPERATIVE, MAN.
BRING IT UP AGAIN, MATT. LOOK, I CAN ALWAYS HOPE, SO LAY OFF THAT TOPIC, PLEEEEASE.
YOU DON'T KNOW WHEN TO QUIT, DO YOU?
I AM CURIOUS MELLOW. LISTEN, JACKSON, I JUST WANT ROB TO BE SURE HE'S DOING THE RIGHT THING.
IT'S A LITTLE LATE IN THE GAME FOR HIM TO START SECOND-GUESSING.
TRUE.
NOT HAVING MUCH FUN, ARE YOU?
I LOVE THOSE GUYS, EVEN MATT, BUT SOMETIMES...
ALL I'M SAYING IS MATT CHOSE THE WRONG SCAB TO START PICKING AT.
WHAT IS IT YOU LIKE ABOUT MATT, AGAIN?
THE AGE-OLD QUESTION. LOOK, YOU'VE GOTTA GET TO KNOW MATT. UNDER ALL THE HYPER-MANIC BULLSHIT, HE'S A REALLY SWEET GUY. HE'D DO ANYTHING FOR YOU.
HE'S JUST NOT QUITE POTTY-TRAINED, YOU KNOW?

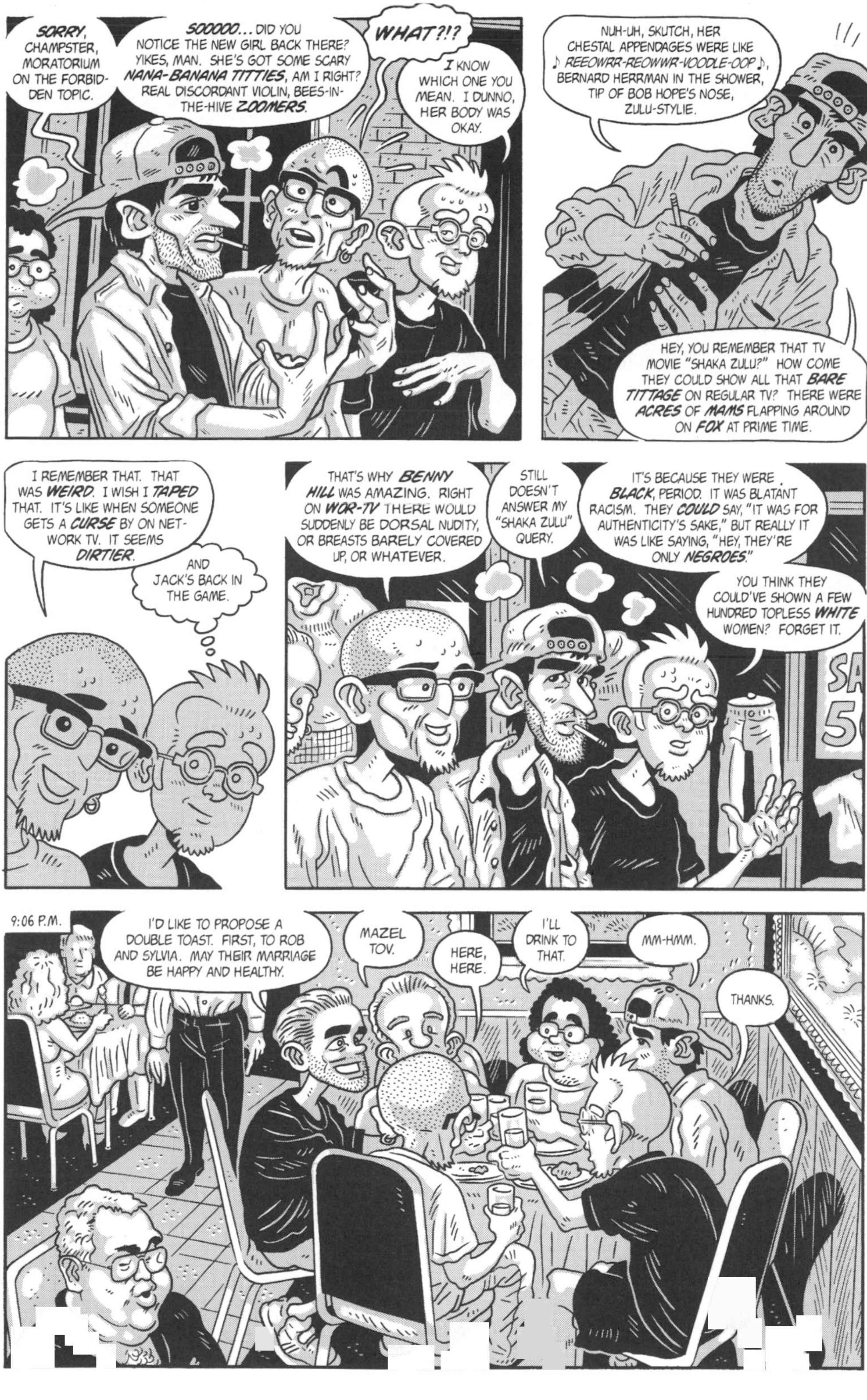
SORRY, CHAMPSTER, MORATORIUM ON THE FORBIDDEN TOPIC.
SOOOOO... DID YOU NOTICE THE NEW GIRL BACK THERE? YIKES, MAN. SHE'S GOT SOME SCARY NANA-BANANA TITTIES, AM I RIGHT? REAL DISCORDANT VIOLIN, BEES-IN-THE-HIVE ZOOMERS.
WHAT?!?
I KNOW WHICH ONE YOU MEAN. I DUNNO, HER BODY WAS OKAY.
NUH-UH, SKUTCH, HER CHESTAL APPENDAGES WERE LIKE ♪ REEOWRR-REOWWR-VOODLE-OOP ♪, BERNARD HERRMAN IN THE SHOWER, TIP OF BOB HOPE'S NOSE, ZULU-STYLIE.
HEY, YOU REMEMBER THAT TV MOVIE "SHAKA ZULU?" HOW COME THEY COULD SHOW ALL THAT BARE TITTAGE ON REGULAR TV? THERE WERE ACRES OF MAMS FLAPPING AROUND ON FOX AT PRIME TIME.
I REMEMBER THAT. THAT WAS WEIRD. I WISH I TAPED THAT. IT'S LIKE WHEN SOMEONE GETS A CURSE BY ON NETWORK TV. IT SEEMS DIRTIER.
AND JACK'S BACK IN THE GAME.
THAT'S WHY BENNY HILL WAS AMAZING. RIGHT ON WOR-TV THERE WOULD SUDDENLY BE DORSAL NUDITY, OR BREASTS BARELY COVERED UP, OR WHATEVER.
STILL DOESN'T ANSWER MY "SHAKA ZULU" QUERY.
IT'S BECAUSE THEY WERE BLACK, PERIOD. IT WAS BLATANT RACISM. THEY COULD SAY, "IT WAS FOR AUTHENTICITY'S SAKE," BUT REALLY IT WAS LIKE SAYING, "HEY, THEY'RE ONLY NEGROES."
YOU THINK THEY COULD'VE SHOWN A FEW HUNDRED TOPLESS WHITE WOMEN? FORGET IT.
9:06 P.M.
I'D LIKE TO PROPOSE A DOUBLE TOAST. FIRST, TO ROB AND SYLVIA. MAY THEIR MARRIAGE BE HAPPY AND HEALTHY.
MAZEL TOV.
HERE, HERE.
I'LL DRINK TO THAT.
MM-HMM.
THANKS.

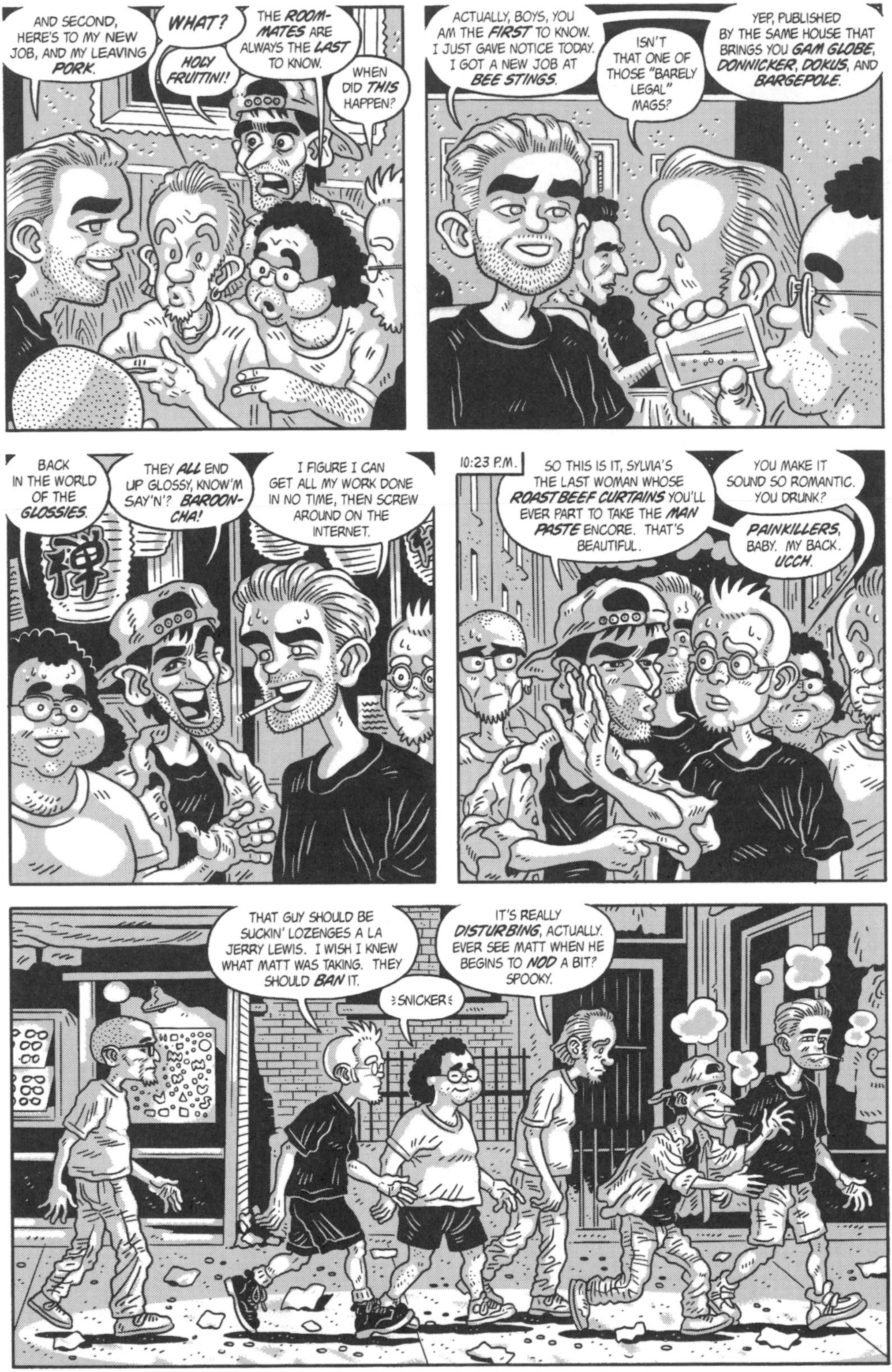
AND SECOND, HERE'S TO MY NEW JOB, AND MY LEAVING PORK.
WHAT?
HOLY FRUITINI!
THE ROOM-MATES ARE ALWAYS THE LAST TO KNOW.
WHEN DID THIS HAPPEN?
ACTUALLY, BOYS, YOU AM THE FIRST TO KNOW. I JUST GAVE NOTICE TODAY. I GOT A NEW JOB AT BEE STINGS.
ISN'T THAT ONE OF THOSE "BARELY LEGAL" MAGS?
YEP, PUBLISHED BY THE SAME HOUSE THAT BRINGS YOU GAM GLOBE, DONNICKER, DOKUS, AND BARGEPOLE.
BACK IN THE WORLD OF THE GLOSSIES.
THEY ALL END UP GLOSSY, KNOW'M SAY'N'? BAROON-CHA!
I FIGURE I CAN GET ALL MY WORK DONE IN NO TIME, THEN SCREW AROUND ON THE INTERNET.
10:23 P.M.
SO THIS IS IT, SYLVIA'S THE LAST WOMAN WHOSE ROASTBEEF CURTAINS YOU'LL EVER PART TO TAKE THE MAN PASTE ENCORE. THAT'S BEAUTIFUL.
YOU MAKE IT SOUND SO ROMANTIC. YOU DRUNK?
PAINKILLERS, BABY. MY BACK. UCCH.
THAT GUY SHOULD BE SUCKIN' LOZENGES A LA JERRY LEWIS. I WISH I KNEW WHAT MATT WAS TAKING. THEY SHOULD BAN IT.
SNICKER
IT'S REALLY DISTURBING, ACTUALLY. EVER SEE MATT WHEN HE BEGINS TO NOD A BIT? SPOOKY.

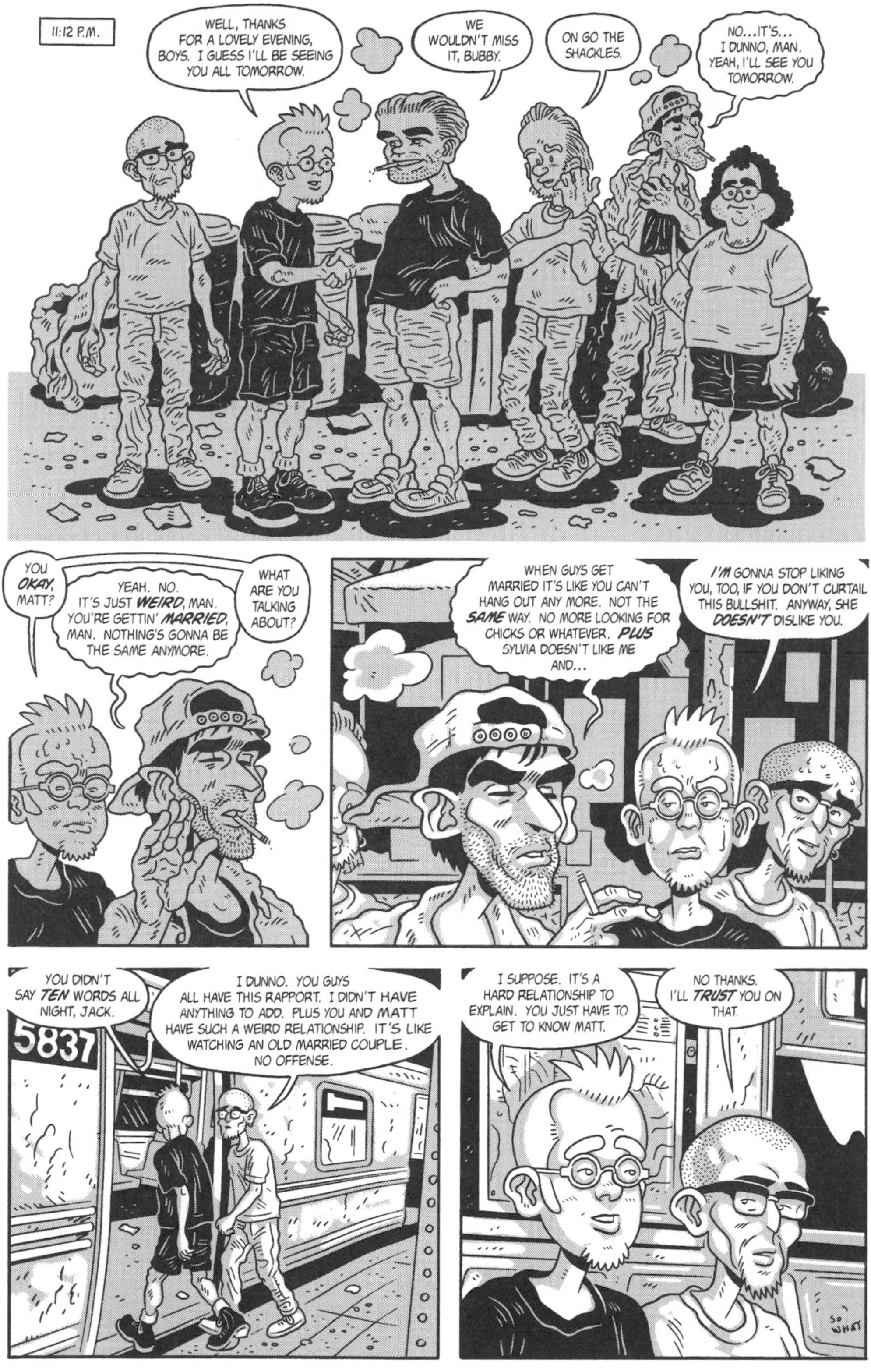
11:12 P.M.
WELL, THANKS FOR A LOVELY EVENING, BOYS. I GUESS I'LL BE SEEING YOU ALL TOMORROW.
WE WOULDN'T MISS IT, BUBBY.
ON GO THE SHACKLES.
NO...IT'S... I DUNNO, MAN. YEAH, I'LL SEE YOU TOMORROW.
YOU OKAY, MATT?
YEAH. NO. IT'S JUST WEIRD, MAN. YOU'RE GETTIN' MARRIED, MAN. NOTHING'S GONNA BE THE SAME ANYMORE.
WHAT ARE YOU TALKING ABOUT?
WHEN GUYS GET MARRIED IT'S LIKE YOU CAN'T HANG OUT ANY MORE. NOT THE SAME WAY. NO MORE LOOKING FOR CHICKS OR WHATEVER. PLUS SYLVIA DOESN'T LIKE ME AND...
I'M GONNA STOP LIKING YOU, TOO, IF YOU DON'T CURTAIL THIS BULLSHIT. ANYWAY, SHE DOESN'T DISLIKE YOU.
YOU DIDN'T SAY TEN WORDS ALL NIGHT, JACK.
5837
I DUNNO. YOU GUYS ALL HAVE THIS RAPPORT. I DIDN'T HAVE ANYTHING TO ADD. PLUS YOU AND MATT HAVE SUCH A WEIRD RELATIONSHIP. IT'S LIKE WATCHING AN OLD MARRIED COUPLE. NO OFFENSE.
I SUPPOSE. IT'S A HARD RELATIONSHIP TO EXPLAIN. YOU JUST HAVE TO GET TO KNOW MATT.
NO THANKS. I'LL TRUST YOU ON THAT.
SO WHAT

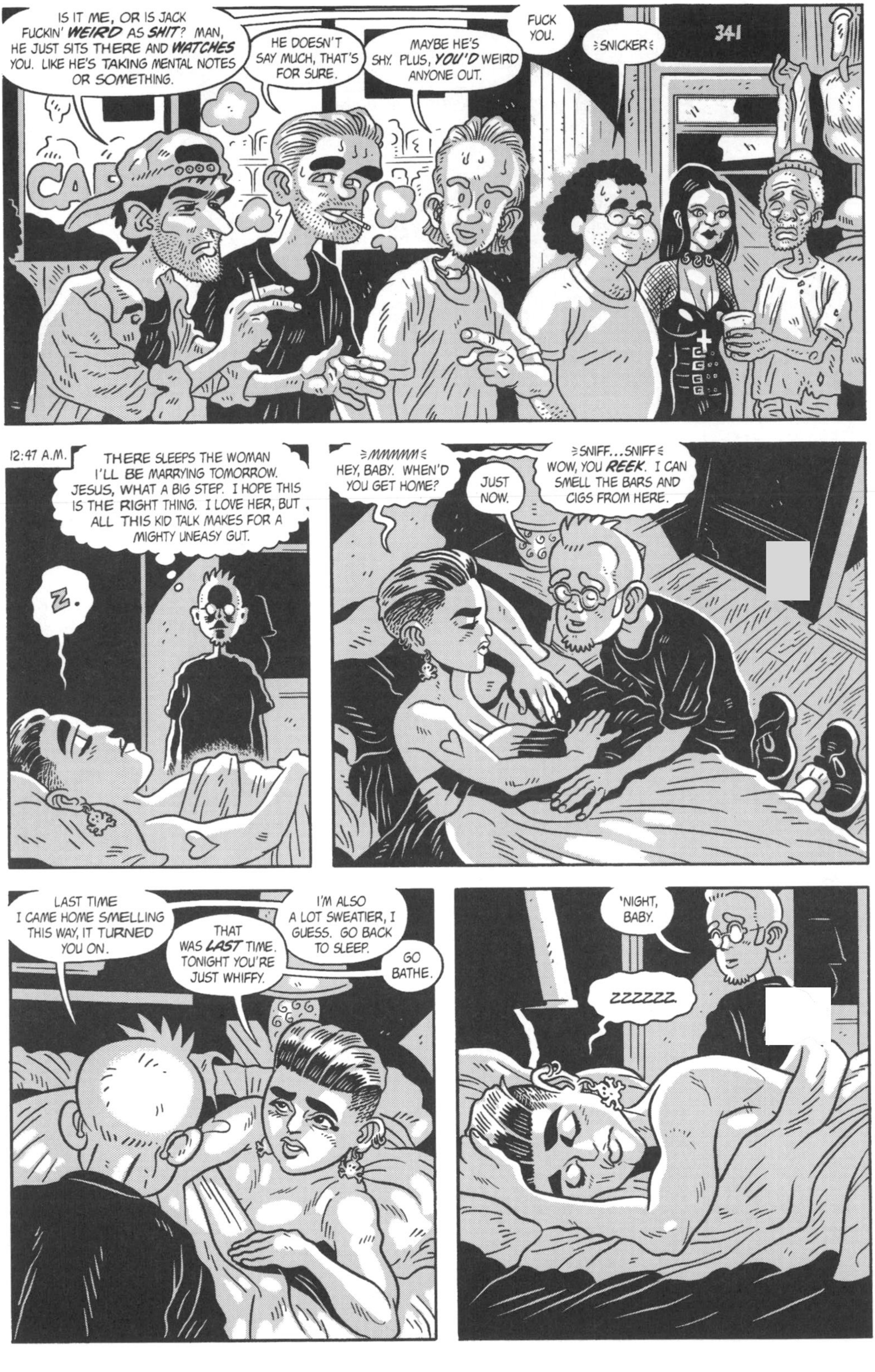
IS IT ME, OR IS JACK FUCKIN' *WEIRD* AS *SHIT*? MAN, HE JUST SITS THERE AND *WATCHES* YOU. LIKE HE'S TAKING MENTAL NOTES OR SOMETHING.
HE DOESN'T SAY MUCH, THAT'S FOR SURE.
MAYBE HE'S SHY. PLUS, *YOU'D* WEIRD ANYONE OUT.
FUCK YOU.
≷SNICKER≷
341
12:47 A.M.
THERE SLEEPS THE WOMAN I'LL BE MARRYING TOMORROW. JESUS, WHAT A BIG STEP. I HOPE THIS IS THE RIGHT THING. I LOVE HER, BUT ALL THIS KID TALK MAKES FOR A MIGHTY UNEASY GUT.
Z.
≷MMMMM≷
HEY, BABY. WHEN'D YOU GET HOME?
JUST NOW.
≷SNIFF...SNIFF≷
WOW, YOU *REEK*. I CAN SMELL THE BARS AND CIGS FROM HERE.
LAST TIME I CAME HOME SMELLING THIS WAY, IT TURNED YOU ON.
THAT WAS *LAST* TIME. TONIGHT YOU'RE JUST WHIFFY.
I'M ALSO A LOT SWEATIER, I GUESS. GO BACK TO SLEEP.
GO BATHE.
'NIGHT, BABY.
ZZZZZZ.

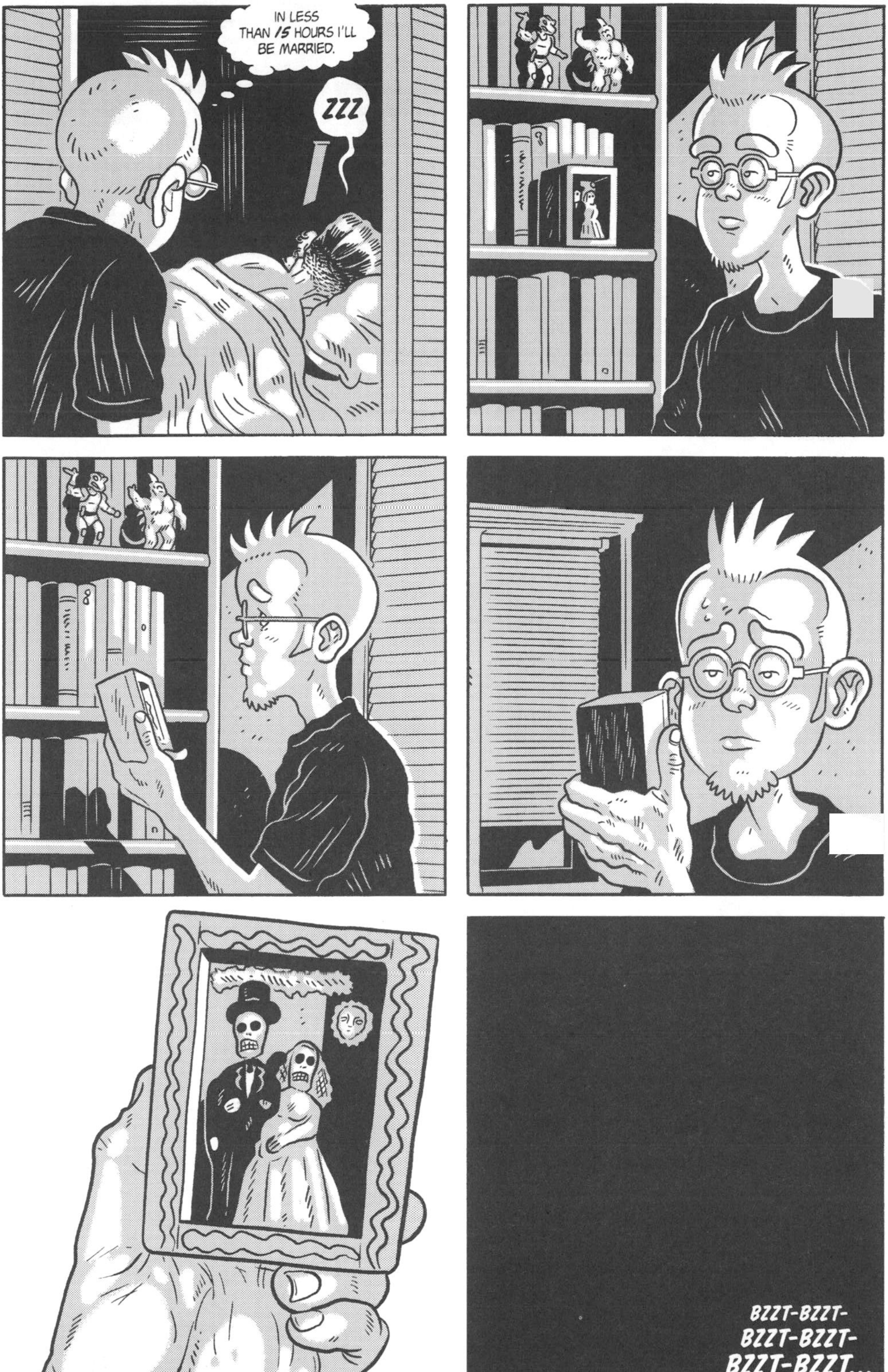
IN LESS THAN 15 HOURS I'LL BE MARRIED.
ZZZ
BZZT-BZZT-
BZZT-BZZT-
BZZT-BZZT...

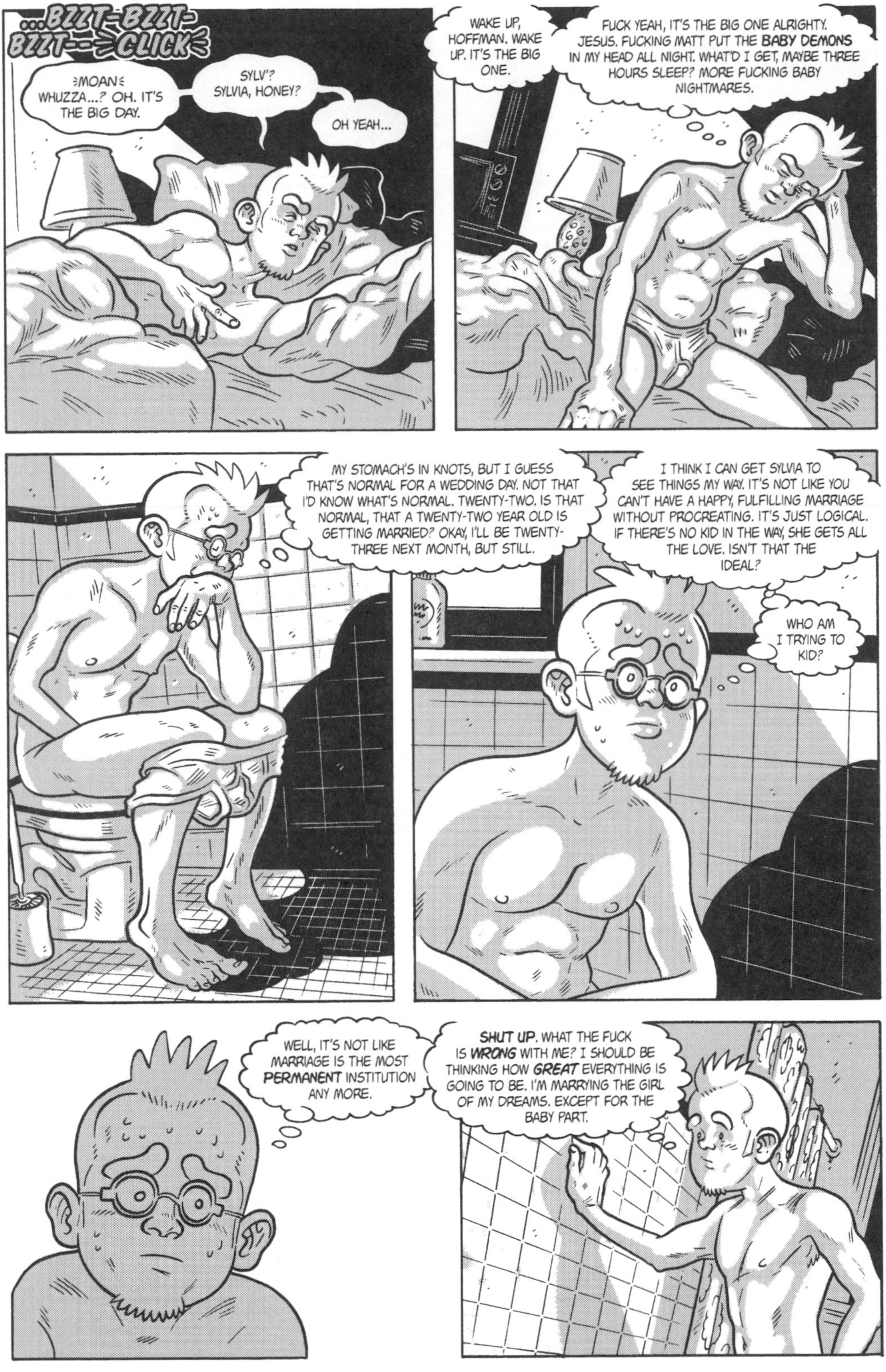
...BZZT-BZZT-BZZT--CLICK
MOAN WHUZZA...? OH. IT'S THE BIG DAY.
SYLV'? SYLVIA, HONEY?
OH YEAH...
WAKE UP, HOFFMAN. WAKE UP. IT'S THE BIG ONE.
FUCK YEAH, IT'S THE BIG ONE ALRIGHTY. JESUS. FUCKING MATT PUT THE BABY DEMONS IN MY HEAD ALL NIGHT. WHAT'D I GET, MAYBE THREE HOURS SLEEP? MORE FUCKING BABY NIGHTMARES.
MY STOMACH'S IN KNOTS, BUT I GUESS THAT'S NORMAL FOR A WEDDING DAY. NOT THAT I'D KNOW WHAT'S NORMAL. TWENTY-TWO. IS THAT NORMAL, THAT A TWENTY-TWO YEAR OLD IS GETTING MARRIED? OKAY, I'LL BE TWENTY-THREE NEXT MONTH, BUT STILL.
I THINK I CAN GET SYLVIA TO SEE THINGS MY WAY. IT'S NOT LIKE YOU CAN'T HAVE A HAPPY, FULFILLING MARRIAGE WITHOUT PROCREATING. IT'S JUST LOGICAL. IF THERE'S NO KID IN THE WAY, SHE GETS ALL THE LOVE. ISN'T THAT THE IDEAL?
WHO AM I TRYING TO KID?
WELL, IT'S NOT LIKE MARRIAGE IS THE MOST PERMANENT INSTITUTION ANY MORE.
SHUT UP. WHAT THE FUCK IS WRONG WITH ME? I SHOULD BE THINKING HOW GREAT EVERYTHING IS GOING TO BE. I'M MARRYING THE GIRL OF MY DREAMS. EXCEPT FOR THE BABY PART.

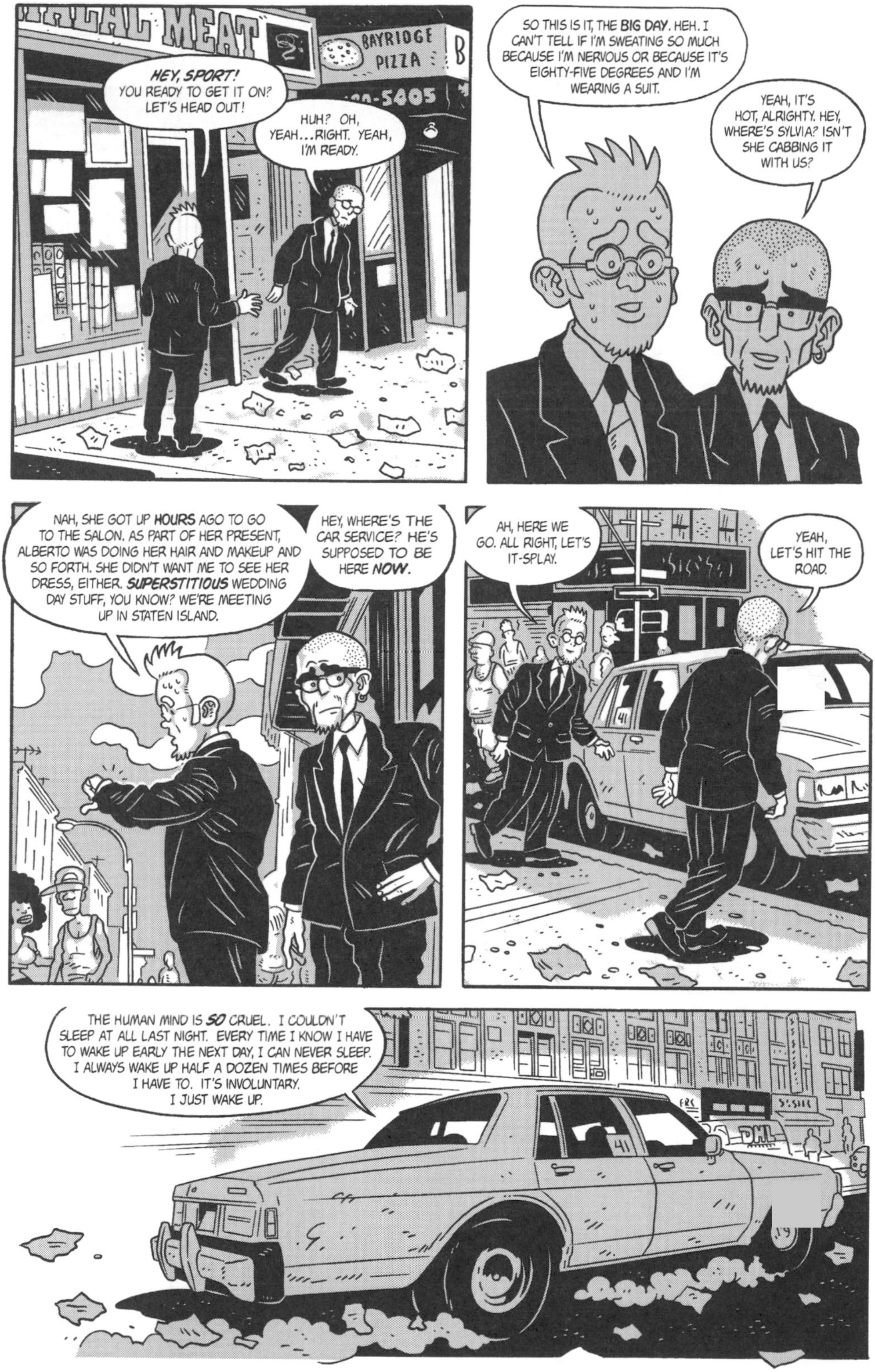
MEAT
BAYRIDGE PIZZA
HEY, SPORT! YOU READY TO GET IT ON? LET'S HEAD OUT!
HUH? OH, YEAH...RIGHT. YEAH, I'M READY.
SO THIS IS IT, THE BIG DAY. HEH. I CAN'T TELL IF I'M SWEATING SO MUCH BECAUSE I'M NERVOUS OR BECAUSE IT'S EIGHTY-FIVE DEGREES AND I'M WEARING A SUIT.
YEAH, IT'S HOT, ALRIGHTY. HEY, WHERE'S SYLVIA? ISN'T SHE CABBING IT WITH US?
NAH, SHE GOT UP HOURS AGO TO GO TO THE SALON. AS PART OF HER PRESENT, ALBERTO WAS DOING HER HAIR AND MAKEUP AND SO FORTH. SHE DIDN'T WANT ME TO SEE HER DRESS, EITHER. SUPERSTITIOUS WEDDING DAY STUFF, YOU KNOW? WE'RE MEETING UP IN STATEN ISLAND.
HEY, WHERE'S THE CAR SERVICE? HE'S SUPPOSED TO BE HERE NOW.
AH, HERE WE GO. ALL RIGHT, LET'S IT-SPLAY.
YEAH, LET'S HIT THE ROAD.
THE HUMAN MIND IS SO CRUEL. I COULDN'T SLEEP AT ALL LAST NIGHT. EVERY TIME I KNOW I HAVE TO WAKE UP EARLY THE NEXT DAY, I CAN NEVER SLEEP. I ALWAYS WAKE UP HALF A DOZEN TIMES BEFORE I HAVE TO. IT'S INVOLUNTARY. I JUST WAKE UP.
DHL

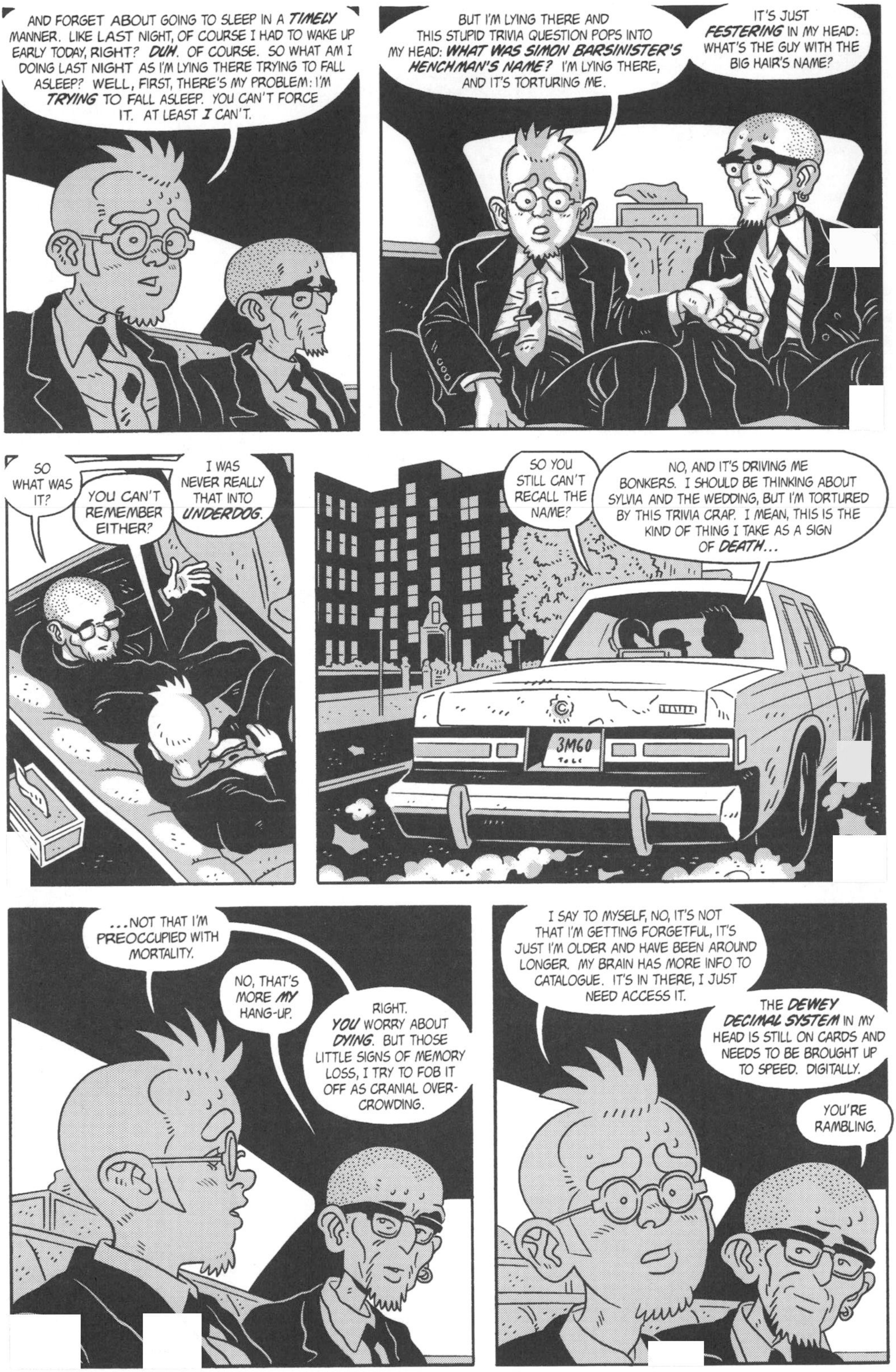
AND FORGET ABOUT GOING TO SLEEP IN A TIMELY MANNER. LIKE LAST NIGHT, OF COURSE I HAD TO WAKE UP EARLY TODAY, RIGHT? DUH. OF COURSE. SO WHAT AM I DOING LAST NIGHT AS I'M LYING THERE TRYING TO FALL ASLEEP? WELL, FIRST, THERE'S MY PROBLEM: I'M TRYING TO FALL ASLEEP. YOU CAN'T FORCE IT. AT LEAST I CAN'T.
BUT I'M LYING THERE AND THIS STUPID TRIVIA QUESTION POPS INTO MY HEAD: WHAT WAS SIMON BARSINISTER'S HENCHMAN'S NAME? I'M LYING THERE, AND IT'S TORTURING ME.
IT'S JUST FESTERING IN MY HEAD: WHAT'S THE GUY WITH THE BIG HAIR'S NAME?
SO WHAT WAS IT?
YOU CAN'T REMEMBER EITHER?
I WAS NEVER REALLY THAT INTO UNDERDOG.
SO YOU STILL CAN'T RECALL THE NAME?
NO, AND IT'S DRIVING ME BONKERS. I SHOULD BE THINKING ABOUT SYLVIA AND THE WEDDING, BUT I'M TORTURED BY THIS TRIVIA CRAP. I MEAN, THIS IS THE KIND OF THING I TAKE AS A SIGN OF DEATH...
3M60
...NOT THAT I'M PREOCCUPIED WITH MORTALITY.
NO, THAT'S MORE MY HANG-UP.
RIGHT. YOU WORRY ABOUT DYING. BUT THOSE LITTLE SIGNS OF MEMORY LOSS, I TRY TO FOB IT OFF AS CRANIAL OVER-CROWDING.
I SAY TO MYSELF, NO, IT'S NOT THAT I'M GETTING FORGETFUL, IT'S JUST I'M OLDER AND HAVE BEEN AROUND LONGER. MY BRAIN HAS MORE INFO TO CATALOGUE. IT'S IN THERE, I JUST NEED ACCESS IT.
THE DEWEY DECIMAL SYSTEM IN MY HEAD IS STILL ON CARDS AND NEEDS TO BE BROUGHT UP TO SPEED. DIGITALLY.
YOU'RE RAMBLING.

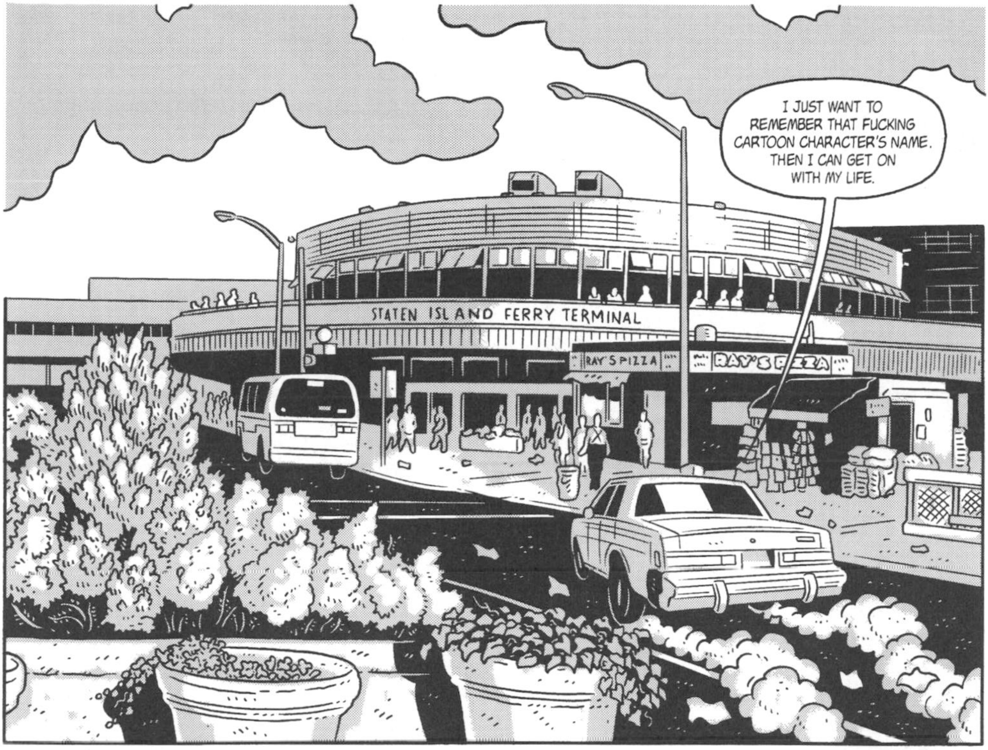
I JUST WANT TO REMEMBER THAT FUCKING CARTOON CHARACTER'S NAME. THEN I CAN GET ON WITH MY LIFE.
STATEN ISLAND FERRY TERMINAL
RAY'S PIZZA
RAY'S PIZZA

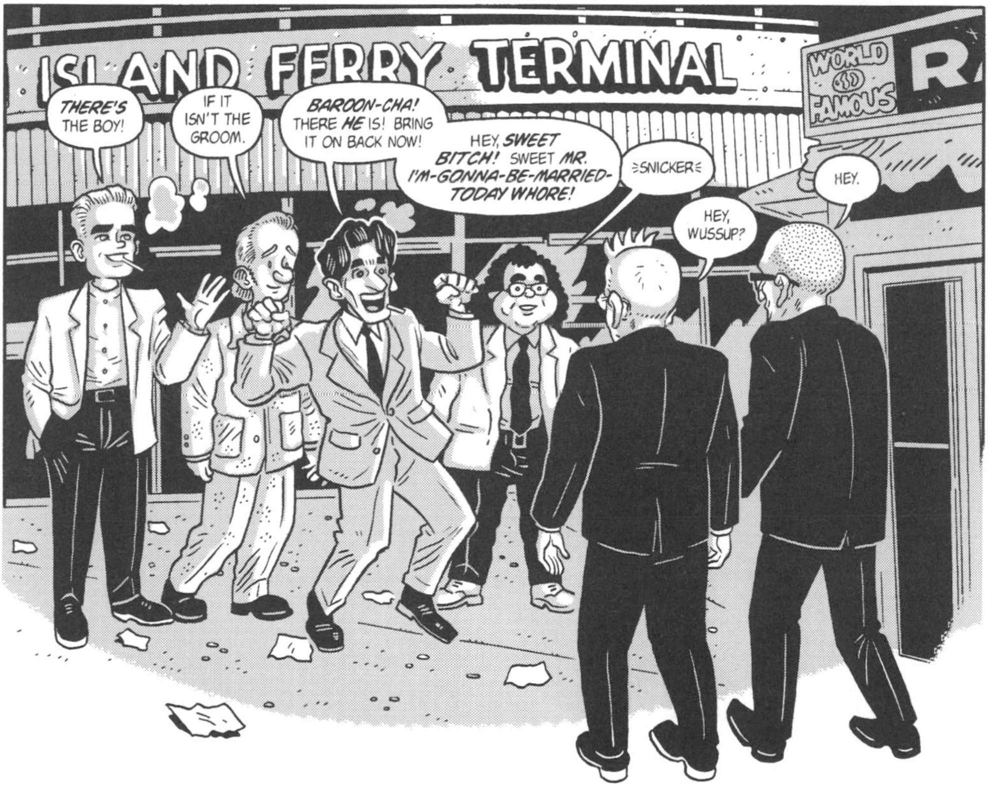
ISLAND FERRY TERMINAL
WORLD FAMOUS
THERE'S THE BOY!
IF IT ISN'T THE GROOM.
BAROON-CHA! THERE HE IS! BRING IT ON BACK NOW!
HEY, SWEET BITCH! SWEET MR. I'M-GONNA-BE-MARRIED-TODAY WHORE!
SNICKER
HEY, WUSSUP?
HEY.

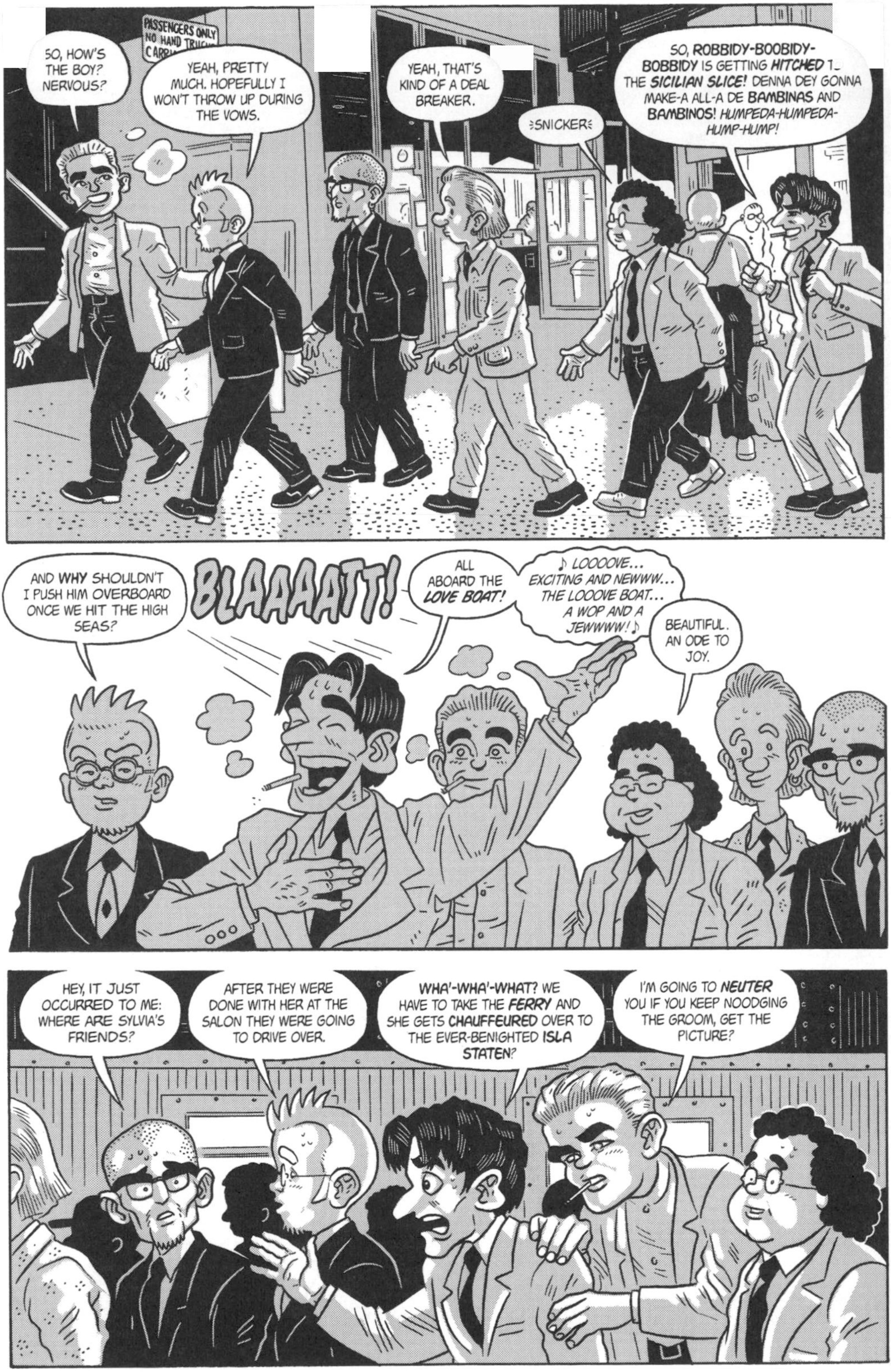
PASSENGERS ONLY
NO HAND TRUCKS
SO, HOW'S THE BOY? NERVOUS?
YEAH, PRETTY MUCH. HOPEFULLY I WON'T THROW UP DURING THE VOWS.
YEAH, THAT'S KIND OF A DEAL BREAKER.
SNICKER
SO, ROBBIDY-BOOBIDY-BOBBIDY IS GETTING HITCHED TO THE SICILIAN SLICE! DENNA DEY GONNA MAKE-A ALL-A DE BAMBINAS AND BAMBINOS! HUMPEDA-HUMPEDA-HUMP-HUMP!
AND WHY SHOULDN'T I PUSH HIM OVERBOARD ONCE WE HIT THE HIGH SEAS?
BLAAAATT!
ALL ABOARD THE LOVE BOAT!
♪ LOOOOVE... EXCITING AND NEWWW... THE LOOOVE BOAT... A WOP AND A JEWWWW! ♪
BEAUTIFUL. AN ODE TO JOY.
HEY, IT JUST OCCURRED TO ME: WHERE ARE SYLVIA'S FRIENDS?
AFTER THEY WERE DONE WITH HER AT THE SALON THEY WERE GOING TO DRIVE OVER.
WHA'-WHA'-WHAT? WE HAVE TO TAKE THE FERRY AND SHE GETS CHAUFFEURED OVER TO THE EVER-BENIGHTED ISLA STATEN?
I'M GOING TO NEUTER YOU IF YOU KEEP NOODGING THE GROOM, GET THE PICTURE?

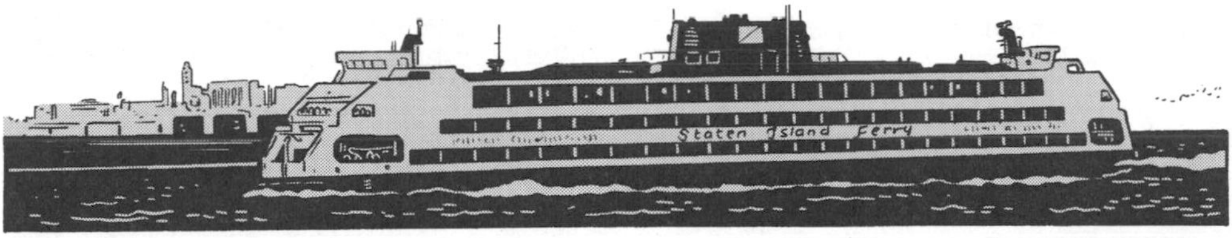
Staten Island Ferry

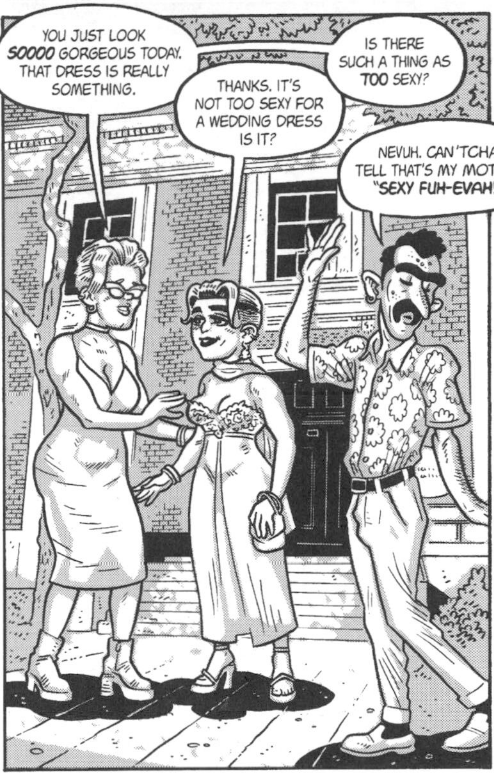
YOU JUST LOOK SOOOO GORGEOUS TODAY. THAT DRESS IS REALLY SOMETHING.
THANKS. IT'S NOT TOO SEXY FOR A WEDDING DRESS IS IT?
IS THERE SUCH A THING AS TOO SEXY?
NEVUH. CAN'TCHA TELL THAT'S MY MOTTO? "SEXY FUH-EVAH!"

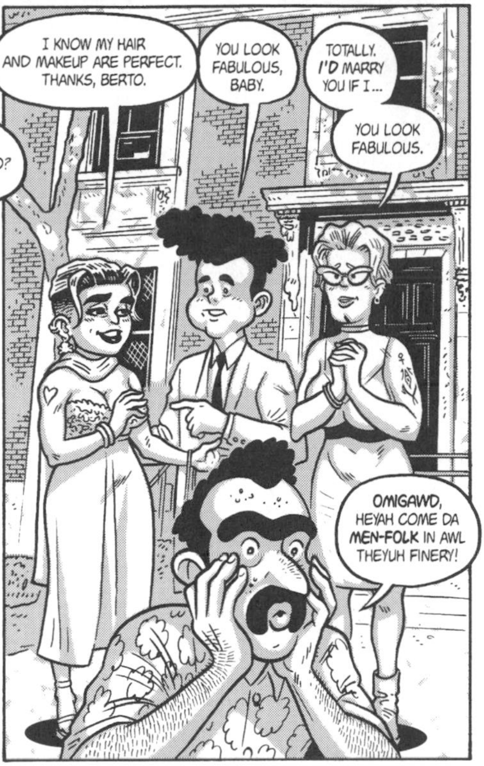
I KNOW MY HAIR AND MAKEUP ARE PERFECT. THANKS, BERTO.
YOU LOOK FABULOUS, BABY.
TOTALLY. I'D MARRY YOU IF I...
YOU LOOK FABULOUS.
OMIGAWD, HEYAH COME DA MEN-FOLK IN AWL THEYUH FINERY!

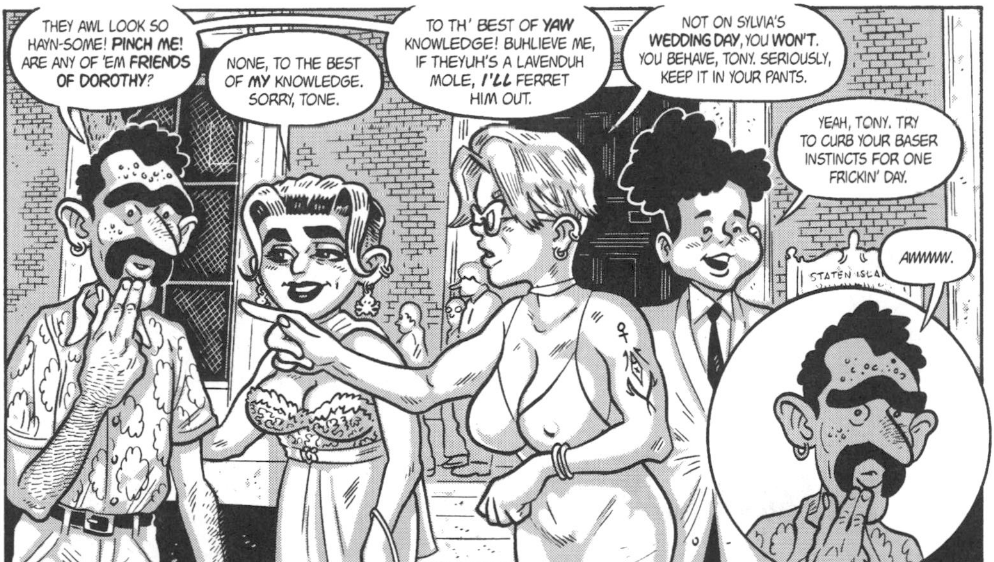
THEY AWL LOOK SO HAYN-SOME! PINCH ME! ARE ANY OF 'EM FRIENDS OF DOROTHY?
NONE, TO THE BEST OF MY KNOWLEDGE. SORRY, TONE.
TO TH' BEST OF YAW KNOWLEDGE! BUHLIEVE ME, IF THEYUH'S A LAVENDUH MOLE, I'LL FERRET HIM OUT.
NOT ON SYLVIA'S WEDDING DAY, YOU WON'T. YOU BEHAVE, TONY. SERIOUSLY, KEEP IT IN YOUR PANTS.
YEAH, TONY. TRY TO CURB YOUR BASER INSTINCTS FOR ONE FRICKIN' DAY.
AWWWW.

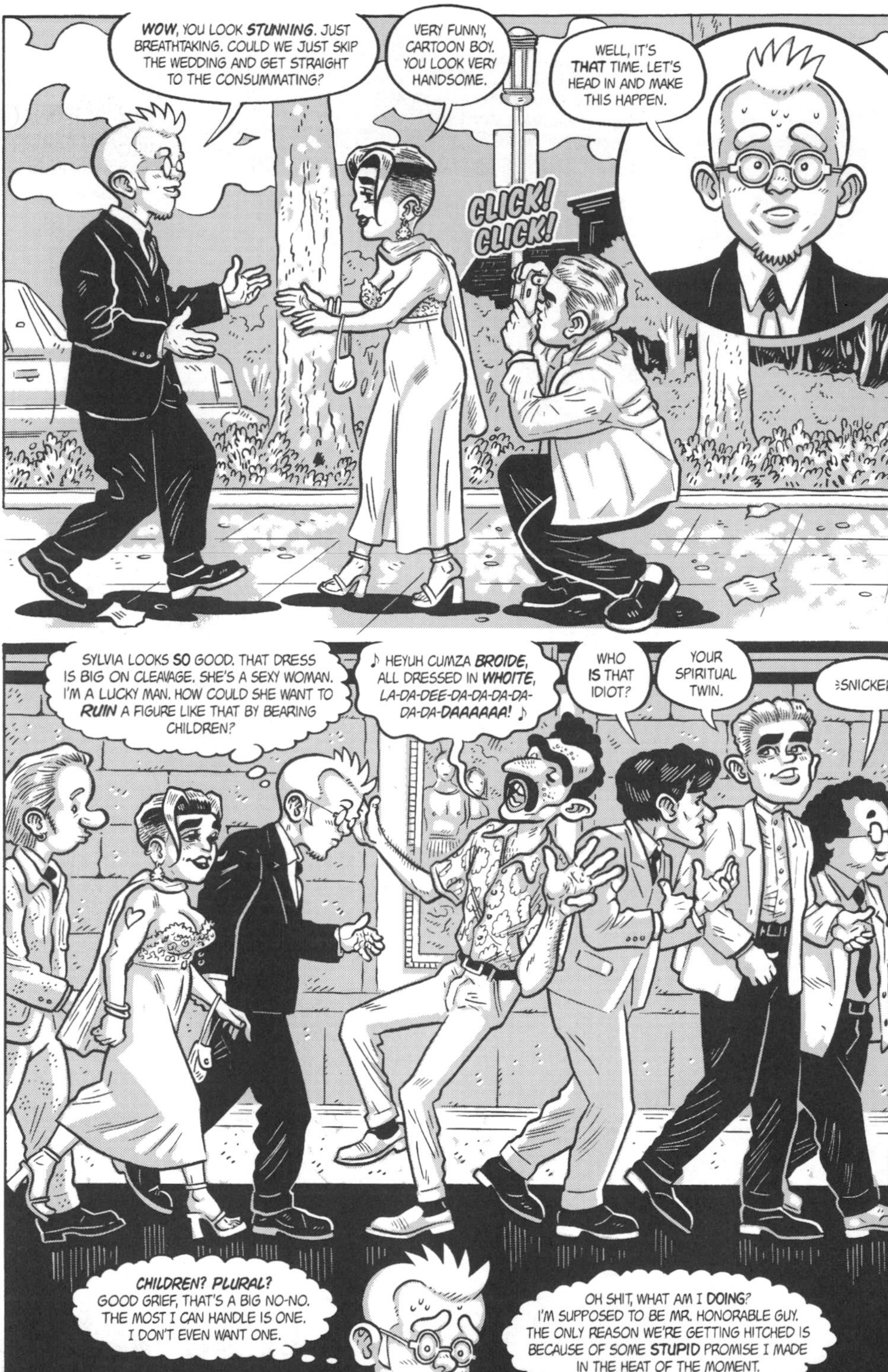
WOW, YOU LOOK STUNNING. JUST BREATHTAKING. COULD WE JUST SKIP THE WEDDING AND GET STRAIGHT TO THE CONSUMMATING?
VERY FUNNY, CARTOON BOY. YOU LOOK VERY HANDSOME.
CLICK! CLICK!
WELL, IT'S THAT TIME. LET'S HEAD IN AND MAKE THIS HAPPEN.
SYLVIA LOOKS SO GOOD. THAT DRESS IS BIG ON CLEAVAGE. SHE'S A SEXY WOMAN. I'M A LUCKY MAN. HOW COULD SHE WANT TO RUIN A FIGURE LIKE THAT BY BEARING CHILDREN?
♪ HEYUH CUMZA BROIDE, ALL DRESSED IN WHOITE, LA-DA-DEE-DA-DA-DA-DA-DA-DA-DAAAAAA! ♪
WHO IS THAT IDIOT?
YOUR SPIRITUAL TWIN.
SNICKER
CHILDREN? PLURAL? GOOD GRIEF, THAT'S A BIG NO-NO. THE MOST I CAN HANDLE IS ONE. I DON'T EVEN WANT ONE.
OH SHIT, WHAT AM I DOING? I'M SUPPOSED TO BE MR. HONORABLE GUY. THE ONLY REASON WE'RE GETTING HITCHED IS BECAUSE OF SOME STUPID PROMISE I MADE IN THE HEAT OF THE MOMENT.

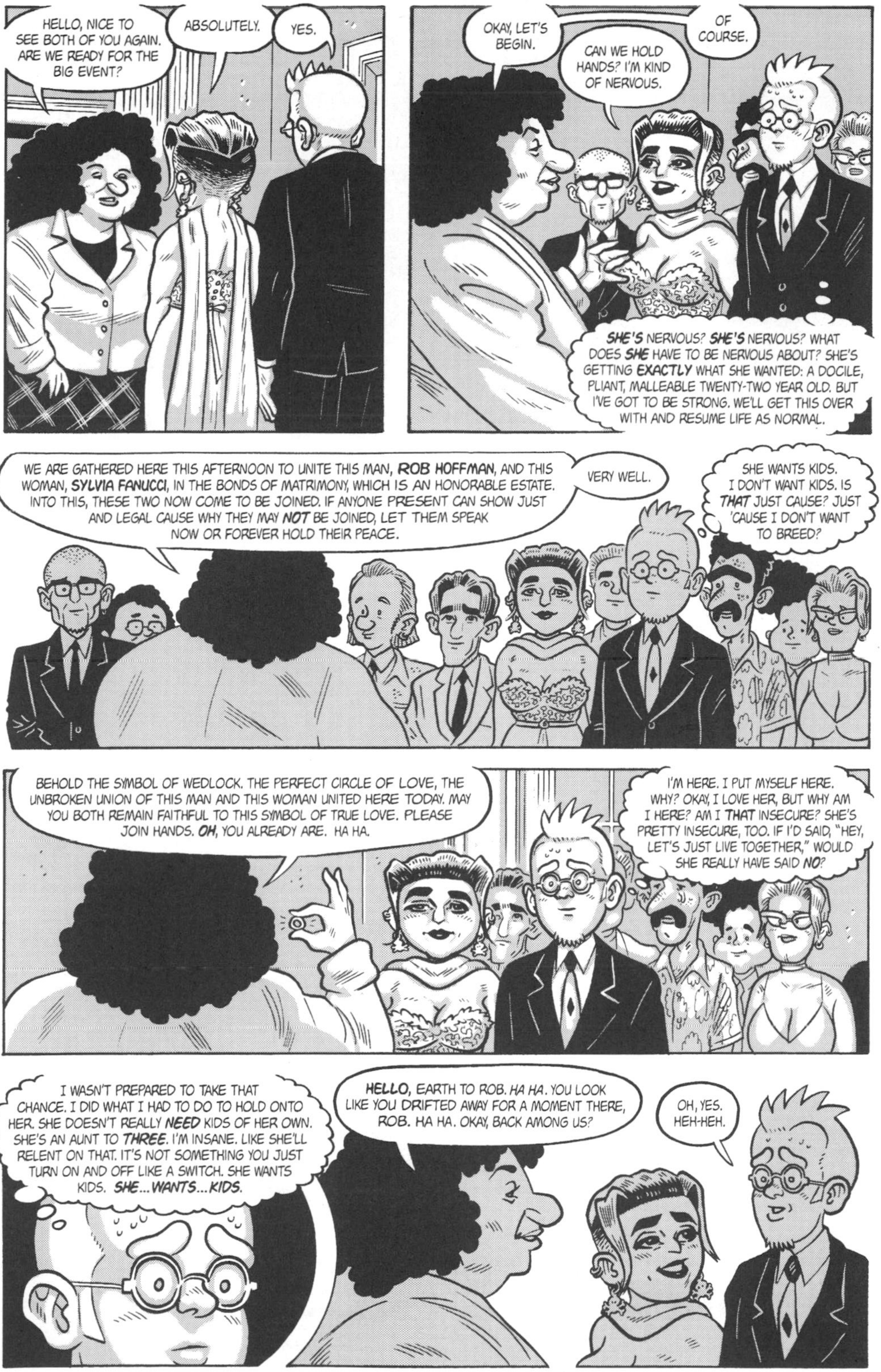
HELLO, NICE TO SEE BOTH OF YOU AGAIN. ARE WE READY FOR THE BIG EVENT?
ABSOLUTELY.
YES.
OKAY, LET'S BEGIN.
CAN WE HOLD HANDS? I'M KIND OF NERVOUS.
OF COURSE.
SHE'S NERVOUS? SHE'S NERVOUS? WHAT DOES SHE HAVE TO BE NERVOUS ABOUT? SHE'S GETTING EXACTLY WHAT SHE WANTED: A DOCILE, PLIANT, MALLEABLE TWENTY-TWO YEAR OLD. BUT I'VE GOT TO BE STRONG. WE'LL GET THIS OVER WITH AND RESUME LIFE AS NORMAL.
WE ARE GATHERED HERE THIS AFTERNOON TO UNITE THIS MAN, ROB HOFFMAN, AND THIS WOMAN, SYLVIA FANUCCI, IN THE BONDS OF MATRIMONY, WHICH IS AN HONORABLE ESTATE. INTO THIS, THESE TWO NOW COME TO BE JOINED. IF ANYONE PRESENT CAN SHOW JUST AND LEGAL CAUSE WHY THEY MAY NOT BE JOINED, LET THEM SPEAK NOW OR FOREVER HOLD THEIR PEACE.
VERY WELL.
SHE WANTS KIDS. I DON'T WANT KIDS. IS THAT JUST CAUSE? JUST 'CAUSE I DON'T WANT TO BREED?
BEHOLD THE SYMBOL OF WEDLOCK. THE PERFECT CIRCLE OF LOVE, THE UNBROKEN UNION OF THIS MAN AND THIS WOMAN UNITED HERE TODAY. MAY YOU BOTH REMAIN FAITHFUL TO THIS SYMBOL OF TRUE LOVE. PLEASE JOIN HANDS. OH, YOU ALREADY ARE. HA HA.
I'M HERE. I PUT MYSELF HERE. WHY? OKAY, I LOVE HER, BUT WHY AM I HERE? AM I THAT INSECURE? SHE'S PRETTY INSECURE, TOO. IF I'D SAID, "HEY, LET'S JUST LIVE TOGETHER," WOULD SHE REALLY HAVE SAID NO?
I WASN'T PREPARED TO TAKE THAT CHANCE. I DID WHAT I HAD TO DO TO HOLD ONTO HER. SHE DOESN'T REALLY NEED KIDS OF HER OWN. SHE'S AN AUNT TO THREE. I'M INSANE. LIKE SHE'LL RELENT ON THAT. IT'S NOT SOMETHING YOU JUST TURN ON AND OFF LIKE A SWITCH. SHE WANTS KIDS. SHE... WANTS... KIDS.
HELLO, EARTH TO ROB. HA HA. YOU LOOK LIKE YOU DRIFTED AWAY FOR A MOMENT THERE, ROB. HA HA. OKAY, BACK AMONG US?
OH, YES. HEH-HEH.

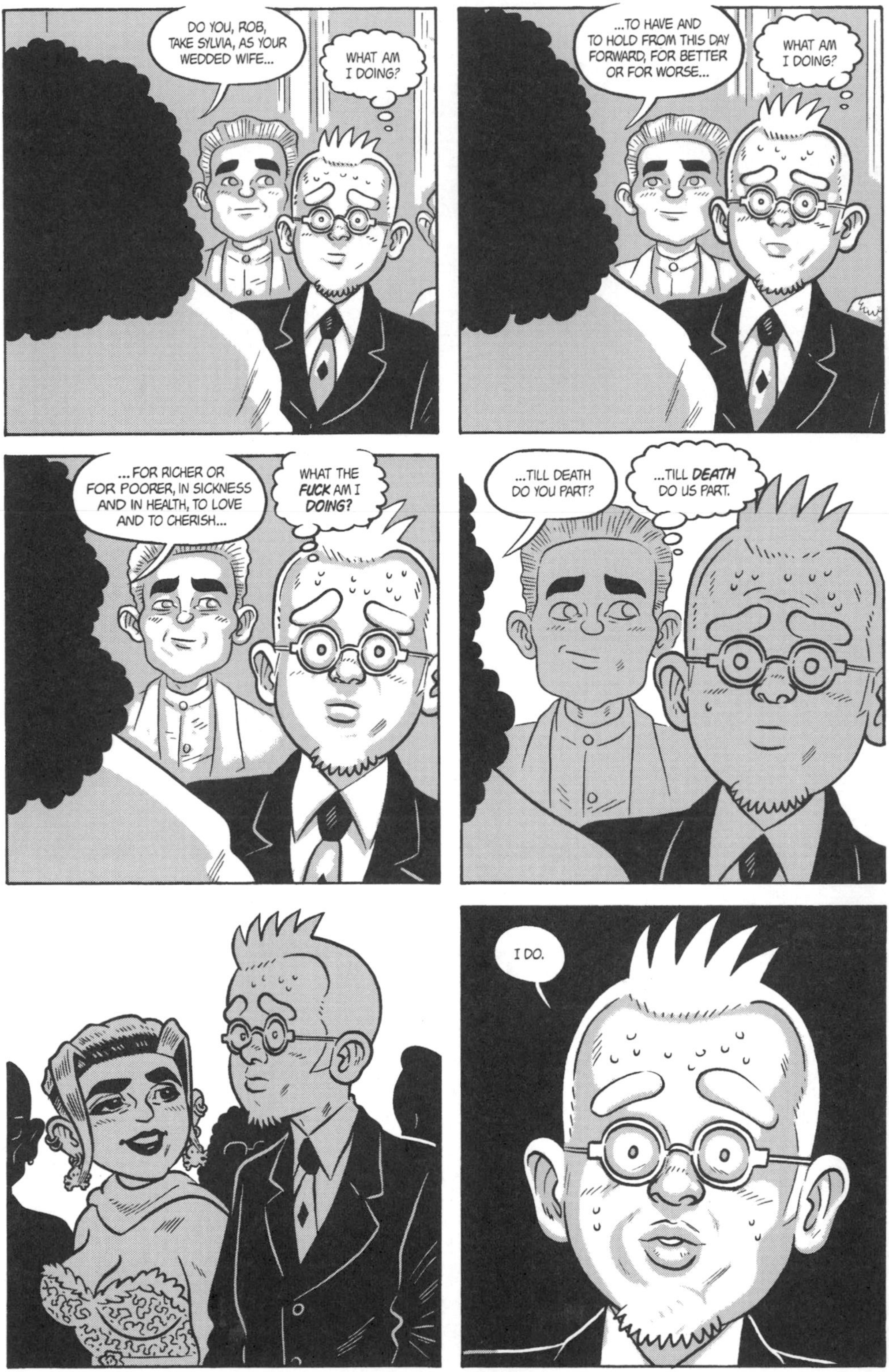
DO YOU, ROB, TAKE SYLVIA, AS YOUR WEDDED WIFE...
WHAT AM I DOING?
...TO HAVE AND TO HOLD FROM THIS DAY FORWARD, FOR BETTER OR FOR WORSE...
WHAT AM I DOING?
...FOR RICHER OR FOR POORER, IN SICKNESS AND IN HEALTH, TO LOVE AND TO CHERISH...
WHAT THE **FUCK** AM I **DOING?**
...TILL DEATH DO YOU PART?
...TILL **DEATH** DO US PART.
I DO.

# From *Minimum Wage* to *Beg the Question*

TEN YEARS IS A LONG TIME. Okay, not in the cosmic sense, but in the span of a human lifetime a decade can be pretty significant. So it was, in late 1994, that I decided to embark upon what has been – to date – the signature work in my comics career. That sounds a bit grandiose, but *Minimum Wage*, more than anything else I ever did, put me on the map. It might have been a smallish blip, but the map now had a town called Fingerman, population one. How my exemplary efforts on *Teenage Mutant Ninja Turtles* didn't get me there earlier remains a mystery. *Ha-ha?*

Anyway.

Prior to *Minimum Wage* I was ever at work refining my style. Style is a dangerous thing (as is over-refinement, but we'll get to that in a moment). All through my art school days fellow students would defend their mediocre efforts by stating a tad too stridently, "But that's my *style*." Perhaps. But mostly it was bad or lazy work. I've always endeavored to do good work. Whether I've accomplished it is debatable, but never for lack of effort. The thing is, up to the point of *Minimum Wage* good work always meant work that came hard. I'd doodle in the margins and those drawings always had a freshness and vitality, but they came too easily. Couldn't be good work if it came easily.

Wrong.

As I neared my thirtieth birthday, fresh off the miniseries *White Like She*, I was at a turning point. While I was proud of the work I'd done on that series, it had been just that: WORK. Hard work. I slogged through *White Like She* and hated almost every minute of doing it. I was experimenting with a style that involved heavy usage of photo reference. I'm not of the school of thought that photo reference is a bad thing. The late, great Will Eisner was not a fan of photo reference, but my other late, great mentor, Harvey Kurtzman, was. Harvey believed in doing one's homework.

Well, homework is one thing, but slavish adherence to photo reference is another. That was *White Like She*. Attempting a stylized realism, I became addicted to, and crippled by, my need for photos. If I didn't have an exact pose, I'd shoot it.

Ridiculous. I began to question every line I put to paper that wasn't based on a photo. I was also refining the life out of my art. It was grueling and I think the art has a stiffness and joylessness I've never before or since witnessed in my work. At any rate, I finished the project but I knew that something had to give.

Plus, as noted, I was just about to turn thirty.

I needed to give myself a special gift to take the sting out of that milestone, and that gift was deciding to do something in my sketchbook quick-and-easy style, the method my friends had been encouraging me to do for years. I'd always done fictional comics. *White Like She* was social science fiction. Most of the rest was done for men's magazines, stuff for kids (*Cracked*), and licensed stuff (*TMNT*).

Years ago, during a row with my first wife, she dismissed my work because it was all fictitious escapist fare. She said "real art" was about truth and reality, not made up junk. Though I didn't agree completely and still don't, it stuck with me. It took our divorce, the passage of time and the love and support of someone new[1] (who, I'm happy to say, I have also just celebrated another decade milestone with: ten years of marriage) to take Mrs. Bob #1's advice and embark on doing something real.

Sort of.

In the interest of telling a story that involves characters based on real people, fictionalization is a pretty important safety valve – for both legal and creative reasons — as are the conflation of people and events, screwing with chronology, and leaving stuff out that's nobody's business. Strict autobiography wasn't what I wanted to do with *Minimum Wage*. I wanted to do an impression of my salad days, not an historical document. I wanted to take people from one point in my life and mix them with ones from another. I also wanted to leave some individuals and other stuff out. Omission is a great tool (see: legal and creative reasons).

And I have to say it: *Rob isn't me.* Yeah, right. Okay, so he's pretty much me, but not exactly. He's an *impression* of me. Consider him the Fred Travalena version of me. Am I dating myself? Danny Gans? Never mind. The same goes for the others depicted herein. They're heightened versions, distortions, but none very well disguised, I'm afraid.

---

1. Upon whom Sylvia is *not* based.

The first installment of Rob and Sylvia's saga was released in 1995 as *Minimum Wage, Book One*, a 72-page "pilot" that led to the comic-book series, which ran for ten issues. *Minimum Wage* never reached as big an audience as I'd hoped it would, and I'm not entirely sure why. Someone suggested that the level of anxiety was too sustained. It was funny, yes, but not comfortably funny like a sitcom.

Maybe, *but that's my style.*

I know part of it was that comic-book retailers are generally pretty conservative and have limited resources and shelf space. Some cautioned me that the frank depiction of sex might put off some retailers (and potential readers), but I wasn't going to compromise. Sex was integral to the story. It wasn't gratuitous (and having made a career of depicting completely gratuitous sex for many years, I think I know the difference).

Who knows why some things click and others don't, especially in pop culture? But *Minimum Wage* reached a really smart audience – quality, not quantity. They found it and responded to it, and for that I am truly grateful. I've met and even become friends with some very cool people because of this epic. I don't want to overstate my plight – it sold pretty well, just not mega, like I'd have preferred.

To return to the art for a moment, a strange metamorphosis occurred during the execution of the series. I started off with the idea in mind of keeping it loosey-goosey, real unpolished. But I realize I have an innate penchant for polish (like some folks have a penchant for huffing spray paint fumes from a paper bag). As the series wore on, the "Schulz Effect" happened in reverse. My freely sketched proto-Rob and Sylvia became more and more detailed, more realistic. It's for this reason that I incorporated some small vignettes from the first *Minimum Wage* book (still in print and still a vital part of this tale), but newly drawn for this edition (Jack's cow brain eating, for one).

As is, none of the pages in this volume are as they appeared during *Minimum Wage*'s serial run. Every page – nearly every single panel – is extensively retouched[2] and futzed with (think of me as the George Lucas of comics; actually, better yet, *don't*). It had to be. In a serial you can get away with a gradual change in appearance.

---

2. Eagle-eyed readers will note that a few panels in this paperback edition are different than the hardcover. Somebody stop me, please. I almost guarantee the European editions – should there be any – will have further revisions. Is this some form of OCD? All qualified diagnosticians please send their assessments to my publisher.

It's like aging; you don't notice it day to day. But put all the chapters together in their original form and the inconsistency is distracting. The book needed to be retooled. Plus, Rob was too ugly. How could I allow my paper-thin stand-in to be so unattractive? My dad once commented, "he looks like an old man." And he was right. So, Rob got younger (and better) looking in *Beg the Question*. That my dad despises the title is another matter, but one upon which I won't dwell.

There's still more story to tell, and I hope to do so someday, perhaps in some other medium (hello, TV producers?). I've done all I want to do with Rob and Sylvia and the rest of the gang in comics form. Comics were the most expedient way to tell their tale up to this point.

Who knows what the future holds?

Not even Criswell.

– Bob Fingerman, NYC 2005